BRITISH
POLITICAL
LEADERS

BRITISH POLITICAL LEADERS

A BIOGRAPHICAL DICTIONARY

Edited by Keith Laybourn

A B C CLIO

Santa Barbara, California   Denver, Colorado   Oxford, England

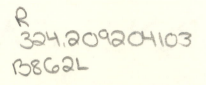
Library of Congress Cataloging-in-Publication Data

British political leaders : a biographical dictionary / edited by Keith
Laybourn.
    p. cm.
Includes bibliographical references and index.
    ISBN 1-57607-043-3 (hardcover : alk. paper); 1-57607-570-2 (e-book)
    1. Politicians—Great Britain—Biography—Dictionaries. 2.
Statesmen—Great Britain—Biography—Dictionaries. 3. Great
Britain—Politics and government—Dictionaries. I. Laybourn, Keith.
    DA28.4 .B65 2001
    941'.009'9—dc21
                        2001003877

06 05 04 03 02 01   10 9 8 7 6 5 4 3 2 1

This book is also available on the World Wide Web as an e-book. Visit abc-clio.com for details.

ABC-CLIO, Inc.
130 Cremona Drive, P.O. Box 1911
Santa Barbara, California 93116-1911

This book is printed on acid-free paper ∞.
Manufactured in the United States of America

CONTENTS

PREFACE AND ACKNOWLEDGMENTS

This book is a biographical listing of the 198 British leaders who filled the top four offices of state and the post of secretary of state for the colonies between 1730 and the present. The entries are arranged in alphabetical order either by birth name or by title—whichever the given individual was best known by. For example, the third Marquess of Salisbury is listed as Lord Salisbury rather than as Robert Arthur Talbot Gascoyne-Cecil. In contrast, William Pitt, the Elder, also known as the "Great Commoner," is listed by his given name rather than as the first Earl of Chatham. The same style is adopted for others such as Benjamin Disraeli, who was also the first Earl of Beaconsfield from 1876, and Philip Snowden, who became Viscount Snowden of Ickornshaw in 1931.

Although the titles of prime minister, foreign secretary, home secretary, and chancellor of the exchequer evolved gradually after 1730, we have applied these titles consistently to the entire period in order to make each leader's role more immediately apparent to readers. The post of prime minister previously was that of First (thus, prime) Lord of the Treasury. William Pitt, the Elder, was the sole exception to this rule: He never commanded the monarch's favor, a majority in the Commons, or control of the Treasury. Yet, as secretary of state for the Southern Department (that is, home secretary), he dominated two administrations between 1756 and 1761, while the Duke of Newcastle filled the post of First Lord of the Treasury. Nevertheless, in this period, Pitt was regarded as the prime minister. The titles of secretary of state for foreign affairs and of secretary of state for home affairs first emerged in 1782. Prior to that, the same two posts were those of secretary of state for the Northern Department and secretary of state for the Southern Department, respectively. The four statesmen who performed the function of secretary of state for the American colonies in the eighteenth century are also profiled in this volume.

The idea for this collection of biographies came from Robert Neville, of ABC-CLIO, who was a tireless helper during its preparation. I was substantially aided in the writing by five others, including Kit Hardwick, whom I particularly thank for his willingness to track down information about some of the lesser political figures—always more difficult to profile than the political giants. In addition, I would like to thank all of the library staff who aided us in our research, most obviously those at the University of Huddersfield, Leeds Central Library, and the Central Library, Huddersfield.

The main sources used in the preparation of the individual biographies are cited at the end of each. More generally, *The Dictionary of National Biography, Dictonary of Labour Biography, Dod's Parliamentary Companions,* and *Who's Who* provided background information, particularly for the lesser-known political figures.

ABBREVIATIONS

AC   secretary for the American colonies
CE   chancellor of the exchequer
FS   foreign secretary
HS   home secretary
M.P.   member of Parliament
PM   prime minister

NOTES ON THE BRITISH POLITICAL AND EDUCATIONAL SYSTEM

Titles of nobility, which can be inherited through the male line or can be conferred by the monarch, are, in order of increasing importance, baronet, baron, viscount, earl, marquess, and duke.

All English peers are entitled to sit in the House of Lords, the upper House of Parliament; but in order to prevent the House of Lords being swamped by an influx of peers, the acts of union (Scotland in 1707 and Ireland 1800/1801) provided for election of only specified numbers of representative Scottish and Irish peers.

Local municipal elections and elections for the European Parliament normally occur on fixed schedules in Britain. However, the prime minister can call a general election for Parliament at any time within the five-year period following the previous general election. They are not subject to the fixed dates of election that face incoming presidents of the United States. Parliamentary by-elections, that is, elections to fill vacancies in particular constituencies, can be held at any time, following the death or resignation of the particular member of Parliament for that constituency.

University degrees in Britain normally are awarded in the following categories, in ascending order: Pass, Third Class Honours (3rd), Lower Second Class Honours (2.2), Upper Second Class Honours (2.1), and First (1st). Oxford and Cambridge have also in the past conferred Fourth Class Honours, often for the nonacademic aristocrat who attended university in the eighteenth and early nineteenth centuries, and Double First Class Honours have been awarded for people doing very well in two subjects.

Public schools in Britain refer to the fee-paying schools to which the rich sent their sons and, later, their daughters. They are the equivalent of American private schools. The state schools in Britain (what are called public schools in the United States)—the schools meant for the working classes—are often referred to as elementary schools, school board schools, or municipal schools, according to the period being dealt with.

A

Aberdeen, Earl of (Sir George Gordon [Hamilton-Gordon])
(1784–1860) [PM, FS]

The fourth Earl of Aberdeen was prime minister at the time of the Crimean War when military action was going badly, and he was replaced by Palmerston, who saw the war to its relatively successful conclusion. Aberdeen's failed ministry blighted his political career. Yet before the Crimean War he had generally been regarded as a solid and reliable leader, unlikely to draw Britain into the dubious foreign escapades that Palmerston enjoyed.

George Gordon was born in Scotland on 28 January 1784, the eldest son of George, Lord Haddo, and Charlotte Baird. His father died in 1791, and his mother took him and her six other children to England, where they came under the protection of Henry Dundas, later Lord Melville. His mother died in 1795, and as Lord Haddo, at the age of 14 and under Scottish law, he chose Dundas and William Pitt (the Younger) as guardians. It was Pitt, the Tory prime minister, who became Aberdeen's lifelong hero.

Lord Haddo was educated at Harrow and then at St. John's College, Cambridge, shortly after becoming the fourth Earl of Aberdeen in 1801, on the death of his grandfather. In 1803–1804, during the Peace of Amiens period of the French and Napoleonic Wars, he made a grand tour of Europe and the Near East, visiting Constantinople, Troy, and Greece. As a result of his touring he gained an interest in antiquities and was president of the Society of Antiquities between 1812 and 1846.

On his return, Aberdeen attended to his estates in Scotland and frequented the social circuit in London, particularly Bentley Priory, where he met Catherine Hamilton, eldest daughter of the Marquess of Abercorn, whom he married in 1805. They had three daughters and a son who died shortly after birth. Catherine died of tuberculosis in 1812. In 1815 George married Lady Hamilton, the widow of the Marquess of Abercorn's heir, and took on responsibility for running the Abercorn estates in Ireland for Lord Abercorn's infant grandson, Aberdeen's stepson. George had four sons and a daughter by his second wife. Lady Hamilton died in 1833.

Aberdeen's political career was unpromising at first. Pitt, the Younger, died in 1806, and the possibility of political patronage disappeared. However, Aberdeen was elected as a representative peer for Scotland to the Parliament in England in 1806, 1807, and 1812, and he accepted the offer to become British ambassador to Austria between 1813 and 1814. He witnessed much of the Napoleonic wars and was horrified by the death and destruction he saw on the battlefield after the battle of Leipzig. His main task as ambassador was to secure Britain's place in the councils of Europe and to prevent Russia, Austria, and Prussia from coming to terms with Napoleon before Lord Castlereagh, the foreign secretary, took over the diplomatic negotiations.

In 1815 he was raised from a baron to a viscount, becoming Viscount Gordon in the United Kingdom peerage. This ensured him a permanent place in the House of Lords. However, his first taste of high office did not occur until 1828, when he became chancellor of the Duchy of Lancaster, minister without portfolio, in the Duke of Wellington's government. He was given the task of assisting the incompetent Lord Dudley at the Foreign Office. Once the Canningites, including Dudley, resigned from the Wellington government, Aberdeen was appointed foreign secretary. In this post he pursued a policy of neutrality in the Portuguese civil war and fell into line with Wellington in attempting to keep Greek gains in the war of independence against the Ottoman Empire to a minimum, for fear that the collapse of the Ottoman Empire would increase Russian influence in the eastern Mediterranean. Aberdeen was more sympathetic than the prime minister toward the demands for Greek independence, but he and Wellington were at one in recognizing Louis-Philippe's new government in France in order to ensure the stability of France. They also called a London conference to deal with the issue of Belgian independence from Holland, an issue that Palmerston spent nine years settling in the 1830s.

Aberdeen became secretary of state for war and colonies in Sir Robert Peel's brief administration (1834–1835) and served as foreign secretary in Peel's Tory government (1841–1846). In these two posts his main task was to restore the good relations with both the United States and France that had been jeopardized by Palmerston's cavalier foreign policy in the 1830s. In the case of the United States he tried to placate American fears about the intent behind British ships intercepting slaving ships that were raising the American flag illegally, and negotiated fixed boundaries between Canada and the United States with respect to Maine and New Brunswick and, in 1846, Oregon. In the case of France he pursued a policy of cooperation that became known as the *entente cordiale,* a phrase coined at Haddo House in the autumn of 1843. This development was unusual for a Tory administration; it was usually the Whigs who supported good relations with France.

The repeal of the Corn Laws in 1846 split Peel's government and let in the Whigs under Lord John Russell. The Tories in opposition were divided between the Peelites, who favored free trade, and the protectionists, who were led by Lord Stanley (later Earl of Derby). Aberdeen remained loyal to Peel but gravitated to Stanley when it became clear that Peel had decided that never again would he form a government. However, the Tory Party was united against Palmerston, whose defense of the Portuguese Jew Don Pacifico's dubious claims to British citizenship and compensation for properties destroyed in anti-Semitic riots in Greece had led Britain to send a fleet to blockade Piraeus, the port of Athens. On 1 July 1850 there was an orchestrated attack upon Palmerston in both the Lords and the Commons, although it was powerfully answered by Palmerston, and the thrust of the attack evaporated with Peel's death the following day.

In 1852 the general election reduced the Peelites to a rump of 30 or so in the Commons, but neither the Whigs nor the protectionist, anti-Free Trade Tories could form a majority government without them. Aberdeen played an important part in the negotiations between the Peelites and the Whigs that were leading to the formation of a new party, which Aberdeen wished to call the Liberal Conservative Party, a party detached from the Tory protectionists. Although Lord John Russell did not like the loss of the name Whig and ultimately opposed the move, it was these negotiations that laid the basis for the Liberal Party that emerged in the 1860s and 1870s. The Whigs and Peelites formed a coalition government under Aberdeen in December 1852, the ministerial posts being equally divided between the two factions.

Aberdeen's new government had Lord Palmerston as home secretary, William Gladstone as chancellor of the exchequer, and Lord John Russell as foreign secretary for a couple of months until he was replaced by the Earl of Clarendon. This was an impressive lineup of political talent, but its potential for change and parliamentary reform was thwarted by the Crimean War. The war itself was an unfortunate outcome of a general confusion in international affairs at this time. The Russians had been happy with the continued prospect of a weak Ottoman Empire on their southern border until France began to press the claims of the Catholic "Latin" clergy in the Ottoman Empire. The French pretensions prompted Russian counterclaims in behalf of the Orthodox Church, followed by the Russian occupation of Moldavia and Wallachia (modern Romania) and the so-called massacre at Sinope, in which the Russian fleet sank a Turkish naval squadron. Although the naval encounter at Sinope was probably accidental, the British feared that Russia was preparing to seize Turkey's Black Sea coast. Aberdeen sent the British fleet to accompany the French fleet into the Black Sea, attempting to force the Russian fleet to return to its base at Sebastopol. When the Russians refused to withdraw to Sebastopol, Britain and France declared war on Russia at the end of March 1854.

The resulting Crimean War progressed badly at first, with the loss of a vital supply fleet in a storm in November 1854 and other military reversals. In the end the British government became unpopular with the press and the public, and as a result Aberdeen resigned following a defeat in the Commons in February 1855. At that point Aberdeen effectively withdrew from political life, although he occasionally advised Lord Clarendon about foreign policy and did contemplate returning as prime minister during a political crisis in 1858. He died on 14 December 1860, his political contribution overshadowed by the military setbacks of the Crimean War.

Keith Laybourn

See also: Canning, George; Castlereagh, Viscount; Clarendon, Earl of; Disraeli, Benjamin; Dudley, Viscount; Dundas, Henry; Gladstone, William Ewart; Grey, Lord; Melbourne, Viscount; Palmerston, Lord; Peel, Sir Robert; Russell, Lord John; Wellington, Duke of
References and Further Reading: Chamberlain, Muriel E., 1983, *Lord Aberdeen: A Political Biography* (London and New York: Longman); Conacher, J., 1968, *The Aberdeen Coalition 1852–1855* (London: Cambridge University Press); Iremonger, Lucille, 1978, *Lord Aberdeen: A Biography of the Fourth Earl of Aberdeen* (London: Collins).

Addington, Henry (Viscount Sidmouth)
(1757–1844) [PM, CE, HS]

Henry Addington was born on 30 May 1757, the son of Mary Hiley and Anthony Addington, a country doctor who owned a small estate in Oxfordshire and who was personal physician to the Earl of Chatham. Educated at Winchester and Brasenose College, Oxford, he trained as a lawyer at Lincoln's Inn, a law school, and entered the House of Commons in 1784 as M.P.

for Devizes. He made little impact, however, until under the patronage of William Pitt, the Younger, a family friend, he gained high office. This provoked George Canning's comment that "Pitt is to Addington as London is to Paddington." Nevertheless, he became an effective speaker of the House of Commons in 1789, winning respect for his common sense, courtesy, and fair-mindedness.

An uncompromising Anglican, Addington won the confidence of George III and was the king's choice to succeed the Younger Pitt as prime minister after Pitt's unexpected resignation over the issue of the emancipation, or establishment of equal and political rights, of Roman Catholics in Ireland in March 1801. Addington remained in office until April 1804—much longer than critics such as George Canning had predicted—combining the office of prime minister with that of chancellor of the exchequer. His ministry is often characterized, with some justification, as a lackluster administration devoid of men of genius and debating talent. Addington himself proved ponderous at the dispatch box, but he appealed intuitively to the backbench country gentlemen whose prejudices he shared. His cabinet contained ministers with sound executive ability, including three future prime ministers, but his appointment of his brother Hiley Addington, his cousin, and two of his brothers-in-law to minor office exposed him to charges of nepotism from George Canning.

His ministry speedily concluded negotiations for peace with France at Amiens in March 1802, to the immense relief of the mercantile classes, but he incurred criticism for making too many concessions to the French, and the peace was short-lived. However, he proved a capable chancellor of the exchequer, and his sound fiscal management laid the foundations for war finances during the next 12 years. He abolished income tax following the Peace of Amiens but retained the high wartime customs and export duties. When the war with France was resumed he reintroduced income tax, but simplified its collection by adopting the principle of deductions at source, raising proportionately higher yields from a lower rate of tax than his predecessor, Pitt. He instituted annual budgets and

1803 cartoon by James Gillray showing Addington, saying "Who's afraid? . . . ," and Napoleon facing each other defiantly across a narrow channel (Library of Congress)

proved able to forecast revenue with extraordinary precision. He consolidated the Sinking Funds to facilitate reduction of the national debt and reviewed the Civil List expenditure, transferring responsibility for government departmental salaries and for the colonial and consular services from the Crown to Parliament. He also enhanced the status of the prime minister by securing an agreement with the king that the latter would not deal directly with ministers without prior consultation with the prime minister. After the resumption of the war Addington came under increasing pressure from the Fox-Grenville coalition and eventually from Pitt himself, and he ultimately resigned in May 1804. He had been criticized for strengthening the militia and volunteers at the expense of the regular army, although his essentially defensive strategy was adopted by successive governments for the next 12 years. Moreover, he had dealt effectively with the threat of insurrection posed by the Despard conspiracy in 1803, and during his administra-

tion army morale began to improve as a result of reforms introduced by the Duke of York.

Later Addington achieved a temporary reconciliation with Pitt, serving as Lord President of the Council in his second ministry from January until July 1805 with a peerage as Viscount Sidmouth. He also served in the "Ministry of All the Talents" from 1806 to 1807, initially as Lord Privy Seal and subsequently as Lord President of the Council. While out of office in 1811 he introduced a highly controversial bill into the House of Lords to control the activities of Nonconformist preachers (that is, those Protestants who did not adhere to the established Church of England). The bill was widely regarded as an assault on religious liberty and was defeated without a vote after nearly 700 petitions had been presented against the measure. He resumed office as Lord President of the Council in Spencer Perceval's administration in March 1812. He served more notoriously as home secretary under Liverpool from 1812 to 1822, during which period he succeeded in maintaining public order—a difficult task before the existence of a police force—through an effective if controversial system of intelligence gathering; by temporarily imprisoning radical leaders; and by increasing the summary powers of magistrates.

Sidmouth dealt severely with Luddism in 1812 but showed some sympathy for those engaged in industrial disputes after 1815, though he disapproved of attempts to exploit distress for political ends and was convinced that concessions made to popular pressure would produce instability. He sanctioned the last and longest suspension of the Habeas Corpus Act (which guaranteed trial by jury) in 1817 and introduced four of the coercive Six Acts of 1819, although their repressive impact has been exaggerated. He was no alarmist, and had the Manchester magistrates in 1819 followed his advice and refrained from confronting the large crowds assembling in protest, the Peterloo massacre might have been avoided. However, the government's public congratulation of the magistracy and the military for "their prompt, decisive and efficient measures for the preservation of public 'tranquillity'" seemed insensitive in the aftermath of the massacre and further alienated public opinion. Sidmouth's spies subsequently exposed the potentially dangerous Cato Street conspiracy of 1820, which aimed to assassinate the entire cabinet. When serious rioting occurred in the capital during George IV's abortive attempt to divorce his estranged wife, Queen Caroline, in 1820–1821, Sidmouth himself led a troop of life guards, or soldiers, in defending his property, which was mobbed on several occasions.

He resigned shortly afterward as home secretary, but he remained in the cabinet for two years as a minister without portfolio, largely because George IV wished it. After leaving office Sidmouth opposed both Catholic emancipation and parliamentary reform in 1829 and 1832. He remarried in 1823 after the death of his first wife, Mary, daughter of Lord Stowell, and enjoyed a long period of retirement. He died in his late eighties on 15 February 1844.

John A. Hargreaves

See also: Canning, George; Liverpool, Earl of; Pitt, William (the Younger)
References and Further Reading: Ziegler, Philip, 1965, *Addington* (New York: John Day).

Akers-Douglas, Aretas (Viscount Chilston)
(1851–1926) [HS]

Aretas Akers was born on 21 October 1851, the only son of the Rev. Aretas Akers, of Malling Abbey, and Francis Maria, formerly Brandram. He was educated at Eton and then at University College, Oxford. In 1875 he was called to the bar, the same year as he inherited estates in both Kent and Scotland and assumed the additional name Douglas in recognition of his benefactors. He also married Adeline Mary, daughter of Horatio Austin Smith, in 1875.

After his marriage he was encouraged to take an active part in county politics, and in 1880 he was elected as Conservative M.P. for East Kent. From 1885 he represented the St. Augustine's parliamentary constituency of Kent until his retirement in 1911. Akers-Douglas rose quickly in Conservative ranks, becoming an opposition whip in 1883. In 1885 he was appointed patronage secretary to the Conservative ministry of Lord Salisbury. After a brief interlude, William Gladstone formed a government, and Akers-Douglas was, from 1886 to 1892, appointed to the Treasury. He became a member of the Privy Council in 1891.

Akers-Douglas served as chief whip in the opposition period from 1892 to 1895, but with Salisbury in office again in 1900 he became minister of works, and he continued in this post until 1902. In this role he was responsible for the ceremony associated with the coronation of King Edward VII at Westminster Abbey in 1902. In 1902 he became home secretary during the Conservative administration of A. J. Balfour, filling the role from August 1902 to December 1905 without controversy or ostentation. With the emergence of a Liberal government, confirmed in office by the 1906 general election, he was to play no further part in politics. He became the first Viscount Chilston in 1911, and later, Baron Douglas. He died on 15 January 1926.

Keith Laybourn

See also: Balfour, Arthur James; Salisbury, Lord
References and Further Reading: Ramsden, John, 1978, *The Age of Balfour and Baldwin* (London: Longman).

Althorp, Henry (John Charles Spencer; self-styled Viscount Althorp; Earl Spencer)
(1782–1845) [CE]

John Charles Spencer, the eldest son of George John Spencer, the second Earl Spencer, and Lavinia, the eldest daughter of Charles Bingham, was born on 30 May 1782 at Spencer House, St. James's, London. Owing to his father's political life and his mother's social activities, he was somewhat neglected, and he was taught to read by a Swiss footman employed by his mother.

Althorp was a shy though fairly intelligent boy at Harrow and was more given to country pursuits than to academic life. In 1798, despite a desire to go into the navy, he was given a private tutor for two years before entering Trinity College, Cambridge, in January 1800. Although he spent considerable time on hunting and racing while at Trinity, he managed to graduate with an M.A. in 1802. His brief grand tour of the continent seems to have given him no polish; he was bored with works of art and failed to properly learn French.

Thus equipped, Spencer entered public life as Tory M.P. for Oakhampton in 1804, as a supporter of William Pitt, the Younger. He failed to be elected for Cambridge in 1806 but was elected briefly to represent St. Albans before gaining the Northamptonshire seat in November 1806; he held the latter seat until he succeeded to the earldom 28 years later. He rarely attended the House of Commons, preferring to remain in Northamptonshire and to ride with the Pytchley hunt. Although he had been born a Tory and had supported Pitt, under the influence of Charles James Fox he became a Whig committed to preventing the monarchy from exceeding the limits of the parliamentary framework.

Althorp married Esther Acklom in 1814. On the cessation of the Napoleonic Wars in 1815 he became increasingly concerned with the plight of the working classes and the need to reduce taxation and reform parliamentary representation. He became at this time something of an expert on financial matters. However, the death of his wife in childbirth in 1818 left him a broken man, and he retired again from Parliament.

Althorp eventually returned to public life to lend his support to the shoemakers of Northampton, who opposed a leather tax in 1812; to work for parliamentary reform and for a reform of the county court system aimed at facilitating the recovery of small traders' debts; and to oppose any extension of the protective Corn Laws. His public service culminated in his appointment as leader of the advanced Whigs, who believed in radical social reforms, in 1830.

After his election to the House of Commons in 1830, Althorp immediately announced a number of proposals for reform. When the Duke of Wellington's ministry fell, Althorp reluctantly joined Lord Grey's government and chose the chancellorship of the exchequer and the leadership of the House of Commons as the posts in which he could be most useful, but stipulated that in the event of Grey's death he should not be required to take over the leadership. As chancellor he made only marginal reductions to expenditure and protected the pension of George IV from the serious cuts that many Whigs favored.

Althorp also worked amicably with Lord John Russell on the Reform Bill; he took over responsibility for it completely on 10 August 1831; and with some modifications to placate the Lords, he carried the bill in Parliament on 4 June 1832. Again, however, he became a reluctant parliamentarian, and he resigned from the government on 7 July 1833; but he was persuaded by a massive vote of confidence to continue in office when Grey was replaced by Melbourne. On 10 November 1833 his father died, and his succession to the earldom in 1834 became the opportunity he sought to retire finally from public life and to work to restore the family fortune. He spoke tellingly in 1843 in favor of the repeal of the Corn Laws. He died on 1 October 1845, after being taken ill during the Doncaster races.

Althorp's position among English statesmen is unique. With moderate abilities he gained the trust and respect of friends and opponents by his simple truthfulness and his patent lack of ambition combined with a desire to do what was right. He stepped from obscurity to high office yet remained determined to quit high office at the earliest opportunity.

Kit Hardwick

See also: Fox, Charles James; Grey, Lord; Melbourne, Viscount; Pitt, William (the Younger); Russell, Lord John; Wellington, Duke of
References and Further Reading: Brock, Michael, 1973, *The Great Reform Act of 1832* (London: Hutchinson); Newbould, Ian, 1990, *Whiggery and Reform, 1830–1841: The Politics of Government* (Stanford, CA: Stanford University Press).

Anderson, Sir John (Viscount Waverley)
(1882–1958) [CE, HS]

Although he was recognized in his day as a brilliant politician who invariably rose to the top of every political tree he climbed, Sir John Anderson's major political contributions are often forgotten because they coincided with World War II, when military action occupied the national interest. Today his name is perhaps most familiar to Londoners from the backyard air-raid shelter design that he advocated during the war years.

Sir John Anderson was born on 8 July 1882 in Edinburgh. His father, David Anderson, ran a shop in Princes Street Arcade and later was hired as director of Valentines, the postcard makers of Dundee. Sir John was educated at George Watson's College, Edinburgh, and at Edinburgh University, where he studied chemistry. This led him to Leipzig University, then the leading center for the study of chemistry. He returned to Edinburgh for a year in 1904, studying economics and political science to prepare himself for the civil service entrance exams. He seems to have moved in this direction in order to earn a decent income with which he could support a family. (He married Chrissie Mackenzie in 1907.)

He took the examination in the summer of 1905 and passed it with exceptionally good marks. As a result he was appointed to the Colonial Office in London, but he never traveled to any of the British colonies during his six and a half years in that department. In 1913 he was moved to Lloyd George's new National Insurance Commission, which was run by Sir Robert Morant. A year later he was appointed secretary of the National Insurance Commission. From there he was eventually transferred to become secretary of the new Ministry of Shipping, which in 1917 and 1918 addressed the issue of shipping losses during World War I. In 1919 he became secretary of the Ministry of Health, which also embraced housing, local government, and the poor law; and in October 1919 he was made chairman of the Inland Revenue.

For the next seventeen years, Anderson filled one administrative post after another. On 16 May 1920 he accepted the joint permanent undersecretaryship of the Irish Office, and in March 1922 he became permanent undersecretary at the Home Office, serving under seven home secretaries over the next ten years. In 1931 he accepted the governorship of Bengal, which was one of three such positions in India (Bengal, Bombay, and Madras) reserved for politicians and administrators. He filled this post from 1932 to 1937 with admirable success, considering that his area, which included Calcutta, contained a potentially combustible mixture of population that was 60 percent Muslim and 40 percent Hindu. He also survived an assassination attempt in 1934. After his return to Britain in December 1937, his career underwent a dramatic shift.

Ramsay MacDonald had died in November 1937, leaving vacant one of the three seats reserved for the representatives of graduates of Scottish universities. Anderson ran for this seat as a supporter of the National government, which was a government that brought together Conservative and some Labour and Liberal M.P.s in the 1930s, and declared "I am not a Party man." He pronounced himself an independent and a non-Conservative, but after his election he proved the opposite. He gave his first speech in the House of Commons in June 1938, on the issue of air-raid precautions. This speech set the tone of his work for the next two and a half years, for the home secretary (Samuel Hoare) asked him to preside over a small parliamentary committee to prepare for the evacuation of nonessential workers in the event of war. This committee reported in July 1938, and its recommendations led Anderson to be designated as civil regional commissioner for London and the home counties in September 1938. At this point he was made Lord Privy Seal in Neville Chamberlain's government, which meant that he had a seat in the cabinet, and he was given the additional title of minister of defense. As a result, Anderson instigated the production of the famous Anderson shelter, with its corrugated circular roof, which became a feature in many backyards over the next few years. (The shelter was actually designed by Sir William Paterson.) About 1,500,000 of these structures had been manufactured and made available by September 1939.

At the beginning of the war, Anderson changed places with Hoare—who reverted to the sinecure of Lord Privy Seal—and became home secretary and minister of home security. Despite this promotion, Anderson did not become a member of Neville Chamberlain's war cabinet. He continued in that post for another five months after Winston Churchill formed his wartime coalition government in May 1940. However, as home secretary Anderson proved vulnerable on two issues.

The first was the internment of enemy aliens, mainly refugees. Anderson arranged for tribunals to examine their cases, as a result of which very few people were interned. However, in the summer of 1940, when the threat of the German invasion of Britain was high, he overreacted and interned many in the Isle of Man. It is clear that most of those who were interned were anti-Nazi; Colonel Josiah Wedgwood stated in the House of Commons on 22 August 1940 that after some gallant but fatal action by resistance fighters on the continent, "the next of kin have been interned." Anderson's vulnerability was further exposed on 7 September 1940 when the London blitz began and he stated his opposition to underground shelters, which he believed would be expensive and unnecessary. He was removed from the Home Office on 8 October 1940 and replaced by Herbert Morrison. However, he was then made a member of the war cabinet (of eight) and chair of cabinet committees, with the title of Lord President of the Council. He fulfilled this role for almost three years until, with the death of Kingsley Wood in September 1943, he was appointed chancellor of the exchequer.

Anderson presented two budgets, in April 1944 and April 1945, neither of which was particularly memorable or innovative. In the 1944 budget, with income tax at ten shillings to the pound, surtax rising up to five shillings more, and indirect taxes already heavy, he merely extended the pay-as-you-earn (PAYE) arrangements instituted by his predecessor. His 1945 budget was virtually the same.

The Labour victory in the 1945 general election brought Anderson's ministerial career to an end. However, he remained in the House of Commons, asserting his political independence but accepting a position in the Conservative shadow cabinet. He also rejoined many of the boards of directors he had previously been connected with, most notably that of Imperial Chemical Industries, and became chairman of the London port authority in January 1946. He left the House of Commons in 1950, his university seat having been abolished by Labour. He vainly hoped that it would be restored by the Conservatives, who came to power in 1951; but when this was not done, he accepted the title of viscount, the normal level of rank awarded to an ex-chancellor of the exchequer and home secretary, in 1952. Over the next five years, he attended the House of Lords regularly, was associated with numerous public bodies, and, in 1952, became chairman of the Royal Commission on the Taxation of Profits and Incomes. However, he became ill in 1957 and died at the beginning of January 1958. A few days before his death, the Order of Merit was conferred on him as he lay in the hospital. He responded, "The civil service will be pleased about this." This remark was apt, as most observers will remember him as a civil servant rather than a politician.

Keith Laybourn

See also: Asquith, Herbert Henry; Baldwin, Stanley; Campbell-Bannerman, Sir Henry; Chamberlain, Neville; Churchill, Sir Winston; Hoare, Sir Samuel; Lloyd George, David; Morrison, Herbert; Wood, Sir Kingsley

References and Further Reading: Jenkins, Roy, 1998, *The Chancellors* (London: Macmillan); Wheeler-Bennett, John W., 1962, *John Anderson, Viscount Waverley* (New York: St. Martin's).

Asquith, Herbert Henry (Earl of Oxford and Asquith) (1852–1928) [PM, CE, HS]

The career and reputation of Herbert Henry Asquith are strikingly comparable to those of Sir Robert Peel. The circumstances of his resignation as prime minister in 1916 closely resemble those of Peel's resignation in 1846, and the relationship of Asquith to the Liberal Party thereafter recalls that of Peel to the Tory/Conservative Party after 1846. Both men have been revered and both reviled.

Like Peel, too, Asquith came from a northern industrial family, though a less wealthy one. He was born on 12 September 1852, the second of two sons and five children of Joseph Dixon Asquith, owner of a woollen mill at Morley, near Leeds. After Joseph's sudden death in 1860, his widow, Emily—a chronic invalid—took her four surviving children to Huddersfield, where her father, William Willans, was a prominent citizen with national Liberal and Congregationalist connections. When her father died in 1863, Emily moved to Sussex, and the boys were entrusted to the care and support of her eldest brother, John, in London. When John returned to Yorkshire, the boys were boarded with a London family. They were excellently taught at the City of London School. Asquith was an outstanding pupil and exhibited "intellectual effortlessness" throughout his academic career. In 1870 he won a scholarship to Balliol College, Oxford, where he was an all-around success: he excelled in Union debates, rowed, and played golf; gained "easy firsts" and prizes in his degree examinations in classics; and was made a fellow of his college.

He retained his fellowship until 1881, but in 1875 he moved to London to practice as a lawyer, and in 1877, at age 25, he married Helen Melland, daughter of a Manchester physician. Despite their precarious finances, the couple lived in some style, and between 1878 and 1887 four children were born. Meanwhile,

Herbert Henry Asquith, 1914 (Library of Congress)

Asquith became involved in Liberal politics and was elected to the 1886 Parliament as M.P. for East Fife, which he was to represent continuously for 32 years. His lucid and trenchant speeches brought him prominence in Parliament and success in his profession. The course of his life was changed by two events in 1891 and 1892: In November 1891 his wife died; and after the 1892 general election he became home secretary in Gladstone's fourth ministry. In that office, in the Gladstone and the succeeding Rosebery government of 1894–1895, Asquith was notably successful as a cautious reformer. Politically he moved away from the Radical Liberalism of his Nonconformist background, and personally and socially his lifestyle changed when in 1894 he married Margot Tennant, who, in complete contrast to his first wife, was a socialite. Henceforth, Herbert became Henry, and he shed what remained of his Congregationalist puritanism to enjoy London's high society and the country-house life.

This lifestyle was expensive, and Asquith was forced to resume his legal practice when the 1895 general election brought a Conservative government to power. He was, therefore, content to see Henry Campbell-Bannerman replace Rosebery as Liberal leader. Like Campbell-Bannerman, striving to hold the party together, he was a moderate on issues that divided it: Irish Home Rule and the Empire. He was more "Liberal Imperialist" than "pro-Boer," a term that applied to the crisis building up in South Africa, where Dutch-descended Boer farmers were in conflict with British *Uitlanders*. War broke out in October 1899, and in the general election of 1900 the Liberals were in disarray; the Conservatives (also called "Unionists" because they opposed Irish Home Rule) again triumphed. In June 1901, Campbell-Bannerman uncharacteristically exacerbated the Liberal turmoil by denouncing British treatment of the Boers as "methods of barbarism." Asquith now became the moderating influence in the party against the extremist pro-Boers.

The Liberals' fortunes revived in 1902, more because of Conservative/Unionist policies than their own. They could unite against Balfour's Education Act, which "put Church schools on the rates," that is, local government taxes; then, in 1903, against Joseph Chamberlain's "protective tariff" campaign to favor Empire trade. The Unionist government collapsed in December 1905, and Campbell-Bannerman headed a Liberal cabinet in which Asquith was chancellor of the exchequer. After the ensuing 1906 general election, the Liberals and their Irish Nationalist and Labour allies held a Commons majority of 400. Asquith presented three budgets with the underlying goals of "Peace, Retrenchment and Reform." His greatest achievement as chancellor, for which he has not been given due credit, was state provision of old-age pensions. On Campbell-Bannerman's death, in April 1908, Asquith's succession as prime minister was unchallenged.

As premier, Asquith was a coordinator and facilitator rather than an innovator. In the cabinet his authority was unquestioned, and he dominated in the Commons by his clarity of mind and force of argument, disdaining the demagogic and the sentimental. Outwardly calm and imperturbable, he felt a compulsive need to relax through voracious reading and socializing, especially in the company of young ladies; he indulged in copious and indiscreet correspondence with a series of women. His government established new principles of state responsibility for social justice that provided the basis for a welfare state. The great legislative issues for Liberals were education, temperance, land reform, Welsh Church disestablishment, and Irish Home Rule; and when in 1908–1909 the cabinet divided over naval and military expenditure in the face of German rearmament, a looming clash with the House of Lords was a welcome diversion from mounting internal tensions.

The finance bill resulting from Lloyd George's budget of 1909—because it proposed new taxes, especially one on land—was unprecedently rejected by the Lords. A consequent general election in January 1910 left Asquith's government dependent upon Irish and Labour votes to command a Commons majority. The Lords did not pass the 1909 budget until April, and Asquith was under pressure to reduce their powers. At that point, Edward VII died, and Asquith had to persuade a reluctant George V—after yet another indecisive general election, in December 1910, and rowdy scenes in Parliament—to agree to create enough new peers, if necessary, to overcome the Lords' opposition to a bill to reduce their constitutional powers. This bill became the Parliament Act of August 1911.

By then Asquith faced new crises on the industrial front. From 1910 to 1913 there was a continuous sequence of strikes by miners, dockers, and railwaymen, which generated fierce class hatred and damaged the economy: 40,980,000 working days were lost in 1912. Because it depended on Irish Nationalist Party M.P.s' support, the government also had to reactivate its Home Rule policy, which renewed the prospect of civil war in Ireland. In March 1913 there was a "mutiny" of Ulster Protestant army officers, which Asquith countered by imposing obedience, against the wishes of the king and protests by the Unionists. In his handling of these domestic crises, Asquith has been both lauded for his statesmanship and denounced for his inertia.

Even more critical were the problems abroad that brought war in 1914. These began with German aggression in Morocco in 1905–1906, renewed in 1911, which intensified the Anglo-German "naval race." Now, in addition to divisions over domestic issues, there were cabinet splits on the financing of rearmament and on involvement in the Balkans crisis that pitted Britain, in alliance with tsarist Russia as well as France, against Germany and Austria-Hungary. Only German violation of Belgian neutrality allowed Asquith to lead a partly pacifist Liberal Party into a war that was more enthusiastically supported by the opposition. And the prime minister's calm and deliberate disposition, his tendency to "wait and see," made him seem unsuited to leadership in wartime.

Popular discontent at the government's inaction and incompetence developed as the war dragged on. In Asquith's re-formed cabinet of August 1914, Lord Kitchener, the country's most famous soldier, became war minister, but according to David Lloyd George and others, he proved "a terrible muddler." Asquith lost prestige by repeating Kitchener's false assurance that there was no shortage of shells. He erred in establishing a war council that was too large and unwieldy. The adoption of a strategy of attacking Turkey when stalemate set in on the Western front produced the disastrous amphibious operation to capture the Dardanelles and the Gallipoli Peninsula. This and the scandal of the munitions shortage precipitated a crisis by May 1915 and the formation of a coalition cabinet, containing Unionists and one Labour member, as a gesture of national unity. For a cabinet riddled with intrigue, the chief war issue became that of conscription. Kitchener's greatest achievement had been to create a volunteer army of two and one-half million by March 1916. Liberals were opposed ideologically to compulsory service and felt betrayed when Asquith's inner war council of three Liberals and two Unionists pushed a conscription bill through Parliament.

From May on, Asquith was under siege. The Gallipoli fiasco had ended in January 1916; after the April 1916 "Easter Rebellion" of Irish republicans in Dublin, Asquith bungled the chance to solve the Home Rule problem; the Somme offensive in France, begun in July, ended in disaster—and the death of Asquith's eldest son—by November; and at sea, the brief clash of battleships off Jutland only made the Germans turn to their more effective submarines. On 5 December, Asquith was forced to resign when he was outmaneuvered in war cabinet intrigues by the only Liberal in the group of five—David Lloyd George—and by the Unionist leader, Andrew Bonar Law. Lloyd George became prime minister. Exhibiting the qualities of wartime leadership Asquith had lacked, he became a virtual dictator and "the man who won the war."

Henceforth, Asquith's reputation suffered more and more by comparison. His one attempt to challenge in Parliament the government's conduct of the war left him discredited and Lloyd George triumphant. When the war ended in November 1918, Lloyd George called an election, in which Liberal candidates were divided between "Asquithian" and "coalition" camps (the latter supporting Lloyd George in coalition with the Unionists). In a landslide defeat, Asquith lost his own seat, and only 29 noncoalition Liberals remained, not all of whom were "Asquithian." Lloyd George, leading 129 "coalition Liberals," could have claimed the party leadership, had he so wished.

Asquith returned to the Commons in a by-election at Paisley in February 1920, but he made little impact, and attempts at reconciliation with Lloyd George to reunite Liberal resources foundered on Asquith's distractions and ineptitude and on mutual suspicion. In October 1922, the Unionists rejected Lloyd George's leadership, and in the ensuing general election, the Liberal factions fought separately, and both unsuccessfully. Further puny attempts at reunion were made in a general election in 1923. Asquith and Lloyd George campaigned together to defend free trade, the one issue on which they agreed. Labour was now the main party of the left, and MacDonald's government of January 1924 was sustained by Liberal votes. But when MacDonald called an election in October, the Liberals won only 40 seats, and Asquith lost his own seat for the last time.

This humiliation effectively ended his political career. With no hope of returning to the Commons, he accepted the earldom of Oxford and Asquith. Public disputes with Lloyd George scandalized Liberal M.P.s and supporters. Asquith suffered strokes in 1926 and 1927, which impaired his powers. He retired in October 1926 and died on 15 February 1928, leaving a reputation achieved in peacetime by outstanding intellectual powers but tarnished by the succession of defeats since 1916.

John O'Connell

See also: Bonar Law, Andrew; Campbell-Bannerman, Sir Henry; Gladstone, William Ewart; Lloyd George, David; MacDonald, James Ramsay; Peel, Sir Robert; Rosebery, Lord
References and Further Reading: Asquith, Herbert H., 1928, *Memories and Reflections,* 2 vols. (Boston: Little, Brown); Jenkins, Roy, 1964, *Asquith* (London: Collins); Koss, Stephen, 1976, *Asquith* (New York: St. Martin's); McCallum, Ronald B., 1936, *Asquith* (London: Duckworth); Spender, John A., and Cyril Asquith, 1932, *The Life of Lord Oxford and Asquith* (London: Hutchinson).

Attlee, Clement
(Earl Attlee of Prestwood)
(1883–1967) [PM]

On Attlee's death in 1967, the *Times* concluded that he was "one of the least colorful but most effective of the British Prime Ministers of this century." Indeed, as prime minister he presided over the granting of independence to India, the formation of the North Atlantic Treaty Organization (NATO), the development of Britain's modern welfare state, and the formation of the National Health Service. His impact upon the Labour Party, which he led from 1935 to 1955, was similarly dramatic, to the extent that prominent figures in the declining Labour Party in the 1980s looked back longingly on the Attlee era, gradually developing a mythology around this reticent and unassuming leader.

Clement Richard Attlee was born at Putney on 3 January 1883, the seventh child of Henry Attlee and Ellen (Watson). He was raised in an upper-middle-class family and educated at Haileybury School, a public school (equivalent to an American private school) founded by the East India Company, between 1896 and 1901, where he enjoyed cricket and literature. He then went to University College, Oxford, emerging with a second-class degree (British degrees are scaled First Class, Second Class [often Upper and Lower], Third Class, and Fail) in history. At this point he drifted into law, the profession of his

father, and became a barrister in 1906. However, in October 1905 he went to Haileybury House, a boys' club in the East End of London, and by 1907 he had become manager of the club. He also had joined the Stepney branch of the Independent Labour Party, and in doing so had abandoned both his legal career and his political commitment to the Conservative Party. From this point on, Attlee sought a career in politics. He promoted the Poor Law Minority Campaign of Sidney and Beatrice Webb, campaigned for the trade unions during the Dock Strike of 1911, and lectured on trade unionism at Ruskin College, Oxford. His hopes of a political career were interrupted by World War I. Attlee joined the South Lancashire regiment of the army, serving in Gallipoli, Mesopotamia, and France. When the war ended, he held the rank of major. He soon joined the London School of Economics as a lecturer, a position he held until 1923.

The end of the war was also the beginning of Attlee's rise within the Labour Party. His first elective post was as councillor for Stepney. He was elected mayor of Stepney in 1919. In 1922 he won the Limehouse constituency, which he represented in Parliament until it was reorganized in 1950 (after which he represented West Walthamstow, until 1955). Now an M.P., Attlee rose quickly in the Labour ranks. He became private secretary to Ramsay MacDonald, the Labour leader, and was appointed undersecretary of state for war in the Labour government that MacDonald formed in 1924. When the first Labour government collapsed at the end of 1924, he was an active M.P. and was placed on the Simon Commission, which was set up in 1927 to examine constitutional changes in India. While serving on the commission, Attlee became an ardent supporter of a gradual movement toward Indian self-government. His involvement in this commission prevented him from assuming office immediately on the formation of the second Labour government in 1929; but in May 1930, he replaced Oswald Mosley as chancellor of the Duchy of Lancaster. Attlee used this post, which entailed no departmental responsibilities, to develop an economic policy that appeared as a memorandum entitled "The Problems of British Industry"; but the

Prime Minister Clement Attlee on a visit to Washington, D.C., 1945 (Library of Congress)

paper was ignored. Attlee was also postmaster-general for a short time in this second Labour government.

The collapse of the second Labour government in August 1931, followed by a disastrous general election result for Labour, propelled his political career forward, for he was one of only two Labour M.P.s with ministerial experience who were elected to the House of Commons, the other being Sir Stafford Cripps. Despite Attlee's prominence, he was a follower rather than a leader; his attempts to reshape Labour policies in the 1930s led Hugh Dalton to suggest that he was "a small person with no personality, nor real standing in the Movement." Small man or not, Attlee acted as deputy leader of the Labour Party between 1931 and 1935, first under Arthur Henderson and then under George Lansbury. When Ernest Bevin, the great trade union leader, forced Lansbury to step down as leader just before the November 1935 general election, it was Attlee who became interim leader. After the general election Attlee defeated Herbert

Morrison and Arthur Greenwood in the leadership contest. He remained Labour leader for the next 20 years.

Attlee's style of party leadership gave preference to collective decision making instead of top-down policies and initiatives. He did not shape events in the way Dalton did in moving Labour toward public ownership; nor did he shape attitudes toward the need for rearmament as an aspect of foreign policy, as did Ernest Bevin. Nevertheless, he nudged the Labour Party in the directions that both Dalton and Bevin had defined. Attlee outlined this new Labour Party strategy in his books *The Will and the Way to Socialism* (1935) and *The Labour Party in Perspective* (1937). However, given that many trade unionists were Catholics and concerned about the reported murders of Catholic priests in Spain, he trod a careful line, supporting nonintervention in the Spanish Civil War in 1936 and early 1937 and gradually moving toward support for the Spanish republican government. By 1938 he was determinedly opposed to the National government's (between 1931 and 1940 the National government united Conservative, Labour, and Liberal M.P.s) policy of appeasing Hitler and to the 1938 Munich agreement that effectively abandoned Czechoslovakia to Germany. He showed that he could make decisions when needed; and for the Labour Party he proved an ideal neutral force to balance the rival political claims of Herbert Morrison, Hugh Dalton, Arthur Greenwood, Stafford Cripps, and Ernest Bevin.

Although Attlee was often seen as Labour's temporary leader before 1939, this attitude changed during World War II. He decided that Labour would support Winston Churchill in his wartime administration from May 1940, and he informed the Labour Party Conference of 1940 that "the world that must emerge from this war must be a world attuned to our ideals." Thus he supported both national unity and social change, although the latter issue became his priority. Indeed, he forced Churchill to allow the publication of the Beveridge Report on social insurance in December 1942, threatening to withdraw from the coalition if this was not done. On this and most issues he was successful, and in the wartime cabinet he was often the unflappable figure keeping it together, serving as Lord Privy Seal between 1940 and 1942, secretary of state for dominions affairs (1942–1943), Lord President of the Council (1943–1945), and, officially from February 1942, deputy prime minister. Although Attlee's cabinet position gave rise to criticism from Labour's left wing—most obviously from Harold Laski and Aneurin Bevan—he managed to retain the strong support of Ernest Bevin, who ensured that there was no real wartime challenge to Attlee's position as Labour leader.

The general election of July 1945 was Attlee's finest hour. Appearing calm and responsible in the face of Churchill's infamous radio broadcast that compared the Labour Party's policies to those of the Gestapo, Attlee presided over a Labour landslide victory, which had seemed possible since 1942. He accepted office immediately, ignoring the Labour Party directive of the 1930s that such a decision should be decided by the party as a whole, and he fought off a last-minute attempt by Morrison to push himself forward as Labour leader and, thus, prime minister. Attlee then astutely created a cabinet of great talents, some of whom could not stand each other's company, by playing to their strengths. He neutralized the political opposition of Aneurin Bevan by making him minister of health, invoked the negotiating skills of Ernest Bevin by making him foreign secretary, appeased Dalton by making him chancellor of the exchequer, and called upon the organizational skills of Morrison by making him Lord President of the Council with responsibility for the introduction of a program of public ownership. The end product is what Kenneth Morgan has called the most hyperactive peacetime government of the twentieth century. Indeed it was, introducing a wide-ranging program of public ownership, which included the coal industry and the railways; establishing the National Health Service (NHS), based upon public control that Aneurin Bevan had envisaged; and creating the modern welfare state, based upon the insurance principles advocated by William Beveridge in 1942. Attlee also gave some of the younger talents, such as Hugh Gaitskell and Harold Wilson, their first ministerial responsibilities in both junior and senior posts.

The Attlee governments experienced both successes and failures. The country was practically bankrupt as a result of World War II and had to borrow money from the United States. The conditions on which this aid was provided helped to create the economic crisis of 1947, during which Cripps attempted to engineer the removal of Attlee. There was a dollar-gap crisis in 1949, which saw the devaluation of the pound. Nevertheless, about 30 percent of British industries and services were nationalized by 1948, exports increased enormously, and the NHS and the social insurance system came into existence in the summer of 1948.

Attlee did not play a direct role in all of these achievements. His only significant personal involvement was in the field of foreign affairs, where he speeded up the process by which India was given independence on 15 August 1947, replacing Archibald Wavell as viceroy with Earl Mountbatten, who was more committed to fixing the date for independence, and attempting to keep India within the Commonwealth. He also supported Ernest Bevin in opposing the Soviet Union, bringing the Americans onto the world stage through the creation of the North Atlantic Treaty Organization in 1949, building up the United Nations, and deciding (in 1946) to build a British nuclear weapon.

However, by 1949 the first Attlee government was facing serious difficulties. The weakness of the pound on the international money markets forced its devaluation. There was widespread trade union unrest, and the nationalization of the coal industry gave rise to a major political battle. Within government circles there was also conflict over the cost of the NHS, particularly between Bevan and Morrison. With his term of office almost at an end, Attlee called an election in March 1950, which Labour won narrowly, with a margin of only 15 seats. Attlee's second administration proved equally contentious. Although Bevan was moved to the post of minister of labor, he was unhappy at the prospect that prescription charges might be imposed on NHS patients and he was also embroiled in further conflict with Hugh Gaitskell and Herbert Morrison over the succession to Attlee as Labour leader. In the end Bevan, along with Harold Wilson and John Freeman, resigned from the government in April 1951. The turmoil within the Labour government was plain for all to see, and Labour's appeal was further diminished by the deaths of both Bevin and Cripps. Thus Attlee called a general election for October 1951. Although Labour gained the largest total number of votes ever achieved by any political party, the Conservative Party, which won more seats, formed the new government.

Attlee was Labour leader, and thus leader of the opposition, from 1951 to 1955. This was a period of intense conflict between the 50 or 60 "Bevanites," who supported Bevan in demanding that the party implement more public ownership, and the right wing of the party, led by Hugh Gaitskell and Anthony Crosland, which thought the party should abandon public ownership. The conflict weakened the party, which lost the 1955 general election. Attlee intended to resign as Labour leader at this point but was persuaded to stay on until December 1955, when he was replaced by Hugh Gaitskell. He was given a peerage, becoming the first Earl Attlee of Prestwood, and settled down to a retirement in journalism. He died on 8 October 1967, was cremated, and had his ashes interred in Westminster Abbey.

Attlee could rightly claim to be one of the greatest twentieth-century British prime ministers. His first administration saw the granting of independence to India and the creation of the modern British welfare state, either of which would have marked him as an exceptional talent.

Keith Laybourn

See also: Bevin, Ernest; Churchill, Sir Winston; Cripps, Stafford; Crosland, Tony; Dalton, Hugh; MacDonald, James Ramsay; Morrison, Herbert; Simon, Sir John; Wilson, Harold
References and Further Reading: Attlee, Clement R., 1935, *The Will and the Way to Socialism* (London: Methuen); Beckett, Francis, 1996, *Clem Attlee: A Biography* (London: Richard Cohen); Morgan, Kenneth, 1984, *Labour in Power* (Oxford: Clarendon Press); Pearce, Robert, 1996, *Attlee* (London: Longman); Pimlott, Ben, 1986, *The Political Diary of Hugh Dalton, 1918–40, 1945–60* (London: Cape); Tirastsoo, Nick (ed.), 1991, *The Attlee Years* (London: Pinter Publishers).

B

Baker, Kenneth
(1934–) [HS]

Throughout the 1980s and early 1990s, Kenneth Baker was one of the leading Conservative politicians, filling several ministerial posts before becoming home secretary in November 1990. He was closely associated with Margaret Thatcher's drive to privatize publicly owned monopolies, such as British Telecom and the water industry, and with the controversial abolition of the Greater London Council and the Inner London Education Authority. As education secretary he initiated highly controversial changes that saw the emergence of the local management of schools (LMS) at the expense of Local Education Authority control. He also chaired the Conservative Party between 1989 and 1990, a period of internal party dissension that resulted in the resignation of Thatcher. Thus, he was a leading and active participant in British politics during one of its most turbulent periods.

Kenneth Wilfred Baker was born in Newport, Wales, in 1934, the son of Wilfred Michael Baker, a civil servant, and Amanda Baker (née Harries). His father moved to London in 1939 but moved back to work in Liverpool during World War II, living at nearby Southport. After the war the family moved to Twickenham, London, and the young Kenneth won a place at Hampton Grammar School; from there, he moved on to St. Paul's, a school to which the rising middle classes had sent their sons since its foundation in 1509. After graduating, he did his national service in the army and then enrolled at Magdalen College, Oxford, where he obtained a second-class honors degree in history. He then became a trainee at the Shell Oil Company and from there moved on to several other, smaller firms. He eventually joined the Minster Trust, a City of London investment trust. From there he moved on to become managing director of a clothing company. In 1962 he met Mary Muir, whom he later married. It was at this point that Baker began to cultivate an interest in politics, serving on the ward committee of Twickenham Conservative Association and becoming a member of the Twickenham Borough Council in 1960.

From that base, Baker moved into national politics. After unsuccessfully contesting the Poplar seat in London, he won election to Parliament representing the Acton constituency in a parliamentary by-election in March 1968. Although he lost his seat in the 1970 general election, he won the London seat of St. Marylebone in a parliamentary by-election later in 1970. Thereafter, he gradually began to rise in Conservative ranks. He gained his first post in March 1972 in the Edward Heath government (1970–1974), when he was made parliamentary undersecretary to the Civil Service Department, a department designed to improve the efficiency of public administration. This was a junior post that trained him in the internal workings of government administration. His experience there was relatively brief, as the Heath government was defeated in the general election of February 1974. It is clear that Baker was not fully in sympathy with Heath but was more in tune with Margaret Thatcher, the subsequent Conservative leader. When she became prime minister, in May 1979, his political career took off.

In January 1981 Baker was made minister of information technology in what became Thatcher's first administrative reshuffle after her assumption of the office of prime minister, an occasion dubbed by journalists and political observers "the night of the long hatpin." Baker's main function was to prepare British technology for the microchip revolution that was about to occur, diverting money into the new electronic technologies. He also announced, in April 1981, the objective of getting a microcomputer into every school, with the government paying 50 percent of the cost. In addition, he was involved in completing the process of introducing the British Telecommunications Bill, which would pave the way for ending the monopoly of British Telecom (a section of the post office) over British communications. The latter task was accomplished with the sale of 51 percent of British Telecom to the public at the end of 1984.

Baker was elected to represent the Dorking constituency in the June 1983 general election, a move forced on him by the breakup of his old constituency, and retained his post as minister of information technology in Thatcher's new administration. However, in September 1984 he was moved and became minister for local government. In this role, his main battle was with Ken Livingstone, a left-wing figure in the labor movement, and his supporters, who had gained control of the Greater London Council (GLC) in 1981 and had used its financial resources to reduce the fares on London Transport by 25 percent. Skirmishes between Kenneth Baker ("Blue Ken") and Ken Livingstone ("Red Ken") became a regular feature of London and British politics in 1984 and 1985, which eventuated in the passage of the "Abolition" Bill ending the existence of the GLC in 1985. In fact, this was but one of three major battles Baker fought. The second was the rate-capping of 20 Labour inner-city councils whose expenditures were exceeding government budgetary guidelines. The most prominent of these was Liverpool, which had fallen into the hands of Militant Tendency councillors who were in the left wing of the Labour Party and who wished to use the party for revolutionary socialist objectives. The Liverpool council was dominated by Derek Hatton, its rather brash deputy leader, who committed Liverpool to increased spending and set a tax rate inadequate to meet the financial costs. The conflict raged throughout 1985 and early 1986, until the Liverpool council agreed to set a "legal" budget. Thirdly, Baker was in-

volved in the development of the idea of a Community Charge, essentially a poll tax, to replace the standard system of rates (this idea later led to the downfall of Thatcher). In 1984 and 1985, Baker presided over a review group that suggested that council rates should not be based upon the size of property but upon a locally based charge levied on every person over the age of eighteen, thus ensuring that every citizen would contribute to local services and that councils would be responsive to the demands of their local community.

Baker became environment secretary in September 1985, which brought with it a seat in the cabinet. This was a brief, nine-month appointment, during which Baker focused on the concerns of the inner cities and, in February 1986, announced plans to privatize the water industry. By May 1986 he had been appointed education secretary, in charge of the Department of Education and Science.

Baker's period of service as education secretary was both momentous and embattled, since he decided to tackle education on all fronts. His driving forces were the twin themes of standards and choice. Concerned that Britain's educational standards were falling behind those of foreign competitors and that only 12 percent of Britain's eighteen-year-olds went on to higher education, he introduced a national curriculum and extended the provision of higher and further education. Believing that parents should have a choice in what schools they sent their children to, he attempted to revive choice through the creation of alternative schools. He also tried to weaken the control of the Local Education Authorities (LEAs) by introducing the local management of schools (LMS), which allowed head teachers (similar to American principals) and governors (elected unpaid directors) to manage their own school budgets. In addition, Baker removed the Burnham arrangements for organizing teachers' pay and replaced them with a pay review body, thus effectively cutting off the negotiating rights of teachers' unions. He also established the basis for a network of 15 city technology colleges.

Baker's introduction of a national curriculum laying out what should be taught in schools, and his institution of national testing in English, math, science, and other subjects, evoked controversy, as did his announcement in April 1987 that "we can no longer leave individual teachers, schools or local education authorities to devise a curriculum children should follow" (Baker 1993, p. 192). Under his leadership, separate committees were set up to work out the various subjects taught in the different stages of the various curriculum patterns. As part of these new arrangements Baker mandated five days of training per year for teachers, which subsequently became known as "Baker Days."

Baker was committed to the principle on which the 1944 Education Act was based: that pupils should be educated in accordance with the wishes of their parents. Recognizing that only parents with money had a choice of which schools to send their children to, he sought to create the possibility of the parents of children at a school voting to opt out of the state system through ballots and gaining grant-maintained status (direct funding from the government) for their operation, but running their own affairs, without local authority control, in educating to the national curriculum (similar to charter schools in the United States). Baker also instigated the 1988 Education Act disbanding the Inner London Education Authority, an agency that he felt had had a stranglehold on public education. School inspection was placed in the hands of Ofsted, a new government oversight agency created to examine the standards of teaching. All of these actions evoked as much opposition as support. The national curriculum was opposed by many teachers and parents, usually on the grounds that it limited teachers' and students' prerogatives.

Reflecting recently on his actions as education secretary (in an interview with the *Guardian,* 16 September 1999), Baker candidly admitted: "I took away all the negotiating rights from the unions. It was quite brutal stuff. It was absolutely extreme stuff. . . . I would have reduced LEAs to dealing with special educational needs and not much else. I put them on a course to wither in the vine. I have no regrets. My sins are of omission rather than commission." He said that he had wished to challenge the com-

prehensive system of schooling: "I would have liked to bring back selection but I would have got into such controversy at an early stage that the other reforms would have been lost." Thus, stealth was essential: "I was not going to take the comprehensive system head-on. I'd had the teachers' strike, the national curriculum, you can't take on yet another great fight. So I believed that if I set in train certain changes they would, er, have a cumulative beneficial effect." He felt that offering parents a choice of schools would cause the poorer schools to close and other necessary changes to take place.

In the realms of higher and further education, Baker advocated rapid expansion; and indeed, whereas only one in eight children received higher education in 1980, the figure had risen to one in five by 1990. The problem was that even in improving these ratios, and in setting a target of one in three for 2000, he, like his predecessors Mark Carlisle (1979–1981) and Keith Joseph (1981–1986), aimed at the same time to reduce radically the funding that the government paid for each student. Universities found student numbers increasing on a vast scale, but had little money with which to deal with this flood. There were staff and student protests at these developments—particularly at Baker's insistence that the cost of student education should be cut by replacing student grants with student loans, the first of which were made available for the academic year 1990–1991. Baker and his department were strongly opposed by what Baker called the "reactionary forces in education—the National Union of Students, the Labour Party, the Liberal Party, and the Tory Reform Group" (Baker 1993, p. 240).

Baker's style in the education and other ministerial posts he held was clearly confrontational. He was as driven by his own ideological approach as were the extreme socialists whom he condemned. Consultation was not his habit, and the advice he sought was that which supported his own position. It is fair to describe him as a most unpopular education secretary, particularly among what he dubbed the "reactionary" forces—that is, the majority of the British electorate.

Much to the relief of many educationists, Baker was asked to become the Conservative Party chairman on 25 July 1989, retaining his position within the cabinet as chancellor of the Duchy of Lancaster, a post that carried no ministerial responsibility. The party chairmanship was no easy brief; Baker had problems with some of the other leading political figures in the party—most notably with Michael Heseltine, Nigel Lawson, and Sir Geoffrey Howe—and encountered setbacks in the implementation of the Community Charge. Throughout the final days of the Thatcher administration, Baker remained one of the prime minister's most faithful supporters. Reflecting on Thatcher's decision in November 1990 to resign, Baker commented, "A great leader of our country, a very great Prime Minister, had been struck down by a collective loss of nerve among her colleagues" (Baker 1993, p. 409).

Thatcher supported John Major for the subsequent Conservative leadership, and Major was duly elected as Conservative leader and thus prime minister of the Conservative government. Baker loyally supported this action and was rewarded with an appointment to the office of home secretary on 29 November 1990, a post that he held until the general election of April 1992. During Baker's tenure in this post, in late 1990, the Criminal Justice Bill put forward by his predecessor to ensure greater consistency in sentencing and punishment was successfully passed. Baker was deeply involved in his duties as home secretary and was particularly active in supporting the police, in initiating the privatization of prisons, and in promoting the National Lottery. His biggest embarrassment was the escape of two Irish Republican Army (IRA) terrorists from Brixton Prison on 8 July 1991. An inquiry revealed security weaknesses at Brixton as well as a failure to take preventive measures despite prior knowledge that the two prisoners intended to escape. Given that these were flaws in operations rather than demonstrable indicators of policy weakness, Baker felt that there was no reason to resign. Nevertheless, he did resign following Major's victory in the general election of April 1992; refusing the post of secretary of state for Wales—an appointment that must

have seemed a demotion to a man who had long been a member of the inner cabinet circle—Baker returned to the back benches.

Baker was at the center of British politics during the Thatcherite years when change was afoot. However, he will be remembered more for his confrontational style as education secretary and for the fact that he instigated several measures of privatization than for his more modest performance as home secretary.

Keith Laybourn

See also: Clarke, Kenneth; Heath, Edward; Howe, Sir Geoffrey; Lawson, Nigel; Thatcher, Margaret
References and Further Reading: Baker, Kenneth, 1993, *Kenneth Baker: The Turbulent Years: My Life in Politics* (London: Faber and Faber).

Baldwin, Stanley (Earl Baldwin of Bewdley) (1867–1947) [PM, CE]

Stanley Baldwin was a major figure in British politics in the years between the two world wars. He was leader of the Conservative Party from 1923 to 1937; prime minister on three occasions, from 1923 to 1924, 1924 to 1929, and 1935 to 1937; closely associated with the defeat of the General Strike in 1926; and involved in the early days of the "appeasement" policy toward Hitler in the mid-1930s. Although frequently attacked by contemporaries for his lack of effort, and damned by Michael Foot and others as one of the "guilty men" of appeasement in 1940, in more recent times he has been recognized as a great political leader who managed both to defeat Labour in the 1920s and to modernize the Conservative Party during the interwar years, identifying his party with "one-nation paternalist Conservatism." Indeed, it is now acknowledged that Winston Churchill and other political figures viewed Baldwin as a formidable opponent.

Stanley Baldwin was born on 3 August 1867, the only child of Alfred Baldwin, a Worcestershire ironmaster, and Louisa MacDonald. He was educated at Harrow and at Trinity College, Cambridge, after which he worked in his father's business. He married Lucy Ridsdale in 1892. At first, he appeared to be destined for a career as an ironmaster; indeed, since his father

Prime Minister Stanley Baldwin standing between Austen Chamberlain (left) and Winston Churchill, 1925 (Library of Congress)

was an M.P., it fell increasingly to him to run the family business. It was during these formative years that he developed many of the skills and attitudes that he would employ in his later political life. He was a paternalistic employer and sought good relations with workers; he had developed sound business acumen. Having been raised in semirural Worcestershire, he also cultivated a love for the English countryside. The last of these interests he greatly developed, in the nostalgic society of the years immediately following World War I, in a series of lectures and books about "Englishness," which he associated with an idyllic rural and semirural society, a lost land of repose, where harmony and understanding resided. Many of his lectures and books emphasized the notions of Englishness and of a "golden age of paternalism" in which peace and industry, and close relations between workers and employers, had flourished. He sought to preserve the "mythical" values of the past in the new industrial world; and he clearly associated these values with the Conservative Party.

Baldwin entered Parliament as the Conservative M.P. for Bewdley in 1908, winning a by-election resulting from a vacancy left by the death of his father. He went on to represent the Bewdley seat until 1937, when he left the Commons and was ennobled as the first Earl Baldwin of Bewdley. He made no significant political impact until 1917, when he was given the post of joint financial secretary to the Treasury, which he held until 1921. He subsequently became president of the Board of Trade. In 1922, however, he came into conflict with Lloyd George, whom he described as "a dynamic force . . . a very terrible thing," and expected that his political career would come to an end. However, at the Carlton Club of the Conservative Party it was decided that the party would withdraw from the Lloyd George coalition government. Austen Chamberlain, who opposed this move, resigned as conservative leader and was replaced by Andrew Bonar Law. In October 1922, Bonar Law became prime minister, and he appointed Baldwin chancellor of the exchequer. As a result of ill health, Bonar Law retired both as Conservative Party leader and prime minister in May 1923, and Baldwin was appointed Conservative leader, and thus prime minister, in his place. Within just two years he had risen from obscurity to the highest political office in the land.

At one time it was fashionable to criticize Baldwin as an indolent fellow who had risen by good fortune alone. Writing in the 1950s, C. L. Mowat depicted him as one of the political pygmies of the age; and G. Young, a biographer, was positively hostile toward Baldwin. Yet these views can no longer be sustained, especially in the light of *Baldwin: A Biography,* a monumental work written by Keith Middlemass and John Barnes and published in 1969, as well as more recent works by Stuart Ball and Philip Williamson (listed below, in *References and Further Reading*). These books present a tougher image of Baldwin. He is described as a modernizer within the Conservative Party, and a powerful leader who always kept control by retaining the confidence of the majority of the party's center. Apparently, Baldwin was committed to capitalism, and he sought to limit government commitments to subsidizing British industry. He was also committed to parliamentary politics, in a way that Lord Curzon, the alternative candidate for Conservative leader and prime minister in 1923, would not have been.

Baldwin was faced with the need to reunite the party in 1923 and to bring Austen Chamberlain and former supporters of Lloyd George back into the fold. There was also the need to tackle the serious economic problems of unemployment, which was still running at well over one million, and foreign protectionist tariffs. It thus made both political and economic sense to advocate protectionist measures, even more so since it was rumored that Lloyd George was about to advocate protectionism. Therefore, in October and November 1923, Baldwin presented a number of such measures in the campaign prior to the 1923 general election. However, the election saw the loss of the Conservatives' large majority. Given

that no party had won an overall majority, Baldwin tried to form a government; but the King's Speech (the program of the incoming government read out by the monarch to Parliament) was defeated on the issue of protectionism, and thus the Labour Party was asked to form a minority government, with the support of the Liberals.

The Conservative setback was short-lived, and Baldwin returned to head a new Conservative government after the general election of 1924. For just over four and a half years, Baldwin's Conservative government attempted to transform the work and responsibilities of local government and to tackle the economic problems of the nation. There was little change. Unemployment remained above the "intractable million," and implementation of the much-praised local government reforms was gradual. Yet Baldwin gained some kudos from his handling of the General Strike of 1926. This strike had occurred as a result of a wage and hours dispute in the coal industry, a dispute that was only temporarily resolved in July 1925 by the provision of a nine-month coal subsidy from the government and by the formation of the Royal Commission on the Coal Industry under the chairmanship of Sir Herbert Samuel. The dispute remained unresolved; the coal strike began at the end of April 1926, when the subsidy ran out; and the Trades Union Congress (TUC) supported the miners with a nine-day general strike of vital workers. In the end, however, the TUC called off the strike unconditionally. Baldwin was credited with having been both firm and fair in seeking a resolution of the dispute.

Nevertheless, by 1929 Baldwin's star was on the wane, and his "Safety First" slogan in the May general election did not deceive the public, which perceived a lack of ideas on the part of the departing Conservative government. Baldwin had attempted to capture the middle ground of British politics, but his detestation of Lloyd George (who had become the Liberal leader again in 1926, although he was never given that title) prevented him from coming to terms with the Liberals. Without Liberal support, Baldwin was forced to relinquish office to MacDonald, and the second Labour government was formed.

This defeat, however, put Baldwin under pressure from the press barons, Lords Beaverbrook and Rothermere, who set up the Empire Party in direct opposition to the Conservative Party. Although in the short run the Empire Party was a major challenge, claiming to have attracted 170,000 members and capturing two Conservative seats in parliamentary by-elections, it had ceased to be an important political force by March 1931.

In the financial crisis of August 1931, which brought an end to the second Labour government, Baldwin agreed to serve as Lord President of the Council (effectively deputy prime minister) under Ramsay MacDonald in the National government. After the October 1931 general election, Baldwin led the largest political party in Parliament, commanding about two-thirds of parliamentary seats. He could have easily replaced MacDonald but was more intent upon keeping the coalition together. He was particularly concerned with developing a bipartisan line on India—a concern that led to the implementation of Sir Samuel Hoare's 1935 Government of India Act.

In June 1935 Baldwin replaced MacDonald, becoming prime minister a third time, and won a comfortable victory in the November 1935 general election. From then onward he was mainly concerned with the threat of fascism emanating from the continent, and with the political crisis leading up to the abdication of Edward VIII. He was forced to sack Hoare as foreign secretary in December 1935 because of the public reaction against the Hoare-Laval Pact, an abortive effort by Britain and France to satisfy Italy's imperial ambitions in Africa by sacrificing to it half of Abyssinia. The cabinet was forced to reject the pact and to demand Hoare's resignation.

The abdication crisis was precipitated by Edward VIII's determination to marry American divorcée Mrs. Wallis Simpson—a union forbidden under British law, which did not allow the marriage of a monarch to a divorcée. The constitutional issues raised by the possibility of such a marriage on the one hand and by the monarch's impending abdication on the other were discussed and resolved away from the public glare throughout October and November 1936, and though widely discussed in the American and European press, were largely ignored by the British press. This silence ended on 2 December 1936 when the Bishop of Bradford (A. W. F. Blunt) remarked upon the situation at a diocesan conference. The issue was immediately picked up by the British press. Because the planned marriage was creating a major constitutional crisis and evoking a public outcry, Edward VIII decided to abdicate on Saturday, 5 December, and Baldwin made arrangements for the formal announcement to the House of Commons on 10 December 1936, royal assent to abdication being given on 11 December 1936. Although Baldwin's part in these events has been criticized, it would appear that he acted with remarkable aplomb, for it is doubtful whether the British public and Parliament would have been willing to accept the marriage of their king to a divorcée any more than the current British public would be inclined to accept Prince Charles marrying a divorcée and ascending to the throne.

In 1936 Baldwin suffered a nervous breakdown but recovered sufficiently to deal with the abdication of Edward VIII. Neville Chamberlain became acting prime minister after Baldwin decided to resign with the coronation of George VI in May 1937. He was ennobled the same year, becoming the first Earl Baldwin of Bewdley. His prestige was somewhat dimmed when in 1940 Michael Foot and others produced a book entitled *The Guilty Men,* in which they accused Baldwin of having contributed to the outbreak of World War II by having failed to face up to Hitler and fascism; however, recent reevaluation (see Middlemass and Barnes, and Ball) of Neville Chamberlain's role in these events has called into question the accusation leveled against Baldwin. Baldwin died on 14 December 1947.

Keith Laybourn

See also : Chamberlain, Neville; Churchill, Sir Winston; Curzon, Lord; Eden, Sir Anthony; Hoare, Sir Samuel; Lloyd George, David; MacDonald, James Ramsay
References and Further Reading: Baldwin, Stanley, 1971, *On England, and Other Addresses* (Freeport, NY: Books for Libraries Press); Ball, Stuart, 1988,

Baldwin and the Conservative Party: The Crisis of 1929–1931 (New Haven, CT: Yale University Press); Hyde, Harford M., 1973, *Baldwin: The Unexpected Prime Minister* (London: Hart-Davis MacGibbon); Middlemass, Keith, and John Barnes, 1969, *Baldwin: A Biography* (London: Weidenfeld and Nicolson); Ramsden, John, 1978, *The Age of Balfour and Baldwin: 1902–1940* (London: Longman); Williamson, Philip, 1992, *National Crisis and National Government: British Politics, the Economy and Empire, 1926–1932* (Cambridge: Cambridge University Press); Williamson, Philip, 1999, *Stanley Baldwin: Conservative Leadership and National Values* (Cambridge: Cambridge University Press); Young, George, 1952, *Stanley Baldwin* (London: Hart-Davis).

Balfour, Arthur James (Earl of Balfour)
(1848–1930) [PM, FS]

Balfour was a Conservative prime minister before he held any other senior post in government. His premiership was not particularly impressive, and he is remembered more for his subsequent career and his immense pragmatism in a period of fundamental social and political change.

Arthur James Balfour was born on 25 July 1848 in Whittingehame, East Lothian, in Scotland. He was the eldest son of James Maitland Balfour, a Scottish landowner. His mother was Louise Blanche Cecil, the daughter of the second Marquess of Salisbury and the sister of the third Marquess of Salisbury; her brother later served three times as prime minister. Balfour was educated at Eton and Trinity College, Cambridge, where he studied moral sciences.

Balfour's political career began in 1874 when he became M.P. for Hertford, a seat that he represented until he became M.P. for Manchester East in 1886. He held the latter seat until 1906 when he became M.P. for the City of London, which he represented until 1922, when he was raised to the House of Lords as the first Earl of Balfour. Despite his family's political connections, his political career was slow in taking off; not until the 1880s did he begin to make a mark. At that point he became a member of the "Fourth Party," a group of Conservatives, including Lord Randolph Churchill, who had de-

cided to attack Gladstone directly, given the failure of Sir Stafford Northcote, the Conservative leader, to do so. In the mid-1880s, however, Balfour transferred his loyalty to Lord Salisbury, his uncle, who became prime minister in June 1885. As a result Balfour became the president of the Local Government Board. In 1886, following Gladstone's short-lived third ministry, which fell over the issue of Irish Home Rule, he became secretary of state for Scotland. Within four months he had entered the cabinet. In March 1887, after the resignation of Sir Michael Hicks Beach, he became chief secretary for Ireland, a role that earned him a reputation for toughness and gained him the respect of the loyalist community.

With the death of W. H. Smith in October 1891, Balfour became First Lord of the Treasury and leader of the Commons. (The first title was often associated with the prime ministership in the eighteenth and nineteenth centuries, but was often separated from it in the nineteenth century.) He held these posts until 1892, when Salisbury's government fell, and was returned to them between 1895 and 1902, in Salisbury's next government. In these posts, Balfour was effectively the leader of the Conservative government in the Commons and without departmental responsibilities. As a result he occupied his time with Ireland and foreign policy. He believed that Catholics in Ireland would accept their country's continued existence within the United Kingdom as long as their economic and social conditions were improved, and he therefore promoted the reforming Irish Local Government Act of 1898 and a series of land purchasing schemes, including the Wyndham Irish Land Act of 1903. In foreign policy, he hoped to encourage alliances to shore up Britain's position as a great power, but he had failed to secure any such arrangements before the Boer War began in October 1899.

The Boer War was unpopular in Britain, but the Salisbury government was still able to win the general election of October 1900. When the Boers surrendered in the summer of 1902, Salisbury resigned as prime minister. He was replaced by Balfour, the only acceptable Conservative leader, given that Balfour's two rivals, the

Duke of Devonshire and Joseph Chamberlain, were old Liberal Unionists who had split from Gladstone in the mid-1880s over the issue of Home Rule. Balfour inherited a Conservative and Unionist government that was deeply divided on the issues of education and free trade versus protectionism.

The 1902 Education Act, which owed a great deal to Balfour, proved contentious; although it removed 3,500 school boards and replaced them with 328 local education authorities (LEAs), and rationalized the education system, it offended religious Dissenters and Nonconformists. David Lloyd George led resistance to the act in 1902, advocating that opponents should refuse to pay the proportion of the education tax that would be used by the LEAs to support Church of England schools. This development was serious in that it united Liberals against the act; but it also presented a more direct threat to the Conservative and Unionist Party. Joseph Chamberlain, a Unitarian, depended upon the Dissenters' votes in his Birmingham constituency. This fact proved divisive within the Conservative and Unionist alliance; but Chamberlain's advocacy of Imperial Preference and protection (a preference for goods from the British Empire and protectionist measures against the rest of the world) proved even more contentious.

In 1903, Chamberlain began his campaign to protect British industries from unfair competition, to extend social reform, and to build up a network of imperial preference. He was opposed by some Unionists (the "Unionist Free-Fooders") and by Balfour, who attempted to steer a middle course. Balfour's solution was to use the threat of protection to force protectionist countries to negotiate; and he outlined this strategy in his pamphlet *Insular Free Trade*. However, it did not solve his government's problems, for Chamberlain resigned in order to advocate protectionism, and C. T. Ritchie, chancellor of the exchequer, resigned in order to protect it. Other fiscal debates also created tensions within Balfour's government.

Despite its lack of internal cohesiveness, Balfour's government could claim some political achievements. It passed the 1902 Education Act, which formed the basis of the twentieth-century British education system. It attempted to respond to the weakness of the British military machine, exposed by the Boer War, by moving to reform the navy and by creating an army general staff; and it organized the Committee of Imperial Defence. Britain's foreign relations were also improved when Lord Lansdowne, the foreign secretary, negotiated the Anglo-Japanese alliance and the Anglo-French entente.

Nevertheless, with an ailing government, Balfour resigned in December 1905, defying the divided Liberals to form a government. Henry Campbell-Bannerman did precisely that, and his government was confirmed in office at the subsequent general election, which reduced the number of Unionist seats to a mere 157. In the process, Balfour lost his Manchester East seat, although he was soon elected to represent the City of London, in a by-election in February 1906. From then until 1911, Balfour led the Conservatives/Unionists in the House of Commons, led the opposition to Lloyd George's "people's budget," and was prepared to form a minority government so as to enable the new king, George V, to sidestep the Liberal threat of creating a mass of new peers in order to ensure that the House of Lords would pass the Liberal reform legislation. Toward that end Balfour ordered his supporters in the Lords not to oppose the Liberal Party's Parliament Bill. The Unionist Party rebelled at Balfour's action, mounting a "BMG" (Balfour Must Go) campaign, and Balfour was replaced by Andrew Bonar Law in November 1911.

Nevertheless, Balfour, then 64 years of age, continued in political life. He was invited by Herbert Asquith, the Liberal prime minister, to be a member of the Committee of Imperial Defence. In the wartime coalition government formed in May 1915, he became First Lord of the Admiralty, and in December 1916 he became foreign secretary in David Lloyd George's wartime administration, holding the post until 1919. In many respects, as he had at the Treaty of Versailles in 1919, he played second fiddle to Lloyd George. However, the most famous event of this period, the "Balfour Declaration," was entirely his own doing. On his personal initiative he announced, in November 1917, that the

Jews would be promised a "national homeland." The question of Jewish settlement in Palestine would dominate the next three decades in British foreign policy.

In October 1919, Balfour became Lord President of the Privy Council, although the title meant that the Lord President organized the various committees, or subcommittees, of the cabinet. Also around this time he was deeply involved in negotiations with Japan and the United States, in connection with the Washington Naval Treaty of 1922. In May 1922 he became the first Earl Balfour and entered the House of Lords. Convinced of the need for a coalition government, Balfour left office when Lloyd George was replaced as prime minister by Andrew Bonar Law; he did not return until April 1925, when he was offered the post of president of the council by Stanley Baldwin. In this office he was involved in discussions about the relationship of the United Kingdom to its dominions, and also attempted to encourage scientific research through the Medical Research Council and several other, similar bodies. He eventually stood down from political office in June 1929, and he died less than a year later, a few months short of his eighty-second birthday, on 19 March 1930.

Balfour was an aloof and distant politician whose political opportunities arose partly as a result of his connection with the Cecil family and the patronage of his uncle Lord Salisbury. Nevertheless, he recognized that the political climate was changing and that the extension of democratic voting to the working classes meant that aristocratic rule could not survive. Although his premiership resulted in no major successes other than the controversial 1902 Education Act, his later political career was a model of pragmatism. In 1911 he recognized that the House of Lords could not continue to block Lloyd George's "people's budget," the means of financing many Liberal social reforms. During World War I, he recognized the need for a David Lloyd George to move Britain toward democratic government. He likewise foresaw that there would be an overwhelming demand for a Jewish state. In the end, Balfour, who never won a general election, was possibly the first Conservative prime minister and party leader who was driven more by political pragmatism than political principle.

Keith Laybourn

See also: Asquith, Herbert Henry; Baldwin, Stanley; Bonar Law, Andrew; Campbell-Bannerman, Sir Henry; Churchill, Lord Randolph; Disraeli, Benjamin; Gladstone, William Ewart; Hicks Beach, Sir Michael; Lansdowne, 5th Marquess of; Ritchie, C. T.; Salisbury, Lord
References and Further Reading: Egremont, Max, 1980, *Balfour: A Life of Arthur James Balfour* (London: Collins); Mackay, Ruddock, 1985, *Balfour, Intellectual Statesman* (Oxford: Oxford University Press); Ramsden, John, 1978, *The Age of Balfour and Baldwin* (London: Longman); Searle, Geoffrey, 1990, *The Quest for National Efficiency: A Study in British Politics and Political Thought, 1899–1914* (London: Ashfield Press); Shannon, Catherine, 1988, *Arthur James Balfour and Ireland, 1874–1922* (Washington, DC: Catholic University of America Press); Zebel, Sydney, 1973, *Balfour: A Political Biography* (Cambridge: Cambridge University Press).

Barber, Anthony (Lord Barber of Wentbridge) (1920–) [CE, FS]

Barber was a Conservative politician who filled two of the highest offices of state. However, he was unfortunate in being in office under two governments—those of Lord Home and of Edward Heath—that faced serious financial difficulties and industrial unrest. As a politician he left little imprint upon the Conservative Party.

Anthony Perrinott Lysberg Barber was born on 4 July 1920, the son of John Barber. He was educated at Retford Grammar School and at Oriel College, Oxford University. On graduating from the university, he trained in law, and he became a member of the bar in 1948. In 1950 he married Jean Patricia Asquith; she died in 1983, and in 1989 he married Rosemary Youens.

Barber began his political career as Conservative M.P. for Doncaster in 1951, retaining the seat until 1964. Defeated in the 1964 general election, he won the Altrincham and Sale parliamentary by-election in 1965 and retained that seat until 1974. He was a promising politician and rose quickly in the political hierarchy. He served as Conservative whip from 1955 to 1958, parliamentary private secretary to Prime Minister Harold Macmillan between 1958 and 1959, and then economic secretary to the Treasury, a post he held until 1963. He was, briefly, foreign secretary, being appointed by Macmillan in 1962 but replaced when Sir Alec Douglas Home became prime minister in October 1963. Douglas Home moved Barber to the Ministry of Health the year preceding Labour's 1964 general election. In opposition Barber became chairman of the Conservative Party (1967–1970). When Edward Heath formed his Conservative government in June 1970, Barber was appointed chancellor of the Duchy of Lancaster. Within a month, Iain Macleod, the incumbent chancellor of the exchequer, had died, and Barber replaced him for the duration of the Heath years (until 1974).

As chancellor of the exchequer, Barber faced increasing unemployment; the total rose to more than one million in 1972—which was the highest level since the end of World War II. In order to reflate the economy, he significantly increased government spending and reduced taxes (measures popularly referred to as the "Barber Boom"), attempting to control inflation through a voluntary prices and incomes policy. When voluntary measures failed to bring inflation under control, he sought to impose compulsory wage and price caps. Resistance from trade unions—particularly from the miners, who struck for wage increases beyond the government-imposed limits—brought an end to the Heath government. At this point Barber left the Commons, was elevated to the House of Lords as Lord Barber, and entered banking. His political career never fulfilled its early promise.

Keith Laybourn

See also: Eden, Sir Anthony; Heath, Edward; Macleod, Iain; Macmillan, Harold
References and Further Reading: Campbell, John, 1993, *Edward Heath* (London: Cape); Harris, R., and B. Sewill, 1975, *British Economic Policy, 1970–74: Two Views* (London: Institute of Economic Affairs).

Baring, Sir Francis Thornhill (Lord Northbrook)
(1796–1866) [CE]

Francis Thornhill Baring was born in Calcutta, India, on 20 April 1796, the eldest son of Sir Thomas Baring, who was the the second Baron Baring. He was educated at Winchester and at Christ Church, Oxford, graduating with a double first class honors degree (that is, a degree taken in two subjects instead of one and reaching the top class level) in 1817. He married Jane, the youngest daughter of the Hon. Sir George Grey.

His political career began in 1826 when he was elected as a Whig to represent Portsmouth, a seat he kept until 1865. He was committed to constitutional reform and to the subjection of the monarch to Parliament. He was Lord of the Treasury from November 1830 until June 1834, and joint secretary to the Treasury from June to November 1834 and from April 1835 to September 1839. He became chancellor of the exchequer in August 1839, a post he held until September 1841. This was a turbulent period in his life; his first wife had died in 1838, and in September 1841 he married Lady Arabella Georgina Howard, second daughter of the Earl of Effingham. His budget proposals, which were published in a pamphlet in 1841, had evoked strong criticism from Sir Robert Peel. The formation of the Peel government brought his tenure in this post to an end; but he did later serve as First Lord of the Admiralty, between 1849 and 1852, in Lord John Russell's Whig ministry. Thereafter, he played little part in politics.

Baring became the third Baron Thornhill in 1848 and Lord Northbrook in January 1866. He died on 6 September 1866. Since then his political achievements have drawn little attention from historians.

Keith Laybourn

See also: Grey, Lord; Melbourne, Viscount; Peel, Sir Robert
References and Further Reading: Newbould, Ian, 1990, *Whiggery and Reform, 1830–1841: The Politics of Government* (Stanford, CA: Stanford University Press).

Barrington, Viscount (William Wildman Barrington) (1717–1793) [CE]

William Wildman Barrington, the second Viscount Barrington, was the eldest son of John Shute, the first Viscount Barrington. He was educated privately by Mr. Graham, father of Sir Robert Graham, one of the barons of the Court of Exchequer. At the age of eighteen years he traveled to Geneva and, after a short residence there, made a grand tour of the continent. After his return to England (on 21 February 1738), he was elected as M.P. for Berwick-upon-Tweed in March 1740, just in time to oppose the administration of Sir Robert Walpole, whose political power terminated with the first session of the new Parliament in 1741. Barrington represented Berwick until 1754, and Plymouth from 1754 to 1778.

In 1745 Barrington put forward a plan for a new national militia whose units were to be based on the parish. In the autumn of that year, he visited Dublin to take his seat as an Irish peer. He was appointed a lord commissioner of the admiralty on 22 February 1746, and on 14 December was appointed to a committee being formed "to manage the impeachment" of Simon, Lord Lovat, for high treason—a proceeding that ended in Lovat's conviction and execution. Barrington subsequently wrote a paper justifying the conduct of the admiralty board. His paper on quarantine in 1751 also received considerable attention. In 1754 he was appointed Master of the Great Wardrobe and in the same year was elected to Parliament as member for Plymouth. He was sworn a member of the Privy Council on 11 March 1755 and was again elected to represent Plymouth after his acceptance of the office of secretary at war on 21 November 1755. This post involved the preparation of army expense estimates for Parliament, as well as the issue of orders for troop movements, although major troop movements were always arranged by the secretaries of state.

On 21 March 1761 Barrington was appointed chancellor of the exchequer, succeeding Mr. H. B. Legge. Barrington held this office until he replaced George Grenville as treasurer of the navy. He continued in that position until he resumed office as secretary at war, on 19 July 1765, at the king's express wish. Barrington remained in this office until 16 December 1778, when in recognition of his long public service he was awarded a pension of £2,000. The Civil List was relieved briefly of the expense of this pension in January 1782, when Barrington was appointed joint postmaster general; but the pension was renewed at the king's insistence when Barrington was removed from office the following April. Barrington died on 1 February 1793 and is commemorated by a memorial in the chancel of Shrivenham Church, Berkshire.

Kit Hardwick

See also: Bute, Earl of; Devonshire, Duke of; Grenville, George; Rockingham, Marquess of; Shelburne, Earl of; Walpole, Sir Robert
References and Further Reading: Black, Jeremy (ed.), 1990, *British Politics and Society from Walpole to Pitt, 1742–1789* (Basingstoke, UK: Macmillan).

Bathurst, Henry (Earl Bathurst) (1762–1834) [FS]

Henry Bathurst was born 22 May 1762, the son of Henry, the second Earl of Bathurst, who was then lord chancellor, and his second wife, Tryphena. He was married in April 1789 to Georgina, daughter of Lord George Henry Lennox, and succeeded to the family honors with his father's death on 6 August 1794. He was M.P. for Cirencester between 1783 and 1794, and from 1790 until his death was a teller of the exchequer. Bathurst, a personal friend of William (the Younger) Pitt's, also was Lord of the Admiralty between 1783 and 1789, Lord of the Treasury from 1789 to 1791, and commissioner of the Board of Control between 1793 and 1802. On the formation of Pitt's second ministry in 1804, he accepted the mastership of the mint, with responsibility for the coinage of the realm. He was subsequently president of the Board of Trade, under the Duke of Portland (1807–1809) and under Spencer Perceval (1809–1812), holding the mastership of the mint concurrently. From October to December 1809 he served as foreign secretary, but his tenure was too brief to achieve anything of substance, other than support for Wellington's military campaign in Spain.

His longest period of office was in Lord Liverpool's ministry (1812–1827), when he occupied the responsible position of secretary for war and the colonies. He ended his political career in the Duke of Wellington's ministry (1828–1830), as Lord President of the Council (the Privy Council). He was made a K.G. (Knight of the Garter) in 1817. He deserves credit for his support of Wellington during the war in Spain; but as a Tory of the old school, he was bitterly opposed to the Great Reform Act and took no active part in Parliament after its passage in 1832. He died on 27 July 1834.

Kit Hardwick

See also: Liverpool, Earl of; Perceval, Spencer; Portland, Duke of; Wellington, Duke of
References and Further Reading: Gray, Denis, 1963, *Spencer Perceval: The Evangelical Prime Minister, 1762–1812* (Manchester: Manchester University Press).

Bedford, Duke of (John Russell)
(1710–1771) [HS]

John Russell, the fourth Duke of Bedford, was born on 30 September 1710, the second son of Wriothesley Russell, the second Duke of Bedford, by his wife Elizabeth Howland. Educated at home, John completed a grand tour of Europe when he was 19. He married Lady Diana Spencer, the daughter of the third Earl of Sunderland and sister of Charles, third Duke of Marlborough, in 1731. After Lady Diana died in 1735, he married Gertrude Leveson-Gower, daughter of John, Earl Gower, in 1737. Russell entered politics in 1732, and was preparing to run for Parliament when his brother died and he became the fourth Duke of Bedford.

In the House of Lords he became a strong opponent of Sir Robert Walpole, supporting the position of the Tory group led by John Carteret. He was also opposed to the presence of 16,000 Hanoverian troops in British pay. After Walpole retired, Henry Pelham formed his ministry. John Carteret attempted to draw Bedford into government. In December 1744, Bedford became First Lord of the Admiralty and a member of the Privy Council in the process. In 1745 he became Lord Justice of Great Britain, colonel of a regiment raised to oppose the Jacobite rebellion of 1745. He also served in many other administrative posts.

Bedford became secretary of state for the Southern Department in February 1748 (1747, under the old calendar) and held that position until 13 June 1751. He resigned because he was constantly in conflict with the Duke of Newcastle, Henry Pelham's brother, in the Pelham administration. Although he was not particularly hostile to the Pelham administration, he could not be persuaded by Henry Fox, who became secretary of state for the Southern Department in 1755, to rejoin the government, although many of his close political friends did so. Nevertheless, he became lord lieutenant of Ireland in 1757. He remained in that post until 1761, dealing with serious riots in Dublin in 1759 and 1760 (when it appeared that there might be a legislative union between England and Ireland), and deterring a French expedition in February 1760 that aimed to help the rebellion.

On retiring from office, he joined Lord Bute in seeking a speedy conclusion to the Seven Years' War (1756 to 1763) with France. He remained controversially connected with British politics; he was strongly opposed to the repeal of the Stamp Act, and he demanded that the American colonists accept the will of the British government. He refused many offers of government posts, and by the beginning of the 1770s was withdrawing from politics. He died on 15 January 1771.

Keith Laybourn

See also: Bute, Earl of; Carteret, John; Fox, Henry; Newcastle, Duke of; Pelham, Hon. Henry; Pitt, William (the Elder); Walpole, Sir Robert
References and Further Reading: Browning, Reed, 1975, *The Duke of Newcastle* (New Haven, CT: Yale University Press).

Bevin, Ernest
(1881–1951) [FS]

Ernest Bevin was one of the greatest British trade union leaders of the twentieth century. He was a prominent member of the Trades Union Congress (TUC) at the time of the General Strike in 1926 and was an influential figure in the reshaping of Labour Party policy during the 1930s. Yet his greatest claims to fame are his service as minister of labor between 1940 and 1945, overseeing the organization of labor resources in Winston Churchill's wartime government; and as foreign secretary in Clement Attlee's Labour government, from 1945 to 1950. In this latter role he was instrumental in the formation of the North Atlantic Treaty Organization (NATO) in 1949, thus helping to shape international politics for the next 50 years.

Ernest Bevin was born at Winsford, in Somerset, on 7 March 1881, although some sources suggest 9 March. He was the illegitimate son of an agricultural laborer, raised by his mother until her death, when he was eight, after which he was raised by his half sister in Devon. He received little formal education, and began working on a farm at the age of 11. At the age of 13, he moved to Bristol to live with his half brother. He became a soft rounds drinksman (a mineral water deliveryman) and an active lay preacher in the Baptist Church. Indeed, it was in the Church that he gained valuable experience as a public speaker. Bevin also became involved in the Bristol Socialist Society. It was about this time that he married Florence Townley. The couple had one child, Queenie, who was born in 1914.

Bristol, with its outlying docks, was still an important seaport at this time, and Bevin, because of his concern for the unemployed and his work on Ramsay MacDonald's Right to Work Movement in 1908, was drawn into helping to organize the dockers and carters. In 1910 he was asked to organize the carters for the Dock, Wharf, Riverside, and General Labourers' Union, better known as the Dockers' Union. He increased the local membership significantly, and by 1914 he had risen to become one of the three national organizers of the Dockers' Union. Seeing that employers' organizations were uniting and getting much stronger, he became convinced that trade unions needed to organize together more effectively.

Toward this end he advocated the reform of the TUC's organization to include a General Council, which would give more centralized industrial direction to the trade union movement. He also pushed forward with the amalgamation of 14 different unions into the Transport and General Workers' Union in January 1922.

For much of the interwar period, Bevin was the dominant British trade union leader. He organized the General Strike, which lasted for nine days in May 1926, ensuring that there was some semblance of discipline in the last-minute arrangements of the TUC to support the miners, who had been locked out by their employers. He attempted to influence the economic policy of Ramsay MacDonald's second Labour government, of 1929 to 1931, by acting on the Economic Advisory Council and the Macmillan Committee; but he found that his influence was limited—not least in August 1931, at the time of the financial crisis that brought about the collapse of the second Labour government. He published his own expansionist program for tackling unemployment in the pamphlet *My Plan for 2,000,000 Unemployed* (1932). This program advocated the raising of the school-leaving age and the lowering of retirement age as well as policies to generate immediate work. The pamphlet did not attract the widespread attention he had hoped for. He had more success with his Labour Party activities. The National Council of Labour (formerly the Joint Council of Labour) brought the executives of the Parliamentary Labour Party, the Labour Party, and the TUC together to attempt to coordinate the policies of the British labor movement. Bevin steered this organization into a discussion of the need for public ownership, or the socialization of industry, in the 1930s, as well as in the need to direct Labour's foreign policy. In debates about British rearmament to deal with the threat of European fascism, Bevin first encouraged the Council to oppose rearmament; but later, in the wake of the Spanish Civil War and the powerful demonstration of air power by the German Luftwaffe when it bombed Guernica, Spain, in 1937, he reversed his position and began to advocate rearmament. He was also a formative influence on the Amulree Committee (Committee on Holidays with Pay), which, in 1938, recommended that workers should receive at least one week's annual holiday with pay.

Bevin saw himself as a trade union leader and not as a political figure. He felt that politicians—particularly intellectual middle-class ones—were people "who stab you in the back."

As a result he remained unshaken by his failure to secure a parliamentary seat in both the 1918 and 1931 general elections. However, with the formation of Winston Churchill's wartime coalition government, in May 1940, Bevin was offered the post of minister of labor and national service by Churchill. In fact the M.P. for Central Wandsworth stood down, and Bevin was elected to that seat, retaining it until 1951. In his new role, Bevin organized the whole country behind the war effort, thereby winning the esteem of Winston Churchill. His scheme to increase the number of coal miners in the country by directing young men—some of them schoolboys—to the mines gave rise to the term "Bevin Boys."

Toward the end of World War II, when victory in Europe had been achieved, the Labour Party convincingly won the 1945 general election. Bevin supported Attlee against the rival claims of Herbert Morrison to be the Labour leader and prime minister, and was rewarded by the post of foreign secretary in Attlee's postwar Labour governments. He was much respected as foreign secretary, particularly within the Foreign Office, which now found itself with an increased role in world affairs. He provided the Foreign Office with importance through his support of the Marshall Plan of 1947, whereby financial assistance was given to Western Europe, and through his pressure to secure the formation of the North Atlantic Treaty Organization (NATO) in 1949. Indeed, in this role he sought to preserve Britain's status as a world power, to work with the United States, and to oppose the threat posed both to Eastern and to Western Europe by the Soviet Union. In particular, he worked hard to defeat the Soviet Union's air blockade of Berlin in June 1948. He also attempted, unsuccessfully, to act even-handedly in dealing with the rival interests of the Jewish immigrants and the native Palestinians over the future of Palestine. In the end he was forced to allow the creation of the state of Israel in January 1949 and to preside over the ignominious withdrawal of British troops. He had underestimated American support for the Jews, and in the end, fell victim to what has been referred to by Morgan (1984, p. 2) as "the endless imbroglio of Palestine."

Bevin was seriously ill in his later years and decided to resign as foreign secretary on 19 February 1951. He then became Lord Privy Seal, which involved no departmental responsibilities; but he left government altogether less than a month later, on his seventieth birthday. He died on 14 April 1951.

Bevin was a great trade union leader, an impressive minister of labor, and a much-praised foreign secretary, although the last stage of his career has come under much criticism from the Labour left in the past 50 years. The Keep Left Group, the Bevanites, and Labour M.P.s such as Barbara Castle, Richard Crossman, and Ian Mikardo were all critical of his role in the formation of NATO and wary of a foreign policy that brought Britain into too close an alliance with the United States. Yet, whatever one's assessment of the results, there is no doubt that Bevin was profoundly influential as foreign secretary.

Keith Laybourn

See also: Attlee, Clement; Baldwin, Stanley; Churchill, Sir Winston; Morrison, Herbert
References and Further Reading: Bullock, Alan, 1960 and 1967, *The Life and Times of Ernest Bevin,* 2 vols. (London: Heinemann); Bullock, Alan, 1983, *Ernest Bevin: Foreign Secretary 1945–1951* (Oxford: Oxford University Press); Morgan, Kenneth O., 1984, *Labour in Power 1945–1951* (Oxford: Oxford University Press); Weiler, Peter, 1993, *Ernest Bevin* (Manchester: Manchester University Press).

Bexley, Lord
(Nicholas Vansittart; Baron Bexley)
(1766–1851) [CE]

Nicholas Vansittart was born in London on 29 April 1766, the fifth son of Henry Vansittart, governor of Bengal, and Emilia, daughter of Nicholas Morse, the governor of Madras. After his father's death in 1770, he was raised by two uncles. He was educated at Mr. Gilpin's school at Cheam and at Christ Church, Oxford, gaining a B.A. in 1787 and an M.A. in 1791. He went to Lincoln's Inn in 1788 and was called to the bar in May 1791, but practiced law only a short time before pursuing a career in politics.

In 1793 he published the pamphlet *Reflections of an Immediate Peace,* in which he argued for the continued necessity of war against the French. He also wrote and published other political pamphlets in support of William Pitt, the Younger. He entered the House of Commons as Tory M.P. for Hastings in 1796 and continued to sit in the House of Commons for the next 26 years, being elected for Old Sarum in 1802, Helston in 1806, East Grinstead in 1812, and Harwich in 1812. He became the first Baron Bexley in 1823.

In 1801, Vansittart was given the responsibility of leading a British mission to the court of Denmark, with the goal of improving British-Danish relations. Although the mission was unsuccessful, on his return Vansittart was appointed joint secretary to the Treasury, a post he held until 1804. He was briefly, and unsuccessfully, chief secretary for Ireland in 1805. In 1806 and 1807, Vansittart again held the post of secretary to the Treasury. When Spencer Perceval formed a government in 1809, he offered Vansittart the post of chancellor of the exchequer, partly in the hope of attracting the influential Lord Sidmouth's supporters in the Commons—a group to which Vansittart belonged—into his government. Vansittart rejected the offer in favor of opportunities in the private sector, where he went on to develop a formidable reputation as a financier. However, with the assassination of Perceval in 1812 and the formation of a new administration under Lord Liverpool, Vansittart accepted a second offer to become chancellor of the exchequer.

Vansittart served in that post from 20 May 1812 until 1823, a difficult period in British finance. His early budgets were concerned with raising money for the war effort; toward that end, in 1814 he raised customs charges by 25 percent. Once the Napoleonic wars were over, however, he was faced with a Parliament that was reluctant to continue with some of the wartime tax measures. Indeed, in 1816 he lost rather more revenue than he expected when the Commons voted against continuing with the property tax, and he had to resort to increasing the soap tax to make up the deficit. This event led to his being caricatured in cartoons as "Startling Betty," appearing in a washtub. His later budgets aimed to raise money—to the tune of £5 million

per year—to reduce the national debt. In 1823 he resigned as chancellor of the exchequer and was made chancellor of the Duchy of Lancaster—effectively, a minister without a ministry; he was also awarded the title of first Baron Bexley and a seat in the House of Lords. He continued in his post until 1828, when the Duke of Wellington became prime minister.

The rest of Bexley's life was taken up with religious and charitable activities. He served as president of the British and Foreign Bible Mission, and presided over the inauguration of King's College, London, in 1831. He died on 8 July 1851, leaving no heir; although he had married Catherine Isabella, the second daughter of Lord Auckland, in 1806, the couple had remained childless, and Catherine had died in 1810.

Keith Laybourn

See also: Liverpool, Earl of; Perceval, Spencer; Pitt, William (the Younger); Wellington, Duke of
References and Further Reading: Brock, William, 1967, *Lord Liverpool and Liberal Toryism* (Hamden, CT: Archon Books); Cookson, J. E., 1975, *Lord Liverpool's Administration: The Crucial Years, 1815–22* (Hamden, CT: Archon Books).

Blair, Tony
(1953–) [PM]

Blair became leader of the Labour Party on 21 July 1994 and Labour's new prime minister on 1 May 1997, ending an eighteen-year period of Conservative rule during which the Labour Party despaired of ever forming another administration. After becoming Labour leader, he pursued his "New Labour" policy of the "Third Way," using both public and private resources to encourage economic growth and enhance social welfare. In effect, he abandoned Labour's traditional commitments to public ownership, full employment, and close association with the trade unions.

Anthony Charles Lynton Blair was born 6 May 1953 into a Conservative family. His father, Leo, was a law lecturer and a Conservative activist in northeast England. The young Tony was educated at Fetters College, a leading Scottish public (equivalent to an American private school) school, and studied law at St. John's College, Oxford. While at Oxford, he became both a confirmed member of the Church of England and an adherent to the views of Christian ethical socialists such as R. H. Tawney. He graduated from Oxford in 1975, and in 1976 he was called to the bar at Lincoln's Inn. He practiced law until 1983, specializing in employment and industrial law. He married Cherie Booth, a barrister at Queen's Counsel, in 1980. The couple have three sons and a daughter, the last being Leo, who was born on 20 May 2000, giving Blair the distinction of being the first prime minister in 150 years to have a child born while in office.

Blair first entered Parliament in June 1983, at the age of 30, as M.P. for Sedgefield. He had previously lost a contest for the Beaconsfield seat, in a parliamentary by-election in 1982. He soon revealed a talent for financial and economic matters, and was promoted to the opposition's front-bench team for the Treasury in 1985. In 1987 he became the Labour Party's spokesperson on trade and industry with special responsibility for consumer affairs and the City (of London). He was elected to the shadow cabinet in 1988 and was appointed shadow secretary of state for energy. In the following year he was made shadow secretary of state for employment, and forged a new industrial relations policy that ended Labour's support for the closed shop and backed the retention of Conservative legislation on strike ballots and secondary action. He also supported Neil Kinnock's other reformist policies—most obviously, his commitment to Europe; his advocacy of multilateral rather than unilateral nuclear disarmament; and his insistence on wider democratic involvement in the Labour Party, even at the expense of the trade unions.

Following Labour's defeat in the general election of 1992, he was appointed shadow home secretary by John Smith, Labour's new leader. In this role, he successfully wrested the law-and-order mandate away from the Conservatives, his slogan being "Tough on crime, tough on the causes of crime." In September 1992 he was elected to Labour's National Executive Committee, the ruling body of the Labour Party. He was elected Labour leader on 21 July 1994, following the sudden death of John Smith in May.

Blair, perhaps more than any other Labour leader, has been a modernizer. He was determined not to be constricted by the old Labour culture, sensing that change was more necessary than ever since traditional mass industry had given way to lighter industry and services. The traditional working-class workforce had changed enormously and declined. Blair maintained that the Conservative Party had been successful since it was seen as the party that opposed state control and that Labour was seen as the party linked with trade unionism, the state, ethnic minorities, and social security claimants. He felt that such perceptions had to be changed. The "New Labour" Party he was to lead needed to cultivate a moderate image. It needed to accept some of the changes that the Conservatives had introduced and to convince voters that it would not raise taxes, favor the trade unions, overspend, and build up debts. In other words, it had to remove the demons of "Old Labour."

The symbol of the shift from "Old Labour" to "New Labour" was the removal of the traditional Clause Four of the Labour Party Constitution, which committed Labour to common ownership of the means of production; to social justice; and to full employment. Blair announced his intention to reject the old Clause Four at the 1994 Labour Party Conference and to praise the successes of capitalism. Soon afterward, he presented a new Clause Four that committed Labour "to work for a dynamic economy, serving the public interest, in which the enterprise of the market and the rigour of competition are joined with the forces of partnership and cooperation . . . with a thriving sector and high quality public services" (Laybourn 2000, p. 134). In addition, the clause contained vague references to a just society, security against fear, equality of opportunity, and related issues. The idea of redistribution of wealth and income within British society had effectively been rejected.

At a special Labour Party Conference held on 29 April 1995, which was seen by the press as a test of Blair's ability to deal effectively with the trade unions, he won support for his new Clause Four by just under two-thirds of the vote. Blair had won a mandate for reform of the Labour Party, and the press and media recognized this as his personal triumph. He had tackled and tamed trade-union opposition, driven by the realization that he and the Labour Party would not be taken seriously by the public if the proposal were defeated.

"New Labour" rejected the Keynesian social democracy of "Old Labour" according to which the state should intervene to promote economic growth and ensure employment. Instead, Labour committed itself to the pursuit of low inflation through the increased powers of the Bank of England, and prepared to use interest rates in the same fashion as the Thatcher and Major governments had done. This meant that progressive taxation was ruled out and that Labour's past commitment to redistributing income and wealth was at an end.

These views were confirmed in a book written in 1996 by Peter Mandelson and Roger Liddle, two of Blair's spin doctors, which was entitled *The Blair Revolution: Can New Labour Deliver?* The authors wrote: "New Labour has set itself a bold task: to modernize Britain socially, economically and politically. In doing so it aims to build on Britain's strengths. Its mission is to create, not to destroy. Its strategy is to move forward from where Margaret Thatcher left off, rather than to dismantle every single thing she did." According to the authors, New Labour's approach was based upon five insights: the need for people to feel secure; investment, partnership and top quality education for all; the recognition of the potential of government; "One Nation socialism" going beyond the battles of the past between private and public interests; and, further, the need to unite public and private activities in the ideal of social cooperation.

The commitment to partnership between public and private sectors, the "Third Way," has been the fundamental characteristic of New Labour's strategy. This approach was not obvious from the start of Blair's leadership; it only became evident later, as signs of it repeatedly emerged in policy and in Blair's willingness to cut across the political barriers for advice and help. To the media and the public, Blair was more immediately the man who had stood up to the unions and abandoned nationalization. His personality, charm, and communication skills quickly endeared him to the British electorate and the Labour Party. His draft manifesto *New Labour, New Life for Britain* was overwhelmingly endorsed by the Labour Party Conference in October 1996. The subtler implications of his policy were not immediately detectable.

On 1 May 1997, Blair led the Labour Party to a sweeping victory in the general election: It won 44.4 percent of the vote, a total of 419 seats, and held a majority of 179 seats over the other political parties. He had successfully presented the modernization of the Labour Party as a precursor to the modernization of Britain: "New Labour, New Britain." Once in office, Blair moved quickly to establish his New Labour credentials. From the start, he decided to strengthen the center of government. Peter Mandelson was appointed minister without portfolio inside the Cabinet Office to coordinate the work of government departments, and a strategy committee of the cabinet was set up under Blair's own chairmanship. The Labour government also introduced a new ministerial code requiring that all media contacts and policy initiatives by ministers be cleared in advance by the prime minister.

In order to strengthen control further, Blair pressed the Labour Party Conference of 1997 to adopt *Partnership into Power,* a document that set out a radical program to reform the party's decision-making processes. In this program, the Party Conference lost its control over party policy to a 175-strong National Party Forum that would discuss policies, in a two-year revolving cycle; and the party's National Executive Committee (NEC) was altered. The women's section of the NEC was to be abolished and trade union representatives reduced from 17 to 12, although 6 were to be women. Three places on the NEC were to be reserved for members of the Labour government (or Party) appointed by the party leader/prime minister, and another, for the leader of the Labour group in the European Parliament. Six were to be set aside for representatives elected by postal ballot of all members. These changes weakened the Labour Party Conference, reduced the power of the trade unions, and strengthened Blair's hand as Labour leader.

Riding high on a groundswell of popular

support, Blair responded with a number of other initiatives. There was a veritable rush of activity to recognize the European Social Charter and to change the management of the national economy. In relation to Northern Ireland, Blair offered Sinn Fein a meeting with British officials involved in the peace process, without the precondition of a renewed cease-fire.

Blair's "New Labour" Party, in applying its philosophy, focused on five main areas. First, it sought to communicate with the public and to present a better image of Labour policies than it had previously. It also emphasized that there would be a greater openness in government. Secondly, it sought to apply market-led forces to its economic and social strategies, with an emphasis being placed upon the state acting as an enabler rather than simply as a provider. Thirdly, its emphasis is essentially pro-European and pro-American. Fourthly, it is committed to brokering a peace in Northern Ireland. Fifthly, it has essentially stressed the need for constitutional reform in such areas as the electoral system, the devolution of government, and changes in the House of Lords.

Ostensibly, New Labour is about communication and more open government. Blair has emerged as the great communicator and as a populist leader. This was most evident in August and September 1997, in the aftermath of the death of Diana, Princess of Wales, when his style effectively tapped into the popular mood.

The market-led nature of New Labour's approach, the second feature of Labour's new strategy, has also been blatantly obvious in the budgets of Gordon Brown (particularly in the "welfare-to-work" program that emerged in Brown's 1997 budget) and in more recent proposals to reform the welfare state. Indeed, the philosophy behind New Labour seems to be to reduce social need through an alliance between the state and the private sector. This approach was outlined in some detail by Blair on 18 March 1999, in the context of a government pledge to establish a 20-year program to eradicate child poverty. Blair suggested that a modern welfare state should be "active, not passive, genuinely providing people with a hand-up, not a hand-out." Indeed, he argued that

The third way in welfare is clear: not to dismantle it or to protect it unchanged but to reform it radically, taking its core values and applying them afresh to the modern world. . . . Poverty should not be a birthright. Being poor should not be a life sentence. We need to break the cycle of disadvantage so that children born into poverty are not condemned to social exclusion and deprivation. . . .

There will always be a mixture of universal and targeted help. But one is not superior or more principled than the other. (Laybourn 2000 p. 143, quoting *The Guardian*, 19 March 1999)

In effect, Blair's statement stressed that the state under New Labour would become an enabler as well as provider, helping people into jobs as well as ensuring the protection of their interests. It was now in partnership with, not hostile to, private industry.

Thirdly, New Labour is committed to Europe. In government it has followed through on that commitment, recognizing that the European Economic Community is responsible for half of British exports and about three million jobs in Britain. Indeed, in October 1997, Gordon Brown announced that the British government favored eventual entry into the European Monetary Union, albeit not in the lifetime of Blair's first Parliament, and only if agreed to by referendum.

The British political and military alliance with the United States is obvious. It was particularly evident in Blair's constant support for Bill Clinton, the U.S. president, in containing Saddam Hussein and Iraqi military expansion and in dealing with the rump Yugoslav government and the Kosovan refugee crisis through 1999. Indeed, during the crisis in Kosovo, Blair took a leading role in organizing the NATO action against the Serbian-dominated rump Yugoslav state.

Regarding Ireland—the fourth major area of its activity—the Blair government offered Sinn Fein, the Irish Republican political party, a meeting with officials to discuss the preconditions for a renewed cease-fire in May 1997. By July 1997, the Irish Republican Army (IRA) had

Prime Minister Tony Blair meeting with a Kosovan Albanian refugee couple at the Macedonian border, May 1999 (AFB/Corbis)

declared a cease-fire and Sinn Fein representatives were allowed to enter Stormont, although not allowed to be involved in the peace negotiations. In October 1997, Blair met with Gerry Adams, the Sinn Fein leader, and full-scale negotiations began. After many political twists, Blair focused the minds of all and gained an agreement on the Irish peace process, including provision for a Northern Ireland assembly, a North-South Ministerial Council of the Isles. There remains, however, the issue of implementing the agreement and the problem of decommissioning of arms, which the Irish Republican army seems reluctant to deliver, a vital part of the "Good Friday Agreement" of 1998.

The fifth major commitment of New Labour has been to constitutional and electoral reform. This commitment was first proclaimed in the queen's speech in May 1997. In June it was announced that the Liberal Democrats were being invited to take seats on the Cabinet Committee

to discuss constitutional reform and other mutual interests. In December 1998 the Electoral Reform Commission was set up under Lord Jenkins, the former Labour minister and cofounder of the SDP (Social Democratic Party). Lord Jenkins was set the task of devising a system of proportional representation for the Westminster elections, in preparation for a referendum on the issue. In October 1998, Blair accepted the commission's recommendation of an alternative Vote Top-Up System of proportional representation for parliamentary elections; and in June 1999, the elections for European M.P.s took place, based upon a system of proportional representation, with electors voting for parties instead of individuals.

Blair's Labour government also moved to create both a Scottish and a Welsh assembly in 1999, which allows for a greater representation of national minority interests in an attempt to undermine the demands for political independence in both Scotland and Wales. In addition, it has initiated steps to modernize the monarchy and discussions about replacing the House of Lords with an assembly largely made up of life-time peers, and a much-reduced number of hereditary peers, a category that eventually would be phased out.

One might well describe the Blair government as hyperactive. Indeed, it is fair to argue that Blair has achieved the objective he set himself, at the 1997 Labour Party Conference, of making his administration, as he said, "one of the great reforming governments in British history." Certainly, there have been constitutional, economic, and welfare reforms in abundance. Most certainly, the direction of British politics has been changed.

As Britain enters the twenty-first century, it is led by a Labour government with a zeal for reform. It is offering a wider participation in politics, more regional and local decision making, closer links with Europe, a modern political society, and above all, the Third Way in British politics—uniting the state and private industry in tackling the social and economic problems of the nation. The Blair government is thus far removed from its predecessors, with less dependence upon the trade unions and less emphasis upon the state intervening in the economy to ensure full employment. In capturing "middle England" and the middle classes, Labour under Blair has loosened its traditional bonds. Labour is no longer the class-based party of 1918, nor even the more loosely based trade union party of 1983. However, the support from "middle England" cannot always be relied upon; the fuel crisis of mid-September 2000, when truck drivers and farmers blockaded fuel depots and almost brought Britain to a halt in a week, exposed the volatility of the British voter, as opinion polls indicated that Labour's support had fallen from about 44–46 percent to about 34–36 percent. The Labour government has recovered popular support; but the fuel crisis has revealed that the class vote that was taken for granted in the past cannot be relied on in the new, less class-based politics.

Keith Laybourn

See also: Brown, Gordon; Cook, Robin; Major, John; Straw, Jack
References and Further Reading: Anderson, Paul, and Nyta Mann, 1997, *Safety First: The Making of New Labour* (London: Granta); Blair, Tony, 1996, *New Britain: My Vision of a Young Country* (London: Fourth Estate); Laybourn, Keith, 2000, *A Century of Labour: A History of the Labour Party, 1900 to 2000* (Stroud, UK: Sutton); Mandelson, Peter, and Roger Liddle, 1996, *The Blair Revolution—Can New Labour Now Deliver?* (London: Faber and Faber); Panitch, Leo, and Colin Leys, 1997, *The End of Parliamentary Socialism: From New Left to New Labour* (London: Verso); Rentoul, John, 1992, *Tony Blair* (London: Warner Books).

Bonar Law, Andrew
(1858–1923) [PM, CE]

Andrew Bonar Law was prime minister for barely six months, in 1922 and 1923, but was a tremendously important political figure in the decade leading up to his premiership. He became the Conservative leader in October 1911, revitalizing and reorganizing the party, and was an important supporter of David Lloyd George from 1916 until 1922, when he replaced him as prime minister. He was also the first person of colonial birth and upbringing to become prime minister, and also the first person of a relatively humble, middle-class background to rise to the top of "the greasy pole" of Conservative politics.

Bonar Law was born at Kingston, New Brunswick, Canada, on 16 September 1858, the fourth child of the Rev. James Law, a Presbyterian minister, and Elizabeth Kidston. He was educated at Gilbertfield School, Hamilton. His father was from Portuish in North Antrim, Ireland, and returned there in 1877. Bonar Law himself had left Canada in 1870 to join his mother's prosperous family business connection in Glasgow and Helenburgh, completing his education at Glasgow High School. In 1874 he joined a merchant bank owned by his brothers, the Kidston brothers, and, at the age of 27, in 1885, he bought a partnership in the iron firm of William Jacks. In 1891 he married Annie Pitcairn, who died in 1909.

He began his parliamentary career as Unionist M.P. for Blackfriars Glasgow in 1900 but was defeated there in January 1906. In May 1906 he was elected to the "safe" (strong Unionist) Dulwich seat. By this time he had become the leader of the Unionist section of the Conservative and Unionist party and he gave up his seat to contest the much more marginal Manchester Northwest seat in December 1910, in the Unionist free-trade heartland. His move misfired, but he was elected for Bootle, also in Lancashire, in a parliamentary by-election in March 1911. Finally, he contested and won the Glasgow Central seat in 1918, which he held until his death in 1923.

In politics, Bonar Law was identified with the two major issues of tariff reform and Ulster Unionism. The latter arose from his Irish Presbyterian background. His tariff reform interests, however, emerged from the fact that as a Canadian by birth he was attracted by the imperial tariff preference arrangements advocated by Joseph Chamberlain at the beginning of the twentieth century. As a businessman he was also fully aware of the imperfect nature of the free-trade policy that the Liberals and the Conservatives were still advocating. In any case, he believed that the revenue from protective measures could also be used to finance the social legislation needed to ameliorate the social conditions of the British working class. Driven by this interest, his first speech before Parliament, in February 1901, was in defense of Joseph Chamberlain and Cecil Rhodes; and on 22 April 1902, he spoke in favor of Sir Michael Hicks Beach's duty on corn.

This brought him to the forefront of national politics and earned him the parliamentary secretaryship at the Board of Trade, which gave him an ideal position from which to press for imperial preference. He spoke in favor of the Sugar Bounty Convention and supported Chamberlain's imperial preference campaign when it was launched in May 1903. He lost his seat in the Liberal landslide in the 1906 general election, but he was found the "safe" Dulwich seat in May 1906. With the illness and retirement of Joseph Chamberlain, Bonar Law and Austen Chamberlain were at the head of the 157 Unionist M.P.s who dominated the much-diminished Conservative and Unionist Party at this time.

Although Bonar Law was seen as an extreme tariff reformer, a "whole-hogger," he was also pragmatic and advocated the holding of a referendum on the matter. He realized that there was no possibility of revoking the 1911 Parliament Act, passed by the Liberals to restrict the legislative blocking abilities of the House of Lords. Having been reelected to Parliament in 1911 after a brief absence, he was elected leader of the Unionists in November 1911, following the resignation of Arthur Balfour. Since the Unionists were still divided between those advocating protection and those committed to free trade, the possibility of an electoral disaster remained strong. Ever the pragmatist, Bonar Law dropped his commitment to a referendum on tariff reform at a shadow cabinet meeting in April 1912; and although the same meeting indicated the need for a food tax, he accepted that this would have to be submitted independently to the electorate. As such, then, tariff reform became less important to the Unionist cause.

Bonar Law still maintained his commitment to tariff reform but now placed greater emphasis on maintaining the Union with Ireland, so as to keep his forces together in their desire to defeat the Liberal Party. He pressed the issue of Ulster Unionism from 1911 until the all-party truce in July 1914, on the eve of World War I. He endorsed the Ulster Unionist opposition to an Ireland separate from Britain, both in his speeches and in his support for the military-style drilling that took place at the Balmoral demonstration on 9 April 1912, as well as in the Blenheim Pledge of 29 July 1912, when he could not conceive of limits to the lengths he would go to in order to protect Ulster. Although he seemed to be contemplating the possibility of some type of direct attack on parliamentary sovereignty, he was prepared to compromise in favor of some form of exclusion for Ulster from any Home Rule bill for Ireland. These issues dominated the Parliamentary debates of early 1914, when there was discussion of amending the army act to prevent British military intervention in Ulster.

It was only the outbreak of World War I, in August 1914, that put an end to the internecine strife in British politics—strife that was evident as late as 23 July 1914, in the Buckingham

Palace talks. Nevertheless, six weeks after the outbreak of war, on 15 September, the domestic political truce was temporarily halted. Asquith had put forward the third Home Rule bill on the statutes, but suspended its implementation until the end of the war. Bonar Law reacted badly, leading his party out of the Commons. In the wake of the Easter Rising, he was also involved in negotiations organized by David Lloyd George to find a settlement; but when these failed he was placed in the embarrassing position of dividing his party. He came to accept that Home Rule would occur, and therefore, in 1920, he supported the fourth Home Rule bill —the Government of Ireland Bill. He gave the Anglo-Irish treaty of December 1921 his support, comforted by the knowledge that the Northern Unionists would not be coerced and, indeed, would be guaranteed their own territory, which subsequently came to be known as Northern Ireland.

World War I was the other major issue that dominated Bonar Law's political career. He led the patriotic opposition to the Liberal government from August 1914 to May 1915, when he was drawn into a coalition government under Asquith, serving as secretary of state for the colonies. He continued to lead the Conservative and Unionist Party, although he was under serious attack from Edward Carson and was becoming increasingly disillusioned with Asquith's running of the war effort. When Asquith resigned, on 5 December 1916, Bonar Law advocated his replacement by David Lloyd George, to whom he became deputy leader. He also accepted the post of chancellor of the exchequer. From then onward, he acted as Lloyd George's junior, retaining the post of chancellor until January 1919. He then assumed the role of leader of the Commons until March 1921.

As chancellor of the exchequer he was a member of the war cabinet, mainly responsible for organizing the financing of the war effort. He replaced short-term loans with long-term war loans, which raised £2 billion between January and March 1917. In October 1917 he announced the issue of war bonds for an unlimited amount, which was also successful. He was barely involved in the details of the war, but gave Lloyd George his strong support at times when Lloyd George's authority was being challenged.

At the end of World War I, Bonar Law and the Conservative and Unionist Party could have won the 1918 general election, given that the Liberal Party was divided and the Labour Party was still emerging. Yet Bonar Law decided to support the continuation of a coalition government under the premiership of David Lloyd George. Why he did this has been subject to speculation, ranging from the fact that the coalition had won World War I to the possibility that the coalition would ensure that the Liberals remained divided, and the fact that the 1918 Representation of the People Act had tripled the electorate, which also was influenced by the knowledge that the coalition had won the war. In any event, the coalition government won 474 seats, and thus had a majority of 252 seats.

In the new coalition government, Bonar Law moved from the post of chancellor of the exchequer to that of Lord Privy Seal, and he remained leader of the House. He was one of the signatories of the Treaty of Versailles on 28 June 1919, although he played little part in the negotiations. Bonar Law had endured a number of personal tragedies including the death of his two sons in the war in 1917, and he himself was in ill health. As a result he retired as Conservative leader in 1921, although he remained an M.P.

In October 1922 the Conservative Party, despite the opposition of Austen Chamberlain, its new leader, decided to withdraw its support from David Lloyd George because of a range of policy issues and scandals. Lloyd George resigned, and Bonar Law, now reinstated as the leader of the Unionist Party, agreed on 23 October 1922 to allow his name to be put forward for prime minister. His premiership lasted little more than six months, and his government failed to tackle the three main issues of the day: American loans and German reparations, high unemployment, and a shortage of housing. He resigned on 19 May 1923, suffering from cancer of the throat, and died on 30 October 1923.

Bonar Law's career leaves the impression that he lacked ambition. Despite his rhetoric, which marked him as a trenchant Unionist, he was a pragmatic politician. His political record was, nevertheless, impressive. He was a most effective chancellor of the exchequer, a powerful leader of the Unionist Party, and a formidable leader of the House of Commons. He could also be ruthless, if needed, being prepared to ditch the coalition government in December 1915 and again in October 1922. He was certainly one of those politicians who combined the almost contradictory tendencies of ambition and deference. Dubbed the "unknown prime minister" by Robert Blake, Bonar Law's lasting contribution to politics is that he reorganized the Conservative and Unionist Party at a time when it looked as though they, rather than the Liberals, might disintegrate.

Keith Laybourn

See also: Asquith, Herbert Henry; Baldwin, Stanley; Balfour, Arthur James; Chamberlain, Austen; Hicks Beach, Sir Michael; Lloyd George, David
References and Further Reading: Blake, Robert, 1955, *The Unknown Prime Minister: The Life and Times of Andrew Bonar Law, 1858–1923* (London: Eyre & Spottiswoode); Blake, Robert, 1985, *The Conservative Party from Peel to Thatcher* (London: Metheun); Ramsden, John, 1978, *The History of the Conservative Party: The Age of Balfour and Baldwin* (London: Longman).

Bridgeman, W. C. (Viscount Bridgeman)
(1864–1935) [HS]

William Clive Bridgeman was born on 31 December 1864, the son of the Rev. Orlando Bridgeman, third son of the second Earl of Bradford. He was educated at Eton and at Trinity College, Cambridge. An able cricketer, he became president of the Marylebone Cricket Club (MCC) in 1931. He married Caroline Parker in 1895. He began his political career as Conservative M.P. for the Northern (Oswestry) division of Shropshire between 1906 and 1929. He developed into a substantial political figure, although he was never a politician of the first order.

Bridgeman saw himself as a "Disraelian" Conservative, interested in social reform. He was an active backbencher who became a junior opposition whip between 1911 and 1915, becoming a government whip in the wartime

coalition of Herbert Henry Asquith. Between June and December 1916, he was a chief whip, as parliamentary secretary to the Treasury. He gained this post toward the end of Asquith's premiership, and lost it when David Lloyd George became prime minister. However, within a few weeks he had been appointed parliamentary secretary to the newly created Ministry of Labour, a post he held until January 1919, when he became parliamentary secretary to the Board of Trade. About eighteen months later, in August 1920, he became parliamentary secretary for the mines, the government having taken over control of the mines in 1917. He held this post until 1922, although the government had handed the coal mines back to the owners on 1 April 1921. When Andrew Bonar Law formed his new Conservative government, in October 1922, Bridgeman was appointed home secretary. He continued in this post under Stanley Baldwin until the first Labour government was formed, in January 1924.

Bridgeman left little impact on domestic policy; and even as he was emerging as a grandee of the Conservative Party, he does not appear to have possessed outstanding leadership qualities. Out of office during the first Labour government, he returned as First Lord of the Admiralty between 1924 and 1929, when he was recognized to be a true patriot. He retired from the House of Commons after Labour's victory in May and June 1929, having been awarded the title of viscount and thus promoted to the House of Lords. He died on 14 August 1935.

Keith Laybourn

See also: Asquith, Herbert Henry; Baldwin, Stanley; Bonar Law, Andrew; Lloyd George, David
References and Further Reading: Middlemass, K., and J. Barnes, 1969, *Baldwin: A Biography* (London: Weidenfeld and Nicolson); Williamson, Philip (ed.), 1988, *The Modernisation of the Conservative Politics: The Diaries and Letters of William Bridgeman, 1904–1935* (London: Historians' Press).

Brittan, Sir Leon
(1939–) [HS]

Leon Brittan was born on 25 September 1939, the son of Joseph and Rebecca Brittan. He was educated at Haberdasher Aske's school before entering Trinity College, Cambridge University. He then pursued a legal career, was called to the bar, Inner Temple, in 1962, and later obtained other legal honors. He married Diane Peterson in 1980.

Brittan's political career began in 1974 when he became M.P. for Richmond, Cleveland, and Whitby. He also served as M.P. for Richmond from 1986 to 1988. Above all, he is remembered as being one of the new Thatcherite M.P.s who rose to power and influence in the early 1980s, although he himself later diverged from Margaret Thatcher's hostile line on the European Economic Community.

Brittan became chief secretary to the exchequer in January 1981 and held that post until June 1983. He then became home secretary in Thatcher's second administration, holding the post between June 1983 and September 1985. He was a fairly routine home secretary but was regarded as rather "wet" by Thatcher, who proceeded to blame him for the poor presentation of government policy that she believed had led to the defeat of a number of members of her government in the parliamentary by-election of 1985. After the election, Brittan was effectively demoted to the post of minister of trade, a post he held for four months.

However, this period did produce one major controversy, when he and Thatcher decided that the only way to rescue the Westland company, which manufactured helicopters, was to force it into partnership with the American firm Sikorsky. Michael Heseltine, the British defense secretary, objected to this approach, instead favoring the construction of a rival European consortium to rescue the company, and waged an open campaign against the Thatcher and Brittan line in December 1985 and January 1986. At this point Thatcher got Solicitor General Sir Patrick Mayhew to write a letter complaining about "material inaccuracies" in Heseltine's campaign. Brittan arranged to have this letter "leaked" by Downing Street, and within hours, selective passages were in the hands of the press association. The next day, the *Sun*'s front page featured a picture of Heseltine with the headline "You Liar." Mayhew was outraged at the leak of what he regarded as an internal and confidential letter, and he demanded an immediate inquiry into the source of the leak, even threatening Thatcher with the police if she refused. A few days later she acceded to an inquiry; and on 9 January, she informed the Cabinet that all future statements about the Westland issue had to be cleared by her office. Heseltine was not prepared to accept this restraint and walked out of the cabinet, immediately holding a press conference condemning Thatcher's style of government. Brittan subsequently misled the House of Commons on important details of the affair and had to apologize. He resigned on 24 January 1986, admitting that his continued role in government would weaken its effectiveness.

Later in 1986, Brittan was rewarded with a knighthood. He became a member of the European Commission in 1989, and served as vice-president of the commission between 1989 and 1993 and again in 1995. He continues to work with the European Commission.

Keith Laybourn

See also: Thatcher, Margaret
References and Further Reading: Evans, Brendan, 1999, *Thatcherism and British Politics, 1975–1999* (Stroud, UK: Sutton).

Brooke, Henry (Lord Brooke of Cumnor) (1904–1984) [HS]

Henry Brooke was born on 9 April 1903, the younger son of Leonard Leslie Brooke, an author and illustrator of children's books, and his wife, Sybil Diana. He was educated at Marlborough College and Balliol College, Oxford, and declined a fellowship at Balliol. In 1927 and 1928 he worked at a Quaker settlement for the unemployed in the Rhondda Valley, in South Wales. He joined the staff of the *Economist* in 1929 and was a member of the Conservative Party's Research Department between 1930 and 1938. He also edited the journal *Truth* for a short time.

Brooke was a member of the London County Council in the 1930s and entered Parliament after winning a parliamentary by-election at Lewisham West in 1938, retaining the seat until

1945. From 1946 to 1948, he was the last deputy chairman of the Southern Railway Company. In 1950, however, he returned to Parliament as member for Hampstead, holding the seat until 1966. In 1954 he became financial secretary to the Treasury, and in 1957 became minister of housing and local government in Harold Macmillan's Conservative government. His main role seems to have been to tackle the smog pollution that frequently blighted London and to maintain the rapid pace of new housing construction promised by the Conservative government.

In October 1961 Brooke became the first chief secretary of the Treasury, with the responsibility for control of public expenditure; then, paymaster general; and in 1962, home secretary. His main activity in the latter role seems to have been to adopt a harsh attitude toward immigration. However, he lost his post with the formation of Harold Wilson's Labour government in October 1964, and he also lost his parliamentary seat in the 1966 general election. He was then raised to the House of Lords, as life peer, becoming Lord Brooke of Cumnor. He spoke on the Conservative front bench for a time but was forced to retire later, due to physical debilitation caused by Parkinson's disease.

Brooke died on 29 March 1984, leaving behind his wife, Barbara Muriel, whom he had married in 1933. She had become a life peer in her own right in 1964 and had joined him on the Conservative front bench at that time. Rarely has a man-and-wife team occupied such a high position in British politics.

Keith Laybourn

See also: Eden, Sir Anthony; Home, Sir Alec Douglas; Macmillan, Harold
References and Further Reading: Lamb, Richard, 1995, *The Macmillan Years, 1957–63: The Emerging Truth* (London: John Murray); Macmillan, Harold, 1973, *At the End of the Day* (London: Macmillan).

Brown, George
(Lord George-Brown of Jevington)
(1914–1985) [FS]

George Brown was one of the most outrageous figures in British politics in the 1960s. A "colorful" character known for his short-tempered outbursts and his liking for alcohol, he was nevertheless a modestly effective foreign secretary for eighteen months in Harold Wilson's Labour government of the late 1960s, before his ill-tempered resignation in March 1968, in which he accused Wilson of forming a presidential-style government and going above the heads of his cabinet colleagues. His parliamentary career was brought to an end in 1970, when he lost his Belper seat in the general election.

Alfred George Brown was born on 2 September 1914, in the Peabody Buildings in Lambeth, London. His father, of Irish extraction, also had been born in London and made his living driving a Lyons truck, delivering cakes. The young George was educated at an elementary school on Gray Street, Blackfriars, from which he went to West Square Central School, a school for working-class children who showed academic promise. His father lost his job in the General Strike of 1926. He later managed to get work by driving a newspaper van for the *Evening Standard,* but his periods of unemployment meant that George was often raised in poverty. Yet George enjoyed his early life and was greatly influenced by Father Sankey—a High Church Anglican and the brother of Lord Sankey, who was in charge of a Royal Commission on Coal in 1919—who was priest at St. Andrew's-by-the-Wardrobe (Brown 1972, p. 24). Influenced by him, Brown remained a lifelong Anglican.

Brown first gained employment in the purchasing department of a firm of merchants and general manufacturers in the City of London. When that job was eliminated, he moved on to the fur department of the John Lewis stores. From there, at the age of 22, he became a full-time officer in the Transport and General Workers' Union (TGWU), which gave him exposure to a wide range of tasks in trade union and political work. In 1927 he married Sophie Levine. During World War II he continued with his work at TGWU.

At the end of the war, Brown was sponsored by TGWU as a candidate for Parliament and was selected for the Belper constituency. He was elected to Parliament in July 1945, in Attlee's landslide Labour government, and was immediately appointed parliamentary private secretary (PPS) to George Isaacs, the minister of labor and national service. He held this post until 1947. This was followed by other minor appointments; he became PPS to the chancellor of the exchequer in 1947, joint parliamentary secretary to the Ministry of Agriculture and Fisheries between 1947 and 1951, and joint parliamentary secretary to the minister of works between April and October 1951. Brown, following the defeat of the Labour government in the general election of October 1951, became the Labour spokesman for defense in the shadow cabinet. In this period, he was greatly affected by the internal politics of the Labour Party, which pitted Bevanite socialists, with their demand for an extension of public ownership, against the Gaitskellites, with their desire to remove Clause Four, the Labour Party's commitment to public ownership, from the party's constitution. This contest and battles over nuclear disarmament and membership in the European Economic Community continued to divide the party. In general, Brown tried to rise above the internecine conflict.

Harold Wilson's victory in the 1964 general election brought Brown to the forefront of politics. He was immediately given the new post of first secretary of state and secretary of state for economic affairs (a single post), a position he held from 1964 to 1966. The Department of Economic Affairs (DEA), which he thus headed, was an experiment that failed. It was intended to recast the machinery of government to meet the needs of the late twentieth century, and to introduce social accountancy into British politics in place of the financial accountancy of the Treasury. The problem was that even as the new Labour government was trying to develop the social requirements of the modern age, it was facing serious economic, trade, and financial difficulties that were forcing it back into the Treasury's fold. As a result, Brown's national plan, which contained a prices and incomes policy, was falling under a hailstorm of criticism toward the end of 1965 from both employers and trade unions. The DEA declined further in 1966, as it became clear that the prime minister was reluctant to allow it to operate free from Treasury control. Brown also came to be identified with a minority group in the government that favored devaluation rather than major cuts in expenditures. He offered to resign in August 1966 but was recommended to the post of foreign secretary, which he accepted on 11 August 1966, just after the third reading of his Prices and Incomes Bill. The DEA lingered on, but its functions were eventually swallowed up by other departments.

Brown spent an eventful eighteen months at the Foreign Office before resigning. He had to deal with the Arab-Israeli War of June 1967, prompted partly by the Egyptian closure to Israeli ships of the Strait of Tiran, which prevented access via the Gulf of Aqaba to the Israeli port of Eilat. During the months preceding these events, Brown had tried to improve relations between Egypt and Israel by personal interventions with the Russians. However, these attempts were to no avail. He was also concerned with the issues of European integration, the Vietnam War, and the U.S.-Soviet Cold War. Indeed, he attempted to get President Lyndon Johnson to halt the mass bombing of Vietnam.

Brown was a somewhat unusual foreign secretary and was known for his occasional gaffes. However, his resignation on the night of 14–15 March 1968 was entirely voluntary and was caused by disagreement on a matter of principle: He objected to the prime minister's pattern of acting unilaterally and often without the knowledge of the ministers. His letter of resignation to Harold Wilson, on 15 March 1968, made it clear that he took exception to "the way this Government is run and the manner in which we reach our decisions."

The particular incident that sparked the dispute was Wilson's decision to ask the queen, at a hurriedly called, late-night meeting of the Privy Council, to announce a bank holiday to meet the American request to discuss international financial arrangements and to steady the chaotic gold situation that then existed in the international markets. Calling a bank holiday would shut the banks and stop financial maneuvering. Brown's resignation was also sparked by the government's decision to deny South Africa certain categories of arms, including Buccaneer aircraft, at a time when British industry needed orders and when British interests in the southern part of Africa needed protection. Brown felt that the provision of such arms would not jeopardize black interests in South Africa and that his own position on the issue had been undermined.

On 18 March, Brown took the opportunity to make a personal statement on his resignation to the House of Commons "in order to deny some of the wilder speculations and exaggerations." Mentioning the gravity of the financial situation, he stated: "It is in just such a situation that it is essential for Cabinet Government to be maintained if democracy is to be assured, and equally it is [in] just such a situation that the temptation to depart from it is at its greatest. Power can very easily pass not merely from Cabinet to one or two Ministers, but effectively to sources quite outside the political control altogether." He added: "My purpose in the action I have taken is not to challenge the Prime Minister or to set out to lead a left-wing revolt against the Cabinet.... I do, however, feel most strongly that if the authority and success of this Government is to be reestablished, as, indeed, it must be, then the basis on which they take decisions must be changed and their communication within the Government and with those outside must be really improved."

George Brown's departure from the government created some problems, since he had been deputy leader of the Labour Party since 1960, and normally the deputy leader would be a member of a Labour government. Brown consulted Harold Wilson about his continuing in this post, but Wilson did not seem to care one way or the other. As a result Brown continued in that post, feeling that there was no obvious successor and believing that his resignation would only open up new wounds and arguments within the party. He wrote to Douglas Houghton, chairman of the Parliamentary Labour Party, on 26 March 1968, suggesting that he would stay on despite the anomalous situation in which he found himself, in order to ensure Labour's victory at the next general election.

Brown remained deputy leader of the Labour Party until 1970 but lost his seat in the general election of June 1970. He was made a life peer, becoming Lord George-Brown of Jevington, in

1970. He continued to play a marginal role in Labour's political activities but left the party to form a social democratic organization in 1976. He died in 1985.

Keith Laybourn

See also: Gaitskell, Hugh; Wilson, Harold
References and Further Reading: Brown, George, 1971, 1972, and 1975, *In My Way* (London: Gollancz).

Brown, Gordon
(1951–) [CE]

Brown is a leading figure in Tony Blair's Labour government, which came to power in May 1997, and one of the architects of the "Third Way" philosophy on which are based the Labour government's efforts to draw upon both public and private institutions in order to secure industrial growth and social provision.

James Gordon Brown was born in Glasgow on 20 February 1951, and was educated there at Kirkcaldy High School. He later attended Edinburgh University, where he obtained a Ph.D. in 1982. Before entering Parliament, he was a lecturer at the University of Edinburgh, between 1975 and 1980, and a journalist for Scottish Television, becoming head of Scottish Television's Current Affairs department between 1980 and 1983. He is the author of *The Red Paper on Scotland* (1975); *Scotland, the Real Divide* (1983); *Maxton* (1986); *Where There Is Greed* (1989); *Values, Visions and Voices* (1989); *John Smith: Life and Soul of the Party* (1994); and *An Anthology of Socialism* (1995). He is also a member of the Transport and General Workers' Union (TGWU).

Gordon Brown's parliamentary career began in 1983 when he was elected as M.P. for Dunfermline East, a seat he has represented ever since. He rose quickly in Labour circles. He was a member of the Scottish Labour Party executive between 1977 and 1983; chairman of the Labour Party's Scottish Council between 1983 and 1984; and chairman of the Labour Party in Scotland in 1987. He performed the roles of Labour's shadow chief secretary to the Treasury between 1987 and 1989 and shadow secretary of trade and industry between 1989 and 1992, before serving as shadow chancellor of the ex-

Gordon Brown delivering a speech at the Labour Party Conference in Brighton, 25 September 2000 (Reuters NewMedia, Inc./Corbis)

chequer between 1992 and 1997. Also in 1992 he became a member of the National Executive Committee of the Labour Party. With Labour's victory in May 1997, he was appointed chancellor of the exchequer, and he committed his efforts to maintaining controls on public expenditure at the same time as targeting education and health for increased financial expenditure, and encouraging New Labour's "Third Way" policy of cooperation between the private and public sectors of the economy.

This New Labour approach has emerged in Brown's overall economic strategy. He announced that the Bank of England, rather than the government, would take responsibility for setting interest rates through a new monetary policy committee. In June 1997, task forces were established on the National Health Service (NHS), efficiency, and youth justice.

The market-led nature of New Labour's approach—the second feature of Labour policy—was, of course, blatantly obvious in Brown's 1997 budget, particularly in the program officially titled "Welfare to Work." It was also evident in the statement, in November 1998, that pledged that there would be a fundamental reform of the welfare state and that proposed a tax credit scheme for poor working families. In December, as part of that strategy, the government pressed forward with a reduction in the benefits for single parents, which led 47 Labour M.P.s to vote against the action, on a three-line whip, and 14 others to abstain. The Labour government in fact won by 457 votes to 107, with the support of the Conservatives.

In January 1998, as part of this new strategy, the Blair government did announce a New Deal for the unemployed between the ages of 18 and 24 years. The program offered work with subsidized private employers, education or training, self-employment, or a variety of other alternatives, with the goal of eliminating unemployment by the twenty-first century. And in March 1998, Brown announced a redistributive budget strategy that included the introduction of tax credits for working families, starting in October 1999; a disabled persons tax credit; increases in child benefits; subsidies for employers to take on the long-term unemployed; and extra spending in many other areas. It seems that New Labour has attempted to soften the side effects of its compromise with market forces (i.e., increasing socioeconomic inequalities) by redistributing income.

Gordon Brown has been as responsible as Tony Blair for the implementation of the policies of New Labour. Until September 2000 these policies seemed to be working. However, the fuel crisis of mid-September 2000, caused by truck drivers and farmers blockading the fuel depots, led Labour to lose almost a quarter of its support in the opinion polls; Brown's intransigent stand against reducing the tax on gasoline was almost as emphatic as that of Tony Blair. The general election of 7 June 2001, however, returned the Labour Party to office with a majority just short of its landslide victory of 1997. It would appear that the fuel crisis of September–October 2000 was not such a vital factor in the election when compared with the perception of the electorate that Conservative Party policies were far too right-wing.

Keith Laybourn

See also: Blair, Tony; Cook, Robin; Straw, Jack
References and Further Reading: Anderson, Paul, and Nyta Mann, 1997, *Safety First: The Making of New Labour* (London: Granta); Panitch, Leo, and C. Leys, 1997, *The End of Parliamentary Socialism: From New Left to New Labour* (London: Verso).

Bruce, Henry Austin
(Lord Aberdare)
(1815–1895) [HS]

Henry Austin Bruce, the first Baron Aberdare, was born on 16 April 1815 at Duffryn, Aberdare, in Wales, the second son of John Bruce and his wife, Sarah. He was educated at Swansea Grammar School and then went on to work in a legal practice run by his uncle, the later Lord Justice Bruce. In 1837 he became a barrister through Lincoln's Inn. He retired early, in 1843, to visit Italy and Sicily for his health. In 1847 he became a magistrate for Merthyr Tydfil and Aberdare.

Bruce's political career began in 1852 when he was elected Liberal M.P. for Merthyr Tydfil. In November 1862 he was appointed undersecretary of state for the Home Department in Lord Palmerston's government. In April 1864 he became vice president of the Council on Education, and a member of the Charity Commission, serving in the latter capacity until 1866.

In November 1868, Bruce was defeated at Merthyr Tydfil, but he won a seat in Renfrewshire on 25 July 1869, whereupon William Gladstone invited him to be home secretary in his Liberal government. As home secretary (1869–1873) his main work seems to have been to reduce the number of public houses and to introduce stricter licensing hours for the consumption of alcohol in public houses, imposing an 11 P.M. curfew in the provinces and a midnight curfew in London. He also became embroiled in the debates about the disestablishment of the Church of England in England and Wales. In 1873 he became Lord President of the Council and was raised to the House of Lords as Lord Aberdare. However, he was forced to resign as lord president in 1874, when Disraeli replaced Gladstone as prime minister.

For the rest of his life, Aberdare gave his time to educational, economic, and social issues. He was president of the Royal Historical Society from 1878 to 1892 and chairman of the National Africa Company. He was also committed to extending education in Wales, encouraging the introduction of the Welsh Intermediate Ed-

ucation Act of 1889 and acting as president of University College, Cardiff, when it was formed in 1881. In 1893 he was also appointed chairman of the Royal Commission on the Aged Poor. He died on 25 July 1895.

Keith Laybourn

See also: Gladstone, William Ewart; Palmerston, Lord

References and Further Reading: Feuchtwanger, E., 1975, *Gladstone* (London: Allen Lane); Jenkins, Roy, 1995, *Gladstone* (London: Macmillan).

Bute, Earl of (John Stuart)
(1713–1792) [PM, FS]

The first Scot to head the Treasury, Bute was perhaps the most reviled leading minister in British history. He was attacked not least for being Scottish; English graphic satires during and long after his ministry almost invariably featured tartan plaids and starveling Scots along with the jackboot, which was the usual visual pun on his name.

Of Scottish royal blood, Bute was the scion of the family of Stuart, seated for centuries on the Isle of Bute. He was lucky in a companionable marriage, contracted in August 1736 with an intelligent and devoted woman, the daughter of the celebrated Lady Mary Wortley Montagu (both Lady Mary and her husband, Edward Wortley Montagu, disapproved of the match). In 1761, after nearly 25 years of marriage, Bute's wife (also Mary Wortley Montagu) inherited a fortune of well over one million pounds from her father, and soon afterward, a good estate from her mother.

Early in his adult life, between 1737 to 1741, Bute served as one of the 16 elective Scottish representative peers; but for the 20 years after that, he eschewed Parliament to follow a political career centered on the court and family of Frederick, Prince of Wales. Having met the prince by chance in 1747, Bute was soon drawn into his circle and became an indispensable friend and adviser to his household. Bute was an imposing and handsome man, tall and well built, who had often acted in private theatricals and took a keen interest in the visual arts. His greatest and most sustained passion, though, was botany. He worked closely with Princess

Augusta during the 1750s and 1760s in shaping the initial layout and choosing the plant collection for Kew Gardens. The gardens begun under Frederick's patronage became a center of horticultural experimentation and botanical display, around which was organized the larger park created under George III, which survives today.

Bute became a Gentleman of the Prince's Bedchamber in October 1750, and though Prince Frederick died in March 1751, Bute was retained by his widow out of a friendship that scandal later magnified into an affair. Bute became increasingly close to the young Prince George, later George III. The prince's official tutor was Lord Waldegrave. Although Bute sought this post, he was temporarily prevented from attaining it by opposition from George II; in 1755 he did become official tutor, and he had a great influence on the young prince in the years before his accession to the throne. No doubt due to the insistence of Princess Augusta and against the express wishes of the king and of the Duke of Newcastle (who was then prime minister), Bute was appointed Groom of the Stole in October 1756. Under his close supervision, Prince George shook off the habits of indolence that had dismayed Waldegrave, and applied himself to historical, scientific, and architectural studies. The power of the influential tutor over the prince's household became increasingly evident in October 1760, with the death of George II and the accession of the prince, who called Bute his "dearest friend."

The new king opened his reign on a note of military victory and optimism, but in Horace Walpole's summary, "a passionate, domineering woman, and a Favourite without talents, soon drew a cloud over this shining prospect" (Walpole, 1985). Bute was immediately sworn a member of the Privy Council and took the appointments of Groom of the Stole and First Gentleman of the Bedchamber. The Newcastle-Pitt ministry was forced to allow Bute to attend all cabinet meetings, though his posts were not parliamentary but solely within the royal household. He was the most important member of the king's household, and, it was feared, the man to whom the king intended to entrust his government.

Over the next few years, the main struggle at the center of politics was the fight to control and limit the influence of Bute, to prevent him from becoming prime minister and shaper of policy. His and the king's greatest inclination was to secure peace by withdrawing from the Seven Years' War, which by 1760 had brought popular victories and great overseas conquests. In May 1761, Bute once more entered Parliament as a Scottish representative peer. Earlier, in March, he had secured an appointment as secretary of state for the Northern Department (foreign secretary). The Earl of Holderness, who had held this post since 1754, was given a royal pension of £4,000 to step down. Newcastle and William Pitt (the Elder) remained in office, but were coming under increasing pressure to negotiate an end to the war they had so successfully conducted. By the end of that year, secretly from the other ministers and answering only to the king, Bute was conducting negotiations with France in preparation for Britain's withdrawal from the war and abandonment of its ally, Prussia.

Bute was pressuring the king to take in more Tories to the ministry—a principled stand but one that would have alienated large numbers of electors, as would any attempt to drop Pitt. When Pitt was forced from office in October 1761, Bute was mobbed on his way to Parliament. On 26 May 1762, the Duke of Newcastle, having never enjoyed the confidence of the young king, finally resigned, and the next day Bute replaced him as First Lord of the Treasury (prime minister). Henry Fox was brought in to manage the Commons for the court party, and used bribery and bullying of M.P.s on an unprecedented scale to win votes in favor of a peace settlement. Former supporters of the Duke of Newcastle were purged from office. The so-called Massacre of the Pelhamite Innocents in 1762–1763 affected not only members of Parliament but even supporters of Newcastle and Pitt in county and local offices. Disgruntled Whig politicians, with the benefit of secret advice and covert funds, actively propagated the myth that the king was a despot; at the same time, Bute was popularly depicted as the lover of the dowager princess and a favorite who dominated the young king.

The Peace of Paris was signed on 10 February

1763 and proved vastly unpopular, the rumor being that Bute must have been bribed by the French to even consider giving back the productive sugar islands in return for the snowy wastes of Canada and the unpopulated woods of North America west of the Mississippi. The withdrawal from the war on what were seen to be disadvantageous terms inflamed opposition sentiment. Soon after the unpopular Peace of Paris, Bute's ministry imposed a tax on cider, which predictably caused such a storm that his political position became untenable. He resigned on 9 April 1763 and was forced also to retire from the court, in order to persuade the remaining ministers that he really was removed from the king's counsels. On 28 September he also resigned his court office of Keeper of the Privy Purse, but was still denounced by both the public and politicians as the "minister behind the curtain." He carried on a correspondence with the king until 1765, when his successor, George, Earl Grenville, extracted a promise from the king that he would never again consult with Bute. The Grenville ministry threatened to resign *en masse* if the king continued to communicate with Bute.

With this, Bute really did withdraw from active politics, and the king ignored his pleas to be allowed to join Pitt's 1766 ministry. When his last royal friend, the dowager princess, died in 1772, Bute retired from all social activity outside of his family circle, and pursued his naturalist studies, publishing a book, *Botanical Tables,* in 1785. In 1780, he left the House of Lords. Yet the "Bute myth" was so entrenched that the former royal favorite continued to be blamed for almost every policy failure and every reversal that occurred. Graphic satires during the War of American Independence continually depicted him as the source of the nation's ruin— a good ten years after he had lost his influence on policy and his audience with the king. Bute carried on as before with his private life, spending part of the year in London and part in Scotland, until his death in March 1792.

Philip Woodfine

See also: Fox, Henry; Grenville, George; Le Despenser, Lord; Newcastle, Duke of; Pelham,

Hon. Henry; Pitt, William (the Elder); Rockingham, Marquess of

References and Further Reading: Brewer, J., 1973, "The Misfortunes of Lord Bute: A Case Study in Eighteenth-Century Political Argument and Public Opinion," *Historical Journal* 16: 3–44; Brewer, John, 1976, *Party Ideology and Popular Politics at the Accession of George III* (Cambridge: Cambridge University Press); Brown, Peter D., and Karl W. Schweizer (eds.), 1982, *The Devonshire Diary, William Cavendish, Fourth Duke of Devonshire, Memoranda and State of Affairs, 1759–1762* (London: Office of the Royal Historical Society, University College London); Schweizer, Karl M., 1988, *Lord Bute: Essays in Reinterpretation* (Leicester: Leicester University Press); Walpole, Horace, in John Brook (ed.), 1985, *Memoirs of King George II* (New Haven, CT: Yale University Press).

Butler, Richard Austen (Lord Butler of Saffron Walden) (1902–1982) [CE, FS, HS]

Richard Austen Butler, often known by the acronym RAB, was a Conservative politician who filled all the major offices of government save one—that of prime minister. Gradually over the years, his name became almost a household word, strongly identified with a belief in and a commitment to a postwar economic and political consensus that, in the opinions of some, dominated British politics until 1979: a brand of politics dubbed "Butskellism," based upon an extension of his name into an "ism" as in the form of socialism or communism.

Butler was born in 1902, at Attock Serie in the Punjab, India, into a family with connections both to the imperial service and to the University of Cambridge. His father was the distinguished administrator Sir Montague Butler. Richard Butler was educated at Marlborough College and the University of Cambridge, where he became president of the University Union in 1924 and fellow of Corpus Christi College between 1925 and 1929. In 1926 he married Sydney Courtauld, heiress to the fortunes of the famous family that dominated the British chemical industry, and therewith obtained a financial settlement guaranteeing him £5,000 per year for life, tax free. The financial security he derived from this marriage encouraged him to pursue a political career, and he became Conservative M.P. for Saffron Walden in 1929, holding that seat until his retirement from the House of Commons in 1965.

Butler gained early promotion up the political ladder. In the National governments of 1931 to 1940 he became undersecretary for India (1932–1937), parliamentary secretary to the minister of labor (1937–1938), and then undersecretary for foreign affairs (1937–1941), a post he kept in the wartime government of Winston Churchill. Since Lord Halifax, the foreign secretary on the eve of World War II, was in the House of Lords, Butler became the principal spokesman on foreign affairs in the House of Commons. For this reason he came to be associated with the policy of appeasement advocated by Neville Chamberlain and Lord Halifax, and was identified as one of the politicians who were prepared to hand over Czechoslovakia to Hitler through the Munich agreement of 1938.

On leaving the Foreign Office in 1941, Butler became president of the Board of Education (1941–1944) and then minister of education (1944–1945) in Churchill's wartime administrations. In these roles he was responsible for the introduction of the 1944 Education Act, which laid down the postwar system of education in England and Wales, raising the school-leaving age to 15 and formalizing the tripartite system of secondary education—grammar schools, central schools, and modern secondary schools—and free secondary education for all. In 1945 he also briefly served as minister of labor in Churchill's outgoing government.

The 1945 general election brought a landslide victory to the Labour Party. In opposition, Butler became chairman of the Conservative Research Department between 1945 and 1951, and helped to change the Conservative Party from a monetarist into a Keynesian interventionist party. In 1947 he chaired the body that drafted the Industrial Charter of 1947, which committed the reluctant Churchill and the party to accept the need for government intervention in the economy and to support most aspects of the Labour Party's welfare state. In this sense, he helped to create the political consensus that seems to have dominated both Labour and Conservative governments on such issues. With the formation of another Churchill administration, following the general election of 1951, Butler became chancellor of the exchequer.

As chancellor, between 1951 and 1955, Butler was able to consolidate the development of this political consensus. His first two budgets were popular ones. However, he found that there were problems both in allowing high wage increases in the economy and seeking to build the 300,000 houses per year that the Conservative government had promised in its manifesto. By 1955 he was facing serious difficulties, which forced him to raise interest rates; nevertheless, he reduced income tax by 6d (2.4p) in the pound, in the electioneering 1955 budget. The tax reduction helped win the general election for Sir Anthony Eden, but Butler had to bring in a revised budget at the end of the year to control expenditure and staunch the run on the pound. This persuaded Eden to remove Butler as chancellor and to make him both the leader of the House of Commons (1955–1961) and Lord Privy Seal (1955–1959). He continued in those posts when Eden was replaced by Harold Macmillan, following the Suez Crisis in which the United States forced both British and French troops to withdraw from the Suez Canal in 1956. Although he played little part in the Suez affair, he had advocated that British, French, and Israeli forces attack Egypt instead of merely occupying the canal zone.

Butler did not enjoy the best of relations with Macmillan, having had hopes of being prime minister himself in 1957. Nevertheless, Macmillan did add to his duties by making him home secretary—a post he filled from January 1957 to July 1962—as well as chairman of the Conservative Party from 1959 to 1961 and deputy leader of the Conservative Party from 1962 to 1963. He was also First Secretary of State and minister in charge of the Central African Office between 1962 and 1963. He was removed from this last post in 1963, but in October 1963, in the government of Sir Alec Douglas Home, he was made foreign secretary; he held that post until October 1964. Home had replaced Macmillan as prime minister, having benefited from Macmillan's personal backing. Butler temporarily took over the day-to-day running of the government in 1963, while Macmillan was having an operation for prostate cancer; but that was as near to becoming prime minister as he ever came, although he had sought such an opportunity in 1957 and again in 1960.

Once the Labour government was formed in October 1964, Butler decided that his political career was at an end. He left the Commons in 1965 and was raised to the House of Lords as Lord Butler of Saffron Walden in 1965. From that point on, he contented himself with an academic career, acting as master of Trinity College, Cambridge, between 1965 and 1978. He died on 8 March 1982.

Many contemporaries have suggested that Butler was always a good second-in-command; Macmillan himself suggested that "he lacked the last six inches of steel" necessary for leadership. Indeed, this judgment seems fair, given that Butler was generally a less-than-spectacular minister. Nevertheless, his ushering in of the Education Act of 1944 and his advocacy of economic and political consensus—"Butskellism"—have ensured him a political reputation that extends beyond mere partisan politics. Indeed, once described as "both irrepressible and unapproachable," he was one of the most progressive Conservative leaders.

Keith Laybourn

See also: Chamberlain, Neville; Churchill, Sir Winston; Eden, Sir Anthony; Halifax, Lord; Home, Sir Alec Douglas; Macmillan, Harold
References and Further Reading: Butler, Lord, 1971, *The Art of the Possible* (London: Hamilton); Cosgrave, Patrick, 1981, *R. A. Butler: An English Life* (London: Quartet Books); Howard, Anthony,

C

Callaghan, James (Lord Callaghan of Cardiff)
(1912–) [PM, CE, FS, HS]

Callaghan is the only twentieth-century politician to have filled all four top offices of state, and given this unique position in British politics he cannot be seen as the political lightweight he is sometimes considered to be. Although his three years as Labour prime minister, between 1976 and 1979, left the Labour Party weaker than it had been for a generation, he was, according to Denis Healey, second only to Clement Attlee in the pantheon of Labour prime ministers. Indeed, it may well be argued that even though he is often represented as a proponent of "Old Labour"—with its emphasis upon trade unionism, working-class politics, nationalization, and expansionary Keynesian economics—he was in many ways a pioneer of Tony Blair's New Labour/Third Way approach, in which public ownership was abandoned and a closer relationship between the private and public sectors was sought.

Leonard James Callaghan was born on 27 March 1912, the younger child of James Callaghan and Charlotte Cundy. He was brought up in a working-class district of Portsmouth during and just after World War I, and was educated at Portsmouth Northern Secondary School. His father, a coast guard, died in 1921, after which the family faced difficult financial circumstances. However, James did well at school and gained entry into the civil service. His mother ensured him a strict, puritanical upbringing by sending him to the local Baptist church, but in later life he invested more faith in socialism. In Portsmouth, with its strong naval tradition, he also grew up in a strongly patriotic atmosphere.

Callaghan rose quickly in the Inland Revenue section of the civil service. He soon became a prominent member of the tax officers' union, and by the age of 24 he was an assistant secretary in the Inland Revenue Tax Federation. He had already joined the Labour Party in 1931. In 1936 his Labour Party membership and his commitment to trade unionism spurred him to raise money for the Republican side in the Spanish Civil War. He married Audrey Moulton in 1938.

During World War II, he prepared a pamphlet on Japan for the Royal Navy, and served on an aircraft carrier in the Far East but did not see any enemy action. During the war he became a staunch supporter of the social change many expected from the "People's War."

By 1945 Callaghan was a strong believer in trade unionism, with which he was closely associated until the 1960s; an experienced negotiator; a member of the Labour Party; and a committed advocate of social reform. In the 1945 general election he won the Cardiff South seat for Labour and represented the seat in its many forms (Cardiff Southeast, 1950–1983; Cardiff South and Penarth, 1983–1987) until his retirement from the House of Commons in 1987, when he became Lord Callaghan of Cardiff and entered the House of Lords.

By any standard Callaghan had a distinguished political career. However, his early career as a backbencher and junior minister did not suggest that he would be a future Labour leader. At first he was a rather troublesome backbencher, attacking Ernest Bevin's anti-Soviet foreign policy; and in 1947, he became involved in the backbench rebellion that forced the proposed period of national military service to be reduced. He became a junior minister in the

Ministry of Transport in October 1947 and acted as parliamentary and financial secretary of the admiralty between 1950 and 1951. It was at this point that he revealed himself to be both a popular and an able politician. Although he was prone to hasty comments, he always supported government decisions once they had been made. He continually sought the middle ground between the extreme views within the Labour Party. This was evident in the 1950s, when he steered a middle course between Hugh Gaitskell's reformism and Aneurin Bevan's more immediate demands for socialism and public ownership. He was also an independent thinker: he was identified with the trade unions, which rejected Gaitskell's attempt to get the Labour Party Conference to abandon public ownership; but he was opposed to the Campaign for Nuclear Disarmament and was a convinced supporter of the North Atlantic Treaty Organization (NATO).

Recognizing Callaghan's abilities, Gaitskell, the new Labour leader from 1955, gave him the post of shadow colonial affairs spokesman in December, which Callaghan filled until 1961. In this role he dealt successfully with the conflict in Cyprus and the Mau Mau guerrilla activities in Kenya, earning the respect of many prominent Africans (such as Kenneth Kaunda and Julius Nyerere, who later became national leaders). Callaghan encouraged a coherent policy of progressive and constitutional change in all African nations of the British Commonwealth. In 1961 he was promoted to Labour's shadow chancellor of the exchequer. This gave him greater visibility, to such an extent that when Gaitskell died in 1963, Callaghan was possibly third in the Labour hierarchy, behind only Harold Wilson and George Brown. After Wilson became Labour leader and won the 1964 general election, Callaghan was appointed chancellor of the exchequer, a position he filled from 1964 until 1967.

Callaghan was not the most successful or fortunate of chancellors. He inherited a large balance-of-payments deficit from Reginald Maudling, the previous, Conservative chancellor, and was forced to introduce deflationary budgets to curb this deficit. By July 1966 it was clear that this tactic had failed, and the country found itself in the midst of a massive balance-of-payments crisis. The situation did not improve from there. In 1967 the Arab-Israeli War caused an oil crisis, and the seamen's strike placed further strain on the faltering domestic economy. On 1 November 1967, Callaghan was forced to devalue the pound to $2.40. At this point, Callaghan resigned in favor of Roy Jenkins. However, although his reputation was damaged by the currency devaluation, he was still a major figure within the Labour Party, having been elected its treasurer the previous month as a result of the votes of the mining, engineering, and transport unions. He also was appointed home secretary, taking up Roy Jenkins's old post.

As home secretary, from 1967 to 1970, Callaghan was not considered a great success, although he later handled anti-Vietnam protests, and policing in general, with some success. However, he made his mark as a leader in two ways at this time. First, he resisted, on behalf of the unions, the attempt of Harold Wilson and Barbara Castle to apply the White Paper *In Place of Strife* to British industrial relations. This proposal was eventually withdrawn; but if it had garnered the necessary support, strike action would have been restricted by legal penalties.

Second, Callaghan dealt intelligently with the growing instability in Northern Ireland. Responding to the violence in Londonderry's Bogside and Belfast's Falls Road areas in 1968 and 1969, he set forth a program of civil rights measures, described in his "Downing Street declaration." He also abolished the paramilitary "B specials" and reformed the traditionally Protestant-dominated Royal Ulster Constabulary.

After Labour's defeat in the June 1970 general election, Callaghan again found himself in the opposition camp. At 58 years of age, it might have seemed that his career in British high politics was at an end. However, with Roy Jenkins's resignation as deputy leader of Labour because of his pro-European views, and with George Brown's having lost his seat, Callaghan was the most likely alternative to Wilson as Labour leader. He allied himself with the trade unions in opposing Edward Heath's move to impose legal sanctions on trade unions and their strike activities, and he adopted the anti-Euro-

James Callaghan outside 10 Downing Street in 1964 (Hulton-Deutsch Collection/Corbis)

pean attitudes of many trade unionists. When Labour returned to power in March 1974, Callaghan became foreign secretary.

Callaghan was a determinedly political foreign secretary, holding almost daily meetings on the government's position with Harold Wilson, and he performed well on most occasions. He played an important part in negotiating the Helsinki accords with the Soviet Union and was on friendly terms with U.S. Secretary of State Henry Kissinger and with German Chancellor Helmut Schmidt.

Britain had entered the European Economic Community (EEC) under Edward Heath, and Callaghan took up the task of renegotiating Britain's membership. He had always doubted the economic arguments for joining the EEC, and on political grounds he favored NATO and the Commonwealth. He managed to obtain some trading concessions for the Commonwealth countries and the pegging of the United Kingdom's budgetary contribution to the EEC. This saw the Labour government through the referendum in 1975, in which there was a two-to-one vote in favor of Britain's continued membership in the EEC.

His outstanding performance in this arena made Callaghan seem a natural successor to

Wilson when the latter resigned as Labour leader and prime minister in March 1976. Roy Jenkins withdrew from the leadership contest, and Michael Foot had insufficient support to be a genuine contender. Thus Callaghan became the fourth Labour prime minister, on 5 April 1976. He inherited a minority government, which had lost its majority on the same day, with the defection of John Stonehouse. Remarkably, the new government lasted three years.

Callaghan ran his cabinet in an open fashion, involving all of its members in policy making, thus avoiding the "kitchen cabinet" arrangements (where a few cabinet minsters made the decisions) with which Wilson had steered government policy. Nevertheless, he faced great difficulties from the start. He headed a minority government and was therefore forced to make a pact in 1977 with the Liberal Party led by David Steel in order to ensure a working parliamentary majority. Callaghan's government, through Denis Healey, was also involved in securing a loan agreement of £3,900 million from the International Monetary Fund in December 1975, in return for imposing cuts on government spending. In the end, the cuts were not too severe, and the economy recovered quickly from the 1976–1977 crisis. Government reserves improved, and the economy was buoyant by the summer of 1978. Yet there would be no going back to the spending policies that had been used to tackle unemployment in the past; Callaghan had informed the Labour Party Conference of October 1976 that Britain could no longer spend its way out of recession.

It was at this point that matters took a turn for the worse. Callaghan began to alienate his traditional base of support in the trade unions by suggesting that pay increases should be pegged at about 5 percent. This provoked many trade unions, particularly in the service sector but also in road haulage, into strike action in the "winter of discontent" of 1978 and 1979. The situation was not helped by his reported statement in the *Sun* newspaper in Feburary 1975, on returning from an international conference in Guadeloupe: "Crisis? What crisis?" There were also other disasters. For instance, on 1 March 1979 the referendums on devolution in

Wales and Scotland went badly—devolution was overwhelmingly rejected in Wales and only narrowly accepted in Scotland. The Liberals deserted the Labour government, and on 29 March the government was defeated in the Commons by one vote. Callaghan's government was defeated at the general election in May 1979 and replaced by a Conservative one led by Margaret Thatcher. Callaghan remained Labour Party leader until his resignation in 1980, when Michael Foot took his place. Callaghan nonetheless remained in the House of Commons until 1987, attaining recognition as the longest-serving M.P., "the Father of the House," in 1983. In 1987 he was raised to the House of Lords.

Although he is often described as a traditional figure who represented the interests of Old Labour and of the trade unions, Callaghan was far from that. He was a pragmatic politician who was prepared to move ahead with the times, and his speech to the Labour Party Conference in October 1976 almost anticipated the New Labour approach of Tony Blair.

Keith Laybourn

See also: Attlee, Clement; Blair, Tony; Cripps, Stafford; Dalton, Hugh; Jenkins, Roy; Maudling, Reginald; Wilson, Harold

References and Further Reading: Callaghan, James, 1987, *Time and Chance* (London: Collins); Donoughue, Bernard, 1987, *Prime Minister: The Conduct of Policy under Harold Wilson and James Callaghan* (London: Cape); Jefferys, Kevin (ed.), 1999, *Leading Labour: From Keir Hardie to Tony Blair* (London: I. B. Tauris); Morgan, Kenneth O., 1997, 1999, *Callaghan: A Life* (Oxford: Oxford University Press).

Campbell-Bannerman, Sir Henry (1836–1908) [PM]

If Andrew Bonar Law can be described as the "unknown prime minister" of the Conservative and Unionist Party, then Henry Campbell-Bannerman was the "unknown prime minister" of the Liberal Party. Both men were politicians of conviction and pragmatism. Both enabled their divided parties to heal, and both exuded an amiable and diffident approach to politics, although Bonar Law sometimes gave the impression of being an uncompromising Ulster Unionist. In the end, both had their political careers cut short by untimely deaths. Campbell-Bannerman, unlike Bonar Law, can claim to have presided over an impressive administration. Among the members of his short-lived government were Herbert Henry Asquith, David Lloyd George, and Winston Churchill, who later introduced the immensely influential Liberal social reforms of 1906 to 1914.

Campbell-Bannerman was born on 7 September 1836, the second son of James (later, Lord Provost Sir James) Campbell and Janet Bannerman, and was raised in a strict Presbyterian household. He was educated at Glasgow High School and at the universities of Glasgow and of Cambridge. At the age of 22 he joined his family's prosperous retail firm, and he became a partner two years later. In 1860, he married Charlotte Bruce. In 1868, he changed his name to Campbell-Bannerman on inheriting an uncle's estate in Kent. Later he also came to own an estate in Scotland.

Campbell-Bannerman entered politics in 1868, when he became M.P. for Stirling District Burghs, a constituency he represented in Parliament until his death in 1908. Throughout the late nineteenth century, he became an increasingly prominent political figure within the Liberal Party. He served as financial secretary of the War Office in Gladstone's first administration, between 1871 and 1874, and fulfilled the role again between 1880 and 1882. He was parliamentary and financial secretary to the admiralty from 1881 to 1884, and Chief Secretary for Ireland between 1884 and 1885. He served briefly in 1886 as secretary of war, a post he occupied again between 1892 and 1894. Following the retirement of Gladstone and the resignations of Lord Rosebery (1894–1896) and Sir William Harcourt (1896–1898), in 1899, he became leader of the Liberal Party. He held this position until shortly before his death in 1908. As party leader, he was a great critic of Lord Salisbury and the Conservatives in their conduct of the Boer War.

Campbell-Bannerman's major task as Liberal leader was to unite the party. The Boer War had divided its leading figures into three main camps. Men such as Lord Rosebery and Herbert Henry Asquith, who were Liberal Imperialists, opposed the Boers; another group, including Campbell-Bannerman, was pro-Boer; and the third group was attempting to strike a balance between the two. Campbell-Bannerman managed to outflank the Liberal Imperialists by appointing Asquith to mount an attack on the Unionist campaign for tariff reform. In 1905 the leading Liberal imperialists attempted to rid themselves of Campbell-Bannerman by having him elevated to a position in the House of Lords (via the Relugas Pact), but failed. Campbell-Bannerman responded by appointing the three conspirators (Asquith, Sir Edward Grey, and R. B. Haldane) to senior ministerial posts.

Campbell-Bannerman formed a Liberal administration in December 1905, which was endorsed in the 1906 general election by a Liberal landslide victory. His appointment as prime minister was a landmark in British politics, for he was the first prime minister to have risen primarily from business rather than land and the first who was not an Anglican. The diversification of British politics in the twentieth century had begun.

Unlike many previous holders of this post, Campbell-Bannerman was more an enabler and a moderator than an instigator of reform. Indeed, his approach was very much like that adopted by Clement Attlee in later years—that of a leader who managed and negotiated among his various talented ministers. He was careful to ensure that the various sections of the party were well represented and supported his administration. In addition to the Liberal Imperialists, mentioned above, there were Gladstonian Liberals (John Morley, Ripon, Herbert Gladstone, and Campbell-Bannerman himself), a number of Whigs (Elgin and Crewe), and a number of radicals (Lloyd George, John Burns, and Winston Churchill). The party was thus balanced, and some important legislative measures were introduced, including the Education Act of 1906 (regarding school meals) and the Education Act of 1907 (medical provision). He also supported self-government for the Boers, as he had done between 1899 and 1902. He overturned the trades' dispute bill that his ministers had prepared in 1906, replacing it with a

Labour backbenchers' bill revoking the financial penalties imposed upon striking trade unions by the Taff Vale Case of 1900–1901.

This last action was a reflection of his intent to embrace the Labour Party rather than to reject it. Indeed, it was as leader of the Liberal Party that he endorsed the Lib-Lab Pact of 1903 hammered out by Herbert Gladstone, Liberal chief whip, and Ramsay MacDonald. The agreement was reciprocal, allowing both parties 30 seats in which there would be either no Liberal or no Labour opponent. This may have helped the Liberal Party, but it certainly was an important breakthrough for the Labour Party (at the time, known as the Labour Representation Committee).

In failing health, Campbell-Bannerman resigned as prime minister on 3 April 1908; he died on 22 April. Today few remember his premiership, although it directly encouraged a cooperative early relationship between the Liberal and Labour parties. Campbell-Bannerman did much to heal the divisions within Liberalism that had emerged in the late nineteenth century.

Keith Laybourn

See also: Asquith, Herbert Henry; Gladstone, William Ewart; MacDonald, James Ramsay; Rosebery, Lord; Salisbury, Lord
References and Further Reading: Harris, J. F., and C. Hazlehurst, 1970, "Campbell-Bannerman as Prime Minister," *History* 55; Rowlands, Peter, 1968, *The Last Liberal Governments: The Promised Land, 1905–10* (London: Barrie & Rockliff); Russell, Alan K., 1973, *Liberal Landslide: The General Election of 1906* (Hamden, CT: Archon Books); Wilson, John, 1973, *CB: A Life of Sir Henry Campbell-Bannerman* (London: Constable).

Canning, George
(1770–1827) [PM, CE, FS]

George Canning was born on 11 April 1770 at Marylebone, London, the son of George Canning, the eldest son of an Irish landowner, who had been disinherited for his improvident marriage to a penniless young girl, Mary Ann Costello. George Canning, Sr., died in 1771, leaving his widow and infant son destitute. Mary Ann subsequently became an actress and lived with actor Samuel Reddish, by whom she had five children. She later married another actor, by whom she had five more children. Fortunately, George Canning was adopted at the age of eight by a wealthy uncle, Stratford Canning, and was educated at Hyde Abbey School, Winchester (1778–1782), and Eton (1728–1787), thus imbibing some of the family's Whig principles (and hence sharing their initial enthusiasm for the French Revolution). After graduating from Christ Church College, Oxford (1787–1791), where he was awarded the Chancellor's Prize for Latin verse, he entered Lincoln's Inn to learn law; but he was never called to the bar, and he soon decided on a political career.

In July 1792, increasingly disillusioned by the excesses of the French Revolution, he became a protégé of William Pitt, the Younger, who secured his election to Parliament for the pocket borough of Newtown, Isle of Wight, and then procured for him the undersecretaryship of state for foreign affairs in January 1796. In 1799 he left the Foreign Office and was appointed a commissioner of the Board of Control for the government of India. In May 1800 he was promoted to the office of joint paymaster of the forces and appointed a privy councillor; and in July 1800 his marriage to a wealthy heiress, Joan Scott, by whom he had four children, brought him financial security. Regarding himself as a Pittite rather than a Tory, he left office when Pitt unexpectedly resigned in 1801 over the issue of Roman Catholic emancipation. However, he later dissociated himself from Pitt because of Pitt's support for Henry Addington as prime minister. Canning gave up the seat of Wendover, which he had represented since 1796, and purchased election as M.P. for the Irish borough of Tralee. Pitt's declining support for Addington by 1803 revived his friendship with Canning, and Canning was appointed treasurer of the navy in Pitt's last ministry. He was disappointed not to have obtained a cabinet post, but was assured by Pitt in December 1805 that he would be promoted to the cabinet in the new year.

Canning was consequently devastated by Pitt's death in January 1806 and the resignation of his ministerial colleagues. Nonetheless, he returned to office as foreign secretary in March 1807, serving under the ailing Duke of Portland. He directed the controversial seizure of the neutral Danish fleet at Copenhagen in July 1807 in order to prevent it from falling under French control; launched the Peninsular War in response to growing French aggression in 1808; and initiated the ill-fated Walcheren expedition in 1809. He held Viscount Castlereagh responsible for the catastrophic failure of the landing at Flushing and the evacuation of Corunna, and insisted on his dismissal. The two men quarreled. Later, they fought a duel on Putney Heath, in which Canning, who had never before in his life fired a pistol, was wounded in the thigh. They both then resigned from office.

When George III appointed Spencer Perceval prime minister in 1809, Canning declined to serve in the new administration; and even after Perceval's assassination in 1812, Canning remained out of office on account of his continuing support for Roman Catholic emancipation. Seeking to strengthen his team in the House of Commons, Lord Liverpool subsequently adopted a neutral line on this issue and effected a reconciliation between Castlereagh and Canning. Castlereagh even expressed a willingness to allow Canning to return to the Foreign Office, but Canning declined because Castlereagh insisted on remaining leader of the House of Commons. Canning did return to the cabinet as president of the Board of Control in 1816, but refused to act with his cabinet colleagues on the matter of the queen's divorce in 1820, and resigned his post. Allegations that Canning had been the lover of Princess Caroline, which he "neither owned nor denied," made George IV suspicious of him, and the king refused to allow Liverpool to bring him back into the cabinet six months later.

Indeed, only Castlereagh's suicide as Canning was about to set sail for Calcutta to become governor general of India enabled him to become foreign secretary and leader of the House of Commons in August 1822. Canning was less than enthusiastic about this change in his fortunes, proclaiming that he would rather have acted as "an absolute monarch" in India than be returned to the cabinet as "a buffeted minister." However, he won acclaim for his liberal policies at the Foreign Office between 1822 and 1827, which were well attuned to British commercial interests and popular with the middle classes,

and which influenced the course of British foreign policy throughout the nineteenth century.

He carried further Castlereagh's abandonment of the Congress system, instructing the Duke of Wellington, Britain's representative at the Congress of Verona, to refuse British support for French intervention in Spain to restore King Ferdinand VII; but this refusal did not prevent a French invasion in 1823–1824 with the goal of restoring the reactionary ruler to his throne. Canning nonetheless succeeded by diplomatic intervention in maintaining a pro-British government in Portugal in 1824. He also supported the movement for independence among the former Spanish American colonies in 1824–1825, calling "the New World into existence to redress the balance of the Old" and opening up Latin American markets for British exports. However, a proposed joint Anglo-American declaration that neither London nor Washington would condone the transfer of Spain's former South American colonies to any other power came to nothing, leaving President Monroe to take unilateral action through the celebrated Monroe Doctrine. Canning's intervention in the Greek War of Independence in 1826 ultimately secured freedom for the Greeks from Turkish domination and prevented Russian aggrandizement from upsetting the European balance of power; but he died before the controversial allied naval victory at Navarino Bay in October 1827.

Canning's policies differed little in substance from those of his predecessor. The differences were more of presentation and style. He was more forthright and less diplomatic than Castlereagh had been. He was also more aware of the value of public opinion in strengthening his influence and authority abroad, releasing long extracts from his speeches to the press and explaining his policies at length in the House of Commons and at large public meetings. His speeches were noted for their wit and sarcasm, and he has been judged the greatest orator of the age after the deaths of Pitt and Fox. The famous French historian Elie Halévy, contrasting Canning's style with that of his predecessor at the Foreign Office, declared, "A poet had succeeded the man of prose."

By February 1827, when Liverpool suffered his stroke, Canning was the most senior minister in the House of Commons but was perceived as a potentially divisive leader on account of his support for Roman Catholic emancipation. He was also mistrusted by George IV, although ultimately the king had no other option than to offer him the premiership. When George IV finally received Canning on 10 April 1827, the Duke of Wellington observed that Canning "stood with a watch in his hand giving the King half an hour to make him Prime Minister."

After Canning's appointment in April 1827, seven members of Liverpool's cabinet, including Wellington and Peel, resigned at once, together with about forty other ministers, and Canning was obliged to form a coalition of liberal Tories and conservative Whigs. Only four months after he inaugurated a program of progressive reforms (embracing reform of the Corn Law but not of Parliament), Canning, who was already a sick man when he took office, died at Chiswick House, London, on 8 August 1827.

Renowned for his brilliant oratory and polemics, Canning had appeared indefatigable to his contemporaries, often working from breakfast until late at night without food. This habit may have contributed to his notoriously irritable temperament, which led to frequent disagreements with his colleagues. Although Canning was despised by many Tory aristocrats and Whig political opponents for his unconventional upbringing—Earl Grey famously averred that he took it as axiomatic that "no son of an actress should become Prime Minister of England"—his political influence was nevertheless considerable and enduring. His disciples included William Huskisson and Lord Palmerston, and he was also much admired by William Gladstone. Indeed, the historian A. J. P. Taylor once pronounced in his famous BBC television series of the 1960s that Cannning was "the most striking personality in public life between Chatham and Churchill."

John A. Hargreaves

See also: Addington, Henry; Castlereagh, Viscount; Liverpool, Earl of; Perceval, Spencer; Pitt, William (the Younger); Portland, Duke of

References and Further Reading: Dixon, Peter,

1976, *George Canning: Politician and Statesman* (New York: Mason/Charter); Hinde, Wendy, 1973 and 1989, *George Canning* (London: Collins).

Carr, Robert (Lord Carr of Hadley) (1916–) [HS]

Robert Carr was home secretary in the Conservative ministry of Edward Heath in the early 1970s; but he was regarded as a "wet" soft-liner, and never gained office in Margaret Thatcher's Conservative ministry, formed in 1979. Carr was born on 11 November 1916, the son of Ralph Edward Carr and his wife Katie Elizabeth. He was educated at Westminster School and at Gonville and Caius College, Cambridge. He then worked for a number of firms from 1938 onward, acting as director of the Metal Closures Group between 1964 and 1970 and as chairman of Cadbury-Schweppes PLC between 1978 and 1989.

Carr became Conservative M.P. for Mitchum in 1950 and represented it until he became M.P. for Carshalton in 1974, retaining that seat until 1976. He rose through the junior ministerial positions in the various Conservative governments of the 1950s. He became parliamentary secretary in the Ministry of Labour and National Service on 20 December 1955 and continued in that role in the governments of both Sir Anthony Eden and Harold Macmillan, until 14 April 1958. In 1963 he was appointed secretary of state for employment but lost his post when Labour won the general election in October 1964. When Edward Heath formed his Conservative government in 1970, Carr became secretary of state for employment, then acted as Lord President of the Council and leader of the House of Commons between April and November 1972. He was then promoted to the post of home secretary, which he held until February 1974.

Carr was regarded as a "wet" (a weak political character) in the early 1970s, at a time when right-wing Conservatives were beginning to discuss denationalization and more private involvement in social welfare and less state provision.

When Margaret Thatcher became Conservative leader in 1975, she was determined to abandon some of her leading political supporters, in-

Robert Carr (right) with Edward Heath, c. 1974 (Hulton-Deutsch Collection/Corbis)

cluding Peter Walker, Robert Carr, Geoffrey Rippon, Paul Channon, and Nicholas Scott. Carr was not invited into Thatcher's shadow cabinet and he was instead created Baron Carr of Monken Hadley in 1975. Since then he has been mainly involved in business.

Keith Laybourn

See also: Eden, Sir Anthony; Heath, Edward; Macmillan, Harold
References and Further Reading: Evans, Brendan, 1999, *Thatcherism and British Politics, 1975–1999* (Stroud, UK: Sutton).

Carrington, Lord (Peter Carrington; Baron Carrington)
(1919–) [FS]

Known as a distinguished diplomat, Lord Carrington rose to fame as the first foreign secretary in Margaret Thatcher's government, formed in 1979. He resigned from the government as a re-

sult of the Argentinian invasion of the Falkland Islands in 1982 but maintained a reputation as a formidable international statesman in the 1980s and 1990s.

Peter Alexander Rupert Carrington was born on 6 June 1919 and was educated at Eton and Sandhurst. He inherited his title in 1938, but decided to pursue a career in the army, and proceeded to distinguish himself in the military service during World War II. He married Iona McClean in 1942.

After the war he became a banker and became increasingly active in the House of Lords and in government. He was parliamentary secretary to the Ministry of Agriculture and Fisheries between 1951 and 1954, in Churchill's government, and performed the same role for the Ministry of Defence between 1954 and 1956, under both Churchill and Eden. He was then made high commissioner of Australia (1956–1959), returning to Britain to become

First Lord of the Admiralty, a post he held from 1959 to 1963. After that, he became leader of the House of Lords in 1963, where he headed the opposition between 1964 and 1970.

Carrington's political career was on hold while the Labour governments were in office in the mid- and late 1960s; but on the formation of Edward Heath's Conservative government, in 1970, he became the secretary of state for defense, a post he held until 8 January 1974, when he became secretary of state for energy, a post he served in only until March 1974. While holding these important positions in government, he was also chairman of the Conservative Party Organization (1972–1974). Edward Heath persuaded him and other prominent Conservatives that the February 1974 general election could be won on a "who governs Britain" appeal—challenging the electorate to choose between a Conservative government and the coal miners and trade unionists, who were seeking to force the government to abandon wage controls. In the end, the Labour Party, which was the largest party but had no overall majority, formed the government.

Carrington was out of office for five years but still maintained a high profile within the Conservative Party, and when Margaret Thatcher won the 1979 general election, he became her foreign secretary. This was the high point of Carrington's political career, and he gained a formidable reputation in international diplomacy. However, the Argentinian invasion of the Falklands ended this chapter of his career.

The dispute over the Falkland Islands arose as a result of one of the Foreign Office ministers, Nicholas Ridley, having presented to the House of Commons a proposed lease-back arrangement under which sovereignty would pass to Argentina. This suggested that the British government was not interested in retaining the Falkland Islands and a foothold in the South Atlantic. As a result, the Argentinian military junta mounted an invasion of the islands. Lord Carrington accepted responsibility for the debacle and resigned in April 1982.

Despite this setback in his political career, Carrington's formidable knowledge of defense and international diplomacy did not go to waste. From 1984 to 1989 he served as secretary

general of NATO (the North Atlantic Treaty Organization), and subsequently, in 1991 and 1992, he became the main European peace negotiator in dealing with the civil war within the former Yugoslavia. Since then he has been absent from the international political stage.

Keith Laybourn

See also: Heath, Edward; Thatcher, Margaret
References and Further Reading: Bruce-Gardyne, J., 1984, *Mrs. Thatcher's First Administration* (London: Macmillan); Evans, Brendan, 1999, *Thatcherism and British Politics 1975–1999* (Stroud, UK: Sutton); Seldon, Anthony, and Stuart Ball, 1996, *The Heath Government 1970–1974: A Reappraisal* (London: Longman); Thatcher, Margaret, 1993, *The Downing Street Years* (New York: Harper-Collins).

Carteret, John (Earl Granville) (1690–1763) [FS, HS]

John Carteret, the first Earl Granville, was one of the leading political figures of the early eighteenth century. He was famed for his influence over kings George I and II and for his opposition to Robert Walpole, the first British prime minister.

John Carteret was the eldest son of George, first Baron Carteret, by his wife, Lady Grace, daughter of the first Earl of Bath. He was born on 22 April 1690 and succeeded to the baronetcy at five years of age. He was educated at Westminster School and at Christ Church, Oxford.

Carteret took his seat in the House of Lords on 25 May 1711. From the start he supported the Protestant succession, which brought George I to the throne. In recognition of his support, he was appointed one of the gentlemen of the bedchamber to George I. He also held a succession of other administrative posts, including that of bailiff of the island of Jersey in 1715.

Carteret's mother inherited large estates in Bath in 1711, becoming Viscountess Carteret and then Countess Granville in 1715. Carteret married Frances, the only daughter of Sir Robert Worsley, in 1710. After her death in Hanover in 1743, he married Lady Sophia Fermot, the second daughter of Thomas, the first Earl of Pontefract.

Carteret was a Whig, committed both to reform and to a constitutional monarchy, and in 1717, the year when the Whigs fragmented, he joined the Sunderland faction. In 1719 he became ambassador extraordinary and minister plenipotentiary to the queen of Sweden. In that post he ensured continuing freedom of trade in the Baltic, mediated between Sweden and Denmark to achieve a treaty, and brought about peace between Sweden, Prussia, and Hanover in March 1720. He played a similar role in France before being appointed secretary of state for the Southern Department (equivalent to the post of home secretary) by Sir Robert Walpole, the First Lord of the Treasury and the prime minister, in March 1721 (1720, on the old calendar), fulfilling this role until April 1724.

Carteret and Walpole were unable to work together; and Carteret—who was the only minister who could converse with George I, who spoke only German—decided to form his own party and challenge Walpole. However, Walpole and Charles Townshend (Viscount Townshend, 1674–1730), Walpole's main supporter, won the battle. As a result, Carteret lost his post in April 1724 and became lord lieutenant of Ireland, serving there until 1730. Although Carteret was strongly criticized by Dr. Swift in the latter's *Drapier's Letters* in 1724, even Swift acknowledged that Carteret showed greater finesse in Irish affairs than had many of his predecessors.

On returning from Ireland, Carteret joined William Pulteney in mounting a staunch opposition to Walpole. Indeed, he put forward a resolution in the House of Lords, on 13 February 1741, demanding the removal of Walpole from his "presence in the counsels for ever." This resolution was defeated by 108 votes to 59, and a similar motion was also defeated in the House of Commons. However, a year later Walpole resigned and Carteret became secretary of state for the north in the ministry of Spencer Compton, the first Earl of Wilmington. In this role, he generally supported the domestic policies of Walpole but in foreign policy slavishly supported the Hanoverian succession; using his influence over George II, he committed Britain to supporting Hanover's military activities. This period was popularly referred to as "the drunken administration." It came to an end with the death of

Wilmington. Henry Pelham, who became the new prime minister, defeated Carteret, who had just succeeded to the title of Earl Granville in the cabinet to become prime minister. Carteret still had a degree of influence over the king, and in 1746 he and Lord Bath attempted to form a new ministry; but they gave up the effort after only three days. However, the king prepared the way for Carteret's reconciliation with Pelham, which allowed the former to become Lord President of the Council in 1750. The Duke of Newcastle offered Carteret the chance of forming a ministry in 1756, but he declined, and gradually, largely as a result of ill health, he began to withdraw from the center stage of politics. He died at Bath on 2 January 1763.

Keith Laybourn

See also: Compton, Spencer; Newcastle, Duke of; Pelham, Hon. Henry; Walpole, Sir Robert
References and Further Reading: Dickinson, H. T., 1973, *Walpole and the Whig Supremacy* (London: English Universities Press); Owen, John, 1957, *The Rise of the Pelhams* (London: Metheun).

Castlereagh, Viscount (Robert Stewart; Marquess of Londonderry) (1769–1822) [FS]

Viscount Castlereagh was a great statesman of the nineteenth century whose reputation rose on the issue of foreign policy but declined with his role as spokesman of home policy after the Napoleonic Wars. He was also known for his commitment to the Irish and English Union and his advocacy of a widening of Catholic rights.

Castlereagh was born Robert Stewart on 17 June 1769, the eldest surviving son of Robert Stewart, the first Marquess of Londonderry, and his first wife, Lady Sarah Frances, the second daughter of Francis Seymour Conway, Marquess of Hertford. He was educated at Armagh in Ireland, and then at St. John's College, Cambridge. He visited Paris, Geneva, Rome, and Vienna in 1788 and 1789, and on returning to Ireland in 1790 he contested and won one of the County Down seats in the Irish Parliament— but at a cost of £60,000, which nearly ruined his family. At the outbreak of the French wars in 1793 he became lieutenant colonel of the Lon-

Castlereagh; lithograph based on the painting by T. Lawrence (Library of Congress)

donderry militia. On 9 June 1794 he married Lady Emily Anne, the youngest daughter and coheiress of John Hobart, the second earl of Buckinghamshire.

Stewart generally voted with the Tories when he was able to attend sessions of the Irish Parliament, and was firm in his belief in the necessity of a parliamentary union between England and Ireland as well as of the removal of restrictions against the Catholics. He later served as M.P. for Tregony (1794–1796) in the English Parliament and as M.P. for Orford, Suffolk (1796–1797). With his father's elevation to an earldom in 1796, he became Lord Castlereagh; and in 1797, he was appointed to the chief secretaryship of Ireland. In this capacity he ordered the arrest of the United Irishmen who had rebelled against English rule in 1798 with the help of French troops. Shortly afterward he was involved in pressing for the Act of Union between Ireland and England and also for a degree of Catholic emancipation. The Act of Union was passed in 1800; but the king's refusal to make any significant concessions to the Irish Catholics led Castlereagh to resign in 1801, fol-

lowing the example of William Pitt, the Younger, who had resigned as prime minister over the same issue. Castlereagh held no official position in Henry Addington's ministry but was given the responsibility of conducting through Parliament two Irish measures—the Suppression of Rebellion Act and the Suspension of Habeas Corpus, the right of trial with a jury.

After the Act of Union of 1800, Castlereagh sat in the House of Commons for County Down until 1805, when he was defeated in the parliamentary election. He was elected for Boroughbridge, in Yorkshire, in January 1806. He was subsequently elected as M.P. for Plympton Earl in Devon in November 1806 and for County Down again in 1812, 1818, and 1820. On succeeding to the Irish peerage, he was elected for Orford in April 1821. This almost unbroken period of tenure in the English Parliament projected him forward in a succession of governments, particularly on foreign policy.

Encouraged by William Pitt, Castlereagh joined Addington's administration as president of the (East India) Board of Control in 1802, which gave him a seat in the cabinet. In cabinet he spoke increasingly on foreign policy, almost acting as Pitt's mouthpiece. After Pitt formed a new government in 1804, Castlereagh was given the additional post of secretary of war in 1805. On Pitt's death he lost these responsibilities; but in 1807 he again became secretary of war, this time in the Duke of Portland's ministry. In this post he supported Arthur Wellesley's military campaigns in Spain and Portugal, during the Peninsular War. He also mounted his own illfated expedition of 40,000 troops and naval personnel to capture the island of Walcheren, off Holland, in an attempt to get France to divert its troops from other theaters of war. The expedition was mounted in July 1809 but had failed by September. As a result there was cabinet pressure for him to move from the post of secretary of war to that of Lord President of the Council. George Canning, the foreign secretary, was behind the attempt to remove Castlereagh; and Spencer Perceval, the new prime minister, showed Castlereagh the letters Canning had written to him on the subject. An incensed Castlereagh challenged Canning to a duel on

Putney Heath on 21 September 1809. Canning was slightly wounded in the thigh, and both men were forced to resign from the government.

Castlereagh returned to office as foreign secretary on 28 February 1812, in the latter days of Spencer Perceval's ministry, and remained in that post under Lord Liverpool until his death in 1822. Initially, his main responsibility was to secure the alliance against Napoleon, dealing with the rival interests of Austria, Russia, Prussia, and other allied powers involved in the conflict. When the Congress of Vienna was called in September 1814, he and his brother Sir Charles, then Lord Stewart, represented Britain. Castlereagh's main concerns were to limit France to its prerevolutionary borders, to restore the Bourbons to the throne, and to restrict the growing power of Russia—for which purpose he sought the creation of a Polish state and of the German confederation. In the end he had to compromise. In the case of Poland, for instance, instead of an independent Polish state to act as a buffer, the Prussians were given a defensible border against Russia; the Russian claims to Austrian Poland were reduced; and the tsar maintained control of Warsaw and its province. The negotiations were, however, interrupted by Napoleon's campaign of 1815, and the Treaty of Vienna was not signed until June 1816, by which time Napoleon had been subdued and imprisoned on the island of St. Helena.

Castlereagh was then at the peak of his influence; but later his popularity declined to the point of expiry. This decline was partly because he was the government spokesman on home policy in the House of Commons, while Lord Sidmouth, the home secretary, was in the House of Lords. Among the many oppressive social and political measures he introduced to control the radical agitation of the time was the ending of trial by jury through the suspension of the Habeas Corpus Act in 1817. Castlereagh also introduced into the House of Commons the severe Six Acts in the wake of the Peterloo "Massacre" of 1819 to restrict the holding of reform meetings and give magistrates additional power to search for arms; and it was his head, as well as Sidmouth's, that the Cato Street conspirators proposed to carry on pikes through the streets of

London if their uprising was successful. As far as foreign policy was concerned, Castlereagh's main concern was to pursue a policy of nonintervention and conciliation. For instance, he would not allow Britain to become involved in the revolutions that occurred in Spain, Portugal, and Piedmont in 1820 and 1821.

Castlereagh became Lord Londonderry after the death of his father on 11 April 1821. By this point the enormous work burden and a number of health problems, particularly gout, were beginning to take their toll. It seems that his mind also was going: on 12 August 1822 he committed suicide by cutting his throat with a penknife; an inquest found him to have been of unsound mind. He was subsequently buried in Westminster Abbey, on 20 August 1822.

By any standards, Castlereagh was one of the greatest of British politicians. He helped defeat the Irish uprising of 1798, organized the Union of England and Ireland in 1800, played a major part in the defeat of Napoleon, and helped ensure the balance of power in Europe through the Treaty of Vienna.

Keith Laybourn

See also: Addington, Henry; Canning, George; Grenville, Lord; Liverpool, Earl of; Perceval, Spencer; Pitt, William (the Younger)
References and Further Reading: Turner, Michael, 2000, *The Age of Unease* (Stroud, UK: Sutton).

Cave, Sir George (Viscount Cave of Richmond, Surrey)
(1856–1928) [HS]

Sir George Cave was one of the many political figures who gained high office as home secretary as a result of their legal rather than political skills. He was born in London on 23 February 1856, the second of five sons of Thomas Cave, later Liberal M.P. for Barnstaple. He was educated in Caen in France, at Merchant Taylors' School and at St. John's College, Oxford, where he obtained a first-class honors degree. He went to the bar by the Inner Temple in 1880 and began to practice law as a junior barrister. In 1885 he married Anne Estelle Sarah Penfold. He made steady progress in his legal career, and after 24 years of practice, took silk (became King's Counsel) in 1902.

Cave's political career began in local politics, as a member of the Surrey County Council. Eventually, in 1906, he was elected as Unionist (Conservative) M.P. for the Kingston Division of Surrey, a seat he held until he entered the House of Lords in 1918. His twelve years in the House of Commons were hectic ones, in which the prewar Liberal governments of Henry Campbell-Bannerman and Herbert Henry Asquith challenged the constitution and introduced state-supported Liberal social reforms. Cave was in opposition until Asquith formed the wartime coalition government in May 1915 and made him his solicitor general in November 1915. This appointment ended when David Lloyd George replaced Asquith as prime minister in December 1916 and made Cave home secretary. Cave fulfilled this role until January 1919, both from the House of Commons and the House of Lords, dealing with issues of censorship, control of aliens, and military service.

At the end of World War I, in 1918, Cave became the Lord of Appeal. In this capacity he and a committee examined the trade boards formed in 1909, which had the power to fix wages in industries where sweated labor was endemic. The boards were under attack from the association of British chambers of commerce and from the press. From 24 October 1922 until January 1924, and from 6 November 1924 until 28 March 1928, Cave served as lord chancellor. The brief interval between these two periods was a result of the formation of Ramsay MacDonald's Labour government in 1924.

Cave filled many other roles and served on many committees. In addition, he was elected chancellor of the University of Oxford in 1925, beating Lord Oxford and H. H. Asquith in the process. He died on 29 March 1928, shortly after being granted an earldom.

Keith Laybourn

See also: Asquith, Herbert Henry; Baldwin, Stanley; Bonar Law, Andrew; Lloyd George, David
References and Further Reading: Cave, Lady, 1931, *Lord Cave: A Memoir* (London: J. Murray); Turner, John, 1992, *British Politics and the Great War: Coalition and Conflict, 1915–1918* (New Haven, CT: Yale University Press).

Cavendish, Lord John
(1732–1796) [CE]

Lord John Cavendish—fourth son of the third Duke of Devonshire and brother of William Cavendish, the fourth Duke of Devonshire and prime minister—was born on 22 October 1732 and educated at Peterhouse, Cambridge, where he obtained an M.A. degree in 1753. In April 1754 he was elected to the House of Commons for the parliamentary seat of Weymouth and Melcombe Regis, which he continued to represent until 1761, when he was elected for Knaresborough. He was appointed one of the lords of the Treasury in 1765, in the ministry of the Marquess of Rockingham, but left office with his leader in little more than a year. From 1763 to 1784, Cavendish represented the city of York. Following Rockingham's return to office, he was appointed chancellor of the exchequer on 27 March 1782, the same day as he was sworn in as a member of the Privy Council. When Rockingham died on 1 July 1782, Cavendish refused to serve under the Earl of Shelburne and resigned jointly with Charles James Fox and other members of Rockingham's party. He returned briefly to the chancellorship under the Duke of Portland, between April and December 1783, after which the coalition collapsed and William Pitt, the Younger, took power. Cavendish lost his parliamentary seat in 1790 and was out of politics for four years; but he returned as M.P. for Derbyshire in 1794 and again in 1796. Cavendish never married, and he died at his brother's house at Twickenham on 18 December 1796. He had been a thoroughly honorable and upright man with a taste for the literary and for country pursuits, both of which outweighed his parliamentary ambitions.

Kit Hardwick

See also: Fox, Charles James; Pitt, William (the Younger); Portland, Duke of; Rockingham, Marquess of; Shelburne, Earl of
References and Further Reading: Cannon, John, 1969, *The Fox-North Coalition: Crisis of the Constitution, 1782–1784* (London: Cambridge); Hoffman, Ross, 1983, *The Marquess: A Study of Lord Rockingham, 1730–1782* (New York: Fordham University Press); O'Gorman, Frank, 1975, *The Rise of Party in England: The Rockingham Whigs, 1760–1782* (London: Allen & Unwin).

Chamberlain, Austen
(1863–1937) [CE, FS]

Although often overlooked in comparison to his father, Joseph, and his brother, Neville, Austen Chamberlain was a successful politician whose principled stand in opposing the Conservative Party's removal of David Lloyd George from office in 1922 led to his resignation as Conservative leader, denying him the opportunity of becoming prime minister. Very much manufactured to become a leading politician by his father, in the end he lost out to his half brother Neville, who became prime minister and is notoriously associated with the Munich agreement of 1938. Austen's formality—he was among the last in the House of Commons to abandon the traditional top hat—and his shyness combined to give him an aloof and distant appearance, which made it difficult for him to attract widespread popular support. In the end, given his political pedigree, he was never able to rise above the role of a natural second in politics. Indeed, he is the only Conservative leader of the twentieth century, other than the untested present incumbent William Hague, not to become prime minister.

Joseph Austen Chamberlain was born in Edgbaston, Birmingham, on 16 October 1863, the son of Joseph and Harriet (formerly Kenrick) Chamberlain, who brought him up as a Unitarian. He was educated at Rugby from 15 years of age, and was then sent to Trinity College, Cambridge. Thereafter he traveled the Continent and acquired a good command of French, which placed him in good position later in life for a role as British foreign secretary. On his return home, Austen continued to live, in some elegance, in Birmingham.

He first ran for public office as a candidate for the Border Boroughs in Scotland. Later, he entered the House of Commons as M.P. for the East Worcestershire constituency, representing the Liberal Unionists, who had defected from William Gladstone's faction (favoring Home Rule for Ireland) in 1886. Austen represented that seat until 1914, when he took over his father's seat of Birmingham West, standing as a Conservative. He represented that seat until his death in 1937, thus serving in the House of Commons for an uninterrupted period of 45 years.

From the start, Austen made steady progress in parliamentary politics. He became a Liberal Unionist whip in 1892 and spent five years as civil lord of the admiralty in the Conservative government, between 1895 and 1900. Following the 1900 general election, he became financial secretary to the Treasury, and in 1902—when A. J. Balfour replaced Lord Salisbury as Conservative prime minister—he was appointed postmaster general, thus joining the cabinet hierarchy (albeit in its lowliest seat). Austen therefore was a member of the same cabinet in which his father served as colonial secretary. However, in 1903, Joseph Chamberlain resigned in order to pursue his campaign for tariff reform (in other words, protectionist measures), which had divided the Conservative Party. At the same time C. T. Ritchie, the free-trade-favoring chancellor of the exchequer, resigned, and in order to keep the Conservative Party and government together, Balfour appointed Austen chancellor of the exchequer.

In his role as chancellor, Austen introduced two budgets: In his 1904 budget he attempted to deal with a deficit by raising income tax from 11d (4.6p) to one shilling (5p) on the pound and increasing the duty on tea. His 1905 budget, introduced in a period of improving trade, restored the tea duties to their former level.

When the Liberals returned to power, Austen was out of office. From the end of 1905 until 1915, he took over from his father, who had had a stroke in 1906, as leader of the tariff reform movement. Austen also married Ivy Dundas, the 27-year-old daughter of a retired army colonel, in 1906.

It was during this period that he almost became leader of the Conservative and Unionist Party. He opposed Lloyd George's "people's budget" of 1909; participated in the constitutional discussions about changing the powers of the House of Lords; and found himself in conflict with Balfour, the Conservative leader, over the issue of tariff reform, which Balfour declared he would not introduce without a referendum. After a turbulent period of political and constitutional debate, Balfour decided to resign in November 1911. Austen, who had become more favorably disposed to Balfour (as Balfour also was to him), was then the leading candidate for the post of Conservative and Unionist leader. Yet both he and Walter Long withdrew from the contest in favor of Andrew Bonar Law, in order to keep the party together. Austen thus gained a reputation both as a gentleman and as a political loser. Revealingly, on Balfour's resignation in November 1911, Austen wrote: "I wish there was another Balfour clearly superior to us, and obviously marked out for the post. How gladly I would play second fiddle to him" (Thorpe, 1980).

The outbreak of World War I brought Chamberlain back to the center of British politics. He became secretary of state for India in the May 1915 coalition government. This was not a role he enjoyed, for he had little knowledge of India. He found himself at loggerheads with the viceroy, who although he was in principle subordinate to the secretary of state for India, was actually appointed by the monarch. He himself fell under criticism for the failure of British and Indian troops to push up the Tigris in Mesopotamia. As a result he resigned in 1917, against the wishes of Prime Minister David Lloyd George. After a period of recuperation, he returned to the cabinet in April 1918 as minister without portfolio—a position that involved no departmental responsibilities but that gave him a seat in the six-member war cabinet. Following the formation of the postwar coalition government, Austen became chancellor of the exchequer for the second time, a post he held from 1919 to 1921.

As chancellor during this period Austen faced a situation where the scale of British indebtedness was vastly greater than it had been before World War I. His 1919 budget was, therefore, an attempt to restore sound finance mainly by increasing taxation (by £110 million). His 1920 budget was even more draconian, increasing revenues from taxation by up to £200 million above the normal government revenues of about £1.2 billion. A large proportion of this revenue came from charges on excess profits, although the sudden collapse of the postwar boom meant that the revenue targets were never met. Still, the government enjoyed a financial surplus. The 1921 budget was introduced by his successor as a result

of his move to become Lord Privy Seal, leader of the House of Commons, and leader of the Conservative Party. Despite the worsening economic situation, this budget continued to deflate the economy in order to strengthen the pound.

With Andrew Bonar Law suffering poor health in March 1921, it was clear that Austen would be his successor as Conservative leader. Austen's tenure was short-lived, however, since the Conservative Party, at its Carlton Club meeting on 19 October 1922, decided to end the coalition and remove Lloyd George as prime minister. Austen was opposed to this action but found that the meeting was swayed by Stanley Baldwin, who spoke eloquently about Lloyd George in unflattering terms, characterizing him as "a dynamic force"—that is, "a very terrible thing: it may crush you but it is not necessarily right." Austen resigned as Conservative leader, and Bonar Law replaced him, thus becoming prime minister of the new Conservative government. When Bonar Law fell ill in May 1923, however, Stanley Baldwin became both Conservative leader and prime minister. Austen had difficulty reconciling himself to this development, which had brought Baldwin, a mere financial secretary to the Treasury, to the post of prime minister in little more than two years.

Baldwin attempted to mend his relationship with Austen when, after the interlude of the first Labour government, Baldwin returned to office as prime minister of the Conservative government of 1924 to 1929. He gave Austen the post of foreign secretary and associated it with the position of deputy prime minister. It was in this role, in which Baldwin gave him a free hand, that Austen secured his greatest political successes. Meeting with his French and German counterparts, he concluded the Locarno Pact of 1925, whereby Britain and Italy guaranteed Germany's western frontiers with Belgium and France. Similar nonaggression pacts were concluded with Czechoslovakia and Poland. For his efforts to bring Germany back into the international community while also protecting French frontiers, Austen received the Nobel Peace Prize and a knighthood in 1925. Locarno was, however, swept away by Hitler's expansionism in the 1930s.

Once again in the opposition, between May 1929 and August 1931, Austen began to reconsider his political future. He had hopes of again being foreign secretary in a future Conservative government. At the same time, he began to encourage and support the career of his half brother, Neville Chamberlain. He attempted as far as possible to steer clear of the political campaign being waged by press barons Lord Rothermere and Lord Beaverbrook to have Baldwin replaced as Conservative leader, even though he was attracted by their emphasis on protectionism and the creation of an Empire Free Trade Area. For his discretion he was offered the post of First Lord of the Admiralty in August 1931; but he decided to retire from office following the general election of October 1931, clearing the way, as he saw it, for Neville's becoming chancellor of the exchequer.

Austen enjoyed his period on the back benches. He acquired a number of directorships of various companies and pursued a range of activities that were sufficiently remunerative to provide him with a comfortable income. He declined the offer of a second appointment as foreign secretary in 1935, and died on 16 March 1937, a month before his half brother became prime minister.

Aloof, arrogant, and lacking supreme political ambition, Austen Chamberlain has always suffered by comparison with his father and half brother. His father had groomed him for political greatness, but he never truly saw himself as prime minister. He conceded to Bonar Law in the Conservative and Unionist leadership election in 1911, when he might have won, and unwisely gave up the Conservative Party leadership in 1922, when remaining party leader would have guaranteed him the position of prime minister. In the end, a lack both of will and of guile marked him as a politician of the second rather than the first rank.

Keith Laybourn

See also: Baldwin, Stanley; Balfour, Arthur James; Bonar Law, Andrew; Chamberlain, Neville; Lloyd George, David; Salisbury, Lord
References and Further Reading: Dutton, David, 1986, *Austen Chamberlain: Gentleman in Politics* (New Brunswick, NJ: Transaction Books); Jenkins, Roy, 1998, *The Chancellors* (London: Macmillan); Self, Robert (ed.), 1996, *The Austen Chamberlain Diary Letters* (London: Cambridge University Press); Thorpe, D. R., 1980, *The Uncrowned Prime Minister* (London: Darkhorse Publishing).

Chamberlain, Neville
(1869–1940) [PM, CE]

Neville Chamberlain was one of the most controversial of Britain's prime ministers, being closely associated with the attempt to secure peace in Europe through the "appeasement" of the European dictators, the climax of which was reached at the Munich conference in September 1938. In 1940, when this policy failed, he was dubbed by Michael Foot and other writers of a famous pamphlet one of the "guilty men." More recent writers have attempted to understand his actions, rebut this charge, and revive his reputation.

Arthur Neville Chamberlain was born on 18 March 1869, the eldest child of Joseph Chamberlain and his second wife, Florence Kenrick. His father had been the leader of the Unionist section of the Liberal Party, which had split over Home Rule in 1886; and his elder half brother, Austen, was leader of the Conservative Party between 1921 and 1922. Austen was guided toward a career in politics, but Neville was directed toward a business career and spent the years 1890 to 1897 on Andros Island in the Bahamas, presiding over a family business venture in growing sisal. On his return, until 1911, it was the family business activities that dominated his life.

Neville's move into politics occurred gradually. He was elected as a city councillor for Birmingham in 1911, and served as lord mayor in 1915–1916, during World War I. It was at this stage that he was drawn into the war effort because of his municipal experience. When David Lloyd George took over the premiership from Herbert Henry Asquith, Neville Chamberlain was offered the post of director-general of national service in December 1916, with responsibility for the supply of civilian manpower to industry. However, he had no parliamentary seat, was soon at odds with Lloyd George, and was forced to resign in the summer of 1917. This outcome led to a lifelong hostility between Chamberlain and Lloyd George. It was also at this point that the loss of a close family friend convinced Chamberlain that war was to be avoided in the future, if at all possible.

Chamberlain began his parliamentary career in 1918 when he was elected as M.P. for Birmingham Ladywood, a seat he held until 1929. From 1929 until 1940 he was M.P. for the neighboring Edgbaston seat. Ostensibly, he was a supporter of Lloyd George's coalition government; but he had little real enthusiasm for it, and his political career did not take off until Andrew Bonar Law replaced Lloyd George as prime minister in October 1922, at the head of a Conservative government. This political shift was opposed by Neville's half brother Austen, who lost his position as leader of the Conservative Party.

Neville was appointed first to various junior ministerial posts, eventually joining the cabinet in March 1923 as minister of health. His main achievement in the latter role was the passing of the Housing Act of 1923, which provided substantial financial incentives for private developers to build houses on speculation. For a few weeks, at the end of 1923 and the beginning of 1924, Chamberlain became chancellor of the exchequer, but he lost his post with the election of Ramsay MacDonald's first Labour government in January 1924. However, when the Conservatives returned to office at the end of 1924, Chamberlain again became minister of health, having rejected the offer of the post of chancellor of the exchequer.

In the next four and a half years, Chamberlain pursued a massive rationalization program in which he sought to provide a better financial basis for local government; to introduce a contributory scheme for pensions; and to arrange for the transfer of the Poor Law to local government through the Local Government Act of 1929. This last objective was deemed necessary because of the government's problems in controlling the lavish expenditures of boards of guardians of the Poor Law as well as those of the Labour-controlled local borough and city councils. The government had fought a protracted battle over this issue with the Poplar borough council throughout the 1920s and with Labour-

dominated boards of guardians during the General Strike of 1926. The second Labour government, which came to power after the May 1929 general election, resolved the conflict by means of the Poor Law Act of 1930.

With the defeat of the Conservative Party in the 1929 general election, Chamberlain occupied himself with the politics of the Conservative Party. He chaired the party's newly formed research department; acted as chairman of the party from June 1930 to March 1931; shaped the future economic thinking of the party; and, in March 1931, helped resolve the differences between Lord Beaverbrook, the press baron, and Stanley Baldwin, which had led the former to organize the Empire Party to compete with the Conservative Party. At about this time, Chamberlain passed on a memo to Baldwin from Robert Topping, who was the party's senior official, recommending that Baldwin resign as party leader. Indeed, for a time it appeared that Chamberlain might replace Baldwin as Conservative leader. However, the party seems to have accepted the adage "Better the Devil you know than the Neville you don't"; and relations between Chamberlain and Baldwin soon returned to normal. Shortly afterward, in August 1931, Chamberlain was deeply involved in the negotiations that led to the end of Ramsay MacDonald's second Labour government and the formation of the National government.

Chamberlain accepted the post of chancellor of the exchequer in the National government in November 1931, after the departure of Philip Snowden, and he occupied that office until May 1937, when he became prime minister. He proved a pragmatic chancellor, although he was much criticized for the slowness of the two National governments in tackling the country's high rate of unemployment. Nevertheless, he presided over a slow economic recovery, which was assisted by the economic decisions he made early on. Most obviously, he introduced the protectionist measures his father had sought 30 years before, and pushed ahead with the idea, if not the reality, of an Empire Free Trade Area at the Ottawa Conference of 1932. Although not all of his economic policies were completely successful, British interest rates did fall to 2–3 per-

Prime Minister Neville Chamberlain, standing between Sir Neville Henderson (left) and Adolf Hitler, in Hitler's hotel room, Godesberg, Germany, October 1938 (Library of Congress)

cent as a result of his fiscal policy, which helped stimulate a boom in private housing construction and in the new consumer industries (of cars and electrical goods) in the 1930s. Nevertheless, high rates of unemployment persisted, and he and the government faced significant criticism from Lloyd George over the limited financial support his government had put forward in the Special Areas Act of 1934.

Stanley Baldwin was often ill throughout 1936, as a result of which Chamberlain became acting prime minister. It was at this stage that he began to encourage the gradual rearmament of the country and the expansion of the Royal Air Force, at a pace that would not damage the fragile British economy. Chamberlain had become the obvious—indeed, the only—candidate for prime minister; and when Baldwin resigned,

Chamberlain took office on 28 May 1937. Chamberlain was not a natural leader. He had a reputation as a cold-hearted administrator, and although he was a stubborn and persistent politician and a good debater, he was a limited orator. Yet his strengths outweighed his weaknesses, and he dominated the cabinet. He ran his administration with the support of an inner cabinet consisting of Sir John Simon, Sir Samuel Hoare, and Lord Halifax, who replaced Sir Anthony Eden as foreign secretary in February 1938 because of Eden's opposition to Chamberlain's appeasement policies toward Hitler and Mussolini. Hitler and Germany were Chamberlain's greatest political problems from then onward.

With the goal of territorial expansion, Hitler was preparing to send German troops eastward, into Austria, Czechoslovakia, and Poland. Emphasizing the "German nature" of Austria (a thinly veiled threat), Hitler successfully bullied Austrian politicians into submitting to the Anschluss—the absorption of Austria into "Greater Germany"—on 13 March 1938. Chamberlain does not seem to have been too perturbed at this development, but was more concerned about German claims on Czechoslovakia. Britain had promised France that it would protect the borders of Czechoslovakia; but Hitler was demanding that the large German community there, particularly that in the Sudetenland, be allowed to vote on whether or not to join Germany or to remain within Czechoslovakia. He announced a deadline of 1 October 1938 for agreement on this. Chamberlain, after making three trips to meet with Hitler personally in September 1938, eventually conceded to Hitler's demands on 30 September 1938, in the infamous Munich agreement. A year later, however, as a result of Germany's invasion of Poland in September 1939, Britain declared war on Germany.

The great concern of British politicians was how to deal with Hitler's expansionist activities. The British armed forces were weak, and it did not seem likely that the League of Nations would be able to act in concert to restrain Hitler. Indeed, it had obviously failed to prevent Italy's invasion of Abyssinia in the mid-1930s. Realistically, there were only three alternative actions that might maintain peace—to seek collective security through the League of Nations, to form an alliance with powers opposed to the German and fascist states, or to pursue appeasement. The first was instantly rejected. Indeed, Chamberlain asked the question, in the House of Commons on 7 March 1938: "What country in Europe today if threatened by a large Power can rely upon the League of Nations for protection?" His answer was "None."

The second alternative seemed unlikely; for although Britain had an alliance with France, Chamberlain was unwilling to develop an Anglo-Soviet alliance. That left the third alternative: appeasement.

Chamberlain's pursuit of appeasement has, of course, been subject to intense scrutiny. The authors of *The Guilty Men* (1940) suggested that Chamberlain had stumbled into war because he naively believed that Hitler could be appeased. Instead of facing up to Hitler, he gave him everything he asked for, and thus ironically hastened the onset of war. Keith Feiling attempted a modest defense of Chamberlain from such accusations in *The Life of Neville Chamberlain* (1946). Since then, there have been mixed responses to Chamberlain. Martin Gilbert and Richard Gott were critical of his action in *The Appeasers* (1963); but in a later book, *The Roots of Appeasement* (1966), Gilbert was more positive about Chamberlain's "honourable quest" to maintain peace. Indeed, since the late 1960s, the availability of new records has led to the defense of Chamberlain, suggesting that he was far from naive and cowardly, that appeasement was the only realistic policy available to him, and that this policy was widely supported by the British public. David Dilks has been foremost in defending Chamberlain's reputation in this respect, suggesting that he did the best that was possible given that Britain needed time to build up its defense capability, and that he was prepared to defend Poland.

More recently, however, these revisionist views have been challenged. Ian Colvin has suggested that Chamberlain was naive in his personal diplomacy; Chamberlain's problem was that in pursuing appeasement he ignored the other alternatives that might have prevented war. Richard Cockett stated that Chamberlain

"GOOSE-STEPPING, NEVILLE?"

"Goose-stepping, Neville?" U.S. cartoon, c. 1939 (Library of Congress)

manipulated the "free press" in such a way as to give the impression that both the government and the nation were united in support of appeasement, when neither was. R. A. C. Parker has gone further still, asserting that Chamberlain ruled out alternatives to appeasement that might have secured peace. Recently, P. Shen suggested that the whole appeasement process began in 1931, after the Japanese invasion of Manchuria, and was pursued by successive prime ministers in the hope of gaining time to build up Britain's military strength. Clearly, the debate will continue.

After the outbreak of World War II, Chamberlain continued to serve as prime minister. However, both the Liberal Party and the Labour Party refused to serve in his wartime ministry, even though Anthony Eden and Winston

Churchill, staunch prewar critics, did serve. At first, Chamberlain adopted the defensive strategy of building up the armed forces and avoiding offensive action; but rising public pressure forced his ministry to attempt to block the flow of iron ore from Scandinavia to Germany. When British forces failed to prevent the subsequent invasion of Norway, the Labour Party, the Liberal Party, and some sections of the Conservative Party came together to remove Chamberlain as prime minister. Following several heated debates in the House of Commons, the government majority fell from 240 to 81, and Chamberlain resigned on 10 May 1940. He was replaced by Winston Churchill at the head of an all-party government. However, he continued in government as Lord President of the Council (responsible for the various cabinet committees), with a seat on the war cabinet, and as leader of the Conservative Party until his declining health forced him to resign. He died of cancer on 9 November 1940.

Keith Laybourn

See also: Asquith, Herbert Henry; Baldwin, Stanley; Bonar Law, Andrew; Churchill, Sir Winston; Eden, Sir Anthony; Halifax, Lord; Hoare, Sir Samuel; Lloyd George, David; Simon, Sir John Allsebrook
References and Further Reading: Aster, S., 1989, "'Guilty Men': The Case of Neville Chamberlain," in Boyce, Robert, and Esmonde Robertson (eds.), *Paths to War* (Basingstoke, UK: Macmillan); Charmley, John, 1989, *Chamberlain and the Lost Peace* (London: Hodder and Stoughton); Cockett, Richard, 1989, *Twilight of Truth: Chamberlain, Appeasement and the Manipulation of the Press* (London: Weidenfeld and Nicolson); Colvin, Ian, 1971, *The Chamberlain Cabinet* (London: Gollancz); Dilks, David, 1984, *Neville Chamberlain: Pioneering and Reform, 1868–1940*, vol. 1 (Cambridge: Cambridge University Press); Dilks, David, 1987, "'We Must Hope for the Best and Prepare for the Worst': The Prime Minister, the Cabinet and Hitler's Germany 1937–9," *Proceedings of the British Academy;* Feiling, Keith, 1946, *The Life of Neville Chamberlain* (London: Macmillan); Fuchser, Larry W., 1982, *Neville Chamberlain and Appeasement* (London: Norton); Gilbert, Martin, 1966, *The Roots of Appeasement* (London: Weidenfeld & Nicolson); Gilbert, Martin, and Richard Gott, 1963, *The Appeasers* (London: Weidenfeld & Nicolson); Jefferys, Kevin, 1991, "May 1940: The Downfall of Neville Chamberlain," *Parliamentary History* 10; Macleod, Iain, 1961, *Neville Chamberlain* (London: Frederick Muller); Parker, Robert A. C., 1993, *Chamberlain and Appeasement: British Policy and the Coming of the Second World War* (Basingstoke, UK: Macmillan); Shen, Peijian, 1999, *The Age of Appeasement: The Evolution of British Foreign Policy in the 1930s* (Stroud, UK: Sutton).

Chesterfield, Earl of (Philip Dormer Stanhope) (1694–1773) [FS]

Philip Dormer Stanhope—statesman, wit, and famous letter writer—was the grandson of Philip Stanhope, the third Earl of Chesterfield, and his wife Elizabeth, daughter of George Saville, Marquess of Halifax. He was born in London on 22 September 1694, was educated privately, and spent a year at Trinity Hall, Cambridge, before being named Gentleman of the Bedchamber to the Prince of Wales, later King George II.

In the same year, 1715, he also entered the House of Commons as Whig member for St. Germans, Cornwall. Soon afterward he left for Paris. When he returned later that year, he tried to steer a middle course between the Prince of Wales, his main benefactor, and King George I, in order to sustain his political career. Through his court connections, he became a close friend of Lord Bolingbroke and the poets Pope and Swift. He also befriended Henrietta Howard, the mistress of Prince George, thus incurring the enmity of George's wife, Princess Caroline.

He was elected M.P. for Lostwithiel in 1722 but lost that seat in 1725; meanwhile, he had secured a minor advancement because of his general support of the king, being captain of gentleman-pensioners between 1723 and 1725. He quarreled with Sir Robert Walpole and rejected the latter's offer of the Order of the Bath. After his father died on 27 January 1726, he became the fourth Earl of Chesterfield and entered the House of Lords.

The death of George I in 1727 brought the previous Prince of Wales, George II, to the throne, and the Earl of Chesterfield was given the post of Lord of the Bedchamber. He also was made privy councillor in 1728. Shortly afterward, he became English ambassador to the

Netherlands, headquartered in The Hague. There he indulged in amorous affairs with various ladies, including Mlle. du Bouchet, who gave birth to his illegitimate son in 1732. In the course of his ambassadorial service, Chesterfield negotiated the marriage of the Prince of Orange (the Dutch royal house) with Anne, princess royal of England. Temporarily reconciled with Walpole, for whom he had the highest regard as a parliamentarian (Franklin 1993, p. 114), Chesterfield became K.G. (Knight of the Garter) and Lord Steward of the Household in 1730. He also played a role in the negotiating and signing of the treaty with Spain and Holland, guaranteeing the Pragmatic Sanction in 1731, before retiring from the embassy in 1732.

Chesterfield was dismissed from the Lord Stewardship for opposing the Excise Bill in 1733, although he had previously supported Robert Walpole's proposal to maintain a standing army of about 18,000 men. He also incurred the displeasure of George II by marrying Petronilla Melusina von der Schulenburg (who had been created the Countess of Walsingham in her own right in 1722), the daughter of George I by his mistress, the Duchess of Kendal, in 1733. In fact, this seems to have been a marriage of political convenience, for he lived next door to his wife for most of the rest of his life and lived with his mistress, Lady Francess (Fanny Shirley). His marriage worsened his relations with the royal family. The estrangement became complete after he succeeded in wresting a settlement of £20,000 from the Crown in return for abandoning legal proceedings on behalf of his wife's mother over a legacy bequeathed to her by George I. Cool relations persisted between Chesterfield on one side and Walpole and George II on the other, often flaring up into overt conflicts in Parliament.

Chesterfield made a witty speech in 1737 (published in 1749) against a bill for licensing theaters. A particular fan of contemporary French writers, he visited Voltaire while in Brussels in 1741, and frequently sought the company of men of letters in Paris.

In the late 1730s he was particularly active in supporting a British war with Spain over trading differences, forcing Robert Walpole to abandon his hopes for peace. The naval operations went badly, and eventually, in 1742, brought about Walpole's resignation as prime minister and his transfer to the House of Lords as the Earl of Orford.

Though instrumental in the fall of Walpole, Chesterfield remained leader of the opposition in the House of Lords. Having received a legacy from the dowager Duchess of Marlborough in return for his political and personal support in 1744, he could have retired to a life of leisure; but instead he joined the ministry of Henry Pelham (after George Carteret retired in 1744) as envoy to The Hague, where he induced Holland to take part in the war of Austrian succession in 1745. He then became an excellent viceroy in Ireland between 1745 and 1746, where he not only kept the country quiet by his tolerant policies but also encouraged national industries.

Chesterfield served as secretary of the Northern Department (this post became that of foreign secretary after 1782) between 1746 and 1748. In this post, alas, his pacific policy was thwarted by his colleague the Duke of Newcastle, who was secretary of state for the Southern Department (home secretary) and the elder brother of Prime Minister Pelham. Chesterfield resigned in 1748. Thus ended his official career in government; he rarely became involved in politics thereafter.

Nevertheless, Chesterfield was instrumental in bringing England into line with the continent of Europe by his introduction of a bill to reform the calendar in 1751. The Gregorian calendar of 1582 was thus finally accepted in England in 1752, replacing the Julian calendar. Compensation for the ten "lost" days resulted in the tax year beginning on 5 April instead of Lady Day, 25 March, as it had formerly been.

In his own time Chesterfield was perhaps best known for his letters to his illegitimate son, which he wrote almost daily from 1737. These were published posthumously in 1774 and were hugely popular; they went into an eighth edition within three years of publication.

In the mid-1750s, Chesterfield became increasingly involved in patronage of the arts and of letters, though he was famously reviled by Dr. Johnson for having declined to sponsor his dictionary. Chesterfield gave Johnson's dictionary a generous review in 1754; but Johnson did not respond in kind, writing instead of Chesterfield that he taught "the morals of a whore and the manners of a dancing-master." Chesterfield maintained a regular correspondence with Voltaire and other French friends; and in 1755, he was elected to the Académie des Inscriptions, a literary society. His posthumous reputation was much injured by the hostility of several leading contemporaries; but subsequent publications of his writings show his immorality to have been greatly exaggerated and his worldliness—and in today's terms, his political correctness—to have been tempered by a warmhearted humanity. Chesterfield was that rare thing: an English intellectual of international standing who was yet sufficiently English to hide his intellect under a cloak of indolence and urbanity. His last words, spoken when an old friend came to visit him, were "Give Dayrolles a chair." He died immediately afterward, on 24 March 1773.

Kit Hardwick and Keith Laybourn

See also: Newcastle, Duke of; Pelham, Hon. Henry; Walpole, Sir Robert

References and Further Reading: Franklin, C., 1993, *Lord Chesterfield: His Character and Characters* (Aldershot: Scolar).

Childers, Hugh
(1827–1896) [CE, HS]

Hugh Culling Eardley Childers was born in London on 25 June 1827, the son of the Rev. Eardley Childers (who died in 1831) and his wife, Maria Charlotte Smith. Hugh was educated at Cheam School from 1836 until 1843, went to Wadham College, Oxford, in May 1845, and graduated from Trinity College, Cambridge, in 1850. After graduation he married Emily, third daughter of G. J. A. Walker of Norton, Worcestershire, and moved to Melbourne, Australia, to pursue a career in the colonies. In 1852 he became auditor general there, with an impressive salary of £1,200 per year. In 1853 he helped found Melbourne University and became its first vice-chancellor. He filled many other posts in Australia, but drifted back to Britain in 1857, determined to pursue a political career.

Childers became Liberal M.P. for Pontefract in 1859, being elected to this two-member seat with another Liberal candidate. In the House of Commons he campaigned to end penal transportation to Australia. His efforts gained him the attention of Lord Palmerston, who made him a civil lord of the admiralty. In 1865 he was appointed financial secretary to the Treasury, a post in which he developed a friendship with William Ewart Gladstone, then chancellor of the exchequer. When Gladstone formed his first administration in 1868, Childers was appointed First Lord of the Admiralty and was admitted to the Privy Council. In this capacity he introduced new regulations for promotion and retirement in 1870 and improved the management of dockyards. On health grounds, he retired from office in March 1871, although he returned as chancellor of the Duchy of Lancaster in August 1872, also being reelected as M.P. for Pontefract the same month. However, he again retired from office in 1873 and remained out of mainstream politics until 1880, when Gladstone returned to power after the fall of Disraeli's government of 1874 to 1880.

Gladstone appointed his old friend Childers secretary for war. In this post Childers was responsible for dealing with the Transvaal War in 1881 and the Egyptian campaign in 1882. He also produced a scheme for army reforms in 1881, which led to the formation of regiments by the territorial principle, extended the period of enlistment, and made better use of militia and volunteer forces. His success led Gladstone, then prime minister and chancellor of the exchequer, to offer him the post of chancellor of the exchequer. In this capacity Childers moved immediately to reduce taxation. In his 1883–1884 budget, income tax was reduced from 6d (2.4p) on the pound to 5d (2p). However, his 1885–1886 budget proved controversial because he had to increase taxation in order to prepare for a possible war with Russia; he was forced to raise income tax from 5d to 8d on the pound and to postpone paying off the national debt through the Sinking Fund. This budget plan generated so much opposition that the Revenue Bill was defeated and Childers had to resign as chancellor of the exchequer.

Childers maintained a loyal friendship with Gladstone despite this reversal, and he encouraged Gladstone's advocacy of Home Rule for Ireland in 1885. Childers lost his Pontefract seat in January 1886 but won South Edinburgh and became home secretary in Gladstone's brief ministry of 1886. He was elected for South Edinburgh again in June 1886; but failing health led him to seek warmer climes in Europe and in India. He retired from active politics at the 1892 general election but continued to play a role in public service until his death on 29 January 1896. He is remembered today not as a first-rate politician but as an efficient and effective administrator.

Keith Laybourn

See also: Gladstone, William Ewart; Palmerston, Lord
References and Further Reading: Matthew, Henry C. G., 1995, *Gladstone, 1875–1898* (Oxford: Clarendon Press).

Churchill, Lord Randolph
(1849–1895) [CE]

Lord Randolph Churchill, the father of Winston Churchill, was a prominent politician whose physical decline owing to syphilis led to an early death. He was a brilliant parliamentary figure within the Conservative Party who never quite reached the political heights that many expected of him.

Randolph Churchill was born on 13 February 1849, the son of the seventh Duke of Marlborough, and was raised at Blenheim Palace. His political career began in February 1874 when he was elected as M.P. for Woodstock, the family borough. Shortly afterward he was married in Paris to a 20-year-old American, Jennie Jerome, the daughter of a wealthy New York financier named Leonard Jerome. Jerome gave his daughter a dowry of about £40,000 (about £2 million, at today's rate of exchange)—a generous gift that nonetheless did nothing to keep the couple from a lifetime of indebtedness.

At first, Churchill was barely involved in parliamentary politics, and in 1876 he was to be found acting as private secretary to his father when he became viceroy to Ireland in 1876. It was during this period that Lord Randolph developed close associations with a variety of influential Irish friends—affiliations that led him to make a speech in 1877 that was construed as critical of British rule and favorable to Irish Home Rule.

Churchill neglected his parliamentary duties in the 1870s; he attended only three of the 217 parliamentary divisions (votes) on foreign affairs between 1874 and 1880. He squeaked by with a scant majority of 60 votes at the 1880 general election, but held onto his Woodstock seat, and began to cultivate a reputation as a witty and effective parliamentary speaker. He described Gladstone as "an old man in a hurry," and suggested, referring to Gladstone's tree-cutting exploits, that "the forest laments so that Mr. Gladstone may perspire." The first day in Parliament after the 1880 general election, Churchill spoke out against Charles Bradlaugh, the atheist member for Northampton, who had won a seat in the 1880 general election and three subsequent by-elections but was not permitted to enter the House of Commons; in particular, Churchill attacked one of Bradlaugh's pamphlets that was critical of the royal family. This was a speech intended to help restore Churchill's relations with the Prince of Wales, which had reached an ebb in 1876. Bradlaugh responded by protesting at the fact that the Duke of Marlborough was still receiving a pension of £4,000 per year (worth more than £200,000, at current values)—a pension that had been awarded long ago, to the first Duke of Marlborough, for his military victories at the beginning of the eighteenth century.

Churchill also developed a reputation for quarreling with some of the leading figures within the Conservative Party, not least with its leader, Lord Salisbury. Indeed, during this period he supported an eclectic group of issues—opposing religious intolerance in 1880, attacking the Gladstone government's Egyptian invasion with the fervor of an anti-imperialist, and flip-flopping on the Coercion Acts (passed to maintain public order in Ireland) and Irish Home Rule in his Belfast speech in February 1886.

In these years Churchill seemed at his clever best, making excellent speeches and coining devastatingly original epithets. Although his inconsistent approach to politics and his propensity for intrigue alienated many of his Tory colleagues, he nevertheless served briefly at the India Office during the Salisbury administration of 1885. In the general election at the end of 1885, he was defeated by John Bright in the Central Division of Birmingham; but since he was nominated and elected for the South Paddington seat in London, his parliamentary career was uninterrupted. This meant that he was able to play a significant part in opposing Gladstone over Irish Home Rule, until Salisbury formed his second government in mid-1886.

Churchill was clearly something of a loose cannon, being tremendously inconsistent in his political stance. This may have been partly due to the stress and strain of his private life. He appears to have contracted syphilis in 1883, and he was effectively separated from his wife, who spent most of her time in London alongside Count Kinsky, an Austrian diplomat. He drank excessively and smoked heavily. His health and temperament were poor, and those around him thought he might be on the verge of a nervous breakdown. Nevertheless, Salisbury appointed him chancellor of the exchequer on 3 August, a post in which he lasted a mere five months, until December 1886, when he resigned because of opposition in the cabinet to his budget proposals.

Churchill was one of only two nineteenth- and twentieth-century chancellors (the other being Iain Macleod, who died within five weeks of taking office) who never presented a budget. However, it is known what he would have done had his term of office lasted longer. He had proclaimed himself a convinced free trader, and had retreated from some of the protectionist statements he had made in 1885 and 1886, committing himself to providing £5 million of new money to lubricate local government reform, and earmarking a similar sum to reduce income tax from eightpence (3.4p) to fivepence (2.2p) on the pound; and death duties were to be simplified. However, his budget proposals evoked much criticism when they were presented to the cabinet in December 1886. It seems that Joseph Chamberlain had convinced him over dinner that Gladstone was going to withdraw his commitment to Home Rule, aiming to reunite the Liberals and Liberal Unionists. After a dinner with Lord Salisbury, the Prince of Wales, and George Joachim Goschen, followed by a dinner with Queen Victoria, Churchill decided to resign his post. He made a resignation speech in the House of Commons on 31 January 1887 and then went off to tour North Africa and Italy, remaining abroad until March 1887.

Thereafter, Churchill remained in Parliament, but his speeches over the next four years became confused and ineffective as his health declined. He died in January 1895, at the age of 45. Although he had been considered a potentially great politician in his early years, he had achieved relatively little.

Keith Laybourn

See also: Gladstone, William Ewart; Salisbury, Lord
References and Further Reading: Foster, Robert F., 1981, *Lord Randolph Churchill: A Political Life* (Oxford: Clarendon Press); James, Robert R., 1951, *Lord Randolph Churchill* (London: Hamilton).

Churchill, Sir Winston
(1874–1965) [PM, CE, HS]

Winston Churchill's career was one of the longest and most distinguished in British parliamentary history, extending continuously from 1900 to 1964, with the exception of a break between 1922 and 1924. Throughout his parliamentary career he was nearly always in the public eye.

Until 1940 his highest ambitions remained unfulfilled, despite his having led eight separate government departments between 1908 and 1929 and his having flip-flopped from Conservative to Liberal and then back to Conservative again. There was always a suspicion about Churchill's political reliability, and he was in the political wilderness throughout the 1930s. Nevertheless, his position and reputation were restored in 1940, when he replaced Neville Chamberlain as prime minister.

Churchill is best remembered as the statesman who led Britain to victory in World War II. Although he served again as prime minister between 1951 and 1955, nothing he did then or later surpassed his wartime leadership, the crowning glory of his political career.

Winston Leonard Spencer Churchill was born on 30 November 1874, the son of Lord Randolph Churchill and Jennie Jerome and the grandson of the seventh Duke of Marlborough. He was educated at Harrow and at Sandhurst, where he was trained for a career in the army. From 1895 to 1900 he was in the army, serving in India and fighting in the Battle of Omdurman in the Sudan in 1898. He left the army to work as a journalist during the Boer War, during which he was captured and escaped. Thereafter his life was devoted to politics.

Churchill failed to win a parliamentary by-election in 1899, but was elected as Conservative M.P. for Oldham in 1900. Upset by Joseph Chamberlain's protectionist campaign, Churchill, a firm believer in free trade, joined the Liberal Party in 1904. He successfully contested the Northwest Manchester seat in 1906 but lost it in 1908 and then switched to Dundee, which he represented until 1922. Switching his party affiliation, he gained a junior ministerial post in Henry Campbell-Bannerman's Liberal government.

On Campbell-Bannerman's death in April 1908, H. H. Asquith succeeded him as prime minister. Asquith made Churchill president of the Board of Trade and gave him a seat on the cabinet. In this role Churchill worked closely with David Lloyd George, the chancellor of the exchequer, in pressing forward with old-age pensions (1908), labor exchanges (1909), and other Liberal welfare legislation. In February 1910 he became home secretary, a post he held until October 1911. He was most controversial in this role, particularly when he sent troops into South Wales, which led to two deaths at Tonypandy, and in his involvement in the Sidney Street siege, in 1911, which involved East European revolutionaries.

In 1911 Churchill became First Lord of the Admiralty. Whereas he earlier had opposed increases in naval expenditure as president of the Board of Trade, he now found himself demanding naval expansion and clashing over this issue with Lloyd George, his former political mentor. The conflicts caused by his interference in naval operations led many to vilify him for the failure of the Gallipoli campaign in early 1915. When the first coalition government was formed, under Asquith in May 1915, the Conservative members demanded Churchill's removal from the admiralty. He spent six months as chancellor of the Duchy of Lancaster, effectively as a minister without a department, and then went to the western front as a battalion commander.

Lloyd George's replacement of Asquith as prime minister in December 1916 split the Liberal Party, leaving Lloyd George a limited group of supporters from which to draw in forming his administration. In spite of continued vehement Conservative hostility toward Churchill, Lloyd George brought Churchill back to become minister of munitions in July, a post he held until January 1919. Between 1919 and 1921, Churchill served as secretary of war and air, and then as colonial secretary from February 1921 until October 1922. He was a close confidant of Lloyd George, as well as friendly with F. E. Smith (the Earl of Birkenhead) and R. S. Horne, who were among the most influential operators in Lloyd George's coalition government. However, this government collapsed in 1922, and Bonar Law replaced Lloyd George. Churchill lost his Dundee seat at the subsequent 1922 general election.

With a divided and defeated Liberal Party as his platform for political power, Churchill gradually moved toward "Constitutionalism," and was adopted by the Conservatives for the safe seat of Epping. He was elected to Parliament in 1924 and represented Epping for forty years. When Baldwin became prime minister at the end of 1924, Churchill was given the post of chancellor of the exchequer, a post he retained until May 1929. As a free trader he was committed to balancing the budgets, like his Labour counterpart Philip Snowden in 1924. He also returned Britain to the gold standard, which was synonymous with free trade, in April 1925—even though the process saw the pound reflated by 10 percent in order to raise it to its prewar parity with the dollar. He was also a particularly belligerent opponent of the Trades Union Congress (TUC) during the General Strike of 1926, refusing to accept TUC demands for protection of miners' wages. During this time he also acted as editor of the *British Gazette*—a role that Lloyd George described as a first-class indiscre-

Prime Minister Winston Churchill (left) with President Franklin D. Roosevelt and Marshal Joseph Stalin at Yalta, February 1945 (Library of Congress)

tion "clothed in the tawdry garb of third-rate journalism." After the strike was suspended by the General Council of the TUC, Churchill attempted to achieve a settlement by bringing the coal owners and the coal miners together; however, he could budge neither side. He commented that he had never met a more stubborn and pigheaded set of men than the coal miners—until he met the coal owners.

With the Conservative defeat at the May 1929 general election, Churchill moved into the political wilderness for 11 years. He began to write a biography of Marlborough and an Anglo-American history, returning to his journalistic roots, and traveled the world. He neglected Parliament and was frequently in conflict with the Conservative Party due to his opposing the bipartisan attitude toward India and supporting Edward VIII during the abdica-

tion crisis of 1936. He was also at odds with the Conservative Party on the Spanish Civil War. At first he supported the fascist cause in Spain; later, realizing that a fascist Spain allied with fascist Germany and Italy would surround France, he began to fear that France would be invaded and Britain would be drawn into war. As a result he opposed Franco in Spain and demanded British rearmament and the development of the Royal Air Force. He was most certainly a minority voice in the Conservative Party until the Munich agreement of 1938 effectively sacrificed Czechoslovakia to Germany in order to maintain peace. At this stage Churchill forged an alliance with Anthony Eden, by then a Conservative dissident, to oppose appeasement.

On 3 September 1939 Britain declared war on Germany. Churchill was called into Neville Chamberlain's wartime administration as First

Lord of the Admiralty. He typified the "bull-dog" spirit to such an extent that when Chamberlain resigned in May 1940 it was clear that Churchill was the only possible replacement; Churchill had already effectively taken over the defense side of the cabinet in April. Indeed, the Labour Party insisted upon Churchill as prime minister before it would join the wartime coalition in May 1940. Churchill's reputation as a tough and tenacious leader was enhanced by the groundswell of public support to continue the fight following the fall of France. His close friendship with Franklin D. Roosevelt led to significant help for Britain even before the United States joined the war. Churchill's meetings with Roosevelt and Stalin were key in forming the alliance that would win the war and prepare the way for a peaceful postwar world.

In 1945, after the victory had been won in Europe but before Japan had surrendered, Churchill decided to call a general election. As a successful wartime leader, he expected to win, even though the Gallup polls had indicated a strong lead for Labour since about 1942. It was thus a shock when he was defeated. Although Churchill was leader of the opposition between 1945 and 1951, he had less interest in British politics than in the world stage. As a staunch believer in empire, he opposed Britain's withdrawal from the Indian subcontinent as well as from the other far-flung corners of the British Empire. His sense of the direction of world political affairs at this time was well reflected in his famous speech, made on 15 March 1946, at Fulton, Missouri, in which, referring to Soviet expansion in Eastern Europe, he coined the phrase the "Iron Curtain." Churchill appears to have anticipated the development of the Cold War between the "Communist Bloc" and the "Western Bloc."

Churchill became prime minister again in October 1951. During his next four years in office he attempted to reconstruct some of the wartime unity that had characterized his first administration, tendering an olive branch to the Liberals and deciding not to revoke nationalization except in the case of the iron and steel industry. He aspired to the role of great world leader and sought an international agreement to reduce postwar tensions.

For his service to Britain, Churchill was awarded a knighthood in 1953. He also suffered a stroke in July 1953; from then onward, until his eventual resignation in 1955, he had limited influence. In reality it was Sir Anthony Eden who ran the day-to-day operation of government during this time; Eden officially became prime minister in 1955. After 1955, Churchill gradually withdrew from politics, although he did not retire from the House of Commons until 1964. He died in 1965.

Had Churchill retired from politics in the 1930s, he would have been remembered as a modestly successful politician who had secured some claim to fame through his involvement with Lloyd George in building up the Liberal government's welfare state between 1906 and 1914. Given his great talent, that might have been considered something of a failure. World War II gave him a better opportunity to prove his leadership abilities and to build a reputation as one of the most successful British politicians of the twentieth century.

Keith Laybourn

See also: Attlee, Clement; Baldwin, Stanley; Bevin, Ernest; Bonar Law, Andrew; Chamberlain, Neville; Eden, Sir Anthony; MacDonald, James Ramsay
References and Further Reading: Addison, Paul, 1992, *Churchill on the Home Front: 1900–1955* (London: Pimlico); Blake, Robert, and William R. Louis (eds.), 1993, 1996, *Churchill* (New York: W. W. Norton); Cannadine, David (ed.), 1996, *Blood, Toil, Tears and Sweat: The Speeches of Winston Churchill* (London: Penguin); Charmley, John, 1993, *Churchill: The End of Glory* (London: Hodder & Stoughton); Gilbert, Martin, 1971–1988, *Winston S. Churchill*, 8 vols. (London: Heinemann); Rhodes James, Robert (ed.), 1974, *Winston S. Churchill: His Complete Speeches, 1897–1963* (New York: Chelsea House Publishers); Robbins, Keith, 1991, *Churchill* (London: Longman); Stansky, Peter (ed.), 1973, *Churchill: A Profile* (New York: Hill and Wang); Taylor, A. J. P., et al., 1969, *Churchill: Four Faces of the Man* (London: Allen Lane).

Chuter-Ede, James Chuter (Lord Chuter-Ede)
(1882–1965) [HS]

James Chuter Chuter-Ede was born on 11 September 1882 in Epsom, Surrey, the son of James

Ede, a grocer, and Agnes Mary Chuter. He was educated at Epsom National School, Dorking High School, Battersea Pupil Teachers' Centre, and then at Christ's College, Cambridge, for which he had won a scholarship. However, he could not afford to complete his degree and he moved on to become an assistant master in various elementary schools in Surrey until 1914. During World War I, he served as a sergeant in the East Surreys and Royal Engineers.

Also during the war, he became a staunch Labour supporter, and in 1918 he stood as Labour candidate for the parliamentary division of Epsom. He lost this election but became Labour M.P. for Mitcham in 1923, following a parliamentary by-election; he did not retain this seat for long, losing it in the general election of December 1923. He returned to Parliament in 1929, as Labour M.P. for South Shields, holding the seat until Labour's heavy political defeat in 1931. However, he was again Labour's M.P. for South Shields from 1935 to 1964.

It was during World War II that Chuter-Ede first obtained ministerial experience. Between 1940 and 1945 he was parliamentary secretary in the Ministry of Education in Sir Winston Churchill's wartime administration, and he was closely involved in the passing of the 1944 Education Act, which ensured secondary education for all. The high point of his political career occurred between 1945 and 1951, when he served more than five years as home secretary in Clement Attlee's Labour governments. In this role he sponsored numerous bills on parliamentary representation and criminal justice.

The latter interest consumed most of his time in this period, largely because of the controversy surrounding capital punishment. Ede opposed a private members' bill, one put forward by a member of Parliament rather than the government, that advocated the suspension of capital punishment for a five-year experimental period. That clause was approved in the House of Commons but rejected in the House of Lords, giving Ede an opportunity to propose a compromise arrangement restricting capital punishment to a number of specific offenses. This clause also was defeated in the House of Lords, however, and the measure was dropped

from the Criminal Justice Bill. Nevertheless, Chuter-Ede had the government set up a royal commission on capital punishment. After the commission submitted its report to the Conservative government in 1955, Chuter-Ede voted in favor of a proposed measure to suspend capital punishment, but the measure was not carried.

In this area Chuter-Ede was greatly influenced by the fact that while serving as home secretary, he had denied a reprieve to Timothy John Evans, who had been convicted of murdering his wife, and that it had later become evident that the mass murderer John Christie, who lodged in Evans's house, was most probably the actual culprit. Although Chuter-Ede had come to believe that the public would never vote in a plebiscite to accept such a radical measure as suspending capital punishment, he nonetheless was disturbed by the permanence of capital punishment, which prevented miscarriages of justice from being rectified. He adamantly opposed capital punishment. Despite the defeat of the 1955 measure, Chuter-Ede himself proposed a second measure in 1956 to suspend the death penalty. The proposal was carried in the House of Commons and eventually led to the Homicide Act, which restricted capital punishment to specific types of murder. This had been Ede's compromise suggestion of 1947.

While serving in the Attlee governments, Ede also became deputy leader of the Labour Party, effectively deputy prime minister, in 1947, and was for a few months in 1951 the leader of the House of Commons. The defeat of the Labour government of 1951 brought his ministerial career to an end. In 1964 he was made a life peer, becoming Baron Chuter-Ede. He died on 11 November 1965. Although most political commentators today would not rank Chuter-Ede among the truly great political figures of the twentieth century, he is generally held in high regard for his performance as home secretary and his role in restricting capital punishment.

Keith Laybourn

See also: Attlee, Clement; Churchill, Sir Winston
References and Further Reading: Morgan, Kenneth, 1984, *Labour in Power* (Oxford: Clarendon Press).

Clarendon, Earl of (George William Frederick Villiers; Baron Hyde)
(1800–1870) [FS]

George William Frederick Villiers was born in London on 12 January 1800, the eldest son of George Villiers and his wife, Theresa, the only daughter of John Parker, first Baron Boringdon. He entered the diplomatic service while little more than a boy and in 1820 became attached to the British embassy in St. Petersburg, Russia. In 1823 he became a commissioner of customs, and between 1827 and 1829 he was employed in Ireland dealing with the unions of the English and Irish excise boards. Throughout the early 1830s he was involved in negotiating a commercial treaty with France and acting as envoy to Madrid.

Villiers married Katherine, the eldest daughter of Walter James Grimston, the first Earl of Verulam, on 4 June 1839. Shortly afterward, on the death of his uncle on 22 December 1839, he succeeded to the earldom and became the fourth Earl of Clarendon. A Whig committed to constitutional government and reform, he joined Lord Melbourne's ministry in 1840 as Lord Privy Seal and was sworn in as a member of the Privy Council. Soon afterward he became chancellor of the Duchy of Lancaster. Disturbed by Lord Palmerston's aggressive foreign policy, he was almost happy to leave office with the fall of the Melbourne ministry in July 1841.

At this stage in his life Clarendon appears to have adopted a liberal attitude toward Ireland and to have been a firm believer in free trade. In Lord Russell's ministry he became lord lieutenant of Ireland in 1847. While acting in this role, he was forced to use more coercion than he would have liked in order to deal with the Irish famine, the Young Ireland movement, and the Smith O'Brien uprising. He found that his policies offended both Catholic and Protestant interests; his life was threatened, and he became almost a prisoner in Dublin Castle. Nevertheless, he continued in this office until 1852.

He was offered the post of foreign secretary on Palmerston's fall in December 1851, but refused. In 1852, when Lord John Russell and Lord Palmerston were in serious conflict, during a brief Conservative ministry led by the Earl of Derby, it was suggested that Clarendon might be a good candidate for Whig prime minister when the political tide turned. However, this never occurred, and it was Lord Aberdeen who became Whig prime minister at the head of a coalition government between 1852 and 1855. Lord John Russell, who was foreign secretary, resigned in February 1853, creating a new opening for Clarendon.

Clarendon served as foreign secretary for five years, until February 1858. During this period there was a great deal of friction between Russia and Turkey over control of the Crimean peninsula. When it looked as though Russia planned an expansion into Turkey, the British and French governments ordered their respective national fleets to the Black Sea. After the British and French clashed with the Turkish fleet at Sinope, war in Crimea became inevitable. Clarendon went to Paris in February and March 1856 to conclude a peace settlement with the Russians. He successfully negotiated a treaty that demonstrated to the Turks, by the Russian concession of lands, that Britain was a trustworthy ally.

Clarendon gained further prestige in 1855 when the Whig Lord Aberdeen resigned as prime minister and it was not at all clear whether Lord John Russell, a Whig, or Lord Derby, a Tory, would succeed him. Acting as adviser to Queen Victoria, Clarendon suggested that Lord Palmerston, a Whig, might be able to form a ministry. Palmerston accepted the post, and Clarendon continued as foreign secretary until Palmerston's government fell in 1858 and was replaced briefly by Lord Derby's second Tory government. When the Whig/Liberals returned to office in 1859, once again under Palmerston, Lord Russell claimed the post of foreign secretary. Clarendon refused Palmerston's offer of another post, and instead, for the next six years, he fulfilled a number of other public duties for both Queen Victoria and the British government. Clarendon did later return to office as foreign secretary when Russell formed a ministry in 1865, following the death of Lord Palmerston; but it was a very brief period of service, from November 1865 until July 1866.

In December 1868 the Liberals returned to office under William Ewart Gladstone, and Clarendon became foreign secretary for a third time. During this period his main achievement was to obtain a settlement between Britain and the United States on the issue of Alabama and other outstanding territorial claims. The convention of 14 January 1869 established that territorial claims by British and American citizens would be settled by private litigation. The U.S. Senate, however, refused to ratify this agreement, and negotiations continued.

Clarendon died unexpectedly on 27 June 1870 and was buried at Watford in Hertfordshire. His contemporaries recognized this Liberal aristocrat as one of the great foreign secretaries of the nineteenth century, his training and early experiences having made him highly suitable for the post. He might not have had the reputation and vigor of Palmerston; but he was a diplomatic, solid, and reliable advocate of peace and of British interests abroad.

Keith Laybourn

See also: Aberdeen, Earl of; Derby, 14th Earl of; Gladstone, William Ewart; Melbourne, Viscount; Palmerston, Lord; Russell, Lord John
References and Further Reading: Chamberlain, Muriel, 1987, *Lord Palmerston* (Washington, DC: Catholic University of America Press); Conacher, J., 1968, *The Aberdeen Coalition: 1852–1855* (London: Cambridge University Press); Conacher, J., 1987, *Britain and the Crimea, 1855–56: Problems of War and Peace* (New York: St. Martin's).

Clarke, Kenneth
(1940–) [CE, HS]

Throughout the 1980s and 1990s Kenneth Clarke represented the left wing of the Conservative Party, opposing the right-wing, anti-European tendencies of Margaret Thatcher and some sections of the John Major government. Defeated in the 1997 Conservative leadership elections by William Hague, he has nevertheless since then sought to challenge the Conservative Party's tendency to present an anti-European image. Although popular with the British electorate, he has never won the hearts of Conservative Party activists.

Clarke was born on 2 July 1940, the son of a Nottingham miner who had left the mines to open a jeweller's shop. He was educated at Nottingham High School and at Trinity College, Cambridge, where he was chairman of the Cambridge University Conservative Association. He was later chairman of the Conservative Federation of Students. He was admitted to the bar through Gray's Inn in 1963, and married Gillian Mary Edwards the following year.

In 1970, after failing to win the Mansfield parliamentary seat in 1964 and 1966, he became Conservative M.P. for Rushcliffe. He soon began to rise through the junior ministerial ranks, becoming assistant whip (1972–1974) and then lord commissioner at the Treasury (1974) in the ministry of Edward Heath. After a break of five years, he continued to climb the political ladder during the years of the Thatcher and Major governments. He became parliamentary secretary on transport in 1979, minister of health in 1982, and paymaster general and minister of employment in 1985. He served as chancellor of the Duchy of Lancaster and as minister of trade between 1987 and 1988; as secretary of state for health between 1988 and 1990; and as secretary of state for education and science between 1990 and 1992. He reached the top echelon in 1992, becoming home secretary.

In all these roles, Clarke was a brusque, nononsense imparter of Thatcherite views, although he had a pro-Europe attitude that brought him into conflict with large sections of his party. A savvy political operator, Clarke sensed in November 1990 that it was time for Thatcher to resign as Conservative leader and prime minister, and he forthrightly told her so.

Clarke became chancellor of the exchequer in May 1993, succeeding Norman Lamont. His appointment alarmed many in the party's right wing who felt that the balance of Major's cabinet was tilting away from full-blooded Thatcherism. Ironically, by the autumn of 1993, some of these same right-wingers were so disillusioned by Major's leadership that they were beginning to promote Clarke as a future Conservative leader. One right-winger approvingly cited Clarke's aggressive approach to the issue of European union, even though this right-winger was highly skeptical of Europe himself, quoting

Clarke's comment, "What I think is that they're a bunch of complete f—rs and if only I didn't have a majority of seventeen I'd kick their heads in" (Evans 1999, p. 181). Clarke was seen at this stage by many elements as the "only natural leader when the party cries out for one" (Evans 1999, p. 181). Such speculation was ended at the Conservative Conference of 1993, however, when Clarke declared that any "enemy of John Major is an enemy of mine" (Evans 1999, p. 181). As chancellor he introduced cautious budgets that continued to impose restrictions on government spending. Gordon Brown, who succeeded him in May 1997 when Tony Blair formed his Labour government, also continued this tight control of spending for two years.

Clarke has continued to be prominent in Conservative politics. He was outbid for the Conservative leadership position by William Hague in 1997 and has since become increasingly isolated from the mainstream Conservative Party. His pro-European policy is at odds with the views being put forward by the present Conservative leadership.

Keith Laybourn

See also: Heath, Edward; Lamont, Norman; Major, John; Thatcher, Margaret
References and Further Reading: Evans, Brendan, 1999, *Thatcherism and British Politics, 1975–1999* (Stroud, UK: Sutton).

Clynes, John Richard
(1869–1949) [HS]

John Richard Clynes was born in Oldham on 27 March 1869, the eldest son of Patrick Clynes, an Irish farm worker who had emigrated to Lancashire and found employment there as a gravedigger for the town corporation, and of Bridget Scanlon. John attended elementary school until he was ten years of age and then began work as a piecer (a job in the cotton-spinning process) in the cotton textile trade. He became a "big piecer" in 1883. In 1891 he became a full-time district organizer of the National Union of Gas Workers and General Labourers, a union for the unskilled, and acted as its president between 1912 and 1937. He was first president and then secretary of the Oldham Trades Council between 1892 and 1912, and secretary

of the Lancashire Piecers' Union from 1896. He regularly attended meetings of the Trades Union Congress for his unions as well as various international trade union meetings.

Clynes was a socialist and a founding member of the Independent Labour Party (ILP), which was formed at St. George's Hall, Bradford, in January 1893; he also attended the international Socialist Congress held at Zurich that year. Clynes also married Elizabeth, the daughter of Owen Harper, in 1893. His marital affiliation did not impair his socialist activities. He was active in the ILP and the Labour Representation Committee (LRC), later the Labour Party, which was formed in 1900, and was a member of the LRC/Labour national executive committee between 1904 and 1930.

Clynes began his parliamentary career when he became M.P. for the Manchester Northeast constituency in 1906, holding the seat until 1945, except during the years from 1931 to 1935, following Ramsay MacDonald's defection from Labour. In fact Clynes retired at the age limit set by trade union rules. In the House of Commons he held many different posts. He was vice-chairman of the Parliamentary Labour Party (the Labour Party is the party throughout the country, while the Parliamentary Labour Party is the organization that brings M.P.s together in the House of Commons) in 1918 and chairman in 1921. As chairman, he was effectively Labour leader, although that title did not come into use until 1922, when Ramsay MacDonald defeated Clynes in the leadership contest that followed the 1922 general election.

Clynes's ubiquity within Labour ranks helped him obtain high office. Although he had warned Labour against joining Asquith's wartime coalition government in May 1915, Clynes himself accepted membership in the Food Commission in 1917, and in 1918 he became a member of the Privy Council and the Controller of Food. He was opposed to Labour's withdrawal from Lloyd George's coalition government in November 1918 but accepted the Labour Party's decision to do so. He was out of office until January 1924 when, having moved a vote of no confidence in the Baldwin government in January 1924, he became deputy leader of the House of Commons and Lord Privy Seal in MacDonald's first Labour government.

The first Labour government lasted barely ten months, and it was almost five years before Labour came to office again. In the interlude Clynes worked to enable the miners, mine owners, and the government to achieve a compromise that would avoid industrial conflict. He failed in that effort, but got his union to give its full backing for the nine-day General Strike of May 1926, when almost two million trade unionists struck in support of the miners.

In June 1929 the second Labour government was formed and Clynes became home secretary. In this role he attempted to introduce prison reform, promoted the cotton-trade enquiry, and made the decision to refuse Trotsky, the Russian revolutionary, permission to settle in Britain. He attempted to introduce a bill for electoral reform, but it was doomed by the economic crisis of the summer of 1931 and the collapse of the second Labour government in August. Clynes was offered the leadership of the Labour Party after MacDonald's defection but refused the offer. Instead, he spent more time building up his union, now known as the National Union of General and Municipal Workers, which had almost 500,000 members when he retired as its president.

Clynes retired from Parliament in 1945, at age 75, and lived frugally on his trade union pension at Putney, in London. He died on 23 October 1949. He was a much-respected figure in Labour circles and tremendously active in Labour's trade union and political organs. His defeat by Ramsay MacDonald in the contest to become Labour leader in 1922 is a likely indicator that although he was a brilliant administrator he lacked the oratorical skills essential for effective leadership. His strong trade union credentials guaranteed him a high place in Labour's ranks but could not guarantee him the position of leader and prime minister, although he had anticipated such an outcome at the beginning of 1922.

Keith Laybourn

See also: MacDonald, James Ramsay; Snowden, Philip
References and Further Reading: Clynes, John R., 1937, *Memoirs,* 2 vols. (London: Hutchinson);

Clynes, John R., 1940, *When I Remember* (London: Macmillan); Jefferys, Kevin (ed.), 1999, *Leading Labour: From Keir Hardie to Tony Blair* (London: I. B. Tauris).

Compton, Spencer (Earl of Wilmington) (1673–1743) [PM]

Compton is more often remembered for the brief period when he had the chance of being prime minister and did not take it than for the slightly longer period, at the very end of his life, when against his own wishes he finally took charge of the Treasury (but not of the ministry). When George II inherited the crown on 11 June 1727, Compton was briefly spoken of in political circles as Sir Robert Walpole's successor as head of government; Compton had been head of the household and treasurer to George II before the latter became king, from 1715 to 1727. But Compton lacked the political will and self-confidence to accept the post of First Lord of the Treasury, much less to bring his friends from the opposition into government with him. Within days of George's accession to the throne, it was clear that Walpole would continue in office. When the new king required a King's Speech to dissolve the old Parliament—a routine political step—it was Walpole and not Compton who had the experience and skill to write it.

Walpole mollified his rival, and removed a possible opponent from the Commons, by having Compton created Baron Wilmington on 8 January 1728, and further elevated on 14 May 1730, with the titles of first Earl of Wilmington and Viscount Pevensey. From May to December that year, Compton was Lord Privy Seal; and in the same year he also attained the post of Lord President of the Council, which brought with it considerable influence. He continued in this role until he became First Lord of the Treasury in 1742.

Compton was not a first-rank politician, and he had the misfortune of attracting the contempt of some of the most-quoted pundits of this period. Lord Hervey derided Compton for his passivity during the succession crisis, describing him as "just as well satisfied to be bowing and grinning in the antechamber . . . as if he had been dictating in the closet, sole fountain of court favor at home, and regulator of all the national transactions abroad" (Sedgwick 1931, p. 40). If he lacked the instincts of a politician, though, Compton was an able parliamentarian and a natural courtier.

The second surviving son of the third Earl of Northampton, Compton was born into a Warwickshire family noted for its support of the Crown. He first entered Parliament as a Tory, becoming M.P. for Eye in June 1698. He soon joined the Whigs. He lost his borough seat in the Tory triumphs of the election year 1710. He was already associated with Walpole, and acted with him that year in the impeachment of the extremist High Church Tory Henry Sacheverell. Compton served as M.P. for East Grinstead from 1713 to 1715, and from 1715 to 1728 served as member for the county of Sussex. From 1715 to 1727 he was an able, formal, and industrious speaker of the House of Commons, keeping his position even when, from 1717 to 1720, he was in opposition, together with Walpole and Viscount (Lord) Townshend. His position as speaker was at the time considered compatible with the lucrative office of paymaster general, which he also occupied from 1722 to 1730. Compton's long association with George II as prince and as king was an important element in his political longevity, although Lord Hervey could never understand by what talents or persuasions this "plodding heavy fellow" had managed to gain influence over the king.

When Walpole fell, Wilmington was appointed First Lord of the Treasury on 16 February 1742. The "Patriot" opposition coalition of Whig and Tory was expected to sweep into office and introduce a new era of cross-party cooperation and pure government. In the event, though, the Tories were left in opposition, the Whig leader William Pulteney went to the House of Lords as the Earl of Bath, and many of Walpole's associates continued in office. Wilmington had done nothing to save Walpole, but he was not overtly associated with the opposition and owed his place mainly to George II.

The office of prime minister had not yet developed into a fixed institution, and Wilming-ton was not seen as the head of the administration; that position was viewed as belonging to Pulteney's leading associate, John Carteret, secretary of state for the north. Like Wilmington's, Carteret's standing came from his influence over George II, whose Hanoverian predilections in foreign policy he encouraged. Carteret was gradually outmaneuvered by the Duke of Newcastle and his brother Henry Pelham; and after Wilmington's death, Pelham, as First Lord of the Treasury and chancellor of the exchequer, became the acknowledged leading minister.

The last phase of Wilmington's political career brought him no more credit among political observers than he had previously enjoyed: to a vain and ambitious young Whig, Charles Hanbury Williams, he was that "old, dull, important lord." Wilmington was not a leader and statesman of the first rank but a steady career politician. His industry and his ceremonious and complaisant manner served him well both as speaker and as courtier, despite the sallies of political wits. A lifelong bachelor, he was expected to leave his Sussex estates, worth over £3,000 per year, to John, Lord Sackville. On his death in office on 2 July 1743, however, his entire estate was left to his nephew, the fifth Earl of Northampton.

Philip Woodfine

See also: Newcastle, Duke of; Pelham, Hon. Henry; Pulteney, Sir William; Townshend, Charles (Viscount Townshend); Walpole, Sir Robert
References and Further Reading: Sedgwick, Romney (ed.), 1931, *Memoirs of the Reign of King George II* (London: Eyre & Spottiswoode); Sedgwick, Romney (ed.), 1970, *The History of Parliament: The House of Commons, 1715–1754* (New York: Oxford University Press); Thomas, Peter D. G., 1971, *The House of Commons in the Eighteenth Century* (Oxford: Clarendon Press).

Conway, Henry Seymour
(1721–1795) [FS, HS]

Henry Seymour Conway was the nephew of Sir Robert Walpole and sat as an M.P. for various pocket boroughs in the British Parliament from 1741 to 1784. Concurrently he pursued a military career, being present at several battles, including Culloden in 1745, where he was aide-de-camp to the Duke of Cumberland. He rose to the rank of lieutenant general in 1759 but was dismissed in 1764 for opposing what he felt were arbitrary measures put forward by King George III and his ministers in their attempts to suppress John Wilkes and his freedom-of-the-press campaign.

Conway was secretary of state for the Southern Department between July 1765 and May 1766, in the George Grenville administration. Subsequently, he was secretary of state for the Northern Department between 1765 and 1768, in the administrations of the second Marquess of Rockingham and the first Earl of Chatham, William Pitt. Conway was also lieutenant general of the ordnance between 1767 and 1772. He was promoted to general in 1772, and to field marshal in 1793. He was also governor of Jersey, where he occasionally resided, from 1775 until his death in 1795. Conway opposed the prosecution of the American war between 1775 and 1781, but nevertheless became commander in chief of the British army in 1782. He held that post until 1784, when he resigned after launching a personal verbal attack on William Pitt, the Younger.

Kit Hardwick

See also: Grenville, George; Pitt, William (the Elder); Pitt, William (the Younger); Rockingham, Marquess of
References and Further Reading: Black, Jeremy (ed.), 1990, *British Politics and Society from Walpole to Pitt* (Basingstoke, UK: Macmillan).

Cook, Robin
(1946–) [FS]

Robin Cook became foreign secretary in Tony Blair's Labour government in May 1997. Despite his critics, most observers recognized that he was a most capable occupant of this post. Nevertheless, he came in for severe criticism in 1998, when he left his wife, Margaret, by whom he had two sons, and married his secretary. In early January 1999, Margaret savaged him in a memoir, *A Slight and Delicate Creature,* which suggested that he had had former lovers and had

Robin Cook addresses the United Nations General Assembly, 20 September 1999 (AFP/Corbis)

sold out his Old Labour credentials to New Labour in order to improve his career prospects. In other words, he became "coarsened and hardened" as time progressed, and gradually became estranged from his family.

Robin Cook was born on 28 February 1946 in Bellshill. He was educated at Aberdeen Grammar School; the Royal High School, Edinburgh; and the University of Edinburgh, where he obtained an M.A. (with honors) in English literature. Between 1970 and 1974 he was a Workers' Education Association tutor. He was also a keen follower of horse racing and wrote a weekly column for the *Glasgow Herald*.

Cook entered politics as an Edinburgh city councillor between 1971 and 1974. Then he entered Parliament as M.P. for Edinburgh Central, representing that constituency from 1974 to 1983; since 1983, he has represented Livingston. He rose quickly in the Labour Party and assumed many important leading posts. He was a member of Labour's Treasury team between 1980 and 1983, party leadership campaign manager for Neil Kinnock in 1983, opposition spokesman on European affairs in 1983 and 1984, and campaigns coordinator for the Parliamentary Labour Party between 1984 and 1986. He was also the opposition's spokesman on the City of London Stock Exchange between 1986 and 1987, shadow secretary for health from 1987 to 1992, and shadow secretary of state for trade and industry between 1992 and 1994. He was also campaign manager for John Smith in the Labour leadership contest in 1992. In 1994 he became shadow secretary of state for foreign affairs, which ensured that he would assume the role of foreign secretary, or secretary of state for foreign affairs, when Labour came to power in May 1997.

On accepting the office of foreign secretary in 1997, Cook announced that the new Labour government would pursue an "ethical foreign policy" and would not sell weapons to dictatorial goverments that disregarded human rights; but this policy seems since to have been abandoned. In May 1997, he also announced that the United Kingdom would sign the European Social Charter. In addition, Cook pursued a policy in support of the United States military

campaigns against Iraq and Yugoslavia. More recently, in 2000, he presided over Britain's intervention to restore order in Sierra Leone.

Keith Laybourn

See also: Blair, Tony; Straw, Jack
References and Further Reading: Cook, Margaret, 1999, *A Slight and Delicate Creature* (London: Weidenfeld & Nicolson); Panitch, Leo, and Colin Leys, 1997, *The End of Parliamentary Socialism: From New Left to New Labour* (London: Verso).

Cripps, Sir Stafford
(1889–1952) [CE]

Richard Stafford Cripps, always known as Stafford Cripps, was one of the Labour Party's most controversial political figures. He rose quickly to become the party's deputy leader, was subsequently expelled, and later, when restored to party membership, became Clement Attlee's chancellor of the exchequer—the famous "Austerity Cripps"—in the first postwar Labour government. Throughout his political career he excited critical comment because of his arrogance and certitude, evoking comments such as "There but for the grace of God goes God." Nevertheless, he was particularly important in leading the Labour left in the 1930s and in acting as British ambassador to Moscow at the beginning of World War II.

Cripps was born on 24 April 1889, the fifth child of Charles Alfred Cripps—later the first Lord Parmoor, who was Lord President of the Council in the first two Labour governments of 1924 and 1929–1931—and of Theresa Potter, sister of the famous socialist writer and activist Beatrice Potter (later Webb). Cripps was educated at Winchester and at University College, London, where he intended to become a research chemist. However, he decided to follow both his father and grandfather into a legal career. He married Isobel Swithinbank in July 1911 and became a barrister shortly afterward, in 1913.

Cripps's legal career was interrupted by World War I, during which he drove a truck for the Red Cross, having been barred from military service on medical grounds. In 1915 he took a position in the Ministry of Munitions, in the explosives department. At the end of the war he returned to

A cartoon satirizing the 1949 British devaluation policy enacted by Parliament, featuring Secretary of State Ernest Bevin physically supporting a rattled Stafford Cripps, who drops his briefcase (Library of Congress)

the legal profession and quickly established a successful practice, mainly in patent and compensation cases. In 1926 he became the youngest King's Counsel in the British bar. His legal work for the London county council soon brought him to the attention of Herbert Morrison, who persuaded him to join the Labour Party in 1929. Cripps was appointed solicitor general in Ramsay MacDonald's Labour government in October 1930, and was knighted in 1930.

Cripps entered Parliament as Labour M.P. for East Bristol via the 1931 general election, which brought MacDonald's National government to power and reduced the Labour Party to 46 M.P.s from more than six times that number in 1929. Cripps's obvious ability, in the context of the much-reduced Labour Party, allowed him to rise to the top of Labour politics within months of his entering Parliament.

From the beginning of his parliamentary career, Cripps argued that Labour's gradualist approach to socialism was dead. He adopted a more assertive approach to socialism, demanding the introduction of measures to ensure the swift transfer of the means of production to public ownership under a future Labour government. Toward this end he cofounded the Socialist League in 1932—a body of ex-members of the Independent Labour Party and the Labour left—and through it sought to unify the various British socialist groups, including the Independent Labour Party and the Communist Party of Great Britain, against the rising challenge of fascism. The forlorn hope was that the Labour Party might eventually adopt socialist unity to fight fascism. Instead, the Labour Party, of which he was deputy leader at the time, forced the Socialist League to disband in 1937. Cripps meanwhile rechanneled his efforts into the launching of the *Tribune,* a left-wing journal, in January 1937.

Labour's hostility to other socialist and nonsocialist parties did not permanently prevent Cripps from attempting to form a broader organization. Indeed, he mounted a Popular Front movement, to bring together all those who opposed fascism, in 1938 and 1939. Cripps demanded the removal of the government of Neville Chamberlain; spoke out against appeasement; and issued the "Cripps Memorandum" on the need for a Popular Front against fascism. His renewed call for a political organization that was opposed by the Labour Party led to Cripps's expulsion from the party in early 1939.

At the beginning of World War II, Cripps acted as an unofficial government envoy as he toured China, India, and the Soviet Union, an action promoted by Lord Halifax. Churchill made Cripps British ambassador to the Soviet Union in May 1940, a post he held until January 1942. His job was to improve relations with the Soviet Union and to get it to support Britain in the war effort. This was no easy task, given the existence of a nonaggression pact between Germany and the Soviet Union; but the German invasion of the Soviet Union (Operation Barbarossa) in the summer of 1941 changed matters. The Soviet Union entered the war on the side of the Allies, and Cripps returned to Britain in 1942 to such popular acclaim that there was some speculation that he might replace Churchill as prime minister. Cripps was quickly admitted to the war cabinet; but Churchill soon sent him off to India to secure an accommoda-

tion with the nationalist leaders there, and when Cripps returned empty-handed, Churchill removed him from the war cabinet to the more marginal post of minister of aircraft production.

In 1945, Cripps was readmitted to the Labour Party and was given the post of president of the Board of Trade in Attlee's first postwar Labour government, where he was primarily responsible for rationing. He was also involved in an unsuccessful cabinet mission to India in 1946. At this stage it was clear that he was among those pushing for Ernest Bevin to replace Attlee; but Attlee cleverly headed off this coup by placing Cripps at the head of the newly created Ministry of Economic Affairs. After Hugh Dalton resigned as chancellor of the exchequer, that office was combined with the Treasury, and Cripps was promoted to the post of chancellor of the exchequer in 1947.

In this role Cripps introduced three deflationary budgets between 1948 and 1950, in which he attempted to control the level of welfare spending, particularly on Aneurin Bevan's National Health Service. He also introduced a voluntary wage freeze and a limit on dividends, and announced the devaluation of the pound in September 1949. Ill health led to Cripps's resignation in October 1950 and his move to Zurich, where he died eighteen months later.

Cripps had led a distinguished albeit checkered political career. In the various roles of leader of the Labour left in the 1930s, opposer of appeasement, and proactive British ambassador in Moscow, he won huge recognition and support. Unfortunately, in later years his obvious administrative and political skills were overlooked as his name came to be associated with austerity and devaluation.

Keith Laybourn

See also: Attlee, Clement; Bevin, Ernest; Churchill, Sir Winston; Dalton, Hugh; MacDonald, James Ramsay

References and Further Reading: Bryant, Chris, 1992, *Stafford Cripps the First Modern Chancellor* (London: Hodder & Stoughton); Cooke, Colin, 1957, *The Life of Richard Stafford Cripps* (London: Hodder & Stoughton); Morgan, Kenneth O., 1984, *Labour in Power* (Oxford: Clarendon Press); Morgan, Kenneth O., 1987, *Labour People* (Oxford: Oxford University Press).

Crosland, Tony
(1918–1977) [FS]

Tony Crosland was a leading British socialist thinker of the post–World War II years, and one of the leading revisionists within the Labour Party in the 1950s. He held a number of ministerial posts in Labour governments in the 1960s and 1970s, most prominently, albeit briefly, that of foreign secretary.

Charles Anthony Raven Crosland was born on 28 August 1918 in Sussex and was educated at Trinity College, Oxford, where he at first focused on the classics and then settled on economics. His academic life was interrupted by World War II, during which he became an officer in the Royal Welsh Fusiliers and served in North Africa. He returned to Oxford after the war, becoming chairman of the Democratic Socialist Club, president of the Oxford Union, and a member of the national executive of the Fabian Society. He became a tutor and lecturer in economics at Oxford in 1947. However, he abandoned his academic career in 1950 to become M.P. for South Gloucestershire. He lost that seat in 1955 but established his prominence within the Labour Party by publishing a book titled *The Future of Socialism* in 1956.

Regarded as a key document of Labour revisionism, this work built upon his article in the *New Fabian Essays,* published in 1952, in which he had attempted to balance a theoretical analysis of socialism with its practical application. His writings stressed that Labour's socialism should not be simply about nationalization and the provision of welfare benefits but should seek the eradication of persistent, gross inequalities of wealth (not income), reform of the educational system, and creation of a less confrontational system of industrial relations. *The Future of Socialism* developed these ideas further, stressing that socialist aims were essentially ethical and moral, and sprang from the ideals of liberty, fellowship, social welfare, and equality. To establish these principles, particularly equality, resources and wealth must be redistributed in society through social expenditure and progressive taxation. This, it was argued, could be achieved with ease because society had mastered production and could sustain economic growth.

It followed that the public ownership of the means of production, Labour's famous Clause Four, was no longer essential to the development of socialist policy. However, it was essential that there should be educational reform to create the new egalitarian type of society; the 11-plus exam, and the selective and discriminatory secondary provision that followed it, must be eliminated. At this time, children were tested for their intelligence quotient (IQ) at the age of eleven and then assigned to different grades of school, namely, grammar schools, technical schools, or secondary modern schools.

Crosland's views were taken up by Hugh Gaitskell, who argued that educational reform and taxation were more likely to achieve ethical socialism than public ownership. Gaitskell attempted, unsuccessfully, to get the Labour Party Conference of 1959 to remove Clause Four from the party's constitution, as he felt that this clause was the basis of Labour's unpopularity in the 1959 general election. However, trade union opposition ensured that on this, as on other issues, the Labour Party leadership would not get its way.

In 1959 Crosland was elected to Parliament as the M.P. for Grimsby. During this period he supported Gaitskell's campaigns to revoke Clause Four and to ensure that the Labour Party abandoned its policy of unilateral nuclear disarmament. However, the momentum of revisionism faded in 1963 when Gaitskell died and was replaced by Harold Wilson, a pragmatic and more compromising Labour leader. As a result, Crosland was given middling government posts rather than the higher posts he might have expected under Gaitskell.

Crosland was Wilson's minister to the Department of Economic Affairs in 1964 before serving as secretary of state for science and education between 1965 and 1967. In this latter role he was largely responsible for Circular 10/65, which requested that all local authorities consider plans for a comprehensive reorganization of education. This circular created controversy, as it made clear that Crosland meant to replace the selective grammar schools with all-embracing, comprehensive schools.

Crosland was president of the Board of Trade between 1967 and 1969, and secretary of state for local government and regional planning between 1969 and 1970. In June 1970 the Labour Party was defeated in a general election, and Crosland was in the opposition until 1974. However, during that period, and particularly between 1972 and 1974, it is clear that he was pushing forward arguments within the party in favor of a future Labour government seeking Britain's entry into the European Economic Community, although he compromised on this issue from time to time.

In Wilson's 1974 Labour government, Crosland was appointed secretary of state for the environment. This was a post of only middling importance, but it gave him a seat on the cabinet. When Wilson resigned, Crosland entered the party leadership contest but came in last out of six candidates, polling a mere 17 votes in the first ballot, in an election that eventually resulted in James Callaghan's installation as Labour leader. Despite this outcome, Callaghan promoted Crosland to foreign secretary, a post he held from April 1976 until his death on 19 February 1977, during which his main concern was dealing with Ian Smith's declaration of independence for Rhodesia.

During the last year of his life, Crosland began to rethink again the revisionist ideas he had first put forward in the 1950s. The deepening economic crisis in 1976 had forced Denis Healey, the chancellor of the exchequer, to seek a loan from the International Monetary Fund. The loan was obtained, but at the cost of massive cuts in government expenditures. At this juncture, Prime Minister Callaghan spoke of the fact that the party was over and that vast inputs of investment and expenditure in the economy could not be expected in order to ensure that there was continued full employment. The Keynesian expansionist policies that Labour had adopted since 1945 were now unaffordable. The redistribution of income and wealth that the Labour government had promised the trade unions in 1974 in return for a "social contract" controlling wage demands would not be achieved. The Crosland idea was also dead. Economic growth could not ensure high social expenditure and the redistribution of income and wealth, because it could not be sustained.

Crosland was a successful politician and an effective cabinet minister, but above all he is remembered for being a great socialist thinker. His book *The Future of Socialism* is still regarded as one of the most influential socialist tracts of the twentieth century, although its demands for the redistribution of wealth no longer form a major plank in New Labour strategy. Crosland's lasting legacy is his commitment to Britain's being a society of equals rather than the "parade of dwarfs and giants" described in the *Guardian* (28 July 1997) in the aftermath of the Thatcher and Major administrations.

Keith Laybourn

See also: Blair, Tony; Callaghan, James; Heath, Edward; Thatcher, Margaret; Wilson, Harold
References: and Further Reading: Brivati, Brian, 1996, *Hugh Gaitskell* (London: Richard Cohen); Crosland, Charles A. R., 1956, *The Future of Socialism* (London: Jonathan Cape); Crosland, Charles A. R., 1962, *The Conservative Enemy* (London: Jonathan Cape); Crosland, Charles A. R., 1974, *Socialism Now* (London: Jonathan Cape); Crosland, Susan, 1982, *Tony Crosland* (London: Jonathan Cape); Jefferys, Kevin, 1999, *Anthony Crosland: A New Biography* (London: Richard Cohen).

Cross, Sir Richard Assheton (Viscount Cross)
(1823–1914) [HS]

Richard Assheton Cross was born at Red Scar, near Preston, Lancashire, on 30 May 1823, the third son of William Cross and his wife, Ellen, the eldest daughter of Edward Chaffers of Liverpool. He was educated at Rugby while Thomas Arnold was headmaster, and at Trinity College, Cambridge. He was called to the bar through the Inner Temple in 1849 and began to practice law, operating on the northern circuit. He was active mainly in Preston, where he built up a considerable legal business. He married Georgiana, the third daughter of Thomas Lyon of Appleton Hall, near Warrington, Lancashire.

Cross became Conservative M.P. for Preston in 1857, but often acted independently of the party. He gave up that seat in 1862, along with his legal practice, upon the death of his father-in-law, whose position in Parr's Bank at Warrington he subsequently filled. Parr's Bank performed well during the Cotton Famine of the early 1860s (the lapse in cotton supply was caused by the American Civil War), developing a limited liability within banking, and Cross became chairman in 1870.

Cross returned to the House of Commons in 1868 as a Conservative M.P. for Southwest Lancashire, defeating William Ewart Gladstone in the process. Nevertheless, Gladstone found another seat and formed a ministry. When Benjamin Disraeli became prime minister in 1874, he made Cross home secretary. Cross had achieved this post without first having gone through the customary junior ministerial ranks, and in that respect he was a rarity.

As home secretary Cross was immensely successful. It has been said that Disraeli was either above or below mere matters of detail; but Cross was not, and it was his task to fulfill the pledges of social reform made by Disraeli in the 1874 general election. Cross shaped the principles of social reform that dominated Disraeli's ministry of 1874 to 1880. He introduced the Licensing Act of 1874 and the Artisans' Dwelling Act of 1875, permitting local authorities to pull down slums and replace them with suitable houses. He was also responsible for a variety of factory acts. Most important in this arena were the Factory Act of 1875, which dealt with the employment of women and children in textile factories, and the 1878 Factories and Workshops Act, which codified and consolidated existing legislation in response to a royal commission set up in 1876. In 1875, Cross introduced the Conspiracy and Protection of Property Act, which reinforced the law against violent intimidation of striking workers, stating that any action legal in law if taken by one person would also be legal if taken by two or more. The Master and Servant Act of 1875 made any breach of contract a civil offense for both parties; previously it had been a criminal offense for workers and a civil offense for employers.

Cross was in opposition from 1880 to 1885, and his political influence was eclipsed by the rise of a new breed of Conservative politician, exemplified by Lord Randolph Churchill. Nevertheless, Cross served briefly as home secretary between June 1885 and February 1886, in the government of Lord Salisbury, before he was transferred to the India Office and raised to the peerage as Viscount Cross of Broughton-in-Furness with a seat in the House of Lords. He remained at the India Office until 1892. He became Lord Privy Seal in 1895, retaining the position until 1900, and then retiring from politics in 1902. After that he rarely appeared in the House of Lords. He died on 8 January 1914.

Cross fulfilled many other roles in his life, acting as an ecclesiastical commissioner and working in the interests of the Church of England. Nevertheless, he will be best remembered as the reforming home secretary who, in the 1870s, attempted to improve the social welfare of the working classes in whom Disraeli had placed so much hope of building up working-class Toryism.

Keith Laybourn

See also: Disraeli, Benjamin; Gladstone, William Ewart; Salisbury, Lord
References and Further Reading: Smith, Paul, 1967, *Disraelian Conservatism and Social Reform* (London: Routledge & Kegan Paul).

Curzon, Lord (George Nathaniel Curzon; Marquess of Kedleston; Earl Curzon; Marquess Curzon) (1859–1925) [FS]

George Nathaniel Curzon was a Conservative politician and statesman who narrowly missed becoming Conservative leader and thus prime minister in the early 1920s. Instead, Stanley Baldwin became prime minister, probably ensuring a popular vote for Conservatism across social classes, which Curzon's aristocratic and antidemocratic attitudes might not have done in the years following the tripling of the electorate (which went from 7 million to 21 million in 1918, the year the Franchise Act was passed).

Curzon was born 11 January 1859, the eldest child of the Rev. Alfred Nathaniel Holden Curzon, fourth baron Scarsdale and rector of Kedleston, and his wife, Blanche. The family lived at Kedleston Hall in Derbyshire. He was privately tutored and then sent to a private school operated by the Rev. Cowley Powles, at Wixenford in Hampshire, before entering Eton, where he remained until 1878. He was a successful scholar at Eton, where he gained a passion for the study of the "mysteries" of the East. He then went to Balliol College, Oxford, where he addressed the Oxford Union on the Afghan question and helped form the Canning Club with other young Conservatives. In 1880 he became president of the Oxford Union. Although he showed great intellectual powers, he finished disappointingly, with second-class honors. Toward this and much else he deliberately cultivated an aloof attitude, which was to characterize him for the rest of his days. After graduating from Oxford, he toured Greece, Turkey, and Egypt. By 1884 he was writing reviews and articles to supplement the meager allowance he received from his father.

Curzon's political career began in 1885 when Lord Salisbury, the new prime minister, invited him to be his assistant private secretary. Curzon's attempt, soon thereafter, to win a parliamentary seat for South Derbyshire in the general election of autumn 1885 ended in defeat; in 1886, however, he won the Southport seat. In Parliament he espoused a brand of Tory democracy tinged with imperialism, thus effectively defining himself as a Disraelian type of Conservative, very much in the mold of Lord Randolph Churchill, Conservative chancellor of the exchequer around that time. Curzon began traveling abroad widely, visiting the United States, China, Afghanistan, and other countries between 1887 and 1894. During this period he met Mary Victoria Leiter, the daughter of an American millionaire, whom he married in 1895. He also wrote extensively about his travels.

In 1891 Lord Salisbury made Curzon undersecretary at the India Office; but in the 1892 general election the Salisbury government was defeated, and Curzon resumed his travels. When Salisbury returned to office in 1895, he offered Curzon the post of parliamentary undersecretary for foreign affairs, with responsibility for representing the Foreign Office in the House of Commons (Salisbury, as both prime minister and foreign secretary, was in the House of Lords). At this point Curzon, at the age of 36, was sworn in as a member of the Privy Council. He held his government post for three years, although he was unhappy about the passive way in which Salisbury dealt with the imperial colonies and handled foreign affairs. He wanted a more aggressive policy to protect the interests of the Empire. Nevertheless, he determinedly presented Salisbury's policy, as one contemporary politician stated, in the manner of "a divinity addressing black-beetles."

Curzon's style was more suited to more imperial roles, and he acquired one such toward the end of 1898 when, having just become the Marquess of Kedleston, it was announced that he would replace Lord Elgin as viceroy of India. He left Britain on 15 December 1898 and arrived in Calcutta on 3 January 1899 to begin his term of office. He immediately declared that he would operate in an even-handed manner; and he indeed showed his lack of favoritism on many occasions, particularly in castigating the British army regiment that was responsible for an assault on a native woman (the "Rangoon outrage" of September 1899).

Curzon instituted tariffs to shield the Indian economy against sugar imports. He also pursued a policy aimed at securing the northwest frontier through tribal arrangements rather than military ventures. He presented himself as something of a reforming viceroy, personally tackling the famine problem of 1900 and addressing issues of education, land, and financial matters. His tendency to criticize the army over incidents with the native population, and his pressuring of the British government to assert its influence over Afghanistan and Tibet at a time when the British government wanted no such involvement, began to sour his reputation as viceroy. Despite these tensions, however, his period of office was extended in January 1904.

Curzon decided that several of the larger and more unwieldy provinces of India should be split into smaller units, and set about doing so. In 1905, he created a new province in Bengal, covering 106,000 square miles and including 18 million Muslims and 12 million Hindus. As a result, he lost his popularity with "Indian opinion." While in Britain on home leave, Curzon found himself in conflict with Lord Kitchener, who had been appointed commander in chief of the Indian army on Curzon's advice but who had begun to chafe at the notion that he shared command with the Indian government and thus with the viceroy and the India Office. Curzon and Kitchener eventually reached a compromise. But Curzon was further annoyed when in July 1905 the India Office sent in to the Indian government a supply representative responsible for communications between the India Office and the Indian government without consulting him, and he resigned.

Curzon returned to Britain in December 1905, on the very day that Balfour's Conservative government was replaced by Henry Campbell-Bannerman's Liberal government. For the next eleven years he experienced political and domestic disappointments. His work in India was not honored, and he retired to the south of France. After his wife died on 18 July 1906, he returned to his home at Hackwood Park, Basingstoke, to raise his three daughters. He became chancellor of the University of Oxford in 1907, president of the Royal Geographical Society in 1911, and served as a trustee of the National Gallery during this time. He also wrote memoirs of his travels. He did not seek to enter the House of Commons again but instead became an Irish representative peer and entered the House of Lords. In 1911, on the coronation of George V, he was created Earl Curzon of Kedleston, Viscount Scarsdale, and Baron Ravensdale.

On 27 May 1915, with the formation of H. H. Asquith's wartime coalition government, Lord Curzon was given the title of Lord Privy Seal; but the post involved no major political responsibilities. In early 1916 he was assigned responsibility for the Shipping Control Committee, and in May he became president of the Air Board, which was designed to harmonize the conflicting interests of the army and the navy.

With the fall of Asquith in December 1916, Curzon became a member of the inner war cabinet, Lord President of the Council, and leader of the House of Lords (1916–1925) in David Lloyd George's wartime administration. In 1917, he married again, to Grace, the daughter of Joseph Monroe Hinds, onetime United States minister in Brazil. In his new roles in government, Curzon opposed a commitment to a Jewish homeland; favored the creation of an Arab state; and was opposed to the Montague-Chelmsford report (1918), which advocated the development of a parliamentary government in India. Curzon feared that such action in India would be detrimental to the British Empire.

Curzon became foreign secretary in Lloyd George's postwar coalition government in October 1919 and remained in that position through the Andrew Bonar Law and Stanley Baldwin governments until January 1924. However, he was unhappy with the negotiations that Lloyd George conducted at Versailles in 1919 and with other foreign developments. Curzon negotiated a treaty between Britain and Persia in August 1919, which placed Britain in control of the Persian army and finances; but the treaty was revoked by the Persians the moment British troops left, and in February 1923, the Persians concluded a treaty with the Russians. Britain's control of the Middle East was thus challenged.

Curzon's negotiations with Egypt were far more successful. Britain had made Egypt a protectorate in 1915, and in November 1919 the Milner Commission was sent to Egypt to establish how the protectorate could be reconciled with the independence movement of Zaghlul Pasha. Curzon negotiated to create an alliance between Britain and Egypt in place of the protectorate, but the British cabinet could not agree on terms. In the final event, Curzon got the British cabinet to agree, in January 1922, that Egypt would become independent provided that Egypt accept British interests in Sudan and the Suez Canal, and Britain's right to protect Egypt from external interference.

Curzon clashed with Lloyd George also on the conflict between Greece and Turkey. Curzon wanted the Greeks to occupy the European side of the Dardanelles, and the Turks to occupy the Asiatic side. Lloyd George seems to have adopted an anti-Turkish stance in secret negotiations conducted with Greece. In the end the French withdrew from Chanak, on the Asiatic side of the neutral zone, leaving the British to defend the position alone until the emergence of an armistice. The British public was alarmed at the situation, and Curzon was even more alarmed that decisions were being made behind his back. In the end, therefore, he joined with the Carlton Club of the Conservative Party in agreeing to ditch Lloyd George and form a Conservative administration under Bonar Law.

Curzon continued as foreign secretary in the new administration and soon found himself at the European Conference at Lausanne, negotiating in Britain's behalf from a position of renewed strength. The British retention of Chanak, from which the French had retreated, had given the Turks great respect for British determination. Even though the Lausanne Conference failed to settle the conflict between Greece and Turkey over the control of the Dardanelles and the straits between them, Curzon gained some of the concessions he wanted and the respect of the Turks. British interests were thus reasonably protected.

On 21 May 1923 Bonar Law resigned as prime minister on the grounds of ill health. Curzon, who had become Marquess of Curzon in 1921, fully expected that he would be Bonar Law's successor. He was duly called to London to meet with King George V; however, in London he was informed that the post had been offered to Baldwin. Crushed by this news, he neverthe-less offered Baldwin his support. Continuing as foreign secretary, he successfully renegotiated the 1921 trade agreement with the Soviet Union, but he failed to ease the tensions between France and Germany over German reparations.

Curzon's term as foreign secretary came to an end in 1924, with the fall of the Baldwin government. At that point he was determined to resign. In November 1924 a second Baldwin government was formed and he was again offered the post of foreign secretary; but this time he refused it, accepting instead the position of Lord President of the Council. He continued in that role until his death on 20 March 1925.

Able, egotistic, and aloof, Curzon was nonetheless one of the dominant political figures of his day. The lengthy hiatus in his early political career, however, prevented him from reaching the heights to which he aspired.

Keith Laybourn

See also: Asquith, Herbert Henry; Bonar Law, Andrew; Lloyd George, David
References and Further Reading: Parker, James G., 1991, *Lord Curzon: 1859–1925* (New York: Greenwood Press).

D

Dalton, Hugh (Lord Dalton)
(1887–1962) [CE]

Hugh Dalton became one of the most prominent Labour figures during the 1930s, following the disastrous general election of 1931, which saw the Parliamentary Labour Party reduced to about a sixth of its former size. Later, he became a member of Winston Churchill's wartime coalition government, and served as the first chancellor of the exchequer in Attlee's postwar Labour government.

Edward Hugh John Neale Dalton was born at Neath, in Glamorgan, Wales, on 26 August 1887, the son of the Rev. Canon J. N. Dalton, an Anglican cleric and sometime tutor to the sons of Queen Victoria. Hugh Dalton was educated at Eton and then at King's College, Cambridge, where he studied economics under John Maynard Keynes. There, in 1907, he joined the Fabian Society, which was committed to the gradual extension of public control over industry. After completing his degree he began to study law; but before long, he accepted a Hutchinson research scholarship at the London School of Economics between 1911 and 1913. He married Ruth Fox in 1914 and became a barrister, called to the bar on 6 May 1914, having studied law at Middle Temple since the autumn of 1910.

During World War I, Dalton served in the army and in the royal artillery. Toward the end of the war, he saw battle in Italy. On his discharge from the military, he accepted a post as lecturer at the London School of Economics, teaching economics. He was later appointed the Sir Ernest Cassell Reader in Commerce at the University of London (1920–1925) and reader in economics at the University of London (1925–1936). He combined this academic career with an increasing involvement in the Labour Party and in Parliament.

In the early 1920s he was active in developing the policies of the Labour Party. In October 1924, he was elected as M.P. for the Peckham Division of Camberwell. Later, in 1929, he switched to and won the Durham seat of Bishop Auckland, which he held until 1931; after a brief hiatus, he held this seat again from 1935 to 1959. He rose rapidly in Labour ranks, becoming a member of the party's national executive committee in 1925. His prominence earned him a key position in the second Labour government of 1929 to 1931, when he became an undersecretary to Arthur Henderson in the Foreign Office.

With the collapse of the second Labour government and the disastrous 1931 general election, Dalton found himself both out of government and out of Parliament. During this period, between 1931 and 1935, he built up his power base within the Labour Party, and became deeply involved, alongside Herbert Morrison, in the development of economic planning within the party. Indeed, Dalton was the powerhouse behind Labour's new, moderate policies of socialist economic planning.

Essentially Fabian and gradualist in outlook from the outset, Dalton had joined the New Fabian Research Bureau and, after a trip to the Soviet Union, had become convinced of the need for planning. He then pressed forward his ideas for planning to redistribute wealth and income in Britain, and for tackling the horrendous problem of unemployment, to the various committees of the Labour Party. In his Labour Party pamphlet *Socialism and the Condition of the People* (1933), he asserted that planning had to be a well-planned rush. His ideas were elaborated further in *For Socialism and Peace* (1934), which committed the Labour Party to a program of nationalization, and in various other documents. The ideas that emerged were reshaped under his direction into a short manifesto called *Labour's Immediate Future,* which was adopted at the Labour Party Conference in 1937. This program document committed Labour to a policy of limited nationalization, in more detailed and specific terms than had previously been adopted. Effectively, it provided the blueprint for the postwar Labour governments of Attlee.

Dalton was also instrumental, along with Ernest Bevin, in turning Labour away from the pacifist policies of George Lansbury, the Labour leader between 1932 and 1935, and into a party prepared to support rearmament and to stand up to the European fascist dictators. This was evident in *International Policy and Defence,* adopted by the Party in 1937.

In the 1935 general election, Dalton was elected as Labour M.P. for Bishop Auckland. From then onward he was able to exert his influence within the Parliamentary Labour Party as well as within the Labour Party. He was friendly with Herbert Morrison, whom he supported in the 1935 leadership contest against Attlee, and with Hugh Gaitskell and many of the other up-and-coming young members of the party.

Dalton's prominence ensured that he was projected forward for greater honors when the Labour Party joined Winston Churchill's wartime coalition government in May 1940. Dalton was minister of economic warfare between 1940 and 1942, bearing responsibility for the economic blockade of Germany, and was president of the Board of Trade between 1942 and 1945, dealing with issues such as rationing and reconstruction. In this latter role, he was responsible also for the Distribution of Industry Act (1945), which was designed to relocate industry in economically depressed areas.

After Attlee's postwar Labour victory of 1945, Dalton was appointed chancellor of the exchequer and charged with overseeing the reconstruction of the postwar British economy. In this role, he encouraged cheap money and presided over the nationalization of various industries and services, including the Bank of England. Although he was committed to socialist planning, he was unable to implement many new policies because the economy was weak. Postwar Britain was partly dependent on an American loan, and it faced serious economic crisis in 1947 due to a condition of the American loan making sterling convertible/payable in gold and bullion, which ensured that Britain's gold and bullion reserves, as well as the American loan, were quickly dissipated. Dalton was forced to suspend convertibility in August 1947.

Dalton was, by any standards, an effective chancellor given the economic problems he faced. However, he was forced to resign in November 1947 for having revealed the contents of the next year's budget to a journalist before presenting the budget proposal to the House of Commons. He did return to the cabinet in 1948 as chancellor of the Duchy of Lancaster (responsible for European affairs), and as minister of town and country planning between 1950 and 1951.

After Labour's defeat in the 1951 general election, Dalton gradually withdrew from his previous dominant position within the party. He lost his seat in the 1952 elections for the party's national executive committee and withdrew from the party's parliamentary committee. By the mid-1950s he was acting the role of elder statesman in the party, attempting to shape and influence Hugh Gaitskell and Anthony Crosland. He was created a life peer in 1960 as Lord Dalton, and died in February 1962.

Dalton's life was a remarkable mixture of academic achievement and political guile. It was also characterized by sharp contrasts. Having shaped Labour's initial commitment to nationalization, Dalton drifted away from that position in his later years as he encouraged the socialist ideas of Hugh Gaitskell and Anthony Crosland. Nevertheless, he will be remembered as a politician of immense intellectual ability and as a chancellor of the exchequer of talent and commitment, albeit limited by the economic problems of postwar reconstruction in the mid- and late 1940s.

Keith Laybourn

See also: Attlee, Clement; Bevin, Ernest; Churchill, Sir Winston; Crosland, Tony; Gaitskell, Hugh
References and Further Reading: Dalton, E. Hugh, 1953, *Call Back Yesterday* (London: Frederick Muller); Dalton, E. Hugh, 1957, *The Fateful Years* (London: Frederick Muller); Dalton, E. Hugh, 1962, *High Tide and After* (London: Frederick Muller); Pimlott, Ben, 1985, *Hugh Dalton* (London: Cape); Pimlott, Ben (ed.), 1986, *The Political Diary of Hugh Dalton* (London: Cape); Pimlott, Ben (ed.), 1986, *The Second World War Diary of Hugh Dalton* (London: Cape).

Dartmouth, Earl of (William Legge)
(1731–1801) [AC]

William Legge, second Earl of Dartmouth, was born 21 June 1731, the younger son of George Legge, Viscount Lewisham, and of Elizabeth, daughter and heiress of Sir Arthur Kaye. His father died in 1732 and his mother then married Francis, seventh Baron North and subsequently Earl of Guildford, who died in 1745. William was educated at Westminster School and at Trinity College, Oxford, gaining an initial degree in 1749 and an M.A. in 1751. His grandfather died in 1750, after which he became the second Earl of Dartmouth upon his return from a foreign tour with Frederick (later Lord) North. He took his seat in the House of Lords in 1754, and he married Frances Catherine, the only daughter and heiress of Sir Charles Gunter Nicholl, on 11 June 1755.

At first, Dartmouth was barely active in the House of Lords. He served briefly as president of the Board of Trade and Foreign Plantations in the Marquess of Rockingham's administration in 1765, but resigned with the formation of the Duke of Grafton's ministry in 1766. He was again given office in Lord North's ministry (1770–1782), in August 1772, when he succeeded Lord Hillsborough as secretary of state for the colonies and as president of the Board of Trade and Foreign Plantations. He retained these positions until November 1775, when he became Lord Privy Seal.

In his colonial role Dartmouth sought to understand the American colonists; Benjamin Franklin acknowledged that Dartmouth was "a truly good man, and wishes sincerely a good un-derstanding with the colonies, but does not seem to have strength equal to his wishes" (Bigelow 1879, p. 154). Dartmouth generally supported Lord North's conciliatory policy on the American colonies, but in 1775 he carried a bill for restraining the trade of the American colonies. Even while out of office he was deeply involved in the question of the independence of America, rejecting the Duke of Grafton's attempt at conciliation in 1776 and advocating the use of an "overpowering force" to settle the issue of American independence.

After leaving his colonial post in 1775, he continued as Lord Privy Seal; but he gave that post up in 1782, when Lord North resigned as prime minister. From April to December 1783 he served as Lord Steward of the Household—his last office. He died in 15 July 1801.

Kit Hardwick and Keith Laybourn

See also: Grafton, Duke of; North, Lord
References and Further Reading: Bigelow, John (ed.), 1879, *Life of Benjamin Franklin* (Philadelphia: Lippincott); Whiteley, Peter, 1997, *Lord North: The Prime Minister Who Lost America* (London: Hambledon).

Derby, 14th Earl of (Lord Derby; Hon. Sir Edward George Geoffrey Smith Stanley)
(1799–1869) [PM]

Lord Derby was prime minister of two Whig governments and one Conservative government. Perhaps because his tenure in each case was brief, he is often overlooked in political histories. His ministries were nevertheless important. When Benjamin Disraeli unveiled a statue dedicated to Derby in Parliament Square in 1874, he summed up Derby's career with a pithy comment that went straight to the point: "He abolished slavery, he educated Ireland, he reformed Parliament."

Edward George Geoffrey Smith Stanley was born on 29 March 1799, the eldest son of Edward Smith Stanley, the thirteenth Earl of Derby, and of Charlotte Margaret Hornby. He was heir to some of the largest estates in the country; but his father and he were so generous to the workers on their estates that they left debts of more £500,000 and £680,000, respectively, on their deaths. Edward, the fourteenth Earl, admittedly also incurred debts as a result of his extensive racing interests. Edward was educated at Eton and at Christ Church, Oxford. In 1825 he married Emma Caroline, second daughter of Edward Bootle Wilbraham, later the first Lord Skelmersdale.

Stanley began his political career as a Whig committed to reform and to the monarchy working through Parliament, serving as M.P. for Stockbridge between 1822 and 1826. He was, successively, M.P. for Preston between 1826 and 1830, M.P. for Windsor from 1831 to 1832, and M.P. for North Lancashire between 1832 and 1844. As a parliamentarian he was considered a fine orator, "the 'Darling of Debate,' and a Whig liberal and an 'old constitutional Whig'" (Eccleshill and Walker 1998, p. 162). His early posts in government were all in the service of Whig administrations. He was undersecretary of state for the colonies in George Canning's administration in 1827, and served as chief secretary for Ireland (1830–1833) and secretary of state for the colonies (1833–1834) in Earl Grey's ministry.

As chief secretary for Ireland, Stanley's main task was to construct an Irish policy in the wake of the Catholic emancipation of 1829, by which Catholics were allowed to stand for the House of Commons and to join public bodies. His greatest success here was the passing of the Irish Education Act of 1831, which permitted children of all religious persuasions to attend government-funded schools. As secretary of state for the colonies his main achievement was laying the groundwork for the abolition of slavery, which occurred in August 1833, shortly after he had left office as a result of Lord John Russell's intention to appropriate Irish church lands for nonreligious purposes. At that point he abandoned the Whigs and voted on independent lines.

He refused an offer to join Sir Robert Peel's Tory/Conservative ministry in 1835 but gravitated toward the Conservative Party as time went on. He sat with the Conservative opposition in the House of Commons from 1835, and was eventually rewarded with the post of secretary of state for the colonies in Peel's ministry, fulfilling this role from 1841 to 1844. His main concern

seemed to be to support the Canadian Corn Bill of 1844, which did not please the protectionist section of the Conservative Party. He gave up his ministerial post after being raised to the House of Lords in 1844, as Baron Stanley. He remained politically active, and opposed Peel's decision to repeal the Corn Laws in 1845 and 1846, although he agreed they should be temporarily suspended because of the Irish famine.

Lord (Baron) Stanley emerged as leader of the new, protectionist Conservative Party in 1846. Since he was in the House of Lords, he found it difficult to control affairs in the House of Commons; but in 1849, Benjamin Disraeli began to perform that role. Stanley gradually moved the Conservative Party away from its staunchly protectionist stance, recognizing that this stance was unlikely to generate broad support. There were moments, as in 1851, when he might have cooperated with the Peelite free traders to become prime minister, but this did not occur. However, in 1852, the collapse of Lord Russell's Whig administration allowed the Earl of Derby—as he was commonly known after the death of his father in 1851—to operate a government between February and December 1852. It was a minority government and remained so even after the general election of July, and it soon collapsed. It was replaced by Lord Aberdeen's Whig and Peelite coalition, the forerunner of the Liberal Party.

Derby became prime minister once again, from February 1858 until June 1859, as a result of Palmerston's defeat on the Conspiracy to Murder Bill provoked by the Orsini plot against the French emperor, which had been hatched in Britain. Derby operated from the House of Lords, and Disraeli acted as leader of the House of Commons and chancellor of the exchequer. However, as in 1852, Derby's Conservative government was a minority one, remained in the minority after the June 1859 general election, and failed to achieve much. Having suffered frequent bouts of gout, Derby resigned shortly after the 1859 general election.

Palmerston was prime minister from 1859 until 1865, maintained in power by an annual agreement with Derby not to challenge him unless his policies diverged significantly from those acceptable to the Conservative Party. This arrangement lasted until 1865, when Palmerston increased his majority at the general election. However, Palmerston's unexpected death in October 1865 led to the formation of the short-lived government of Lord Russell, which foundered in June 1866 over the issue of parliamentary reform. As a result Derby formed his third and last government, which would last until 1868.

On becoming prime minister, Derby announced that "nothing, certainly, would give him greater pleasure than to see a very considerable portion of the class now excluded admitted to the franchise," but stressed the need for caution. In failing health, Derby passed on the responsibility for passing the Reform Act of 1867 to Disraeli, whose brief was to bring about household suffrage rather than the manhood suffrage demanded by the National Reform League. Derby realized that only a bill offering householders the vote could pass through both the House of Commons and the House of Lords. His proposal was moderate, giving all taxpaying householders the vote, along with £10 lodgers in the boroughs and £12 occupants (that is, those paying rates on these levels of assessment) in the counties; still, this reform was, as he said in the House of Lords, "a great experiment" and a "leap in the dark."

Derby was replaced as prime minister by William Ewart Gladstone, the Liberal leader, in 1868, at which time he also retired as Conservative leader in favor of Disraeli. He died on 23 October 1869.

Keith Laybourn

See also: Aberdeen, Earl of; Disraeli, Benjamin; Gladstone, William Ewart; Liverpool, Earl of; Palmerston, Lord; Peel, Sir Robert; Russell, Lord John; Wellington, Duke of
References and Further Reading: Derby, Edward H., and John R. Vincent, 1978, *Disraeli, Derby and the Conservative Party: Journals of Lord Stanley, 1849–1869* (Hassocks, UK: Harvester Press); Eccleshill, Robert, and Graham Walker, 1998, *Biographical Dictionary of British Prime Ministers* (London: Routledge); Jones, Wilbur, 1956, *Lord Derby and Victorian Conservatism* (Oxford: Basil Blackwell); Smith, Francis, 1966, *The Making of the Second Reform Bill* (Cambridge: Cambridge University Press); Stewart, Robert,

1971, *The Politics of Protection: Lord Derby and the Protectionist Party, 1841–1852* (London: Cambridge University Press).

Derby, 15th Earl of (Edward Henry Stanley; Lord Stanley) (1826–1893) [FS]

Edward Henry Stanley was the eldest son of Edward George Geoffrey Smith-Stanley, the fourteenth Earl of Derby, who was prime minister on three occasions in the mid-nineteenth century. Edward's mother was Emma Caroline, the second daughter of the first Lord of Skelmersdale. Born on 21 July 1826, Edward was educated at Rugby under the famous headmaster Dr. Thomas Arnold, and at Trinity College, Cambridge.

Stanley's political career began in March 1848, when he contested the Lancaster parliamentary seat, losing by six votes. He then went on tour to the United States and was elected as M.P. for Kings Lynn, which he represented from 1848 until 1869, when he became the fifteenth Earl of Derby. Although Stanley was more than capable as a politician, his political career rested partly upon his father's political prominence. In March 1852, the younger Stanley became undersecretary for foreign affairs in his father's ministry. His main responsibility was to deal with Bengal, in India. He resigned along with the other members of his father's government in December 1852 but continued to speak frequently in the House of Commons on Indian affairs. Lord Palmerston offered him the post of colonial secretary in 1855, but he did not return to government until the second Derby government of 1858, when he became colonial secretary and then president of the Board of Trade. After the passage of the India Bill in 1853, he was appointed first secretary for India.

In 1859, Stanley was out of office again, following the collapse of his father's second government. He continued to debate Indian matters in the House of Commons and was also associated with events in Greece. The Greeks had expelled their king and had offered the throne to Alfred (later Duke of Saxe-Coburg and Gotha), the second son of Queen Victoria, who refused it. At that point, in 1863, they offered the throne to Lord Edward Stanley, who also declined it.

Lord Stanley, 1867 (Library of Congress)

Stanley returned to high office again in his father's third ministry, formed in 1866. He became foreign secretary on 6 July 1866, remaining in that office throughout the ministries of his father and of Benjamin Disraeli, until the end of November 1868. As foreign secretary, his main concern was to avoid British military involvements abroad, particularly in a future European war. Although Stanley did commit Britain to the Abyssinian campaign of 1868, he maintained neutrality in the wars of Prussia, Italy, and Austria and mediated between France and Prussia. He also referred to arbitration the British and American dispute over Alabama. While he was out of office, between 1868 and 1874, Stanley's personal position changed. He became the fifteenth Earl of Derby on his father's death in 1869, inheriting a debt of about £680,000 (which hung over him for the rest of his life), and married Mary Catherine, second daughter of George, the fifth Earl De La Warr, on 5 July 1870.

Derby resumed his role as foreign secretary when Disraeli formed his second ministry, in February 1874. For Derby this was an uneasy period in office: Disraeli was much more committed to expansionism than was Derby, and the two were often in disagreement—the Suez Canal project being a prime example of a policy with which Derby was not completely comfortable. With regard to Russo-Turkish relations, Derby, nonetheless, did pursue a policy supportive of Turkey, which Disraeli saw as a potential buffer to Russian expansionism; but Derby also advocated Turkish reforms at the Constantinople Conference in December 1876. He continued to advocate British support to Turkey throughout 1876 and 1877, when the British population was equally divided between those who supported Turkey and those who objected to the Bulgarian atrocities perpetrated by the Turks. Derby's support for the Turks continued throughout the Russo-Turkish war, which he attempted to bring to an end. However, Derby resigned on 28 March 1878, when it looked as though Disraeli would send a fleet to protect Turkey and thus provoke a war with Russia.

In 1877, referring to middle-class opposition to government policy, Derby had commented, "Unfortunately the Premier neither understands nor likes the middle class." This comment echoed a remark made earlier by Disraeli—that "the middle classes would always be against war; but unfortunately the middle classes did not govern" (Vincent 1994, pp. 413, 457). In the end, Disraeli refused the British fleet permission to go beyond the Dardanelles; but Derby had already left office.

From that point onward, Derby became increasingly alienated from Conservative politics due to disagreements over foreign policy, and he eventually left the Conservative Party in March 1880. He joined the Liberal Party and was quickly accepted as one of its leaders. He served as colonial secretary in Gladstone's second ministry, between December 1882 and 1885. In this role he encouraged a British withdrawal from the Sudan and a reduction of involvement in South Africa through a conciliatory agreement with the Boers. Indeed, his policy was aimed at reducing Britain's imperial involvements throughout the world. In the turbulent political events surrounding Irish Home Rule in 1885 and 1886, Derby split with Gladstone and became a Liberal Unionist leader in the House of Lords.

Derby remained active in politics throughout his life. He presided briefly over the first session of the Royal Commission on Labour, which was convened in 1892, before his death on 21 April 1893.

Derby was both a man of principle and an astute politician. Raised in the Conservative tradition but a Liberal by temperament and predilection, he maintained a firm commitment to a nonexpansionist foreign policy. Had it not been for the divisive issue of Irish Home Rule, no doubt he also would have remained a member of the Liberal Party.

Keith Laybourn

See also: Derby, 14th Earl of; Disraeli, Benjamin; Gladstone, William Ewart
References and Further Reading: Derby, Edward H., and John R. Vincent, 1978, *Disraeli, Derby and the Conservative Party: Journals of Lord Stanley, 1849– 1869* (Hassocks, UK: Harvester Press); Jenkins, Roy, 1995, *Gladstone* (London: Macmillan); Vincent, John (ed.), 1994, *A Selection from the Diaries of Edward Henry Stanley, 15th Earl of Derby (1826– 1893): Between September 1869 and March 1878* (London: Royal Historical Society).

Devonshire, Duke of (Sir William Cavendish)
(1720–1764) [PM]

William Cavendish had what might be described as a birthright to a place in politics, as the scion of a monarchist landed family that since 1688 had been a bulwark of the Revolution Settlement and the Whig party. Staunchly loyal to the Crown and to the Whig "old corps," he could also be loftily independent as befitted a wealthy grandee. The Cavendishes of Chatsworth and Hardwick, extensive landowners in Derbyshire, had been earls of Devonshire (a nominal county title, for they held no land there) since the early seventeenth century, and the dukedom was granted the family by William III in 1694. The second duke was a zealous supporter of the Hanoverian succession, and from 1714 to 1764 without a break, the dukes of Devonshire were given the honor of being lords lieutenant of Derbyshire. Cavendish's father, the third duke, was a loyal supporter of Sir Robert Walpole and served as lord lieutenant of Ireland

from 1737 to 1745; he also had family ties with the Duke of Newcastle and the latter's brother Henry Pelham.

When William Cavendish came of age in 1741 as marquess of Hartington, he was at once elected M.P. for Derbyshire, a seat that he held for ten years. At the outset of his political career he acted vigorously to rally support for Walpole in the disputed elections that led to the minister's fall in February 1742. In November 1742, Hartington was selected by Pelham to move the Address of Thanks in reply to the King's Speech—an honor that marked him as a staunch ministerial supporter.

In March 1748, Hartington entered into a marriage that had been arranged years earlier, with Lady Charlotte Elizabeth Boyle, daughter and heir of the third Earl of Burlington. Hartington's own parents had made a love match, his mother Catherine Hoskins being merely of modest gentry stock, and she separated from her husband in protest at the strategic match he had struck for his son. Nonetheless, Hartington's was a happy marriage, bearing out the comment of Lady Mary Wortley Montague: "I do not know any man so fitted to make a wife happy: with so great a vocation for matrimony, that I verily believe if it had not been established before his time, he would have had the glory of the invention." The marriage also brought a great access of land and political power—not only property in London and Ireland but a huge Yorkshire acreage and the nomination of the two M.P.s for Knaresborough.

His father's retirement from the royal court in 1749 did not hold back Hartington's career. In April 1751, on the death of Frederick, Prince of Wales, he was offered the post of tutor to Frederick's son, the future Prince of Wales, which he declined. In June 1751, Pelham secured for him the more prestigious court post of Master of the Horse, which carried a place in the cabinet. In order to accept it, Hartington had to quit his Commons seat and enter the Lords, taking his father's barony of Cavendish. Pelham died in March 1754, and Cavendish continued on the fringes of high politics as a supporter of Newcastle and of his good friend Henry Fox. On Christmas Eve 1754 came the devastating blow of his young wife's death, and Cavendish was left to bring up four young children. In March 1755 he was appointed lord lieutenant of Ireland, despite his being an Irish landowner, with the mission of bringing to heel the increasingly restless Dublin Parliament. In December of that year, Cavendish's father died and he inherited the title of fourth duke of Devonshire.

In May 1756 he left his Irish post to return to Westminster politics, at the beginning of the Seven Years' War. The loss of Minorca in June that year led Henry Fox to resign his post as secretary of state for the Southern Deparment (home secretary) in October rather than defend the ministry's record in the new session of Parliament. Newcastle, who then headed the ministry, had lost public confidence and needed the support of William Pitt, the Elder, in order to form a stable government. The king, however, disliked and distrusted Pitt; and Pitt in turn would not join any ministry that included Fox, and therefore refused to support Newcastle.

To resolve this impasse, at Pitt's suggestion, Devonshire was called away from Chatsworth to take the Treasury; as a Whig stalwart, he could take over without losing the support of Newcastle's many "old corps" followers. Newcastle and Lord Chancellor Hardwicke resigned on 5 November 1756, and on the next day Devonshire became First Lord of the Treasury, with Pitt as his secretary of state for the south. This arrangement was from the first meant to be temporary; Devonshire had told the king that he would act only for this one parliamentary session. A grateful George II nominated him Knight of the Garter on 18 November, and the ceremonial installation took place in the following March.

As acting prime minister, Devonshire presided over the war effort, in which the most notable domestic development was the court martial and execution of Admiral Byng for having failed to relieve Minorca. The king continued to resist Pitt's dominance, but such was Pitt's popularity in the country that George was unsuccessful in his attempt to create an alternative ministry under Fox in the spring of 1757. In late June 1757 Devonshire was happy to step down, becoming lord chamberlain and a member of the cabinet in the new, compromise ministry led by Newcastle, with Pitt conducting the war as secretary for the south.

Though he found his court attendance as lord chamberlain tedious, Devonshire served on, supporting the Crown, even after the accession in 1760 of a new young king who did not favor him or his Whig allies, the Dukes of Newcastle and Bedford. The rising power of Lord Bute and the difficulties of negotiating an acceptable peace, together with various maneuvers to ease Pitt out of the ministry, fill the Duke's fascinating political diary for the years from 1759 to 1762. Pitt resigned in October 1761, Bute taking the seals as secretary of state. On 26 May 1762, after a long, losing struggle against George III, Newcastle finally resigned, and Bute became the First Lord of the Treasury.

Instead of leaving office along with his ally and relative Newcastle, Devonshire maintained what he perhaps saw as his natural place at court, frequently discussing political strategy with the king's uncle, the Duke of Cumberland, and trying through him to defeat Bute. He no longer attended meetings of the Privy Council, however; and when in October 1762 George III summoned him to attend a meeting of the cabinet on the peace negotiations, he refused and was immediately dismissed from his post as lord chamberlain. Early in November, the king personally struck out Devonshire's name from the list of privy councillors. A further rebuff was in store, when in February 1764 Devonshire was dismissed from the lord lieutenancy that his family had held so long. In October he suffered a stroke and went to try the cure at the famous German town of Spa, where he died on 2 November 1764, leaving four children between the ages of 10 and 14.

Philip Woodfine

See also: Fox, Henry; Newcastle, Duke of; Pelham, Hon. Henry; Pitt, William (the Elder)
References and Further Reading: Brown, Peter, and Karl Schweitzer (eds.), 1982, *The Devonshire Diary: William Cavendish, Fourth Duke of Devonshire, Memoranda on State Affairs, 1759–1762* (London: Royal Historical Society); Namier, Sir Lewis, 1961, *England in the Age of the American Revolution* (London: Macmillan);Pearson, John, 1983, *Stags and Serpents: The Story of the House of Cavendish and the Dukes of Devonshire* (London: Macmillan).

Disraeli, Benjamin
(Earl of Beaconsfield)
(1804–1881) [PM, CE]

Benjamin Disraeli, the first Earl of Beaconsfield, was the most unusual and unconventional "great figure" in British public life in modern times. He was of Italian Jewish parentage, yet became leader of the Conservatives, the party that upheld the landowning interests and the established Church of England.

He was born in London on 21 December 1804, the second child and eldest of the three surviving sons of Isaac and Maria D'Israeli. His parents both rejected Judaism, and Benjamin was baptized into the Anglican Church at the age of 12, almost by accident. He thus avoided the social handicap of being Jewish in Britain at that time. Inherited wealth allowed Isaac to lead a leisured life as a writer and, from 1828, as a country squire in Buckinghamshire.

Benjamin received little formal education but read widely in European literature in his father's library. In his twenties and thirties he incurred heavy debts as the result of a disastrous newspaper venture and Stock Exchange gambling (investment speculations); he also produced the first of his voluminous writings. He traveled widely in Europe, the Mediterranean, and the Near East; had a prolonged nervous breakdown; and became notorious in London society for his flamboyant appearance, his dandyish lifestyle, and his affairs with married women. Disraeli ran for Parliament twice as a Radical and twice as a Tory before being elected as one of the two M.P.s for Maidstone in 1837, at Queen Victoria's accession. When his fellow M.P. died, he married his widow, Mary Ann Lewis, who was 12 years his senior. He had married for money; but Mary Ann was "a perfect wife" until her death in 1872. After that event, Disraeli consoled himself with the 54-year-old Lady Bradford. At the age of 40, largely because of his reputation for flouting social conventions, Disraeli seemed to have no prospect of holding political office.

But in 1846 the political scene was transformed by Sir Robert Peel's decision to repeal the Corn Laws, which until then had guaranteed English landowners and farmers a market for their grain crops that was free of competition

Benjamin Disraeli, c. 1860 (Library of Congress)

from imports. In 1841 Peel had led the Tories, or Conservatives, to their first triumph in a general election since the Great Reform Act of 1832. Disraeli was disappointed not to have been given office—which he had requested from Peel—but had supported the government until Peel became convinced, in view of a potato blight and famine in Ireland, that the Corn Laws should be repealed. It was Disraeli who led the assault in the House of Commons that brought down Peel's government and split the Conservatives. The "Peelite" minority, led by Gladstone, gradually joined with the Whigs and Radicals to form the Liberal Party. The Conservatives did not command a majority in the Commons again till 1874.

Between 1846 and 1851, the Conservatives were led from the House of Lords by Viscount Stanley, fourteenth Earl of Derby; in 1851, Disraeli was reluctantly accepted as their leader in the Commons. In 1852, the Whig cabinet broke up and Derby formed a Conservative government in which Disraeli was chancellor of the exchequer. This government did not survive Gladstone's attack on Disraeli's budget; and for the rest of the decade, the Conservatives found it difficult to establish their distinctiveness from the conservative-minded governments of Aberdeen (1852–1855) and Palmerston (1855–1858). Unexpectedly, Palmerston's government fell in 1858, and a second Derby-Disraeli government was formed. However, the Conservatives were defeated in a general election in 1859, and Palmerston was elected to head a government of Whigs, Radicals, and Peelites. Palmerston died in 1865, and Russell succeeded him as head of government. Gladstone, leader of the Commons, introduced a parliamentary reform bill, but it was defeated, and a third Derby-Disraeli ministry was formed.

The widening of the franchise (the right to vote) had been a leitmotif of politics in the 1860s. In 1866 and 1867, Disraeli persuaded the Cabinet to "dish [outmaneuver] the Whigs" by introducing its own reform bill. Derby fell ill, and Disraeli, on his own initiative, took "a leap in the dark" and accepted amendments that extended the vote to urban working-class men, embodied in the 1867 Reform Act. Derby retired, having arranged with the Queen that Disraeli should succeed him as prime minister. Having "climbed to the top of the greasy pole," Disraeli, by laying on the flattery "with a trowel," became even more influential with the queen; but in the 1868 general election, the Liberals, led by Gladstone, swept to power.

Disraeli's fortunes, political and personal, sank to an ebb. In 1872, his wife died. Yet two public speeches he made, in Manchester and in London—in which he committed his party to uphold the Crown and the Church, defend the Empire, and "elevate the condition of the people"—reasserted his leadership. Although it was mainly Gladstone's alienation of middle-class voters by his radical reforms that brought about the collapse of the Liberal government and its defeat in the 1874 election, ushering in the first Conservative parliamentary majority since 1841, Disraeli's improvements in the Conservative Party's organization also contributed to these events.

Until 1879, with Gladstone in semiretire-

ment, Disraeli dominated the political scene, even after he went to the House of Lords as Earl of Beaconsfield in 1876. But he lacked the driving energy of Peel or Gladstone. He let his ministers run a government of departments; he himself had too little interest in, and control over, the details of government. He was frequently ill and sometimes fell asleep in cabinet meetings. His closeness to and flattery of the queen—his "Sovereign Mistress" and "the Faery"—may have improperly influenced his policy. His reputation was further harmed by subsequent public revelations of his private disparagement of her.

It is a myth that Disraeli implemented in his second ministry the "Tory democracy" outlined in the novels he had written in the 1840s. There were important measures of social reform—in public health and housing, in empowering trade unions and safeguarding friendly societies—but these were the work of his ministers. Nor were these measures especially "Tory," or in any sense forerunners of the "welfare state."

Disraeli did take a personal interest in two pieces of legislation that had religious implications. He disapproved of clauses in the 1876 Education Act that favored schools supported by the High Church or "ritualist" wing of the Church of England; and he supported a Public Worship Act that restricted "ritualism" (Catholic ceremonies). His sympathies, like the queen's, were "Low Church" and strongly "anti-Popery." He also promoted an agricultural holdings act in 1875 that compensated tenants for improvements they made on land they rented. This was what Gladstone's Irish Land Act of 1870 had sought to do, in very different conditions, for Irish peasants. However, Disraeli did nothing to relieve the growing distress in Ireland, which he never visited. He was fortunate that the trouble brewing in Ireland did not bubble over into revolt in his time.

Disraeli's greatest successes as prime minister were in foreign and imperial affairs. In 1875 he gained popularity with the purchase for the British government of a large minority of shares in the Suez Canal Company, with money borrowed from the Jewish bankers, the Rothschilds, claiming that this would secure the route to India, "the jewel in the Crown"; and his popularity was further strengthened by the passage of the Royal Titles Act (1876), in which Queen Victoria was proclaimed "Empress of India." He also won kudos for dealing with the "Eastern Question," the problem of "the sick man of Europe"—that is, the Turkish Empire. The immediate problem was Turkish misrule over the provinces in the European part of the empire, peopled mainly by Serbs and Bulgarians, who like the Russians were Orthodox Christians. When the Serbs of Herzegovina rebelled in midsummer of 1875, the powers of the Three Emperors' League (Germany, Austria-Hungary, and Russia) intervened, demanding reforms.

Disraeli, fearing that Russia would gain control of Constantinople—and that this outcome might threaten British rule in India—sent a fleet to the Dardanelles to support the Turkish fleet. This encouraged Turkey and helped bring about the Russo-Turkish War in April 1877. The first rustlings of conflict were heard in May 1876, when reports surfaced that Turkish irregulars had committed atrocities against Bulgarians. At first Disraeli disbelieved the reports of massacres, but they were later confirmed, at which point Gladstone launched a campaign to drum up political support for driving the Turks "bag and baggage . . . from the province they have desolated and profaned." Disraeli (now Lord Beaconsfield) survived the resulting political onslaught and the rift in his cabinet by riding a wave of mass patriotism ("jingoism" was the word coined at the time). When negotiations between Russia and Turkey broke down over Russian attempts to control Turkey, Russia invaded Turkey and advanced on Constantinople. Crisis came in January 1878, when the British fleet was ordered to Constantinople. At this point the Russians ceased hostilities but forced Turkey in return to accept the Treaty of San Stephano. Beaconsfield succeeded in having this agreement revoked at the Congress of Berlin, though in fact the negotiating was done by his new foreign secretary, Lord Salisbury. The Treaty of Berlin, signed in July 1878, was the pinnacle of Disraeli's career: he had brought back, he claimed, "peace with honour," and in the process had acquired Cyprus for Britain, strengthening the link with India.

The mood of triumph soon changed, however, as 1879 was a calamitous year for Britain abroad. British forces were massacred in battles in Afghanistan and Zululand, South Africa, which Gladstone denounced as "Beaconsfieldism" (Disraelian adventurism) in his "first Midlothian campaign" of speeches in his new Edinburgh constituency. Britain at this time was in a deep economic depression; and whereas Peel's repeal of the Corn Laws in 1846, which Disraeli had so lambasted, had left British agriculture flourishing, it would never recover from Beaconsfield's failure to protect it at this juncture. A general election in April 1880—in which the ailing and failing Beaconsfield made no attempt to counter the attacks in Gladstone's "second Midlothian campaign"—resulted in catastrophic defeat for the Tories. Yet Beaconsfield rallied. He even began to write a novel in which the main character was based on Gladstone; and he was spiritedly leading his party in denouncing Liberal radicalism until just before his death on 19 April 1881.

Historians have differed over the political importance of Disraeli. Robert Blake, although acknowledging Disraeli's political failures up to the 1860s, believes that as a parliamentarian Disraeli was "one of the half a dozen greatest in our history" (Blake 1966, p. 764), and that although other Conservative leaders have worked harder for their party, "none has left a deeper impression upon it" (Blake 1966, p. 765). John Vincent is less convinced of Disraeli's greatness, although he described him as "the greatest leader of the opposition modern Britain has known" (Vincent 1990, p. 6). Vincent points out that Disraeli led his party in opposition, and political failure, longer than anyone else in British politics and that his reputation rests upon the slender period of six years in office from 1874 to 1880. He maintains that Disraeli's achievments in office are slender in comparison with the accomplishments of Sir Robert Peel, whose career Disraeli helped curtail, or with those of Disraeli's archrival Gladstone. What then is Disraeli's place in British history?

Disraeli was exceptional among conservative thinkers. He was optimistic about society, believing that social harmony, not class conflict, was the natural state of affairs; and he was skeptical about what political action could achieve, regarding politics as "a great game," and his own role as that of an "adventurer." His one guiding principle was belief in the party as the vehicle for political action. Perhaps his greatest achievement was to revive and hold together the Conservative Party; in death, he became the party idol he had never been in life. He is unique in his continuing hold over his party's devotion: no other Prime Minister has had such an influence. Myths about him still persist: that he was a great popular leader, a social reformer, a "Tory democrat," a visionary of Empire.

Whatever one's view of Disraeli's achievements and failures, it must be remembered that he was always unlucky with the state of the economy: He missed the era of mid-Victorian prosperity, in 1850–1873, and instead came to office during the depression of 1879–1880. "'Hard times' . . . has been our foe," as he said to Salisbury. Secondly, he constantly battled the handicap created by the fact that the Tories were a natural minority: there were more Liberals than Tories. Disraeli grasped the need to formulate an alternative "political culture" to challenge the Whig Liberals' natural monopoly on power. His achievement was the rescue of the Conservative Party from being a permanent minority. But although he was a great party leader, Disraeli was not a great prime minister, for he failed to command the political agenda as had Peel, Gladstone, Attlee (in establishing the welfare state in 1948), and Thatcher (in breaking trade union power in the 1980s).

John O'Connell

See also: Aberdeen, Earl of; Attlee, Clement; Derby, 14th Earl of; Gladstone, William Ewart; Palmerston, Lord; Peel, Sir Robert; Salisbury, Lord; Thatcher, Margaret
References and Further Reading: Blake, Robert (Lord Blake), 1966, *Disraeli* (London: Eyre & Spottiswoode); Ramsden, John, 1998, *An Appetite for Power: A History of the Conservative Party since 1830* (London: HarperCollins); Shannon, Richard, 1992, *The Age of Disraeli, 1868–1881: The Rise of Tory Democracy* (London: Longman); Stewart, Robert M., 1978, *The Foundations of the Conservative Party, 1830–1867* (London: Longman); Vincent, John, 1990, *Disraeli* (Oxford: Oxford University Press).

Dowdeswell, William
(1721–1775) [CE]

William Dowdeswell was born in 1721, the son of William Dowdeswell and his second wife, Anne Hammond, into a rich Worcestershire family that owned considerable property around Tewkesbury. William was educated at Westminster School and then at Christ Church, Oxford, although he does not appear to have received a degree. He also went to the University of Leyden, where he was associated with many future political figures, including Charles Townshend (1725–1767) and John Wilkes. He then toured Italy, Sicily, and Greece. On his return to England in 1747 he married Bridget, the fifth and youngest daughter of Sir William Codrington, the first baronet, and was elected to Parliament for the family borough of Tewkesbury. He retained this seat until 1754, but was then out of Parliament until 1761, when he became M.P. for the county of Worcester, representing it until his death.

In the House of Commons, Dowdeswell was an active, landed Whig, opposing the Cider Act in 1764 and demanding the reduction of naval expenditure in 1765. As a result he was invited to be the chancellor of the exchequer when Lord Rockingham formed his ministry in 1765. He held that post, which included membership in the Privy Council, from July 1765 until August 1766. He succeeded George Grenville as chancellor, inspiring Bishop Warburton to opine, "The one just turned out never in his life could learn that two and two made four; the other knew nothing else" (*Dictionary of National Biography,* p. 1290). Others were similarly critical, although Dowdeswell does appear to have had a reasonable understanding of economics.

He lost his office with the breakup of the Rockingham ministry in 1766 and refused to accept offers of office in the subsequent ministries. However, he remained active while out of office, forcing through a bill to reduce land tax from four shillings to three shillings on the pound, much to the annoyance of Charles Townshend (1725–1767), his successor as chancellor. Indeed, he remained an active M.P. for the rest of his life. He became ill in 1774 and died on 6 February 1775.

Kit Hardwick and Keith Laybourn

See also: Grenville, George; North, Lord; Pitt, William (the Elder); Rockingham, Marquess of
References and Further Reading: Langford, Paul, 1973, The First Rockingham Administration, 1765–66 (London: Oxford University Press); O'Gorman, Francis, 1975, The Rise of Party in England: The Rockingham Whigs, 1760–1782 (London: Allen and Unwin).

Dudley, Viscount (John William Ward; Earl of Dudley of Castle Dudley, Staffordshire; Viscount Dudley and Ward)
(1781–1833) [FS]

John William Ward was the only child of William, third Viscount Dudley and Ward, and his wife, Julia, second daughter of Godfrey Bosville of Thorpe and Gunthwaite in Yorkshire. He was born on 9 August 1781 and educated by private tutors. He then went to Oriel College, Oxford, in 1799, and graduated with a B.A. from Corpus Christi College on 16 June 1802, obtaining his M.A. in 1813. In 1802 he became a resident pupil of Dugald Stewart, along with Lord Lansdowne, Lord Palmerston, and Lord Ashburton.

Ward's political career began in 1802, when he became M.P. for Downton in Wiltshire. He was a follower of William Pitt (the Younger), and George Canning was his close friend. Ward supported Lord Grenville in 1804 and Charles James Fox, and was subsequently a firm supporter of Canning. On 1 August 1803 he stood for Worcestershire in a by-election and was elected without opposition. In 1806 he was elected M.P. for Petersfield, in Hampshire, and in 1807 he became M.P. for Wareham, in Dorset. In 1812 he became M.P. for Ilchester, in Somerset; and in 1819, after being out of Parliament for six months, he became M.P. for Bossiney, in Cornwall. He retained that seat until 1823, when he succeeded to his father's peerage.

Although he was a member of the House of Commons for almost 21 years, Ward spoke rarely and refused a number of junior posts. Therefore, when George Canning appointed him foreign secretary in April 1827 (a post he held until May 1828), Ward had no prior experience of government. Ward became the Earl of Dudley on 24 September 1827.

As foreign secretary he did little more than carry out Canning's decisions; and though he continued for a time as foreign secretary in the government of the Duke of Wellington in 1828, he resigned with other Canningites, including Lord Palmerston and William Huskisson, in May 1829. While foreign secretary he was mainly concerned with Greece, and he signed a treaty with France and Russia on 6 July 1827 for the pacification of that country. After his retirement from the office of foreign secretary, he never held public office again. His only other notable activity was that he vehemently opposed the Reform Bill in 1831 and 1832.

In his later years Dudley was forgetful of mind and began conducting conversations with himself. He was eventually put under restraint at Norwood, in Surrey, where he suffered a stroke and died on 6 March 1833.

Kit Hardwick and Keith Laybourn

See also: Canning, George; Grenville, George; Palmerston, Lord; Pitt, William (the Younger); Wellington, Duke of
References and Further Reading: Dixon, Peter, 1976, Canning: Politician and Statesman (London: Weidenfeld and Nicolson); Hinde, Wendy, 1973, George Canning (London: Collins); Rolo, Paul J. V., 1965, George Canning (London: Macmillan).

Duncannon, Viscount (John William Ponsonby; Earl of Bessborough)
(1781–1847) [HS]

John William Ponsonby was born on 31 August 1781, the eldest son of Frederick, the third Earl of Bessborough, and his wife, Lady Henrietta Frances Spencer, second daughter of the first Earl Spencer. The family held large estates in Ireland. In early life John bore the courtesy title of Lord Duncannon. He went to Christ Church, Oxford, completed his education there in 1799, and obtained an M.A. in June 1802. He married Lady Maria Fane, the third daughter of John, tenth Earl of Westmoreland, on 11 November 1805.

Duncannon's political career began in 1805, when he entered the House of Commons as

Whig M.P. for Knaresborough. In 1806 and 1807 he represented Higham Ferrers, and between 1812 and 1826, Malton. In 1826 he won the Irish seat of Kilkenny, despite the opposition of Daniel O'Connell, the leader of the campaign for Catholic emancipation. He also narrowly won Kilkenny again in the 1831 general election. In 1832 he was elected M.P. for Nottingham.

Politically committed to Catholic emancipation and parliamentary reform, he was one of the leading Whig Radicals of his day. He acted as chief whip for the Whigs, and along with Lord Durham, Lord John Russell, and Sir James Graham, he prepared the Reform Bill of 1830. In February 1831 he was appointed by Lord Grey as the First Commissioner of Woods and Forests, and became a member of the Privy Council. He then became home secretary when Lord Melbourne, his brother-in-law, became prime minister in July 1834, largely as a result of pressure from the now more favorably inclined O'Connell. On 18 July 1834 he became Baron Duncannon of Bessborough and then continued in office when Sir Robert Peel became prime minister in December 1834. He returned to the post for woods and forests in April 1835, when Melbourne became prime minister again, and was also Lord Privy Seal until 1839. He also was responsible for the designs of the new houses of Parliament around that time.

Duncannon became the Earl of Bessborough in February 1844, and in 1846 he was appointed lord lieutenant of Ireland. He was friendly at that time with Daniel O'Connell, and he performed well in his Irish post. He died in that post on 16 May 1847, while at Dublin Castle.

Keith Laybourn

See also: Grey, Lord; Melbourne, Viscount; Peel, Sir Robert
References and Further Reading: Newbould, Ian, 1990, *Whiggery and Reform, 1830–1841* (London: Macmillan).

Dundas, Henry (Viscount Melville) (1742–1811) [HS]

Henry Dundas was born on the 28 April 1742, son of Robert Dundas, Lord Arniston, and was educated at Edinburgh High School and Edinburgh University. He pursued a legal career and became a member of the Faculty of Advocates (an independent, professional organization) in 1763 and solicitor general for Scotland in 1706. From 1774 to 1790, except for a few months in 1782 when he sat for Newtown, on the Isle of Wight, he was M.P. for Midlothian. As lord advocate from 1775 to 1783, he supported an amendment for the repeal of the Massachusetts charter in 1778 and carried the resolution for the recall of Warren Hastings from India in 1782. Nevertheless, he defended Hastings's Rohilla War in 1786. He later spoke in favor of the East India Company in 1793. He also served as lord rector of Glasgow University between 1781 and 1783; as keeper of the Scottish signet in 1782; and as chancellor of St. Andrews University in 1788. He was awarded an honorary doctorate of law at Edinburgh University the following year. He was also M.P. for Edinburgh from 1790 to 1802.

Dundas filled many of the important posts of state. He was treasurer of the navy between 1782 and 1783 and from 1784 to 1800, and a member of the Privy Council. He was home secretary between 8 June 1791 and 10 July 1794, president of the Board of Control between 1793 and 1801, and secretary for war between 1794 and 1801.

It was during this period of his greatest influence that he took on the responsibility of protecting the seven children of the late Lord Haddo. The children had been taken to England from Edinburgh by Haddo's wife, Charlotte Baird, who subsequently died in 1795. Dundas ensured that the children were looked after in England and brought them to the attention of William Pitt, the Younger, then prime minister. The eldest child, George Gordon, became Lord Haddo in 1798, and exercising his right under Scottish law to choose his own curators (guardians), named Pitt and Dundas. Lord Haddo became the fourth Earl of Aberdeen in 1801 and served as prime minister be-

Prime Minister William Pitt and subordinate ministers Dundas and Thurlow portrayed as the witches from Macbeth, *contemplating a moon composed of the profiles of Queen Charlotte and King George III (Library of Congress)*

tween 1852 and 1855, and he always remembered the help that Pitt and Dundas provided in his youth.

Dundas was responsible for planning and executing the Egyptian Campaign of 1801, against the opinion of both Pitt and the king. Nevertheless, he became Viscount Melville of Melville and Baron Dunira in 1802. He served as First Lord of the Admiralty from 1804 to 1805; but in the latter year he was accused of financial corruption, removed from the rolls of privy councillors, and impeached for mishandling of public funds. Though he was found guilty of negligence, he was subsequently acquitted of the more serious charge of corruption and was restored to the Privy Council in 1807. He died on 28 May 1811.

Kit Hardwick and Keith Laybourn

See also : Pitt, William (the Younger)
References and Further Reading : Eccleshall, Robert, and Graham Walker, 1998, *Biographical Dictionary of British Prime Ministers* (London and New York: Routledge).

E

Eden, Sir Anthony (Earl of Avon)
(1897–1977) [PM, FS]

Sir Anthony Eden is invariably remembered for his involvement with the Suez Canal Crisis in 1956, when Britain and France, with the aid of Israel, invaded Egypt in response to the decision of Colonel Nasser to nationalize the Suez Canal Company. The ignominious withdrawal of British and French forces in the face of American pressure led to Eden's resignation on grounds of ill health. The Suez Crisis was an unfortunate end for a politician who had a reputation as a diplomat of some distinction.

Robert Anthony Eden was born on 12 June 1897, the third son of Sir William Eden and Sybil Gray, although there is some suggestion that his father actually may have been the politician George Wyndham. Anthony had an unhappy childhood and did not enjoy his time at Eton, but distinguished himself in World War I, winning the Military Cross and becoming the youngest brigade major in the British army. After the war he enrolled at Christ Church, Oxford, where he obtained a first-class honors degree in oriental languages. In 1923 he married Beatrice Beckett.

Eden's political career began in 1923 when he became Conservative M.P. for Warwick and Leamington, a seat he held until his retirement from the House of Commons in 1957. He performed a number of junior roles in Stanley Baldwin's Conservative government of 1924 to 1929. He was parliamentary private secretary to the parliamentary undersecretary at the Home Office between 1924 and 1926, and fulfilled the same role at the Foreign Office in 1926, until his promotion to parliamentary private secretary to the foreign secretary (Sir Austen Chamberlain), a post he held between 1926 and 1929.

He rose further in the National government of the 1930s, becoming parliamentary undersecretary at the Foreign Office between 1931 and 1933, Lord Privy Seal between 1933 and 1935, and minister without portfolio for League of Nations affairs in 1935. By 1935 he had gained wide political experience and was developing expertise in foreign affairs.

Eden's formidable political reputation is based on his role as foreign secretary, a position he held on three occasions. He was first appointed to that post in 1935 and resigned from it in 1938. That led his name being associated with that of Winston Churchill in his opposition to the "appeasement" policies of Neville Chamberlain, which seemed to be drawing Britain into war. Whether Eden actually objected to appeasement seems open to question, for he was reluctant to oppose the remilitarization of the Rhineland in 1936. His resignation also can be attributed to a fit of pique at Neville Chamberlain's interference in Anglo-Italian affairs. Whatever the situation, Eden's reward for being seen as an anti-appeaser was that he became Churchill's foreign secretary from December 1940 until the end of World War II in 1945, which involved him in extensive diplomatic work.

It has been suggested that Eden enjoyed a close working relationship with Churchill during the war years, like that of father and son. However, recent evidence suggests that the two were often bitter rivals. Attempting to see the Soviet point of view on major issues, Eden often clashed with Churchill, and he was on the verge of resigning his post on a number of occasions. This conflict was revealed after the war, when Eden privately indicated his strong disapproval of Churchill's attack on communism in his "Iron Curtain" speech at Fulton, Missouri, in 1946.

Sir Anthony Eden (left) and John Foster Dulles in New York, 1956 (Library of Congress)

Eden was out of office between 1945 and 1951, under Attlee's Labour governments. During these years Eden aspired to become the Conservative leader but found his way blocked by Churchill, who refused to step down despite defeats in the 1945 and 1950 general elections.

The return of Churchill's Conservative government in 1951 once again brought Eden the post of foreign secretary. As he had in wartime, he often found himself in conflict with Churchill over foreign policy. Nonetheless, he managed three major accomplishments. First, he helped organize the Geneva Conference of 1954, which ended the conflict between the French and communists in Indochina. Secondly, he brokered the 1954 agreement with Egypt for the withdrawal of British troops from the Suez Canal Zone in 1956. Thirdly, he was influential in forcing France to accept that West Germany could rearm under the auspices of the North Atlantic Treaty Organization (NATO).

Eden succeeded the ailing Churchill as Conservative leader on 6 April 1955 and led the Conservative Party to a general election victory the following month. As prime minister, he gained world attention by arranging a trilateral summit (of the United States, Britain, and the Soviet Union) at Geneva in July 1955 to help improve international relations. There was some Western optimism (in Britain and the United States) that the Soviet leadership was different after the death of Stalin in 1953. In fact, Eden's efforts to mediate between the Americans and the Soviets proved of limited value, but he invited Nikolai Bulganin and Nikita Krushchev to make a state visit to Britain in 1956. Unfortunately, the Soviet invasion of Hungary in October/November 1956 put an end to efforts to improve East-West relations.

In other areas, Eden's premiership faced increasing problems. A deep financial crisis was developing in 1955. R. A. Butler, Churchill's chancellor of the exchequer, had introduced an expansionist budget immediately before the May general election but was forced by expansionary pressures to introduce an emergency deflationary budget in October 1955. Eden replaced Butler with Harold Macmillan in December 1955. Macmillan attempted to impose further deflationary measures in 1956, but they seem to have achieved little.

The final months of Eden's premiership were dominated by the Suez Crisis, an event that generally has blighted assessments of his political achievements. The crisis arose partly out of Eden's beliefs that Britain could continue to be a major player in international politics alongside the United States and the Soviet Union, and that Britain was not necessarily dependent upon the United States. In 1944, as wartime foreign secretary, Eden had been determined to preserve Britain's involvement in the Middle East irrespective of American interests. This situation continued throughout his tenure as foreign secretary during the 1950s. John Foster Dulles, the U.S. secretary of state, was equally adamant that the United States would not be seen to be involved in any act of imperialist aggression. The two approaches clashed during the Suez Crisis.

The Suez Canal had been controlled by a company based in Paris. However, at the end of 1955, Gamal Abdel Nasser led Egypt into an arms deal with Czechoslovakia, a communist-dominated country, and mounted an aggressive campaign against British interests in the Middle East. Then, on 26 July 1956, he nationalized the Suez Canal Company, aiming to use the canal revenues to finance the Aswan Dam project, which both the British and the Americans had refused to finance. Nasser's action annoyed the French, and Eden felt that Britain's access to the oil supplies of the Middle East was seriously threatened. Action had to be taken.

It is clear that the Egypt Committee of the British cabinet was discussing the need to restore the Suez Canal to international control by the end of July 1956 and that its concern was also to topple Nasser from power in Egypt. It is also evident that the United States made its opposition to military intervention in Egypt perfectly clear. Regardless, Eden was drawn into a plan whereby Israel would invade Egypt and British and French forces would intervene by invading and occupying the Canal Zone. The

Israelis invaded Egypt on 29 October 1956, and following an Anglo-French ultimatum the following day demanding that both sides withdraw their troops from the Canal Zone, the Anglo-French invasion began on 31 October 1956 and culminated in the landing of a task force at Port Said on 5 November 1956. The United Nations demanded a cease-fire throughout the whole affair, the Soviet Union supported Egypt, and the United States refused to give support to sterling, which had come under speculative pressure. Faced with strong opposition to their actions, Britain and France agreed to a cease-fire and a humiliating withdrawal of their forces on 6 November 1956.

Why Eden became involved in the Suez fiasco has been a matter of debate. David Carlton suggests that Eden's actions were motivated by the desire to distract the British from their domestic problems; Robert Rhodes James believes that Eden acted in order to counter the Soviet Union's growing influence in the Middle East. There is also some doubt about how much the cabinet knew about the plan to involve Israel in the invasion of Egypt. Richard Lamb suggests that Eden misled the cabinet; in contrast, Carlton asserts that no minister could rightly claim he had been deceived.

Eden had suffered ill health throughout his life. His health had been further weakened in 1953 when a bile duct operation had gone wrong. He appears to have been ill throughout 1956 and to have decided for that reason to resign on 9 January 1957. Yet ill health was merely the pretext for his resignation; the Suez Crisis was the determining factor. His political reputation had been greatly damaged as a result of Suez. Furthermore, the fact that he had misled the House of Commons on 20 December, by denying collusion with Israel, was bound to be exposed in the fullness of time.

Eden left the House of Commons in 1957 and was ennobled in 1961 as the first Earl of Avon. He died on 14 January 1977. His obituary writers recognized that he was the last British prime minister to have believed that Britain was still a great power. Suez exposed his belief as an illusion.

Keith Laybourn

See also: Attlee, Clement; Baldwin, Stanley; Chamberlain, Austen; Chamberlain, Neville; Churchill, Sir Winston; Macmillan, Harold
References and Further Reading: Carlton, David, 1981, *Anthony Eden: A Biography* (London: Allen Lane); Dutton, David, 1996, *Anthony Eden: A Life and Reputation* (London: Arnold); James, Robert Rhodes, 1986, *Anthony Eden* (London: Weidenfeld & Nicolson); Lamb, Richard, 1987, *The Failure of the Eden Government* (London: Sidgwick & Jackson);Rothwell, Victor, 1991, *Anthony Eden: A Political Biography 1931–1957* (Manchester: Manchester University Press).

Egremont, Earl of (Sir Charles Wyndham [or Windham])
(1710–1763) [HS]

Sir Charles Wyndham was born on 19 August 1710, the son of Sir William Wyndham, of Orchard-Wyndham, Somerset, and his first wife, Katherine, daughter of Charles Seymour, sixth Duke of Somerset. He was educated at Westminster School and Christ Church, Oxford. He entered the House of Commons as Tory M.P. for Bridgwater in 1735, lost his seat there in 1741, but was then returned for Appleby. He had become a Whig by that time, and supported the proposal to take Hanoverian troops into British pay. In June 1740 he succeeded to his father's baronetcy and Somerset estates, and was elected to represent the family borough of Taunton in 1747. (He was elected also for Cockermouth, but preferred the Somerset seat.) In 1750 Wyndham inherited the Cumberland and Sussex estates of his maternal uncle Algernon, the seventh Duke of Somerset, together with his titles of Earl of Egremont and Baron Cockermouth. In 1751 he married Alicia Maria, daughter of George Carpenter, second Baron Carpenter of Killaghy, and sister of the first Earl of Tyrconnel.

The second Earl of Egremont was not the most able of politicians and, in the character of the age, owed much of his political success to preferment and family connections. But he did take advantage of political opportunities that arose. On 22 March 1751 he moved the House of Lords address of condolence to the king on the death of Frederick, Prince of Wales. In the same year he was appointed lord lieutenant of

Cumberland. He also acquired a political reputation, although he was very rarely involved in political debates.

In 1757, Egremont was asked to become secretary of state in the ministry that James Waldegrave, second Earl Waldegrave, was attempting to form, but he declined the offer. He was then involved in several other political ventures before becoming secretary of state for the Southern Department (home secretary), replacing William Pitt, the Elder, in October 1761. He remained in that post for a little less than two years, through the governments of the Duke of Newcastle, the Earl of Bute, and George Grenville, the last of whom happened to be his brother-in-law.

In this new role, Egremont was involved in dealings with Spain aimed at ensuring that the Spanish agreement with France—the Bourbon family compact—would bring no detriment to English interests. At this time, and until 1782, both the secretaries of state for the Southern and Northern departments could deal with foreign as well as domestic policy. In 1762 he was further involved in developing peace negotiations with France, opposing the Earl of Bute's peace-at-any-price approach in ending the Seven Years' War. Nonetheless, Egremont did cede some territory to Spain to appease the French, agreeing to give up Florida in return for the recently acquired Havana in modern-day Cuba.

The terms of the peace settlement, and the rival approaches adopted by various members of the succession of ministries under which Egremont served, led him into many conflicts—in particular, with the Earl of Bute; John Russell, the fourth Duke of Bedford; and Sir William Petty, the second Earl of Shelburne. The conflict with Shelburne arose from Egremont's pressing for all British territories in North America to be included in the new province of Canada—a move that Shelburne vehemently opposed.

Egremont's position was strengthened in April 1763 when George Grenville, his brother-in-law, was persuaded to become prime minister. This was a short-lived ministry, however, during which Egremont's main task seems to have been to order the arrest, imprisonment, and prosecution of John Wilkes, the beacon of liberty at this time, for publishing issue number

45 of *North Briton*. Egremont died at the beginning of September 1763. His contemporary and more recent critics have denied his parliamentary ability and pointed to his avarice, and few political observers would rank his political skills above the ordinary.

Kit Hardwick and Keith Laybourn

See also: Bute, Earl of; Grenville, George; Newcastle, Duke of; Pitt, William (the Elder); Shelburne, Earl of

References and Further Reading: Lawson, Philip, 1984, *George Grenville: A Political Life* (Manchester: Manchester University Press).

Ellis, Welbore (Baron Mendip)
(1713–1802) [AC]

Welbore Ellis, a minor figure in eighteenth-century British politics, is known today primarily for having served as the last secretary of state for the American colonies. He was born on 15 December 1713, the younger son of the Right Rev. Dr. Welbore Ellis, Bishop of Meath, and of Diana, daughter of Sir John Briscoe of Broughton, Northamptonshire. Educated at Westminster School and Christ Church, Oxford, he was elected, after some dispute, to the House of Commons as M.P. for Cricklade in the 1741 general election. Thereafter he occupied a number of posts in government. He was appointed Lord of the Admiralty in Henry Pelham's administration in February 1747, promoted to the Treasury board, and elected to represent the joint boroughs of Weymouth and Melcombe Regis in 1747.

He held these various offices until December 1755, when he resigned his seat in the House of Commons in favor of an appointment as vice treasurer of Ireland. He became a member of the Privy Council in 1760; he was elected jointly with John Wilkes to represent the borough of Aylesbury in 1761; and he was appointed secretary at war in December 1762, a post that conveyed the responsibility of representing military fiscal needs to the House of Commons.

Upon the formation of the government of the Marquess of Rockingham in 1765, Ellis resigned as secretary at war and became joint vice-treasurer of Ireland, a post that he held until September 1766. In the 1768 general election,

he was returned as M.P. for Petersfield and became vice-treasurer of Ireland a third time, despite his deep opposition to Lord North's motion for the repeal of the American tea duty. In 1774 he was returned for his old constituency at Weymouth. He resigned the office of vice-treasurer in March 1777, and was appointed treasurer of the navy in June 1777. He was again returned as M.P. for Weymouth in 1780.

Toward the end of Lord North's ministry, on 11 February 1782, Ellis was appointed secretary of state for the American colonies. His tenure in this post was brief; he resigned in March 1782, when the Marquess of Rockingham became prime minister. Nevertheless, he continued to take an active part in politics, opposing William Pitt, the Younger, who was prime minister and chancellor of the exchequer between 1783 and 1801. Ellis was returned again for Weymouth in 1784. He was defeated in 1790, but won a by-election at Petersfield in April 1791. He was created Baron Mendip, of Mendip, in the county of Somerset, on 13 August 1794, but he never spoke in the House of Lords. He died at his house in Brook Street, Hanover Square, London, on 2 February 1802 and was buried in the north transept of Westminster Abbey. Ellis had married twice: first, Elizabeth, the daughter of Sir William Stanhope, in 1747; and following Elizabeth's death in 1761, Anne, the daughter of Hans Stanley of Paultons, near Romsey, in Hampshire, in 1765. There were no children by either marriage.

Although Ellis was no great politician, he provided effective support in the 1750s to more prominent leaders, such as Henry Fox, the later Lord Holland. (Indeed, Horace Walpole, the son of Sir Robert Walpole, described Ellis as Fox's "Jackal.") He also served efficiently in many offices, including—albeit briefly—that of secretary of state for the American colonies.

Kit Hardwick and Keith Laybourn

See also: North, Lord; Pelham, Hon. Henry; Pitt, William (the Younger); Rockingham, Marquess of
References and Further Reading: Whiteley, Peter, 1997, *Lord North: The Prime Minister Who Lost America* (London: Hambledon Press).

Estcourt, Thomas H. S. S.
(1801–1876) [HS]

Thomas Henry Sutton Sotheron Estcourt was born on 4 April 1801, the eldest son of Thomas Grimston Bucknall Estcourt, of Estcourt, in Gloucestershire, who was Tory M.P. for Devizes from 1805 to 1827 and M.P. for Oxford University between 1827 and 1847; and of Eleanor, daughter of James Sutton, of New Park, Wiltshire. He was educated at Harrow and at Oriel College, Oxford, where he graduated with a first-class honors degree in classics in 1822, at the same time as his friend Lord Ashley, later the seventh Earl of Shaftesbury. Estcourt then completed a grand tour of Europe.

After returning home, he became M.P. for Marlborough in 1829. In 1830 he married Lucy Sarah, the only daughter of Admiral Frank Sotheron, of Kirklinton, Nottinghamshire, and Darrington Hall, Yorkshire. In 1839 Estcourt inherited the latter estate and for a time adopted the name Sotheron in place of Estcourt (he re-assumed his paternal name in 1855). In 1835 he became M.P. for Devizes, a seat that he held until 1844, when he was returned without opposition as M.P. for North Wiltshire. He held the North Wiltshire seat until 1865.

He was considered a talented Tory M.P. but seemed disinclined to hold office. In 1858 he did agree, at the request of the fourteenth Earl of Derby, to become president of the Poor Law Board; he was also sworn in as a member of the Privy Council. He proved an efficient politician, and he briefly succeeded Spencer Walpole as home secretary in March 1859. This office ended in June 1859, however, with the collapse of the Derby ministry. Estcourt willingly retired from office; and in 1863 he withdrew entirely from public life as a result of illness. He died childless on 6 January 1876, leaving his property to a younger brother and a nephew. Today he is a largely forgotten political figure.

Keith Laybourn

See also: Derby, 14th Earl of
References and Further Reading: Jones, Wilbur, 1956, *Lord Derby and Victorian Conservatism* (London: Basil Blackwell).

F

Fox, Charles James
(1749–1806) [FS]

Charles James Fox was born in London on 24 January 1749, the third son of Henry Fox, first Baron Holland. His Stuart forenames reflected the family's connection with the former royal house, as his great-grandfather had been a page to King Charles I on the scaffold in 1649—though his father had, according to Fox's biographer J. G. Mitchell, learned to love the Hanoverians. Despite a deep and lasting mutual devotion between father and son, Fox junior's political career was characterized by his implacable opposition to the royal interference that he saw as presaging a wish by King George III for an absolutist rule such as was widespread in continental Europe at the time.

Charles Fox was a precocious boy whose appetites both for scholarship and for debauchery were seemingly limitless. These tendencies were hugely encouraged by his doting father; the only restraint on the boy came from his mother, who often compared him unfavorably with William Pitt, the Younger, who she predicted would be a thorn in Charles's side as long as he lived. Many of Fox's later circle were contemporaries from his school days at Eton, where he developed a capacity for friendship and a love of classical languages. At age 12 he was writing love verses in Latin to his cousin Lady Susan Fox Strangeways—who coincidentally, and perhaps significantly, was also much admired by the young George III. Though he subsequently went to one of the more academically demanding colleges at Oxford—not then a place universally renowned for scholarly rigor—it was not to offer him much further stimulation than Eton. France was to be his real university. As his school friend Carlisle later wrote, when Fox's father introduced him to Paris at age 15 he "talked French admirably and employd [sic] it in declaiming against Religion with a fashionable grace that would have charmed Voltaire himself." In France, he also learned to gamble for high stakes and was initiated into adult life by a certain Madame de Quallens of "high fashion." A subsequent extended visit to France during 1767–1768 allowed Fox to meet Voltaire, Gibbon, and many others who were to play key roles in the subsequent revolutions in America and in France, and at the same time confirmed him as a libertine and a dandy. His tour gave him all the "philosophy," friendships, and fashion that would mark him out, on his return to London, as a man of the world.

In 1768, at age 19, Fox became M.P. for Midhurst. He immediately made his mark—ironically, in light of his subsequent career—by speaking against the champion of democratic liberty, John Wilkes. He became Lord of the Admiralty under Lord North in 1770, but resigned in 1772, before rejoining the administration as Lord of the Treasury ten months later. Fox's independence made him many enemies. He publicly humiliated his leader, Lord North, whose behavior he thought too timid. This was too much for the king, who insisted on Fox's removal from office.

After his dismissal Fox played a leading role in the opposition to Lord North's American policy. His shift of allegiance, which was probably influenced by Edmund Burke, a Whig who later wrote about the French Revolution, led him into the mainstream of oligarchic Whiggery, which sought precedence for the constitution and Parliament over the king.

Between 1774 and 1782, American independence became a political issue of increasing con-

"The reconciliation between Britannia and her daughter America," a cartoon showing America as an Indian rushing to the arms of Britannia, while a Spaniard and a Frenchman try to pull her away. Charles James Fox, recently appointed secretary of state for foreign affairs, points out these actions to the Lord of the Admiralty (right). (Library of Congress)

cern to Fox. Referring to his "illustrious friend" George Washington, he spoke out strongly in favor of the rights of colonies to be self-governing. Indeed, the buff and blue of Washington's army were adopted as the colors of the Fox club. Fox and his followers supported the Americans because they believed that if George III succeeded in imposing despotism in America, he would soon attempt to impose a similar regime in England. Between November 1776 and January 1777, Fox was in Paris, where he met rebel American diplomats including Benjamin Franklin, who befriended him. Fox had further inside information from his former gambling chum John Burgoyne, who led one of the British armies, and from another soldier, Richard Fitzpatrick, who informed Fox that his old friend Lafayette wished to be remembered to him. Fox was proud of his American connection, and with some justification, for he was much better informed about current developments than was Lord North. As the American crisis deepened, Fox became the government's severest and most telling critic, speaking out

publicly against the prosecution of the American War, until peace was finally secured in 1783.

North's government fell in March 1782, and Fox became foreign secretary under the Rockingham-Shelburne administration. It soon became apparent to Fox that Shelburne was George III's cat's-paw, working from within to destabilize the government. With the illness and subsequent death of Rockingham in July 1782, the hostility between Fox and Shelburne came to a head. Fox saw France as England's greatest enemy and sought to isolate it diplomatically by forming an alliance with Russia and Prussia as well as by wooing the American rebels away from their French allies. He was convinced that to give the Americans independence freely and with good grace was in England's best interests politically. In addition, once America ceased to be a colony, it would come within Fox's remit, which would facilitate his broader European peace negotiations. At the time, Shelburne had jurisdiction over the colonies, including America, and was blocking Fox's attempts to secure peace terms with France.

When the cabinet vote went against American freedom, Fox immediately resigned. But this move was politically ruinous for him: Instead of his resignation being perceived as a protest against the king's undermining of the administration, it appeared to many to be motivated by the fact that he had not been given a more prominent position on the death of Rockingham. Fox had challenged the king's right to appoint whom he chose, maintaining that a parliamentary majority should decide the matter, and nominating the Duke of Portland to head the new administration—which would not include Shelburne. Fox cast about for new allies in his fight against the king. He finally secured a coalition with Lord North, his old chief, in February 1783, and by a majority of more than 100 votes Shelburne was forced out of office. Fox had won the battle. He underlined his victory by presenting the king with a complete cabinet list; for the first time in history, an English monarch had been deprived of all influence in the composition of his government.

George III was determined to regain the upper hand, and in June 1783 he tried to drive a wedge between North and Fox over the debts of his son, the Prince of Wales, which Parliament was invited to repay. North had no sympathy for the prince, but Fox was deeply embarrassed by the affair. Himself a gambler and a bankrupt, Fox was widely seen as the prince's mentor in dissipation. The prince backed down, and Fox was temporarily off the hook; but in the next parliamentary session the king struck again. The East India Company was notoriously corrupt, and Fox had proposed to bring India within the government's direct control; toward that end, on 27 November 1783, he had secured from the Commons a substantial vote in favor —229 to 120. On 15 December, the Lords, bowing to pressure from the king, defeated the bill by eight votes. The king's maneuvering was now exposed and his position desperate; but being determined to get rid of Fox, he appointed the young William Pitt prime minister. Contrary to Fox's expectations, the House of Commons grew weary of his constant blocking of Pitt's proposals, and his supporters gradually drifted away. The king finally settled the matter

by dissolving Parliament in March 1784—even though it had three years left to run—and plunging the country into the most acrimonious election of the century. Fox was eventually returned to Westminster, but he had become embittered and disenchanted. His subsequent career was marred by his vacillation between reluctance to attend the House of Commons at all, and longing for revenge against Pitt and the others who had wronged him and flouted the constitution.

In the summer of the same year Fox bought a villa in Surrey that was to be his home for the rest of his life. He settled there with his most recent lover, Mrs. Armistead, whom he married in 1795. He made occasional contributions to public life during the next two decades. He attacked Warren Hastings and moved for his impeachment in 1786–1787; moved to repeal the Corporation and Test acts in 1790; and opposed Pitt on most issues other than reform, especially on his policy toward the French Revolution. Fox interviewed Napoleon Bonaparte in 1802 during a tour of France and the Netherlands, and made a three-hour speech in favor of peace in 1803. He was proposed as a member of a coalition with Pitt when Addison died in 1804 but was vetoed by the king. He finally became foreign secretary again in 1806 under Lord Grenville. That year, shortly before his death, he proposed the abolition of slavery.

Fox was a very clever man of great charm who cared little for personal critics or for personal power. He lived very much on his own terms, and to his many friends he was enormous fun to be with. Much loved in his lifetime, he was deified almost immediately after his death. His importance and rarity as a politician lay in the fact that he valued friendship and loyalty more than the exercise of power, though he saw more clearly than most of his contemporaries the importance of keeping power within constitutional bounds.

Kit Hardwick

See also: Grenville, Lord; North, Lord; Pitt, William (the Younger); Rockingham, Marquess of; Shelburne, Earl of
References and Further Reading: Mitchell, L. G., 1997, *Charles James Fox* (Oxford and New York:

Oxford University Press); Schweitzer, David, 1991, *Charles James Fox, 1749–1806: A Bibliography* (New York: Greenwood).

Fox, Henry (Baron Holland)
(1705–1774) [HS]

To many of his contemporaries, Henry Fox was a political adventurer whose prime interest was building up the family fortune through his use and abuse of political power. Yet most would also concede that he was a formidable debater and an effective politician if not a great orator. He was born on 28 September 1705, the younger son of Sir Stephen Fox by his second wife, Christian, the daughter of the Rev. Francis Hope. Fox was educated at Eton, where he was a contemporary of William Pitt, the Elder. He quickly earned a reputation as a reckless gambler and was forced to go abroad to avoid financial embarrassment. This reputation dogged him throughout his life; and when he married Lady Georgiana Caroline Lennox, the eldest daughter of Charles, second Duke of Richmond, on 2 May 1744, he did so without the consent of her parents, who were not reconciled to the marriage for many years. Lady Caroline became Baroness Holland, of Holland, Lincolnshire, in the British peerage, on 6 May 1762. Fox had four sons, one of whom was the famous and immensely politically active Charles James Fox.

Henry Fox's parliamentary career began in February 1735 when he became M.P. for the borough of Hinden, in Wiltshire. He was a Whig and quickly attached himself to Robert Walpole, becoming surveyor-general of works in 1737. In 1741 he was returned as M.P. for the borough of Windsor, which he represented until 1761. He resigned from office in 1742, with the fall of Walpole, but became Lord of the Treasury in August 1743, in the ministry of Henry Pelham. In May 1746, he was appointed secretary at war; in this post he was responsible for presenting military and naval estimates to the House of Commons. He became a member of the Privy Council in July 1746. He continued as secretary at war after Pelham's death in 1754, under the leadership of Pelham's brother, the Duke of Newcastle.

Although he served in a Whig administration, Fox often joined forces with William Pitt, the Elder, the Tory leader, in attacking government ministers. However, after Fox became leader of the House of Commons and then secretary of state for the Southern Department (the post of home secretary, after 1782) in November 1755, he began to identify more closely with Newcastle. Fox resigned in November 1756, suspecting that Newcastle was going to blame him for the loss of the Mediterranean island of Minorca; but he was soon followed by Newcastle himself. The king asked Fox to form a ministry with Pitt, but the latter declined, whereupon the Duke of Devonshire formed a ministry with the help of Pitt.

In 1757, Fox was persuaded to become paymaster-general, a post that did not include a seat in the cabinet but that allowed him to amass a large fortune. He held this post until the fall of the Grenville ministry in October 1762 and managed to secure its continuance under the ministry of Lord Bute, although in return he had to agree to serve as leader of the House of Commons. He sought, and obtained through bribery, the support of the House of Commons for the Treaty of Paris in 1763, claiming as his reward the title of Baron Holland of Foxley, Wiltshire. He continued to hold the profitable post of paymaster-general until May 1765. He was reluctant to give up this lucrative position, the true value of which was suggested in 1769 by a petition to the king, brought by the Lord Mayor of the City of London, in which Fox and other ministers were attacked for having misappropriated "unaccounted millions" of pounds. Proceedings were initiated against Fox to recover some of this money, but they were stopped by a warrant from the Crown. Fox died at Holland House, near Kensington, London, on 1 July 1774.

Keith Laybourn

See also: Bute, Earl of; Devonshire, Duke of; Grenville, George; Newcastle, Duke of; Pelham, Hon. Henry; Pitt, William (the Elder); Walpole, Sir Robert
References and Further Reading: Browning, Reed, 1975, *The Duke of Newcastle* (New Haven, CT: Yale University Press).

G

Gaitskell, Hugh
(1906–1963) [CE]

Hugh Todd Naylor Gaitskell was born on 9 April 1906 and was educated at Winchester and at New College, Oxford, where he was influenced by G. D. H. Cole, the famous socialist thinker and writer. He obtained a degree in economics from New College. He worked briefly as an adult education tutor in Nottingham in the late 1920s; and in the 1930s he became part of a London group of intellectual socialists advocating Keynesian economics. During World War II, as a trained economist who spoke German, Gaitskell served at the Ministry of Economic Warfare. After the war, he worked at the Board of Trade, as personal assistant to Hugh Dalton.

Gaitskell was elected to Parliament in 1945 as M.P. for South Leeds. He was appointed parliamentary secretary to the minister of fuel and power, and he helped organize the nationalization of the gas industry. He also encouraged the Labour government to devalue the pound in 1949. After the general election of 1950, he was appointed Labour's chancellor of the exchequer, in place of Sir Stafford Cripps. In that post he grappled with the problems of the rising costs of rearmament, provoked both by the Korean War and by his strong support for the Anglo-American alliance. He came into conflict with Minister of Labour Aneurin Bevan (who previously had been minister of health and housing) over the issue of imposing prescription charges on the health service (such charges later were introduced under the subsequent, Conservative, government), which Bevan rejected. This led to the resignation of Aneurin Bevan and Harold Wilson in April 1951, deeply dividing the Labour Party between left and right factions (with the left supporting Bevan). The government, which could no longer muster a solid majority, was thus forced into a general election later that year and was defeated by Winston Churchill and the Conservative Party.

In December 1955, Gaitskell replaced Clement Attlee as Labour leader. Gaitskell's leadership proved intensely controversial and divisive. He opposed the Anglo-French invasion of Suez in 1956; advocated multilateral, rather than unilateral, disarmament; and favored what he felt was a more ethical approach to socialism, at the expense of the extension of public ownership. As a right-wing revisionist, he advocated the creation of equality through high social expenditure financed out of economic growth—very much along the lines outlined by Anthony Crosland in his book *The Future of Socialism* (1956). His attempt in 1959 and 1960 to amend Clause Four, the public ownership clause of the Labour Party's constitution, was opposed by many major trade unions. These unions also favored unilateral disarmament, in opposition to his multilateral approach. Gaitskell was defeated on the armament issue at the Scarborough Conference of the Labour Party in 1960, after which he announced his decision "to fight and fight again" against the resolution favoring unilateral disarmament. At the Blackpool Conference in 1961 it was his pressure that helped reverse the unilateral resolution. Gaitskell also upset many of his supporters in 1962 by opposing Britain's entry into the Common Market (now known as the European Union) at a time when many in the party thought Britain should move in that direction.

While at the height of his powers, Gaitskell died in London on 18 January 1963. He is remembered for his assertive and confrontational style of leadership, which was not always in tune with the working-class sentiments of the Labour Party in his day. His objective of revising the Labour Party constitution was stalled because of trade union opposition but has since been carried forward—and developed further than he envisaged—by Neil Kinnock and Tony Blair.

Keith Laybourn

See also: Attlee, Clement; Blair, Tony; Churchill, Sir Winston; Cripps, Stafford; Dalton, Hugh; Wilson, Harold
References and Further Reading: Brivati, Brian, 1996, *Hugh Gaitskell: A Biography* (London: Richard Cohen); McDermott, Geoffrey, 1982, *Leader Lost: A Biography of Hugh Gaitskell* (London: Leslie Frewin); Williams, Philip M., 1979, *Hugh Gaitskell: A Political Biography* (London: Cape).

Gilmour, Sir John (Baron Gilmour of Lundin and Montrave)
(1876–1940) [HS]

Sir John Gilmour was born at Montrave, in the parish of Scoonie, Fife, Scotland, on 27 May 1876. He was the second, but the eldest surviving, son of Sir John Gilmour and his wife, Henrietta, second daughter of David Gilmour of Quebec City. He was educated at Trinity College; Glenalmond; Edinburgh University; and Trinity Hall, Cambridge. He became an officer of the Fife and Forfar Yeomanry during the Boer War and was a member of Fife county council from 1901 to 1910. He married Mary Louise Lambert in 1902; and in 1920, a year after her death, he married Violet Agnes Lambert, his first wife's younger sister. Also in 1920, he inherited the title of Baron Gilmour of Lundin and Montrave.

Gilmour unsuccessfully contested the East Fife constituency as a Unionist against Herbert Henry Asquith in January 1906, but he was elected M.P. for East Renfrewshire in January 1910, holding the seat until 1918, when he won the Pollock Division of Glasgow—a seat he held until his death.

Gilmour fought in World War I, during which he distinguished himself in battle. After the war, in 1919, he began to gain political experience in a succession of junior government appointments. Between 1919 and 1922, and again in 1924, he was a Scottish Unionist whip.

In 1921 he was appointed junior Lord of the Treasury, becoming a member of the Privy Council in 1922 and in 1924 secretary for Scotland (this post was renamed secretary of state for Scotland in 1926). He held the latter post until June 1929, when James Ramsay MacDonald's second Labour government came to power, at the same time acting as rector of Edinburgh University from 1926 to 1929.

With the formation of MacDonald's National government of 1931, Gilmour became minister of agriculture and fisheries. In September 1932 he became home secretary, a post he held until June 1935. His relations with MacDonald, however, were stiff and formal. The two men had clashed over the release of Oscar Slater, a German Jew who had been found guilty of murdering an elderly spinster, Miss Gilchrist, in her flat in Glasgow in December 1908. After a campaign by Sir Arthur Conan Doyle, the author of the Sherlock Holmes stories, and the revelation of new evidence, Ramsay MacDonald forced Gilmour to arrange for Slater's release from prison in November 1927. Their relations had become even more strained when Gilmour attempted to introduce a wheat quota (in other words, protectionism) while he was minister of agriculture in 1931 and 1932. MacDonald and Gilmour seem to have maintained a respectful distance from each other between 1931 and 1935, and Gilmour left the National government in 1935.

In 1937, while out of office, he presided over a departmental committee appointed to inquire into the organization of the various departments of the Scottish government; the decisions of this committee were introduced in 1939. His only other post in government was that of minister of shipping, which he held from October 1939 until his death on 3 April 1940. Although Gilmour had proved a fine administrator and a major figure in Scottish affairs, he never achieved the status of a first-class politician.

Keith Laybourn

See also: Baldwin, Stanley; Chamberlain, Neville; MacDonald, James Ramsay
References and Further Reading: Marquand, David, 1977, *Ramsay MacDonald* (London: Cape).

Gladstone, Herbert (Viscount Gladstone)
(1854–1930) [HS]

Apart from acting as home secretary between 1905 and 1908, in the hyperactive period of Liberal prewar legislation, Herbert Gladstone is best known for being the son of William Ewart Gladstone, the dominant Liberal prime minister of the late nineteenth century, and for playing a role in the secret Liberal-Labour pact or electoral deal of 1903. He was no mean politician, although he pales into insignificance when compared to his father.

Herbert John Gladstone was youngest of the four sons (of a family of eight children) of William Ewart Gladstone and his wife, Catherine, the elder daughter of Sir Stephen Glynne, eighth baronet, of Hawarden, Cheshire. He was born on 7 January 1854, at 12 (now 11) Downing Street, which was then the family home, as his father was chancellor of the exchequer. He was educated at Eton, and in 1872 enrolled at University College, Oxford, where he obtained a third class in classics in 1874 and a first class in modern history in 1876. From 1877 until 1880 he was a history lecturer at Keble College.

Herbert Gladstone began his political career in April 1880, when he contested, unsuccessfully, the Conservative county constituency of Middlesex. In May he became M.P. for Leeds— a seat vacated by his father, who had won both Leeds and Midlothian but had opted for the latter. Herbert represented Leeds until 1885; and after the reorganization of the constituencies, West Leeds, from 1885 until he became a peer (as Viscount Gladstone) in 1910. He secured the West Leeds seat through the influence of Sir James Kitson, a local industrialist and prominent figure in the Leeds Liberal organization; and it was felt that Kitson's adoption for the nearby West Riding constituency of Colne Valley in the 1890s was a return favor.

Once in the House of Commons, he acted as one of his father's private secretaries until 1881, when he was appointed a Liberal whip and a junior Lord of the Treasury. In 1882 he visited Ireland, which was then undergoing various troubles, and became sympathetic to the cause of Irish Home Rule. Indeed, in an interview with journalists in December 1885 he committed the political indiscretion of revealing that his father was intending to take up the issue of Irish Home Rule in opposition to the intention of Lord Salisbury's Conservative government to introduce limited self-government. The incident of the "Hawarden kite," as it was popularly called, taught him the need for political discretion, which later became characteristic of his relations with the emergent Labour Party.

In his father's Liberal government of 1886 to 1892, he was first appointed financial secretary at the War Office, and later, undersecretary at the Home Office, under H. H. Asquith. He became a privy councillor in 1894 and First Commissioner of Works in Lord Rosebery's Liberal government of 1894 to 1895. The Liberal Party was then out of office for ten years, during which time he became Liberal chief whip in 1899, playing a major part in keeping the Liberals together over the issue of the Boer War at the turn of the century.

In 1901, he married Dorothy Mary, the daughter of Sir Richard Horner Paget, first baronet, of Cranmore Hall, Somerset. Continuing with his political duties, he was particularly preoccupied with the concern that the newly formed Labour Representation Committee, soon to become the Labour Party, might undermine the Liberal progressive vote. He secretly arranged with Ramsay MacDonald in 1903 a pact whereby both the Liberal and Labour parties undertook not to put candidates up against each other in thirty seats each. This was a factor in the return of 377 Liberal M.P.s in the January 1906 general election but was even more significant in permitting Labour to secure 29 seats in the House of Commons.

Gladstone had worked closely with Sir Henry Campbell-Bannerman, who had become prime minister in December 1905. He was immediately appointed home secretary, and held that post until April 1908, when he was replaced by Winston Churchill shortly after the resignation and retirement, as a result of serious ill health, of Campbell-Bannerman in favor of H. H. Asquith as prime minister. In this role Gladstone had to fulfill the promises of legislation made by the Liberal Party in opposition, and he was personally involved in carrying 22 bills through Parliament. The most important of these were the Workmen's Compensation Act (1906), the Eight Hours Act (for miners, in 1908), and the Trades Boards Act (1909). He was also responsible for setting up the Court of Criminal Appeal in 1907 and for the Probation of Offenders Act (1907), the Prevention of Crime Act (1908), and the Children's Act (1908), which codified existing legislation on children. These three pieces of legislation together created the Borstal system and children's courts. Toward the end of his period in office, his political skills were further challenged by the often violent campaign for female suffrage.

In December 1909, Gladstone was appointed governor-general and high commissioner of the Union of South Africa, which had been formed as a result of the South Africa Act of 1909. In early 1910 he gave up his seat in the House of Commons and was raised to the peerage as Viscount Gladstone. He arrived at Cape Town, in South Africa, in May 1910, where he quickly won the support of the Boers, the Dutch white population, by his sympathetic attitude toward Home Rule. Indeed, he called upon General Botha to form a constitutional government for the Union and arranged for the Duke of Connaught, acting on behalf of King George V, to open the first South African Parliament. Gladstone faced difficulties when Botha resigned over cabinet differences in 1912, but he encouraged Botha to form a new government. In 1913, with public order coming under threat from various industrial disputes, he was forced to introduce martial law in the Johannesburg area. Despite these problems, he had won the respect of the British and Dutch in South Africa, who regretted his departure in July 1914.

After returning to Britain, which by then had become embroiled in the European war, Gladstone became treasurer of the War Refugees Committee and devoted himself to dealing with Belgian refugees in Britain. Around this time, he also became preoccupied with protecting his father's reputation, and distracted by frequent traveling. He was never fully attuned to the new Liberal Party that had emerged after 1916. Nonetheless, he did work at Liberal headquarters in 1922 and 1923 to reorganize the declining Party; and he supported Lord Grey of Fallodon, often known as Sir Edward Grey, in the Liberal Council, formed in December 1926. He was also involved in work for the League of Nations. He died on 6 March 1930, survived by his wife; the couple had had no children. Apart from his family connections, Gladstone today is most remembered for his record as an active and forthright politician and as a more than able home secretary.

Keith Laybourn

See also: Asquith, Herbert Henry; Campbell-Bannerman, Sir Henry; Gladstone, William Ewart; Grey, Sir Edward

References and Further Reading : Mallet, Sir Charles E., 1932, *Herbert Gladstone: A Memoir* (London: Hutchinson); Marquand, David, 1977, *Ramsay MacDonald* (London: Cape); Robbins, Keith, 1971, *Sir Edward Grey: A Biography of Lord Grey of Fallodon* (London: Cassell); Rowlands, Peter, 1968, *The Last Liberal Governments: The Promised Land, 1905–10* (London: Barrie & Rockliff).

Gladstone, William Ewart
(1809–1898) [PM, CE]

William Ewart Gladstone was the dominant parliamentarian of the Victorian age and one of the giant characters in British history. Endowed with tremendous physical and mental energy, he was driven by his belief that he owed a duty to God to use the powers bestowed on him to good purposes. Religion was central to his life, and this is fully revealed in the diary he kept for seventy years—from age 15—as "an account book of all the all-precious use of time." He read the Bible daily, often in (classical) Greek, and over his lifetime, he read nearly 20,000 books in Greek, Latin, French, German, and Italian, as well as English.

By descent entirely Scottish, he was born on 29 December 1809, the fourth son, and fifth of the six children, of John and Anne (née Robertson). His father, a prosperous Liverpool merchant involved in trade with the West Indies, where he owned slaves, was a friend and supporter of George Canning, and himself served as an M.P. from 1818 to 1827. Conjoined with the political background of Canningite Liberal Toryism, which prevailed in the Gladstone household, was a religious atmosphere of Evangelical piety. From this Gladstone retained always a deep sense of his own sinfulness. From his semi-invalid mother and his elder sister Anne, who died early, he derived an idealized view of saintly womanhood.

In 1821, Gladstone was sent to Eton, where despite the irreligious atmosphere he was happy and developed close friendships. There, and at Oxford, he was an outstanding scholar. His mind was a highly efficient machine for absorbing and ordering knowledge. He gained a "double first" degree in classics and mathematics while developing his debating skills. He maintained a strong attachment to Oxford throughout his life. It was there, and during an extended visit to Italy, that his religious adherence changed from the Evangelical Anglicanism of his family to the Catholic wing of the Church of England. At Oxford, too, he had evolved from his family's "Liberal Toryism" to become an ultra-Tory opponent of parliamentary reform. With such views he became an M.P. in December 1832.

Gladstone's abilities quickly impressed the Tory leader, Peel, who, accepting the consequences of the Great Reform Act (1832), was re-molding his party into that of Conservatism. Gladstone's first parliamentary speech was in opposition to the 1833 Slavery Abolition Bill, but he was sufficiently attuned to Peel to be made a junior minister, at barely 25 years, in the minority government of 1834–1835. In the following, opposition years, he married Catherine Glynne, who was to bear him eight children (she was to outlive him by two years, and her family home, Hawarden, was to become his own). He also wrote a book on church-state relations. Reviewing this work, the great Whig historian T. B. Macaulay called Gladstone "the rising hope of those stern, unbending Tories" who followed "a leader . . . whose moderate opinions they abhor."

Peel was Gladstone's political mentor, and Gladstone became his fellow-Lancastrian's political heir. In 1841, Peel became the first Conservative prime minister and made Gladstone vice-

William Ewart Gladstone, 1867 (Library of Congress)

president of the Board of Trade. In 1843, he appointed Gladstone president of the Board of Trade and a cabinet minister. For Peel, whose supporters were mainly landowners, the period 1844–1845 was one of crisis, brought on by his conversion to free trade and by the need—because of the potato blight and famine in Ireland—to repeal the Corn Laws, which protected British agriculture from foreign imports. He tried to avoid splitting his party over the Corn Law repeal by resigning, but the Whig leader, Russell, declined to take office and instead handed back the poisoned chalice to Sir Robert. Gladstone could not defend Peel from Disraeli's onslaught in early 1846, because he had resigned in 1844 over an abstract matter of conscience, and although he was back in the cabinet, he had lost his Commons seat in the consequent by-election. The Conservative Party was shattered, and after Peel's death in 1850, Gladstone led the "Peelites" as a dwindling group until they joined the emergent Liberal Party in 1859.

In these years Gladstone experienced religious and emotional crises. He took to venturing out at night to try to convert London prostitutes. He did this so openly that no scandal attached to him. But he endangered his reputation, and there was "a powerful element of sexual temptation" involved, to which he succumbed and for which he underwent penitential exercises.

Yet this was also the time when he emerged to front-rank eminence in the House of Commons. After Peel's resignation in 1846, Russell headed a Whig government in which Palmerston was foreign secretary; and Gladstone clashed with both. In 1850 he ridiculed Palmerston's demand that the Greek government provide compensation to "Don Pacifico," a Spanish-born Jew, by then of Portuguese nationality. Don Pacifico, who had been born in Gibraltar and held a British passport, had been living in Athens, where one day his house was ransacked (Palmerston used this situation to demand compensation). Then, in 1851, Gladstone denounced Russell's attempt to prevent the Pope's restoration of Catholic bishoprics in Britain. These episodes were, however, landmarks in Gladstone's progression from Conservatism to Liberalism.

A further stage was marked when he became chancellor of the exchequer in a coalition government of Whigs and Peelites headed by Aberdeen, in December 1852. Gladstone's budgets of 1853 and 1854 laid the basis of his reputation as one of the greatest chancellors, and established the Treasury's role as the controlling finance department of the British government. Aberdeen was forced to resign in 1855 because of the incompetent conduct of the Crimean War, and Gladstone resigned with him. He made a decisive break with his past in declining to join Derby's Conservative government in 1858; and in 1859 he committed himself to the Liberal Party, a conjunction of Whigs, Radicals, and Peelites, by joining Palmerston's cabinet as chancellor. His budgets from 1859 to 1865 completed Britain's transition to free trade. Gladstone's speeches in these years were popular, and he became known as "the people's William," as a sign of affection.

The death of Palmerston in 1865 removed an obstacle to parliamentary reform. In the party warfare that accompanied a sequence of fran-chise bills, Gladstone was outmaneuvered by Disraeli, whose Conservative measure became the Second Reform Act of 1867. But it was Gladstone's Liberals who swept to victory in the 1868 election.

"My mission is to pacify Ireland" was how Gladstone received the queen's summons to become prime minister. Gladstone was a man of many words, but these few encapsulate both his strength and his weakness. He guided through Parliament two bills dealing with Ireland. But although his was one of the greatest reforming ministries of the century, Gladstone was detached from, or even hostile to, reforms like the 1870 Education Act, the University Tests Act (1871), and the Ballot Act (1872). His Irish Church Disestablishment Act ended the imposition of the Church of England as the established church of Catholic Ireland; and his Irish Land Act was a valiant failure to redistribute land from English owners to Irish peasants. By 1872, Disraeli could mock the cabinet as a "row of exhausted volcanoes"; but he waited for it to exhaust itself further. Gladstone, his difficulties compounded by deteriorating relations with the queen, resigned in 1874 and withdrew from politics, though remaining an M.P.

He was aroused from retirement by the "Bulgarian horrors"—Turkish massacres of Bulgarian subjects—to play out, from 1876 to 1880, "the greatest setpiece drama in Victorian politics." Gladstone spoke to audiences of up to 30,000 and became an unprecedentedly popular idol, denouncing Disraeli's "forward policy" here and in wars against the Zulus and Afghans as "Beaconsfieldism." This crusade culminated in the popular frenzy of the "Midlothian campaigns"—Gladstone's speeches in his new Edinburgh constituency. On this wave of popularity, the Liberals were swept back to power in 1880, and Gladstone—against the will of the queen, who thought him a "half-mad firebrand"—returned to the premiership.

But appearances were deceptive. "The people's William" had become the "Grand Old Man" (GOM), who was no social radical. Moreover, although he had scarcely mentioned Ireland during the campaign, this subject was to dominate his second ministry. Gladstone postponed domestic reform and overcame distractions in South Africa and Egypt to concentrate on Irish grievances. His Irish Land Act of 1881, passed against the background of his own illnesses, obstructions from others in Parliament, and violence in Ireland, began the process of solving that country's problems, but did not satisfy Parnell, the Irish Nationalist leader. The government did nonetheless achieve franchise reform in the Acts of 1884–1885, which laid the basis for the present democratic electoral system with its single-member constituencies.

Though Gladstone still dominated the Commons, his government was torn by dissension; and after the 1885 election, the number of seats held by the Irish Nationalists exceeded the Liberals' majority over the Conservatives. Convinced that justice demanded self-government for Ireland, Gladstone hoped that the Conservatives, helped by the votes of the Irish M.P.s, would provide it. But they opposed Home Rule for Ireland, and he was left to try to secure it without their help. In June 1886, his Home Rule bill was defeated in the Commons. Of the 333 Liberal M.P.s, only 229 supported it. In the election that followed, the Conservatives were returned to power, and—apart from the Liberal government of 1892 to 1895—the Liberals, the naturally dominant party, were divided and out of office for nineteen years.

Gladstone was so dominant a figure that he remained Liberal leader for eight more years. Derided by Disraeli as "an old man in a hurry," he stayed, he said, for "one fight, the best and the last." He had little interest in the many reforms proposed by his colleagues, many of which he dismissed as "socialism." Achieving Home Rule depended on a "union of hearts" between Irish Catholic followers of Parnell (who was a Protestant) and the English Nonconformist supporters of Gladstone, a High Church Anglican. But the fall in 1890 of Parnell, who was rejected by both Nonconformists and Catholics after being cited in the O'Shea divorce suit, left Gladstone with a Home Rule majority of only forty after the 1892 election. His second Home Rule bill passed through the Commons but was overwhelmingly defeated in the Lords. At this point, at age 85, deaf and nearly blind, he resigned as prime min-

ister—to the unconcealed relief of Queen Victoria. He remained an M.P. until 1895, however, completing 62 years in the Commons.

For 30 years before his death on 19 May 1898, Gladstone had been a cult figure. Though he had no "common touch," he was the first great parliamentary orator to address mass meetings; he brought the masses into the political system, although most members of his vast audiences had no opportunity to hear his words, and would not have understood them even if they had heard them. He was a great and uniquely Victorian statesman, both in terms of the number of years he held office during the queen's reign and in the context of the importance he attached to religion in what was a profoundly religious era.

But hindsight provides a different scale by which to judge him than the one his contemporaries had. As prime minister, he enjoyed certain advantages (for example, he never faced the crisis of war), and he suffered from certain limitations ("Gladstonianism"—his policies of "peace, retrenchment, and reform"—was, by the 1890s, anachronistic and inadequate). Gladstone made many mistakes, and if he had been active later, in the age of investigative journalism, those mistakes might well have taken a far greater toll on his political effectiveness. Like Peel, he sacrificed his party for the greater cause; but unlike Peel, he failed in his mission. Nonetheless, a number of his policies are still relevant today, as are his views of the United Kingdom—in particular, of the nature of empire—and of the comity of European nations. He himself was an example of this comity: a Scot born and educated in England and residing in Wales; and he had proposed for Ireland a formula that would have settled Anglo-Irish relations. In his antipathy for jingoism and his freedom from racism, he can be seen now as ahead of his time, rather than as having outlived it.

John O'Connell

See also: Aberdeen, Earl of; Canning, George; Derby, 14th Earl of; Palmerston, Lord; Peel, Sir Robert; Russell, Lord John
References and Further Reading: Birrell, Francis, 1933, *Gladstone* (London: Duckworth); Feuchtwanger, E. J., 1975, *Gladstone* (London:

Allen Lane); Jagger, P. J., 1991, *Gladstone: The Making of a Christian Politician* (Allison Park, PA: Pickwick Publications); Jagger, Peter J. (ed.), 1998, *Gladstone* (London: Hambledon); Magnus, Philip, 1954, *Gladstone* (London: Murray); Matthew, Henry C. G., 1986, *Gladstone, 1809–1874* (Oxford: Oxford University Press); Matthew, H. C. G., 1995, *Gladstone, 1875–1898* (Oxford: Oxford University Press); Morley, John, 1903, *Life of Gladstone* (New York and London: Macmillan); Shannon, Richard, 1982, *Gladstone*, vol. I: *1809–1865* (London: Hamilton).

Goderich, Viscount
(Hon. Frederick John Robinson; Earl of Ripon)
(1782–1859) [PM, CE]

Frederick John Robinson was born in London on 30 October 1782, the second of the three sons of the second Baron Grantham, foreign secretary under Shelburne, and of Lady Mary Yorke. He was educated at Harrow and at St. John's College, Cambridge. In 1802 he entered Lincoln's Inn to train in the law, but was never called to the bar. In 1803 he became private secretary to his cousin the Earl of Hardwicke, who was then lord lieutenant of Ireland. In 1806 he entered Parliament as Tory M.P. for the Irish borough of Carlow, and a year later he became M.P. for Ripon, a seat that he held for twenty years. He was appointed undersecretary for war and the colonies in April 1809, but resigned his post in September, together with his mentor Castlereagh. He was brought back into the Perceval administration of 1810 to 1812 and remained continuously in office until 1828.

He became a loyal supporter of Lord Liverpool, and from 1813 to 1817, acted as joint paymaster-general of the land forces. He accompanied Castlereagh to the continent for the Vienna peace negotiations. In 1814 he married the daughter and heiress of the Earl of Buckinghamshire, Lady Sarah Hobart, a notorious hypochondriac who became neurotically obsessed with her husband's safety. At Lord Liverpool's request, he introduced, "with great reluctance," the notorious Corn Law Bill of 1815, after which his home was besieged by angry mobs, and in the ensuing fracas two assailants were killed. He broke down in tears while re-

porting the incident to the House of Commons, earning the unflattering nickname of "Blubberer." In 1812, Liverpool appointed him vice-president of the Board of Trade, and in 1818, president. The latter post was the first of a large number of ministerial appointments that he filled in an active career that lasted until 1846.

Robinson was appointed chancellor of the exchequer in the government reshuffle that followed Castlereagh's suicide. During his period in this office, between 1823 and 1827, he became associated, along with William Huskisson at the Board of Trade, with policies designed to balance the national budget and increase freedom of trade through the lowering of customs duties and fiscal reform. Although no more able a financier than his predecessor, Nicholas Vansittart (Lord Bexley), who had left him a handsome legacy of nearly £5 million in excess revenue, he was a better communicator and a more popular figure in the House of Commons. With trade recovering, Robinson was able to budget for an even greater surplus of £7 million, which, after allowing for the £5 million earmarked for debt redemption, gave him £2 million for tax reductions, enabling him to slash the window tax by half. Budget surpluses in 1824 and 1825 allowed him to lower duties on a whole range of consumer goods and raw materials for industry, including iron, coal, wool, silk, hemp, coffee, wine, and rum. Despite the lowering of duties, rising consumption and a greater volume of trade kept the revenue buoyant and facilitated further fiscal reform, so that when the financial crisis of 1825 and the subsequent recession of 1826 brought the first phase of economic recovery to a halt, Robinson was still able to anticipate a small revenue surplus for 1827. During this period he acquired two further nicknames, Prosperity Robinson and Goody Goderich, from William Cobbett. Applied sarcastically by the radical journalist on account of the chancellor's unwarranted optimism on the eve of the economic crisis of 1825, they have since been appropriated by historians to underline the success of his policies in generating economic improvement in the early 1820s. Robinson, a devout Christian and patron of the arts, also directed revenues from Austria's partial repayment of a

British war loan into grants to build new churches, restore Windsor Castle, and found the National Gallery. Robinson also was a cautious supporter of Roman Catholic emancipation.

Grief-stricken by the death of his 11-year-old daughter Henrietta after a painful illness, and increasingly anxious about his wife's health, he contemplated quitting politics altogether in 1826. In April 1827 he was created Viscount Goderich and appointed secretary of war and the colonies, and leader of the House of Lords, in George Canning's short-lived ministry. He proved less effective in the House of Lords than he had been in the House of Commons. Nevertheless, he was persuaded by George IV to succeed Canning as prime minister, following the latter's sudden death in August 1827.

Goderich was indecisive, unassertive, and incapable of holding together the lukewarm and fractious cabinet, which was deeply divided on domestic and foreign policy. The appointment of the ultra-Tory J. C. Herries as chancellor of the exchequer, under pressure from the king, alienated the Canningites and Whigs in Goderich's administration and fueled continuing controversy around Roman Catholic emancipation, which divided the Whigs and Tories. These divisions were further exacerbated by new issues arising from the Eastern question, following the Anglo-French destruction of the Turkish fleet at Navarino Bay in October. When he resigned in January 1828 after less than five months in office, Goderich became the only prime minister ever to resign without having appeared in Parliament as the holder of that office. William Huskisson observed that Goderich had been reduced to "a most pitiful state." However, it was Huskisson himself who first lost his nerve and resigned, after a bitter quarrel with Herries, in the belief that the government would simply collapse as soon as the new session of Parliament began. George IV, fearing a further lurch toward the Whigs, eased Goderich out of office in January 1828.

Goderich was not offered a post in the Duke of Wellington's government, and he gradually drifted closer to the Whigs. After a grudging conversion to parliamentary reform, he joined Earl Grey's Whig administration as secretary of war and the colonies, and was thus responsible for implementing the government's policy of abolishing slavery in the colonies. He agreed, reluctantly, to exchange this post for that of Lord Privy Seal in 1833. He was compensated with the new title of Earl of Ripon, but found himself an increasingly peripheral figure, and a year later left government altogether with Stanley, Graham, and Richmond, in opposition to Irish church reform. Their departures, mocked by the Irish nationalist Daniel O'Connell as the "Derby Dilly," precipitated the fall of Grey's government a few weeks later and added another humiliating sobriquet to the Earl of Ripon's collection.

He returned to the Conservative Party later in 1834 and took office for the last time in Peel's second administration as president of the Board of Trade (1841–1843) and president of the Board of Control (1843–1846). He supported Peel's overhaul of customs duties, which paralleled his own in the early 1820s, and the revision of the sliding scale on corn. He resigned with Peel in 1846 and remained a Peelite after 1846, making his last speech in the Lords on Irish affairs in 1847. He died from influenza at Putney Heath, London, on 28 January 1859.

The personal ridicule to which he was subjected throughout his political career, and the ignominy of his failed premiership—dismissed by Disraeli in *Endymion* as a "transient and embarrassed phantom"—have ensured that he has been treated somewhat contemptuously by posterity. However, as Norman Gash has argued, the malicious epithets of "Goody Goderich" and "Blubberer" suggest "a more foolish man than he actually was." On the whole, he was a capable administrator unable to withstand the strains of the highest office during the post-Liverpool era, when Tory Party unity was rapidly disintegrating.

John A. Hargreaves

See also: Bexley, Lord; Canning, George; Castlereagh, Viscount; Disraeli, Benjamin; Herries, John Charles; Liverpool, Earl of; Peel, Sir Robert; Perceval, Spencer; Shelburne, Earl of
References and Further Reading: Jones, Wilbur D., 1967, *"Prosperity Robinson": The Life of Viscount Goderich, 1782–1859* (London: Macmillan; New York: St. Martin's).

Gordon Walker, Patrick Chrestien (Baron Gordon-Walker; Lord Gordon Walker of Leyton)
(1907–1980) [FS]

Patrick Chrestien Gordon Walker, later Baron Gordon-Walker, was born 7 April 1907, at Worthing. He was the elder son of Alan Lachlan Gordon Walker—a Scottish judge of the supreme court of Lahore (in the Indian civil service)—and his wife, Dora Marguerite Chrestien. He was educated at Wellington College and won a scholarship to Christ Church, Oxford. Narrowly missing first class honors in history in 1928, he nevertheless became a history tutor at Christ Church in 1931. He then spent a year at German universities, becoming fluent in German and developing a hostility toward both the Nazis and the Communists in Germany and elsewhere in Europe. His father's Fabian socialist commitment to gradual social change also influenced him greatly.

He married Audrey Muriel Rudolf, who was born in Jamaica, in 1934, and she encouraged his later commitment to the ideal of a British multiracial Commonwealth of nations. His political activities began in 1935, when he was defeated in his first parliamentary election, running for the Oxford City seat. He chose not to run for the Oxford by-election of 1938 in favor of the master of Balliol, A. D. Lindsay, an independent progressive. By this time, Gordon Walker had become a passionate advocate of the Popular Front against fascism, fearing the threat of fascist expansionism from the continent. During World War II, his knowledge of the German Social Democrats (Nazis) and the German language made him an important contributor to the BBC's propaganda war against Germany. In 1944 he landed with the invading Allied troops and became chief editor for Radio Luxembourg, which was the main Allied radio station at the end of the war.

Gordon Walker's parliamentary career began in October 1945, when he was elected to Parliament in a by-election for the Birmingham seat of Smethwick. As a respected democratic socialist, he progressed rapidly through the political ranks of Clement Attlee's postwar Labour governments. In 1946 he became parliamentary secretary to Herbert Morrison, who was then deputy prime minister and Lord President of the Council; and in 1947, a junior minister, as undersecretary of state to the commonwealth relations office. In this role he went to India and negotiated with Jawaharlal Nehru to try to keep the newly independent country within the Commonwealth. After the 1950 general election, he joined the cabinet as secretary of state for Commonwealth relations, being admitted to the Privy Council at the same time. He was committed to a multiracial Commonwealth. However, he was criticized for his refusal to recognize (Sir) Seretse Khama—who was married to an Englishwoman, Ruth Williams—as head of the Bamangwata, the dominant tribe of Bechuanaland (as Botswana was then known), and thus Bechuanaland. He also was criticized for planning to set up a Central African Federation despite opposition from blacks in Nyasaland, and from Northern and Southern Rhodesia. This move was ill-fated, and the federation was dismantled by the Conservative government that replaced Labour in 1951.

With Labour out of office for thirteen years (1951–1964), Gordon Walker remained Labour's main spokesman on international affairs with regard to the Commonwealth and Europe. Politically, he was close to Hugh Gaitskell, the new Labour Party leader from 1955, supporting him on the need to modernize the party and to amend Clause Four, the clause in the Labour Party's constitution committing it to public ownership; and opposing unilateral nuclear disarmament. When Gaitskell died in 1963, Gordon Walker refused to become a candidate for the leadership of the Labour Party. Harold Wilson, the new party leader, appointed him shadow foreign secretary. Labour came to power in the general election of October 1964, but Gordon Walker lost his Smethwick seat, a victim of the racist attacks leveled against him for his having opposed the Conservative Commonwealth Immigration Act of 1962. Nonetheless, Wilson made him foreign secretary, in the expectation that he would be reelected to the House of Commons in a forthcoming parliamentary by-election. However, in January 1965 he was defeated in a by-election for the East End London seat of Leyton. With this failure, his brief period as foreign secretary, which had extended from October 1964 to January 1965, came to an end. He remained out of Parliament until 1966.

When he returned to the House of Commons in 1966, having secured an 8,000-vote majority for Leyton, he rejoined the Labour cabinet first as minister without portfolio (1966–1967), and then, from 1967 to 1968, as secretary of state for education and science. However, he never returned to the high political position that he had once occupied. In 1974, he was made a life peer (as Lord Gordon Walker of Leyton) and thus acquired a seat in the House of Lords. From 1975 to 1976 he served as one of the British members of the European Parliament. He died in London on 2 December 1980, an almost forgotten political figure whose career as foreign secretary was blighted by his unfortunate political defeat in a parliamentary election dominated by racist attacks.

Keith Laybourn

See also: Attlee, Clement; Gaitskell, Hugh; Wilson, Harold
References and Further Reading: Pimlott, Ben, 1992, *Harold Wilson* (London: HarperCollins).

Goschen, George Joachim (Viscount Goschen)
(1831–1907) [CE]

George Joachim Goschen is one of the least remembered of all chancellors of the exchequer, although he was a man of solid and reliable political abilities. He was descended from a German family of printers and publishers based in Bremen and Leipzig. His father, William Henry Goschen, the third son of the founder of this business, emigrated to England in 1814 and married an Englishwoman. William Henry moved into merchanting and finance activities and founded the enormously successful merchant banking business of Frühling and Goschen, which became a rising force in the City of London.

Thus George Joachim Goschen was born on 10 August 1831 into a prosperous, City-based merchant banking family. At first, he seems to have received little formal education; but he

spent three years, between the ages of 11 and 14, at a school in Germany before going to Rugby, the famous public school (similar to an American private school), where he rose to become head (or senior) boy. He then went to Oriel College, Oxford, where he obtained a first class degree and became president of the Oxford Union. As a reward for his academic successes, his father gave him £2,000 (more than £100,000, at modern values).

From Oxford, Goschen went to a counting house and into merchant life. He was sent to Colombia for two years to look after the interests of the family firm. On his return in 1857 he married Lucy Dalley, and he lived happily with her until her death in 1898. He rose quickly in the City of London, joining the Court of the Bank of England at the age of 27. He became a leading figure in the family firm and in 1861 gained some fame through the publication of his book *The Theory of Foreign Exchange*, a practical guide to the working of the City of London.

Goschen's political career began in 1863 when he was elected to one of the four City of London parliamentary seats. He held that seat until 1880, advocating Liberal policies, pushing forward the interests of City financiers and merchants, and opposing aristocratic privilege. He supported the extension of the franchise and the removal of religious discrimination from university as well as public life. He also attempted to protect the City of London from the loss if its privileges; but inconsistently, he also favored democratic local government reform throughout Britain. He was committed to the concept of Englishness; generally sympathetic to imperialism, although not at ease with Disraeli's flashy jingoism; and opposed to Home Rule for Ireland—unusual attitudes for a Liberal to take. These views, particularly the last, led him to ditch Liberalism in 1885–1886 and to become a Unionist ally of the Conservative Party.

As a Liberal he nonetheless advanced quickly in his political career. Lord John Russell, the prime minister who took over after Palmerston's death, made him vice-president of the Board of Trade in 1865. Almost before he could do anything in that role, he was raised to the post of chancellor of the Duchy of Lancaster. Although the Russell government came to an end in June 1866 without Goschen having achieved much, two and a half years later Gladstone offered Goschen the post of president of the Poor Law Board (soon to become the Local Government Board, and in the twentieth century, the Ministry of Health and the Ministry of Housing and Local Government) in his first government. In this role Goschen sought to establish a more uniform, rational, and democratic structure for local government but was equally determined that the poor would have no control over the administration of the Poor Law. In particular, he is famous for having introduced the Goschen Minute of 1869, which tightened up the outdoor relief provision (money given to the poor living outside the Poor Law institution and in the community) of the Poor Law and dramatically reduced the number of applicants over the next twenty years.

In 1871, Gladstone made him First Lord of the Admiralty—an appointment that led to the mocking jingle "Goschen has no notion of the motion of the ocean." It is believed that this jingle inspired W. S. Gilbert, of Gilbert and Sullivan fame, to pen the satirical representation of the First Lord in *HMS Pinafore*. Goschen's inability to reduce naval expenditure eventually provoked Gladstone into the rash decision to dissolve Parliament in 1874—an action that backfired, resulting in a victory for Disraeli's Conservative Party in the subsequent general election.

While in opposition, Goschen was connected with various proconsular roles, most obviously in negotiation for the Council of Foreign Bondholders with the Egyptian government in 1876, at a time when the khedival government looked likely to default on payment. He also spent a year in Constantinople (1880–1881), with the purpose of exerting pressure on the Turkish sultan to observe the conditions of the Congress of Berlin with regard to Greece, Montenegro, and Armenia.

In 1880 Goschen switched parliamentary seats from the City of London to Ripon. By the time of the 1885 general election the Ripon seat was altered, and he was elected instead for the Edinburgh East seat. During this period he was still a Liberal but refused various posts offered

him in Gladstone's governments. By the mid-1880s he was becoming disenchanted with the Liberal Party, and had effectively split with it over the question of Home Rule. As a result of this he was asked to act as chancellor of the exchequer in Lord Salisbury's Conservative government at the end of 1886, after Lord Randolph Churchill left that office in an infamous act of petulance. Goschen was thus appointed chancellor on 14 January 1887. He remained in that post until 17/18 August 1892, although he was the only Liberal in an otherwise Conservative cabinet.

Goschen was a solid, rather than innovative, chancellor. His main achievement was in establishing the principle and practice of paying 2.75 percent, and later 2.5 percent, on the core of the national debt from 1888 on, instead of the 3 percent previously paid. He introduced six rather conventional budgets, the first four being introduced in a period of prosperity. He was also the last chancellor to keep the budgeted expenditure below £100 million, although he committed future chancellors to much higher expenditures by financing the commitment to build seventy ships for the navy between 1889 and 1894. Convinced that the traditional means of raising income, such as duties on tobacco and alcohol, were exhausted, he believed the taxation base had to be widened, preferring indirect as opposed to direct taxation. As chancellor, Goschen also appears to have been involved in saving the Baring Bank from collapse in 1890 by offering government intervention, although the precise extent of this commitment is unknown.

In 1892 Gladstone and the Liberals replaced Salisbury's Conservative government. Goschen was thus out of office for three years. When Salisbury formed another government in 1895, he again offered Goschen the post of chancellor of the exchequer. However, Goschen turned this down in favor of a return to the Admiralty. As First Lord he began a campaign to build up the strength of the navy, increasing the number of personnel from 61,000 in the early 1870s to 85,000 in 1895 and 112,000 in 1900.

At the end of 1900, Goschen was raised to the House of Lords as Viscount Goschen, although he would have preferred an earldom. He was now practically semiretired from politics. Beginning in 1903, he occupied the post of chancellor of Oxford University for three years. He remained active up to his final days, and died in his sleep in 1907.

Goschen was an unusual and able politician, a fervent free trader and a right-wing Liberal who, because of his opposition to Home Rule, found himself chancellor of the exchequer in a Conservative government. The national finances were in good hands with Goschen, although he might have been constrained in his work by his need to represent the interests of the City of London.

Keith Laybourn

See also: Churchill, Lord Randolph; Gladstone, William Ewart; Harcourt, Sir William; Salisbury, Lord
References and Further Reading: Jenkins, Roy, 1998, *The Chancellors* (London: Macmillan).

Goulburn, Henry
(1784–1856) [CE, HS]

Henry Goulburn, who became a competent Conservative chancellor of the exchequer, was the eldest son of Munbee Goulburn and his wife, Susannah, the eldest daughter of William Chetwynd, fourth Viscount Chetwynd. Henry was born in London on 19 March 1784 and educated at Trinity College, Cambridge. He contested and lost the Horsham seat for the Tories in the May 1807 general election but petitioned against his defeat and was awarded the seat in February 1808. Thereafter, his political rise was swift. He became undersecretary at the Home Department in February 1810, in the government of Spencer Perceval, and became undersecretary for war and the colonies in August 1812. At the general election of October 1812 he was returned for the seat of St. Germans; and in July 1814 he was appointed one of the commissioners responsible for negotiating a peace with the United States. He married the Hon. Jane Montagu, the third daughter of Matthew, fourth Lord Rokeby, on 20 December 1811.

Goulburn was M.P. for West Looe from 1812 to 1826. He became a member of the Privy Council in 1821, being appointed at that time chief secretary to the Marquess Wellesley, then lord lieutenant of Ireland. Since Goulburn had previously opposed Plunket's Roman Catholic Disability Removal Bill, which had been passed in the House of Commons during the previous session, he was unpopular with the Irish Roman Catholics. Nevertheless, in March 1823 he introduced the Irish Tithe Composition Bill, to raise money to help relieve the poorer classes in Ireland. In February 1825 he pressed the House of Commons to impose a bill to suppress unlawful societies in Ireland for three years; but the bill had little impact. In 1826 he unsuccessfully contested the seat for Cambridge University and was eventually elected to represent the city of Armagh constituency—a seat he held until 1831. He resigned the post of chief secretary of Ireland when George Canning became prime minister in 1827. He was subsequently appointed chancellor of the exchequer in January 1828, in the Duke of Wellington's new government.

Now in the upper echelons of government, Goulburn began to make his impact. He continued to oppose Catholic emancipation. As chancellor, he introduced three budgets, in 1828, 1829, and 1830. The first two were uncontentious, but the 1830 budget became the focus of controversy because it allowed the excise board to grant beer-selling licenses to anybody, and thus destroyed the monopoly of the great brewers. Goulbourn's period as chancellor came to an end with the defeat of Wellington's ministry in November 1830.

Goulbourn was elected as M.P. for Cambridge in 1831, representing it until his death in 1856; but he did not return to office again until the formation of Sir Robert Peel's first cabinet in December 1834, when he became home secretary. He held that office for about four months, until the Peel ministry was defeated in April 1835. He became chancellor of the exchequer again when Peel formed his second ministry in September 1841, and held that post until 1846. Goulburn's budgets began to reduce interest rates on government stocks, thus permitting the reduction and removal of tariffs. Reluctantly, he supported Peel's moves to repeal the Corn Laws; and he resigned when the Conservative government collapsed over that issue in 1846. He remained in the House of Commons but played a limited role in politics from then until his death on 12 January 1856. Contemporary political opinion recognized that he had been a good chancellor of the exchequer.

Keith Laybourn

See also: Peel, Sir Robert; Wellington, Duke of
References and Further Reading: Gash, Norman, 1972, *Sir Robert Peel: The Life of Sir Robert Peel after 1830* (London: Longman).

Grafton, Duke of
(Augustus Henry Fitzroy)
(1735–1811) [PM, FS]

The second, but first surviving, son of a naval captain who died at the siege of Cartagena in 1741, Augustus Henry Fitzroy, Duke of Grafton, has sometimes been seen as an archetype of the eighteenth-century Whig grandee. Wealthy, meticulous in his dress, and persuasive in address and manner, he came into political life as though by right, as soon as he had left behind him the experiences of Oxford and the grand European tour. Yet he was no passionate career politician, and devoted much of his energies to farming, hunting, and the breeding of racehorses: he won the Derby three times. A founding member of the Jockey Club, he was also part of the political scene at Brook's and White's club. He had firm religious convictions, and when he was appointed chancellor of the University of Cambridge in 1769 he refused the usual honorary doctorate of laws because he could not subscribe to the Church of England. He became a Unitarian, a member of a dissenting intellectual elite from whose ranks came a number of constitutional reformers; and in later years he wrote two serious works advocating "rational Christianity."

At age 21, in December 1756, Fitzroy entered Parliament as a member for the family seat of Bury St. Edmonds; but he left the Commons in May 1757, when he succeeded his grandfather (who had raised him) as the third Duke of Grafton. In his early political life he was a supporter both of the Duke of Newcastle and of William Pitt (the Elder), and he spoke out strongly against Lord Bute and the terms of the

Peace of Paris in 1763. In July 1765 he took up the post of secretary of state for the Northern Department at the unusually early age of 29; but he resigned this post the following May, in protest of the continued exclusion of Pitt. In July 1766, Rockingham was dismissed and Pitt agreed to form a ministry, in which he himself took the role of Lord Privy Seal. The more obvious job of First Lord of the Treasury was pressed upon Grafton, not yet 31, who soon found himself having to deal with a divided coalition while Pitt concerned himself less and less with the business of political management.

Separated from his first wife in January 1765, Grafton was living openly with Anne Parsons, a well-known "woman of the town"—a liaison that elicited critical comment from his colleague Charles Townshend (1725–1767). As Pitt's health worsened, Grafton gradually took on more responsibilities, until by the summer of 1767 he was serving as the de facto head of administration. He managed temporarily to strengthen the government by bringing in the Bedford Whig faction and by persuading Lord North in October of that year to become chancellor of the exchequer. However, he badly mishandled the government's campaign in the election of spring 1768—an election made mandatory by the terms of the Septennial Act—in large part, due to the distractions of his private life. His estranged wife, Anne, eloped with John Fitzpatrick, Earl of Upper Ossory, by whom in August of 1767 she had a child; and Grafton had scandalized polite society by appearing publicly with his mistress. The anonymous critic Junius, who in 1769 began savaging the Grafton ministry in print, reflected scornfully on the election period: "The prime minister of Great Britain, in a rural retirement, and in the arms of faded beauty, had lost all memory of his Sovereign, his country and himself."

With the election so negligently handled, the new Parliament of May 1768 saw no improvement in the government's majority, despite the support of the Crown as well as all the other resources a ministry typically enjoys. Nonetheless, when Pitt (now Lord Chatham) resigned in October 1768, it was Grafton who was invited to head the new ministry, becoming prime minister officially as well as in practice. Junius continued to allege that Grafton neglected his duty and showed an excessive dedication to private pleasures; but the main thrust of his attack was the clumsy handling of the Wilkes affair, which became the central controversy surrounding Grafton's time in office.

Expelled from the House for blasphemy and seditious libel in 1764, Wilkes had returned from outlawry and exile in Paris to stand for election in the large open constituency of Middlesex. Denied parliamentary privilege, he was sentenced for his earlier seditious libel to two years in King's Bench prison, where crowds of supporters gathered, riotously demonstrating. Wilkes appealed on various technicalities against his sentence, and stood for by-election in Middlesex—an election necessitated by his imprisonment. He was duly reelected, but the Commons annulled the election. Wilkes's rhetorical skill in linking his cause with ancient English liberties generated massive popular support, which culminated in the demonstration in St. George's Fields on 10 May 1768, in which ten of his followers were killed by soldiers called out by the magistrates. In February 1769, Wilkes was expelled from the House, only to be reelected in the ensuing by-election and expelled again.

Twice more the Parliament responded in this manner, which was tantamount to proclaiming to the volatile and proud Middlesex electorate that they had no influence whatever at the polls. In April 1769, Colonel Henry Luttrell contested the Middlesex by-election on behalf of the government. The Commons declared Wilkes's candidacy invalid and Luttrell legally elected, although Luttrell received only a sixth of the votes cast. Horne Took's Society of Supporters of the Bill of Rights, which was formed initially to find ways of paying off Wilkes's debts, triggered a wave of petitions and reform agitation, which gave new force and significance to extraparliamentary politics.

The ministry's unpopularity over the handling of Wilkes, and the unexpected way in which a personal cause had swollen into a widespread antigovernment campaign for liberties and reform, made it harder for Grafton to control his cabinet. In the spring of 1769 the min-

istry also had to sort out the American problem caused by Towshend's intensely unpopular taxation measures, which brought in little revenue but were designed to push the colonists into accepting the principle of Westminster taxation. Grafton wanted to repeal all the duties, but he was overruled in May by a cabinet majority voting to retain, for the sake of the principle, the duty on tea.

The divisions and ineffectiveness of the ministry became increasingly apparent, as did Grafton's indolence in office, which worsened after his remarriage. He was divorced from Anne Liddell, his first wife, by an act of Parliament in March 1769, and in June he married Elizabeth Wrottesley, with whom he enjoyed an affectionate and full family life (the couple had 13 children over the years). By the middle of January 1770, the ministry had been further weakened by the resignation of Granby and the dissent of Lord Chancellor Camden, who was dismissed by the king. Grafton persuaded Charles Yorke, son of the famous Lord Chancellor Hardwicke and a supporter of Rockingham, to accept Camden's post; but three days later, afflicted by remorse at his betrayal of his family by joining their political enemies, Yorke killed himself. At the end of that month, execrated in the press, disillusioned, and powerless, Grafton resigned. He was succeeded by Lord North.

In June 1771, under pressure from North and the king, Grafton accepted the office of Lord Privy Seal. In serving in North's ministry, he sought as before to promote moderate policies toward the American colonists. In November 1775 Grafton spoke out boldly in the House of Lords against government policy, advocating a complete rescinding of all legislation imposed upon the colonists since the end of the Seven Years' War. This was too much for George III, who demanded his resignation the next day. Over the next few years, Grafton gradually aligned himself with Lord Rockingham, and in March 1782 he accepted the appointment of Lord Privy Seal when Rockingham became prime minister. He continued in that post under Shelburne after Rockingham died in July of that year; but he resigned in February 1783, when the Duke of Rutland was brought into the cabinet without consultation with leading ministers. Thereafter Grafton retired to country pursuits, to enjoy matrimony, horse racing, and religious observations and study. He died in March 1811.

Philip Woodfine

See also: Bute, Earl of; Newcastle, Duke of; North, Lord; Pitt, William (the Elder); Rockingham, Marquess of; Shelburne, Earl of; Townshend, Charles (1725–1767)
References and Further Reading: Anson, Sir William R. (ed.), 1898, *Autobiography and Political Correspondence of Augustus Henry Third Duke of Grafton K.G.* (London: Murray); Cannon, John (ed.), 1978, *The Letters of Junius* (Oxford and New York: Oxford University Press); Langford, Paul, 1989, *A Polite and Commercial People: England, 1727–1783* (Oxford: Clarendon Press; New York: Oxford University Press); Norris, John, 1963, *Shelburne and Reform* (London: Macmillan; New York: St. Martin's);Thomas, Peter D. G., 1963, *John Wilkes: A Friend to Liberty* (Oxford: Clarendon Press; New York: Oxford University Press).

Graham, Sir James
(1792–1861) [HS]

Graham is famous for his service as home secretary in Sir Robert Peel's Conservative ministry in the 1840s, although his political affiliations often fluctuated in this age of major political changes. James Robert George Graham was born in 1792, the son of Sir James Graham and Lady Catherine Stewart, daughter of John, seventh Earl of Galloway. He was raised at Netherby, in Eskdale, in northern England, and was taught at a private school at Daldston, in Cumberland. At age 15, he was sent to Westminster School. In 1810 he enrolled at Christ Church, Oxford, but he left in 1812 to tour Spain and Sicily. While traveling abroad, he was asked to become the private secretary of Lord Archibald Montgomerie, who was on a diplomatic mission at Palermo to dissuade King Joachim Murat from supporting Napoleon. Montgomerie became ill during this mission, and much of the responsibility for diplomatic negotiations fell on Graham's shoulders.

Returning to London in 1814, Graham declared himself a Whig, committed to constitutional reform, in contrast to his father, who was a Tory. In 1818 he won the Hull seat in the general election, at a cost of £6,000, and in 1819 he married Fanny, the daughter of Colonel Callander of Craigforth in Stirlinghire, Scotland. His political career was slow to gather momentum. He became M.P. for St. Ives, in Cornwall, in 1820, but opposed by some of the ratepayers, he retired in 1821 to attend to his father's estates at Crofthead, near Netherby. While indulging in these activities he produced a pamphlet entitled *Corn and Currency,* which pointed to the failure of the protective Corn Laws to regulate prices and to the need for both free trade and free banking. He inherited the Netherby estates on his father's death in 1824; and in 1826 he was returned as a Whig/Liberal candidate for Carlisle, in an election noted for a riot that Graham helped defuse. In 1827 he was returned as M.P. for the county of Cumberland. However, he did not begin to make a mark for himself until 1830, when he moved to reduce the official salaries of government ministers and of privy councillors—a motion of no confidence in the government. The Duke of Wellington's government fell; and in November 1830, Lord Grey, the newly appointed Whig prime minister, gave Graham the post of Lord of the Admiralty. In this role Graham focused on fiscal reform of the Admiralty. He continued in this post through the turbulent period that surrounded the passage of the Great Reform Bill of 1832.

When the Grey ministry fell, Peel offered Graham a position in his new Tory administration—a sure sign that Graham's political position was shifting. He refused the post but did attack some of his former Whig colleagues in the general election of 1835. At this point he seemed to have returned to the House of Commons as an Independent rather than a Whig or Tory; but soon after, he moved across the floor of the Commons to the Conservative opposition benches, to challenge Lord Melbourne's new Whig government. His conversion to Toryism was complete when, in September 1841, he accepted Peel's offer of the post of home secretary, having just been elected to represent the constituency of Dorchester in Parliament.

Graham was home secretary for the entire period of Peel's ministry, from 1841 to 1846, and was a more effective and less aloof politician than he had hitherto appeared to be, although he seems to have lacked tact (e.g., he upset the Scottish Church on the issue of patronage). He also failed to get the 1844 Factory Act passed, in its original form, in which it would have provided schooling facilities for children. In 1844 he was at the center of a storm concerning the secret surveillance by the post office of the correspondence of G. Mazzini, an Italian revolutionary, and others, although censorship of the mail had been permissible under specific circumstances for well over a century. The correspondence of these individuals had been opened on the request of the foreign secretary, Lord Aberdeen, in order to ascertain whether any revolutionary plots were afoot in England. Graham and the government were deeply embarrassed by the public revelation of these official actions. Despite the examination of the issue by a secret committee, the government's right to intercept and open the post was upheld. In 1845 and 1846, Graham supervised relief efforts during the Irish famine, and along with Peel, attempted to convince Parliament to lift the duty on imported corn. The resultant Repeal of the Corn Laws of 1846, along with the defeat of a bill that aimed to put down agrarian crime in Ireland, divided the Conservative Party and led to the collapse of the Peel ministry. Peel resigned in June 1846, and Graham's tenure as home secretary came to an end.

Out of office, Graham was attacked by the protectionist Conservatives, and was loath to return to his Whig roots. As a Peelite he was part of a small band who sat in the opposition benches, across from the Whig government of Lord John Russell. In 1847 Russell offered Graham the governor-generalship of India. He refused it and remained in the House of Commons, as M.P. for Ripon. He also refused the possibility of a post at the Admiralty. After Peel's death (from 1850 on), he was effectively leader of the Peelites. In this role he was courted by Russell and his Whig government, especially in its opposition to the protectionist moves being advocated by Benjamin Disraeli and the Conservatives; but he declined various offers, including the presidency of the Board of Trade.

Lord Derby, the fourteenth Earl, and the Conservatives came to office in 1852, and Graham returned to the opposition benches, becoming, once again, M.P. for the Carlisle seat. However, when Derby's government was defeated and replaced by Lord Aberdeen's coalition government, Graham took up his old post at the Admiralty, to work on improving administrative efficiency. In this role he was responsible for appointing Sir Charles Napier as commander of the British fleet in the Baltic, with orders to block the Russian fleet from access to the Crimean battle zone. Although Napier was unhappy at his relative inactivity, and the Aberdeen government was criticized for the problems and failures that accompanied the Crimean adventure, Graham seems to have escaped most of the criticism. He remained in his post in the government of Lord Palmerston, which was formed in 1855, but resigned soon afterward, along with William Ewart Gladstone, in protest against the establishment of a committee of inquiry into the prosecution of the Crimean War while the war was still being fought.

From then on, Graham played a limited role in politics. His health was suffering, and he was greatly upset by his wife's death in 1857. He died at Netherby on 25 October 1861. He was not, and will not be, remembered as a talented politician or an outstanding home secretary; he was far too contentious. Nevertheless, he was an efficient administrator and one of the great reformers of the Admiralty in the early and mid-nineteenth century.

Keith Laybourn

See also: Aberdeen, Earl of; Grey, Sir George; Palmerston, Lord; Peel, Sir Robert; Russell, Lord John
References and Further Reading: Conacher, J., 1968, *The Aberdeen Coalition, 1852–1855: A Study in Mid-Nineteenth Century Party Politics* (Cambridge: Cambridge University Press); Gash, Norman, 1972, *Mr. Secretary Peel: The Life of Sir Robert Peel after 1830* (Cambridge, MA: Harvard University Press).

Grantham, Lord (Thomas Robinson)
(1738–1786) [FS]

Thomas Robinson, the second Baron Grantham, was foreign secretary for barely ten months and left no imprint on British politics. He was born in Vienna on 30 November 1738, the elder son of Thomas, the first Baron Grantham, and his wife, Frances, the daughter of Thomas Worsley of Hovingham, in North Riding, Yorkshire. He was educated at Westminster School and at Christ College, Cambridge.

In the general election of March 1761 he was elected to the House of Commons for Christchurch, Hampshire, and he represented the borough for nine years. He won some minor roles in government, being appointed secretary to the British embassy to the intended congress at Augsburg in April 1761, and in October 1766, one of the commissioners of trade and plantations. In February 1770 he became vice-chamberlain to the king's household and a member of the Privy Council. He rose to the House of Lords, becoming the second Baron Grantham on the death of his father in September 1770. He was appointed ambassador to Spain in January 1771, and held that post until the outbreak of war between Britain and Spain in 1779. He was then appointed first commissioner of the Board of Trade and plantations in 1780, acting in that role until June 1782, when the board was abolished. The following month he joined Lord Shelburne's ministry as foreign secretary, helping Shelburne negotiate the peace between France, Spain, and America.

He resigned office in April 1783, upon the formation of a coalition government, receiving a pension of £2,000 per year from the foreign office on top of the pension of £3,000 per year that had been granted to his father. In 1784 he became a member of the Privy Council for matters concerning trade. He died on 17 August 1786. He was survived by his wife, Lady Mary Jemima Grey Yorke—the younger daughter and coheiress of Philip, the second Earl of Hardwicke—whom he had married in 1780.

Keith Laybourn

See also: North, Lord; Shelburne, Earl of

References and Further Reading: Scott, Hamish, 1990, *British Foreign Policy in the Age of the American Revolution* (Oxford: Clarendon Press; New York: Oxford University Press).

Granville, Earl (Granville George Leveson-Gower)
(1815–1891) [FS]

Leveson-Gower, the second Earl Granville, served as foreign secretary on three separate occasions. He was not one of the great foreign secretaries of the nineteenth century, but he was effective in the Gladstonian Liberal cause in the 1880s, although many believed that his commitment to peace at all costs would prejudice Britain's international interests.

Granville George Leveson-Gower was born in London on 11 May 1815, the eldest son of Lord Granville Leveson-Gower, first Earl Granville, and was educated at Eton and at Christ Church, Oxford. In 1835 he became an attaché at the British embassy in Paris, under his father. In the general election of 1837 he was elected a Whig M.P. for Morpeth. In 1840 he became undersecretary of state for foreign affairs, but he resigned this post at the fall of the Melbourne government in 1841.

Meanwhile, he had married Maria Louise, the only child of Emeric Joseph, duc de Dalberg, on 25 July 1840. After she died in 1860, he married Castalia Rosalind, the youngest daughter of Walter Frederick Campbell, in 1865.

In 1841 he was elected to the House of Commons for Lichfield. He was raised to the House of Lords after the death of his father in 1846, and in Lord John Russell's Whig government (1846–1852), he was appointed vice-president of the Board of Trade in 1848, and later paymaster of the forces, and was admitted to the cabinet in 1851.

On 26 December 1851, when Lord Palmerston left the Foreign Office, Granville was his successor as foreign secretary—but only for two months, until 21 February 1852, when the Russell ministry collapsed. Granville then accepted the posts of Lord President of the Council and chancellor of the Duchy of Lancaster in the succeeding Aberdeen coalition government. In 1855 he became leader of the House of Lords.

Granville was involved also with many other matters—most particularly, the Crystal Palace Exhibition in 1851 (he was vice president of the commission organizing the exhibition). He also represented Queen Victoria at the coronation of Tsar Alexander II in Moscow on 7 September 1856. He was then so much in favor that upon the resignation of the Derby government in 1859, the queen called on him, rather than Palmerston and Lord John Russell, to form a government. In the end he failed in his efforts to do so and instead accepted the role of Lord President of the Council in Palmerston's ministry. He was once again considered as a candidate for prime minister on the death of Palmerston in 1865 but was passed over.

In December 1868, William Ewart Gladstone appointed him secretary of state for the colonies. In this role Granville ordered the withdrawal of imperial troops from several colonies (e.g., New Zealand and Canada) and presided over the transfer of the Hudson Bay territory to Canada. As leader of the House of Lords at this time he also played an important role in carrying forward the Irish Church and Land Bills of Gladstone's Liberal government.

After the death of Lord Clarendon in July 1870, Granville became foreign secretary for the second time. Holding the post for more than three and a half years, his main concern was to maintain the peace that Gladstone and the Liberals so desired. This meant preserving the neutrality of Britain during the Franco-Prussian War, which began in July 1870, and maintaining the neutrality of Belgium, which had been guaranteed in 1839. After Russia repudiated the Treaty of Paris (1856) in October 1870 and began to assemble a fleet in the Black Sea, Granville called a conference in London in January 1871, at which Russia was criticized, but nothing was done to oppose its actions. Similar concessions were made to the United States and France on international issues. In effect, Granville compromised on every issue in order to maintain the Liberal government's commitment to peace. Disraeli's Conservative government, which came into power in 1874, took a much more aggressive approach.

Out of office from 1874 to 1880, Granville led the Liberal Party in the House of Lords. As Gladstone had retired from party leadership in 1874, many expected Granville to become prime minister after the defeat of the Conservatives in the 1880 general election. In the event, Gladstone came out of retirement, formed a new government, and made Granville foreign secretary.

Once again, Granville sought peace, attempting to temper the aggressive policies of Prussia and Prince Bismarck—although he still managed to offend their enemies, the French. His Suez Canal convention of 1883 was never ratified, because of strong resistance from British shipowners. In addition, his agreement to carve up Africa and Southeast Asia among the European powers meant that British influence would be excluded from the Cameroons and from parts of New Guinea. As a result of his conciliatory approach, he was reputed to be reluctant to protect British interests. When the Liberal government was defeated in 1885, he resigned; and although he supported Gladstone's Home Rule policy in 1886, he did not return to the Foreign Office but accepted the post of colonial secretary in Gladstone's short-lived third ministry. He continued to lead the Liberal Party in the House of Lords until his death on 31 March 1891. He was remembered as an influential politician who narrowly missed becoming prime minister on at least two occasions. Perhaps, as was said of R. A. Butler in the twentieth century, he lacked the final six inches of steel necessary to be the premier.

Keith Laybourn

See also: Aberdeen, Earl of; Gladstone, William Ewart; Melbourne, Viscount; Palmerston, Lord; Russell, Lord John
References and Further Reading: Harrison, Robert, 1995, *Gladstone's Imperialism in Egypt: Techniques of Domination* (London: Greenwood Press); Matthew, Henry, 1986, *Gladstone, 1809–1875* (Oxford: Oxford University Press); ———, 1995, *Gladstone, 1875– 1898* (Oxford: Oxford University Press; Prest, John, 1972, *Lord John Russell* (London: Macmillan).

Grenville, George
(1712–1770) [PM, CE, FS]

George Grenville (born 14 October 1712) was brought into politics by his uncle, Lord Cobham, along with two of his brothers, his cousin

In this cartoon entitled "The repeal or the funeral of Miss Ame-stamp" George Grenville carries a coffin inscribed "Miss Ame-stamp b. 1765 died 1766" (Library of Congress)

George Lyttleton, and William Pitt (the Elder), a cousin by marriage, who together made up the core of the group known as "Cobham's Cubs" and sometimes "the Nepotism." Long frustrated by his unsuccessful rivalry with Pitt, Grenville came into his own at the accession of George III, through the friendship he had cultivated with the influential Lord Bute. Grenville's short tenure in the premiership, though, was overshadowed by the continuing influence of Bute behind the scenes. Today Grenville is chiefly remembered for the episode of the seditious libel of M.P. John Wilkes, and for the passing of the Stamp Act, which provoked widespread protest in the American colonies.

When Grenville was 15 his father died, leaving four sons and three daughters in the care of their mother, Hester Temple, sister of Viscount Cobham. The eldest son, Richard, was publicly designated heir of Cobham's title and Stowe estate, which he inherited in 1749, and along with Pitt and Lyttleton was a founding father in 1735 of Cobham's opposition group of "boy patriots."

George, the second son, joined the group when he was elected M.P. for Buckingham in 1741, making his first known speech in the debate on the 1742 motion for an enquiry into Sir Robert Walpole's conduct of the war. Ambitious for office and responsibility, George followed the Cobhamite line and outwardly supported Pitt, the group's leading member, although inwardly he was often resentful and frustrated.

As Lord of the Admiralty from 1744 to 1747, Lord of the Treasury from 1747 to 1754, and subsequently treasurer of the navy, with short interruptions from then until 1762, Grenville showed his dedication to business and his efficiency, but failed to make a mark as a parliamentary speaker or to build a personal following. Described by Horace Walpole as deceitful and ungentlemanly, he was a career politician who suffered constant disappointments over the places and promotions he thought were his due. He distanced himself progressively from Pitt, on whose lukewarm support he blamed much of his own lack of advancement.

On the accession of George III in 1760, Grenville aligned himself increasingly with the king's favorite, Lord Bute. In 1761, Grenville was brought into the cabinet; and when Pitt resigned in early October, Bute offered Grenville Pitt's former post of secretary of state for the Southern Department. Conscious that he was politically isolated and lacked the connections necessary to success at this level, Grenville refused. He was considered for the speakership of the House of Commons, to which he would have been well suited by his interest in procedures, and which he regarded as "the highest honour that could have befallen me," as well as a safe retreat from the storms and uneasiness to which all other public situations "are unavoidably exposed." Instead he was persuaded by the king to accept the role of leader of the House of Commons.

Despite Bute's support, Grenville's share of royal favor and patronage was still small, though his brother-in-law Lord Egremont was given the vacant secretaryship. In late May 1762 the Duke of Newcastle resigned and Bute became First Lord of the Treasury, on which he offered the chancellorship of the exchequer to Grenville. Instead, Grenville sought and gained the post of secretary of the Northern Department, just vacated by Bute, and promptly differed from his new premier on the peace negotiations that Bute was conducting with France. In October 1762, Bute compelled Grenville to step down both as secretary and as leader of the House of Commons, though he was made First Lord of the Admiralty—a post that his financial needs forced him to accept. An increasingly difficult colleague, Grenville was denounced by Henry Fox, the new leader of the House, as a hindrance to the ministry. In March 1763, Grenville attracted the ridicule of the House when he spoke of the need for new war taxes and wistfully asked where they could be raised. Pitt launched his attack by parodying Grenville's words, citing the old ballad "Gentle Shepherd, tell me where." This refrain was immediately taken up by the opposition benches, which dubbed the hapless Grenville "Gentle Shepherd."

Despite, or even because of, his weak position, Grenville was chosen in April 1763 to become First Lord of the Treasury on Bute's resignation. Fox, who was subject to frequent failures of political nerve, had turned down the post on health grounds, and Grenville seemed the obvious choice to the king and to Bute, who intended to remain a major influence on policy from within the king's closet. Grenville's time in office was dominated by his attempt to remove Bute from the king's counsels and establish the principle that George III should work only with his avowed ministers.

A week after Grenville became prime minister, John Wilkes published the famous issue number 45 of the anti-Bute publication (financed by Temple) titled the *North Briton,* which was an insolent attack on the king's speech from the throne about the Peace of Paris, grossly offensive to the king. Wilkes's arrest under a general warrant brought, in December 1763, a judgment that this form of warrant was an illegal use of executive power. In January 1764, though, Wilkes was expelled from the House; and in February, thanks to the wily attack of the new secretary of state, Lord Sandwich, the House condemned Wilkes as the author of the *North Briton* paper and found it a seditious libel not covered by parliamentary privilege. This apparent resolution of the matter was in fact only a temporary stopping point. In December 1767, Wilkes generated a wave of popular indignation against the House and ministry—a wave that crested in 1774 with his triumphant election as Lord Mayor of London and his reelection as M.P. for Middlesex.

Two other notable political misjudgments marked Grenville's premiership. The first was his extension to the American colonies of the heavy Stamp Duties imposed at home in Britain. First announced in Grenville's March 1764 budget, the proposals were withheld for a year to allow consultation; but they were imposed in March 1765, despite the strongly hostile response that consultation had brought. In the same month, Grenville seriously offended the king by omitting the mention of the dowager princess in the Regency Bill that was necessitated by the king's illness. Though the king tried, as he had before, to dispense with Grenville, it proved impossible for Pitt to form a replacement administration. In late May, the king had to assure Grenville that he would place confidence in him if he continued in office. Using the threat of a mass ministerial resignation, the premier finally managed to obtain assurances that Bute would no longer be consulted "behind the curtain." This was an important victory for the Grenville ministry, establishing the principle that if ministers of the Crown were to do the king's business, they must be the only channel through which people obtained royal patronage and support. The king agreed, but was bitterly resentful of his treatment at the hands of the ministers, and though Bute finally disappeared from the center of politics, he was soon followed by Grenville.

In early July 1765 the Marquess of Rockingham succeeded in forming an administration without Pitt, and Grenville retired to the opposition. His influence suffered a sharp decline in 1769 when, on constitutional grounds, he opposed the expulsion of Wilkes from the Commons. In the spring of 1770, though, he managed to steer through the Commons a bill that regularized the House's procedures for resolving disputed elections of M.P.s. The Election Act, Grenville's last contribution to politics, fittingly arose from his ideals of hard work and his love of parliamentary procedures. He died in November 1770.

Philip Woodfine

See also: Bute, Earl of; Egremont, Earl of; Fox, Henry; Newcastle, Duke of; Pitt, William (the Elder); Rockingham, Marquess of; Walpole, Sir Robert

References and Further Reading: Beckett, John, 1994, *The Rise and Fall of the Grenvilles, Dukes of Buckingham and Chandos, 1710–1921* (Manchester: Manchester University Press); Lawson, Philip, 1984, *George Grenville: A Political Life* (Oxford: Clarendon Press; New York: Oxford University Press); Smith, William J. (ed.), 1852–1853, *The Grenville Papers: Being the Correspondence of Richard Grenville, Earl Temple, KG and the Rt. Hon. George Grenville, Their Friends and Contemporaries* (New York: AMS Press [reprint]); Wiggin, Lewis M., 1958, *The Faction of Cousins: A Political Account of the Grenvilles, 1733–1763* (New Haven, CT: Yale University Press).

Grenville, Lord (William Wyndham Grenville; Baron Grenville of Wotten-under-Bernewood)
(1759–1834) [PM, FS, HS]

William Wyndham Grenville has the dubious distinction of being regarded as a politician who would sacrifice his country for family gain. Indeed, so steeped was he in buying and maintaining family influence that the epithet "Grenvillite" in the nineteenth century connoted one who was mired in corruption. Sir Lewis Namier has suggested that much of early-nineteenth-century politics involved factional conflict over sinecures and pensions rather than ideological differences between Whigs and Tories. Indeed, William was joined by his elder brother George Nugent-Temple Grenville (1753–1813), and by his (William's) nephew Richard Grenville (1776–1839), the first Duke of Buckingham and Chandos, in working from their estate at Stowe to build up a lucrative empire of annual rent rolls and parliamentary boroughs to strengthen their pursuit of public money, positions, and titles. It was from this financial and political base that the Grenvilles built up their power, although only William had the political stature to become prime minister. The *Courier* of 27 January 1806 described the Grenville family as "gorged with places and pensions." This was a reputation that William had difficulty playing down. He adopted a high moral stance that he attempted to maintain throughout his political career. Nevertheless, he did fall into the Grenvillite mold when he secured some sinecures for himself. Most notably, in December 1791 he was appointed ranger and keeper of St. James's and Hyde parks—a position that he exchanged in February 1794 for the more lucrative one of auditor of the exchequer, which was worth £4,000 per year.

William Wyndham Grenville was born on 25 October 1759, the third son and seventh surviving child of George Grenville, who had been prime minister between 1763 and 1765, and Elizabeth Wyndham. He was educated at Eton and at Christ Church, Oxford. In 1780 he was admitted as a student of law at Lincoln's Inn, but he was never called to the bar. In 1792, he married the Hon. Anne Pitt, daughter of Thomas Pitt, first Baron Camelford.

His political career began in 1782 when he became M.P. for Buckingham (1782–1784) and Buckinghamshire (1784–1790), before becoming Baron Grenville and being raised to the House of Lords in 1790. He then filled a large number of junior posts. He was chief secretary for Ireland (1782–1783), paymaster-general (1783–1789), on the Board of Control (1784–1790), president of the Board of Control (1790–1793), a commissioner at the Board of Trade (1784–1786), and vice president of the Board of Trade (1786–1789).

Grenville's first major political role arose when he was elected speaker of the House of Commons in January 1789, being responsible for taking the speeches of William Wilberforce on the need to end the slave trade. This role did not last long: he was appointed home secretary in June 1789, in the government of William Pitt (the Younger), and resigned most of his other posts soon afterward.

He was appointed foreign secretary in 1791. In this role he claimed to be a keen advocate of maintaining the European peace, but feared, with some justification, that the emergence of the new French Republic would threaten war with the rest of Europe. As a result, and as a "Europe man," he was always at the head of those who advocated war in Pitt's cabinet and strongly opposed to Pitt's more pacific line. He was foreign secretary for ten years, until 1801, and during that period was responsible for the Alien Bill of 1792 and thus for the registration and supervision of all foreigners in Britain. In January 1793, he ordered M. Chauvelin, the French ambassador, to leave the country within eight days. In 1795 he introduced the Treasonable Practices Bill and the Seditious Meeting Bill. In 1799 he spoke in the Lords for four hours on union with Ireland; he, like Pitt, believed that a genuine union could be achieved only with the support of the Irish Catholics. Both men left office in February 1801, after the king refused to agree to Catholic emancipation.

While out of office, Grenville took the opportunity to oppose the peace terms with France being discussed in November 1801, which he felt were "fraught with degradation and national humiliation." He constantly attacked the handling of the war by Henry Addington, then prime minister (1801–1804), but he refused to join Pitt's new administration in 1804 without Charles James Fox, whom the king refused to allow into the ministry. This refusal terminated the longstanding friendship between Pitt and Grenville. Nevertheless, when Pitt died in 1806 and Lord Hawkesbury refused to form a ministry, it was Grenville who was asked to form what became known as the "Ministry of All the Talents," comprising the leaders of all the parties that had previously been in opposition to Pitt's government: Grenville was appointed First Lord of the Treasury (prime minister); Fox became foreign secretary; and Lord Sidmouth (Henry Addington) took the office of Lord Privy Seal.

The Ministry of All the Talents was a brief and unsuccessful administration, lasting from February 1806 until March 1807. Grenville's party (sometimes referred to as the Portland Whigs, after a group that had joined the Tory administration of William Pitt in the 1790s), the Foxite Whigs, and the followers of Sidmouth (Henry Addington, until 1805) did not work well together, and the government tended toward disintegration. Grenville and Fox did manage to unite with William Wilberforce to abolish the slave trade in 1806; but such successes were few. In any case, Fox, who led the House of Commons, died in September 1806. In foreign policy, little could be done other than to support the war effort and to play down Britain's embarrassment over its South American and Mediterranean expeditions. The ministry fell in March 1807 because its leading cabinet figures refused to promise King George III that they would not again raise the issue of Catholic emancipation and the access of Roman Catholics to the highest position in the military of the United Kingdom. Effectively, to make concessions to Roman Catholics was to commit political suicide at that moment.

Out of office, Grenville continued to participate in political debates. He opposed the Peninsular War (1809–1814), since he thought military operations in Spain and Portugal were a distraction to the main theater of combat. In

1808 he refused to join Lord Charles Grey in a ministry upon the collapse of the Portland ministry, and both refused to work together again in 1812, despite the assassination of Prime Minister Spencer Perceval. In 1815 Grenville was to be found attacking the protective Corn Bill; in 1817, supporting the Habeas Corpus Suspension Bills (suspending the right to trial by jury); and in 1819, giving support to Lord Grey's Roman Catholic Relief Bill. He continued to dabble in politics until he was partly paralyzed in 1823. Despite his physical handicap, he continued his literary pursuits and remained chancellor of the University of Oxford (1810–1834). He died on 12 January 1834.

Grenville's period as prime minister was far from successful, although he was perhaps one of the few men who could have brought the government's disparate political talents together. As a politician he was a man of contradictions. While attempting to keep the moral high ground, he nevertheless participated in the political corruption associated with gathering sinecures, which dominated late-eighteenth- and early-nineteenth-century British politics. In addition, although he supported repressive measures in some areas, he was a leading opponent of the slave trade and proponent for Catholic emancipation.

Keith Laybourn

See also: Addington, Henry; Fox, Charles James; Grey, Lord; Pitt, William (the Younger); Portland, Duke of

References and Further Reading: Beckett, John, 1994, *The Rise and Fall of the Grenvilles, Dukes of Buckingham and Chandos, 1710–1921* (Manchester: Manchester Unviersity Press); Jupp, Peter, 1985, *Lord Grenville* (Oxford: Clarendon Press; New York: Oxford University Press); Harvey, Arnold D., 1999, *Lord Grenville, 1759–1834: A Bibliography* (Westport, CT: Meckler).

Grey, Lord (Sir Charles Grey; Earl Grey of Howick; Viscount Howick; Baron Grey)
(1764–1845) [PM, FS]

Sir Charles Grey, the second Earl Grey of Howick, is best remembered for leading the Whig opposition for almost a quarter of a century and having only once been in office, in 1806–1807, before becoming prime minister in 1830. His reputation rests largely upon the fact that his government (1830–1834) was responsible for widening the political franchise through the Reform Act of 1832, and for introducing other reforming legislation, including the abolition of slavery, the 1833 Factory Act, and the 1834 Poor Law Amendment Act. An aristocratic Whig who trimmed his radical demands to the political needs of the age, Grey was, by any standards, a major reforming figure in the nineteenth century.

Grey was born at Fallodon, near Alnwick, Northumberland, on 13 March 1764, the son of General Sir Charles Grey, later the first Earl Grey, and his wife, Elizabeth, daughter of George Grey of Southwick, Durham. He was raised into a landed family, which lived at the other family seat, at Howick. He was educated at a preparatory school in London, at Eton, and lastly, at King's College, Cambridge. In 1794 he married Mary Elizabeth Ponsonby, daughter of William Brabazon Ponsonby, later Baron Ponsonby of Imokilly.

His political career began in 1786 when he won a by-election for the parliamentary seat of Northumberland, which he held until 1807, when he was returned to Parliament by means of the influence of the powerful Percy family, on the assumption that he would support the government of William Pitt, the Younger. In fact he was won over to the Whigs by Charles James Fox, and was a Foxite Whig for the rest of his political career. He was opposed to the monarchy, opposed tyrannies abroad, and sought to establish the constitutional freedoms that the Whigs had sought since the Revolution of 1688. He supported Edmund Burke in the Commons impeachment of Warren Hastings for his alleged misgovernment of India. He supported Fox in 1788 in opposing the idea that George III should be replaced by an unrestricted Regency of the Prince of Wales while he, George III, was suffering from mental and physical illness, but did not agree with him in supporting the French Revolution. He was a member of the Whig Club and joined the Society of the Friends of the People, which was committed to furthering

Earl Grey (Library of Congress)

constitutional reform. In 1794 he joined Fox to head a small Whig party of about sixty M.P.s who were committed to various reforms, although not always parliamentary reform; the Whig supporters of Lord Portland joined him in government with Pitt.

The Pitt ministry, supported by the Portland Whigs, opposed all the reforms advocated by the Foxite Whigs. The Foxite Whigs, in turn, battled against the repressive Seditious Meetings and Treasonable Practices Bills, which were carried forward by Lord Grenville, a Portland Whig. In 1801, Grey refused to join the Whig government of Henry Addington (Lord Sidmouth) because it did not offer sufficient promise of reforms (he later referred to this decision as the "happiest escape" he had ever had in his life). Grey was uneasy about the possible alliance of the Foxite Whigs with the Pittite Tories at this stage. He was even less enamored of the coalition of Whigs in 1806 and 1807, assembled within the so-called "Ministry of All the Talents" led by Lord Grenville. Nevertheless, this ministry gave him his only taste of office before 1830; he became First Lord of the Admiralty, and used the opportunity to increase the pay of the navy.

With the death of Fox in September 1806, Grey became the leader of the main body of Whigs in the House of Commons. He resigned along with the government in 1807, when King George III refused to entertain any idea of Catholic emancipation. The experience of this collapse of government left him with an abiding hostility toward royal interference in the political process.

For the next twenty-three years, Grey led the Whig Party in opposition to a succession of Pittite and Tory administrations under Lord Portland, Spencer Perceval, Lord Liverpool, George Canning, Viscount Goderich, and the Duke of Wellington. He represented the constituencies of Appleby and Tavistock in 1807 until he was raised to the House of Lords as second Earl Grey of Howick (he had become Lord Howick on the elevation of his father to the peerage in 1806). His move to the Lords meant that he could no longer easily control the radicals in the Commons, including his own brother-in-law Samuel Whitbread.

At times—for example, in 1809 and in 1812—it looked as though he and Lord Grenville might form a Whig government; and in 1820, he might well have become prime minister. This last opportunity fizzled, largely because Grey wanted a complete change in the political system in order to save the country—an impossibility at that time. As a result he endured opposition, attacking the Tory governments for undermining traditional liberties, the scandal of the "Peterloo Massacre" of 1819, and all the other repressive actions that took place after the end of the Napoleonic War in 1815, including the suspension of the Habeas Corpus Act in 1817, by which trial by jury was denied. He supported Queen Caroline in her conflict with George IV in 1820, thereby gaining popularity with the British public. He found himself unable to accept office until 1830, when George IV died and was succeeded by his brother, the Duke of Clarence as William IV. In the 1830 general election, following the death of George IV, the Whigs secured a majority, and the king asked Grey to form a government. Grey's cabinet contained eight Whigs and four of George Canning's old Conservative followers, and included four future prime ministers: Lord Melbourne, Lord John Russell, Lord Derby, and Lord Palmerston.

Grey's first act as prime minister was to ask Lord Durham, his Radical nephew, and Lord John Russell to draw up a bill that would reform the political system. Although their plan was amended, the result was that 61 boroughs lost all their parliamentary seats and a further 47 lost one seat—these seats being redistributed to large-franchise English counties; to large, unrepresented cities and towns; and to London. The borough franchise was to be made uniform and based upon households taxed at the rate of £10 per year. However, there was to be no manhood suffrage or secret ballot. Grey was largely responsible for this sweeping reform, championing it through the House of Commons and the House of Lords, being convinced that it was the only solution to civil strife. When the bill was defeated in the Lords in 1832, he offered to resign and call another general election. However, fearing a Whig landslide and an overwhelming Whig presence in the Commons as well as the creation of new Whig peers in the House of Lords, the Lords and the king agreed to the reforms without further significant resistance. The "Great" Reform Act of 1832—the most important constitutional change of the early nineteenth century—was thus achieved through Grey's persistence.

Grey's ministry also introduced numerous other reforms. The most important of these was the Factory Act of 1833, which reduced the hours of work for children and created a factory inspectorate. Also important was the Poor Law Amendment Act (1834), which replaced the old law with a new one based on the imposition of a workhouse test and the abandonment of outdoor relief, the payment of an allowance to the poor who were not interred in the workhouse. This act was even more unpopular with laborers and some employers than the Factory Act, and it was strongly resisted in the north of England, where textile workers relied upon outdoor relief to tide them over lulls and interruptions in trade. In 1834, as a result of cabinet splits over the proposed appropriation of Irish Church revenues, Grey decided to resign in favor of Lord

Melbourne, who sustained Whig rule (with a brief hiatus between 1834 and 1835) until 1841. Grey disliked Melbourne, and declined the offer of the post of Lord Privy Seal in his government. Although Grey was more favorably inclined toward the free-trade policies of Sir Robert Peel, Melbourne's Tory successor between 1841 and 1846, Grey played no further, significant role in British politics. He died on 17 July 1845.

Keith Laybourn

See also: Addington, Henry; Derby, 14th Earl of; Fox, Charles James; Grenville, Lord; Melbourne, Viscount; Palmerston, Lord; Pitt, William (the Younger); Russell, Lord John
References and Further Reading: Brock, Michael, 1973, *The Great Reform Act* (London: Hutchinson); Derry, John, 1992, *Charles, Earl Grey: Aristocratic Reformer* (Oxford, UK, and Cambridge, MA: Basil Blackwell); Mitchell, Austin, 1967, *The Whigs in Opposition, 1815–1830* (Oxford: Clarendon Press); Smith, E., 1990, *Lord Grey, 1764–1845* (Oxford: Clarendon Press; New York: Oxford University Press).

Grey, Sir Edward (Viscount Grey of Fallodon) (1862–1933) [FS]

Sir Edward Grey was a Liberal who served as foreign secretary at the outbreak of World War I. Many socialists believed that his "secret discussions" with France in the prewar years drew Britain into the conflagration.

Grey was the son of a landed army officer and a descendant of Lord Grey, the Whig prime minister of the early nineteenth century. He was educated at Winchester and at Balliol College, Oxford. Expelled from Oxford in 1884, he moved into public life, becoming private secretary to Evelyn Baring, the later Lord Cromer, and then to the Liberal chancellor of the exchequer, Hugh Culling Eardley Childers.

Grey's political career began in 1885 when he won Berwick-on-Tweed, a parliamentary seat that he retained until he was raised to the peerage as Viscount Grey of Fallodon in 1916. He was an impressive politician who remained within the Liberal Party during and after the split over the issue of Irish Home Rule, in the mid-1880s. He rose to become a junior minister at the Foreign Office in the Liberal governments of William Ewart Gladstone and Lord Rosebery, between 1892 and 1895. In 1895 he declared his opposition to the French advance in the Sudan, the eventual outcome of which was the Fashoda confrontation between the French and British in 1898.

With the fall of the Liberal government in 1895, he followed Rosebery into the Liberal Imperialist section of the Liberal Party. As a result of this, he found himself supporting the Conservative government's action during the Boer War (1899–1902), Lord Lansdowne's treaty with Japan in 1902, and the entente cordiale with France in 1904. Grey believed that treaties were necessary in order to maintain the balance of power in Europe, and that Britain needed the military strength to enforce its treaties.

At this time the Liberal Party was deeply divided, with Radicals opposing imperialist ambitions and foreign entanglements, the national Liberals accepting the need to protect British interests, and the Liberal Imperialists being concerned with protecting Britain's current and future imperial interests. Consequently, when the Conservative government resigned in December 1905, Grey joined with H. H. Asquith and R. B. Haldane, both Liberal Imperialists, in attempting to replace the Radical Sir Henry Campbell-Bannerman as Liberal leader and thus as prime minister. Despite this intrigue, Grey was appointed foreign secretary, a post he occupied from December 1905 until December 1916.

As foreign secretary, Grey was determined to maintain the balance of power in Europe in order to neutralize Germany's growing military strength and imperialist ambitions. Central to the containment of Germany was Britain's alliance with France, which Grey sought to preserve regardless of difficulties. Indeed, he intervened in the first Moroccan crisis between France and Germany in 1907, while maintaining Britain's alliance with France. Without the knowledge of most of his cabinet colleagues, he developed an Anglo-French military strategy. Fearing that Russia, having been defeated in the Russo-Japanese war of 1904–1905, would seek an alliance with Germany, he cemented the anti-German alliance of Britain, France, and Russia by means of the Anglo-Russian Convention of 1907.

The strategic interests of Britain were far more important to Grey than the Radical Liberal interest in peace, even though in domestic matters he supported women's suffrage, Irish Home Rule, and land reform. Grey saw the maintenance of peace in Europe as vital. Although Britain was not yet formally obligated to its French and Russian allies in 1911, the second Moroccan crisis between France and Germany, which occurred that year, led to a declaration from David Lloyd George that Britain might be obligated to fight alongside France. The subsequent revelation that there had been prior secret discussions between Britain and France caused a split in Asquith's cabinet. Grey continued to struggle to maintain the balance of power within Europe, containing the Balkan Wars with German help in 1912–1913; but the assassination of the Austrian archduke Franz Ferdinand at Sarajevo in June 1914 tested Grey's balancing act beyond its limits.

Grey was unable to persuade Austria-Hungary and Germany to pull back from war with Serbia, Russia, and France; a European war involving Britain thus was inevitable. On the eve of war, Grey spoke, with great effect, in the House of Commons on the balance of power that he had attempted to maintain in Europe but admitted the inevitability of Britain being drawn into the conflict. Although many took this speech as evidence of how Britain had been brought into the conflict by secret discussions, treaties, and understandings, it is clear that Grey had sought to avoid the conflict that was now upon Europe. Once Britain was in the Great War, Grey worked equally hard to draw Italy into the alliance in 1915 and to maintain good relations with the United States.

When Lloyd George replaced Asquith as prime minister in December 1916, Grey was replaced as foreign secretary. He withdrew permanently from the center stage of politics, and devoted the rest of his life to a variety of public duties. Although still active in the Liberal Party, he was most closely associated with the postwar League of Nations. He also served as chancellor of Oxford University from 1928 until his death in 1933.

Keith Laybourn

See also: Asquith, Herbert Henry; Childers, Hugh; Gladstone, William Ewart; Lloyd George, David; Rosebery, Lord
References and Further Reading: Grey of Fallodon, Viscount, 1925, *Twenty-Five Years, 1892–1916*, 2 vols. (New York: Frederick A. Stokes); Hinsley, F. H. (ed.), 1977, *British Foreign Policy under Sir Edward Grey* (Cambridge and New York: Cambridge University Press); Robbins, Keith, 1971, *Sir Edward Grey: A Biography of Lord Grey of Fallodon* (London: Cassell).

Grey, Sir George
(1799–1882) [HS]

Sir George Grey was an efficient home secretary in Lord John Russell's government of the late 1840s and helped the government successfully meet the challenge of Chartism. He was the only son of George Grey, third son of Charles, first Earl Grey. His uncle was Sir Charles Grey, who became second Earl of Howick and was prime minister between 1830 and 1834. George's mother was Mary, daughter of Samuel Whitbread of Bedwell Park, Hertfordshire. His mother was religious and brought him up in a pious manner; he was educated by the Rev. William Buckle before going to Oriel College, Oxford, in 1817. After graduating from Oxford with a first class honors degree in 1821, he intended to seek holy orders, but he decided instead to study law. He was called to the bar in 1826. In 1827 he married Anna Sophia, eldest daughter of Henry Ryder, Bishop of Lichfield, son of the first Earl of Harrowby.

Grey's political career began in 1832 when he was elected to the House of Commons for the newly enfranchised seat of Devonport. He was also later elected M.P. for Northumberland (1847–1852) and for Morpeth (1853–1874). In 1834 he was offered the post of undersecretary for the colonies, under Thomas Spring-Rice. Melbourne's government soon fell; but after a brief interruption, Grey continued in the same post when Melbourne formed a new ministry in April 1835. Grey's main task was to carry out the provisions for the emancipation of slaves in the West Indies. In 1839 Grey was advanced to the post of judge advocate general, which he held until June 1841, when he became, for a few months, chancellor of the Duchy of Lancaster—a cabinet post that involved no departmental responsibility. In 1846 the death of an uncle, Sir Henry Grey, provided him with a family estate at Fallodon, in Northumberland, where he lived for the remainder of his life.

A careful and moderate politician, Grey was appointed home secretary in Lord John Russell's government, a post in which he served from 1846 to 1852. He held the same post on two other occasions (1855–1858 and 1861–1866). His most significant action was to maintain the public order during the Chartist disturbances in London in April 1848, which culminated in the massive Chartist demonstration at Kennington Common on 10 April 1848. He was out of Parliament briefly, losing his Northumberland seat in 1852, but was returned to Parliament in 1853.

In 1854 he accepted the post of secretary of the Colonial Office in Lord Aberdeen's Coalition government. It was Lord Palmerston who gave him the post of home secretary again in his new ministry in 1855. Grey's main task at this time was to maintain internal order and reorganize the police. In this respect, he was substantially responsible for introducing and implementing the 1856 Police Act, which made it compulsory for all counties to have police forces and offered a contribution from government revenues to police forces that won a certificate of efficiency. Grey continued as home secretary until the collapse of Palmerston's ministry in 1858. When Palmerston returned to power, Grey became chancellor of the Duchy of Lancaster in 1859.

Grey returned to the Home Office in 1861. His main challenge during this period appears to have been the cattle plague of 1866. In that year Earl Russell resigned and was replaced by William Ewart Gladstone as prime minister, as a result of which Grey retired from government. Grey resigned from Parliament in 1874, standing down in favor of Thomas Burt, the miners' leader. Grey spent the rest of his life as a country gentleman and died on 9 September 1882.

Grey was a popular figure, with many friends and few enemies. He was not personally ambitious and was content to be an efficient administrator rather than seeking political prominence and prestige.

Keith Laybourn

See also: Aberdeen, Earl of; Melbourne, Viscount; Palmerston, Lord; Russell, Lord John

References and Further Reading: Mandler, Peter, 1990, *Aristocratic Government in the Age of Reform: Whigs and Liberals, 1830–1852* (Oxford: Clarendon Press; New York: Oxford University Press); Prest, J., 1972, *Lord John Russell* (London: Macmillan).

H

Halifax, Earl of (George Montagu Dunk)
(1716–1771) [FS, HS]

George Montagu was born on 5 October 1716, the son of George Montagu Dunk, who was created Earl of Halifax in 1715. The young George was educated at Eton and at Trinity College, Cambridge. He succeeded to the earldom in 1739. The family estates were not large, and George was somewhat profligate; but he had the good luck to marry, in 1741, Anne, the daughter of William Richards, who had inherited the property of Sir Thomas Dunk, a great clothier of Tonge, in Hawkhurst, Kent. She brought him what was in those days a vast sum: £110,000 (more than £11 million at modern values); and he took her name in recognition of this fortune.

In 1748 Halifax was appointed head of the Board of Trade. Although some critics found his manners in this office overbearing, his zeal in forwarding the mercantile interests of his country was universally recognized. In particular the commerce of the American colonies was so greatly extended under his direction that he was sometimes called the "Father of the Colonies"; and the town of Halifax, Nova Scotia, was named after him in recognition of his efforts in founding that colony. In 1751 he proposed that a third secretaryship of state be created for the colonies, including the whole of the West Indies, and that he be appointed to the post; the king refused.

In 1757 Halifax was admitted to the cabinet as president of the Board of Trade and then as lord lieutenant of Ireland in 1761, an office that he held simultaneously with that of secretary of state for the Northern Department in the third Earl of Bute's administration (1762–1763). When Bute was succeeded by George Grenville in 1763, Halifax took over as secretary of state for the south. However, with the demise of the Grenville ministry in 1765, Halifax was dismissed. In January 1770 he was appointed Lord Privy Seal; and exactly one year later, he was reinstated as secretary of state for the Northern Department, under the administration of his nephew Lord North. However, he was considered too old and, according to Horace Walpole, "too sottish" to realize the fact. Halifax's faculties declined rapidly with increasing age, and he died on 8 June 1771 in harness. He was later eulogized by the king as "so amiable a man."

Kit Hardwick

See also: Bute, Earl of; Grenville, George; North, Lord

References and Further Reading: Valentine, Alan, 1967, *Lord North*, 2 vols. (Norman: University of Oklahoma Press); Whiteley, Peter, 1997, *Lord North: The Prime Minister Who Lost America* (London: Hambledon).

Halifax, Lord (Edward Wood; Lord Irwin; Viscount Halifax; Earl of Halifax)
(1881–1959) [FS]

Lord Halifax, a lifelong Conservative, is most famous for his close association with the appeasement policies of Neville Chamberlain when Halifax was foreign secretary, in the late 1930s. The Munich agreement of 1938, which effectively handed Czechoslovakia over to Hitler's Germany, colors attitudes toward him even today.

Edward Frederick Lindley Wood was born on 16 April 1881 into an Anglo-Catholic family, being the son of Charles Lindley Wood, the second Viscount Halifax, and Lady Agnes Elizabeth Courtenay, the only daughter of the eleventh Earl of Devon. Edward was educated at Eton and at Christ Church, Oxford, and was a fellow of All Souls College, Oxford.

He began his political career in 1910 as Conservative M.P. for Ripon, holding the seat until 1925, whereupon he became the first Lord Irwin and was raised to the House of Lords. While an M.P., he filled several junior ministerial positions, being undersecretary for the Colonial Office between 1921 and 1922, president of the Board of Education between 1922 and 1924, and finally, minister of agriculture between 1924 and 1925. At this point he was appointed viceroy of India, a post he held until 1931. This was a period of conflict and violence in India; Wood, who favored dominion status for India, succeeded in reducing the level of violence by making a deal with the leaders of the Indian independence movement.

Returning to Britain in 1931, he entered Ramsay MacDonald's National government as president of the Board of Trade (1932–1935). He filled many other posts in the subsequent National governments headed by Stanley Baldwin and by Neville Chamberlain. In 1935 he was briefly secretary of state for war, and then filled other posts, including those of Lord Privy Seal (1935–1937), leader of the House of Lords (1935–1938, 1940), and Lord President of the Council (1938–1940).

It was as foreign secretary that Halifax drew the most attention. He was seen as an appeaser, given his support of Neville Chamberlain's attempt to control Hitler by conceding to the latter's demands on Czechoslovakia. Nevertheless, Halifax did not attend any of the three meetings that Chamberlain held with Hitler, at Berchtesgaden, Godesberg, and Munich, which led to the notorious agreement. And unlike Chamberlain, Halifax saw Munich as a "horrible and wretched business," resulting partly from British military weakness. In its wake, he pressed for the rapid militarization of Britain and for military guarantees to protect nations such as Poland. He was also one of those who wished to gain an alliance with the Soviet Union—much against the wishes of Chamberlain before the outbreak of World War II.

In the spring of 1940 there was a brief moment when Halifax was considered as a possible replacement for Chamberlain as prime minister, but he wisely deferred to the rival claims of Winston Churchill. In December 1940, Winston Churchill asked Halifax to become British ambassador to the United States, a post that Halifax accepted and held until 1946. In this role he explained to the Americans the serious threat of Hitler's actions and the dire position that Britain was in at the beginning of the war. He also cultivated good relations with President Franklin D. Roosevelt and played a vital role in encouraging the United States' entry into the war.

On returning to Britain in 1946, Halifax retired from politics to his country estates in Yorkshire. He died on 23 December 1959. Despite his wide political experience and diverse public duties, he will always be remembered as an "appeaser."

Keith Laybourn

See also: Baldwin, Stanley; Chamberlain, Neville; Churchill, Sir Winston; MacDonald, James Ramsay
References and Further Reading: Birkenhead, Frederick, Earl of, 1965, *Halifax: The Life of Lord Halifax* (London: Hamish Hamilton); Charmley, John, 1989, *Chamberlain and the Lost Peace* (London: Hodder & Stoughton); Roberts, Andrew, 1991, *The Holy Fox: A Biography of Lord Halifax* (London: Weidenfeld and Nicolson).

Harcourt, Sir William
(1827–1904) [CE, HS]

Sir William Harcourt, dubbed the "Great Gladiator" because of his political style, has attracted little attention from biographers. Yet even though he cannot be described as a politician of the first rank, he was a good parliamentarian and narrowly missed being prime minister.

William George Granville Venables Vernon Harcourt was born in York on 14 October 1827, the son of William Vernon (Harcourt), an Anglican clergyman who was in turn the son of an archbishop of York. As a condition of inheriting large estates in 1830, the elder William Vernon was obliged to take the surname Harcourt; thus, in 1830, the younger William Vernon became William Vernon Harcourt (or W. V. H., as he was commonly known). The family's landed estates eventually passed from the father to William's elder brother, and then to William when he was 76.

Harcourt's mother, Matilda, had been raised in a military family drawn partly from Church of England background. Harcourt did not attend the traditional upper-class private schools, as his father disapproved of them; but he did for a time attend a preparatory school, and he was tutored along with five other boys by Canon Parr, who operated near Salisbury. Harcourt then went on to Trinity College, Cambridge, in 1846, where he studied law and history. He left Cambridge in 1851 with a first class honors degree in classics and mathematics. (He would later return, in 1869, having accepted the Whewell Professorship in International Law, which offered a fellowship and rooms at Trinity College, and would occupy that professorial chair until 1887. These are the years during which he also served as home secretary and as chancellor of the exchequer.)

In 1851, Harcourt became a journalist for the Peelite organ the *Morning Chronicle* and for the *Saturday Review,* while studying law at Lincoln's Inn. He was called to the bar in 1854 and gradually built up a prosperous law practice in the 1850s and 1860s. In 1859 he married Theresa Lister, who died in childbirth in 1861. He did not remarry until 1875 or 1876, when he wedded Elizabeth Cabat Ives, of good, east coast American stock.

Harcourt's deep involvement in politics began in 1859 when, representing the newly formed Liberal Party, he fought for the Kirkcaldy seat against a Whig local squire and coal owner. He was narrowly defeated, and it was another eight and a half years before he contested another seat, but he continued to express his strong concerns about the American Civil War and supported the position of Abraham Lincoln in most of his attitudes. Politically he was a Liberal, but temperamentally he was closer to Disraeli, the Conservative politician who offered him a "safe Welsh [Tory] seat."

Harcourt won a parliamentary seat as a Liberal M.P. for Oxford in the 1868 general election. During the next few years, having declined the offer of a minor government post, he supported William Ewart Gladstone's government but opposed him on the Education Act of 1870, believing that education should be entirely secular. He was also opposed to the way in which the government addressed the issue of the abolition by royal warrant of the sale of army commissions—a measure with which he agreed, in principle. His general support of Gladstone, and his strong legal reputation, brought him the post of solicitor general in the autumn of 1873, a few months before the Gladstone government was defeated in the general election of February 1874. As solicitor general, he gained the title of Sir William Harcourt.

Throughout his political career, Harcourt was generally pro-Gladstone, even in the Home Rule crisis of 1886. He opposed female emancipation and jingoism in foreign and imperial politics. With the Liberal victory in the 1880 general election, he expected to become attorney general; but he was rewarded the more senior post of home secretary, which he filled from 25 April 1880 until 23 June 1885. This post necessitated his reelection for Oxford. He lost his Oxford seat in the parliamentary by-election but obtained a seat at West Derby, where Samuel Plimsoll had resigned and Harcourt ran unopposed.

As home secretary, Harcourt was appalled at the high level of false convictions. He was also increasingly opposed to alcohol, since he felt that it was the cause of much crime. It was Harcourt who set up a special branch of the metropolitan police to maintain surveillance over Irish terrorist activity. As a result, he was fully apprised of Charles Stewart Parnell's relations with Mrs. O'Shea six or seven years before the relationship became public in 1890. While home secretary, Harcourt also was engaged in developing the ill-fated London Bill to democratize the City of London corporation, and in introducing a local government bill to extend more democratic and representative government throughout the country. However, his tenure as home secretary came to an abrupt end with the resignation of Gladstone's government on 9 June 1885.

Throughout the rest of the 1880s and early 1890s, Harcourt was a loyal supporter of Gladstone—unlike half of the previous cabinet—and of Home Rule for Ireland, though more out of a sense of loyalty to Gladstone than from any love of the Irish. As a result, Harcourt was appointed chancellor of the exchequer in Gladstone's third government—the first government committed to Home Rule—in January 1886. He was chancellor for a mere five and a half months, during which he maintained the fiscal status quo, increasing neither taxation nor expenditure. Thereafter, he was out of office for six years, and increasingly took on the more routine business of the Liberal Party, which Gladstone tended to neglect. An international lawyer of some repute, Harcourt now became famous for his robust parliamentary performances. Yet his political fortunes were shaken by the Parnell divorce case (1890), which was also a setback for the Nonconformist-dominated Liberal Party and its Irish Catholic allies in Parliament.

Nevertheless, Harcourt returned to the post of chancellor of the exchequer in the Gladstone government formed on 18 August 1892, remaining in that post until the end of the succeeding Rosebery government in June 1895. It seemed, for a time, that he might be the obvious successor to Gladstone; but after Harcourt wrote an aggressive letter to Gladstone on 12 February 1893 about some of the financial aspects of the second Home Rule Bill, Harcourt's friend John Morley refused to support his leadership claims in the cabinet. Lord Rosebery replaced Gladstone as Liberal leader and prime minister.

As chancellor, Harcourt introduced the 1894 budget, one of the most effective of the nineteenth century. Facing a deficit of about £5 million—largely as a result of increased expenditure on defense—Harcourt reduced debt repayment; increased the beer and spirit duty; and raised income tax from 7d to 8d in the pound (there were 240 pence to the pound at that time), at the same time making allowance for some abatement of tax by introducing graduated direct taxation. He also raised money by ensuring that landed property was subject to the same death duties as those levied on all other property.

Harcourt's budget, which passed through Parliament easily, was one of the few successes of Rosebery's administration, which soon collapsed and was swept away in the general election of 1895. Almost inevitably, Harcourt took over the

party leadership from Rosebery, remaining Liberal leader until 1898. He then moved out of the political limelight, although he was returned for the House of Commons in the 1900 "khaki" general election. He died in the autumn of 1904.

Keith Laybourn

See also: Disraeli, Benjamin; Gladstone, William Ewart; Rosebery, Lord; Salisbury, Lord
References and Further Reading: Gardiner, Alfred G., 1923, *The Life of Sir William Harcourt,* 2 vols. (London: Constable); Jenkins, Roy, 1998, *The Chancellors* (London: Macmillan).

Hardy, Gathorne (Gathorne Gathorne-Hardy; Earl of Cranbrook) (1814–1906) [HS]

Gathorne Hardy was born on 1 October 1814 at the Manor House, Bradford, the son of John Hardy of Dunstall Hall, Staffordshire. His father was the chief owner of Low Moor ironworks in Bradford, judge of the Duchy of Lancaster court at Pontefract, and M.P. for Bradford. His mother was Isabel, the eldest daughter of Richard Gathorne of Kirby Lonsdale, Westmoreland. After attending various preparatory schools and Shrewsbury school, Gathorne attended Oriel College, Oxford, where he obtained a B.A. in 1836, and, in order to vote against Gladstone, an M.A. in 1861, which conferred upon him the right to vote in the university constituency. He married Jane, the third daughter of James Orr, of Ballygowan, Ireland. In 1840 he was called to the bar at the Inner Temple and became a barrister in the northern circuit, where he built up a substantial clientele.

In 1846 Hardy unsuccessfully contested Bradford for the Conservatives. In 1856 he was elected as Conservative M.P. for Leominster, which he represented until 1865. He became undersecretary for the Home Office on 25 February 1858, in Lord Derby's second ministry, under Home Secretary Spencer Walpole. He remained in that office until the fall of Derby's ministry in June 1859.

In 1865 he was returned to Parliament as M.P. for the University of Oxford, opposing Gladstone's reelection; and in July 1866 he was appointed president of the Poor Law Board and a member of the Privy Council in Lord Derby's third ministry. He introduced the 1867 Poor Law Amendment Bill, which established metropolitan asylums for sick and insane paupers, with separate accommodation for smallpox patients. By this time he had become a supporter of Benjamin Disraeli, and reluctantly, of the extension of the franchise brought by the 1867 Reform Bill.

On 17 May 1867, after the Hyde Park riots, Hardy replaced Walpole as home secretary. His immediate concern was to deal with the Irish Fenian threat. Because he did not commute to a life sentence the capital punishment imposed upon the Fenian murderers at Manchester, his life was threatened on several occasions. He resigned along with other members of the Disraeli government in October 1868.

Hardy held many other positions in subsequent Conservative governments. In Disraeli's second ministry he filled the post of secretary of war between 1874 and 1878, preparing for the possibility of a Mediterranean War. In 1878 he became secretary for India, replacing Lord Salisbury, who had gone to the Foreign Office. At this point, on 11 May 1879, Hardy was raised to the House of Lords as Viscount Cranbrook of Hemsted, whereupon he assumed the additional surname of Gathorne. Now at the India Office, he supported the Vernacular Press Act of 1878—which allowed the government to silence any Indian newspapers that promoted disaffection—although he was unhappy with the intent of the bill. He also was in tune with the general concern about Russian expansionism and the restoration of Britain's relations with Afghanistan.

With the collapse of Disraeli's second ministry in 1880, Cranbrook played a less dominant role in politics. He was Lord President of the Council in Salisbury's 1885 ministry, continuing in that role in Salisbury's second ministry, from 1886 to 1892. In 1892 he was created Earl of Cranbrook. Thereafter he offered his services to the Conservative Party as and when required, but he never assumed office again. He died at Hemsted Park on 30 October 1906. A popular politician and a good speaker, he was remembered as a good administrator.

Keith Laybourn

See also: Derby, 15th Earl of; Disraeli, Benjamin; Gladstone, William Ewart; Salisbury, Lord; Walpole, Spencer
References and Further Reading: Blake, Robert, 1969, *Disraeli* (London: Oxford University Press); Grenville, J. A. S., 1964, *Lord Salisbury and Foreign Policy: The Close of the Nineteenth Century* (London: Athlone Press).

Harrington, Earl (William Stanhope)
(1690?–1756) [FS]

William Stanhope earned his high reputation as a diplomat rather than a politician in the early eighteenth century. Nevertheless, he did serve as secretary of state in the ministries of both Sir Robert Walpole and Henry Pelham.

Stanhope was born about 1690, the fourth son of John Stanhope of Elvaston, Derbyshire, and of his wife, Dorothy. He was educated at Eton, where in 1710 he acquired the rank of captain in third foot-guards, after which he served in the military in Spain. In 1715 he was made colonel of a regiment of dragoons, and entered the House of Commons as Whig member for Derby. In August 1717 he was sent to Spain to try to improve relations between the European nations and to present the compensation claims of British merchants to the Spanish monarch. In the war of 1718 and 1719, which saw French and English action against Spain, he was English envoy at Turin. There he volunteered to command French troops against the Spanish and led them in cooperating with the English fleet against Spain. After the war, he returned to Madrid. In 1739 he was awarded the rank of lieutenant general, and in 1747, that of general, although he saw no military action after the 1720s.

After the Spanish War, Stanhope spent seven years as British ambassador in Madrid. During this period, he conducted negotiations for Britain's return of Gibraltar to Spain in return for improved trading relations; but Spain never agreed to British terms. Stanhope also reported home on events surrounding the abdication of Philip V of Spain. Upon returning to Britain in 1727, Stanhope was named vice-chamberlain and privy councillor by George II and was immediately sent as a British representative to the

Congress of Aix-la-Chapelle (which was soon relocated to Soissons). Stanhope still favored Britain's returning Gibraltar, which was then under siege, to Spain. He was involved in the negotiations that led to the Treaty of Seville, on 9 November 1729 (among England, France, Spain, and Holland), which improved British trading relations in return for agreement to the Spanish claims of the succession of control in Tuscany and Parma; but in this treaty the Spanish claim to Gibraltar was ignored. For his efforts, on 6 January 1730 he was awarded the title Baron Harrington of Harrington, Northamptonshire, and the office of secretary of state for the Northern Department (after 1782, this was the office of foreign secretary).

Harrington was at the Northern Department from June 1730 until 12 February 1741 (1742 in the new calendar)—in other words, until the end of Robert Walpole's premiership. Harrington did not work closely with Walpole but maintained his influence by pushing forward policies that favored the Hanoverian interests of George II. In general, King George II and Harrington favored an aggressive, warlike policy, whereas Queen Caroline and Walpole struggled to maintain peace. Toward the end of the 1730s, Harrington began to work with the Duke of Newcastle and Lord Hardwicke in order to promote a war with Spain over trading indiscretions by the Spanish; their efforts led to the famous "War of Jenkin's Ear." In 1741 he also negotiated, behind Walpole's back, a treaty with France for the neutrality of Hanover, again serving the Hanoverian interests of George II.

With the fall of Walpole and the formation of the Spencer Compton (Lord Wilmington) ministry, Harrington resigned from the Northern Department and took up the post of Lord President of the Council, combining it with other lucrative posts, such as the tellership of the exchequer and the post of Lord of Justice.

Compton's death in 1743 led to the formation of the Whig ministry of Henry Pelham. At this point Harrington joined the Pelhamites in opposing the foreign policy of John Carteret, who was as committed to supporting George II's pro-German interests in Europe as Harrington earlier had been. Pelham replaced Carteret with

Harrington, as secretary of state for the Northern Department, on 10 February 1745 (1746 in the new calendar). But Harrington had changed his mind, and he now opposed George II's desire for more extensive military operations against France, especially the idea of some type of Grand Alliance that would further George's Hanoverian interests. Harrington did urge the Dutch to declare war against France; but he also suggested that Britain would not be able to bear the cost of protecting George's German empire. George II attempted to win Harrington over to his cause through Pulteney (Lord Bath), but Harrington remained loyal to Pelham and resigned along with him in February 1746. Both men were returned to office soon after; but Harrington resigned again in October 1746, when his recommendation that Britain accept the French proposals for peace was opposed by the Duke of Newcastle and by Lord Hardwicke.

Harrington was retained by the government as lord lieutenant of Ireland, holding the post until 1751, when he was replaced by his kinsman Philip Dormer Stanhope, the Earl of Chesterfield. During his period in Ireland, Harrington faced agitation led by Charles Lucas (1731–1771) and the beginnings of opposition to English rule within the Irish Parliament. After leaving this office, he played no further part in public affairs. He died on 8 December 1756.

Keith Laybourn

See also: Compton, Spencer; Newcastle, Duke of; Pelham, Hon. Henry; Walpole, Sir Robert
References and Further Reading: Black, Jeremy (ed.), 1984, *Britain in the Age of Walpole* (London: Macmillan); Dickinson, H. T., 1973, *Walpole and the Whig Supremacy* (London: English Universities Press); Owen, John, 1957, *The Rise of the Pelhams* (London: Methuen).

Harrowby, Lord (Dudley Ryder; Baron Harrowby; Earl of Harrowby; Viscount Sandon) (1762–1847) [FS]

Dudley Ryder was born on 22 December 1762, the eldest son of Nathaniel Ryder, first Baron Harrowby, and Elizabeth, daughter of Richard Terrish, bishop of London. He was educated at St. John's College, Cambridge, and began his political career as M.P. for Tiverton in 1784. His junior ministerial career began as undersecretary of state for foreign affairs, in 1789, and continued with his appointments in February 1791 as paymaster of the forces and vice president of the Board of Trade. In 1795 he married Lady Susan Leveson-Gower, the sixth daughter of the Marquess of Stafford. He became Lord Harrowby on the death of his father in 1803.

Harrowby was a Tory and a strong supporter of William Pitt, the Younger. His close association with Pitt, and Harrowby's distinguished record as a junior minister, led to his appointment as foreign secretary in Pitt's government, with a place on the cabinet, in May 1804. However, Harrowby fell ill and left office in December of the same year. After he recovered, he was given the post of chancellor of the Duchy of Lancaster, which entailed no departmental responsibilities but allowed him a seat in the cabinet. He lost office again with the death of Pitt in 1806, but became president of the Board of Trade in 1809, in the ministry of Spencer Perceval. On 20 July 1808 he became the first Earl of Harrowby and Viscount Sandon.

In 1812 he was made Lord President of the Council in Lord Liverpool's government, and he remained in this post through the end of George Canning's government in August 1827. Harrowby resigned in November 1827, during the premiership of the Viscount Goderich (later the first Earl of Ripon), and refused the premiership after Goderich resigned in January 1828. After that, he played a diminishing role in politics. He died on 26 December 1847.

Keith Laybourn

See also: Canning, George; Goderich, Viscount; Liverpool, Earl of; Perceval, Spencer; Pitt, William (the Younger)
References and Further Reading: Dickinson, H. T., 1989, *Britain and the French Revolution, 1789–1815* (Basingstoke, UK: Macmillan).

Healey, Denis (Lord Healey)
(1917–) [CE]

Healey was a gifted Labour politician, one of the most effective representatives of the right wing of the Labour Party in the 1970s and 1980s. An able minister of defense in the 1960s, he was also chancellor of the exchequer during the financial crisis in Britain of the mid- to late 1970s. During the early 1980s, he was deputy leader of the Labour Party, balancing his right-wing views against Michael Foot's left-wing leadership.

Denis Winston Healey was born in Kent on 30 August 1917, to a family of Irish origin. His grandfather, John William Healey, a tailor, had left Ireland for Todmorden, Yorkshire, and his family had established a political presence in that area. Denis's father, Will, was a skilled engineer who had studied on scholarship at the University of Leeds; and Denis's mother, Winnie Powell, was the daughter of a station master. The two had met and married while Will was working in Gloucester. Denis, therefore, came from an educated working-class and lower-middle-class background. His father's literary writings had a great influence on him early on; his father's Irish nationalism did not intrude until much later in Denis's life.

Denis was raised on an estate of temporary wooden huts constructed in Kent during World War I to house workers at the Woolwich Arsenal. The family left Kent in 1922, when Denis's father was appointed principal of Keighley Technical School, on the then substantial salary of £600 per year. At the age of eight, Denis won a scholarship to Bradford Grammar School, and the family moved from the center of Keighley to Riddlesden, on the edge of Ilkley Moor. In October 1936, Denis enrolled at Balliol College, Oxford. In the summer of 1937, while at Oxford, he joined the Communist Party of Great Britain, having become convinced of the need for a popular front of all political organizations against fascism. He was a "bed-and-breakfast" Communist, and remained in the party only briefly. He became chairman of the Oxford Labour Club in the summer of 1939; this group in turn splintered in 1939 and 1940, when Tony Crosland, Roy Jenkins, and Philip Williams founded the Democratic Socialist Party, in opposition to the Stalin-Hitler Pact and in protest against the Soviet attack on Finland. Healey himself did not break with the Communist Party until France capitulated in 1940. After finishing his finals in the summer of 1940, he volunteered for the Keighley Home Guard; met Edna Edmunds, his future wife; and waited to be called up to the Royal Artillery Field Training Unit at Uniacke Barracks, just outside Harrogate in Yorkshire. For the next five years he fought as a soldier in World War II, gradually rising to the rank of major.

Once the war in Europe was over, Healey obtained three months' leave in order to run as Labour candidate for Pudsey and Otley in the general election of July 1945. He was defeated in this staunchly Conservative seat, but had cut the Conservative majority by 10,000, to a mere 1,651 votes. In December 1945 he married Edna and began to work at Transport House as international secretary to the Labour Party. In this position he was one of the leading figures opposing the attempted affiliation of the Communist Party of Great Britain with the Labour Party, and was active in pressing the 1946 Labour Party Conference to amend the party constitution in order to rule out the affiliation of organizations that fielded separate candidates in local or national elections. On the whole, he regarded his effectiveness in this capacity as limited, since the international subcommittee of the Labour Party's national executive was dominated by cabinet ministers who barely bothered to read the papers he prepared.

Nevertheless, one of his primary interests and responsibilities was the formulation of a Labour Party line on Britain's foreign policy, which became increasingly anti-Soviet with the emergence of the Cold War, the Soviet air blockade of Berlin, and the formation of the North Atlantic Treaty Organization (NATO) in 1949. It was Healey who presented Ernest Bevin's foreign policy to the nation. His crowning triumph, however, was the formation of the Socialist International at Frankfurt in June 1950.

Healey began his parliamentary career when he was elected as M.P. for Leeds Southeast in 1952. He then served as M.P. for Leeds East, from 1955 until 1992, after which he was made a life peer, becoming Lord Healey. In that forty-year period he was often at the forefront of Labour politics.

From the start, Healey was to the right of the party, and from 1955 until 1963 he was a staunch supporter of Hugh Gaitskell, a fellow Leeds M.P. and Labour leader. Despite his close connections with Gaitskell, he never became part of his inner circle, which included Tony Crosland and Roy Jenkins, and did not join the Campaign for Democratic Socialism, which was set up by other right-wingers, such as Bill Rodgers and Brian Walden. During this period he became shadow spokesman for foreign affairs, and expressed the Labour Party's incensed opposition to the Suez affair of 1956, when British and French forces invaded the Suez Canal Zone to protect their interests but were forced to withdraw because of international pressure.

In 1959 he was elected to the Labour Party's parliamentary committee, better known as the shadow cabinet, where he occupied his time with international affairs and defense issues. He remained a member of the parliamentary committee for the next twenty-eight years, either in the shadow cabinet or in the cabinet of a Labour government.

Healey became minister of defense in Harold Wilson's Labour government, formed in October 1964. In this post Healey was responsible for the 458,000 members of the British armed forces and for 406,000 civil servants throughout the world. Although he had no prior ministerial experience, his international and defense connections in the 1950s and early 1960s had prepared him for his new role. His six-year period of office is, perhaps, most noted for the fact that he greatly reduced—practically liquidated—Britain's military role outside of Europe. When he took office in 1964, Britain had more troops east of Suez than in Germany, with major bases at Singapore (for Southeast Asia) and at Aden (for Africa and the Middle East). There was also a substantial garrison in Hong Kong. Under Healey's ministry, Britain withdrew from Aden and in July 1968 committed to cutting half of its forces in Singapore and Malaysia by 1970–1971, with the rest being withdrawn a few years later. In January 1969 it was announced that Britain would end its commitment in the Gulf, and that its final withdrawal from Singapore would occur in December 1971.

As minister of defense, Healey was also responsible for continuing the construction of submarines capable of delivering Polaris nuclear

Chancellor of the Exchequer Denis Healey on budget day, 26 March 1974 (Hulton-Deutsch Collection/Corbis)

missiles. As a concession to opponents of the building of the five Polaris submarines, which Harold Macmillan had committed Britain to in 1962, Healey decided to cancel construction of the fifth submarine and to rely on a fleet of four.

The United States at the time was encouraging the European nations to take on more financial responsibility for their own defense. Healey felt that this trend necessitated a joint command system to assure that European forces worked effectively together. General De Gaulle felt that nuclear weapons prevented such a command structure, and France responded by withdrawing from NATO on 7 March 1966. In negotiating with the various interests involved, Healey was part of the process that led NATO to abandon its idea of a massive nuclear response to any Soviet incursion and helped develop the policy of flexible response, which envisaged NATO's using conventional responses to minor incursions and gradually increasing the seriousness of the response only as needed, culminating in the use of nuclear weapons.

Healey felt that his six years as minister of defense were the most rewarding of his political career. Indeed, though his policies were severely criticized by the Conservative opposition, the Conservatives did not reverse the defense cuts east of Suez or order the building of a fifth Polaris submarine when they came to office under Edward Heath (1970–1974). Out of office for four years, Healey returned in 1974 as chancellor of the exchequer, an office that never gave him the same excitement that he enjoyed at the Ministry of Defence. He found the work difficult and frustrating, as Britain faced serious economic difficulties throughout his stewardship.

At the beginning of his chancellorship, Healey led a Treasury that was dominated by the ideas of John Maynard Keynes, an economist who argued that government must spend its way out of an economic slump and reduce spending in periods of economic boom in order to maintain full employment and to prevent inflation. The difficulty was that economic institutions such as trade unions were likely to interfere with such a strategy. Keynesian theory also ignored other events in the world economy—particularly, sharp rises in prices. When Healey took office at the Treasury, Britain was still exporting about 30 percent of its gross domestic product, was deeply involved in international trade, and was particularly dependent upon foreign oil, the price of which had shot up enormously in the previous two or three years. The country was besieged by a rising cost of living, a resultant rise in inflation, falling output, and rising unemployment. The Keynesian solution of tackling rising unemployment by increasing government expenditure, however, was impossible, because there seemed to be no control over the amount of investment that was pumped into the economy and because resources were limited.

As a result, Healey had difficulty estimating how much the government needed to borrow to run the economy in a balanced manner. His 1974 budget underestimated government borrowing requirements by about £4 billion, and his 1976 budget overestimated them by £2 billion. In any case, the government was forced to borrow heavily.

With unemployment rising from 678,000 to 1,129,000 during the course of 1975, the Labour government panicked and introduced an austerity budget that transferred resources from the private to the public sector and reduced public spending for 1977–1978 by £900 million—at a cost of about 20,000 jobs. This was followed by the £6 per week wage increase limit in July 1975. The Labour government decided to impose an incomes policy. Matters grew worse when Healey was forced to approach the International Monetary Fund (IMF) to secure a massive loan. When the deal was struck in December 1975, the Labour government was faced with the necessity of pruning government expenditure by another £2.5 billion in order to secure a loan of £3 billion—which created immense tensions and rival responses within the Labour cabinet.

The ensuing political crisis was the low point of Healey's chancellorship, but it initiated a change of direction in Labour's economic policy. No longer would Labour governments invest on a vast scale to ensure full employment. James Callaghan, who took over from Harold Wilson as prime minister in 1976, stated at the Labour Party Conference of 1976 that

> We used to think that you could spend your way out of recession and increase employment by cutting taxes and boosting Government spending. I will tell you with candour that that option no longer exists, and that insofar as it ever did exist, it only worked on each occasion since the war by injecting a bigger dose of inflation into the economy, followed by a higher level of unemployment as the next step.

Healey and Callaghan had abandoned the economic policies that governments had adopted since 1945. One casualty of this abandonment of Keynesian economic policies was the government's arrangement with the trade unions. Wilson's Labour government had come to power in 1974 with a "social contract" whereby trade unions curbed their wage demands in return for the withdrawal of Conservative legislation on industrial relations and an increase in public spending. The government honored its commitment to withdraw the Conservative legislation but failed to redistribute wealth and income through increased social spending. The terms of the IMF loan mandated severe cuts, which prevented such increases. In the end, Healey helped negotiate three pay rounds in which tight controls over increased expenditure were imposed. As a result, in January 1978, inflation fell below 10 percent for the first time since October 1973, falling to 8 percent by midsummer. Nevertheless, the trade unions felt that they had honored their pledge to accept wage restraint but that the Labour government had not met its part of the bargain.

Industrial tensions mounted, and in the winter of 1978–1979 the conflict reached a high point. In its wake, the Labour government was defeated in the May 1979 general election. Labour's loss of office marked the end of Healey's ministerial career, although he remained M.P. for Leeds East until he was raised to the House of Lords.

From 1980 to 1983, Healey was deputy

leader of the Labour Party, representing the right-wing section in balance to the left-wing influence of Michael Foot, who became Labour leader in 1980. This was a turbulent period. As the Labour Party became increasingly dominated by the Labour left, the party moved toward supporting an extensive program of public ownership. The revolutionary Militant Tendency faction was gaining strength in the party, and some of the Labour right split off to form the Social Democratic Party in 1981. Healey attempted to keep these members of the right within the Labour Party but was unsuccessful, although Labour did begin in 1981 to drift once more to the right, where it remained.

Labour was defeated in the 1983 general election. In the opinion of Healey and Gerald Kaufman, a leading Labour Party front-bench spokesman, Labour's left-wing manifesto had been "the longest suicide note in history" (Laybourn 2000 and 2001, p. 133). After the party's defeat, Healey gave up the post of deputy leader but remained opposition spokesman on foreign and commonwealth affairs, a position that he held from 1980 to 1987. Healey retired from the House of Commons in 1992, when he was raised to the House of Lords.

Healey's career, illustrious as it was, remained somewhat unfulfilled. He was a remarkably talented politician who in other circumstances might have become prime minister. But he was clearly an effective secretary of state for defense; and he is well remembered as the chancellor of the exchequer who presided over some of Britain's worst economic difficulties, in the mid- and late 1970s.

Keith Laybourn

See also: Bevin, Ernest; Callaghan, James; Crosland, Tony; Gaitskell, Hugh; Heath, Edward; Jenkins, Roy; Thatcher, Margaret; Wilson, Harold
References and Further Reading: Healey, Denis, 1989, *The Time of My Life* (London: Michael Joseph); Jefferys, Kevin, 1999, *Anthony Crosland: A New Biography* (London: Richard Cohen); Laybourn, K., 2000 and 2001, *A Century of Labour: A History of the Labour Party, 1900–2000* (Stroud, UK: Sutton): Pimlott, Ben, 1992, *Harold Wilson* (London: HarperCollins).

Heath, Edward
(1916–) [PM]

Heath was prime minister of the controversial and unsuccessful Conservative government of 1970–1974. Amid this government's industrial problems, Heath's major achievement was to secure Britain's entry to the European Economic Community (EEC) with the signing of the Treaty of Accession in 1972, followed by entry in 1973. Since then, Heath has been a determined supporter of the EEC in the face of much skepticism from Conservatives. Removed as Conservative party leader in 1975 and replaced by Margaret Thatcher, he became a determined opponent of the strident, confrontational style of leadership she adopted, particularly after her victory in the 1979 general election. Indeed, his support for the EEC often worked together with his opposition to Thatcherism.

Edward Richard George Heath was born in Broadstairs on 9 July 1916, the first child of William Heath and Edith Pantony. He did not have the traditional wealthy background of Conservative leaders; his father was a carpenter who later ran a small building firm, and his mother had been in domestic service before she married. He won a scholarship to Chatham House School, Ramsgate, a fee-paying grammar school, and then went to Balliol College, Oxford, where he studied politics, philosophy, and economics. While at Oxford he became both president of the Oxford Union and president of the Oxford University Conservative Association. Revealing an early independence of thought, he worked for an anti-Munich candidate in the 1938 Oxford by-election.

During World War II he became a colonel in the Royal Artillery. He then entered the civil service. He was elected M.P. for Bexley in the 1950 general election, and held that seat until 1974, when he became M.P. for Sidcup (1974–1983) and then Old Bexley and Sidcup (1983–).

Heath rose steadily within the Conservative Party and in the governments of the 1950s and early 1960s, becoming chief whip in 1955, minister of labor in 1959, and Lord Privy Seal in 1960. In the latter office he conducted unsuccessful negotiations to arrange for Britain's entry to the EEC, in 1960 and 1961. In 1963 he be-

Edward Heath celebrates becoming the new prime minister after the Tory victory in the 1970 election (Hulton-Deutsch Collection/Corbis)

prepare a political program for a future Conservative government.

Heath's moment came in the general election of June 1970, when he committed the Conservative Party to a policy of modernization aimed at tackling the relative decline of the British economy. His approach was largely designed to release private initiative and enterprise by reducing direct taxation, cutting back on government expenditure, and reforming industrial relations and central and local government administration. It was also linked with the need to negotiate entry into the EEC, which Heath felt would guarantee both Britain's political security and economic competitiveness in its postimperialist days. Armed with these policies, and with the Wilson government facing difficulties with the trade union movement, Heath's Conservative government was elected with a majority of thirty seats.

Heath's premiership foreshadowed Margaret Thatcher's in its demonstrated willingness to challenge political convention by attempting to reduce the government's commitment to the welfare state. Heath developed a reputation for being abrupt, lacking tact, and leading from the front, and his efforts were not as successful as those of other recent British prime ministers. Yet in some areas he showed surprising political skill—for example, on the question of Europe, where he put the question of Britain's entry to the EEC to a free vote in Parliament and obtained the necessary majority (39 Conservative M.P.s voted against entry, but 69 Labour M.P.s ignored the Labour Party whip and voted in favor).

His handling of the immigration issue—an issue that provoked as much controversy as did Britain's entry to the EEC—was less successful. The Conservative manifesto of 1970 had accepted that there would be no further large-scale immigration, and the Immigration Act of 1971 was introduced to ensure that immigration restrictions would be tightened. Heath's agreement to accept 60,000 Ugandan Asians who held British passports and who were threatened with expulsion from Uganda by President Idi Amin evoked serious criticism from Conservative M.P. Enoch Powell, a well-known opponent of immigration, as well as considerable disquiet within the Conservative Party.

came minister of trade, industry, and regional development in Sir Alec Douglas Home's coalition government. It was while in this office that he partially abolished resale price maintenance, which he felt fixed prices too high, at the expense of the customers. This action, which was unpopular with business owners, marked him as a reforming and modernizing Conservative.

After the Douglas Home government was defeated in the 1964 general election, Heath was made shadow chancellor of the exchequer. The following year, he won the Conservative leadership contest against Enoch Powell and Reginald Maudling. Heath's success was probably due to the fact that he was seen as a modern Conservative who might provide an attractive alternative to Harold Wilson's reforming zeal. Nevertheless, Heath was defeated in the 1966 general election. With the Conservatives continuing in the opposition for the time being, Heath decided to set up a large number of policy review groups, to

The dominating theme of Heath's government was efficiency; it introduced many initiatives to reduce public expenditure, creating new, larger departments, such as the Ministry of Trade and Industry and Ministry of the Environment. The government's financial prudence was, however, offset by rising inflation, wage demands, and the failure of high-profile companies such as Rolls Royce, which had to be nationalized, and Upper Clyde Shipbuilders, which had to be subsidized. The Heath government also abolished the prices and incomes board and the Industrial Reorganization Corporation, and was determined to fight excessive public sector wage claims. At first it made attempts to negotiate a voluntary prices and incomes policy. When this policy failed, Heath moved to make the scheme compulsory. The early stages of implementation went well enough, but there were problems at the final stage, when the miners' union decided to ignore the wage guidelines altogether.

The battle over wage limits added to the tensions that had been accumulating since the passage of the Industrial Relations Act of 1971, which had mandated sixty-day cooling-off periods and prestrike ballots. Trade unions and employers refused to cooperate in such measures, and the resultant increase in antagonism between the two groups led to a number of serious industrial confrontations. The coal miners' strike of 1972 created serious difficulties for Heath's government, and the 1973–1974 coal strike broke its back: The government was compelled to introduce a three-day work week in order to save fuel, and the ensuing political fracas forced Heath to call a general election in February 1974, at which his government was defeated.

Heath remained Conservative leader until 1975, when he was replaced by Margaret Thatcher. From then on—particularly after Thatcher became prime minister in 1979—he was very much an isolated political figure in the party, maintaining a commitment to a united Europe while most Conservatives were expressing grave doubts about the EEC. Nonetheless, Heath fulfilled the function of senior statesman and became the "Father of the House" of Commons (i.e., its longest-serving member) in 1992. He retired as an M.P. in June 2001.

Heath will hardly figure in anyone's pantheon of great prime ministers. He was particularly unfortunate in assuming office at a time of rapidly changing economic and political circumstances. His great achievement was that he negotiated Britain's entry into the EEC. His great failure was his inability to deal effectively with industrial relations.

Keith Laybourn

See also: Home, Sir Alec Douglas; Maudling, Reginald; Thatcher, Margaret; Wilson, Harold
References and Further Reading: Blake, Robert, 1985, *The Conservative Party from Peel to Thatcher* (London: Methuen); Campbell, John, 1993, *Edward Heath: A Biography* (London: Pimlico); Holmes, Martin, 1982, *Political Pressure and Economic Policy: British Government, 1970–1974* (London and Boston: Butterworth).

Heathcoat Amory, Derick (Viscount Amory)
(1899–1981) [CE]

Derick Heathcoat Amory, usually referred to as Heathcoat Amory, came late to parliamentary politics and left early; he did not enter Parliament until 1945, and did not become a minister until 1951. But he filled his various posts with such a calm efficiency that when he retired in 1960, some politicians considered him a possible alternative to Harold Macmillan, the Conservative prime minister.

Heathcoat Amory was born on 26 December 1899, the son of Ian Murray Heathcoat Heathcoat-Amory, second Baronet Amory, and his wife, Alexandra Georgina, daughter of Vice Admiral Henry George Seymour. Derick was educated at Eton and at Christ Church, Oxford, where he obtained third-class honors in modern history. He then entered the family silk and textile business at Tiverton.

In 1932 he was elected to the Devon county council, on which he served for twenty years. He was also deeply involved in the Boy Scouts movement and the Federation of Boys' Clubs, and in later life was chairman of Voluntary Service Overseas (1964–1975). During World War II he achieved the rank of lieutenant colonel on the general staff of the Royal Artillery. Toward the end of the war, he landed with the paratroopers at Arnhem and was severely wounded.

In 1945 he became Conservative M.P. for Tiverton, and in 1951 he was made minister of pensions in Winston Churchill's postwar government. In 1953 he was given the more important post of minister of the Board of Trade and was admitted to membership in the Privy Council. He then became minister of agriculture (1954–1958), and subsequently, chancellor of the exchequer (1958–1960). He was successful in both posts, but drew the most attention as chancellor. In that post he replaced Peter Thorneycroft, who had resigned with his Treasury ministers in what Harold Macmillan, then prime minister, called "a little local difficulty," in which Harold Macmillan preferred to pursue a low interest rates policy, while Thorneycroft was attempting to push rates up. Within two months of taking office, Heathcoat Amory had produced a successful budget. For a time it looked as though he might be a possible successor to Prime Minister Macmillan; but he decided to retire at 60, saying that he did not approve of old men continuing to exercise political control.

On his retirement, in 1960, he was created the first Viscount Amory. He subsequently filled many distinguished positions, including those of high commissioner for Canada (1961–1963), chairman of the Medical Research Council (1960–1961 and 1965–1969), and chancellor of Exeter University (1972–1981). He died on 20 January 1981, a much-respected politician whose political skills had enabled him to obtain high political office.

Keith Laybourn

See also: Churchill, Sir Winston; Macmillan, Harold; Thorneycroft, Peter
References and Further Reading: Lamb, Richard, 1995, *The Macmillan Years, 1957–1963: The Emerging Truth* (London: John Murray).

Henderson, Arthur
(1863–1935) [FS, HS]

Arthur Henderson was a major figure from the Labour Party's trade union wing who served as foreign secretary from 1929 to 1931. An archetypal moderate trade unionist and Labour loyalist, he dominated the party for most of the first third of the twentieth century.

Henderson was born in Glasgow, probably on 20 September 1863, to Agnes Henderson, a domestic servant. When he was eight or nine, his mother moved to Newcastle-upon-Tyne, where in 1874 she married Robert Heath, a policeman. Arthur, his elder brother, and his younger sister were brought up as a chapel-going family. At 16, after attending a Salvation Army street meeting, Henderson became a "born-again Christian." He met his wife, Eleanor Watson, at the Wesleyan Methodist mission chapel on Elswick Road, Newcastle. Together they had a long and happy marriage, during which they raised four children.

Henderson was well known as a Nonconformist politician. He began his party involvement as a Lib-Lab within the Liberal Party, and went on to become a key figure in the early Labour Party. In his younger years he also took an active role in his chapel's affairs. Later he was prominent in national Wesleyan bodies, such as the Wesleyan Methodist Union for Social Service and the Brotherhood Movement (of which he was president). Before he was elected to Parliament, he was an active temperance lecturer.

Henderson was also an active trade unionist, and served as president of the Friendly Society of Iron Founders in 1911. His involvement in the union began after he completed an industrial apprenticeship in Newcastle. From his earliest days he was committed to conciliation, not confrontation, in industrial relations. The exceptional skill and moderation he demonstrated during a major local strike in 1894 won him renown. In 1903 he topped a poll to be his union's first parliamentary candidate.

He began his political career as an admirer of Gladstone. He served as a radical Liberal councillor (a member of the City Council) in Newcastle in 1892; and he was nearly one of the two Liberal candidates for the city in the 1895 general election to Parliament (but in the end the members of the Liberal Party declined to endorse him). However, he accepted the offer of the post of Liberal agent in the Barnard Castle constituency. He was both a district councillor

Britain's new home secretary, Arthur Henderson, is introduced to the House of Commons by his two sons, both M.P.'s, March 13, 1924. (Library of Congress)

and a county councillor for Darlington, and became the town's first Labour mayor in 1903.

In moving from the Liberals to the Labour Party, Henderson was following the lead of his union, which was represented at the inaugural conference of the Labour Representation Committee (the forerunner of the Labour Party) in 1900. He remained politically moderate, vehemently opposed to Bolshevism. His victory in the 1903 by-election in Barnard Castle made him the fifth independent Labour M.P. in the House of Commons. The 1906 general election increased the number to thirty. Henderson was chairman of the Parliamentary Labour Party (in effect, leader) from 1908 to 1910, succeeding James Keir Hardie. He held the party leadership position again from 1914 to 1917, following Ramsay MacDonald, who resigned after the outbreak of World War I.

Like other trade union Labour M.P.s, Hen-

derson supported Britain's war effort. He entered the cabinet in Asquith's coalition government, serving first as president of the Board of Education (1915–1916) and then as paymaster general (1916). In Lloyd George's coalition government he was one of the five members of the war cabinet (1916–1917), but he resigned after the prime minister disagreed on whether Britain should support Kerensky's government in Russia, Henderson favoring Kerensky and the Menshevik government rather than a Bolsehvik government that, Henderson felt, might take over in Russia if the British government failed to endorse the Kerensky government.

Freed from the burdens of office, Henderson returned to what he did best, organizing the Labour Party. He was a key figure in revising its policies, providing it with a new, socialist constitution, and reorganizing it as a national party. In 1924 Labour took office for the first time, with Henderson as home secretary. In this role he appeared orthodox and even timid, declining to honor Labour's pledges to reinstate the police who had been dismissed after the strike of 1919. However, he did have responsibility for a wide-ranging factory bill of 143 clauses, which would have remedied many employees' grievances, had it not fallen by the wayside when the government lost office.

Henderson was far more successful as foreign secretary in Ramsay MacDonald's 1929–1931 Labour government. Henderson won admiration at the Foreign Office for his willingness to make decisions and the quietly firm manner in which he ran his department. He carried out Labour's foreign policy, strongly supporting the League of Nations and making great efforts to secure international peace. He also made substantial attempts to end the isolation of Germany and the Soviet Union. He also made efforts to improve Britain's standing with Iraq and Egypt.

After Ramsay MacDonald formed the National government in 1931, Henderson succeeded him as leader of the Labour Party. However, like most Labour politicians, he lost his seat in the 1931 general election. He resigned as leader in 1932. After chairing the World Disarmament Conference in Geneva (1932–1934), he was awarded the Nobel Peace Prize in autumn 1934. He died in London a year later, on 20 October 1935.

Chris Wrigley

See also: Asquith, Herbert Henry; Lloyd George, David; MacDonald, James Ramsay
References and Further Reading: Carlton, David, 1970, *MacDonald versus Henderson* (London: Macmillan); Hamilton, Mary A., 1938, *Arthur Henderson* (London: William Heinemann); Jenkins, Edwin A., 1933, *From Foundry to Foreign Office* (London: Grayson & Grayson); Leventhal, Fred M., 1989, *Arthur Henderson* (Manchester: Manchester University Press); Marquand, David, 1977, *Ramsay MacDonald* (London: Cape); Wrigley, Chris, 1999, *Arthur Henderson* (Cardiff: GPC Books).

Herries, John Charles
(1778–1855) [CE]

John Charles Herries was never a political heavyweight but owed his appointment as chancellor of the exchequer in Viscount Goderich's government (1827–1829) to good fortune and his knowledge of finance. A worthy Tory politician of upright political character, he lacked first-rate political ability and commitment to political life.

Herries was born in November 1778, the son of Charles Herries, a London merchant, and his wife, Mary Ann Johnson. He was educated at Cheam and at Leipzig University, and in July 1797 was appointed a junior clerk in the Treasury. He was soon promoted to the Revenue Department. In 1801 he became private secretary to Nicholas Vansittart (Lord Bexley), who was then joint secretary to the Treasury; and in 1804 he drew up a pamphlet titled *A Reply to Some Financial Misstatements in and out of Parliament* in defense of the government. He became private secretary to Spencer Perceval after the latter became chancellor of the exchequer in the second government of the Duke of Portland (1807–1809).

He also filled a number of posts, most obviously that of assistant to Wellesley-Pole, later the third Earl of Mornington, who had been appointed chancellor of the Irish exchequer in 1811. Herries was appointed commissary in chief in October 1811, in which post he was responsible for raising money for Wellington's armies and for negotiating financial treaties with the allies in Paris in 1814. When that appointment came to an end, in October 1816, Herries was given a pension of £1,350 per year, which was later reduced to £1,200. For the next seven years he filled a number of posts that demanded his financial skills. He also married Sarah, daughter of John Dorington, clerk of the fees of the House of Commons, on 8 February 1814. Until 1823 he was effectively a talented financial administrator married into an administrative family.

In February 1823 he was elected as M.P. for Harwich in a parliamentary by-election and was appointed financial secretary to the Treasury by Lord Liverpool. His financial expertise paid off in 1827, when he was appointed chancellor of the exchequer in Viscount Goderich's short-lived ministry (August 1827–January 1828), becoming a member of the Privy Council in the process. A conflict between Herries and Goderich on one hand and William Huskisson on the other, over the appointment of a chairman to the finance committee, led to the early collapse of the Goderich ministry and its replacement by a ministry led by the Duke of Wellington. In the process, Herries was moved to the post of master of the Mint. He served briefly as president of the Board of Trade in 1830, until Lord Grey's Whig ministry forced the Tories out of office.

He was also secretary at war in Sir Robert Peel's ministry of December 1834 to April 1835. However, his career was by now an extremely checkered one. He retired from the Harwich seat in June 1841 and was defeated in his contest at Ipswich, remaining out of both Parliament and government office until 1847, when he was returned for Stamford as a Tory protectionist. He then gained office as president of the Board of Trade in Lord Derby's government (February to December 1852). However, he retired from Parliament the following year. He died on 24 April 1855, at age 77.

Keith Laybourn

See also: Canning, George; Derby, 14th Earl of; Goderich, Viscount; Liverpool, Earl of
References and Further Reading: Jones, Wilbur D., 1967, "Prosperity Robinson": The Life of Viscount Goderich, 1782–1859 (London: Macmillan).

Hicks Beach, Sir Michael (Viscount St. Aldwyn; Earl Aldwyn) (1837–1916) [CE]

Sir Michael Hicks Beach is one of the least well-known chancellors of the late nineteenth and early twentieth centuries. Yet he was one of the longest-serving chancellors of the exchequer, fulfilling the role in 1885–1886 and again from 1895 to 1902, a period during which he introduced seven consecutive budgets. Toward the end of his life, he was awarded the titles of first (although he was in fact the ninth holder of the title) Viscount St. Aldwyn (in 1906) and of first Earl of Aldwyn (in 1915). The latter title was granted him by a Liberal wartime administration, in recognition of his personal contribution to securing industrial peace.

Michael Edward Hicks Beach was born on 23 October 1837, the son of a landowner with 4,000 acres in Gloucestershire and 8,000 acres in Wiltshire. On his father's death in 1854, he inherited the land and a baronetcy. Ten years later, he was elected for his father's parliamentary constituency of Gloucester East, which he represented between 1864 and 1885, before representing Bristol West between 1885 and 1906. His income came entirely from agriculture. As a result, he faced financial difficulties during the agricultural depression of the late nineteenth century, which forced him to rent out his Williamstrep Park mansion, near Cirencester in Gloucester, and move to the manor house at Netheravon, on his Wiltshire estate. After the latter property was purchased by the War Office for an extension to the Salisbury Plain training area, Hicks Beach moved to the Coln St. Aldwyn Manor in Gloucester. He was always facing financial difficulties and always acted as his own estate manager, even when he was chancellor of the exchequer. While chancellor he was often helped out by private subventions, mainly raised by W. H. Smith, the newsagent. While out of office between 1892 and 1895, he drew a ministerial pension (such pensions were made available to those whose private income was inadequate to maintain their customary social position).

Hicks Beach was educated at Eton, and in 1854 went to Christ Church, Oxford, where in 1858 he obtained a first-class degree from the school of jurisprudence and modern history. In the early 1860s he married Caroline Elwes, but she died in childbirth 18 months later. He married again in 1874, to Lucy, the daughter of Earl Fortescue. The couple later had four children.

In 1864, he was elected M.P. for Gloucester East. He gained his first office in the Derby-Disraeli government of 1866 to 1868, as secretary of the Poor Law Board in 1868, before becoming secretary of the Home Office later that year. He served as chief secretary for Ireland between 1874 and 1878, and gained a place in the cabinet in 1876. In 1878 he moved on to become secretary for the colonies, a post in which he supported Disraeli's aggressive imperialist policies, particularly with respect to the Zulu War in southern Africa in 1878.

Out of office between 1880 and 1885, Hicks Beach used this period to develop his political position within the Conservative Party. He acted as chairman of the National Union (of Conservative Associations), a position he gained because it was felt that he could bring together the Lord Salisbury and Sir Stafford Northcote sections of the Conservative Party. He also made some useful speeches in the House of Commons, and he was responsible for moving a successful amendment to the Finance Bill (in other words, he opposed part of the budget) that brought about the end of the second Gladstone government in June 1885. In the subsequent, Salisbury government, he was made both chancellor of the exchequer and leader of the Commons, holding both posts from 1885 to 1886. It was a short term of office, in which he never introduced a budget—one of only four occasions when a chancellor of the exchequer has not done so. As leader of the House of Commons, he was closely involved in organizing the opposition to Gladstone's Home Rule campaign; and following the formation of a Liberal government in 1886, as leader of the opposition, he was involved in opposing Gladstone's Home Rule bill (for Ireland), although it is clear that he had some sympathy with Home Rule ideas.

The defeat of Gladstone's bill led to a general election and the return of Salisbury at the head of a Conservative administration that enjoyed a substantial parliamentary majority. Hicks Beach had hoped to be chancellor of the exchequer again but was given the post of chief secretary for Ireland—the same post he had occupied 12 years before. It was a brief appointment, since his liberal attitudes toward Ireland conflicted with the harsher tone of the Salisbury administration. An eye disorder saved him from embarrassment by giving him an excuse to resign in March 1887, upon which he was given the post of minister without portfolio (without a department) in the cabinet; however, he later withdrew entirely from the cabinet. When his eyesight improved again, he returned to government as president of the Board of Trade in February 1888, holding the post in a relatively uneventful period, until 1892.

After three years of Liberal administration, between 1892 and 1895, the fourth Salisbury Conservative administration was formed. Hicks Beach was appointed chancellor of the exchequer, and held the post from 1895 until 1902, during which period he introduced seven annual budgets. The first four of these budgets occurred during years of good economic conditions; but the last three were in periods of relative economic decline, during the South African/Boer War.

In his early budgets, those for 1895–1896 and 1897–1898, government expenditure increased from £98 million per year to £118 million; but revenues then were so buoyant that he was able nonetheless to reduce the national debt of about £650 million, by about £7.5 million per year. In contrast, his budgets in a period of growing government income were more cautious. From 1898 onward, he faced rising expenditure, mainly caused by the South African Boer War of 1899 to 1902. Government expenditure rose to £144 million in 1898–1899, £193 million in 1899–1900, and £205 million in 1900–1901. He financed three-quarters of the increased expenditure by government loans and the rest by increasing taxation. Nevertheless, he increased income tax three times, raising it from 8d (3.3p) on the pound to 1s 3d (6.25p), and raised taxes on tobacco, tea, spirits, beer, sugar imports, and coal exports. In 1902 he revived the shilling (5p) "registration" duty on corn and flour imports, which had been removed thirty years earlier.

Hicks Beach's budgets of 1900, 1901, and 1902 were considered conservative, although he did almost double the level of income tax. These budgets did not increase taxation substantially, overall. Income tax levels remained low, in comparison with what was needed in order to enable the government to meet its obligations; and the other taxes that were increased were indirect and were imposed on a narrow range of goods. This gave rise to the comment, "We have a government which dare not tax the poor and will not tax the rich" (Jenkins 1998, p. 99). To make up the difference, Hicks Beach raised substantial loans of £30 million in 1900 and £32 million in 1901.

Hicks Beach decided to resign the chancellorship in the wake of Lord Salisbury's decision to retire in July 1902. He must have realized that unlike many chancellors before him, he had little chance of becoming prime minister, for at that point he was almost 65 years of age. He was apparently content to remain on the Conservative backbench until the end of 1905, opposing Joseph Chamberlain's tariff reform campaign of 1903 to 1905. After he was raised to the House of Lords in 1906, Hicks Beach also opposed the Lords' rejection of Lloyd George's "people's budget" of 1909.

During this time, Hicks Beach was engaged also in numerous financial and industrial activities. He was an alderman of the Gloucestershire county council, and he presided over the Royal Commission on Ecclesiastical Discipline between 1904 and 1906. He died on 30 April 1916, a largely forgotten figure.

Keith Laybourn

See also: Derby, 14th Earl of; Disraeli, Benjamin; Gladstone, William Ewart; Ritchie, C. T.; Salisbury, Lord
References and Further Reading: Jenkins, Roy, 1998, *The Chancellors* (London: Macmillan).

Hillsborough, Earl of (Wills Hill; Viscount Hillsborough; Viscount Kilwarlin and Earl of Hillsborough; Lord Harwich; Viscount Fairford and Earl of Hillsborough; Marquess of Downshire)
(1718–1793) [FS, AC, HS]

Wills Hill, the first Marquess of Downshire and second Viscount Hillsborough, an Irish peerage, is best remembered as secretary of state for the American colonies and a fervent opponent of American independence. He was, later on, secretary of state for the Northern Department at the end of the ministry of Lord North, but his reputation was that of a courtier rather than a statesman. His lack of political understanding led George III to comment that he did "not know a man of less judgment than Lord Hillsborough" (*Dictionary of National Biography,* p. 975).

Wills Hill was born on 20 May 1718, at Fairford, Gloucestershire, England, the son of Trevor, first Viscount Hillsborough, and his wife, Mary. Privately educated, he was first elected to Parliament for Warwick at the May

1741 general election and continued to represent that constituency until he was made an English peer in 1756. He succeeded to his father's Irish peerage in May 1742, as second Viscount Hillsborough. In July 1742 he was appointed lord lieutenant of county Down, and in November 1743 he took up his seat in the Irish House of Lords, becoming a member of the Irish Privy Council in 1746. He married Lady Margaret Fitzgerald, sister of James, first Duke of Leinster, in 1748, thereby consolidating his position in Irish politics. In 1751 he was created Viscount Kilwarlin and Earl of Hillsborough. In 1754 he was appointed comptroller to the household of George II, as a result of which he became a member of the English Privy Council. He gave up that post to become treasurer of the chamber between 1755 and 1756. In November 1756 he was created Lord Harwich, baron of Harwich in the county of Essex, which gave him a place in the British peerage and in the House of Lords.

Harwich's political career moved up a notch when he became president of the Board of Trade and Foreign Plantations in George Grenville's administration, in September 1763. He resigned from this post in 1765, when the Marquess of Rockingham became prime minister at the head of a Whig ministry. This was a trying period for Harwich, as his wife died in 1765. Nevertheless, he returned to office the following year, when William Pitt, the Elder, formed a ministry that Harwich led as Lord Privy Seal. Harwich became president of the Board of Trade again in August 1766, but resigned from the position in December 1767 to serve as secretary of state for the American colonies—the third secretary of state, after those for the Northern and Southern departments—from January 1768 until August 1772. In October 1768 he was married for the second time, to Mary, Baroness Stawell, heiress of Edward, fourth Baron Stawell, and widow of Henry Bilson Legge, a former chancellor of the exchequer.

As secretary of state for the American colonies, Harwich was a firm opponent of American independence. In 1768 he instructed Francis Bernard, the governor of Massachusetts Bay, to rescind the resolution of the Massachusetts Assembly to oppose the "obnoxious taxes" imposed by the British and ordered him to dissolve the Assembly if this were not done. In June 1768, he arranged for a regiment to be sent to Boston. In December he had eight motions passed through the House of Lords condemning the actions of the House of Representatives in Massachusetts Bay and at Boston. When in May 1769 the British cabinet resolved to remove all the "obnoxious taxes" except for the one on tea, he circulated a harsh and ungracious circular to the governors of the American colonies. In August 1772 he resigned his office because he could not agree to a plan of settlement on the Ohio. Almost immediately he was raised to the title of Viscount Fairford and the Earl of Hillsborough. He continued to oppose any concession to the American colonies, vehemently speaking out against the American Conciliatory Bill in 1778. Nevertheless, Lord North asked him to be secretary of state for the Southern Department (home secretary) in 1779. Even in this post Harwich continued to express the view that "the independence of America would never be admitted in that house" (the House of Lords).

Harwich resigned this post with the fall of the North administration in March 1782. His political influence, which was never great, subsequently waned. He was created the Marquess of Downshire, in the Irish peerage, in August 1789. He died on 7 October 1793, at the age of 75.

Keith Laybourn

See also: Grenville, George; North, Lord; Pitt, William (the Elder)
References and Further Reading: Black, Jeremy, 1990, *British Politics from Walpole to Pitt, 1742–1789* (Basingstoke, UK: Macmillan); Whiteley, Peter, 1997, *Lord North: The Prime Minister Who Lost America* (London: Hambledon).

Hoare, Sir Samuel (Second Baronet and Viscount Templewood)
(1880–1959) [FS, HS]

A Conservative politician, Sir Samuel Hoare is best remembered for his role in the controversial Hoare-Laval Pact (1935) and his strong commitment to appeasement before World War II. His actions during this period brought him a reputation as one of the "guilty men" who

failed to check Hitler and who thus paved the way to war.

Samuel John Gurney Hoare was born on 24 February 1880, the elder son of (Sir) Samuel Hoare, later first baronet, M.P. for Norwich (1886–1906), and his wife, Katharine Louisa Hart. He was educated at Harrow and New College, Oxford. At first it looked as though he might carve out a career in banking, for he was a member of an old Norfolk banking family. He was also a landed gentleman by virtue of his marriage to Lady Maud Lygo, the fifth daughter of the sixth Earl of Beauchamp in 1909. Having opted for a career in politics, he unsuccessfully contested the Ipswich constituency in the 1906 general election. In 1910 he was elected Conservative M.P. for Chelsea, a seat he held until 1944.

During World War I, he served as a general staff officer with the rank of lieutenant colonel and conducted military discussions in Russia in 1916 and 1917 and in Italy in 1917 and 1918. After the war he was a prominent figure in Conservative politics and in the Conservative governments. He was one of the Conservative M.P.s who acted to remove David Lloyd George from the premiership of the coalition government in October 1922. Hoare also held numerous ministerial offices between the wars: secretary of state for air (1922–1924, 1924–1929, 1940); secretary of state for India (1931–1935); foreign secretary (1935); First Lord of the Admiralty (1936–1937); home secretary (1937–1939); and Lord Privy Seal (1939–1940). After the fall of Neville Chamberlain from office, in May 1940, Hoare became ambassador to Spain (1940–1944), before being raised to the peerage as Viscount Templewood in 1944.

In the 1920s he did much to popularize aviation. His arrival by air at Gothenburg in 1923, to attend the first international air exhibition, was a first for ministerial travel. And on Boxing Day, in 1926, he and his wife set off in an Imperial Airways de Havilland airplane on the first civilian flight to India, arriving in Delhi on 8 January 1927.

India occupied most of his attention in the early 1930s. As secretary of state for India, he was responsible for the drafting of the Government of India Act in 1935. During the Round Table Conferences on India, he attempted to come to some type of accord with Mahatma Gandhi; and he was a prominent witness when a select committee of both houses of Parliament convened to discuss the outcome of these conferences in 1934 and 1935. Although the resulting Government of India Bill was strongly opposed by Winston Churchill and a small group of dissident Conservatives, it was passed in 1935.

When Stanley Baldwin replaced Ramsay MacDonald as prime minister of the National government, Hoare was made foreign secretary. This was not an easy post: Britain had reduced its expenditure on military forces at the same time as Germany, Italy, and Japan were ignoring the League of Nations and rearming at a rapid rate. Britain's commitment to collective security through the League of Nations meant nothing unless Britain and France were prepared to act together, especially since the United States appeared to have adopted an isolationist policy. Hoare's foreign policy was, therefore, aimed at gaining time for Britain to build up its military strength. Toward that end he negotiated the 1935 Anglo-German Naval Treaty, which permanently fixed German naval strength at 35 percent of the level of British naval forces, although it allowed Germany parity with submarines. Since this treaty was concluded only two months after Germany announced an expansion of its army and the reactivation of its air force, it seemed to some observers to be a British endorsement of German rearmament.

Hoare's next problem was to deal with the Abyssinian crisis. Italy's threatened invasion of Abyssinia over the latter's disputed border with Italian Somaliland created a problem for the League of Nations, which should have acted collectively against Italy. However, the French had made it clear that they would not consider military action against Italy over Abyssinia. In a meeting at the League Assembly on 11 September 1935 Hoare attempted to rally the League by emphasizing the need for collective security: "If the burden is to be borne, it must be borne collectively. If the risks for peace are to be run, they must be run by all." He reaffirmed Britain's support for "the collective maintenance of the Covenant." This statement evoked little support for military action from the other member states of the League of Nations; but a committee of five was set up by the League to negotiate a settlement to the crisis.

A compromise was reached but was later repudiated by Mussolini, who ordered the Italian invasion of Abyssinia in October 1935. The League of Nations then retaliated by imposing limited sanctions against Italy. On behalf of the League of Nations, Britain and France negotiated together to produce the Hoare-Laval Pact. Under this agreement, Abyssinia would maintain access to the sea and sovereignty over some of its territory; but Italy would keep most of the Tigre district, which its troops had occupied, and would have the right to economically develop a large zone of land in the south and southwest of the country. When the plan was leaked to the press, many Conservative M.P.s protested that it was a reversal of Hoare's 11 September speech. As a wave of opposition swelled throughout the country, Baldwin and the cabinet decided not to accept the plan after all, although they had earlier approved its outline. Hoare opted to resign rather than withdraw the plan, largely because he believed that any other course of action would lead Britain into a war with Italy, without the support of France. In any event, Mussolini's Italian fascist state did what it wanted in Abyssinia; the League of Nations was discredited; and, many historians believe, Europe was thereby brought one step closer to World War II.

Hoare returned to Baldwin's government in June 1936, when he was made First Lord of the Admiralty. In May 1937, he was appointed home secretary in Neville Chamberlain's government. His main work in this role was connected with introducing the Criminal Justice Bill in 1938 and 1939, which introduced two new types of prison sentences, corrective training and preventive detention; abolished flogging; and provided for alternative punishments for juvenile offenders.

As one of Chamberlain's closest colleagues, Hoare was invited to join an inner group of four ministers in September 1938 during the events that led to the Munich agreement. Indeed,

Hoare was a great defender of the Munich agreement, since he felt that there was no alternative without French support and with Labour Party and public opinion at home being opposed to military activity. Hoare remained one of Chamberlain's key ministers after the outbreak of war, although he soon resigned the post of home secretary in favor of that of Lord Privy Seal. He subsequently became a member of the war cabinet; and in April 1940 he was appointed secretary of state for the air, for the fourth time. However, he resigned the following month, when Chamberlain was replaced by Winston Churchill. That same month, he was appointed British ambassador to Spain, a post he filled until December 1944. His main task during this time was to secure the release from Spanish prisons of about 30,000 Allied prisoners of war and refugees, which he successfully achieved.

Hoare was named Viscount Templewood about six months before he retired as British ambassador. He rarely spoke in the House of Lords, having effectively retired to his Norfolk estate to build Templewood, a small classical villa. He served as chairman of the Council of Magistrates (1947–1952); as president of the Howard League for Penal Reform (1947–1959); and as chancellor of the University of Reading from 1937 until his death. During these years he was the recipient of many degrees and honors. He died in London on 7 May 1959. Today he is still remembered for his commitment to appeasement.

Keith Laybourn

See also: Baldwin, Stanley; Bonar Law, Andrew; Chamberlain, Neville; MacDonald, James Ramsay
References and Further Reading: Cross, J. A., 1977, *Sir Samuel Hoare: A Political Biography* (London: Cape).

Holderness, Earl of (Robert D'Arcy)
(1718–1778) [FS, HS]

Robert D'Arcy, born in 1718, was the only surviving son of Robert, third Earl of Holderness, and his wife, Lady Frederica, coheiress of Meinhardt Schomberg, third Duke of Schomberg. Robert succeeded to the title of Earl of Holderness as a child in 1722, and was educated at Westminster and at Trinity Hall, Cambridge, though it appears that he never received a degree.

In 1740 he was appointed lord lieutenant of the North Riding of Yorkshire. He undertook various diplomatic roles, attending the king as a lord of the bedchamber in Hanover in 1743, being ambassador to Venice between 1744 and 1746, and serving as minister plenipotentiary to The Hague in 1749. On 21 June 1754 he succeeded John Firth, Duke of Bedford, as secretary of state for the Southern Department under Henry Pelham and became a privy councillor on the same day. He continued in office during the administration of the Duke of Newcastle but was transferred to the Northern Department under the fourth Duke of Devonshire. Holderness resigned the latter post in 1757 but was recalled a few days later, when Newcastle returned to become the First Lord of the Treasury and appointed him to succeed William Pitt, the Elder, in the Southern Department. After the accession of King George III—who reportedly complained that "he had two secretaries, one who would do nothing, and the other who could do nothing" (*Dictionary of Labour Biography*, p. 511)—he was dismissed on 12 March 1761. He played no active part in government after that and died in 1778.

Kit Hardwick

See also: Bedford, Duke of; Devonshire, Duke of; Newcastle, Duke of; Pelham, Hon. Henry; Pitt, William (the Elder)
References and Further Reading: Black, Jeremy (ed.), 1990, *British Society from Walpole to Pitt, 1742–1789* (Basingstoke, UK: Macmillan); Black, Jeremy, 1993, *The Politics of Britain, 1688–1801* (Manchester: Manchester University Press)

Home, Sir Alec Douglas (Earl of Home; Baron Home)
(1903–1995) [PM, FS]

The fourteenth Earl of Home became prime minister thanks in part to the Peerage Act of 3 July 1963, which enabled him to renounce his title and thus to run for a seat in the House of Commons. Home's premiership was a brief, transitional period between the resignation of

Harold Macmillan and the emergence of Edward Heath as leader of the Conservative Party. This was the last gasp of the old Conservative Party, which was being replaced by the newly emerging, more radical and modern type of Conservative leadership.

The Earls of Home (pronounced as Hume) owned substantial estates based upon their mansion at Hirsel, near Coldstream, in Scotland. Alexander Frederick Douglas Home was born on 2 July 1903, the eldest son of the thirteenth Earl of Home and Lady Lilian Lambton. He was educated at Ludgrove before entering Eton (at the same time as George Orwell [Eric Arthur Blair], the famous novelist), and later studied at Christ Church, Oxford. He distinguished himself at cricket, touring South Africa and Argentina, and graduated with a third-class degree in history. He became Lord Dunglass in 1918.

For four years, from 1927 to 1931, he spent his time in managing the family estates, shooting, and fishing. In 1931 he contested and won the South Lanark seat, which he held from 1931 to 1945, and again from 1950 to 1951. In 1936 he married Elizabeth Alington, the daughter of the headmaster of Eton and later dean of Durham.

By the late 1930s, Home had begun to attract political attention. From 1937 to 1940, he served as parliamentary private secretary to Prime Minister Neville Chamberlain, accompanying him in 1938 to the famous Munich meeting with Hitler, which led to Germany's takeover of Czechoslovakia. Like Chamberlain, Home viewed the Soviet Union as a greater danger to British interests than Nazi Germany. Home contracted tuberculosis of the spine in 1940, and therefore was not involved in the wartime administration of Britain. He became an evangelical Christian while in his immobilized state. In later years, he criticized the Yalta treaties among the Soviet Union, the United States, and Britain, which created spheres of influence for the Soviets.

Home (still Lord Dunglass) lost his parliamentary seat in the 1945 general election but regained it in 1950. His father's death in 1951 raised him to the House of Lords as the fourteenth Earl of Home. He intended to retire to his landed estates but was given the post of minister of state in the Scottish Office by Winston Churchill in 1951, in order that the government would have a minister resident in Scotland capable of defusing demands for Scottish Home Rule. Home held this post until 1955, when he became secretary of Commonwealth relations. He subsequently served as Lord President of the Council in 1957 and 1959–1960, deputy leader of the Lords between 1956 and 1957, and leader of the Lords from 1957 to 1960.

Prime Minister Harold Macmillan appointed Home foreign secretary in 1961. In this role he organized Britain's attempt to join the European Economic Community (the Common Market) in 1961, but did little else. When Macmillan fell ill in 1963, the Conservative Party and government split into two camps; the centrist M.P.s supported R. A. Butler for prime minister, and the constituencies supported Lord Hailsham (Quintin Hogg). With no liking for either candidate, Macmillan pressed Home's claim to the office, and Home became both leader of the Conservative Party and prime minister. This process necessitated that he renounce his title and be returned as M.P. for Kinross and West Perthshire; he did so and was duly elected to this seat, which he held from 1963 to 1974.

At first Home's administration was popular, for it heralded the expansion of the universities following the Robbins report on the need for educational expansion; but when Edward Heath, who was then president of the Board of Trade, revoked resale price maintenance and upset many small businesses, the ministry's fortunes went into decline. At this point, in 1964, the balance-of-payments deficit in Britain was spiraling toward £800 million, and Reginald Maudling, then chancellor of the exchequer, seemed unable to check this trend. Home's unguarded remark describing how he used a box of matches to work out economic problems seemed to confirm a general sense that the Conservative government lacked economic expertise. As a result of the rising economic crisis, Home lost the October 1964 general election by seven seats. He stepped down as Conservative leader in 1965, making way for the election of Edward Heath as the new party leader.

Conservative politician and future leader Alec Douglas Home (right) with Prime Minister Neville Chamberlain, 1939 (Hulton-Deutsch Collection/Corbis)

Nevertheless, Home remained active in politics, acting for a time as Heath's foreign affairs spokesman. In 1968 he chaired the Committee on the Constitution for Scotland, which recommended that a Scottish national assembly be established; however, this recommendation was not implemented by the Heath government, which came to power in June 1970. Home was appointed foreign secretary in 1970 and held this post until February 1974. His greatest challenge as foreign secretary was to secure a settlement bringing Southern Rhodesia back into the Commonwealth; but his efforts toward that end were unsuccessful. The only other significant act for which he is remembered today is his expulsion of 108 Soviet spies from Britain in 1973.

Home retired from the House of Commons in 1974 and was raised to the House of Lords once again, this time with the life peerage of Lord Home of Hirsel. His political activity was limited at this stage; but he did work to oppose the Labour Party's devolution campaign for Scotland in February 1979, suggesting that the Conservatives might offer "something better" (though suggesting no alternative). He died on 15 October 1995.

Keith Laybourn

See also: Chamberlain, Neville; Churchill, Sir Winston; Eden, Sir Anthony; Heath, Edward; Macmillan, Harold; Wilson, Harold
References and Further Reading: Dickie, John, 1964, *The Uncommon Commoner: A Study of Sir Alec Douglas Home* (London: Pall Mall Press); Home, Lord Alec, 1976, *The Way the Wind Blows* (London: Collins); Margach, James, 1984, *The Anatomy of Power* (London: W. H. Allen); Young, Kenneth, 1970, *Sir Alec Douglas-Home* (London: Dent).

Horne, Sir Robert Stevenson (Viscount Horne of Slamannan)
(1871–1940) [CE]

Sir Robert was chancellor of the exchequer for the last eighteen months of David Lloyd George's governments of 1916 to 1922. He would barely be remembered today were it not for Stanley Baldwin's memorable description of him as "that rare thing, a Scots cad." However, others among his contemporaries considered

Horne debonair and something of a high-society person; although he never married, he enjoyed the company of smart, fashionable women.

Robert Stevenson Horne was born in February 1871 at Slamannan, a south Stirlingshire mining town in Scotland, where his father was minister of the Presbyterian church. He was educated at George Watson's College and at Glasgow University, where in 1893 he gained a first-class honors degree in mental philosophy. From there he moved on to teach philosophy for a year at the University College of Wales at Bangor. He then returned to Scotland, was admitted to the Faculty of Advocates, and built up a Glasgow-based commercial and shipping legal practice. He became a King's Counsel (K.C.) in 1910. (The title indicates that he was qualified to deal with the major legal cases in the land. At the present time, the same status would be Q.C., or Queen's Counsel, as the title is related to the gender of the current monarch.) During World War I, he worked with Sir Eric Geddes in organizing the railway network behind the front line in France. After the war, he handled labor relations in the dockyards for the Admiralty.

Horne's interest in politics began when he became president of the University Conservative Club. That interest revived in 1910, when he ran twice—unsuccessfully—in the general elections for the seat of Stirling. In December 1918 he won the Glasgow constituency of Hillhead for the Conservatives. He was immediately made minister of labor, and he became one of the few M.P.s to make their first parliamentary speech from the dispatch box on the government side. In March 1920 he became president of the Board of Trade, succeeding Eric Geddes, and in April 1921, chancellor of the exchequer, succeeding Austen Chamberlain. In the latter post he was responsible for two budgets but delivered only one. The 1921 budget was delivered by Austen Chamberlain as Horne's budget, although it largely had been prepared by Chamberlain for Horne, who was engaged in dealing with various industrial disturbances and strike threats at that time. It mattered little in any case who prepared and presented the budget, for it contained few changes in taxation. The only significant item was the creation of the Geddes

Committee, which would report on government expenditure.

Horne's second budget was presented on 1 May 1922. Because of the depression, government expenditure was £57 million below the anticipated level; but government inland revenue tax receipts were also down, by the more substantial sum of £111 million. Given this situation, Horne decided that there would be no attempt to reduce the national debt through repayment via the Sinking Fund, which he proceeded to give away by reducing the standard rate of income tax from six shillings (30p) to five shillings (25p) in the pound. Despite this, the budget was poorly received, particularly by those who saw attempts to pay back the national debt as evidence of financial prudence, and those who felt that he had achieved his budget surplus by financial trickery. Philip Snowden, the great advocate of balanced budgets, and Labour's shadow chancellor, was vehement in his criticism. Indeed, Horne's critics proved correct, since the 1922 budget was among the least financially accurate of all British budgets.

When Andrew Bonar Law formed a Conservative government in October 1922, replacing the coalition government of David Lloyd George, Horne felt obliged to remain loyal to his coalition associates—particularly to Austen Chamberlain, who had stood down as Conservative leader in response to the removal of Lloyd George. Horne was offered the opportunity of being chancellor of the exchequer again when Stanley Baldwin replaced Bonar Law as prime minister in May 1923, but he refused the offer. He thus became a backbencher in the House of Commons until he retired from Parliament in 1937, when he was raised to the House of Lords as the first Viscount Horne of Slamannan. For the rest of his life he was involved in business as well as politics, becoming a director of the Suez Canal Company, and in 1934, chairman of the Great Western Railway Company. He died in 1940.

Although a competent chancellor, Horne seems to have lacked the ambition for a sustained and high-profile political career. His years in the House of Commons and as chancellor left few ripples in British politics.

Keith Laybourn

See also: Baldwin, Stanley; Bonar Law, Andrew; Chamberlain, Austen; Lloyd George, David
References and Further Reading: Jenkins, Roy, 1998, *The Chancellors* (London: Macmillan).

Howard, Michael
(1941–) [HS]

Michael Howard was born on 7 July 1941, the son of Bernard and Hilda Howard. He was educated at Llanelli Grammar School and Peterhouse College, Cambridge, where he became president of the Student Union in 1962. He trained for a career in law and was called to the bar through the Inner Temple in 1964. Indeed, he was counsel to the Crown between 1980 and 1982, and became a Queen's Counsel in 1982. He married his wife, Sandra, in 1975.

Howard entered the House of Commons after the 1983 general election, as M.P. for Folkestone and Hyde. He rose quickly in Margaret Thatcher's Conservative government. He was undersecretary of the Department of Trade and Industry from 1985 to 1987, and minister of state for the Department of the Environment between 1987 and 1990. In John Major's Conservative government he was secretary of state for the Empire and Commonwealth Office between 1990 and 1991, secretary of state for environment between 1992 and 1993, and a rather controversial home secretary from 1993 to May 1997.

His main problem as home secretary was a series of well-publicized breakouts from prisons in 1995. Choosing to interpret these events as indicative of operational failures rather than failures of public policy, Howard chose not to resign and instead attributed responsibility for the breakouts to Derek Lewis, the director of the prison service. In October 1995, after the publication of the Learmont report about one prison breakout, which blamed prison management for the escape, Howard dismissed Lewis. Also during this period many of Howard's immigration and parole rulings were overturned by the courts. These issues worried the Conservatives, since Labour's Tony Blair and Jack Straw projected an image of strength on issues of law and order. Howard's period as home secretary came to an end when Tony Blair formed a

Conservative M.P. Michael Howard speaking at a party conference in 1994 (Sean Aidan, Eye Ubiquitous/Corbis)

Labour government in May 1997, but Howard has remained an active member of the shadow cabinet.

Keith Laybourn

See also: Blair, Tony; Major, John; Thatcher, Margaret
References and Further Reading: Evans, Brendan, 2000, *Thatcherism and British Politics, 1975–1999* (Stroud, UK: Sutton).

Howe, Sir Geoffrey (Lord Howe of Aberavon)
(1926–) [FS, CE]

Sir Geoffrey Howe was one of the leading lights of Margaret Thatcher's "New Conservatism," filling the posts of chancellor of the exchequer and foreign secretary between 1979 and 1989. He resigned from the government in November 1990, and shortly afterward made a resignation speech that contributed to Thatcher's political downfall.

Richard Edward Geoffrey Howe was born on 20 December 1926 at Aberavon, near Port Talbot, in Wales. His father, Edward, who was born in 1890, was a solicitor. The young Geoffrey attended various schools in Port Talbot until, with his brother, he went to Abberley Hill, a preparatory school near Worcester, and from there on to Winchester, the famous public (private in the American sense) school. At the end of World War II, he was conscripted into the British army and served with the Royal Signals Corps.

After three years in the army, he enrolled at Trinity Hall, Cambridge, from which he eventually graduated with an upper second-class honors degree. From Cambridge he progressed toward a legal career, taking the final examinations for the bar in December 1951 and being called to the bar the following year. It was a precarious living at first, and he only managed to survive by virtue of £1,200 that his father had given him. It was at this time that he met Elspeth, the daughter of P. Morton Shand. He and Elspeth were married in August 1953.

Howe's interest in politics began when he joined the Bow Group, formed by Colonel Cecil Joel, secretary of the Constitutional Club and chairman of the Poplar Conservatives, who offered some of the younger talents of the Conservative Party facilities at the Bow and Bromley Constitutional Club (near Poplar Town Hall, on Bow Road, in London). The Bow Group was formed in February 1951. According to Howe, its purpose was to make the "Tory Party fit for *Observer* and *Guardian* readers to live in." Howe ran unsuccessfully as the Conservative candidate for Aberavon in 1955 and 1959. He was elected to Parliament in October 1964, with the relatively secure Conservative seat of Bebington, in the Wirral, south of Liverpool and on the edge of North Wales. Defeated in the 1966 general election, he returned to his legal career. In 1970 he was elected M.P. for Reigate, and in 1974, for Surrey East, which he represented until 1992.

It was in Edward Heath's Conservative government of 1970 to 1974 that Howe gained his first government post—that of solicitor general, a law officer who assists the attorney general—with the specific responsibility of drafting legislation on industrial relations. He was one of the architects of the Industrial Relations Act, which received royal assent on 5 August 1971. This parliamentary act established the National Industrial Relations Court (NIRC), which was to have jurisdiction over most industrial disputes, as well as the powers to advise the secretary for employment to impose a "cooling-off period" in industrial disputes and to require a ballot in cases where an impending strike would seriously affect the economy. The Court could also impose fines on unions engaging in "unfair industrial practices," to use the wording of the 1971 Industrial Relations Act.

On 5 November 1972, Howe was invited to join the cabinet as minister of trade and consumer affairs, with the primary responsibility of controlling prices in the British economy. The next day Heath announced a sixty-day freeze on pay, prices, rents, and dividends, and over the following days Howe was dubbed the "minister for keeping down prices" by the newspapers. Unfortunately, he assumed this role at a time when miners and other workers were attacking governmental limits on wages, and the government was defeated in the general election of February 1974, during a national strike by coal miners.

In the opposition between 1974 and 1979, Howe came into close association with Margaret Thatcher, who had replaced Edward Heath as leader of the Conservative Party. It was thus hardly surprising that she appointed Howe chancellor of the exchequer as she was forming a Conservative government after the general election victory of May 1979. Howe presented his first budget a little over a month later, in mid-June. This budget inaugurated a major shift in postwar budgets, simultaneously reducing direct taxation and increasing indirect taxation. Higher rates of income tax were reduced from between 83 and 98 percent on incomes over £25,000 to 60 percent; the standard tax rate was reduced from 33 pence to 30 pence on the pound; and the general level of value-added tax on goods was raised to 15 percent. This change of approach, which was considered a sign of the "Thatcher Revolution," was part of the process whereby the control of the state would be rolled back and private enterprise encouraged. This process involved a variety of actions, including the ending of exchange controls on the pound in October 1979 and the slashing of £3.5 billion from public spending between 1970 and 1980 (with further substantial cuts thereafter).

The four years when Howe was chancellor, from 1979 to 1983, saw enormous economic policy changes in Britain. The government was progressively reducing public spending and forcing industry to become more competitive.

The result was rapidly rising levels of unemployment—from about one and a quarter million in 1979 to more than three million by September 1982. Nevertheless, inflation fell from a peak of 22 percent in 1980 to 5.4 percent by the beginning of 1983, as a result of "monetarism," the tight control of money and credit. Monetarist policy featured the introduction of the medium-term financial strategy (MTFS), a plan whereby various targets—such as specific levels of monetary growth, public spending, and tax revenue—would be reached by stages over a four-year period. The 1980 budget was the first to lay out the government's MTFS, setting levels for the growth in the circulation of sterling and reducing the public sector borrowing requirement (PSBR, or annual state borrowing) as a proportion of gross domestic product (GDP) from 4. 5 percent (£8.5 million) in 1980–1981 to between 1 and 1.5 percent in 1983–1984.

Howe's 1981 budget was his least popular one. With the British and world economies in depression, the recession reduced tax revenues and increased expenditure in dealing with the unemployed. As a result he increased tax by more than £4 billion in order to reduce the PSBR. These tax increases were achieved by freezing personal allowances, imposing an extra duty on North Sea oil, and increasing the national insurance contributions of employees by 1 percent.

The 1982 budget reduced taxes by £1 billion in 1981–1982 and £3 billion in 1982–1983. Other than that, there was a move toward the idea of privatization, the process whereby nationalized industries were sold off to the public. The 1983 budget, Howe's last, was less controversial than its predecessors in the sense that the economy was beginning to recover and the PSBR was £2 billion less than had been expected. As a result, Howe produced a blatantly electioneering budget that restored the previously slashed 5 percent in unemployment benefits, raised tax allowances about 8.5 percent above inflation, and increased the child benefit (an allowance paid by the state to every family with children under the age of 16 to 18, according to whether or not the children were still dependent) to its highest level ever.

In the five budgets that Howe introduced, he had changed the balance of economic strategy. Direct taxation had been reduced and indirect taxation increased; privatization had begun; and inflation was being tackled by the imposition of strong monetary policy controls and credit control and by reductions in public spending. However, little of this counted in the general election of 1983, which was affected more by Britain's success in the Falklands War and the inept performance of the Labour Party.

In Thatcher's new government, Howe was offered the post of foreign secretary, which he occupied from 1983 to 1989. This was a turbulent time for British foreign policy: To begin with, Britain was operating against a background of increasing tension with the Soviet Union in the early 1980s—especially after the Soviets shot down KAL 007, a Korean civil airliner, in September 1983, at the cost of 269 lives. In the latter 1980s, when Mikhail Gorbachev began actively to pursue a rapprochement between East and West, the atmosphere of tension and uncertainty seemed for a while to increase as the communist regimes in eastern Europe began to topple. In addition, negotiations began in 1984 between Britain and China to ensure the peaceful transfer of Hong Kong and the New Territories to Chinese sovereignty—a process that was to begin in 1997.

In addition to these important developments, Britain at this time was primarily concerned with three key areas of foreign policy. First, it sought to maintain and strengthen the "special relationship" with the United States that had sprung up during the Falklands War. Britain deployed Tomahawk (nuclear) cruise missiles at Greenham Common on 14 November 1983, provoking a strong reaction from the antinuclear lobby. Britain also supported the U.S. Strategic Defense Initiative (SDI, also known as "Star Wars") to place installations in space capable of spotting and destroying nuclear weapons after launch. This special relationship came under stress in October 1983, when U.S. forces invaded Grenada, a Commonwealth country in the West Indies, and expelled Cubans, Russians, and Libyans.

The second major foreign affairs development during Howe's tenure as secretary was the

Anglo-Irish agreement of 1985. The Irish Republican Army (IRA), continuing its guerrilla warfare in Ireland and in mainland Britain, had bombed the Grand Hotel at Brighton on Friday, 12 October 1984, in an attempt to murder the leading government ministers. Within months of the bombing, the Irish and British governments had launched a joint effort to end the violence. Neither government wished to concede ground in its position on Northern Ireland; but after considerable negotiation, they reached an agreement to "work with determination and imagination" to improve cooperation in dealing with terrorism and to reconcile the two competing religious traditions (Catholic Republicanism and Protestant Unionism).

The third key area of British foreign policy was relations between Britain and the European Economic Community (EEC). Toward the end of 1985, the member nations of the EEC agreed to the Single European Act, which was implemented in stages, beginning in 1986, with the aim of creating a single European market by 1992. The single market would include a European Monetary Union, which would provide an exchange-rate mechanism (ERM) whereby currencies would operate within a grid and be kept within both minimum and maximum limits. It is clear that Margaret Thatcher accepted the idea of the single market but was not prepared for the European Monetary System (EMS) and ERM. At the same time it is obvious that both Nigel Lawson (chancellor of the exchequer) and Howe were becoming convinced of the need for the ERM to bolster the pound in foreign markets. Howe seems to have even considered going further with the EMS, believing that Britain should be at the forefront of developments in order to shape the future of Europe.

As a result of these disagreements with Thatcher, Lawson resigned and Howe was removed from the Foreign Office and made leader of the House of Commons and deputy prime minister. Howe's new roles were essentially a demotion in terms of their political importance, and Howe may have made a mistake in declining the post of home secretary, which Thatcher had offered him. Thereafter, Thatcher took every opportunity to demean and undermine

Howe in his new roles; and on 1 November 1990, Howe decided to resign because of the "growing difference which has emerged between us on the increasingly important issue of Britain's role in Europe." On 13 November 1990 he delivered a dramatic resignation speech in the House of Commons, in which he stated: "We have paid heavily in the past for late starts and squandered opportunities in Europe. We dare not let it happen again. If we detach ourselves completely, as a party or a nation, from the middle grounds of Europe, the effects of this will be incalculable and very hard ever to correct."

It was clear that the government was divided at the highest level and that Thatcher's style of leadership was being questioned. Howe, in a clear attack on Thatcher, asked how cabinet unity could be maintained "when every step forward risked being subverted by some casual comment or impulsive answer." In the end, he had faced a "conflict of loyalty" (the title of his biography). Shortly after this speech, on 21 November 1990, Thatcher resigned, her reputation having been wounded not only by Howe's revelations but also by other events. As for Howe, he left the House of Commons in 1992, and soon afterward was made a life peer in the House of Lords, as Lord Howe of Aberavon.

Keith Laybourn

See also: Heath, Edward; Lawson, Nigel; Thatcher, Margaret
References and Further Reading: Howe, Sir Geoffrey, 1994, *Conflict of Loyalty* (London: Macmillan).

Hunt, George Ward
(1825–1877) [CE]

George Ward Hunt was the eldest son of the Rev. George Hunt of Winkfield, Berkshire, and of Emma, the youngest daughter of Samuel Gardiner of Coombs Lodge, Oxfordshire. He was born on 30 July 1825, and was later educated at Eton and at Christ Church, Oxford. Hunt was called to the bar at the Inner Temple in November 1851, and worked as a barrister on the Oxford circuit. However, his real interest was politics.

After unsuccessfully contesting the Northampton seat in 1852 and 1857 as a Conservative,

Hunt entered Parliament on 16 December 1857, as M.P. for the northern division of Northamptonshire, which he represented for twenty years. His electoral victory followed close on the heels of his marriage to Alice, the third daughter of Robert Eden, the Bishop of Moray and Ross.

Hunt served as financial secretary to the Treasury under the fourteenth Lord Derby between July 1866 and February 1868, and then became chancellor of the exchequer when Benjamin Disraeli became prime minister in February 1868. He retired with the end of Disraeli's ministry in December 1868, having accomplished little. He was appointed First Lord of the Admiralty when Disraeli formed a new ministry in February 1874. However, he fell ill in 1877 and died in office, of gout, on 29 July 1877.

Keith Laybourn

See also: Derby, 14th Earl of; Disraeli, Benjamin
References and Further Reading: Blake, Robert (Lord Blake), 1966, *Disraeli* (London: Eyre & Spottiswoode).

Hurd, Douglas (Lord Hurd)
(1930–) [FS, HS]

Hurd's fame lies in his success both as a diplomat and as a politician, as well as a writer of thriller novels. He had risen to such an important political position by 1990 that he ran against John Major that year for leadership of the Conservative Party. (Major won.)

Douglas Richard Hurd was born on 8 March 1930, the grandson of a knight and the son of a baron. He was educated at Eton and at Trinity College, Cambridge. He married Tatiana Elizabeth Michelle Eyre in 1960, and after this marriage was dissolved in 1982, married Judy Smart.

Douglas Hurd first entered politics as political secretary to Edward Heath. He served in this post from 1968 to 1973—starting just before Heath became prime minister and continuing through the first three years of his ministry. In 1974 Hurd became Conservative M.P. for Mid-Oxon, a seat he held until 1983, when he was elected for Witney, which he represented until 1997. He rose through the ministerial ranks quickly, acting as minister of state for foreign affairs between 1979 and 1983, minister of state at the Home Office between 1983 and 1984, and secretary of state for Northern Ireland between 1984 and 1985. Thanks to this broad experience, he vaulted into the post of home secretary in September 1985—a position in which he assumed a high profile and from which he attempted to temper Margaret Thatcher's anti-European stance. On 26 October 1989, he became foreign secretary. In this post his steady diplomatic skills were called into play as Britain joined the United States in an international military campaign against Iraq and its leader Saddam Hussein, in the wake of Iraq's invasion of Kuwait. Hurd held the post of foreign secretary until he retired from government in July 1995, being replaced by Malcolm Rifkind.

At one point, in November 1990, Hurd was jockeying for the leadership of the Conservative Party and the post of prime minister. Thatcher's leadership had been challenged in 1990 by Michael Heseltine, and when she failed to get the number of votes she needed for outright victory, she was advised to step down. Three candidates stood for the second round of the election on 27 November 1990: John Major received 185 votes; Michael Heseltine, 131; and Douglas Hurd, 56. Seeking to weld the Conservative Party and the Conservative government together, Major kept Hurd on as foreign secretary.

In this role Hurd attempted to steer Britain toward a more balanced approach to cooperation with its partners in the European Economic Community (EEC). However, the big issue at play in the early 1990s was the question of a single European currency underpinning the EEC's move toward European Union. Although the Maastricht Treaty of 9–10 December 1991 agreed that the European Monetary Union would be established in 1999, Britain's delegates, including Major and Hurd, secured an opt-out clause, permitting Britain to join when it was finally formed.

Hurd resigned as foreign secretary in 1995 and left the House of Commons in 1997, becoming a life peer, as Baron Hurd, in the House of Lords. Since then he has been connected with the boards of various companies, acting as chairman of British Invisibles since 1997 and as deputy chairman of Coutts & Co. since 1998.

Keith Laybourn

See also: Major, John; Thatcher, Margaret
References and Further Reading: Evans, Brendan, 1999, *Thatcherism and British Politics, 1975–1999* (Stroud, UK: Sutton).

J

Jenkins, Roy
(Lord Jenkins of Hillhead)
(1920–) [CE, HS]

Jenkins has been one of the most controversial political figures of recent times. Having carved out a distinguished ministerial career in the Labour Party, he left Labour in 1981 to form the Social Democratic Party. He combined these activities with the role of president of the European Commission in the late 1970s and leader of the Liberal Democrat peers since 1987. Jenkins is also one of the few politicians who has become an outstandingly good academic writer.

Roy Harris Jenkins was born on 11 November 1920, the son of Arthur Jenkins, a Welsh coal miner who had won a trade union scholarship to Ruskin College, the "working-class" Oxford college, in 1908. Roy was educated at Abersychan Grammar School in Monmouthshire, Wales. Having achieved modest academic success, he went to University College, Cardiff, for six months and received private tuition in the writing of history essays from the historian Dorothy Marshall. As a result of her guidance, Jenkins was able to secure entry to Balliol College, Oxford, which was then the only Oxford men's college with competitive entry for commoners.

While at Oxford, he met both Denis Healey and Anthony Crosland, participated in the activities of the Labour Club, and in the spring of 1940, helped form a breakaway body from the Labour Club, which was known as the Oxford University Democratic Socialist Club. This action was taken in protest against the Soviet invasion of Finland and the procommunist line of the Labour Club. In 1941 he obtained a first-class honors degree. In 1942 he entered the army, joining the 55th Field Regiment, Royal Artillery, and gradually advancing to become one of the code breakers at Bletchley. He married Jennifer Morris at the end of the war and was released from military service in January 1946. He went straight into a post as a junior banker in the City of London. During this period he also wrote an 85,000-word biography of Clement Attlee, with Attlee's approval.

At this point, after one or two narrow misses, Jenkins won the seat of Central Southwark in a parliamentary by-election in 1948. So began what became an illustrious political career. Jenkins served his time as a backbench M.P., in the footsoldiery of the House of Commons, and then became parliamentary private secretary to the minister at the Commonwealth Relations Office. As a result of constituency boundary changes that came into force in 1949, he was forced to seek another seat, and at the 1950 general election he was elected for Stechford, Birmingham, which he represented for Labour until 1976.

At first he was considered an Attlee man, identifying with neither the Labour right nor the Labour left. However, by the mid-1950s he was identifying with Hugh Gaitskell, who became the new Labour leader in 1955. Jenkins's evolution toward Gaitskell's position was revealed in an article titled "Equality" in the *New Fabian Essays,* published in May 1952, in which he argued that nationalization was only a secondary interest of Labour. His polemical and historical writings, such as the *Pursuit of Progress* (1953) and *Mr. Balfour's Poodle* (1954), also had the effect of pushing him more toward the revisionist right wing of Labour and away from the Bevanites, who were suggesting the extension of public ownership and were involved in a daily fight for policies like unilateral nuclear disarmament. Jenkins had become a member of the XYZ dining club of Gaitskellites, part of Gaitskell's "Hampstead set."

It was at this stage that Jenkins also became identified with the cause of European unity. In 1955 he was given a two-year appointment to the Consultative Assembly of the Council of Europe, based at Strasbourg. During his period of office, prior to the Treaty of Rome in 1957, he was involved in the events that led to the formation of the European Economic Community (EEC)/Common Market. He became a strong advocate of European unity and was appalled when Macmillan's Conservative government threw away the opportunity to shape the political development of Europe and opted instead for the European Free Trade Association for countries not associated with the EEC.

After 1957, Jenkins contemplated a life of writing. He produced a number of historical biographies and seemed to be headed toward a journalistic career, especially after his resignation in 1960 from the opposition's front bench, to which he had been appointed in 1959. The failure of Labour to win the 1959 general election led him to become more involved in journalistic work for newspapers and the BBC. But Labour's success in the general election of October 1964 changed his direction.

Jenkins felt no loyalty to Harold Wilson, who had become Labour leader on Gaitskell's death in 1963. Nevertheless, it was under Wilson that he gained political advancement. He became minister of aviation in 1964 and served as home secretary between 1965 and 1967, and as chancellor of the exchequer between 1967 and 1970. In the first of these posts, much of his time was spent in dealing with his French counterpart in developing the Concorde aircraft project.

Replacing Sir Frank Soskice, Jenkins became, at the age of 45, the youngest home secretary since Winston Churchill in 1910. In this role he felt obliged to stand firm on the issue of capital punishment, and to press toward the legalization of homosexuality (which came in 1967). He also attempted to bring about a revolution in the Home Office by bringing in new blood.

In addition to these actions, he was closely associated with three other major initiatives dur-

ing his brief tenure. The first was the controversial decision to reduce the number of independent police forces in Britain from 117 to 49. The second was a commitment to improving race relations in Britain by integrating minority groups into British society. In regard to this effort, Jenkins said: "I define integration, therefore, not as a flattening process of assimilation but as an equal opportunity, accompanied by cultural diversity, in an atmosphere of mutual tolerance" (speech to the National Committee for Commonwealth Immigrants, 23 May 1966 at King's College, Cambridge). The third initiative was a criminal justice bill that included a number of measures to improve legal aid, to ensure that the owners of shotguns were registered, and to investigate whether or not corporal punishment in prison was needed. Perhaps most significantly, the bill also included measures to reduce the rising prison population (then considered intolerably high, at 33,000) by extending parole and restricting the powers of magistrates' courts to imprison for default in payment of fines. All three of these initiatives were proposed and carried through by Jenkins and his successor.

Jenkins's period as home secretary was exhilarating and strenuous, particularly given rising public concern about crime. His tenure was brought to an end by the devaluation crisis of November 1967 and by the ensuing decision of Chancellor of the Exchequer James Callaghan to resign from office. Tony Crosland was widely seen as Callaghan's likely successor; but since Crosland and Wilson did not get along, Jenkins became chancellor instead. This appointment created some tensions between Jenkins and Crosland, who were old friends, since Crosland had assumed that the post was his and since, as president of the Board of Trade, Crosland was expected to work closely with the new chancellor.

Jenkins had inherited a poor economic climate along with the difficult mandate to restore confidence in the British economy. His first task was to formulate a budget that would enable the government to deal with the mounting economic crisis. The 1968 budget introduced measures to increase indirect taxes and impose a surtax on direct income, raising about £923 million in additional revenue. Such deflationary ac-

Roy Jenkins, president of the European Commission, with Margaret Thatcher, May 1979 (Hulton-Deutsch Collection/Corbis)

tion was needed at the time, but it was insufficient to prevent a sterling crisis in November 1968. Financial instability continued throughout 1969. As a result, Jenkins introduced a mini-budget at the end of 1968 that increased indirect taxes by about £250 million. The April 1969 budget also contained measures to raise another £340 million by indirect taxes. With the country experiencing a modest improvement in its trade position that year, Jenkins's 1970 budget made tax cuts of about £150 million in what was effectively a neutral budget.

The Labour government was defeated in the June 1970 general election. This was an obvious setback for Jenkins's political career, but the blow was softened by his election as deputy leader of the Labour Party. It was a period dominated by a split within Labour over a future application by Britain for membership in the EEC. This conflict intensified when the Conservative government pressed forward with the European

Communities Bill. The issue that had so divided Labour was the party's decision to commit a future Labour government to holding a public referendum on the question of Britain's EEC membership. As a result of this decision, Jenkins resigned as deputy leader on 10 April 1972.

In February 1974, he again became home secretary. He seems to have accepted the appointment without great enthusiasm; but back in office, he introduced some important initiatives, most obviously the White Paper on Sex Discrimination, which was promulgated in December 1974. He also had to deal with IRA bombings and other terrorist acts, one of the worst of which was the Guildford bombing of October 1974, in which two public houses were bombed, killing five and injuring many more. The duties of home secretary were demanding, and the issue of Europe was distracting.

By the end of 1974 Jenkins had accepted the inevitability of a referendum on membership in the EEC. When the referendum was held in 1975, the Labour M.P.s were given the freedom to decide their own position. Jenkins was part of the Labour Campaign for Europe, which campaigned strongly up to the June referendum day. The overwhelming victory for the pro-Europe faction was a great relief to him.

When Wilson resigned as prime minister in March 1976, Jenkins was one of six contenders for the positions of Labour leader and prime minister. Although he was a credible candidate, he withdrew from the contest after the first ballot of Labour M.P.s, in order to ensure that James Callaghan, with whom he had not had the best of relationships, was elected rather than Michael Foot. Jenkins remained in Callaghan's government for several months before deciding to leave the Home Office in September 1976. He had been offered the presidency of the European Commission before Wilson's resignation, and now he decided to accept the offer. He took up his new duties at the beginning of January 1977, giving up his Stechford seat in the Commons. He served as president of the Commission until 1981.

His four years in this post were dominated by two issues in particular. The first was his attempt to develop the European Monetary System, which was blocked in November 1978 when Callaghan announced that Britain would not join the EMS. The second was the "Bloody British Question," or BBQ—Britain's attempt to reduce its monetary contribution to the EEC. This latter problem occupied much of 1980, as the attempt was spearheaded by the prime minister of the new, Conservative government, Margaret Thatcher.

On retiring from the European Commission presidency, Jenkins became concerned at the state of the British Labour Party. After Callaghan's defeat in the May 1979 general election and his resignation in 1980, Michael Foot had become Labour leader. At this point the Labour Party had split disastrously between the left and the right—the former wanting a return to the old working-class, trade union–dominated party of public ownership, and the latter denying public ownership and espousing a pro-European standpoint.

Jenkins led a part of the right faction—with Bill Rodgers, Shirley Williams, and David Owen—in issuing the Limehouse Declaration at the end of January 1981 and forming the Social Democratic Party on 26 March 1981. He unsuccessfully contested the Warrington seat in a parliamentary by-election in 1981, but won the Hillhead, Glasgow, seat at the beginning of 1982. This victory positioned him to become leader of the SDP in 1982, when he narrowly defeated David Owen, giving rise to a split within the SDP, which was to persist. At this stage, Jenkins struck an agreement with David Steel, the leader of the Liberal Party, that both men would run in the next general election as coleaders of an SDP-Liberal alliance. If they gained a majority in the House of Commons, Jenkins was to become prime minister. In the end, at the famous Ettrick Bridge Summit, it was decided that since Steel's personal political rating in the opinion polls was higher than Jenkins's, Steel would take a higher profile in the last ten days of the 1983 general election campaign.

The alliance won 22.5 percent of the general election poll of June 1983. Four days later, on 13 June, Jenkins resigned as leader of the SDP in response to Owen's threat to contest his leadership if Jenkins did not step down. Jenkins was replaced by Owen as leader of a parliamentary party of six M.P.s and joint leader of an alliance of 23 M.P.s. Thereafter, he played a limited role in the declining fortunes of the SDP and the alliance. A section of the SDP allied with the Liberals in 1988 to form the Social and Liberal Democratic Party; the rest continued as the SDP under Owen, before collapsing in 1990.

After resigning in 1983 as leader of the SDP, Jenkins played a less prominent role in politics and lost his Hillhead seat in the 1987 general election. However, after receiving the title of Lord Jenkins of Hillhead, he became the leader of the (Social and) Liberal Democrat peers in the House of Lords. Since 1987, he also has acted as unpaid chancellor of Oxford University. He has published about twenty books, and continues to write both historical biographies and polemical pieces.

Keith Laybourn

See also: Attlee, Clement; Callaghan, James; Crosland, Tony; Gaitskell, Hugh; Healey, Denis; Soskice, Sir Frank; Thatcher, Margaret; Wilson, Harold
References and Further Reading: Jenkins, Roy, 1991, *A Life at the Centre* (New York: Random House).

Joynson-Hicks, William (Baron Brentford; Viscount Brentford) (1865–1932) [HS]

William Joynson-Hicks, popularly known as Jix, was home secretary at the time of the General Strike of 1926 and is highly regarded for his service in that post. He was born in Canonbury on 23 June 1865, the eldest son of Henry Hicks, a merchant, and his wife, Harriet. He was educated at Merchant Taylor's School before being articled to a firm of London solicitors in 1882. He became a solicitor in 1887 and built up a considerable practice. In 1894 he met Richard Hampson Joynson, a Manchester silk manufacturer, and his only daughter, Grace Lynn. He married her in 1895 and added the name Joynson to his own name in 1896. He and Joynson were both philanthropic Conservatives, well known and in high standing in Manchester.

Joynson-Hicks showed an interest in Conservative politics and unsuccessfully contested the North Manchester seat in 1900. He also failed to capture the Manchester Northwest seat in 1906, being defeated by Winston Churchill. However, there was a by-election in 1908 after Churchill was appointed president of the Board of Trade, in which Joynson-Hicks was elected M.P. It was during this election that he earned the nickname Jix. He lost his seat in the general election of January 1910 and was defeated in Sunderland in December 1910, but was elected unopposed for Brentford in the by-election of March 1911. In 1918 he was elected M.P. for Twickenham, and he held that seat until he became the first Viscount Brentford in 1929.

As a young M.P., and particularly after 1911, he revealed great interest in the new technologies of aviation, telecommunications, and automobiles. During World War I, he developed a great interest in the Royal Flying Corps, and in 1916 he published *The Command of the Air*. At the end of the war he was created a baronet. He had a secure seat in the House of Commons, but found himself in opposition to David Lloyd George, who headed the coalition government. There seemed little prospect of advancement in his political career, and he busied himself with fringe political interests. He traveled to India in 1920 to investigate the shootings at Amritsar; and upon returning to the House of Commons, spoke in defense of the actions of Brigadier R. E. H. Dyer.

In October 1922, Jix was among the Conservatives who demanded the removal of David Lloyd George, and he was appointed to a number of important posts in the subsequent Conservative governments. In 1922 he was offered the post of parliamentary secretary to the department of overseas trade, in Andrew Bonar Law's ministry; and in March 1923 he was made postmaster and paymaster-general. When Stanley Baldwin became prime minister in May 1923, Joynson-Hicks became financial secretary to the Treasury, as well as a member of the cabinet and of the Privy Council. In August he became minister of health. He was in opposition between June and October 1924, during the first Labour government, but then became home secretary in Baldwin's second ministry, filling this post until May 1929.

His most important task as home secretary was to prepare the government for the General Strike of May 1926. In January 1926 he informed his cabinet colleagues that the government was prepared for a general strike by the Trades Union Congress (TUC) in support of the miners, should it occur. During the strike, between 3 and 12 May, he was responsible for maintaining public order and for disabusing Sir Herbert Samuel, who the TUC wanted to act as an arbiter, of the idea that the government would be bound by any compromise package offered by the TUC. In other words, Joynson-Hicks made it clear that the famous "Samuel Memorandum"—a list of the terms under which the TUC would call off the strike—was unacceptable to the government. He also appealed for special constables to maintain public order.

In 1927 he was responsible for the raid on Arcos Limited, which brought an end to diplomatic relations between Great Britain and the

Soviet Union, which was represented by that firm. In 1928 he was largely concerned with passing the Shops Act, which laid down the conditions of employment for shop assistants, and the Summer Time Act. His political career came to an end in May 1929, however, when he decided not to contest a parliamentary seat and was created Viscount Brentford.

Joynson-Hicks was a strong churchgoer throughout his life. He was a member of the Church Assembly and in 1921 became president of the National Church League. He was prominently involved in the defeat of the Prayer Book measure in Parliament in 1927, and was influential in getting Parliament to reject the amended Deposited Book Measure when it was before the House of Commons in June 1928.

Just a few years after leaving the House of Commons, with his health in decline, Joynson-Hicks died on 8 June 1932. Today he is remembered as a politician of considerable ability and is particularly credited for his early recognition of the potential impact of new technologies on warfare, and for the maintenance of public order during the General Strike of 1926.

Keith Laybourn

See also: Baldwin, Stanley; Bonar Law, Andrew; Lloyd George, David
References and Further Reading: Middlemass, Robert Keith, and Anthony John Lane Barnes, 1969, *Baldwin: A Biography* (London: Weidenfeld & Nicolson).

K

Kimberley, Earl of (John Wodehouse)
(1826–1902) [FS]

The first Earl of Kimberley served as foreign secretary for just fifteen months following his appointment to that post in March 1894, at the advanced age of 68. He was never a popular political figure but was an efficient and effective politician who led the Liberals in the House of Lords after Lord Rosebery's retirement in 1896. He can be counted among the many politicians who gained high office and were subsequently ignored by historians, although his title was used to name a famous diamond town in southern Africa.

Wodehouse was born at Wymondham, Norfolk, on 29 May 1826, the eldest son of the Hon. Henry Wodehouse and his wife, Anne. John was educated at Eton, where he earned a reputation for cleverness, and at Christ Church, Oxford. He succeeded to a baronetcy on his grandfather's death in 1846. On 16 August 1847 he married Lady Florence, daughter of Richard Fitzgibbon, the third and last Earl of Clare.

As Lord Wodehouse, he served as undersecretary of foreign affairs in Lord Aberdeen's coalition government (1852–1854) and in Lord Palmerston's first ministry (1854–1856). He was appointed British minister at St. Petersburg in 1856, at the end of the Crimean War, and held that post until 1858. He was once again appointed undersecretary of foreign affairs in Lord Palmerston's second ministry, holding that post from June 1859 until August 1861. In December 1863 he was sent off to Denmark, ostensibly to congratulate King Christian IX on his accession to the Danish throne but in reality to try to resolve the Schleswig-Holstein territorial dispute; the attempt failed. Wodehouse also served

as undersecretary for India in 1864, and in November of that year was appointed lord lieutenant of Ireland—an appointment he held until the collapse of the Liberal government in June 1866. His main difficulty in Ireland was to deal with the Fenians, a partly rural revolutionary movement. In an attempt to hamper the movement, he took action to suppress the paper the *Irish Press*. At the end of his period of office he was created Earl of Kimberley, Norfolk.

With the formation of the Gladstone government in December 1868, Kimberley became Lord Privy Seal, gaining a place in the cabinet. He succeeded to the Colonial Office in 1870. Here he was most famously involved in the annexation of Griqualand (1871) in southern Africa, as well as for the hoisting of the British flag over the diamond fields of southern Africa and the creation of the township of Kimberley. His administration was also famous for the organization of an expedition to secure British territory in West Africa, on the Gold Coast, which was being threatened by the Ashanti. He was also associated with the creation of the Canadian province of Manitoba from territory formerly known as Rupert's Land.

Gladstone's Liberal government was defeated in 1874 and replaced by Disraeli's Conservative ministry; but Kimberley returned as colonial secretary in 1880, when Gladstone formed another Liberal ministry. Kimberley's main task became the securing of British supremacy in the Transvaal against the demands of the South African Boer settlers, and the creation of settlement areas for the native African population.

In December 1880 the Boers took up arms and formed the South African Republic. Soon after, on 27 February 1881, they defeated the British at the battle of Majuba Hill. Kimberley's response was to insist that armed resistance must cease before a settlement could be negotiated. Operating through President Brand of the Orange Free State, Kimberley then passed proposals for negotiations to the Boer leaders, President Kruger and General Joubert. In the end, peace was settled on the basis of complete self-government for the Boers, within the context of overall British control, with native interests and frontier questions to be settled by a royal commission. Kimberley failed to get the district of Zoutpansberg set aside as a native reserve in the convention of Pretoria in August 1881. This failure to set aside a native reserve was seen as something of a humiliation for the British; but Kimberley stressed that even if the British had conquered the Transvaal, they would not be able to hold it. In December 1882 Kimberley was transferred to the India Office, and he remained there until 1885, his main achievement being the winning of Afghan support for the British in the face of Russian opposition. Briefly out of office in 1885 and 1886, he returned to the India Office in Gladstone's short-lived ministry of 1886.

In 1891 Kimberley became leader of the Liberal Party in the House of Lords. He was appointed secretary for India again in Gladstone's fourth administration, in 1892, simultaneously acting as Lord President of the Council. The pinnacle of his political career came when he was appointed foreign secretary in Lord Rosebery's ministry, in March 1894. He held this post a little longer than fifteen months, but his tenure was undistinguished, as he achieved little beyond a faltering agreement with the Congo Free State. (The latter offered Britain a strip of land along the frontier of German East Africa, but later withdrew the offer due to German opposition.)

After the Liberal government's defeat in the 1895 general election, Kimberley was in opposition for the rest of his life. He resumed the leadership of the Liberals in the House of Lords on the resignation of Lord Rosebery in 1896, remaining unreservedly committed to the Empire. He was generous in his support for Lord Kitchener after the overthrow of the Khalifa at Omdurman; and unlike most members of the Liberal Party, he strongly supported British operations in the Boer War in South Africa. By this time, however, he was ill, and he soon had to relinquish his responsibilities with the Liberal Party in the House of Lords to Lord Spencer, the Liberal deputy leader in Lords. Kimberley died in London on 8 April 1902.

Keith Laybourn

See also: Aberdeen, Earl of; Gladstone, William Ewart; Palmerston, Lord; Rosebery, Lord
References and Further Reading: James, Robert Rhodes, 1963, *Rosebery* (London: Weidenfeld and Nicolson); Matthew, Henry C. G., 1973, *The Liberal Imperialists: The Ideas and Politics of a Post-Gladstonian Élite* (London: Oxford University Press).

L

Lamont, Norman
(Lord Lamont of Lerwick)
(1942–) [CE]

Norman Lamont is most often remembered as the chancellor of the exchequer who was sacked by John Major for the economic mistakes he is supposed to have made, culminating in the infamous Black Wednesday of 16 September 1992, when the pound was ignominiously forced out of the European Exchange Rate Mechanism (ERM). After his dismissal in 1993, he became one of Major's most bitter critics.

Norman Stewart Hughson Lamont was born on 8 May 1942, the son of Daniel Lamont and of Helen Irene. He was educated at Loretto School and at Fitzwilliam College, Cambridge, becoming president of the Cambridge Union in 1964. He was married to Alice Rosemary, daughter of Lt. Col. Peter White, in 1971.

From his university days on, Lamont was steeped in Conservative politics. He was chairman of the Cambridge University Conservative Association in 1963. In 1965 he became personal assistant to the Rt. Hon. Duncan Sandys, the Conservative M.P., and between 1966 and 1968 he was employed by the Conservative Research Department. Between 1968 and 1979 he worked as a merchant banker with N. M. Rothschild & Sons. Between 1970 and 1971 he was chairman of the Coningsby Club, and from 1971 to 1972, chairman of the extreme right-wing Bow Group.

Lamont contested and failed to win the East Hull seat in the general election of June 1970, but won Kingston-upon-Thames in a parliamentary by-election in May 1972, representing it until 1997. His first government appointment was that of parliamentary private secretary to Norman St. John Stevas, M.P. In 1974 he was,

very briefly, minister of arts, before the Edward Heath government ended in early March. He was opposition spokesman on prices and consumer affairs between 1975 and 1976, and filled the same post for industry between 1976 and 1979.

When Margaret Thatcher became prime minister in May 1979, Lamont expected and promptly received a promotion. He served as parliamentary undersecretary at the Department of Energy between 1979 and 1981; as minister of state for industry between 1981 and 1985; as financial secretary to the Treasury from 1986 to 1989; and as chief secretary to the Treasury from 1989 to 1990. Despite his Thatcherite credentials, he was one of four ministers, along with Chris Patten, Malcolm Rifkind, and Kenneth Clarke, who refused to serve with Thatcher if she continued in office in 1990.

Lamont became Major's campaign manager during the Conservative leadership election, and was later appointed chancellor of the exchequer, partly in appreciation of this effort. His major problem in this post was caused by Britain's entering the Exchange Rate Mechanism, whereby sterling was linked in a close relationship to other European currencies as a restraint on market forces. Britain had agreed to enter the ERM in September 1990, Major having persuaded Thatcher not to follow her natural instinct to allow market forces to determine the value of the pound. On Black Wednesday, with European currency values plummeting, hundreds of millions of pounds had to be spent to defend the minimum value of the pound, forcing up the Bank of England interest rate by increments (it was at 15 percent by the end of the day). After spending enormous sums of money in order to defend the pound, Lamont was forced to withdraw the pound from the ERM.

Lamont felt betrayed by Major when he was sacked as chancellor of the exchequer on 26 May 1993. He gave a bilious resignation speech that described Major as being "in office but not in power." He also accused Major of dithering over whether to pull out of ERM on "Black Wednesday" and of holding meetings with pro-Europeans such as Douglas Hurd, Kenneth Clarke, and Michael Heseltine but of avoiding a quick emergency meeting with himself (Evans 1999, p. 181). Naturally, John Major has denied his account of events.

Lamont remained in the House of Commons until 1997, when he became a life peer, as Lord Lamont of Lerwick. He has been a nonexecutive director of N. M. Rothschild & Sons since 1993.

Keith Laybourn

See also: Heath, Edward; Major, John; Thatcher, Margaret
References and Further Reading: Evans, Brendan, 1999, *Thatcherism and British Politics, 1975–1999* (Stroud, UK: Sutton).

Lansdowne, 3rd Marquess of (Henry Petty-Fitzmaurice)
(1780–1863) [CE, HS]

Henry Petty-Fitzmaurice, the third Marquess of Lansdowne, has the distinction of being one of the youngest chancellors of the exchequer. He was also a prominent Whig leader for almost fifty years, although he never quite reached the political heights to which he seemed destined. He was born on 2 July 1780, the only son of William Petty, the second Earl of Shelburne and first Marquess of Lansdowne. His mother was Lady Louise Fitzpatrick, daughter of John, Earl of Upper Ossary. Petty-Fitzmaurice was educated at Westminster School in his youth, and later attended Edinburgh University and Trinity College, Cambridge.

Petty-Fitzmaurice launched his political career in 1802, when he was elected M.P. for Calne. From the start he was a very moderate Whig, committed to ensuring that the monarch was answerable to Parliament, and equally committed to reform. He focused his attention on financial matters, choosing as the subject of his first parliamentary speech the Bank Restriction Act of 1804. In 1806, at the age of 25, he became chancellor of the exchequer in the "Ministry of All the Talents," led by Lord Grenville. This brief ministry lasted little more than thirteen months; but it did permit the new chancellor to raise revenue for the Napoleonic Wars by increasing the property tax from 6.5 percent to 10.0 percent in 1806. He, like many other ministers, resigned in March 1807 when the king attempted to wrest from them a promise not to push for Catholic emancipation.

In 1807 Petty-Fitzmaurice became M.P. for Camelford; but on the death of his half brother in 1809 he was raised to the House of Lords as the third Marquess of Lansdowne. The previous year he had married Lady Louise Emma Fox-Strangeways, fifth daughter of Henry Thomas, Earl of Ilchester.

From 1807 on, Lansdowne played a prominent part in British politics, supporting the abolition of the slave trade and strongly advocating Catholic emancipation. The Lansdowne Whigs gave support to Viscount Goderich, who formed a ministry in 1827, following the death of George Canning; but with the exception of Lansdowne, who became home secretary, they gained only minor government roles in return for their support.

Lansdowne returned to office in 1830 when Lord Grey invited him to become President of the Council after he refused the proffered post of foreign secretary. He continued as Lord President of the Council under Lord Melbourne from 1834 to 1841, with a brief hiatus during the Peel government, in 1834–1835. Out of office from 1841 to 1846, he once again became Lord President of the Council in Lord John Russell's government. When Lord Aberdeen formed a ministry, Lansdowne was too ill to occupy a top office, but he remained in the cabinet without a department. In 1855, Lansdowne advised Queen Victoria to call Lord Palmerston to form a government, although he played no part in its political activities. It was at this point that he refused a dukedom, offered as a reward for his public service. The September issue of *Punch*, the political satirical journal, approved:

Lord Lansdowne won't be Duke of Kerry
Lord Lansdowne is a wise man very
Punch drinks his health in port and sherry.

After 1855, Lansdowne's political activities diminished as he gradually withdrew from politics. He died on 31 January 1863, a distinguished elder statesman who was content to be helmsman rather than captain of the ship of state.

Keith Laybourn

See also: Aberdeen, Earl of; Canning, George; Goderich, Viscount; Grenville, Lord; Liverpool, Earl of; Russell, Lord John
References and Further Reading: Jupp, Peter, 1985, *Lord Grenville* (Oxford: Clarendon); Mandler, Peter, 1990, *Aristocratic Government in the Age of Reform* (Oxford: Clarendon).

Lansdowne, 5th Marquess of (Henry Charles Keith Petty-Fitzmaurice)
(1845–1927) [FS]

Henry Charles Keith Petty-Fitzmaurice was born at Lansdowne House, Berkeley Square, London, on 14 January 1845. He was the eldest son of Henry Thomas, fourth Marquess of Lansdowne, by his second wife, Emily Jane Mercer Elphinstone de Flahault, Baroness Nairne, daughter of the Comte de Flahault and the Baroness Keith and Nairne. While his grandfather was alive and his father was the Earl of Shelburne, he was known as Viscount Clanmaurice.

Clanmaurice received his primary education at a private school in Woodcote, near Reading, and was enrolled at Eton at 13 years of age. During his last months at Eton, he was a senior classmate to the young Arthur James Balfour, who later became prime minister. After graduating from Eton, Clanmaurice attended Balliol College, Oxford. In 1866, before his graduation from Oxford with a lower-second-class honors degree, his father died, and he entered the House of Lords as Lord Lansdowne. He had already become the Earl of Kerry in 1863, with large estates in Ireland, and now acquired even larger estates in both England and Ireland.

As Lord Lansdowne, for much of the rest of his life, he was actively involved in politics. Between 1868 and 1883 he held minor posts in two of William Gladstone's governments. In 1868 he became a junior Lord of the Treasury, and in 1872, undersecretary for war. In 1869 he was married to Lady Maud Evelyn Hamilton, the youngest daughter of the first Duke of Abercorn.

From 1874 to 1880 Lansdowne was in opposition to the government of Benjamin Disraeli, but in 1880 he was appointed undersecretary of state for India in Gladstone's government. As the owner of estates in Kerry, in Ireland, he was opposed to Gladstone's policy of Irish Home Rule. However, before these tensions came to the fore, he was made governor-general of Canada in 1883, a post he held until 1888. In this post he became a great promoter of the Canadian Pacific Railway, which was completed in June 1886.

In 1888, Lord Salisbury, the new Conservative prime minister, asked Lansdowne to become viceroy of India, a post he held until January 1894. He was immediately faced with border disputes with Afghanistan and with an uprising in Manipur, a small native state on the border of Burma, in 1890. He also had to deal with currency disputes and with anti-opium agitation in England in 1892, which threatened some of the revenues of the Indian government.

Because of his split with Gladstone over Home Rule, Lansdowne was now a Unionist politician and was working closely with the Conservative Party. In 1895 he became secretary of state for war in Lord Salisbury's government. His first task was to reorganize the army along the lines of reforms instigated in 1890, which strengthened the power of the secretary of state for war. His next responsibility was to mount a military operation against the Boers after President Kruger precipitated the Boer War in October 1899. However, the operation did not go well, for the British military expedition was unused to fighting the extremely mobile war that the Boers initiated. Frustrated with British military failures, Lansdowne readily accepted the new post of secretary of state for foreign affairs, which Lord Salisbury offered him after the general election of November 1900. In effect, Salisbury had given up trying to act as prime minister and foreign secretary at the same time.

Lansdowne remained foreign secretary for the duration of the governments led by Lord Salisbury and then by Arthur James Balfour, and relinquished the post in December 1905. During his years in this post, he was largely responsible for the signing of the Anglo-Japanese Treaty of 1902 and the Anglo-French Entente of 1904, which was the basis of the alliance at the beginning of World War I. He was also involved in settling two disputes with the United States. Under American pressure, in 1903 he withdrew the British forces that had blockaded Venezuela, and capitulated to the demands of President Roosevelt on the disputed boundaries between Canada and Alaska.

From 1906 to 1916, Lansdowne became the official leader of the Conservatives and Unionists in the House of Lords. This occurred at an active time, since the reforming Liberal governments of December 1905 to May 1915 had accelerated the pace of change. Lansdowne led the opposition to the Education Bill of 1906, to the Old Age Pensions Bill of 1908, and to numerous other Liberal attempts at legislation. However, his main battle was over the "people's budget" introduced by David Lloyd George in 1909.

This budget sought to raise extra money, particularly from land taxes, and was rejected by the House of Lords. This event resulted in the general election of 1910, which weakened the power of the Liberals in the House of Commons; a Constitutional Conference in the summer of 1910; a Parliament Bill aimed at curtailing the powers of the House of Lords; and another general election in December 1910. Still in power, the Liberals threatened to create new "Liberal" peers if the House of Lords did not accept a reduction in its powers to block the finance bill. Eventually, in August 1911, the Parliament Bill was passed, reducing the powers of the House of Lords.

On the eve of World War I, Lansdowne was at the center of events. On Sunday, 2 August 1914, Lansdowne, the new Conservative and Unionist leader Andrew Bonar Law, and several of their close colleagues met at Lansdowne House to offer H. H. Asquith, the Liberal prime minister, their support for Britain's entry into the war in support of France and against

Germany; they were thereby attempting to force the divided Liberal cabinet to commit itself to supporting the French. In May 1915, Lansdowne became a member of the inner committee of Asquith's war cabinet, as a minister without departmental responsibilities. By the end of 1916, however, he was making a plea for peace—an action that might well have contributed to David Lloyd George's replacement of Asquith as prime minister in December 1916. Lansdowne's actions certainly led to his exclusion from Lloyd George's war cabinet, which left him even more time to discuss the need for peace. He published an open letter in the *Daily Telegraph* on 29 November 1917, demanding that the Allies clearly state their war aims, in the desire to bring peace closer. His views were supported by the Independent Labour Party and by Philip Snowden but largely attacked by the government, Parliament, and the press. Lansdowne published two other antiwar letters on 5 March and 31 July 1918.

Lansdowne retired from active politics after World War I, although he publicly expressed some disquiet at the creation of an independent Ireland in 1922. In 1919 he was struck down by rheumatic fever. Ill health dogged him for the rest of his life, and he died on 3 June 1927. He had had a long and distinguished career in British politics, fulfilling many ministerial roles. He was a good administrator and speaker and an efficient foreign secretary, though never quite a top-drawer politician.

Keith Laybourn

See also: Asquith, Herbert Henry; Balfour, Arthur James; Gladstone, William Ewart; Salisbury, Lord
References and Further Reading: Ramsden, John, 1978, *The Age of Balfour and Baldwin* (London: Longman); Roberts, Andrew, 1999, *Salisbury: Victorian Titan* (London: Weidenfeld & Nicolson).

Lawson, Nigel (Lord Lawson) (1932–) [CE]

Nigel Lawson was Conservative chancellor of the exchequer between 1983 and 1989, at the high point of Margaret Thatcher's premiership. An ardent Thatcherite, committed to the privatization of publicly owned industries and the rolling back of the state, he nevertheless resigned on 26 October 1989 over Thatcher's support for the ideas of Alan Walters, an adviser who believed that the British pound sterling should not become subject to the European Exchange Rate Mechanism.

Lawson was born on 11 March 1932 into a middle-class family in Hampstead, London. His father was a small but successful tea merchant in the City of London, and his mother was the daughter of a wealthy senior partner in a firm of stockbrokers. At the end of World War II, he went to Westminster, the famous public school (private in America), where he revealed a talent for mathematics. From Westminster, he went to Christ Church, Oxford, in 1951. Here he studied philosophy, politics, and economics (PPE), and graduated with top honors in 1954. Following his graduation, he spent two years in the national service (navy). In 1956 he joined the *Financial Times* as a feature writer, quickly moving up to become industrial editor, and finally, the chief writer in the *Financial Times*. A little more than four years later, he became the first city editor of the newly formed *Sunday Telegraph*.

In 1963 he took up a post in the office of Prime Minister Harold Macmillan, helping write his political speeches. He served under Macmillan and then Sir Alec Douglas Home until the return of Harold Wilson's Labour government, when he found himself out of a job. He eventually accepted the editorship of the *Spectator*. He was sacked from that post by the owner while unsuccessfully contesting the Labour seat of Eton and Slough in the 1970 general election. He was eventually successful, winning the seat of Blaby in the general election of February 1974. He held that seat until 1992.

By the time Lawson entered Parliament, his economic and political ideas were pretty much decided. Feeling that socialism was confined to a few "consenting adults in private," he opposed the political consensus that had seemed to exist between the political parties since World War II. He was a fervent believer in releasing capitalism from unnecessary state controls and maintained that the Conservative Party had to be a truly nationalistic party in Britain. It was these views that attracted him to Margaret Thatcher, and she to him. Her return as leader of the Conservative Party in February 1975 gave the impetus to his subsequent political career.

Lawson rose swiftly through the political ranks. From backbencher in 1974 he had become an opposition whip by 1976. When Thatcher was elected at the head of a Conservative government in May 1979, Lawson was made financial secretary to the Treasury, reporting to Sir Geoffrey Howe, who was the chancellor of the exchequer, and to John Biffen, the chief secretary. He was thus drawn into advising on Howe's first budget, of 12 June 1979, which reduced the top rates of income tax from 83 percent to 60 percent and almost doubled the value-added tax on many goods, even though the Conservatives had denied during their campaign that they would do this. This budget also signaled an attack on public spending. Currency controls were to be relaxed, allowing upward and downward fluctuations according to market forces.

In 1981 Lawson benefited when the cabinet was reshuffled to secure a Thatcherite majority. He was appointed secretary of state for energy, which carried with it a cabinet position. In this post he dealt with the nationalized industries, particularly coal, gas, and electricity. His main concern seems to have been to prepare for the expected coal strike, which, it was believed, would come once Arthur Scargill replaced Joe Gormley as president of the National Union of Mineworkers in April 1982. It was Lawson who replaced Derek Ezra as chairman of the National Coal Board with Ian McGregor, who was later responsible for moving toward the closure of mines that could not compete in the energy market. These mine closures spawned the year-long miners' strike in 1984–1985.

Well before that strike, Lawson had moved on. Following Thatcher's success in the 1983 general election, she appointed him chancellor of the exchequer, replacing Sir Geoffrey Howe. As chancellor, Lawson had two main objectives. The first was to reform the tax system and lighten the tax burden in Britain. The second was to reform the international financial arrangements in order to encourage greater stability and to exert more influence over inflation. Lawson achieved the first objective, which he had formalized in his medium-term financial strategy (MTFS) while serving under Howe. This strategy provided targets for reducing the supply of money in the economy and reducing the level of government borrowing. In effect it meant reducing some, though by no means all, public spending; reforming the tax system; and reducing the tax burden.

He introduced six budgets between 1984 and 1989, the first five of which abolished certain taxes. For instance, the 1984 budget abolished both the national insurance surcharge and the investment income surcharge. He also removed some tax allowances and arrangements that he saw as anachronistic within a modern tax system: tax relief on life insurance went in the 1985 budget (operative from 1986); tax exemptions on lump sums received as part of a pension deal went in 1985; and the 1988 budget provided tax relief of up to £30,000 per mortgage rather than £30,000 per person (allowing unmarried couples to claim £60,000 relief, whereas married couples typically could obtain only a £30,000 allowance). The most memorable tax change, however, was his reduction of the top rate of income tax to 40 percent, from the 60 percent level set by Howe in 1979.

The economy fluctuated, and the budgets that Lawson introduced were for the most part neutral. The exception to this rule was the budget of 1987, a preelection budget that reduced the standard rate of tax from 29p to 27p on the pound. Britain was plagued by high inflation rates in the mid-1980s, and these rates rose to about 14 percent by 1988, in the wake of the expansionary and inflationary preelection budget of 1987. Yet Lawson's budget was only partly to blame for Britain's inflation problems. International pressures on the pound, which led to immense fluctuations in the value of the pound from time to time, added to inflationary difficulties. In 1984 and 1985 the pound was subjected to immense speculative pressures, which caused its value to fall, particularly in July 1984. There was a minor sterling crisis in 1986; and the pound again succumbed to market pressure following "Black Monday" (19 October 1987) and the Wall Street crash. The cost of British imports soared as the pound fell, further increasing inflationary pressures.

How was Britain to deal with these international pressures?

To Lawson the answer lay in international financial reforms to ensure that currencies were more stable. He had been convinced of this need since the early 1970s. In the mid-1980s the issue came to the fore with the signing of the Single European Act of 1985, which went into force in 1986. The aim of the European Economic Community was to create a single market in Europe by 1992 that eventually would lead to a European Monetary Union (EMU). Lawson was opposed to the overall idea of the EMU but was attracted to the part of this process that involved the member nations of the European Economic Community signing onto a commitment to an exchange rate mechanism (ERM) whereby all participating nations would maintain their currency values within a grid of exchanges, keeping within the agreed top and bottom levels. He felt that this mechanism could bolster the pound against the speculative forays that were affecting it in the 1980s.

On this point his views conflicted with those of Thatcher, who was decidedly anti-European in most matters. Lawson found Thatcher totally opposed to the ERM. The conflict between them came to a head in 1989. In a meeting with Lawson on 3 May 1989, speaking of the ERM, Thatcher stressed that she did not want him to raise the subject again. She added, "I must prevail." Nevertheless, Lawson made a case to the House of Commons on 12 June 1989 for the ERM, stating, "It would reduce exchange rate fluctuations and we would be able to use it to assist us in our anti-inflationary policy." Shortly afterward, on 24 July 1989, Sir Geoffrey Howe, who was associated with Lawson in dealing with Thatcher on the ERM, was relieved of his post as foreign secretary and given the posts of leader of the House of Commons and deputy prime minister. These new positions were less important than the office of home secretary, which he otherwise might have had, and allowed Thatcher to ignore him and belittle him on his way out of government.

At this point, Lawson sensed that his own position was becoming untenable. On 25 October 1989 he spoke with Thatcher again about

Britain's mounting economic problems, and added: "I do not want to talk about Alan Walters now, but we must have a talk about him very soon. There is a problem there" (Lawson 1992). However, it was clear that Thatcher felt that her authority over economic matters would be destroyed if Alan Walters were removed. As a result Lawson resigned on 26 October 1989, suggesting, in his resignation letter, that there needed to be "full agreement between the Prime Minister and the Chancellor of the Exchequer" if economic policy were to be properly handled. His letter further stated, "Recent events have confirmed that this essential requirement cannot be satisfied so long as Alan Walters remains your personal economic adviser." Despite his resignation as chancellor, Lawson remained committed to supporting the government from the backbench.

Thatcher could not give up Walters, but she begged Lawson to remain chancellor. Ironically, less than a year later, on 5 October 1990, Thatcher's government committed itself to joining the ERM the following weekend. Even Walters had come to accept that conditions had changed and that membership in the ERM was more desirable than he had previously believed.

As for Lawson, he remained in the House of Commons until the 1992 general election, after which he was given a life peerage, becoming Lord Lawson in 1992. Since then he has published his massive memoirs, *The View from No. 11* (1992). He remains active in the House of Lords.

Keith Laybourn

See also: Heath, Edward; Home, Sir Alec Douglas; Howe, Sir Geoffrey; Macmillan, Harold; Thatcher, Margaret
References and Further Reading: Lawson, Nigel, 1992, *The View from No. 11: Memoirs of a Tory Radical* (London: Corgi).

Le Despenser, Lord (Sir Francis Dashwood; Baron Le Despenser) (1708–1781) [CE]

Francis Dashwood, Baron Le Despenser, was an ineffective chancellor in the government of the Earl of Bute. He was born in December 1708, the only son of Sir Francis Dashwood, the first baron, and his second wife, Mary, the second daughter of Vere Fane, Baron Le Despenser and fourth Earl of Westmoreland. Francis was educated privately and at Charterhouse. He inherited his father's estates at age 16, and embarked on a life of pleasure and debauchery, being a member of the Beefsteak and Hellfire clubs, and later a leading member of the Dilettante Society. He toured Europe; and while in Russia, masquerading as Charles XII, he attempted to become the lover of Tsarina Anne. On his return to England he joined the household of Frederick Lewis, the Prince of Wales. After his uncle the Earl of Westmoreland was dismissed from his position as colonel of the first troop of horse guards, Dashwood became a strong opponent of Walpole's administration.

Dashwood's parliamentary career began with the 1741 general election, in which he won a seat for New Romney. He opposed Sir Robert Walpole, who was shortly to fall from power; and after Walpole fell, he remained in opposition as a supporter of the Prince of Wales and an opponent of George II's governments. He was returned for New Romney again in both the 1747 and 1751 general elections, and became a supporter of George Bubb Dodington (Lord Melcombe), who was a vehement opponent of Walpole. It was during this period that he married Sarah Gould, the widow of Sir Richard Ellis, the third Baron Wyeham. However, marriage does not seem to have settled him down, for in 1745 he founded the famous brotherhood known as "The Knights of St. Francis of Wycombe," whose motto was "Love and Friendship." There were 24 "monks" in this "Franciscan" order (a denomination based solely on Dashwood's Christian name). Dashwood, acting as grand master, used a communion cup to pour out libations to heathen deities. The group included Frederick, Prince of Wales; the earls of Bute, Sandwich, and Carhampton; Bubb Dodington; and the Duke of Queensbury.

Dashwood was reelected as M.P. for New Romney in 1754. In March 1761 he was returned as M.P. for Weymouth and Melcombe Regis, a seat to which he was reelected in 1762. It was at this point that he began to gain political honors. He was appointed treasurer of the chamber and a privy councillor in March 1761, and became chancellor of the exchequer in June 1762, in the Earl of Bute's ministry. He performed poorly as chancellor, did little of worth, and retired with the Bute ministry on 8 April 1763. Shortly afterward he became the fifteenth Baron Le Despenser. Thereafter he almost disappeared from political activity, although he emerged briefly to denounce John Wilkes, his one-time friend, for his "Essay on Woman." Le Despenser died after a long illness, on 11 December 1781.

Keith Laybourn

See also: Bute, Earl of
References and Further Reading: Black, Jeremy (ed.), 1990, *British Politics and Society from Walpole to Pitt, 1742–1789* (Basingstoke, UK: Macmillan).

Leeds, Duke of (Francis Osborne; Marquess of Carmarthen)
(1751–1799) [FS]

Francis Godolphin Osborne was born on 29 January 1751, the youngest son of Thomas, fourth Duke of Leeds, and his wife Lady Mary Godolphin, heiress of Francis, second Earl of Godolphin. He was educated at Westminster School and at Christ Church, Oxford. He became the Marquess of Carmarthen in June 1767, while at Oxford. In November 1773 he married Lady Amelia, the heiress of Robert D'Arcy, fourth Earl of Holderness. The marriage was brief, and the couple divorced in 1779.

Carmarthen, who was a Welsh M.P. and had no automatic right to enter the House of Lords at Westminster, London, was elected M.P. for Ely, in Suffolk, in 1774. He voted consistently with Lord North's government, except that he voted in favor of the third reading of the bill regulating the government of Massachusetts. In the general election of October 1774, he became M.P. for Helston in Cornwall. Soon afterward, in February 1775, when Lord North began to push for conciliation between Britain and America, Carmarthen spoke out in opposition to this move. Carmarthen lost his seat as a result of a petition, but in 1776 he entered the House of Lords, as Baron Osborne of Kiveton in Yorkshire. He held an appointment as Lord of the Bedchamber until 1777, when he became Lord Chamberlain in the queen's household. In 1778, he became lord lieutenant of the East Riding, in Yorkshire. He remained staunchly opposed to Lord North on the issue of American grievances, and eventually left his official posts in 1780.

Carmarthen remained active in politics and was restored to the lord lieutenancy of East Yorkshire with the formation of the second government of the Marquess of Rockingham in March 1782. At this time he was also appointed ambassador-extraordinary and minister-plenipotentiary to Paris. Before he could take up his new post abroad, William Pitt, the Younger, became prime minister of a Tory administration and appointed him secretary of state for foreign affairs on 23 December 1783. He held this post until April 1791.

The driving force behind his foreign policy was the goal of forming alliances with Russia and Austria and of destroying the existing alliance between Austria and France. He also defended Pitt's commercial treaty with France in 1787. He was married, for the second time, on 11 October 1788, to Catherine Anguish. His personal position was further enhanced in March 1789, when he succeeded his father as the Duke of Leeds; but soon afterward, in April 1791, he resigned his foreign affairs post over the issue of Russian armament.

He remained a staunch supporter of the war against France and strongly opposed Lord Lansdowne's motion in favor of peace in 1794. He was also implacably opposed to parliamentary reform, suggesting in 1797 that it was "a most dangerous remedy to resort to" (*Dictionary of National Biography*, p. 1182). He died on 31 January 1799, a respected aristocratic politician of modest political abilities.

Keith Laybourn

See also: North, Lord; Pitt, William (the Younger); Rockingham, Marquess of
References and Further Reading: Black, Jeremy, 1994, *British Foreign Policy in the Age of Revolutions, 1783–1793* (Cambridge: Cambridge University Press).

Legge, Henry
(1708–1764) [CE]

Henry Bilson Legge, chancellor of the exchequer, was one of the most able financiers of his day. Born on 29 May 1708, to William, first Duke of Dartmouth, and his wife, Lady Anne Finch, daughter of Heneage, the first Earl of Aylesford.

Legge was educated at Christ Church, Oxford. He married the Hon. Mary Stawall in 1750, the heiress of Edward, fourth and last Baron Stawall, and adopted the additional surname of Bilson in 1754, as a result of the will of his father's first cousin, Leonard Bilson, which conferred property on him.

Legge was not an impressive political figure but served in many public offices. In October 1739 he was appointed secretary of Ireland. In 1740 he became M.P. for East Looe, Cornwall. He held the Orford seat in Suffolk from 1741 until 1759, when he switched to the Hampshire seat, which he held until his death in 1764.

A supporter of Robert Walpole and the Whig cause, Legge lost his position in Ireland on Walpole's downfall in 1742. That July, he became surveyor-general of the woods and forests north and south of the Trent. He filled many other minor political posts in his early political career, becoming Lord of the Admiralty in April 1745 and Lord of the Treasury in 1747. In January 1748 he was appointed envoy extraordinary to the king of Prussia, and in 1749 he became treasurer of the navy. He also performed many other roles in the Whig cause.

He first rose to political prominence when he became chancellor of the exchequer in the ministry of the first Duke of Newcastle in April 1754. He kept this post under the Duke of Devonshire, whose short-lived ministry was formed in November 1756 as a compromise, resolving a conflict between William Pitt, the Elder, and the Duke of Newcastle over the conduct of the Seven Years' War (1756–1763). In this post he was best known for having introduced a national lottery to supplement government funds. He was soon out of office, but returned as chancellor of the exchequer in July 1757, in the joint Whig-Tory ministry of Newcastle and Pitt. In this role, wishing to raise money for the war, he raised taxes on houses and windows. He was dismissed as chancellor in March 1761, but continued to represent his constituency in the House of Commons.

Remaining a government outsider from that point on, he staunchly opposed the terms for the settlement of the Seven Years' War. He died on 23 August 1764. Today he is generally remembered as a financier of some ability and a politician of no real consequence.

Keith Laybourn

See also: Devonshire, Duke of; Newcastle, Duke of; Pitt, William (the Elder); Walpole, Sir Robert
References and Further Reading: Black, Jeremy, 1992, *Pitt the Elder* (Cambridge: Cambridge University Press); Browning, Reed, 1975, *The Duke of Newcastle* (New Haven, CT, and London: Yale University Press).

Lewis, Sir George Cornewall
(1806–1863) [CE, HS]

Sir George Cornewall Lewis was a prolific writer and a prominent politician who proved an effective chancellor of the exchequer and home secretary in the Liberal administrations of Lord Palmerston. He was born on 21 April 1806, the elder son of Thomas Frankland Lewis and his first wife, Harriet Cornewall, and was educated at Eton and at Oxford. He then trained in the law and joined the Oxford circuit in 1831. However, owing to ill health, he soon decided to pursue a career in literature, making good use of his command of half a dozen languages. His legal skills also brought him occasional work in public investigations.

In 1833 he was appointed assistant commissioner to inquire and report on the condition of the poor in Ireland, and in 1834 he became a member of a commission of inquiry into religious and other instruction in Ireland. This was followed, in 1836, by his appointment as joint commissioner to inquire into the affairs of Malta, focusing on the political and economic condition of the island and the changes in its laws. In 1839 he replaced his father as one of the Poor Law commissioners of England and Wales. This was a thankless task; during his seven years in this office, he and his fellow commissioners were continually attacked by authorities who wished no changes in the Poor Law structure, and were berated as a result of the inquiry into the management of the Andover workhouse in 1846, a notorious case of cruelty.

In August 1847, Lewis was elected to the House of Commons as Liberal M.P. for Hertfordshire, and that November he became one of the secretaries of the Board of Control in Lord John Russell's first ministry. An able young man, he began to rise in government circles by performing well in a number of junior government posts, most notably those of undersecretary at the Home Department in 1848 and of financial secretary to the Treasury in 1850. He lost his seat in the general election of July 1852 and became, for a time, editor of the *Edinburgh Review*, one of the famous radical journals of the day.

In 1855, following the death of his father, he returned to the House of Commons as M.P. for Radnor boroughs, his father's old seat, and was immediately appointed chancellor of the exchequer in Lord Palmerston's first ministry, becoming a member of the Privy Council in the process. In drafting his first budget, he faced a £23 million deficit—a problem that he surmounted largely by borrowing and by increasing income tax from 14d to 16d in the pound (then 240 pence) and by raising duties on sugar, tea, coffee, and spirits. His 1856 budget also borrowed money to pay for the cost of the Crimean War; but in 1857 he more than halved income tax from 16d to 7d in the pound.

When Palmerston formed his second ministry, in 1859, Lewis was replaced by William Ewart Gladstone as chancellor and in return accepted the post of home secretary. Lewis filled this role until 1861, when he was appointed secretary for war. He died suddenly on 13 April 1863, while serving in this post. As a result of his death, the activity of the House of Commons was suspended for one day.

Keith Laybourn

See also: Gladstone, William Ewart; Palmerston, Lord

References and Further Reading: Chamberlain, Muriel, 1987, *Lord Palmerston* (Cardiff: GPC).

Liverpool, Earl of (Robert Banks Jenkinson; Lord Hawkesbury) (1770–1828) [PM, FS, HS]

Robert Banks Jenkinson was born in London on 7 June 1770, the eldest son of Charles Jenkinson (1727–1808), a Tory politician who had served as secretary at war under Lord North and as president of the Board of Trade under William Pitt, the Younger. His father, the scion of a landed family of Oxfordshire, had become a leading adviser to George III, and in 1791 was raised to the peerage as the first Baron Hawkesbury; in 1796 he was created the Earl of Liverpool.

Robert was educated at Charterhouse and at Christ Church, Oxford. He witnessed the fall of the Bastille in Paris while he was touring France in July 1789 and retained a fear of mob violence throughout his political career. He entered the House of Commons at the age of 20, in 1790, as M.P. for Appleby. He later became M.P. for Rye. He was a strong supporter of the war with France after 1793.

Jenkinson served at the Board of Control for India between 1793 and 1796 and as master of the Royal Mint from 1796 until 1801, when he was appointed foreign secretary by Henry Addington. He was responsible for negotiating the short-lived Treaty of Amiens with Napoleonic France in 1802. Created Baron Hawkesbury in 1803 and succeeding to his father's earldom in 1808, he served as home secretary and leader of the House of Lords in Pitt's second ministry, from 1804 until Pitt's death in 1806, as well as in the Portland administration, from 1807 until 1809. He also proved an efficient secretary for war and colonies under Spencer Perceval between 1809 and 1812, staunchly supporting Wellington's Peninsular campaigns.

When Liverpool became prime minister in June 1812, following the assassination of Spencer Perceval, he was only in his mid-forties but already had a broader base of political experience than most who attained this office. Moreover, he remained in office until 1827, completing the longest tenure of any British prime minister in the nineteenth and twentieth centuries. As prime minister he not only presided over the final defeat of Napoleon at Waterloo and the conclusion of the longest period of warfare in modern British history but also over an era of profound social and economic change. His term of office witnessed spectacular industrial and urban expansion and the most rapid period of population growth in Britain's history.

Liverpool had few interests outside of politics. Self-effacing and serious-minded by nature, he also exhibited a consistency, a dependability, and an ability to compromise that won him the respect of more talented and temperamental ministers who served under him. His parliamentary speeches were well-researched although rarely inspiring, and his arguments were carefully reasoned. He proved a sensitive and effective chairman of cabinet meetings during a significant period in the evolution of cabinet government. He entrusted his cabinet colleagues with considerable responsibility in the management of their ministerial departments, and was in turn rewarded by their loyalty.

Liverpool's failure to secure a majority in the House of Commons for a continuation of the wartime income tax after 1815 placed severe financial constraints on his government; but he strengthened the monetary system by restoring the gold standard in 1819, and prosperity returned in the 1820s. Liverpool responded firmly to the wave of radical discontent that erupted during the postwar recession: He suspended the Habeas Corpus Act in 1817, after which his ministry was satirized by the poet Shelley as "rulers who neither see, nor feel, nor know"; and he introduced the Six Acts of 1819, whose repressive effects have been considerably exaggerated by subsequent critics. He was determined to maintain public order by supporting the local magistracy in the absence of a substantial professional police force, but he was privately critical of the conduct of the Manchester magistrates at the time of the so-called "Peterloo Massacre" in August 1819, when a crowd that had gathered to listen to speeches on parliamentary reform and on the repeal of the Corn Laws was beset by the local militia and soldiery. Moreover, Liverpool had no desire to strengthen the power of the central government. His administration foiled a Jacobin threat to assassinate the cabinet and dealt adroitly with the complexities of the Queen Caroline affair in 1820, although he in-

curred the wrath of George IV, who contemplated dismissing him on account of his sympathy for George's estranged wife.

Liverpool's ministry bowed to pressure from anxious farmers and landowners in imposing the unpopular Corn Laws in 1815. Although Liverpool regarded the Corn Laws as an interim measure to encourage the revival of agriculture, in the short term these laws, combined with a series of bad harvests, drove the average price of corn higher in the years preceding 1819 than it had been at any other period during the whole of the nineteenth century, resulting in widespread distress. Liverpool also showed attentiveness to commercial and manufacturing interests, praising Watt's steam engine as "the greatest and most useful invention of modern times." He endeavored, with limited success, to reduce unemployment in 1817. Liverpool's fundamental commitment to the principles of free trade was revealed in a speech in 1820. In 1826, he expressed a willingness to reduce corn duties; but before a sliding scale for import duties could be introduced, he suffered a paralytic stroke in February 1827 and resigned from office.

In 1941, historian W. R. Brock famously characterized the later period of Liverpool's administration (1822–1827) as "an experiment in Liberal Toryism." During this period his government introduced a series of celebrated domestic reforms designed to reduce the number of capital offenses and rationalize the system of criminal justice—reforms that many historians view as sharply contrasting with the repressive legislation of the period before 1820. However, some historians—notably J. E. Cookson and Norman Gash—have emphasized fundamental continuities in the policies of Liverpool's administration before and after 1822. Gash and Eric Evans also have challenged predominantly negative interpretations of Liverpool's premiership influenced by Disraeli's unsympathetic assessment of Liverpool in 1844 as "the Arch-Mediocrity." Liverpool's qualities as an intelligent and able administrator in his tenure of three of the main offices of state are increasingly recognized. As premier, Liverpool skillfully coordinated the disparate interests and abilities within his party and worked persistently toward broadening his ministry's support in Parliament and in the country. His long, cohesive administration achieved success in times of war and of peace, laying the foundations for a return to prosperity in the 1820s by sound economic management, and for Peel's later remodeling of the Conservative Party.

An Evangelical Protestant, Liverpool insisted that ecclesiastical appointments be made on the basis of merit rather than of patronage. He also strenuously promoted the international prohibition of the slave trade. He opposed, in principle, the granting of Catholic emancipation, but allowed members of his cabinet freedom to follow their own consciences on this potentially divisive issue, enabling protagonists on both sides of the argument—notably Addington (Sidmouth) and Viscount Castlereagh, and later George Canning—to serve under him. Although Liverpool was respected for his integrity, calmness, and good temper, his avoidance of the great issues of Catholic emancipation and parliamentary reform created problems for his party after his death on 4 December 1828. By 1832 the party over which he had presided for so long had virtually disintegrated and had suffered a humiliating defeat in the general election of 1830. His success, which had occurred entirely within the context of the unreformed political system, may also be attributed to the weakness, during the period from 1812 to 1827, of the Whig opposition, as revealed in the general elections of 1818 and 1826.

John A. Hargreaves

See also: Addington, Henry; Castlereagh, Viscount; Perceval, Spencer; Pitt, William (the Younger); Portland, Duke of; Wellington, Duke of
References and Further Reading: Brock, William R., 1941, *Lord Liverpool and Liberal Toryism* (Cambridge: Cambridge University Press); Cookson, J. E., 1983, *Lord Liverpool's Administration, 1815–1822* (Hamden, CT: Archon Books); Evans, Eric, 1989, *Britain before the Reform Act: Politics and Society, 1815–1832* (London: Longman); Gash, Norman, 1984, *Lord Liverpool* (London: Weidenfeld & Nicolson); Plowright, John, 1996, *Regency England: The Age of Lord Liverpool* (London: Routledge).

Lloyd, Selwyn (Lord Selwyn-Lloyd) (1904–1978) [FS, CE]

Selwyn Lloyd is famous as foreign secretary during the Suez Canal crisis in 1956; chancellor of the exchequer in the late 1950s and early 1960s; and a respected speaker of the House of Commons in the 1970s. Although he was not a natural politician, he was nevertheless one of the foremost politicians of his generation in a period of dramatic political change.

John Selwyn Brooke Lloyd was born on 28 July 1904, at West Kirby, Wirral, the son of Sir John Wesley Lloyd, a dentist, and his wife, Mary Rachel Warhurst. He was raised as a Methodist and was educated at Fettes College, Edinburgh, and at Magdalene College, Cambridge. He was president of the Cambridge Students' Union in 1927, became a barrister in 1930, and built up a general common law practice on the northern circuit. He was a member of the Hoylake Urban District Council, in Cheshire, for ten years. He enlisted in the Royal Horse Artillery at the beginning of World War II and rose to the rank of lieutenant colonel in 1941 and brigadier in 1944.

Politically, Selwyn Lloyd had been drawn to the Liberal Party in his early years, due to family connections, but was adopted as a Conservative candidate for Wirral in 1939 and was easily elected for that seat in the 1945 general election. He remained Wirral's M.P. until 1976. Although in his early years his attention was concentrated primarily on building up his legal practice, his political career began to thrive. He was appointed as one of the three parliamentary members on the Beveridge Committee, which inquired into the organization of the BBC in 1949. Selwyn Lloyd produced his own report in 1951 that suggested that the BBC should not have a monopoly in broadcasting and should raise revenue from advertising.

Around this time, Selwyn Lloyd married his secretary, Elizabeth Marshall, the daughter of a solicitor. He was appointed a minister of state at the Foreign Office in 1951, where he worked closely with Sir Anthony Eden, the foreign secretary. He was involved in securing independence for Sudan. In 1954, when Eden was ill, he took on responsibility for the day-to-day activities of the Foreign Office. As a result he became closely involved with Prime Minister Winston Churchill, who in 1954 promoted him to minister of supply.

Six months later, when Eden became prime minister, Selwyn Lloyd was made foreign secretary. His main responsibility was to mobilize an international response to the actions of Colonel Nasser, the Egyptian leader, who had nationalized the Suez Canal on 26 July 1956. To this end Selwyn Lloyd organized an international conference in London in August 1956, at which 18 of the 22 participating countries supported the resolution for an international solution to the Suez Canal crisis that would guarantee Egyptian sovereign rights while establishing the rights of users of the canal. The conference sent Sir Robert Menzies to negotiate with Nasser; but the negotiations proved unsuccessful, perhaps in part because U.S. President Eisenhower had declared that he would only support a peaceful resolution to the issue. The Americans also prevented the British from bringing the matter before the United Nations Security Council, advocating that John Foster Dulles's plan for a Suez Canal users' association should be discussed first.

At this point Selwyn Lloyd tendered his resignation, but he was asked to continue as foreign secretary. On 22 October 1956 he became aware of a French-Israeli plan for military action in the canal zone, and on 26 October Israel attacked. By then, Selwyn Lloyd had begun to prepare for the parachuting of British troops into Suez, an event that occurred on 5 November 1956 and that led to the securing of 23 miles of the canal in one day. Selwyn Lloyd wanted to continue until the whole of the canal was secured; but British action ceased on 6 November, after the British cabinet buckled under pressure from the United States, which was threatening to provoke a sterling crisis. Shortly afterward, Eden resigned and was replaced by Harold Macmillan, who kept Selwyn Lloyd on as foreign secretary. From that point on, their main purpose became to improve Anglo-American relations, through the Bermuda Conference of 1957, and to improve Anglo-Soviet relations, through their visit to the Soviet Union in 1959.

In July 1960 Selwyn Lloyd became chancellor of the exchequer. Faced with inflationary pressures, rising wage demands, and increasing government expenditure, he introduced the "pay pause," a period when no pay increases were allowed. He followed up with a more flexible wage policy that allowed wage increases of up to 2.5 percent. He also set up the National Economic Development Council, dubbed "Neddy," as a discussion forum for trade union representatives, employers, and government. However, his strict financial controls on the economy began to dampen political support for the Conservative Party, as a result of which Macmillan organized a ministerial reshuffle ("the night of the long knives," 13 July 1962). Selwyn Lloyd was one of those who lost their posts.

Aggrieved by these developments, he nevertheless remained an active member of the Conservative Party. He conducted an assessment of the national organization in 1963, after which he recommended changes in the party's selection of candidates, its subscriptions for party membership, and the role of its agents. He also influenced the selection of Lord Home as Conservative leader, and thus prime minister, on the resignation of Harold Macmillan in 1963. As a reward, he was given the posts of Lord Privy Seal and leader of the House of Commons, which he enjoyed for ten months, until Harold Wilson's Labour government came to power. From then until 1966, he was a member of the Conservative shadow cabinet. After the Conservatives returned to government under Edward Heath in 1970, Selwyn Lloyd was made speaker of the House of Commons in 1971. He resigned in 1976 and was given a life peerage. He died on 17 May 1978.

Keith Laybourn

See also: Churchill, Sir Winston; Heath, Edward; Home, Sir Alec Douglas; Macmillan, Harold
References and Further Reading: Fisher, Nigel, 1982, *Harold Macmillan* (London: Weidenfeld and Nicolson); Lloyd, J. S. B., 1976, *Mr. Speaker, Sir* (London: Cape).

Lloyd George, David
(Earl Lloyd-George of Dwyfor)
(1863–1945) [PM, CE]

One of Britain's great wartime leaders, David Lloyd George appeared the most powerful of prime ministers at the end of World War I, yet he fell from office, never to return, in October 1922. He had come to the fore as a great Nonconformist and Radical leader; yet his premiership in Conservative-dominated coalition governments (1916–1922) played an important part in shattering the Liberal Party, on which he depended for power.

Lloyd George was born in Chorlton-upon-Medlock, Manchester, on 17 January 1863. His parents—William George, a schoolteacher, and Elizabeth Lloyd, a domestic servant—were Welsh, and the family moved back to Wales when David was four months old. His father died young of pneumonia in June 1864, and his mother returned to her birthplace in North Wales, Llanystumdwy, where she lived with her mother and her brother Richard. Richard Lloyd, who worked as an unpaid lay pastor for the Disciples of Christ (a Baptist sect) and who had radical political leanings, was a major early influence on David.

David was educated at the village elementary school by his uncle, and later successfully trained to be a solicitor. In 1885 he set up his own practice and this, through his brother William's hard work, financed his early political career (M.P.s were unpaid before 1911). Lloyd George made a name for himself as a local solicitor, lay preacher, temperance lecturer, and activist for various radical pressure groups, and thereby secured the nomination for Caernarvon Boroughs.

He became M.P. for Caernarvon Boroughs in a by-election in April 1890, winning by only 18 votes. He held the constituency in every general election until he was elevated to the House of Lords in the New Year Honours List of 1945 as Earl Lloyd George and Viscount Gwynedd.

He served as a Liberal backbencher until he entered Sir Henry Campbell-Bannerman's government on 10 December 1905. In the 1890s he made his name as a Welsh radical. He came to even greater prominence due to his opposi-

David Lloyd George (right) with French Premier Raymond Poincaré, 1922 (Library of Congress)

tion to the Boer War (1899–1902) and to the Conservative government's Education Bill (1902). He entered the cabinet as the most prominent Nonconformist and Radical politician. As president of the Board of Trade (1905–1908), he made a favorable impression through the business-friendly legislation he brought forward and through his skill in conciliation during industrial disputes.

When Herbert Henry Asquith became prime minister, Lloyd George succeeded him as chancellor of the exchequer (1908–1915). Lloyd George took over from Asquith the passage of the Old Age Pensions Bill through the House of Commons. Subsequently, he and Winston Churchill were the major forces behind the National Insurance Act of 1911. Lloyd George's famous "people's budget" of 1909 provided the financial basis for social welfare reforms and for Britain's naval arms race with Germany. The radical nature of this budget sparked a clash with the House of Lords that did much to revive the Liberal Party's electoral fortunes (which had been waning after its 1906 electoral triumph) in the two general elections of 1910. Lloyd George also tried to revive radical enthusiasm in 1913 with his campaign of local rural areas, which proved to have some electoral appeal to rural workers.

Lloyd George's career was transformed by World War I. He had never been a pacifist, though he had opposed the Boer War and "bloated armaments." As chancellor of the exchequer he had resisted high levels of naval spending, clashing vigorously in December 1913 with his close associate Churchill over the Admiralty's estimates. However, he had shown his determination to resist what he saw as German aggression over a German gunboat being sent to Agadir in Morocco in 1911. In August 1914, when Britain declared war on Germany, he justified this decision with reference to the German invasion of Belgium. By early 1915 he was very much associated with Britain's active organization to secure victory.

Lloyd George took a major political risk in leaving the exchequer in May 1915 to set up a Ministry of Munitions. In this role he built on organizational changes begun by the War Office to ensure a massive supply of armaments. He also displayed again skills that he had used to good effect before the war, in helping resolve industrial disputes. As the war proceeded he became convinced, earlier than most Liberals, of the need for conscription. After the Easter Rising in 1916, Lloyd George nearly secured an Irish settlement. In July 1916, following the death of Kitchener, Lloyd George became secretary of state for war. That autumn his efforts to create a committee for more effective supervision of the war effort led to a political crisis and the resignation of Asquith. Although Lloyd George had aspired to the premiership and had taken pains to ensure he was widely viewed as Asquith's crown prince, it is unlikely that he intended to oust and replace Asquith at this specific time (early December 1916).

Lloyd George was prime minister from 6 December 1916 until 19 October 1922, relying on a multiparty support base. During the war he was supported by most Conservative M.P.s, the Parliamentary Labour Party, and roughly half the Liberal M.P.s. In December 1916 he instituted a small war cabinet (which fluctuated between five and seven members), an efficient cabinet secretariat, and a group of special advisers to himself (located in the so-called garden suburb of 10 Downing Street). He also created new ministries of labor and of pensions and actively sought to bring more businessmen ("men of push and go") into Whitehall.

His wartime premiership depended on his ability to energize the war effort by uniting his disparate supporters. The greatest political threat to his leadership was not Asquith and his Liberal supporters but a potential loss of Conservative support. He risked precisely such a loss in attempting to replace Generals Haig and Robertson, whom he felt were too committed to costly, lengthy offensives on the Western front. He did replace Robertson, but backed off from removing Haig.

Lloyd George emerged from World War I as "the man who won the war" in the eyes of the popular press and probably much of the electorate. He ran in the December 1918 general election backed by coalition Liberals and coalition Conservatives, the Labour Party having withdrawn. His supporters received endorsements ("coupons") from him and the Conservative leader, Andrew Bonar Law. The coalition victory was overwhelming, and Asquith and other leading Liberals who lacked coupons lost their seats. The bitterness that had arisen from the December 1916 split in the Liberal Party worsened; and these hard feelings later undercut Lloyd George's leadership of the reunited party. However, the Conservatives won by a landslide in 1918, winding up with a House of Commons majority in their own right; so it is less surprising that Lloyd George was ousted from the premiership in October 1922 than that he held the coalition together so long.

He was at the peak of his career in 1919, alongside U.S. President Woodrow Wilson and France's Georges Clemenceau as one of the most powerful figures in Paris, determining the peace settlement with Germany (leading to the Treaty of Versailles, which was signed on 28 June 1919). Lloyd George responded to the presence of anti-German feeling in the Conservative press, the Conservative Party, and the electorate, in particular with regard to the "war guilt" clause, the scale of reparations, and boundaries. Yet, nevertheless, Lloyd George did tilt the settlement with Germany in a more liberal direction than Clemenceau and much of the Conservative Party wished.

After 1919, he appeared as a participant at various international conferences in Europe, but these appearances did not enhance his reputation. He was unsuccessful in overcoming French hostility to Germany, bringing Soviet Russia back into European trade, or securing agreements on disarmament. His confrontation with Turkey and support of Greece in Asia Minor (the Chanak Crisis of autumn 1922) damaged his standing in Parliament and contributed to his downfall.

Lloyd George's postwar government also began better in its domestic policy than it ended. Though there was some serious unrest among troops impatient to be demobilized, on the whole his administration achieved a reasonably smooth transition from a wartime to a peace economy. In this it was assisted by a boom in the economy from 1919 until late 1920. In this period the government went some way toward meeting Lloyd George's campaign promise of building "a fit land for heroes to live in." Substantial numbers of houses were built under the 1919 Housing and Town Planning Act, albeit at high cost; a further eight million people were covered by the 1920 Unemployment Insurance Act; and there were further extensions of old age pensions and national health insurance. Even before the war ended, Parliament had passed the important Education Act of 1918.

However, the Conservative majority of the coalition government's supporters were increasingly uneasy about the cost of welfare, especially after the postwar boom ended. They were also keen to decontrol the economy, though in the cases of the railways and coal mines they sought a reorganization of the industries and not simply a return to the prewar pattern of private ownership. Lloyd George backed away from social welfare measures as the government came under pressure from middle-class taxpayers, who voted for "antiwaste" candidates in by-elections. He also sacked the Liberal coalition ministers Christopher Addison and Edwin Montagu. The

severe economic recession of 1921–1922 undercut public expenditure further, and deep cuts in public spending, which undid part of the post-1918 reform, were made under the "Geddes axe" in 1922, when the recommendations of the Committee on National Expenditure began to be implemented.

Lloyd George's leadership of a Conservative-dominated coalition government in itself alienated many of his longtime supporters. In addition, that government had instituted many policies that seemed illiberal, including a wartime military conscription policy that made no allowances for conscientious objectors. Illiberal tendencies also were signaled by Lloyd George's inclusion in his war cabinet of the Ulster Unionist Lord Carson, and of the imperial proconsuls Lord Milner and Lord Curzon. After 1918, many radicals were outraged by the British military intervention against the Bolsheviks in Russia; by the Black and Tan, and the government-sponsored atrocities committed in Ireland; by the support shown by some coalitionists for General Dyer after the April 1919 massacre at Amritsar, India; and by various coercive actions against miners and other trade unionists. Although Lloyd George did secure a settlement in Ireland in 1921 that lasted nearly fifty years, there was increasing distrust of his negotiating skills. His integrity also was damaged by the sale of honors, which his government carried out more brazenly, and with more dubious people being rewarded, than in previous ministries. In the later 1920s both Stanley Baldwin (Conservative) and Arthur Henderson (Labour) made much of being blunt and honest, unlike Lloyd George.

Lloyd George fell from office when the Conservative Party backbenchers revolted against the coalition government. Nearly all of the Conservative coalitionists followed Lloyd George into the political wilderness, as the Peelites had after Sir Robert Peel fell in 1846. Unlike the Peelites, however, most of these coalition Conservatives made their way back to office in a purely Conservative government. In contrast, Lloyd George did not return to office, though he remained a substantial political presence until 1931.

Lloyd George rejoined Asquith and the Liberals in 1923. This Liberal reunion came about when Baldwin made tariffs the prime issue in the 1923 general election. In 1926 Asquith, who was still a Liberal Party leader, and Lloyd George, his deputy leader, fell out over the general strike. Lloyd George was highly critical of the Baldwin government's handling of the strike, whereas Asquith was very critical of the trade unions. When it became clear that the Liberal Party's members were predominantly on Lloyd George's side, Asquith resigned. Lloyd George served as Liberal leader (formally in the House of Commons only) from 1926 to 1931.

Unlike Asquith, Lloyd George was notably receptive to new political ideas in the 1920s. He used the political funds that he had accumulated from the sale of honors (and had placed in trust) to finance a series of major policy studies, beginning with *The Land and the Nation* and *Towns and the Land* (both 1925). The Liberal Industrial Inquiry (1926–1928) involved many of the liveliest Liberal minds, with substantial contributions being made by economist John Maynard Keynes and by Lloyd George himself, and resulted in *Britain's Industrial Future* (1928). A major theme was highlighted in the pamphlet *We Can Conquer Unemployment* and in the 1929 general election campaign. In that election the Liberal vote exceeded the 1924 level of 2.9 million, totaling 5.3 million, and the number of Liberal M.P.s rose from 40 to 59.

Lloyd George supported Ramsay MacDonald's minority Labour government (1929–1931). He was more critical of its cautious conservatism, especially in regard to unemployment and agriculture, than fearful that it would be unduly socialist. However, the Liberal Parliamentary Party began fragmenting during this period, with several right-wing Liberals drifting very close to the Conservative opposition. This presaged the very substantial Liberal Party divisions of the 1930s.

During the political crisis of July 1931, Lloyd George was incapacitated by a prostate operation. In 1931–1935 he operated as an independent Liberal M.P., backed by a small family group of M.P.s that were all relatives of his. In 1933 he again tried to rally Nonconformist opinion behind his own "New Deal." After 1935 he focused much of his attention on foreign affairs as the post–World War I peace treaties unraveled. While briefly impressed by Hitler when visiting Germany in 1936, he became increasingly alarmed by the actions of the fascist dictators. In 1940 he declined Churchill's offer to be Food Controller or British ambassador to Washington. Terminally ill with cancer, but believing he could have an impact on the postwar peacemaking, he accepted an earldom in the New Year Honours List, 1945. So he died as Earl Lloyd-George of Dwyfor and Viscount Gwynedd on 26 March 1945.

Lloyd George was married twice. His first wife, whom he married in 1888, was Margaret Owen (1866–1941), who became a major figure in her North Wales community. They had four children, two of whom became prominent politicians, Gwilym and Megan (1902–1966). In October 1943, Lloyd George married his second wife, Frances Stevenson (1888–1972), with whom he had enjoyed a long and steady relationship since 1913.

Chris Wrigley

See also: Asquith, Herbert Henry; Baldwin, Stanley; Bonar Law, Andrew; Campbell-Bannerman, Sir Henry; Chamberlain, Neville; Churchill, Sir Winston; Lloyd-George, Gwilym; MacDonald, James Ramsay
References and Further Reading: Gilbert, Bentley B., 1987, 1992, *David Lloyd George: A Political Life,* 2 vols. (London: Batsford); Grigg, John, 1973, 1978, 1985, *Lloyd George,* 3 vols. (London: Methuen); Lloyd George, Earl David, 1933–1936, *War Memoirs* (London: Ivor Nicholson & Watson); Morgan, Kenneth O., 1974, *Lloyd George* (London: Weidenfeld & Nicolson); Packer, Ian, 1998, *Lloyd George* (Basingstoke, UK: Macmillan); Pugh, Martin, 1988, *Lloyd George* (London: Longman); Rowland, Peter, 1975, *Lloyd George* (London: Barrie & Jenkins); Wrigley, Chris, 1992, *Lloyd George* (Oxford: Blackwell).

Lloyd-George, Gwilym (Viscount Tenby) (1894–1967) [HS]

Gwilym Lloyd-George was born in Criccieth, North Wales, on 4 December 1894, the younger son and the fourth of the five children of David and Margaret Lloyd George. He was educated at

Eastbourne College and at Jesus College, Cambridge, and during World War I served in the 38th (Welsh) division on the western front in France. He fought on the Somme and at Passchendaele and rose to the rank of major.

After the war, his life became closely linked with the political fortunes of his father. He attended the Paris Peace Conference in 1919, became involved in Liberal politics, and became National Liberal M.P. for Pembrokeshire in the 1922 general election. He retained this seat in 1923 but lost it to the Conservative candidate in 1924. His father made him managing director of United Newspapers in 1925, but he resigned this position in 1926 and became a junior trustee of the National Liberal Political Fund, the "Lloyd George Fund," from which David Lloyd George's political campaigns were financed. (In 1945, Gwilym received the remains of this fund for his own personal use.) He was elected to the House of Commons as M.P. once again in 1929, and he served briefly in Ramsay MacDonald's National government (from September to October 1931), as parliamentary secretary to the Board of Trade.

Throughout the 1930s he was a loyal supporter of his father's policies, and he went with him to visit Hitler at Berchtesgaden in the summer of 1936. However, he was veering toward the Conservative Party, and when war broke out he once again became parliamentary secretary to the Board of Trade, serving under both Neville Chamberlain and Winston Churchill. In February 1941 he became parliamentary secretary to the Ministry of Food, in June 1942, minister of fuel and power. In the latter post he devised new techniques for rationing and helped stimulate coal production. In 1943 he was advocating greater government control of mines, and well before the war ended, the formation of the National Coal Board to regulate coal production.

In 1945 he was returned again as M.P. for Pembrokeshire, but now as a "National Liberal and Conservative." He felt that socialism was a major political menace and that Liberalism was a spent force, and he therefore declined the chairmanship of the Parliamentary Liberal Party following the electoral defeat of Sir Archibald Sinclair. In 1950 he was defeated at Pembrokeshire, but in October 1951 he was returned for the seat of Newcastle upon Tyne (North). His move toward the Conservative Party was confirmed when Winston Churchill, in recognition of his administrative skills, made him minister of food in the new Conservative government. He held this post for three years, from October 1951 to October 1954, during which he presided over the end of food rationing. As a result of his successes, he became home secretary in October 1954, combining the role with that of minister of Welsh affairs. He retained both posts when Sir Anthony Eden became prime minister in 1955. His most important action during this period was to modify the severity of the legal penalty in murder cases through the Homicide Act of 1957 (capital punishment was not abolished).

Gwilym Lloyd-George lost his government post when Harold Macmillan became prime minister in 1957. He subsequently was elevated to the House of Lords as Viscount Tenby (1957), and became more broadly involved in public life. He died on 14 February 1967. He is remembered as a politician of solid political and administrative abilities who managed to escape some of the political shadow cast by his father.

Keith Laybourn

See also: Churchill, Sir Winston; Eden, Sir Anthony; Lloyd George, David; Macmillan, Harold
References and Further Reading: Addison, Paul, 1992, *Churchill on the Home Front 1900–1955* (London: Cape); Wrigley, Chris, 1992, *Lloyd George* (Oxford: Blackwell).

Lowe, Sir Robert (Viscount Sherbrooke)
(1811–1892) [CE, HS]

Robert Lowe is perhaps most famous for his introduction of the revised education code in 1862 and his opposition to the 1867 reform bill, which led him to pronounce in the House of Commons, "We must teach our masters their letters." He was also an impressive chancellor of the exchequer and home secretary in William Ewart Gladstone's Liberal government of 1868 to 1874. Popular with the public, he cut an altogether different figure in Parliament, where he created many political enemies.

Robert Lowe was born at Bingham, Nottinghamshire, on 4 December 1811, the second son of Robert Lowe, the rector of that parish, and Ellen Pyndar, his wife. He went to Winchester College in 1825 and then to University College, Oxford, and graduated in 1833. In 1835 he was elected a Fellow of Magdalen College, Oxford, and the following year he married Georgiana Orred. While at Oxford, he became embroiled in the ecclesiastical disputes that divided academics there in the early 1840s.

At the same time as he was teaching students at Oxford, he also was studying law; and in 1842 he was called to the bar at Lincoln's Inn. From 1842 to 1850 he practiced law in Sydney, Australia, where he was responsible for ending imprisonment as a penalty for debt. He returned to England in 1850 and began to contribute feature articles for the *Times*. He was elected M.P. for Kidderminster in 1852, and held that seat until 1859. He then became M.P. for Calne in the 1859 general election, winning the seat through the influence of Lord Lansdowne, and was offered the vice presidency of the Committee of Council on Education by Lord Palmerston, which effectively meant that he was the government's minister of education.

In this latter role, he was responsible for the introduction of a revised code of educational regulations (the famous Revised Code of 1862), whereby the wide variety of government educational grants was swept away and replaced by a system of payments based on attendance levels and on the ability of pupils to pass standard exams in reading, writing, and arithmetic, the famous "three Rs." This was a controversial measure opposed by many schoolteachers, who saw their salaries reduced, and by some school inspectors, such as Matthew Arnold. Lowe's reputation for controversy may well explain why he did not retain his position in Lord John Russell's ministry, which was formed after the death of Lord Palmerston in October 1866.

Free of government responsibility, Lowe found himself in a position to oppose Russell's reform bill of 1866 (which was passed as the parliamentary Reform Bill of 1867). The bill extended the parliamentary vote to some working men, provoking Lowe to warn his colleagues of the dangers of uncontrolled, uneducated democ-

racy. He felt that he had been "deceived and betrayed" (*Dictionary of Labour Biography*, p. 199), for the franchise in the boroughs had become a household franchise, and that in the counties had been reduced to a £12 limit.

Lowe's own constituency disappeared as a result of the bill, and Lowe subsequently became the first M.P. for the University of London in 1868. He was appointed chancellor of the exchequer on 9 December 1868, in W. E. Gladstone's government, thus becoming, for the first time, a member of the cabinet. He remained chancellor until 10 August 1873 and was generally considered effective and efficient. His 1869 and 1870 budgets were popular due to their reduction of income tax by a penny on the pound; but Lowe faced strong opposition in the Commons to his idea of introducing a tax of a halfpenny per pound on each box of lucifer matches (the United States had introduced a similar tax), and the measure was rejected. In his later budgets he moved to reduce taxes on sugar, to increase income tax allowances, and to further reduce income tax. However, his popularity plummeted after he refused to purchase Epping Forest as a national park for the nation. As a result, he resigned the post of chancellor on 9 August 1873 and accepted that of home secretary. The latter appointment was brief, since Gladstone's ministry was dissolved on 20 February 1874.

Lowe's career as a leading politician was now at an end. In May 1880, when Gladstone and the Liberals returned to power, he was raised to the House of Lords as Viscount Sherbrooke of Sherbrooke, in Warlingham, Surrey. He was rarely involved in the activities of the House of Lords, and gradually drifted out of the public eye. He died on 27 July 1892 an almost forgotten figure, although there is no denying his political importance and the significance of his controversial work in the 1860s.

Keith Laybourn

See also: Gladstone, William Ewart; Palmerston, Lord; Russell, Lord John
References and Further Reading: Simon, Brian, 1960, *Studies in the History of Education, 1780–1870* (London: Lawrence & Wishart).

M

MacDonald, James Ramsay
(1866–1937) [PM, FS]

No twentieth-century British political leader has been more reviled than Ramsay MacDonald, Britain's Labour prime minister in 1924 and from 1929 to 1931. His decision to tender the resignation of the second Labour government and accept the king's commission to form a National government during the financial crisis of August 1931 provoked much animus among his former supporters and sustained the view that he had planned to ditch the second Labour government all along. This act for a long time was considered by many the mark of a traitor, and led William Lawther (M.P.) to remark that MacDonald was "bereft of any public decency" (Laybourn 1988, p. 67). To many Labour activists, the man who had helped form the Labour Party also helped undermine it.

MacDonald was born in Lossiemouth, Scotland, on 12 October 1866, the illegitimate son of Anne Ramsay and, possibly, John MacDonald, a plowman. He was educated at a local school and was expected to become a teacher, but in the 1880s he took up a series of clerical posts in Bristol and in London.

MacDonald acquired wide political experience between 1885 and 1892. He joined the Social Democratic Federation, a quasi-Marxist organization, while in Bristol; he was employed by Thomas Lough, a Liberal Radical M.P.; and he moved in socialist circles. He had ambitions of becoming a Liberal M.P., but his candidature for Southampton was thwarted in 1894 and he joined the Independent Labour Party (ILP), the first major socialist party to be committed to electoral politics, in July 1894. He campaigned as ILP and Labour Electoral Association candidate in Southampton in 1894,

and was thoroughly trounced in the 1895 general election.

During the early 1880s, MacDonald was introduced to Sidney Webb and joined the Fabian Society, a body of largely middle-class socialists committed to gradual social change through parliamentary and municipal politics. He acted as a Fabian lecturer in 1892, touring South Wales, the Midlands, and the Northeast. In 1896 and 1897 he was also a member of the Rainbow Circle, which first met in the Rainbow Tavern on Fleet Street in London, and which brought together a number of collectivist Liberals (e.g., Herbert Samuel) who believed that the old Liberal Party was about to disintegrate. The group published papers and, briefly, the *Progressive Review,* in the hope of encouraging the formation of a new center party in British politics. MacDonald's own hope was that a center party with (ethical) socialist ideas would emerge. This desire, as well as his interest in foreign policy, were the two abiding passions that he pursued throughout his political career.

Marriage to Margaret Gladstone in November 1896 provided MacDonald with the financial security he needed to develop his political career, since his wife brought with her a settlement of up to £300 per year. The couple moved to 3 Lincoln's Inn Fields, London, which later became a base for the Labour Representation Committee (LRC), an alliance of socialists and trade unionists that eventually became the Labour Party. The couple had six children. Margaret died on 8 September 1911.

MacDonald's career began to blossom in the 1890s. He joined the executive committee of the Fabian Society in 1894, and became a member of the national administrative committee of the ILP in 1896. He remained a prominent member of the ILP until World War I, often acting as chairman or secretary. Thereafter, he drifted away from the ILP, although he did not formally resign until May 1930. His contribution to the ILP was significant; but his real claim to fame arose from the fact that he was largely responsible for the early development of the Labour Party.

The Labour Representation Committee was formed in February 1900 and formally changed its name to the Labour Party at the beginning of 1906. MacDonald was its secretary from 1900 to 1912, its treasurer in 1911 and 1912, and chairman of the Parliamentary Labour Party (PLP) from 1911 to 1914. From the start, he was committed to winning trade union support for the embryonic organization and was helped in this respect by the attack on trade union funds represented by the Taff Vale Judgment of 1901. Yet support from the unions was slow in coming. With the party having only four M.P.s in 1903, MacDonald embarked on a series of eight secret meetings with Jesse Herbert, confidential secretary to Herbert Gladstone, the Liberal chief whip, to arrange the "Lib-Lab" pact of 1903. This agreement allowed the Labour Party candidates a straight run against the Conservatives in about thirty parliamentary seats, in return for a similar arrangement for the Liberals. In the 1906 general election, only five of the twenty-nine successful LRC candidates faced Liberal opposition; the arrangement had clearly worked for Labour.

The general election result was a personal triumph for MacDonald, who ran a party that now had strong parliamentary representation, initially led by James Keir Hardie. MacDonald also helped move the party in a gradualist, socialist direction by creating a Socialist Library, a monograph series run by the party, to which he contributed several works that he had authored himself, including *Socialism and Society* (1905) and *Socialism and Government* (1909). The dominating theme of his work was that a form of social Darwinism ensured that private organizations would get bigger, that the state would have to intervene, and that socialism would emerge from the success, not the failure, of capitalism. Because of the influence of MacDonald

and the Webbs during World War I, these essentially Fabian views became the defining influence in the Labour Party after 1918.

From 1906 to 1918, MacDonald was M.P. for Leicester, intermittently secretary of the Labour Party, and for nearly four years, chairman of the PLP. He was strongly criticized for helping lead the Labour Party and the PLP into alliance with the Liberal Party. His reputation for radicalism was restored, briefly (long enough to allow him to win the post of Labour leader in 1922), by his opposition to Britain's involvement in World War I. This attitude evoked venomous attacks on him in the press. The most notable instance of this was the occasion when Horatio Bottomley, editor of *John Bull*, published MacDonald's birth certificate, which revealed that he was illegitimate and that he had been named James MacDonald Ramsay, after his father. Bottomley asserted that MacDonald was both an impostor and a traitor and that he should be taken to the Tower of London and shot at dawn. Hostility toward MacDonald's wartime position led to the loss of his parliamentary seat at Leicester in the 1918 general election and to his defeat in a by-election contest for a Labour seat in 1921.

In the immediate postwar years, having no parliamentary duties, MacDonald concentrated on building up the Labour Party. He was returned to Parliament as M.P. for Aberavon in 1922, and shortly afterward became leader of the PLP, largely as a result of the support of Independent Labour Party (a socialist party that had helped to form the Labour Representation Committee/Labour Party in 1900) M.P.s (who, influenced by the dominant ILP group of M.P.s from Clydeside, voted almost to a man for MacDonald). After Stanley Baldwin failed to win support for his protectionist measures in the 1923 general election, MacDonald was invited to form the first Labour government at the beginning of 1924. It was a minority government and lasted little more than ten months, but because it was the first Labour government, it was an important landmark in the rise of Labour. Within this government, MacDonald was also foreign secretary—the first prime minister to assume that role since Robert Cecil, the third

Prime Minister Ramsay MacDonald responds to the welcome upon his arrival in New York, c. 1925. (Library of Congress)

Marquess of Salisbury—and had performed the same joint roles on three occasions in the late nineteenth century. The defeat of the first Labour government in the general election of 1924 occurred in the inhospitable climate created by the publication of the infamous "Zinoviev letter," which suggested that the Soviet Union was intending to use the Labour Party toward its own revolutionary objectives. Whether this letter was real or a fake seems to have made little difference to the electoral performance of the party; it seemed certain to be, and it was, defeated.

During the next five years MacDonald led a Labour Party to which, according to Philip Snowden, MacDonald was becoming a stranger. Yet in the May 1929 general election, MacDonald was returned for the parliamentary seat of Seaham. At the head of what was now the largest parliamentary party, he formed his second, minority, Labour government in June 1929. Unfortunately, six months later, the markets crashed on Wall Street, and as a result of the ensuing world recession, unemployment rose from about one million to three million in less than two years. The Labour government grossly overspent its budget, precipitating a financial crisis in August 1931. The cabinet attempted to make the spending cuts demanded by the opposition parties but split over the decision to cut the unemployment benefit by 10 percent. MacDonald offered the resignation of his government to King George V but returned with a commission to form a National government that would include both the Conservative and the Liberal parties as well as any "National Labour" support he could muster.

These actions led L. MacNeill Weir to suggest that MacDonald was never a socialist but instead was an opportunist who from the start had schemed to ditch the Labour government one day, and that he was guilty of betrayal. However, David Marquand has suggested that such accusations are, at best, half-truths. Indeed, he argues that MacDonald was probably as good a socialist as any other leading figure in the Labour Party and that he was a principled opportunist (he gave up the Labour leadership to oppose World War I) who did not scheme to replace the Labour government with a coalition, although he may have been guilty of betraying his former Labour supporters.

From 1931 to 1935, MacDonald served as prime minister of a National government that was formed after a landslide victory in the 1931 general election in response to the national economic crisis. MacDonald's power depended on the Conservative Party, which encouraged him to move toward protectionism. During this period, MacDonald indulged his passion for foreign policy by participating in two conferences that took place in 1932—the Geneva Disarmament Conference and the Lausanne Conference, which was concerned with German reparations.

His fortunes then plummeted, as he was attacked both by former colleagues such as Philip Snowden and by new political friends. He went into physical and mental decline and was forced to resign as prime minister on 7 June 1935. Subsequently, he lost his seat at the 1935 general election to Emmanuel Shinwell, who had nominated him as PLP leader in 1922. He was found another seat, for the Scottish Universities, but thereafter played a diminishing role in the activities of the National government. MacDonald died of heart failure on 9 November 1937, while cruising in the Caribbean on the *Reina del Pacifico*. His body was returned to Britain and cremated on 26 November 1937. His ashes were interred in the Spynie graveyard, near Lossiemouth, next to those of his wife.

Keith Laybourn

See also: Baldwin, Stanley; Chamberlain, Neville; Clynes, John Robert; Salisbury, Lord; Samuel, Sir Herbert; Simon, Sir John; Snowden, Philip
References and Further Reading: Barker, Bernard (ed.), 1972, *Ramsay MacDonald's Political Writings* (London: Allen Lane); Laybourn, Keith, 1988, *The Rise of Labour* (London: Edward Arnold); Marquand, David, 1977, *Ramsay MacDonald* (London: Cape); Weir, Lauchlan M., 1938, *The Tragedy of Ramsay MacDonald* (London: Secker & Warburg).

McKenna, Reginald
(1863–1943) [CE, HS]
Reginald McKenna was both home secretary and chancellor of the exchequer consecutively between 1911 and 1916 but left relatively little impact upon either office, except for the fact

that his name is associated with a set of protectionist measures introduced at the beginning of World War I. He was born in London in 1863, of a southern Irish father employed by the Inland Revenue and an English mother who had been educated in France. He was educated at St. Malo, in Brittany; then at Ebersdorf, near Coburg, in middle Germany; and later at King's College School, London. He gained a mathematics scholarship at Trinity Hall, Cambridge, gained a good degree in 1885, and has the distinction of having rowed for Cambridge in its victorious boat race in 1887. He then left Cambridge to become a barrister by studying at Inner Temple.

McKenna's political career began in 1895, when he ran in a parliamentary by-election for North Monmouthshire. He won this seat, and held it in the Liberal cause until 1918. In his early days he was associated with Charles Dilke, the Radical M.P., and he later became a close friend of H. H. Asquith. When the Liberal government was formed in December 1905, under Henry Campbell-Bannerman, he was appointed financial secretary to the Treasury. He became president of the Board of Trade in 1908, the same year that he married Pamela Jekyll, who had had a mildly flirtatious relationship with Asquith before her marriage to McKenna—a connection that enhanced McKenna's social and political standing.

Between 1908 and 1911, as First Lord of the Admiralty, McKenna fought hard in the cabinet for the decision to construct six battleships (the famous Dreadnoughts), an effort in which he had the support of Sir Edward Grey, the foreign secretary. In 1911 McKenna was given the less challenging post, as it proved, of home secretary. It was not a post that excited him; in his three and a half years with the Home Office, the only significant piece of legislation passed was the Welsh Church Disestablishment Bill, which he pushed through Parliament between 1912 and 1914 (as a result of the Great War, it was not implemented until 1920). As home secretary, McKenna was also closely involved in dealing with suffragettes. In particular, he introduced the Prisoners' (Temporary Discharge for Ill Health) Bill—better known as the "Cat-and-Mouse Act"—whereby imprisoned suffragettes who were determined to starve themselves to death would be released and then, once they had eaten, rearrested.

On the eve of World War I, McKenna was resolutely Asquithian in his attitude, favoring a steady response to the wartime situation. He was unhappy about the formation of a coalition government in May 1915, but benefited from the event, receiving the post of chancellor of the exchequer. It appears that Asquith gave him this post because the Liberal majority in government would not have tolerated a Conservative politician committed to tariff reform, and because Asquith wanted to keep the post available for David Lloyd George in case the latter left the Ministry of Munitions.

McKenna produced two wartime budgets. The first, of September 1915, revealed a vast increase in expenditure to £1.59 billion, against an income of £272 million. In order to narrow the gap, he increased tax rates by 40 percent, reduced tax limits, and increased the surtax on the rich. A tax of 50 percent was also imposed on excess profits. The most surprising part of this budget, given that McKenna was a free trader, was the duties levied on imports in order to raise revenue and to discourage imports. In the main, the duties were levied at 33.3 percent. His second budget, of April 1916, made the tax system more complicated, and raised income tax to 5 shillings (25p) per pound for incomes above £2,500. The duty on excess profits went from 50 percent to 60 percent.

McKenna's brief tenure as chancellor was also marred by several other problems. First, he suffered from poor personal relations with Lord Cunliffe, governor of the Bank of England. Second, the debate over military conscription had divided the Liberals in government and soured McKenna's attitude toward David Lloyd George. Some Liberals resigned as a gesture of protest against the reimposition of a policy of conscription and the abandonment of voluntary armed forces, which Lloyd George had championed. McKenna took neither a moral nor a religious line on conscription but opposed it on economic grounds: He believed that Britain could not afford to send a large number of men to the western front. He did not resign over the issue but began to develop a dislike of Lloyd George because of it. Third, when Lloyd George took over from Asquith as prime minister in December 1916, McKenna was quickly replaced by Andrew Bonar Law in a ministerial reshuffle. That put an end to his political career, and he left the House of Commons in 1918 to become chairman of Midland Bank in 1919. He remained in that post until his death in 1943.

McKenna was never a political heavyweight. Despite his financial and commercial abilities, his political career was very much associated with the Asquithian period in British politics. He was always, as Roy Jenkins has suggested, something of a will-o-'the-wisp.

Keith Laybourn

See also: Asquith, Herbert Henry; Campbell-Bannerman, Sir Henry; Lloyd George, David
References and Further Reading: Jenkins, Roy, 1998, *The Chancellors* (London: Macmillan).

Macleod, Iain
(1913–1970) [CE]

Iain Norman Macleod, a leading Conservative politician who died within a month of becoming chancellor of the exchequer, was born at Skipton, in Yorkshire, on 11 November 1913, the son of Norman Macleod and his wife, Annabel. His father was a Scottish doctor who practiced in Skipton but retained his contacts with Scotland by maintaining a small property at Lewis. Iain was educated at Fettes College and at Gonville and Caius College, Cambridge, where he obtained a second-class degree in history. In September 1939 he joined the Royal Fusiliers as a private, and quickly rose through the ranks. In 1941 he married Evelyn Hester Blois. He was involved in the D-Day landings in 1944.

Macleod attempted to win a parliamentary seat for the Outer Hebrides in the 1945 general election but came in last. On demobilization in 1946 he joined the Conservative parliamentary secretariat and began to work his way up within the Conservative Party, becoming an expert on social services. He was elected as MP for Enfield West in 1950, a seat he held until his death in 1970. He quickly became a member of Angus

Maude's One Nation Group, and it was he who edited the group's pamphlet *One Nation* in 1950.

He gained no position in Churchill's government when it came to power in 1951 but earned a reputation as an effective speaker on health. (He once suggested in debate that discussing the National Health Service without Aneurin Bevan "would be like putting on Hamlet with no one to play the part of the First Gravedigger.") He was appointed minister of health in 1952.

In December 1955, following Sir Anthony Eden's rise to the premiership, Macleod entered the cabinet as minister of labor. In this role he announced the ending of national service, the two-year period of military service that was required of all young men by the state, in 1957, and he gained kudos from defeating Frank Cousins and the trade unions involved in the bus strike of 1958.

Macleod had some misgivings over the Suez Crisis of 1956 but was not so closely involved that he felt the need to resign. Moreover, he benefited from Sir Anthony Eden's resignation in favor of Harold Macmillan, with whom he had good relations. In 1959, Macmillan appointed Macleod secretary of state for the colonies, helping speed the move toward independence for Kenya, Tanganyika, Uganda, and Nyasaland. In October 1961, Macleod became chancellor of the Duchy of Lancaster, leader of the House of Commons, and chairman of the Conservative Party organization. However, he was removed from all three positions in 1963, having become unpopular with the right wing of the Conservative Party over the speedy dismantling of the British Empire, and having failed to arrest the declining fortunes of the Conservative government.

From 1963 to 1965, he was the editor of the *Spectator* and wrote extensively on Conservative policies and the Conservative leadership crisis of 1963. With the defeat of the Conservative Party in 1964 he was invited to join the shadow cabinet by Sir Alec Douglas Home, his first brief role being responsibility for dealing with the steel industry. He became shadow chancellor of the exchequer in 1965. With the return of Edward Heath's Conservative government, he was appointed chancellor of the exchequer on 20 June

1970; but he suffered appendicitis and died of a heart attack soon after, on 20 July 1970.

Keith Laybourn

See also: Churchill, Sir Winston; Eden, Sir Anthony; Macmillan, Harold
References and Further Reading: Fisher, Nigel, 1973, *Iain Macleod* (London: Andre Deutsch).

Macmillan, Harold
(Earl of Stockton)
(1894–1986) [PM, CE, FS]

Macmillan was a curiously old-fashioned Conservative prime minister for the 1950s and 1960s, combining an interest in Empire with a commitment to the welfare state. He is associated with the slogan "You've never had it so good," which he devised to mask the fact that Britain was suffering an economic decline relative to other industrial countries.

Maurice Harold Macmillan was born on 10 February 1894, the third child of Maurice Macmillan and Helen Belles, an American. His paternal grandfather was a Scottish crofter, and his father ran a successful book publishing company. The young Harold was educated at Eton and at Balliol College, Oxford. When World War I broke out, he volunteered for the army and entered the Grenadier Guards.

Although seriously wounded in the war, Macmillan recovered. In the immediate postwar years, he went to Canada as an aide to the Duke of Devonshire and later married Dorothy, the Duke's daughter. But it was a marriage that never quite worked, and by the late 1920s Dorothy was involved with Conservative M.P. Bob Boothby. Nevertheless, Macmillan's marriage to Dorothy provided him an entrée into Conservative politics and helped him win the Stockton-on-Tees parliamentary seat in 1924. He held this seat until 1929, lost it in the Labour election victory, and won it again in 1931, holding it until 1945.

Stockton was suffering from economic depression and high unemployment, particularly in the 1930s, and its experiences ensured that Macmillan would press for the "middle way" in British politics, using both state and capitalist intervention to help revive the economy. In pursuit of this goal, Macmillan's name was associated with that of Oswald Mosley and the formation of the New Party in 1931. At this time he was also closely associated with Winston Churchill, who was experiencing a period in the political wilderness within the Conservative Party. Due to Macmillan's association with fringe political interests, his career in the government administration did not begin to take off until World War II.

He first entered office in Churchill's wartime government, between 1940 and 1941, with an appointment as parliamentary secretary at the Ministry of Supply, and soon moved on to the post of undersecretary of state for the colonies. In December 1942, he was given the unique appointment of minister resident at the Allied Force Headquarters in Algiers. His post changed both in location and in responsibility as the Allied forces advanced in North Africa. He dealt with De Gaulle, arranged the Italian surrender, and became U.K. High Commissioner to the Advisory Council for Italy. He also served as resident minister of state in Italy and Greece.

At the end of the war, Macmillan was involved in drafting the Yalta agreement, according to which Russian prisoners of war who were being held in Allied prison camps were to be sent back to the Soviet Union upon their release. That they were being sent to their deaths was an observation made only later, by a number of writers whose reports surfaced shortly after Macmillan's retirement in 1963. Some accused Macmillan of knowingly conspiring to send these Allied prisoners to their deaths (the so-called Klagenfurt Conspiracy).

In Churchill's caretaker government at the end of the war Macmillan was appointed to the post of secretary of state for air. However, he lost his Stockton seat at the general election of 1945. Shortly afterward he returned to the House of Commons as M.P. for the London seat of Bromley, Beckenham, and Penge, which he represented from 1945 until his retirement in 1964. This period of his life was closely associated with the idea that a form of political consensus existed between the major political parties in British politics, particularly in relationship to his commitment to the welfare state.

Prime Minister Harold Macmillan converses with Nikita Khrushchev (left) following Macmillan's disarmament address to the United Nations, 1960 (Library of Congress)

When Winston Churchill formed a Conservative government in 1951, Macmillan became minister of housing and local government, and he set a target of having 300,000 houses built per year. When Sir Anthony Eden replaced Churchill in 1954, Macmillan became minister of defense. After Eden and R. A. Butler, he was widely viewed as the third most important figure within the Conservative Party. Following the 1955 general election he became foreign secretary, but he was quickly appointed chancellor of the exchequer, allowing Butler to move to the Home Office. Macmillan held the post of chancellor until 1957.

Nineteen fifty-six was a key year for Macmillan; to a great extent, it determined his future political prospects. That year, Egypt's leader, Gamal Abdel Nasser, nationalized the Suez Canal, which until then had been controlled by a company based in Paris. The British and French felt that Nasser's action would threaten their interests in the Middle East and the Far

East. In response, Eden set up a committee—of which Macmillan was a member—to develop with the French a joint plan for retaking the canal. Both Britain and France felt that the industrialized world would share their outrage at Nasser's act, but they were mistaken; only Israel was prepared to participate in military action against Nasser. Following an Israeli invasion of the canal zone, British and French military forces entered the arena. These events provoked an immediate run on the pound and a financial crisis, which forced the British to accept U.S. demands to withdraw in favor of United Nations forces. The collusion between the Israeli, French, and British forces was played down in government statements, and Macmillan announced that Britain was withdrawing its forces because the job was done.

There was dissension within Conservative ranks because of the military withdrawal; and although Macmillan was deeply involved in the events, Prime Minister Eden took the brunt of criticism. When Eden fell ill and was admitted to the hospital (his place temporarily being filled by Butler), Macmillan turned his mind to the succession. On 22 November 1956, both Butler and Macmillan addressed the 1922 Committee, the committee of the Conservative back-benchers in the House of Commons. The response to Macmillan was animated; to Butler, lukewarm. On 9 January 1957, Eden indicated to the queen his intention to resign on the grounds of ill health. The next day, Macmillan was appointed prime minister.

Floating on the support and indulgence generally available to new prime ministers, Macmillan quickly overcame the embarrassment of the Suez withdrawal. He restored relations with President Dwight Eisenhower and obtained a soon-to-be obsolete missile system from the United States. One of the high points of this honeymoon period was the Nassau agreement of December 1962, by which U.S. President John F. Kennedy agreed that the United States would supply Britain with a number of Polaris submarines. Macmillan presented himself as a statesman who could deal with the Russians, and he was involved in various conferences to ease East-West tensions, the most important being the Nuclear Test Ban Treaty of July 1963. Although Macmillan was successful in most efforts, he nevertheless failed in his bid, mounted in August 1961, to get Britain to join the Common Market. Also, in touring Africa in 1960, where colonialism was giving way to national movements, he detected "the winds of change" blowing across Africa, which would bring about the end of the British Empire and the decline of British influence.

On economic and social matters, Macmillan was a fervent believer in the need to maintain the welfare state, even if Britain's economic situation was not solid enough to support more than a minimalist welfare state provision. Yet as chancellor of the exchequer between 1955 and 1957, he had achieved little in this area. As prime minister, he opposed the anti-inflation measures of his first chancellor, Peter Thorneycroft, who wished to make cuts in the welfare budget. This conflict led to the resignations of Thorneycroft, Nigel Birch, and Enoch Powell in January 1958. Derick Heathcoat Amory re-

placed Thorneycroft. Under Heathcoat Amory the economy expanded too rapidly, and Britain was facing inflation by the late 1950s. Nevertheless, Macmillan won the 1959 general election with a much misquoted statement, revived during the election from a speech he had made in 1957: "Let's be frank about it; most of our people have never had it so good."

In the early 1960s, however, his government faced mounting criticism for a lackluster economic performance. Macmillan sacked one-third of his cabinet, including Selwyn Lloyd, on the "night of the long knives" in March 1962. This event evoked barbs from many observers, including Jeremy Thorpe, the Liberal leader, who quipped, "Greater love hath no man than he lay down his friends for his life." Harold Wilson, now the leader of the Labour opposition, joked, with some exaggeration, that half the cabinet had been sacked—"the wrong half, as it happened" (Eccleshall and Walker 1998, p. 327). The notorious Profumo affair added to the government's unpopularity, and Macmillan's ensuing health problems eventually brought his administration down.

John Profumo, a junior minister at the War Office, had been consorting with Christine Keeler, a prostitute, who was also associating with Captain Ivanov of the Russian Embassy. Profumo's offense was compounded when he gave false assurances to Macmillan and the House of Commons that there had been no "impropriety" (i.e., that he had divulged no secrets to Keeler). When evidence of security breaches surfaced, the scandal and political embarrassment were multiplied.

On 9 October 1963, facing surgery for cancer of the prostate (which he had the following day, with good results), Macmillan wrote to the queen, offering his resignation. The offer was accepted, and Macmillan was replaced by Lord Home (Sir Alec Douglas Home).

In 1984, Macmillan was ennobled as the first Earl of Stockton, although he had done nothing to endear himself to Margaret Thatcher and her administration. (The previous year, for example, he had made a public statement likening Thatcher's privatization to "selling off the family silver.") He died on 29 December 1986.

Macmillan was an able prime minister and a formidable political leader, with a streak of ruthlessness. He was also something of a transitional figure, presiding over Britain's declining empire, being committed to defense and also wishing to preserve the welfare state. These approaches were largely conditioned by his experiences in connection with the Empire, with unemployment, and with appeasement during the 1930s. He was no innovator; the word *illusion* comes more readily to mind than does *innovation* as a description of his term in office. The idea that all was well with Britain, when it clearly was not so, was an illusion that his successors could not afford to perpetuate.

Keith Laybourn

See also: Butler, Richard Austen; Chamberlain, Neville; Churchill, Sir Winston; Eden, Sir Anthony; Heathcoat Amory, Derick; Home, Sir Alec Douglas; Lloyd, Selwyn; Thorneycroft, Peter
References and Further Reading: Carlton, David, 1981, *Anthony Eden: A Biography* (London: Allen Lane); Carlton, David, 1989, *Britain and the Suez Crisis* (Oxford: Basil Blackwell); Clarke, Peter, 1991, *A Question of Leadership* (London: Penguin); Eccleshall, Robert, and Graham Walker (eds.), 1998, *Biographical Dictionary of British Prime Ministers* (London: Routledge); Evans, Harold, 1981, *Downing Street Diary: The Macmillan Years, 1957–1963* (London: Hodder & Stoughton); Horne, Alistair, 1988, *Macmillan, 1894–1956* (London: Macmillan); Howard, Anthony, 1987, *RAB: The Life of R. A. Butler* (London: J. Cape); Knight, R., 1986, "Harold Macmillan and the Cossacks: Was There a Klagenfurt Conspiracy?" *Intelligence and National Security* 1: 234–254; Lamb, Richard, 1995, *The Macmillan Years, 1957–63: The Emerging Truth* (London: John Murray); Macmillan, Harold, 1933, *Reconstruction: A Plea for National Unity* (London: Macmillan); ——, 1966, *Winds of Change, 1914–1939* (London: Macmillan); ——, 1967, *The Blast of War, 1939–1945* (London: Macmillan); ——, 1969, *Tides of Fortune, 1945–1955* (London: Macmillan); ——, 1971, *Riding the Storm, 1956–1959* (London: Macmillan); ——, 1972, *Pointing the Way, 1959–1961* (London: Macmillan); ——, 1973, *At the End of the Day, 1961–1963* (London: Macmillan); ——, 1984, *War Diaries* (London: Macmillan); Pimlott, B., 1988, "Is the Postwar Consensus a Myth?" *Contemporary Record* 2 (Summer): 12–14; Sampson, Anthony, 1967, *Macmillan: A Study in Ambiguity* (London: Allen Lane); Turner, John, 1994, *Macmillan* (London: Longman).

Major, John
(1943–) [PM, CE, FS]

John Major is something of a political enigma. He emerged, with limited political experience, to become the Conservative leader and prime minister in 1990; successfully fought off many political challengers to his position throughout the early and mid-1990s; and was heavily defeated in the 1997 general election, after which he promptly resigned as Conservative leader and immediately faded into political obscurity. Kenneth Baker has suggested that Major published his autobiography in 1999 in order not to be ranked alongside Sir Anthony Eden, Neville Chamberlain, and Arthur James Balfour as one of the Conservative Party's least successful premiers in the twentieth century (*Observer,* 7 October 1999). However, Baker, in a more generous vein, also asserted, "For a Brixton [in London] lad to spend longer in Number 10 than either Asquith or Lloyd George is no mean feat" (*Observer,* 7 October 1999).

John Major was born 29 March 1943, the younger son of Abraham Thomas Ball (who later adopted Major as his stage name) and his second wife, Gwendolyn Minny Coates. John's father was a master bricklayer in his early life; a juggler, acrobat, and comedian in midlife; and a businessman in his later years. John's mother also worked in the theater. John was educated at Rutlish Grammar School, left school at 16 to work as a clerk, and eventually ended up working in the banking sector.

His political career began early. He helped form the Brixton branch of the Young Conservatives in 1965 and was elected to the Lambeth borough council in 1968, where he eventually became chairman of the housing committee. He married Norma Johnson, a teacher, in 1970. He was unsuccessful in his candidature for Camden, St. Pancras North, in 1974, but became M.P. for Huntingdonshire in 1979, holding the seat until 1983, when he became M.P. for Huntingdon, which he has represented ever since.

He rose swiftly in the Conservative ranks and was appointed private secretary to the minister of state at the Home Office in 1981. Successively, he was assistant whip, whip (1983–1985), undersecretary of social security (1985–

John Major in September 1996, at the last Conservative Party conference before the 1997 general election (Sean Aidan;Eye Ubiquitous/Corbis)

1986), minister of state at the Department of Health and Social Security (1986–1987), and chief secretary to the Treasury (1987–1989).

Having served in these junior and middle-level government posts, Major then rose swiftly to the top in a little more than 16 months, between July 1989 and November 1990. During that period he filled the posts of foreign secretary (July–October 1989); chancellor of the exchequer (October 1989–November 1990); and prime minister (November 1990–May 1997), having defeated both Douglas Hurd and Michael Heseltine in the 1990 Conservative leadership contest to replace Margaret Thatcher, who had resigned after failing to secure the required first ballot majority over Heseltine. Although Major was an astute politician and a good administrator, he also benefited from a stroke of political good fortune—as he himself realized. According to Baker, Major opened his first cabinet meeting in 1990 with a rhetorical question, asking almost musingly, with a diffident smile, "Well, who would have thought it?" (*Observer*, 7 October 1999).

Indeed, many were surprised at the ease with which he moved upward through the Conservative Party and the Conservative government. Before he became prime minister, few knew where he stood in the political spectrum; it was clear only that he shared with Thatcher a loathing of inflation and a commitment to rolling back the welfare state. In other policy areas, however, he was more open to persuasion, more willing to gain consensus, and less driven by a fixed ideology. His pragmatism led him to drop the poll tax that Thatcher had introduced as a way of financing local government; and he was less confrontational with Europe than Thatcher had tended to be. Yet he gained a reputation for toughness through his support for the Gulf War in 1991, when the United States, Britain, and other nations drove Saddam Hussein's forces out of Kuwait. Major's determination was even more evident in his support of Boris Yeltsin in Russia in 1991. His victory in the 1992 general election also indicated that he was more than a caretaker prime minister.

Nevertheless, Major faced numerous problems

within his party, particularly over Europe. Major's position on Europe stressed the need to protect British interests. However, within his party were many skeptics who were opposed to any measures that might lead to European integration. Major signed the Maastricht Treaty in December 1991, which edged Britain toward some measures of integration. However, Britain was blown off course in September 1992 when the sterling crisis led to its withdrawal from the European Exchange Rate Mechanism. Major pressed ahead with a parliamentary bill to ratify the Maastricht Treaty; but it was not passed in Parliament until the end of 1994, and only then over opposition from the Euro-skeptics, eight of whom had the Conservative whip withdrawn (but were restored to the party within four or five months) and one of whom resigned from the party. They objected to the larger financial contribution that Britain would have to make to the European community as well as moves toward integration.

As a result of this conflict, the narrow Conservative majority in the House of Commons disappeared; and in December 1994, the government was defeated in the vote on increasing the value-added tax on domestic fuel. This proved an embarrassment for Major's government, which was already reeling from political divisions and scandalous allegations of extramarital affairs, gay sex, and abuses of parliamentary privilege. After two Conservative M.P.s were accused of accepting cash in return for tabling parliamentary questions, the Committee for Standards in Public Life (headed by Lord Nolan) had moved to ban paid advocacy by M.P.s and to require the disclosure of incomes earned from services offered as an M.P. The findings and recommendations in the Nolan report divided Conservative M.P.s; and further scandals had deepened the public's perception of widespread corruption in British politics. In 1996, the publication of a report by Sir Richard Scott on the actions of junior ministers in deciding guidelines for the export of arms-related equipment to Iraq placed even more pressure on Major's government.

Such pressures had forced Major to resign as party leader in summer 1995, provoking a leadership contest in which he was one of the candidates. (The final straw had been his meeting, in June 1995, with more than 50 Euro-skeptic Conservative M.P.s—the "Fresh Start Group"—who seemed to have little respect for his position.) In the event, John Redwood was his only opponent, and Major won the contest by 218 votes to 89 votes (22 Conservative M.P.s failed to register a vote, for a variety of reasons). The Euro-skeptics continued nonetheless to pressure Major to take a tougher line on European integration and the single European currency; and Kenneth Clarke, the chancellor of the exchequer and a strong pro-European, threatened to resign if he did so.

Despite the obvious difficulties faced by Major's governments (1990–1992, 1992–1997), there were some achievements on other fronts. Major was praised for his handling of the conflict in Northern Ireland—in particular, for his brokering of the "Downing Street declaration" in December 1993, whereby he and Prime Minister Albert Reynolds of Ireland attempted to persuade the "men of violence" on both sides to enter the democratic process. This effort led to a cease-fire in 1994 by the Irish Republican Army and loyalist paramilitary groups, and the publication in February 1995 of a consultative document for a future government in Northern Ireland. So began the movement toward power-sharing that developed further under Tony Blair.

Nevertheless, the Conservative government's failures seemed to outnumber its successes, and the Conservatives were trounced in the general election of 1 May 1997, which brought Tony Blair to power in a landslide victory for the Labour Party. The general election campaign had seen the Conservative Party split, with about two-thirds of its more than 320 M.P.s declaring their firm opposition to the idea of a single currency for Europe. After the electoral defeat, Major kept his parliamentary seat; but he has remained a relatively quiet figure on the Conservative backbench, making an occasional announcement in favor of closer ties between Britain and the rest of Europe.

Keith Laybourn

See also: Baker, Kenneth; Clarke, Kenneth; Howard, Michael; Lamont, Norman; Lawson, Nigel; Thatcher, Margaret

References and Further Reading: Junor, Penny, 1996, *John Major: From Brixton to Downing Street* (London: Penguin); Major, John, 1999, *John Major: The Autobiography* (London: HarperCollins).

Malmesbury, Earl of (James Howard Harris)
(1807–1889) [FS]

James Howard Harris was born on 25 March 1807, the eldest son of James Edward Harris, the second Earl of Malmesbury, and his wife, Harriet Susan, daughter of Francis Bateman Dashwood. He was educated at a private school at Wimborne and at Eton and then at Oriel College, Oxford, where he obtained a degree in 1827, and finished his education with a tour of the Continent. He married Lady Emma Bennet, the only daughter of the fifth Earl of Tankerville, on 13 April 1830. Soon afterward he went into politics. His campaign for the Portsmouth parliamentary seat failed in 1838, but he was elected for Wilton in 1841. A few months later, after his father's death, he inherited the earldom in September 1841, and was raised to the House of Lords.

Malmesbury was a Conservative protectionist, and he helped organize the protectionist cause in the House of Lords after the collapse of Sir Robert Peel's Conservative government, which was occasioned by the act repealing the Corn Laws in 1846. He served as foreign secretary in the government of the fourteenth Earl of Derby from February to December 1852. In this role, he quickly accepted the peaceful intention of Napoleon III's second empire in France and attempted to maintain good relations with France. He was soon out of office with the failure of the Derby ministry but returned with the formation of another Derby government in February 1858. He held the office of foreign secretary again until June 1859, and during this period was mainly concerned with ensuring peace among France, Austria, and the Italian states, as the latter were increasingly asserting their rights of political independence. He attempted at first to get both Austria and France to evacuate the Roman states and to modify their controls over all of the Italian states; but he adopted a policy of strict neutral-

ity after war broke out in May 1859, still offering his services in the cause of peace.

For the rest of his life Malmesbury remained a prominent Conservative politician in the House of Lords. He was Lord Privy Seal between 1866 and 1868, became leader of the House of Lords in 1868, and was once again Lord Privy Seal between 1874 and 1876. He died on 17 May 1889.

Keith Laybourn

See also: Derby, 14th Earl of; Disraeli, Benjamin
References and Further Reading: Jones, Wilbur, 1956, *Lord Derby and Victorian Conservatism* (Oxford: Basil Blackwell); Stewart, Robert, 1971, *The Politics of Protection: Lord Derby and the Protectionist Party, 1841–1852* (London: Cambridge University Press).

Mansfield, Lord (William Murray; Earl of Mansfield)
(1705–1793) [CE]

William Murray, the first Earl of Mansfield, was a formidable politician who is remembered for his service as lord chief justice. He was born on 2 March 1705, the fourth son of David, fifth Viscount Stormont, and his wife, Margery. The family were Jacobites with a high ideal for royal authority; but throughout his life William strove to distance himself from their political views, and in that he was successful.

Murray was educated at Westminster College and at Christ Church, Oxford, where he obtained a degree in June 1723. He married Lady Elizabeth Finch, seventh daughter of the second Earl of Nottingham. He was called to the bar at Lincoln's Inn in 1743, and embarked on a legal and political career that was to last a lifetime.

In 1742 he became M.P. for Boroughbridge, in Yorkshire. In November of that year, Spencer Compton, the first Earl of Wilmington, invited him to become solicitor general and King's Counsel. Wilmington died in 1743, but Murray continued in office under Henry Pelham, the new prime minister. On 6 December 1743 he spoke in the House of Commons against the disbandment of the Hanoverian mercenaries and in favor of the Habeas Corpus Suspension Bill (suspending the right to trial). In 1747 he became leader of the House of Commons.

Cartoon (London, May 1, 1775) showing George III and Lord Mansfield, seated on an open chaise drawn by "Obstinacy" and "Pride," about to lead Britain into an abyss represented by the war with the American colonies (Library of Congress)

However, the Jacobite sympathies of his family haunted his political career: In February 1753, rumors spread around the cabinet that he had once raised a toast to the Jacobite claims to the British throne, which had led to the Jacobite rebellions of 1715 and 1745.

After the death of Pelham in 1754 Murray became attorney general in the government of the Duke of Newcastle, Pelham's elder brother. In 1756 he became lord chief justice and was created Baron Mansfield of Mansfield, in the county of Nottinghamshire. He also served in the government of William Cavendish, the Duke of Devonshire, and was made a member of the Privy Council. He was briefly chancellor of the exchequer, between April and June 1757 (from the time when H. B. Legge resigned as chancellor, until Legge returned to that post).

For most of the rest of his life Mansfield was involved in politics, although his prime interest was to act as lord chief justice. He was briefly chancellor of the exchequer again from 11 September to 6 October 1767, before Lord North took over that post, North combining the post with that of prime minister between 1770 and 1782. Mansfield became speaker of the House of Lords in 1770.

Mansfield was involved in the trial of John Horne (later Horne-Tooke) for sedition, and played a role also in many other important trials. As a result of his legal work he was granted the title of Earl of Mansfield. Two years later, while Mansfield was giving a speech in the House of Lords, William Pitt, the Elder (Lord Chatham), was suddenly taken seriously ill, and Mansfield is said to have shown "ostentatious indifference" to Pitt's condition. Mansfield himself fell ill on 4 June 1778 and resigned as lord chief justice. He died on 20 March 1793. He is remembered as an impressive debater in his time, second only to Chatham.

Keith Laybourn

See also: Compton, Spencer; Devonshire, Duke of; Legge, Henry; Newcastle, Duke of; Pelham, Hon. Henry; Pitt, William (the Elder)
References and Further Reading: Brown, Peter, and Karl Schweizer (eds.), 1982, *The Devonshire Diary: William Cavendish, Fourth Duke of Devonshire,*

Memoranda on State Affairs (London: Royal Historical Society); Owen, John, 1957, *The Rise of the Pelhams* (London: Methuen).

Matthews, Henry (Viscount Llandaff)
(1826–1913) [HS]

Henry Matthews was a controversial home secretary in Lord Salisbury's Conservative ministry of 1886 to 1892 and was much attacked by the Radical press. He was born on 13 January 1826 in Ceylon, the son of Henry Matthews, a judge, and Emma Blount. He was raised a Catholic and was educated at the University of Paris and then at the University of London. He won a law scholarship in 1849 and was called to the bar at Lincoln's Inn in 1850. In the following years he built a substantial legal practice, which he maintained throughout his parliamentary career. He acted as counsel in various celebrated trials, such as the Tichborne case (1869).

Matthews entered the House of Commons in 1868, having won the borough of Dungarven for the Conservatives. He favored Irish Home Rule, voting with W. E. Gladstone and the Liberals on the Irish Disestablishment Bill (1869). Indeed, he lost his seat to a supporter of Irish Home Rule in 1874 and failed to win it back in 1880. In the 1885 and 1886 general elections, he was elected M.P. for East Birmingham. Also in the latter year, as a result of his personal friendship with Lord Randolph Churchill, he was appointed home secretary, thus becoming the first Catholic cabinet minister since the passing of the Catholic Emancipation Bill in the late 1820s. This meant that the ecclesiastical patronage of his office, which involved dealing with the offices and titles of the Church of England, was handled by the First Lord of the Treasury. However, he proved a poor home secretary, being likened to a "French dancing master" by one critic (*Dictionary of National Biography*, p. 2786).

Between 1886 and 1892, Matthews was involved in many difficult legal cases (such as the Lipski case in 1886 and the Miss Cass case in 1887); and his decisions in these cases were ridiculed by Henry Labouchere in *Truth* and by W. T. Stead in the *Pall Mall Gazette*. His handling of the Miss Cass case evoked such strong parliamentary opposition that he offered his resignation, although it was refused by Salisbury. He also earned the hostility of a substantial proportion of the working class when he supported Sir Charles Warren, the commissioner of police, in his attempts to put an end to the use of Trafalgar Square for open-air meetings in the weeks leading up to "Bloody Sunday" (13 November 1887). The deaths of two in the crowd, from injuries sustained during clashes with police and military forces, heightened the tensions.

In the opposition from 1892 to 1895, Matthews did not participate in the debate surrounding Gladstone's introduction of a bill to remove the remaining legal sanctions against Catholics (popularly known as the Russell and Ripon Relief Bill), and he voted against a bill calling for the disestablishment of the Welsh Church. His Conservative politics had obviously tempered his religious convictions. On the return of the Salisbury government in 1895, he was raised to the peerage as Viscount Llandaff. He continued to play a part in politics, though a diminishing one, until his death on 3 April 1913.

Keith Laybourn

See also: Disraeli, Benjamin; Gladstone, William Ewart; Salisbury, Lord
References and Further Reading: Ensor, Robert K., 1936, *England, 1870–1914* (Oxford: Oxford University Press); Marsh, Peter, 1978, *The Discipline of Popular Government: Lord Salisbury's Domestic Statecraft, 1881–1902* (Hassocks, UK: Harvester Press).

Maudling, Reginald
(1917–1979) [CE, HS]

Maudling was a controversial chancellor of the exchequer whose political career was blighted in the 1960s by a British public that felt it had been deceived by his economic forecasts. He was born in London on 7 March 1917, the only child of Reginald George Maudling and his wife, Elizabeth Emilie Pearson. He was educated at Merchant Taylors' School and at Merton College, Oxford, and then trained to become a barrister, being called to the bar at Middle Temple in 1940. The previous year he had married Beryl Laverick. At the beginning of World War II, he

Reginald Maudling (left), Lord Blankenham (center), and Quinton Hogg (right), later Lord Chancellor, during the 1964 general election campaign (Hulton-Deutsch Collection/Corbis)

joined the intelligence section of the Royal Air Force and then became secretary to Sir Archibald Sinclair (an old Liberal leader and later Viscount Thurso), who was then secretary of state for air.

In the postwar years, Maudling began to pursue a political career. He was trumped in his bid for the Heaton and Isleworth seat during the 1945 general election, but soon joined the Conservative parliamentary secretariat, which amalgamated with the party's research department in 1948. During this time, he advised both Winston Churchill and Anthony Eden on financial matters.

In February 1950 he won the Barnet constituency in the general election, representing it until his death in 1979 (in 1974 the constituency was renamed Chipping Barnet). He then became a junior minister, first as parliamentary secretary to the Ministry of Civil Aviation in April 1952, and then as economic secretary from November 1952 until April 1955. In 1955, when Anthony Eden replaced Winston Churchill as prime minister, Maudling was given the post of minister of supply, and therewith membership in the Privy Council; but he was discontented in this ministry, the function of which was merely to act as go-between for customer and supplier. He approved of the British intervention in the Suez Canal in 1956 as "morally correct" and felt no need to resign in the wake of the political defeat of Eden's government.

In 1957 he was appointed paymaster-general, and he remained in this post until 1959, acting at the same time as deputy to the minister of fuel and power. In 1959 he became president of the Board of Trade, in which capacity he argued forcibly against British entry into the Common Market. Indeed, he helped form the European Free Trade Association in November 1959, consisting of Britain, the Scandinavian countries, Portugal, and Switzerland. Yet when Prime Minister Harold Macmillan began to press for British entry to the Common Market in 1961, Maudling became an advocate of Market membership, although he continued to oppose a unified European state.

For nine months, between October 1961 and July 1962, Maudling served as colonial secretary, negotiating a new constitution for independent Zambia. In July 1962 he became chancellor of the exchequer, replacing J. S. B. Lloyd (later Lord Selwyn-Lloyd), from whom he inherited the "pay pause" policy. In February 1963 he continued in the same line, approving a recommendation by the National Economic Development Council that a 4 percent limit on pay increases be maintained. His 1963 budget was considered cautious. Although his 1964 budget called for an increase of £100 million in indirect taxation, that amount was insufficient to curb consumer spending and the influx of imports that was occurring. The economy was moving into a balance-of-payments crisis as the October 1964 general election approached, but Maudling was reluctant to impose harsher constraints in a pre-election budget. In the end, the government was swept out of power, to be replaced by a new Labour administration under Harold Wilson. Maudling later claimed that Wilson's government had inherited a balance-of-payments deficit of only £600 million; but Labour claimed that the actual deficit was closer to £800 million.

In 1965, out of office and with his financial reputation stained, Maudling became deputy leader of the Conservative Party, and he continued in this position until 1972. In 1970, with the formation of Edward Heath's Conservative government, it was almost inevitable that he would become home secretary. His liberal instincts ensured that repatriation became less central to the Immigration Bill he prepared; but the same instincts meant that he was not the right person to deal with the problem of violence between the Catholic and Protestant communities in Northern Ireland. He reluctantly agreed to internment as a means of controlling terrorism; and he recognized the need for a secretary of state for Northern Ireland, separate from the Home Office.

He was forced to resign as home secretary in July 1972, following the bankruptcy of John Poulson, an architect and builder with whom Maudling had had dealings in the 1960s. The Poulson affair was subject to criminal investigation by the metropolitan police, over which the home secretary had jurisdiction. In the course of the investigation, a conflict of interest emerged when it was revealed that although Maudling had received no salary from Poulson, Poulson had contributed generously to a charitable trust favored by Maudling's wife.

Maudling returned briefly to public life when Margaret Thatcher replaced Edward Heath as Conservative leader in 1975, joining her shadow cabinet; but he lost his position in November 1976. He died on 14 February 1979, an effete politician whose career had reached its apex in the early 1960s and thereafter had declined rapidly due to unsound economic forecasts and unwise business dealings.

Keith Laybourn

See also: Churchill, Sir Winston; Eden, Sir Anthony; Heath, Edward; Macmillan, Harold; Thatcher, Margaret
References and Further Reading: Maudling, Reginald, 1978, *Memoirs* (London: Sidgwick and Jackson).

Maxwell Fyfe, Sir David Patrick (Earl of Kilmuir)
(1900–1967) [HS]

David Patrick Maxwell Fyfe, home secretary and lord chancellor, was better known for his legal rather than his political work and was never a political heavyweight; he was appointed home secretary in the Conservative government of the early 1950s largely because of his legal training.

Maxwell Fyfe was born on 29 May 1900 in Edinburgh, the son of William Thomson Fyfe, a school inspector, and Isabella Campbell, a schoolteacher. He was educated at George Watson College, Fyfe, and went to Balliol College, Oxford, where he obtained a third-class degree. He then trained to become a barrister, being called to Gray's Inn in 1922, practicing in Liverpool, and eventually taking silk and becoming a King's Counsel in 1936. In 1925 he married Sylvia Margaret Harrison, the daughter of William Reginald Harrison, a civil engineer from Liverpool, and sister of Rex Harrison, the actor.

He continued with his legal career despite his election as M.P. for the West Derby division of Liverpool in 1935, combining his legal practice in Liverpool with a daily, late-evening attendance in the House of Commons. In 1942 he was appointed solicitor general in Winston Churchill's wartime government. He lost this position with the formation of Clement Attlee's Labour government in 1945; but his successor, Sir Hartley (later Lord) Shawcross, permitted him to continue as deputy chief prosecutor at Nuremberg. In Nuremberg he successfully undermined the dominant courtroom presence of Goering, whom he regarded as "the most formidable witness I have ever cross-examined." While in opposition, he also became a prominent advocate of European unity centered on Strasbourg and strongly advocated the European Convention on Human Rights.

Maxwell Fyfe became home secretary in the Conservative cabinet of Sir Winston Churchill in October 1951. In this role he became a firm advocate of traditional law and order. He also made the controversial decision not to grant a reprieve to Michael Bentley, who was hanged for the murder of a police officer who had actually been shot by Craig, Bentley's accomplice.

In 1954 Maxwell Fyfe became lord chancellor, with the title of Viscount Kilmuir. In this role he polled the cabinet to advise the queen on who should succeed Sir Anthony Eden, after Eden's government lost support due to its handling of the Suez Canal Crisis of 1956. He advised Queen Elizabeth II that Harold Macmillan should be the next Conservative prime minister. He was understandably shocked when Macmillan dismissed him and six other cabinet ministers in the ministerial reshuffle of July 1962. Disgusted by such shabby treatment, he accepted an earldom and refused to play any further part in legal and political affairs; he surrendered his pension and went to work in the City of London. He died on 27 January 1967. He is still remembered as one of the longest-serving of all lord chancellors, although his impact on Britain's legal system was minimal.

Keith Laybourn

See also: Churchill, Sir Winston; Eden, Sir Anthony; Macmillan, Harold
References and Further Reading: Kilmuir, Earl of, David P., 1964, *Political Adventures* (London: Weidenfeld & Nicolson).

Melbourne, Viscount (Sir William Lamb)
(1779–1848) [PM, HS]

An intelligent man of broad political and literary tastes, William Lamb, the second Viscount Melbourne, is best remembered for his tempestuous and unhappy marriage to Lady Caroline Lamb, who was besotted by Lord Byron, and by the fact that he acted as political tutor to Queen Victoria after she ascended to the throne at age 18 in 1837. He both preceded and followed Sir Robert Peel into office; and although his reputation suffers by comparison with Peel, there is no doubt that his ministries did pass important reforming legislation.

William Lamb was born on 15 March 1779, the second son of Peniston Lamb and Elizabeth Milbanke. He was educated at Eton and at Trinity College, Cambridge. He married Lady Caroline Ponsonby, daughter of the third Earl of Bessborough, in 1805, but separated from her in 1825.

His political career began in 1806 when he became M.P. for Leominster. In 1807 he became M.P. for Portarlington. He left the Commons in 1812 but returned as M.P. for Northampton in 1816, and for Hertfordshire from 1819 to 1826. He was also M.P. for Newport in the Isle of Wight in 1827 and for Bletchingley between 1827 and 1829, before succeeding to the viscountcy of Melbourne in 1829, which gave him a seat in the House of Lords.

From the start, Lamb was a Whig, supporting a party that dated to the Glorious Revolution of 1688, when the "irresponsibility of the Crown" was tempered by "responsible ministers" who wished to work through Parliament for reforms including parliamentary reform and Catholic emancipation. Nevertheless, by 1822 he was attacking extraparliamentary activity and was becoming a conservative Whig, or perhaps a liberal Tory.

Lamb accepted his first ministerial post when

he became chief secretary for Ireland in George Canning's brief coalition government of 1827. After Canning's death, he was associated with a liberal Tory group led by William Huskisson and the third Viscount Palmerston; but all three men left the Duke of Wellington's government in 1828. Viscount Melbourne (Lamb gained this title in 1829) returned as home secretary in Lord Grey's Whig government in November 1830, committing himself to the process of parliamentary reform, although he was not its most enthusiastic supporter.

In many respects his early enthusiasm for reform was waning. Indeed, as home secretary he was almost reactionary. He advertised high rewards for anyone bringing to justice the "Swing Rioters" who were burning haystacks throughout the countryside in 1830. He also waged a campaign against trade unionism. Between November 1830 and July 1834, he presided over the prosecution, imprisonment, and deportation to Tasmania of the Tolpuddle Martyrs—agricultural laborers who had assembled illegally in 1834 to discuss ways of raising their wages.

In July 1834, while acting as home secretary, Melbourne became prime minister after Lord Grey's resignation. His natural conservatism and genial style seem to have made him the best candidate; but within four months he had been dismissed by King William IV, mainly due to his attempt to impose Lord John Russell as leader of the House of Commons against the wishes of the monarch. However, the Tories, under Sir Robert Peel, were unable to sustain a government after the general election; and Melbourne, meeting with radical M.P.s and Daniel O'Connell in April 1835, negotiated the "Lichfield House Compact," a troublesome alliance of liberals that formed another administration under Melbourne.

Melbourne's administration of 1835 to 1841 passed many reforming measures, most obviously the Municipal Corporations Act of 1835, which replaced 178 of the corrupt boroughs, which elected M.P.s, with elected municipal corporations with the power to raise rates, or local taxes. This government survived the general election of 1837, when the Tories made gains, but was widely considered too reformist and too closely associated with the Irish. Nevertheless, there was cross-party support for some government measures, such as the law on civil registration of births, marriages, and deaths, which was passed in 1837.

In 1837 Melbourne assumed the responsibility of tutoring the newly crowned Queen Victoria in the responsibilities of monarchy, emphasizing the Whig view that the monarchy should be subject to the will of Parliament. The queen looked upon Melbourne "as a friend and almost a father" (Ziegler 1982, p. 291). When Melbourne was facing the possibility of his ministry's failure in May 1839, he advised Victoria to send for Sir Robert Peel; but the queen was upset by the latter's forbidding demeanor. In the end, the Whig administration survived another two years. However, the administration had by then accumulated a budget deficit of £3 million, which neither of its two successive chancellors of the exchequer, Thomas Spring-Rice and Francis Baring, had been able to reduce. Baring did announce his intention to reduce tariffs on timber, sugar, and corn in order to stimulate trade; but Peel and the Tories opposed the reduction of duties on imported sugar in May 1841, and proposed and carried a motion of no confidence in the government in June 1841, forcing a general election. Melbourne continued to lead the Whigs until he suffered a stroke in 1841, after which he withdrew from politics.

Melbourne has been much maligned in comparison to Peel, but he was an effective politician. Although Melbourne was reluctant to undertake some kinds of reform (being a gentleman landowner, he naturally shared the interests of the landowning classes), his ministries nevertheless played a significant role in introducing a number of reforms. William Gladstone later acknowledged the importance of the legislation that Melbourne's government had enacted, and Benjamin Disraeli also praised his "generally moderate, well-matured and statesmanlike schemes" (Newbould 1990, p. 267). Melbourne's aristocratic Whig politics ensured that radical change was tempered by patriotism and responsibility in the shaping of the early Whig-Liberal party.

Keith Laybourn

See also: Canning, George; Disraeli, Benjamin; Gladstone, William Ewart; Peel, Sir Robert; Wellington, Duke of

References and Further Reading: Mandler, Peter, 1990, *Aristocratic Government in the Age of Reform* (Oxford: Clarendon); Marshall, Dorothy, 1975, *Lord Melbourne* (London: Weidenfeld & Nicolson); Newbould, Ian, 1990, *Whiggery and Reform, 1830–1841: The Politics of Government* (London: Macmillan); Ziegler, Philip, 1982, *Melbourne* (London: Collins).

Morrison, Herbert (Lord Morrison of Lambeth) (1888–1965) [FS, HS]

Alongside Clement Attlee and Ernest Bevin, Morrison was one of the three most powerful political figures in the two Labour governments of 1945 to 1951. His real importance to Labour was as the organizer of the political victory of 1945 and of the nationalization program that emerged. He was also Attlee's deputy, and is considered the finest administrator that the Labour Party has ever produced.

Herbert Stanley Morrison was born in London on 3 January 1888, the youngest of seven children of Henry, a police constable, and Priscilla (Lyon) Morrison. He worked for a time as a shop assistant before carving out a career in politics. He joined the quasi-Marxist Social Democratic Federation in 1907, but left and joined the Brixton branch of the Independent Labour Party (ILP) in 1910. From 1910 to 1913 he was chairman of the Brixton branch of the National Union of Clerks and became more deeply involved in local politics. During these years he developed a clear socialist perspective, advocating public works to deal with unemployment and supporting the women's suffrage movement.

During World War I he adopted an antiwar stance and became closely involved in the ILP's peace activities. Although blind in his right eye—a physical condition that exempted him from military service—he nonetheless attended the Military Service Tribunal to determine whether or not his refusal to enlist was genuine, and agreed to work on the land as a substitute form of war work. He married Margaret Kent, the daughter of a railway clerk, in 1919. The couple had one daughter.

Morrison rose quickly in Labour circles, becoming a member of the Hackney borough council and mayor in 1920 and 1921, respectively. He joined the national executive committee of the Labour Party in 1920. He was also a member of the London county council from 1922 to 1945, becoming its leader in 1939 to 1940. But during these years, his parliamentary activities absorbed most of his attention.

Morrison served three stints as M.P. for South Hackney from 1923 to 1924, from 1929 to 1931, and from 1935 to 1945, before becoming M.P. for East Lewisham (1945–1950) and then for South Lewisham (1950–1959). He was appointed minister of transport in the Labour government of 1929 to 1931, and served as minister of supply for a few months in 1940 before becoming home secretary and minister for home security. He served in the latter post from 1940 to 1945, and as a member of Churchill's war cabinet in 1942. Morrison's finest hour came when he was Lord President of the Council, leader of the House of Commons, and deputy prime minister in Attlee's Labour governments of 1945 to 1951. In 1951 he became foreign secretary; and following Labour's defeat, he continued to act as a deputy leader of the Labour Party, from 1951 to 1955.

By any standards, Morrison's political career was impressive, whether in organizing the London Passenger Transport Board in the 1930s, organizing air raid precautions during World War II, pushing forward bills nationalizing the coal industry and railways in Attlee's postwar Labour governments, or in promoting the Festival of Britain in 1951. He was largely responsible for the formulation of Labour's nationalization program, and his book *Socialization and Transport* (1933) committed Labour to the idea of a corporate public body as the model for state control. He was above all a supreme party organizer, keeping the Labour backbenchers happy by creating subject committee groups examining some aspects of the Labour Party policy. He gave cohesion to the Labour Party and to Attlee's postwar Labour governments.

Nevertheless, there were many personal and political failures in Morrison's life. His first marriage failed, and he appears to have had several flirtations, including one with Ellen Wilkinson. Margaret, his first wife, died of cancer in 1953, and he married Edith Meadowcroft in 1955. Politically, his main setbacks occurred at the hands of Attlee, who defeated him for the Labour Party leadership in 1935, and thwarted his attempts to become leader in 1939 and 1945. Attlee delayed his own retirement long enough to enable Hugh Gaitskell to become leader in 1955. Morrison was disliked by some leading party figures. When someone once suggested that Morrison was "his own worst enemy," Ernest Bevin allegedly retorted, "Not while I'm around." Morrison was also considered by some members of the Labour Party to be out of his depth as foreign secretary.

Morrison stood down as M.P. in 1959, whereupon he was elevated to the House of Lords as Lord Morrison of Lambeth. He was appointed president of the board of film censors in 1960, a post he held until his death on 6 March 1965.

Keith Laybourn

See also: Attlee, Clement; Bevin, Ernest; Churchill, Sir Winston; Cripps, Stafford; Dalton, Hugh; Gaitskell, Hugh
References and Further Reading: Donoghue, Bernard, and G. W. Jones, 1973, *Herbert Morrison: Portrait of a Politician* (London: Weidenfeld & Nicolson); Morgan, Kenneth, 1987, *Labour People* (Oxford: Oxford University Press); Morrison, Herbert, 1933, *Socialization and Transport* (London: Constable);——, 1943, *Looking Ahead* (London: Hodder & Stoughton); ——, 1949, *How London Is Governed* (London: People's Universities Press); ——, 1960, *Herbert Morrison: An Autobiography of Lord Morrison of Lambeth, PC, CH* (London: Odhams Press).

Mulgrave, Lord (Henry Phipps; Earl of Mulgrave; Viscount Normanby)
(1755–1831) [FS]

Henry Phipps was born on 14 February 1755, the second son of Constantine Phipps, Baron Mulgrave of New Ross, and his wife, Lepell Hervey. His elder brother was Constantine John, second Baron Mulgrave. Henry Phipps was educated at Eton and then entered the army in 1775, rising to the rank of captain in 1778.

He joined several regiments, fought in the American wars, was stationed in Jamaica, and attained the rank of colonel in 1790. In 1792 he gained the temporary rank of brigadier general of three regiments sent from Gibraltar to garrison Toulon. He eventually rose to the rank of general in 1809, although his active military career effectively ended in 1801.

During these years Phipps combined his military career with politics. In 1784, Phipps was elected as M.P. for Totnes, and in 1790 became M.P. for Scarborough. By and large he supported the foreign and domestic policies of William Pitt, the Younger, the Tory prime minister, but opposed him on parliamentary reform and the ending of slavery.

In 1792 he succeeded, on the death of his elder brother, to the Irish barony of Mulgrave. On 13 August 1794 he was created a peer of the United Kingdom, with the title of Baron Mulgrave of Mulgrave, Yorkshire. The following year, he married Martha Sophia Maling. During this time he acted as a military adviser to Pitt.

Mulgrave was most critical of the policy of the Addington ministry (1801–1804), which was formed after Pitt's resignation in 1801. Pitt formed his second ministry in June 1804, and Mulgrave became secretary for foreign affairs in January 1805, a post that many in political circles felt was beyond his powers. However, he proved an able debater: In February 1805 he announced Britain's breach with Spain and ably defended the seizure of Spanish treasure ships at Ferrol before war was declared. In January 1806 he presented to Parliament treaties concluded with Russia and Sweden. However, after Pitt died, Mulgrave and most of Pitt's friends resigned on 7 February 1806.

Although out of office during the period of Lord Grenville's "Ministry of All the Talents," Mulgrave returned to office as First Lord of the Admiralty in both the succeeding Portland and Perceval ministries, holding the post from 1807 to 1810. In this role he was responsible for several successful naval expeditions, including the seizure of the Danish fleet; but his actions against the French fleet in 1809 were unsuccessful. In May 1810 he became major general of ordnance. He maintained his membership in the cabinet, through the Perceval and Lord Liverpool ministries, until 1820, although he resigned as major general of ordnance, in favor of the Duke of Wellington in 1818.

After 1812 he spoke rarely in the House of Lords. His attitude toward Catholic emancipation changed over time, and he voted in favor of the measure in 1828. He was created the first Earl of Mulgrave and Viscount Normanby in September 1812. He died on 7 April 1831, a much respected politician and soldier, and a much admired debater.

Keith Laybourn

See also: Addington, Henry; Liverpool, Earl of; Perceval, Spencer; Pitt, William (the Younger); Portland, Duke of; Wellington, Duke of
References and Further Reading: Dickinson, Harry, 1985, *British Radicalism and the French Revolution, 1789–1815* (Oxford: Blackwell).

N

Newcastle, Duke of (Hon. Sir Thomas Pelham-Holles) (1693–1768) [PM, HS]

A wealthy aristocrat, Newcastle was the first British prime minister who had not sat in the House of Commons prior to attaining the top government office. He was also a long-serving and dedicated career politician who loved office and who was much poorer when he left it than he had been when he entered it. His ducal income of around £25,000 a year, arising from his extensive property in 11 English counties, was never enough to support his lavish spending, much of which was aimed at extending his influence and securing him support in elections. He was never free of debt, which haunted him throughout his life. By age 30 he had borrowed at least £100,000, and fifteen years later he had debts of nearly twice that sum.

Newcastle's finances were put into the hands of trustees in 1724, a new and more stringent trust was formed in 1738, and with the aid of his brother Henry Pelham a final Pelham family settlement was agreed in November 1741. However, the discussions between Newcastle and his various estate stewards seem more frequently to have revolved around politics and electioneering than around money. He involved himself energetically and in minute detail in the business of winning electoral support, knowing individually hundreds of voters and people of influence in the constituencies that he directly controlled, and using all of the government resources at his disposal to strengthen his base of support. As secretary of state he was a fount of patronage, granting pardons for convicted criminals at the request of local gentlemen (a frequent demand) and controlling appointments to many minor places. In addition, after he became the government's ecclesiastical minister in 1736, he reveled in the extensive possibilities for patronage within the Anglican church, vetting candidates with an eye both to good churchmanship and solid Whig beliefs. By the time he was 50, Newcastle was the most formidable election manager alive, if only by dint of long and assiduous practice rather than a genius for innovative thinking.

He was born (21 July 1693) the son of Thomas, Baron Pelham of Laughton, and added the name Holles to his own in 1711 when he inherited the estates of his maternal uncle John Holles. In 1713, while still a minor, he inherited the title and estates of his father. Just as Newcastle reached the age of 21, in 1714, George I came to the throne. The king soon showed his appreciation of the loyal activity of this young, wealthy, and devoted Whig. In October 1714 Pelham was created Earl of Clare, a title that gave the name to his estate, Claremont in Surrey, which to the end of his life was his favorite residence. There he kept his celebrated French chef and lavished huge sums on landscaping, employing first Charles Bridgeman and later William Kent. In August 1715 he was elevated to Marquess of Clare and Duke of Newcastle upon Tyne. In April 1717 the young duke took up an important court post as lord chamberlain and in the same month married Lady Henrietta Godolphin, the 16-year-old granddaughter of the Duke of Marlborough. It was a singularly devoted, though childless union: Henrietta like himself was a hypochondriac, and the smallest of her imaginary indispositions was enough, even after forty years of marriage, to justify Newcastle's neglect of official business until she recovered.

In April 1724 Newcastle embarked on the first of his great state employments, as secretary of state for the Southern Department, with responsibilities not only for southern Europe but also for overseas colonies, most importantly those in North America. Occasionally, Newcastle's use of patronage while in this office contributed to effective government, as it did in his sponsorship of William Shirley, a Sussex man and Pelham supporter, as candidate for governor of Massachusetts. Generally, however, the duke practiced what has been called "salutary neglect," leaving the colonists to their own decision-making processes.

Newcastle's main preoccupations were the church and legal administration at home, and the balance of European power abroad. He clung to what has been called the "old system" in diplomacy, in which the maritime and Protestant identities of Britain and the United Provinces made them natural partners, along with some small German states and the Habsburg Empire, which although Catholic, were dynastically opposed to the two other major Catholic powers, France and Spain, both under Bourbon rule. This broad alignment served British interests well for a long time, though Newcastle's failure to see that circumstances had changed in the 1750s was one cause of the country's entry into the Seven Years' War in 1756.

Newcastle was an indefatigably industrious secretary of state, working a full week in his London office, despite his love of Claremont and of food and wines. Paperwork was his obsession, and he preserved even minute scraps of official correspondence and memoranda. At cabinet meetings he reserved one end of the cabinet table for himself, so as to spread out all his papers and to keep a full record of what passed. His passion for documentation, and his need for constant advice and reassurance in letters from his closest colleagues, gave rise to the most extensive and complete record of activity of any British statesman. His surviving papers fill more than 425 volumes in the British Library alone. Historians who have used those papers in detailed studies of diplomacy and political conflict have judged Newcastle more positively than have those who relied more heavily on contemporary descriptions of the duke's fussy and undistinguished manner and his undoubted absurdities.

Anecdote can, however, enrich our understanding of Newcastle's personality. The royal family is said to have nicknamed him Permis because of his excessively deferential way of asking in French, each time he spoke, whether it was permitted to make an observation ("Est-il permis?"). Newcastle also reportedly was so afraid of sleeping in unaired sheets that when visiting strange houses he sent servants to lie in his bed before he would occupy it himself. At the funeral of George II, if Horace Walpole is to be believed, the king's son, "the Duke of Cumberland, who was sinking with heat, felt himself weighed down, and turning round, found it was the Duke of Newcastle standing upon his train, to avoid the chill of the marble." With all his oddities, and despite his good-natured inability to say no to requests (which often led him to make promises and then disappoint petitioners when he could not keep them), the duke was not lacking in shrewdness and political talent. He was certainly hungry for office even in old age, not least because his finances absolutely required that he maintain lucrative employment.

By the late 1730s, Newcastle was developing his independence from Walpole. He headed a parliamentary group that, against the prime minister's wishes, favored war with Spain (which began in October 1739). After Walpole's fall in 1742, the duke and his brother, Henry Pelham, became the leaders, along with Lord Chancellor Hardwicke, of the "old corps" of Whigs who had long controlled the government. In February 1748, at the close of the War of Austrian Succession, Newcastle was transferred to the post of secretary of state for the north, and at the same time took over as leader of the House of Lords, a role for which he was not well suited, as he rarely spoke well enough to lead debates on behalf of the ministry.

In March 1754, when his brother died, Newcastle became First Lord of the Treasury. His misreading of the diplomatic position and his alienation of the Habsburg ruler Maria Theresa contributed to Britain's unfavorable position early in the Seven Years' War, which began in May 1756. Unable to persuade William Pitt, the

Elder, to join him in government, Newcastle resigned in November 1756. At what could have been the end of his career of almost forty years in government, his services were recognized in the granting him of the additional title of Duke of Newcastle-under-Lyme—so devised as to pass the Newcastle name on to his favorite nephew, "Linky," the Earl of Lincoln, when the duke died without issue. At the end of June 1757, Newcastle resumed office as prime minister, bringing Pitt with him as secretary of state for the south. The war effort was newly galvanized by a combination of Newcastle's administrative energy and thoroughness with Pitt's strategic sense and oratory.

With the accession of George III in October 1760, however, Newcastle's days of favor were over. He was required by the new king to manage the general election of January 1761 without any help from the secret service funds. Using his own money and all the influence that remained to a politician who was in his late sixties and obviously soon to be discarded in favor of Lord Bute, Newcastle secured a creditable majority but was increasingly bypassed in decision making as the war was brought to a speedy and by no means favorable end. At the end of May 1762 the duke resigned, loftily refusing a pension despite his enormous debts. His only subsequent role in high politics was as Lord Privy Seal in Lord Rockingham's ministry, from July 1765 to July 1766. He was delighted to be back at the center of affairs and again in control of ecclesiastical patronage. In March 1766 he gave a notably successful speech in the Lords on the repeal of the Stamp Act and the need for change in Parliament's relations with the American colonies. Newcastle finally retired to private life when Rockingham was dismissed from office, and once more he refused an offered pension of £4,000. He suffered a stroke the following year, and died in November 1768, having provided in his will that all his debts must be paid before any legacies could take effect.

Philip Woodfine

See also: Bute, Earl of; Pelham, Hon. Henry; Rockingham, Marquess of; Walpole, Sir Robert
References and Further Reading: Browning, Reed, 1976, *The Duke of Newcastle* (New Haven, CT, and London: Yale University Press); Clark, Jonathan C. D., 1983, *The Dynamics of Change: The Crisis of the 1750s and the English Party System* (Cambridge: Cambridge University Press); Kelch, Ray A., 1974, *Newcastle: A Duke without Money* (London: Routledge & Kegan Paul); Middleton, Richard, 1985, *The Bells of Victory: The Pitt-Newcastle Ministry and the Conduct of the Seven Years War* (Cambridge: Cambridge University Press); Owen, John B., 1957, *The Rise of the Pelhams* (London: Methuen).

Normanby, Marquess of (Constantine Henry Phipps)
(1797–1863) [HS]

A home secretary in the government of Lord Melbourne, Constantine Henry Phipps was the son of Henry Phipps, the first Earl of Mulgrave. He was born on 15 May 1797, and was educated at Harrow and at Trinity College, Cambridge. In 1918 he entered Parliament as M.P. for Scarborough, the seat his father had once represented. That same year, he married Maria, the eldest daughter of Thomas Henry Liddell, the first Lord Ravensworth. He made a successful maiden speech before the Commons in 1819, in favor of Catholic emancipation, a cause that his father had accepted after 1812. Unlike his father, he was also in favor of parliamentary reform. Soon afterward he left the House of Commons to live for a time in Italy.

He returned the House of Commons as M.P. for Higham Ferrers in 1822. His liberal interests drew him to the Whigs, with their emphasis on the control of the monarch through Parliament, and he became a great supporter of George Canning. He became M.P. for Malton in 1826. In 1831 he succeeded his father to the earldom of Mulgrave, with a position in the House of Lords. In 1832 he was appointed captain-general and governor of Jamaica. During his tenure there he was involved in suppressing a rebellion and later in distributing financial compensation to slaveholders whose slaves had been emancipated. He resigned from this office in 1834, in the expectation that Lord Grey would offer him a cabinet post in his new ministry. Instead he was offered the relatively minor post of postmaster-general, which did not entitle him to a role in the cabinet. In July 1834, however, when

Lord Melbourne formed a new ministry, Mulgrave was given the post of Lord Privy Seal, which brought with it a seat in the cabinet.

In 1835, Mulgrave became lord lieutenant of Ireland. In this role he attempted to create more administrative and executive positions for Catholics and to reduce the number of positions controlled by Protestants. Daniel O'Connell, the leading advocate of Catholics' rights and of political independence for Ireland, wrote, "We have an excellent man in Lord Mulgrave, the new lord lieutenant" (*Dictionary of National Biography,* p. 1116). In June 1838, Mulgrave was created the Marquess of Normanby. In February 1839, he became secretary of war and the colonies. In May 1839 the Melbourne ministry was defeated on the Jamaica Bill, and for a short time it appeared that either Sir Robert Peel, of the Conservatives, or Mulgrave would be asked to form a government. In the end, the Melbourne ministry survived and Mulgrave remained at the Colonial Office. On 30 August 1839 he was made home secretary, and he remained in that post until the Melbourne ministry fell in September 1841.

Mulgrave later fulfilled a number of diplomatic roles in other Whig ministries. He was ambassador in Paris from 1846 to 1852, and it was his opposition to Lord Palmerston's hasty recognition of Louis Napoleon as the legitimate leader of France that led to Palmerston's dismissal in 1851. In December 1856, Mulgrave was made minister to the court of Tuscany at Florence, where his strong Austrian sympathies proved an embarrassment. He was recalled to England in 1858 and, for the rest of his life, joined his Tory opponents in opposing the Whig ministry of Lord Palmerston, whom he abhorred. He died on 28 July 1863.

Keith Laybourn

See also: Melbourne, Viscount; Palmerston, Lord
References and Further Reading: Ziegler, Philip, 1982, *Melbourne* (London: Collins).

North, Lord (Hon. Sir Frederick North; Baron; Earl of Guildford)
(1732–1792) [PM, CE, HS]

North was an able administrator, Commons politician, and courtier, but was unfortunate in that he lacked the ability to harmonize and control his administration even as it faced some of the most profound political problems of the century. He became known as the prime minister who lost America. His ministry was marred also by the anti-Catholic Gordon riots and by accusations of corruption and tyranny in the press. Easygoing and amiable but driven by a sense of duty to remain in office, North must often have wished to be back amid the rolling farm landscape and honey-colored stone of his village at Wroxton, near Banbury, dominated by the family seat of Wroxton Abbey.

His father, Francis, who lived to within two years of North's own death, had been for a short time governor to Prince George, later George III, who was six years younger than North. As children the two had been so alike that Prince Frederick jokingly remarked to Francis North that "one of their wives had played her husband false." The North family were well placed in provincial landed society. In May 1756, North, then 22, married 16-year-old Anne Speke, whose father, one of the wealthiest landowners in Somerset, had died three years earlier, leaving her an income of £4,000 a year. The marriage was a successful union of two easy-tempered people, and the couple raised three daughters and four sons.

North did not inherit the earldom until 1790, and thus was able throughout his career to sit in the House of Commons—a tradition that the Commons had come to accept, even demand, as normal practice for the First Lord of the Treasury. The long ministries of Walpole and Pelham had so accustomed the lower house to ministerial leadership from within the Commons that it became difficult for later prime ministers, such as the Duke of Newcastle or Grafton, to steer their governments from the upper house.

North entered Parliament for the family seat of Banbury in 1754, but did not make his first speech until two and a half years later. In 1759 he entered his first administrative post, that of junior Lord of the Treasury, under his distant relative Newcastle. He remained in that office under Bute in 1762 and Grenville in 1763. In November 1763 he was chosen as the Com-

"The curious zebra alive from America!" Cartoon showing a group of men, including George Washington, holding the tail of the zebra and Lord North gripping the reins, trying to guide the zebra, whose stripes feature the names of the thirteen colonies, 1778 (Library of Congress)

mons manager of the case against John Wilkes, despite his reluctance, as he had "personally rather received civilities from Wilkes." After a long and violent day of debate, notable for repeated attacks on the ministry's constitutional position by Pitt, North succeeded in passing his motion that the author of *North Briton* issue number 45 should not be protected by parliamentary privilege. North left office when Rockingham formed a ministry in 1765–1766; but he was recognized as an able and useful organizer, and was made paymaster of the forces when Chatham took office in the summer of 1766. Soon he was being considered for the dual role of chancellor of the exchequer and leader of the House of Commons. He initially refused this post in March 1767 but was compelled by circumstances to accept it.

When Charles Townshend died in October 1767, North became chancellor, and in January 1768 he became leader of the Commons. The latter role required him to be constantly in the chamber, where he rapidly acquired a habit of resting his weak eyes, giving an impression of sleep—which evidently was sometimes all too accurate. "Is there a minister who ever slept so much in Parliament?" complained Isaac Barré in 1770. "He has taken his doze and his nap, while notes have been taken for him." As leader, North was responsible for dealing with the further developments of the Wilkes affair, and in the spring of 1769 he was the driving force behind the decision that Wilkes was ineligible to stand for election. This decision effectively meant that the Middlesex freeholders who voted for him had wasted their votes, and the one-sixth of the votes given to the ministerial candidate Colonel Luttrell were the only valid ones. Many members of the Commons feared that the precedents were unclear and that this new decision would open the way to executive control of Parliament. North himself took the opposite stance, defending the right of Parliament to decide upon elections against the clamor of the people: "Let not Parliament fall into contempt. Let not liberty be established upon the ruin of law." Just as this short-run ministerial victory failed to prevent a long-running agitation for liberty outside Parliament, so did North's next intervention, in the American dispute over taxation. He formed a plan to defuse American anger by rescinding all of Townshend's duties save the one on tea—the only one that produced worthwhile revenues. The tea duty was retained to establish the principle of parliamentary sovereignty.

In January 1770, North became First Lord of the Treasury, succeeding his cousin Grafton. One of the earliest decisions taken by Parliament under the new ministry was the resolution to retain the tea duty. For the next three years, however, the fateful consequences were not apparent, and North enjoyed a period of profit and respect. His wife was given the profitable royal post of Ranger of Bushy Park, and he himself was made a Knight of the Garter, a singular honor for a commoner, and elected chancellor of Oxford University.

It was a period also of hard work, not only at the Treasury but in the Commons, which could not open until he attended in person, which he did each day at about 3 P.M. He had to convey to the House the views of the king and the ministry, carry through in detail all financial business, and lead all significant debates. Thomas has calculated that in the 1768–1774 Parliament North made over 900 speeches, more than twice as many as any other member except the speaker. Toward the end of that Parliament, North went to the rescue of the indebted and desperate East India Company with a Regulating Act that contained some well-judged features. A financial loan was extended to the company, and administrative and legal reorganization were supplemented by the privilege of shipping tea directly into North America without paying the English duty. To the English this arrangement must have seemed unexceptionable, as it would give the Americans cheaper tea, even as it was unlikely to undercut the price of the extensively smuggled product. North was inflexibly determined, however, to retain the principle of parliamentary sovereignty embodied in the duty itself.

The response of the Boston trading community was unexpected and shocking: on 16 December 1773 a large party of Americans in Mo-

hawk disguises sacked East India Company ships in Boston harbor and tipped into the sea about 200 chests full of tea. With sizeable support in Parliament, North decided on a swift and uncompromising response to what he mistakenly thought was localized extremism. In March 1774 Parliament passed the Coercive Acts, which quickly fanned the flames of American resentment by their autocratic interference with the administration of politics and justice in Massachusetts. Nothing could have united the protests of the colonists more quickly, as it proved, than the "Intolerable Acts": North had begun the American Revolution.

Like most of his English political contemporaries, North was slow to realize the force of the American decision for independence, but was quick, and sincere, in offering to accommodate the colonies' grievances. In 1775—too late—he offered the colonists control of their own taxation, provided that British parliamentary sovereignty was preserved. Soon North was immersed in the prosecution of a war that was going badly and that by 1778 was threatening to bring on a major war with France; but despite his repeated offers of resignation, the king insisted that he stay on as premier.

North's personal finances were in a poor condition too, partly due to the costs of electoral management, which his income and estate could not support. In September 1777, George III generously paid his debts to the sum of £20,000, but North was calculated to be in debt by nearly as much again when he resigned in 1782. By 1779 serious unrest had broken out also in Ireland, over unfair restrictions on Irish trade, which led some members of his own administration to resign. In December 1779 North substantially freed Irish trade, and in April 1780 he blunted the edge of Dunning's famous resolution against royal "secret influence," though he could not prevent its being passed by the Commons. Allegations of the growing influence of the Crown through corruption were echoed in charges levied personally against North, who had been the king's leading minister for ten years. His unpopularity was manifest in the Gordon riots of June 1780, when a mob attacked his house on Downing Street, which was saved only by the arrival of the military. Satirical prints depicted him as a second Walpole, an all-powerful "prime minister"—a charge to which he was very sensitive. North insisted that no such office as prime minister existed under the constitution, and he frequently remarked that his was a "government by departments," with each minister being answerable to the king for his own department. Such statements indicate his recognition of his own inability to coordinate and control the individual ministries.

North's period in power did not last long after the surrender of Cornwallis at Yorktown in October 1781, even though the government and naval strategies were finally beginning to bear fruit. In mid-March 1782 North narrowly faced down two parliamentary motions of no confidence, and soon after, he was finally allowed by the king to resign. The next phase of his career would have been hard to predict, as within a year he was organizing a parliamentary opposition to Shelburne with Charles James Fox, the man who had been the loudest and most brilliant critic of North's coercive policies and of the ministers' role as the corrupt agents of royal despotism. North still had a substantial following in the Commons, and he and Fox were able to defeat Shelburne over the peace proposals, which tactically meant that George III had no option but to bring in the Duke of Portland to head a ministry in which the main actors would be Fox and North as secretaries of state. The king disliked Fox and felt betrayed by North, but after weeks of delay he finally called them into office in April 1783. The Fox-North coalition was brought down, appropriately enough, by Fox's insistence on passing his India Bill, designed to bring much-needed reform to the East India Company. Like North's earlier attempt, this one backfired because it triggered reactions, not easy to predict, to the invasion of chartered rights and liberties such as those enjoyed, however corruptly, by the company. George III used his personal influence to defeat the bill, and in December 1783 he dismissed Fox and North with a bluntness and a speed that betrayed his anger at their having "stormed the closet" and gained power for all.

North's followers steadily fell away over the next few years, despite his undiminished skill as a debater. His sight, always very poor, deteriorated sharply in 1787, and by the following year he was all but blind and was rarely present in Commons. Nonetheless, when he was present—for example, when he was called upon in 1788–1789 to lead the opposition argument over the Regency Bill—he could still command the floor. North had never been physically attractive and blithely described himself as one of the ugliest men in England, even before the gross obesity of his later years. Horace Walpole harshly described him in Parliament, with his prominent but near-sighted eyes rolling: "a wide mouth, thick lips and an inflated visage gave him the air of a blind trumpeter." He was, nonetheless, a commanding speaker capable of sharp and witty interventions that typically gained the attention and approval of the members of the House. In his last years he bore his blindness and deteriorating health with humor. He died of dropsy on 5 August 1792.

Philip Woodfine

See also: Bute, Earl of; Fox, Charles James; Grenville, George; Portland, Duke of; Shelburne, Earl of; Townshend, Charles (1725–1767)
References and Further Reading: Butterfield, Herbert, 1949, *Lord North and the People, 1779–80* (London: G. Bell & Sons); Christie, Ian R., 1958, *The End of North's Ministry, 1780–1782* (London: Macmillan); Dickinson, H. T. (ed.), 1998, *Britain and the American Revolution* (London: Longman); Thomas, Peter D. G., 1976, *Lord North* (London: Allen Lane); Valentine, Alan, 1967, *Lord North*, 2 vols. (Norman: University of Oklahoma Press); Whiteley, Peter, 1997, *Lord North: The Prime Minister Who Lost America* (London: Hambledon); Wright, J. (ed.), 1841–1843, *Sir Henry Cavendish's Debates of the House of Commons during the Thirteenth Parliament of Great Britain*, 2 vols (London: Longmans).

Northcote, Sir Stafford (Earl of Iddesleigh)
(1818–1887) [FS, CE]

Sir Stafford Henry Northcote was described as a pure-minded politician by William Ewart Gladstone, who eulogized him in the House of Commons on 27 January 1887. According to Gladstone: "He seemed to be a man incapable of resenting an injury: a man in whom it was fixed habit of thought to put himself wholly out of view when he had before him the attainment of great public objects" (*Hansard*, 27 January 1887). Maybe he was self-effacing; but given that he was hardly the most innovative of politicians, it would appear that he was a natural second in command and was aware of it.

Northcote was born in London on 27 October 1818, the eldest son of Henry Stafford Northcote (1792–1851). After a varied early education, he went to Eton and to Balliol College, Oxford. He then read for the bar and was called to the Inner Temple in 1840. His chambers were located at 58 Lincoln's Inn Fields.

In 1842 he became private secretary to William Ewart Gladstone, who was then vice president of the Board of Trade. In 1843 he married Cecilia Frances, daughter of Thomas Farrer and sister of the first Lord Farrer. Northcote later combined his role as private secretary with that of legal assistant at the Board of Trade, and beginning in 1847, with that of barrister. In 1850 he also became one of the secretaries of the Great Exhibition held at the Crystal Palace in 1851. In 1853 he served on a commission planning the reorganization of the Board of Trade.

Despite his early association with Gladstone—who later headed the Peelite section of the Conservative Party when it formed the new Liberal Party—Northcote remained a Conservative. In 1853 he became M.P. for Dudley. He gave up his seat in 1857 and ran for the North Devon constituency, but was defeated. He returned to Parliament as M.P. for Stamford in 1858. Around this time he developed a close friendship with Benjamin Disraeli, advising him on matters of finance and defense. In 1866 he resigned his Stamford seat and was elected as M.P. for North Devon (a seat he held again in 1868, 1874, and 1880).

He was quickly drawn into Lord Derby's new Conservative ministry as president of the Board of Trade, with a seat in the cabinet. He became secretary for India in March 1867, after which he became convinced of the need to decentralize British government control over the subcontinent. Although out of office between 1868 and 1874, he was deeply involved in international matters. He was present at the opening of the Suez Canal in 1869, and was chairman and then governor of the Hudson Bay Company between 1869 and 1874. He was also a member of the high commission that was dispatched in February 1871 to resolve various disputes between the United States and Britain, connected with Alabama, the Canadian fisheries, and the San Juan boundary. These were amicably settled by the Treaty of Washington on 8 May 1871.

Northcote's career reached its zenith in February 1874, when Benjamin Disraeli formed a Conservative government and offered him the position of chancellor of the exchequer. In his early budgets, Northcote sought to reduce income tax (by 1d in 1874, when there were 240d, or pennies, to the pound) and to reduce the national debt (in 1874 and 1875), his most dramatic move being to pay £28 million of the debt per year through the "Sinking Fund," starting in 1875. However, the financial surpluses of his early years became deficits in 1876, when Britain was in the depths of economic depression and was making preparations for war against the Russians and the Zulus. Faced with a budget crunch, Northcote increased income tax (by 1d) in 1876 and reduced tax allowances. Although he was vigorously attacked by Gladstone for his economic performance in the late 1870s, Northcote did gain a reputation as a solid and conventional chancellor. He also became leader of the House of Commons on Disraeli's elevation to the peerage in 1876.

With the Conservative defeat in the April 1880 general election, Northcote led the Conservative opposition in the House of Commons, first as Disraeli's (Lord Beaconsfield's) lieutenant, and after Disraeli's death in April 1881, as joint leader of the Conservative Party with Lord Salisbury. His cautious leadership led him into conflict with a small group of Conservative supporters known as the "Fourth Party," which included Lord Randolph Churchill, Arthur James Balfour, and Sir John Gorst. Indeed, this caution and self-sacrifice continued in 1885 when he gave way to Lord Salisbury's bid for leadership of the new Conservative government and accepted the sinecure title of First Lord of the Treasury. He was raised to the House of Lords as Earl of Iddesleigh and Viscount St. Cyres on 6 July. As First Lord of the Treasury, he had the task of chairing the Royal Commission on the Depression in Trade, which was examining the industrial depression that was occurring in Britain at that time.

When Gladstone formed his short-lived third administration, in January 1886, Iddesleigh found himself out of office for a short time. In Lord Salisbury's second ministry, Iddesleigh was appointed foreign secretary. He fulfilled that role for about six months, his main concern being to deal with the Bulgarian crisis created by the kidnapping of Prince Alexander of Bulgaria and the claim of the prince of Mingrelia, an ally of Russia, to the vacant Bulgarian throne. Iddesleigh died while in office, on 11 January 1887, at 10 Downing Street, in the presence of Lord Salisbury, his secretary, and two doctors.

Keith Laybourn

See also: Derby, 14th Earl of; Disraeli, Benjamin; Gladstone, William Ewart; Salisbury, Lord
References and Further Reading: Blake, Robert, 1969, *Disraeli* (London: Oxford University Press); Shannon, Richard, 1992, *The Age of Disraeli, 1868–1881: The Rise of Tory Democracy* (London: Longman).

Owen, David Anthony (Baron Owen of the City of Plymouth)
(1938–) [FS]

Owen was a controversial figure in the 1970s and 1980s, not least because of his departure from the Labour Party in 1981 and his involvement in the formation of the Social Democratic Party. This ill-starred venture, which began with the Limehouse Declaration of January 1981, exerted a passing impact upon British politics in the 1980s.

David Anthony Llewelyn Owen was born at Plymouth on 2 July 1938, the son of John Owen, a doctor, and his wife, Molly, who were both of Welsh heritage. David saw little of his father, who was away fighting in World War II; but he was greatly influenced by his Welsh grandfather, the Rev. George Llewelyn (known as Gear). David Owen was educated at Mount House School, Plymouth, and at Bradfield College, near Reading, before going on to premedical studies at Sidney Sussex College, Cambridge. He then went on to St. Thomas's Hospital, in Lambeth, London, to train as a medical doctor. As a doctor, he worked at several hospitals, including the Royal Waterloo Hospital, St. Thomas's Hospital, and the National Heart Hospital.

It was at this stage, noting the poverty in the area near the hospital, that he decided to join the Labour Party, ditching his Liberal upbringing. That was in 1960, when he also joined the Fabian Society, an organization committed to gradual moves toward socialism. Although his first priority for a time remained the practice of medicine, he became Labour M.P. for Plymouth Sutton in 1966, and continued to represent that constituency until 1974. In 1974 he became M.P. for Plymouth Devonport, a seat he held until 1992 (from 1981 on, in behalf of the So-cial Democratic Party). After entering the House of Commons, he continued to work part-time, without pay, at St. Thomas's. He continued his dual-track career even after he became private secretary to the Ministry of Defence (Administration) in 1967. But he had to abandon his medical career in 1968 when he became parliamentary undersecretary for defense—effectively, minister of the navy. While visiting Washington, D.C., on official business, he met Deborah, an American, whom he married on 28 December 1968. She later became a literary agent to many famous authors, including Jeffrey Archer. Owen continued in his ministerial role until the defeat of Harold Wilson's Labour government in June 1970.

From the beginning of his political career, Owen's political leanings were toward the right of the Labour Party mainstream; for example, he espoused a closer connection with Europe than was generally popular within the Labour Party. He later resigned from the Labour opposition's front bench on the issue of Europe. Roy Jenkins, the Labour Party's deputy leader, resigned in April 1972, after the Labour shadow cabinet announced its support for a Conservative back-bench motion demanding a referendum before entry to the European Economic Community (EEC). Owen resigned along with him, believing that Britain must commit itself to the EEC.

Nevertheless, Owen campaigned on the issue of a referendum on Europe in the 1974 general election, and soon found himself restored to government, in what he described as a shabby election victory for the new prime minister, Harold Wilson, for whom he held little respect. Owen became undersecretary of the Department of Health and Social Security in 1974, and soon afterward was promoted to minister of

David Owen arriving at Downing Street, February 1977 (Hulton-Deutsch Collection/Corbis)

state for health and social security. In the latter role he dealt with controversial issues, mounting a campaign against cigarette smoking, tackling the abuses of private clinics, and liberalizing the law regarding abortion. A few months after James Callaghan replaced Harold Wilson as prime minister in April 1976, Owen was asked to become minister of state at the Foreign and Commonwealth Office, as Tony Crosland's deputy, with responsibility for strengthening Britain's financial position within the European Economic Community. With the death of Tony Crosland, in February 1977, Owen became foreign secretary.

Owen's tenure at the Foreign Office (September 1976–May 1979) was, by his own admission, the most enjoyable period of his political life. These were critical months for establishing the basis of Britain's relationship with the EEC. Britain criticized the heavy expense of the EEC's agricultural policy, and James Callaghan announced (in November 1978) that Britain would not join the European

Monetary System. On the issue of Rhodesia, Owen's office issued the Bingham Report (which was published in September 1978), revealing that Shell-BP and Total, two leading oil companies, had helped the illegal, white Rhodesian regime to survive by sanction busting and that the Wilson Labour governments had been aware of this. Owen helped organize the Lancaster House Conference of September 1978, which prepared the way for the ending of white rule in Rhodesia by organizing elections for 1980 that would involve the whole nation and not just the white community.

The control of the spread of nuclear armaments and other issues were also discussed during this period. In 1977 it seemed possible that Argentina might invade the Falkland Islands in the south Atlantic. Much more important was the toppling of the shah of Iran (Persia) in early 1979 by the Ayatollah Khomeini, which undermined Iran's status as a regional power, paving the way for the Russian invasion of Afghanistan at the end of 1979, the Iran-Iraq war between

1980 and 1987, and ultimately the Iraqi invasion of Kuwait in 1990.

With the occurrence of these major geopolitical shifts in the late 1970s, Owen moved to strengthen Britain's capabilities for dealing with the rising military threat. He and James Callaghan sought U.S. approval to replace the Polaris missiles in the British nuclear submarine fleet with more technically advanced Trident missiles from the United States.

Owen's tenure at the Foreign Office came to an end with the May 1979 general election. In the wake of Labour's defeat, the party was deeply divided. On the one hand, the trade unions and the more left-wing sections of the party (such as the Campaign for Labour Party Democracy, Clause IV, Independent Labour Publications, and the Socialist Campaign for a Labour Victory) moved toward an extreme set of policies aimed at extending public ownership. On the other hand, right-wingers, such as Owen and Shirley Williams, wanted to play down public ownership in order to capture more middle-class support for Labour, pushing forward their cause through the Manifesto Group of M.P.s in the House of Commons and the Campaign for Labour Victory. At the Labour Party Conference of 1979, the left put forward three demands—that the conference, and not the M.P.s, select the party Leader; that the conference decide Labour's policies; and that M.P.s be subject to mandatory reselection.

These demands seemed a serious challenge to the position of Labour's right wing. Following the conference there were discussions of these issues, and a committee of inquiry was set up to discuss the constitution of the electoral college for the selection of Labour leaders. In this atmosphere James Callaghan resigned as Labour Party leader in October 1980, and under the old system, with M.P.s alone voting, Michael Foot was selected as Labour leader. The party had clearly moved to the left; and on 25 January 1981, the Council for Social Democracy was formed at Limehouse, London, by four prominent Labour right-wingers—Roy Jenkins, David Owen, Shirley Williams, and Bill Rodgers.

This group, which initially intended to campaign for social democracy, quickly moved to form the Social Democratic Party (SDP) on 6 March 1981. Owen felt that the moment was right for the formation of this party, which not only linked him with his Labour past but also would provide him a "springboard for the future" (Owen 1991, p. 500). Initially, 12 Labour M.P.s and 9 Labour peers joined the SDP; but eventually, 29 Labour M.P.s joined. The SDP's threat to Labour increased in September 1982 with the formation of the Liberal-SDP Alliance; the alliance garnered more than 25 percent of the vote in the 1983 general election, although this gave it only 23 M.P.s, of which only six were members of the SDP.

Roy Jenkins was the first leader of the SDP; Owen was his deputy leader. Owen served as leader himself between 1983 and 1987, and in these years the fortunes of the SDP fluctuated and then plummeted. Owen made his presence known in the House of Commons, although it was suggested that this was a virtuoso performance by a one-man band. Indeed it was, and he resisted attempts to move the SDP and the Liberals into a closer alliance or merger. He wanted the SDP to maintain a distinctive image—notably upon issues like defense, on which he took a hard line, and particularly upon the need to maintain Britain's independent nuclear deterrent.

Tensions with the Liberals steadily mounted as the 1987 general election approached. Owen's political relations with David Steel, the Liberal leader, were civil (they wrote the pamphlet *Partnership and Progress* together) but not close; and in the 1987 general election their joint leadership of the alliance was seen as a disadvantage, especially when Steel seemed to veer toward the left and Owen toward the right. The alliance gained 22.6 percent of the vote in the general election, and only 22 M.P.s. Following this disappointing performance, David Steel suggested a merger of the two parties, a recommendation that was endorsed by the majority of SDP members in a national ballot. As a result Owen resigned from the SDP leadership in 1987. In 1988 he rallied his small band of followers into a party under the same rubric (SDP). The new SDP soon lost both membership and support; its supporters decreased to an estimated 18,000 by 1988. It held what was deemed a successful congress at Scarborough in 1989 but ceased to exist in June 1990.

Thereafter, Owen decided to withdraw from the forefront of British politics. His autobiography, *Time to Declare,* was published in 1991. In 1992 he became a life peer, as Baron Owen of the City of Plymouth. That same year, he was appointed European Community cochairman of the International Conference on Former Yugoslavia. He remains active as a leading international statesman in the cause of peace.

Keith Laybourn

See also: Callaghan, James; Crosland, Tony; Jenkins, Roy; Wilson, Harold

References and Further Reading: Harris, Kenneth, 1987, *David Owen* (London: Weidenfeld & Nicolson); Laybourn, K., 2000, *A Century of Labour: A History of the Labour Party, 1900–2000* (Stroud, UK: Sutton); Owen, David, 1991, *Time to Declare* (London: Joseph).

P

Palmerston, Lord (Henry John Temple; Viscount Palmerston)
(1784–1865) [PM, FS, HS]

Lord Palmerston was one of the great political figures of the nineteenth century, a Whig who was closely identified with Britain's bullish imperial dreams. With his amoral lifestyle and his tendency toward aristocratic government, he is often seen as a politician of the eighteenth rather than the nineteenth century, although his government of 1859 to 1865 is widely considered the first Liberal government in British history.

Henry John Temple was born in London on 20 October 1784, the second but eldest surviving child of Henry Temple, the second Viscount Palmerston, and Mary Mee. He was educated at Harrow; at Edinburgh University, where he became a committed free trader; and at St. John's College, Cambridge. He was married in 1839 to Emily Lamb, the sister of Lord Melbourne and widow of Lord Cowper. He succeeded his father as the third Viscount Palmerston in 1802, inheriting the family's Irish estates in county Sligo but not a seat in the House of Lords (his Irish title was not among those admitted to the Lords under the Act of Union in 1800).

Palmerston's political ideas were greatly influenced by his early experiences. His father encouraged him to travel—an activity that made him into a good linguist and that led him to be caught up in the early stages of the French Revolution in 1792. Although his travels gave him an advantage as foreign secretary later in life, his exposure to the revolution left him with a hatred of social upheaval and a fear of the lower classes.

Palmerston's political career began in 1806 when he (unsuccessfully) contested the Cambridge University seat. In 1807 he won the seat for the borough of Newport, on the Isle of Wight. He served as Junior Lord of the Admiralty from 1807 to 1809, in the Duke of Portland's ministry, and then became secretary at war in the Spencer Perceval ministry, holding the post nineteen years (1809–1828), in the successive ministries of Spencer Perceval, Lord Liverpool, George Canning, and the first Viscount Goderich (later the Earl of Ripon). The latter post involved no great commitment, for it concerned only the financial arrangements between the army and the House of Commons; but it did bring with it a seat in the cabinet during Canning's ministry of 1827. Apart from presenting army estimates to the Commons, Palmerston had little to do, and much of his time was spent with his many mistresses (for which he earned the nickname Cupid). His great love was Emily Lamb, the wife of Lord Cowper; and it was well known that he had fathered her younger children. He married her upon Lord Cowper's death in 1839.

Entering Canning's cabinet was an eye-opening experience for Palmerston; having access to cabinet papers and foreign dispatches, he became deeply interested in foreign affairs. His experience was short-lived, however, for Canning's government fell, and Wellington formed a Tory ministry in 1828. Palmerston, who spoke critically of Wellington's foreign policy, found himself in 1830 serving as foreign secretary in Earl Grey's Whig administration. It was a post he held until 1841, with only a brief break in 1834, when Wellington formed a short-lived government before being replaced by Lord Melbourne.

As foreign secretary Palmerston's main concerns were France and Belgium. The Whigs had traditionally been pro-French, and since Wellington's government had recognized Louis-Philippe after the overthrow of the Bourbons in

Lord Palmerston (Sean Sexton Collection/Corbis)

1830, there was little cause for worry about Britain's relationship with France. There was, however, the problem of Belgium, which had been united with Holland under the Vienna Settlement of 1815, in order to provide a stronger border for France. The Belgians rose against the Dutch in 1830, alleging discrimination, and raised the prospect of Belgium falling under French influence. In order to prevent this, Palmerston organized a conference that met in London between 1830 and 1839 and eventually resolved the issue by gaining international recognition of Belgium as a neutral state.

Palmerston was also involved in developing geopolitical counterbalances elsewhere in Europe. While wishing to counter the Holy Alliance of Russia, Austria, and Prussia, he did not wish to allow France too much influence in Spain and Portugal. Thus he committed Britain to a pact of mutual defense with France, Portugal, and Spain—the Quadruple Alliance of 1834. This move was in turn countered by other developments, mainly involving Turkey, which

was viewed as vulnerable—"the sick man of Europe"—at that time. Mehmet Ali, the ruler of Egypt, had risen against the sultan of Constantinople to claim Syria and potentially the whole Turkish Empire. Palmerston felt that this move was encouraged by the French. He also feared that Turkey would fall under the influence of the Russians after the sultan gained support from Russia through the Treaty of Unkiar Skelesi. In an attempt to defuse both French and Russian interests, Palmerston joined Russia, Austria, and Prussia in supporting the sultan at a convention in July 1840, thus thwarting French ambitions.

Foreign policy became increasingly important at this juncture in British politics. Britain was involved in the famous Opium War, which resulted from Palmerston's insistence that China open up normal trading and diplomatic relations with Britain. Palmerston was also bullish about the need to suppress the international slave trade, and he objected to the fact that Britain's "right to search" was often thwarted when slave ships raised the flag of the United States, a country with which Britain had no treaty guaranteeing this right. Palmerston's complaints about the false use of the American flag increased tensions between Britain and the United States, which were already high due to disputes over the U.S.-Canadian border. Indeed, war between Britain and the United States seemed highly likely by 1841. However, the Melbourne government collapsed in 1841, to be replaced by the Tory administration of Sir Robert Peel; Lord (the Earl of) Aberdeen, the new foreign secretary, moved quickly to mend relations with the United States and with France.

Palmerston served as foreign secretary again between 1846 and 1851, in the ministry of Lord John Russell. Once again, this proved a contentious and volatile period in foreign relations. In 1848 France, Italy, and Germany were convulsed by revolutions. Given fears of an uprising in Ireland at the same time as well as Chartist agitation in Britain, it is not surprising that Palmerston, whose mind had been made up after he witnessed the first French Revolution, assumed a hostile attitude toward these developments. Ironically, he gained a reputation among

European conservatives of being a radical who was prepared to support revolutionary causes.

Such an assessment seems somewhat wide of the mark, although he did show some sympathy for Hungarian and Polish nationalism. Palmerston's abiding concern was to protect British interests; and although he may have had some sympathy for Italian desires for independence from Austria, his prime concern was that Austria's interests should be confined to Germany in order to maintain a balance of power within Europe. At the same time, he was determined not to allow the French into Italy. In 1848, he joined France in an attempt to mediate between the Italians and the Austrians. It was difficult, of course, to balance one interest off against the other; a favor to one nation often disadvantaged another. Many pro-French Whigs were critical of Palmerston's actions, and along with the British royal family, worried about the dangerous and radical, indeed revolutionary, actions that Palmerston seemed to be supporting.

One particular situation created new uncertainties. In 1841 Palmerston had sent the British fleet, under Sir William Parker, to the Mediterranean to encourage the Sicilian rebels to challenge the authority and power of Austria in the Italian states. The fleet became involved in the famous Don Pacifico incident of 1847. Pacifico was a Portuguese Jew who claimed British citizenship and sought compensation for the destruction of his property during anti-Semitic riots in Greece. Taking advantage of this situation, for the Greeks had defaulted on loan payment to Britain, Palmerston had the British fleet blockade Piraeus, the port of Athens, without consulting either with Russia or with France, which with Britain were jointly committed by treaty to guarantee Greek independence. The incident shook the Conservative Party under Lord Stanley (later the fourteenth Earl of Derby) as well as followers of the Peelite (soon to be Liberal) leader Lord Aberdeen, who objected to the resort to gunboat diplomacy over the dubious claims of Pacifico.

Their joint opposition led to a stage-managed debate in the House of Commons on 1 July 1850. Palmerston responded with a four-hour speech in which he made the Don Pacifico incident the centerpiece of his defensive foreign policy, raising the nationalistic stakes by claiming that every British citizen should be able to look to their government for protection much as Roman citizens had looked to theirs 2,000 years before. The Commons supported Palmerston and swept away the opposition led by Sir Robert Peel. The opposition completely disintegrated the next day, when Peel was thrown from a horse and died from his injuries.

Much of Palmerston's success on this occasion as well as previous ones came from the fact that he courted public opinion and was prepared to enter into open debate with his opponents. For instance, in 1847 he debated foreign policy with George Julian Harney, the Chartist leader, in his own constituency of Tiverton during the general election. Nevertheless, public opinion and powerful performances in the Commons did not always save him from the criticism of his political colleagues.

Russell, the Whig prime minister, eventually broke with Palmerston over his policy toward France. The British government had been alarmed by the formation of the French Republic following the fall of Louis-Philippe; but it was divided in opinion about Louis-Napoléon's disbanding of the National Assembly of the Republic in December 1851 and extending his own term as president in what was, in effect, a coup d'état. Without first consulting his political colleagues, Palmerston told the French ambassador that he approved of these actions, and as a result Russell asked for his resignation.

Without Palmerston, however, the Russell government soon fell. It was replaced, for most of 1852, by the government of the fourteenth Earl of Derby (known as Lord Stanley before 1851). However, this administration lasted only from February to December 1852, and was replaced by the Whig-Peelite (increasingly Liberal) administration of Lord Aberdeen, with Palmerston returning as home secretary. In this unfamiliar role Palmerston introduced the Penal Servitude Act, which substituted imprisonment for transportation; a Youthful Offenders Act, which allowed the transfer of juveniles from prisons to reform schools; and some modest extensions of the Factory Acts. Being fearful of the emergent working classes, he opposed any further extension of the parliamentary franchise, and resigned over this issue in December 1853, at a time when crucial cabinet decisions were being made regarding the Crimean War.

It appeared at the time that Russia was intent on carving up the Ottoman (Turkish) empire. In October 1853, Palmerston had expressed a desire to see the British and French fleets sent to the Black Sea to intercept Russian warships, providing a clear warning that Britain and France would not permit Russia to acquire the Ottoman Empire. The British cabinet agreed to this action in December 1853, after the Russian fleet sank a squadron of the Turkish fleet (the "massacre at Sinope"). After declaring war on Russia on 28 March 1854, Britain was debating whether to attack Sebastopol, a strategy strongly advocated by Palmerston. As the disastrous Crimean War continued, a popular outcry arose, demanding that Palmerston be made secretary of state for war. The Aberdeen ministry was defeated on a vote of no confidence in the House of Commons in January 1855, and Palmerston became prime minister by popular demand. He served in the post from 1855 until his death in 1865, with a short hiatus in 1858–1859. As prime minister his immediate concern was to win the Crimean War. Sebastopol fell in September 1855, and the Treaty of Paris of 1856, disappointing as it was to the British public, made the Black Sea a neutral zone and brought an end to the Russian Black Sea fleet.

Palmerston's premiership achieved remarkably little in domestic affairs. He opposed parliamentary reform and slowed the pace of legislative reform generally, the only significant piece of domestic legislation passed during his tenure being the Matrimonial Causes Act of 1857, which allowed divorce to be pursued through the civil courts. Palmerston was much more concerned with foreign affairs, with the war with Persia, and the Indian Mutiny. The Indian Mutiny of 1857 was put down by the use of troops that were en route to China to punish the Chinese for interfering with the *Arrow,* a ship that was probably engaged in illegal activities but that claimed immunity because it was registered as a British ship.

The "*Arrow* incident" led Richard Cobden to organize a cross-party alliance in the House of Commons, which immediately passed a vote of no confidence in Palmerston. As a result, Palmerston called a general election, in which he gained a majority of 85 seats and ousted many of his political opponents, including Cobden, from office. However, the following year Palmerston lost office due to British voters' suspicion that he planned, in the wake of the failed assassination attempt on Napoleon III (the Orsini Plot), to amend British law in order to prevent dissidents who were living in Britain from plotting future acts of insurrection and murder.

Palmerston returned to office in 1859, at the head of a new coalition government that included Lord John Russell and William Ewart Gladstone. Although this was a revival of a coalition that initially had been formed in 1852, Palmerston's second government, which lasted until his death in 1865, is traditionally considered the first Liberal, as opposed to Whig, government, drawing its support from an industrial and free-trade base rather than from reform-minded landowners. Gladstone was attracted into the government by virtue of the fact that Palmerston had dispatched a fleet to Italy to observe developments further to the French pact with Piedmont, including the subsequent Franco-Austrian War.

The dominant issue in Palmerston's second and last ministry was the American Civil War. Although his sympathies lay more with the South than the North, he did attempt to maintain a degree of neutrality. That neutrality was endangered by the *Trent* incident, in which a Northern warship intercepted the British mail steamer *Trent* and removed two Southerners, in response to which Palmerston penned a belligerent dispatch to Abraham Lincoln's government. The tone of the dispatch was softened by the intervention of Prince Albert, the prince consort to Queen Victoria; but Palmerston's reinforcement of British troops in Canada made the basic intent behind the message unmistakable.

Palmerston's final years were absorbed by foreign affairs closer to home. He foresaw the rise of Russia to major power status, and sought the unification of the German states in order to buffer this threat. His government was unintentionally drawn into a quarrel with Prussia, the state which ironically became the catalyst for German unification under Otto von Bismarck. Lord John Russell, who was then foreign secretary, publicly suggested that Britain would support Denmark in its quarrel with Prussia over the duchies of Schleswig and Holstein, using force if necessary. This lost Palmerston's administration much public support and threw it into conflict with a potential ally.

Palmerston died in office on 18 October 1865, two days before his 81st birthday. To the end he was preoccupied with foreign affairs—particularly with maintaining the balance of power in Europe. He was somewhat less interested in domestic affairs, although always concerned about the threat from the "lower orders" and "working classes," which were increasingly demanding a greater say in affairs of state.

Keith Laybourn

See also: Aberdeen, Earl of; Canning, George; Gladstone, William Ewart; Goderich, Viscount; Grey, Lord; Liverpool, Earl of; Melbourne, Viscount; Peel, Sir Robert; Perceval, Spencer; Portland, Duke of; Russell, Lord John; Wellington, Duke of

References and Further Reading: Bourne, Kenneth, 1982, *Palmerston: The Early Years, 1784–1841* (London: Allen Lane); Chamberlain, Muriel, 1987, *Lord Palmerston* (London: Cardiff GPC); Partridge, Michael S., and Karen Partridge, 1994, *Lord Palmerston, 1784–1865: A Biography* (London: Greenwood); Ridley, Jasper, 1970, *Lord Palmerston* (London: Constable); Southgate, Donald, 1966, '*The Most English Minister. . . .': The Policies and Politics of Palmerston* (London: Macmillan).

Peel, Sir Robert
(1788–1850) [PM, CE, HS]

Sir Robert Peel played a cardinal role in nineteenth-century British history, as the founder of modern Conservatism and the political mentor of both Gladstone and Disraeli. His repeal of the Corn Laws became the symbolic dividing line between an age of revolt and an age of stability. Yet he was twice accused of betraying his party, leaving it shattered and excluded from power for thirty years.

He was born on 5 February 1788, at Bury, near Manchester, the third of nine children, and the eldest son, of one of the richest cotton manufacturers in the kingdom. His father became an M.P. in 1790 and was made a baronet by William Pitt, the Younger, in 1800. In 1796 this first Sir Robert moved his family to the country estate of Drayton Manor, near Tamworth, Staffordshire. At Bury and Tamworth the young Peel was educated by the local Anglican vicars; in 1800 he was sent out, "a youth of the most promising talents," to Harrow School. His five years at Harrow were happy and successful, socially and academically. In 1805 he enrolled at Oxford, as a "gentleman commoner" of Christ Church. There he "was fond of athletic exercises," as well as an exceptional scholar. In November 1808 he achieved the prodigious feat of graduating with first-class honors—by public oral examination—in both classical and mathematical studies (a "double first"). The next year, at age 21, he became M.P. for Cashel, in Ireland, a "rotten borough" (that is, corrupt) seat bought for him by his father.

Like his father, Peel was a Pittite Anglican Tory, and thus a supporter of the government headed from October 1809 by Spencer Perceval. He quickly made his mark in the Commons, and in 1810, at barely 22, became an undersecretary for war and the colonies. When the prime minister was assassinated in May 1812, Peel's chief, Lord Liverpool, became prime minister and promoted Peel to the post of chief secretary for Ireland, a position that made him answerable to Parliament (nominally, to the home secretary) for Irish affairs. The chief problem for the British rulers of Ireland at this time was that of Catholic emancipation—i.e., the removal of the civil and political disabilities that the mass of the Irish population endured. Pitt had intended that emancipation should follow the Act of Union of 1800, which had abolished the independent Irish Parliament, but George III refused his approval. Thus Catholic emancipation was also a matter of English politics. Liverpool's cabinet was divided over the issue; but Peel upheld "the Protestant establishment in Church and State" (though he regarded the Scots-Irish Presbyterians of the Orange Order of Northern

Sir Robert Peel, 1830 (Library of Congress)

Ireland as objectionable). The government had no official contact with the Catholic Church in Ireland, but since 1795 it had made a small annual grant to Maynooth College, a Catholic seminary.

Peel's six years as chief secretary established him as a national figure and were marked by events which portended future developments. In 1813, an attempt by leading Irish M.P. Henry Grattan to secure Catholic emancipation was defeated, and the next year Peel suppressed the Catholic Board, a committee formed to promote the Catholic cause in Ireland. This episode was notable as the beginning of personal hostility between Peel and the emerging Catholic Irish leader Daniel O'Connell, who dubbed Peel, rather obviously but misleadingly, "Orange Peel." The endemic problems Peel faced in Ireland were those of law and order and of rural poverty. The Irish countryside was a scene of social warfare waged by secret societies of peasants on the alien landlords' properties. In 1814 Peel established a police force (known as Peelers) to supplement the 25,000 troops on hand. But the social problems—poverty; rural overpopulation; overreliance on a single crop, the potato; the progressive subdivision of landholdings; landlord neglect and peasant resistance—became acute during the 1816 depression. In 1817 Peel cemented his reputation as defender of the Protestant cause by fending off Grattan's second attempt to secure Catholic emancipation. He further bound himself to the cause by becoming M.P. for the Anglican stronghold, Oxford University. That year, 50,000 people died in Ireland from famine and consequent fever, and Peel was still attempting to combat these problems with emergency relief measures when he left Ireland in August 1818, never to return.

He took a rest from ministerial office; but in 1819 Liverpool made him chairman of an important Commons committee to advise on the currency. His report in May proposed that the government should abandon the wartime system of paper money and return to the gold standard; this was accomplished by "Peel's Act." The next year, now 32, Peel married Julia Floyd, one of the great beauties of her time. She provided him with a loving and stable family life and bore him one daughter and five sons.

The postwar years (after 1815) were a time of economic depression, popular disturbance, and government coercion. Through a number of cabinet changes that took place over the years 1821–1823, Peel and the liberal Tories Canning and Huskisson joined the Liverpool government. After his appointment in 1822 as home secretary, Peel brought in legislation for prison reform and made major humanitarian amendments to the criminal law by a series of five acts passed between 1823 and 1827. These mitigated the severity and improved the administration of the criminal code. Yet crime increased, and Peel saw the concomitant need to improve policing. He had been fortunate that his time at the Home Office coincided with an economic upturn from the postwar stagnation; but in 1826 there were widespread riots during a deep trade depression. Troops were used to suppress the rioting, and Peel authorized their commanders' use of spies. The army was the only force available to a home secretary attempting to maintain law and order in the face of popular unrest.

This was equally true in Ireland, for which Peel was again responsible, and where the distress of 1826 was more acute. Peel saw the need for reform of the law imposing compulsory tithing on Irish Catholics for the upkeep of the Anglican Church of Ireland; but his being M.P. for Oxford University acted as a restraint on his attempting to commute these payments. His immediate problem in Ireland was to counter the Catholic Association, founded in 1823 by O'Connell to campaign for emancipation, and financed by subscriptions known as "Catholic Rent." Peel suppressed the association, but it was revived and the pressure for Catholic emancipation increased; and when Liverpool resigned in 1827 and was succeeded by Canning, Peel refused to join the cabinet because Canning favored emancipation. Canning died within six months, and Goderich's government was even more short-lived.

In January 1828, a new government was formed under Wellington, with Peel again in the office of home secretary, still opposing Catholic emancipation. The Whig opposition forced through Parliament a repeal of the Test and Corporation Acts, which in name although not in fact had debarred Protestant Nonconformists from political activity. This made the issue of Catholic emancipation seem more urgent than before. When one of Wellington's ministers had to seek reelection, O'Connell defeated him in the by-election in county Clare, and intensified his campaign of mass meetings demanding emancipation. Peel was the key figure in the cabinet, and in January 1829 he made one of the crucial decisions of his career when he told Wellington, to the dismay of the English Tories, that he would support emancipation because it was inevitable. Soon after, a parliamentary act was passed to remove most Catholic disabilities.

Peel's other lasting achievements during Wellington's ministry were further reforms in criminal law, including the establishment of the metropolitan police. "Bobbies" first appeared in London's streets on 29 September 1829. Thereafter, as Peel's relations with Wellington deteriorated, the fortunes of the government declined. The accession of William IV to the throne brought a general election; and although Peel was still a dominant figure in Parliament, he willingly resigned in November 1830. In his twenty-one years as M.P., he had spent all but five in office. In the remaining twenty he was to be in office for only five.

When the Whigs came into office under the premiership of Lord Charles Grey in 1830, their first ambition was parliamentary reform. Peel conceded that a degree of change was inevitable; although the 1832 Reform Act far exceeded his conception, he accepted it as a final and irrevocable settlement. His party suffered a humiliating defeat in the ensuing general election; but by 1834, Whig reforming zeal was evaporating and party coherence dissolving. In November, William IV dismissed the Whig government and called on Peel to form a government.

Peel used the occasion of the delayed general election to issue the so-called Tamworth Manifesto, which was both a statement to his constituents and a national electioneering appeal, promising "the correction of proved abuses and the redress of real grievances." The document became a landmark in party history, as the manifesto of the new Conservatism. Peel resigned in April 1835, but the Conservative Party remained strong in Parliament, having rooted itself in the constituencies. As the Whig government faltered, Peel's ascendancy in the Commons increased. When Melbourne resigned in 1839, Peel did not insist that the reluctant Queen Victoria change her ladies of the bedchamber, since they were linked to the main political figures of the outgoing Melbourne government; he was confident that the electoral tide would flow to the Conservatives, as it did in the 1841 election.

Peel's second ministry (1841–1846) was one of the most creative and controversial in British history. In 1838, against a background of economic depression, both the mass movement known as Chartism and the middle-class Anti–Corn Law League had been founded.

Peel's immediate problem was that of government finance. His solution—the first peacetime use of income tax—made possible reform of the tariff of import duties, including duty on corn. His 1842 budget reduced duties on 750 of the 1,200 dutiable articles in the book of rates, including a graduated scale on wheat, calculated to give British farmers fair protection. In the century's worst year of starvation he made the rich bear the cost of improving "the condition of England."

The condition of Ireland was much worse. In 1841 O'Connell launched a campaign for repeal of the Union of 1800. This campaign reached a climax in October 1843, when his planned mass meeting at Clontarf was banned and he was arrested. This broke O'Connell's power, but it was no solution to England's problems in Ireland.

Peel's major domestic reforms of 1844—the Bank Charter Act, which guaranteed confidence in the currency by making it convertible into gold; and a Factory Act, which regulated hours and conditions for women and children—and his settlement of the Canadian boundary with the United States in 1845 were offset by trouble with his supporters in Parliament, especially over an increase in the grant to the Maynooth seminary.

Ireland had occasioned Peel's alleged betrayal of his party in 1829 (after he changed his mind about Catholic emancipation). The Irish potato blight in the autumn of 1845 precipitated the party's complete breakup. Heavy rain had ruined crops throughout Europe, and in October the failure of the Irish potato crop resulted in a famine that was to last three years and was the worst social disaster in nineteenth-century Europe. Peel was converted to free trade before the famine occurred; but the famine denied him the time and opportunity to convert his party. Because he could not persuade all of his cabinet, he resigned in December. But the Whig leader, Russell, abandoned any attempt to form a government and "handed back the poisoned chalice to Sir Robert." Despite the "gibes and bitterness" of Disraeli's attacks and the outrage of two-thirds of his own party, Peel, with opposition support, pushed through a bill to abolish, in stages, duties on imported wheat. But he soon resigned, after being defeated on the Irish Coercion Bill.

Peel remained an M.P. but made no attempt to reunite the party. When he died after a riding accident, on 2 July 1850, he was the people's hero who had provided cheap food. Monuments were erected to him throughout the land. Historians still debate his reputation. He sacrificed his party to the national interest. The most conspicuous defender of Anglican ascendancy and the landed interest "betrayed" both. Was he a martyred statesman who created mid-Victorian prosperity, or an unprincipled pragmatist who arrogantly sacrificed Tory interests? Suffice it to point out that when Disraeli revived the party, he did so on Peelite Conservative principles: they were the only viable ones on which to build.

John O'Connell

See also: Canning, George; Disraeli, Benjamin; Gladstone, William Ewart; Goderich, Viscount; Grey, Lord; Melbourne, Viscount; Perceval, Spencer; Pitt, William (the Younger); Russell, Lord John; Wellington, Duke of

References and Further Reading: Beales, D., 1974, "Peel, Russell, and Reform," *Historical Journal* 17; Blake, Robert, 1985, *The Conservative Party from Peel to Thatcher* (Suffolk, UK: Woodbridge); Briggs, A., 1974, "Peel," in Herbert von Thal (ed.), *The Prime Ministers*, vol. 1 (London: Allen and Unwin); Coleman, Bruce, 1988, *Conservatism and the Conservative Party in Nineteenth-Century Britain* (London: Edward Arnold); Eastwood, D., 1992, "Peel and the Tory Party Reconsidered," *History Today* 42; Gash, Norman, 1961, *Mr. Secretary Peel: The Life of Sir Robert Peel to 1830* (London: Longman); Gash, Norman, 1972, *Sir Robert Peel: The Life and Times of Sir Robert Peel to 1830* (London: Longman)(both condensed as Gash, Norman, 1976, *Peel*); Hilton, B., 1993, "The Ripening of Robert Peel," in Michael Bentley (ed.), *Public and Private Doctrine: Essays in British History Presented to Maurice Cowling* (Cambridge: Cambridge University Press); Newbould, I., 1983, "Peel and the Conservative Party, 1832–1841: A Study in Failure," *English Historical Review* 98; Ramsden, John, 1998, *An Appetite for Power: A History of the Conservative Party since 1830* (London: Harper-Collins); Read, Donald, 1987, *Peel and the Victorians* (Oxford: Basil Blackwell); Stewart, Robert, 1978, *The Foundation of the Conservative Party* (London: Longman).

Pelham, Hon. Henry
(1695–1754) [PM, CE]

Henry Pelham, younger brother of Thomas Pelham-Holles, Duke of Newcastle, has the distinction of being the first prime minister to die a commoner. He enjoys the further distinction of being noted for his honesty and personal character in an age when it was difficult for politicians to attain eminence with clean hands. Thanks to the early patronage of Sir Robert Walpole, Pelham was paymaster-general of the forces from 1730 to 1743; yet he did not care to take the usual profits of this lucrative post, which had made the fortunes of other incumbents.

His career was shaped by his loyalties to his brother, the politically ambitious and influential Newcastle, and to Walpole. Newcastle brought Pelham into politics in the county of Sussex, which was electorally dominated by their family, first as a member for the borough of Seaford from 1717 to 1722, and then as one of the two county members from 1722 until Pelham's death.

Pelham was noticed early by Walpole, who in 1721 took him under his wing as one of the lords of the Treasury, gaining the younger man's assistance in the Commons following the South Sea crisis. As Walpole's own power grew, he promoted and, in a sense, trained Pelham, of whom he was said to be fonder than any other man living. In 1724 the protégé was made secretary at war; and when Charles, Viscount Townshend, resigned in 1730, Pelham was given the paymaster's post. Both of these posts had been occupied by Walpole in the early stages of his own career. Until the fall of Walpole in February 1742, Pelham was a loyal lieutenant, increasingly important as both a confidant of the premier and an intermediary between him and Newcastle, when—as happened rather frequently—their relations became strained. In these years Pelham referred to Walpole as his oracle in politics; and he undoubtedly gained greatly from the experience of almost daily analyses of events and people from the mouth of the most successful politician of the day. Being loyal to Walpole and overshadowed by him, Pelham was underestimated by rivals such as Carteret, who contemptuously described him as Walpole's clerk.

Pelham's love of family and private life also ensured that he was less known and talked of than more public characters. His 1726 marriage to the daughter of the Duke of Rutland, Lady Catherine Manners, was a happy one, though they suffered the griefs of many parents of that day: only three of their eight children lived to adulthood, and their two sons died of fever within twenty-four hours of one another, in November 1739. When Walpole resigned, loyalty would not permit Pelham to profit by his mentor's downfall, and he retained his post as paymaster-general even though Walpole urged him to accept the chancellorship of the exchequer. In July 1743, however, when (Spencer Compton, first Earl) Wilmington died in office, George II made Pelham First Lord of the Treasury.

Pelham confidently took control, being also appointed chancellor of the exchequer in November of that year. Leading the ministry in both posts, and acting as its chief spokesman in the Commons, Pelham was in effect prime minister as Walpole had been and inherited the benefit of a core of some 200 M.P.s who had been groomed by Walpole to vote for the Court (the Crown and the King's ministers) on all ordinary occasions.

The Walpole method of maintaining the premiership, in which Pelham was thoroughly schooled, involved balancing the support of the Crown against that of the Commons. The vital element that at first eluded Pelham was the full confidence of the king: a letter survives in which Walpole from his retirement advised his chosen successor on how to handle George II and bring him to accept necessary policies. First, though, Pelham had to remove George's favorite minister, John, Lord Carteret, secretary of state for the north. This he accomplished in two stages. In 1744 the king was persuaded to dismiss Carteret (who was then known as Earl Granville), though the latter continued in favor at court. In February 1746, Pelham and Newcastle led an unprecedented mass resignation of the cabinet, designed to show the king that Granville and his ally Bath did not command a political following sufficient to control the Commons. Having resigned on 10 February, the ministers were reinstated on 13 and 14 February; and Pelham immediately set about undermining the entrenched opposition that had characterized the Walpole years. He attracted some opponents over to the court with places and pensions; and he cut the ground away from the remainder by calling a snap general election a year earlier than normal, in 1747. From then on, he increasingly dominated both the Commons and the royal closet. In 1748, at the end of the War of Austrian Succession, and with six years of Parliament still to run, Pelham had the political resolve to do what Walpole had been unable ever to risk doing: he reduced the interest on the national debt from 4 to 3 percent. This slashed the profits being made by the large City financiers and caused predictable outrage in London, but it paved the way for a reduction of the national debt—a goal cherished by a prime minister who wanted the nation to live as moderately and carefully as he did himself.

By 1750, Pelham and his two closest allies, Newcastle and Hardwicke, were running the government in the way Walpole and his inner circle had done. George II said of them, "They are the only ministers; the others are for show." Pelham's position was strengthened still further in 1751, when the Prince of Wales, figurehead of the opposition, unexpectedly died. From then on, Pelham's power was at its height, despite his recurring health problems and his frequent desire to resign. His abilities were more widely known and respected than ever before, so that he seemed to occupy the position of first minister by right. The king's confidence in him was so high that George told Newcastle in 1752 that in financial matters Pelham was more able than Walpole had been.

Always a reluctant manager of elections, Pelham was preparing the ground for a Whig victory in the spring of 1754, despite an inflammatory disease that had persisted for several months. Taking a sudden turn for the worse, he unexpectedly died on 6 March 1754. He could have wished for no better epitaph than that provided by Lord Chesterfield: "He wished well to the public and managed the finances with great care and personal purity."

Philip Woodfine

See also: Carteret, John; Newcastle, Duke of; Walpole, Sir Robert

References and Further Reading: Owen, John B., 1957 and 1971, *The Rise of the Pelhams* (London: Methuen); Wiggin, Lewis M., 1958, *The Faction of Cousins: A Political Account of the Grenvilles, 1733–1763* (New Haven, CT: Yale University Press); Wilkes, John W., 1964, *A Whig in Power: The Political Career of Henry Pelham* (Evanston, IL: Northwestern University Press).

Pelham, Lord (Thomas Pelham; Baron Pelham of Stanmer; Earl of Chichester)

1756–1826) [HS]

Thomas Pelham, the second Earl of Chichester, was born on 28 April 1756, the eldest son of Thomas Pelham, first Earl of Chichester. He was educated at Westminster School and at Clare Hall, Cambridge, where he graduated with an M.A. in 1775. In the autumn of that year he went to Spain in order to learn Spanish, returning in early 1778 in order to pursue a military career as an officer in the Sussex militia, becoming lieutenant colonel of that regiment in 1794.

Pelham's political career began on 14 September 1780, when he was elected to the House of Commons as M.P. for Sussex. A Whig, he was committed to constitutional reform and control of the monarchy and was closely associated with Charles James Fox and other leading members of the Rockingham faction of the Whigs. In April 1782 he was appointed surveyor-general of ordnance in the government of the Marquess of Rockingham but left that office with the death of Rockingham on 1 July 1782. Nevertheless, the Duke of Portland, who became prime minister of a coalition government in 1783, made Pelham the Irish secretary in the summer of 1783. Pelham resigned from that position on the fall of the Portland government in December 1783 despite the efforts of William Pitt, the Younger, the new prime minister, to encourage him to stay in that office. For the next few years, Pelham was a staunch member of the Whig opposition in Parliament. However, he was drawn back into government with the outbreak of the French Revolution. He was attracted to Pitt's policy of desiring peace but of financing and occasionally militarily supporting Britain's European allies, which many of the older and more moderate Whigs wanted. As a result, Pelham became chief secretary to the lord lieutenant of Ireland. He remained in that post until November 1798, although he had been inactive in office from May 1798 as a result of a severe illness.

Despite his ill health, Pelham remained active in politics. On 22 January 1801 he proposed that Henry Addington should be made the speaker of the House of Commons and on 14 April 1801 promoted a bill to suspend the Habeas Corpus Act, which had guaranteed the right to trial. Pelham was offered, but refused, various offices of state at this time, including the secretaryship at war and the presidency of the Board of Trade. However, Pelham accepted the post of home secretary in the government of Henry Addington, which was formed in March 1801 as a result of the unexpected resignation of the Younger Pitt over the issue of emancipation of Roman Catholics in Ireland. Pelham rose to the House of Lords in July 1801, inheriting his father's title of Baron Pelham of Stanmer on his father's becoming the first Earl of Chichester. Thomas Pelham became the second Earl of Chichester on his father's death in January 1805.

Pelham's relations with Addington were never smooth. While Pelham supported the Treaty of Amiens with the French in early 1802, he was not happy at the fine detail of the settlement and objected that the Home Office was no longer to be responsible for colonial affairs and that he, as home secretary, was not allowed to control all of the patronage connected with Irish affairs. He offered to resign his office in favor of Pitt, when in 1803 Addington was discussing with Pitt the possible return of Pitt to government. The negotiations came to nothing, but Addington removed Pelham from the Home Office to the post of chancellor of the Duchy of Lancaster in July 1803. When Pitt did return to government in May 1804, Pelham was deprived of the Duchy of Lancaster. He then retired from high office; the only other post he took in government was that of joint postmaster-general from May 1807 until 1823, when he became the sole postmaster-general until his death in 1826.

Pelham died on 4 July 1826, leaving a wife, Mary Henrietta Juliana Osborne (daughter of the fifth Duke of Leeds by his first wife), four sons, and four daughters. He is remembered as a kind and careful man but an undistinguished home secretary.

Keith Laybourn

See also: Addington, Henry; Fox, Charles James; Pitt, William (the Younger); Portland, Duke of; Rockingham, Marquess of
References and Further Reading: Ziegler, Philip, 1965, *Addington* (New York: John Day).

Perceval, Spencer
(1762–1812) [PM, CE]

Spencer Perceval was born on 1 November 1762, the second son of Sir John Perceval, second earl of Egmont, and his second wife, Catherine Compton. He was educated at Harrow and at Trinity College, Cambridge. He then trained for the bar at Lincoln's Inn, and began a practice on the midland circuit. In August 1790, although still penniless, he secretly married Jane, daughter of Sir Thomas Wilson, M.P. for Sussex, and the newlyweds set up housekeeping over a carpet shop. The marriage proved particularly happy, and in October 1791 the first of their 12 children was born. Perceval published two pamphlets at the time— one on constitutional issues raised by the impeachment of Warren Hastings, and the other on the practicalities of prosecuting radical agitators—and obtained the Crown prosecution briefs (cases) at the trial of Thomas Paine in 1792 and that of Horne Tooke in 1794. He declined an offer from William Pitt (the Younger) of the chief secretaryship in Ireland in 1795, because the salary would not support his growing family. He remained instead at the bar. In 1796 he became a King's Counsel and was elected M.P. for Northampton, where he was deputy recorder.

An uncompromising supporter of the war with revolutionary France and of the younger Pitt's stern fiscal policy, Perceval refused to accept the label of Tory throughout his political career; he regarded himself first and foremost as a staunch Evangelical. He was highly esteemed by William Wilberforce, whose campaigns for the abolition of slavery and the slave trade he strongly supported. He disapproved strongly of gambling and hunting, favored making adultery a criminal offense, and refused to transact business on Sundays. He considered the primacy of the Church of England essential to the security of the state, and he strongly opposed Pitt's proposal for Catholic emancipation. After Pitt resigned over the issue, Perceval accepted his first ministerial post as solicitor general, in Addington's government, in 1801. Promoted to attorney general in 1802, he successfully conducted the treason trial of Colonel Despard and adeptly defended Addington's ministry in the House of Commons.

He retained office on Pitt's return to power in 1804 but resigned on Pitt's death in 1806, returning to the backbench, where he became a fierce critic of William Wyndham Grenville and Charles James Fox. After the death of Fox, Perceval was invited to join the government but refused, and it was his opposition to the government bill to make concessions to Catholics in Ireland that contributed to the downfall of the "Ministry of all the Talents" in March 1807. He was appointed chancellor of the exchequer, chancellor of the Duchy of Lancaster, and leader of the House of Commons in the Duke of Portland's ministry in 1807. He drafted the Orders in Council designed to counteract Napoleon Bonaparte's Continental System in 1807, which aroused fierce parliamentary opposition, but his budget to cover an estimated expenditure of £49 million was generally approved.

Portland's illness in 1809 prompted some maneuvering for position, which eventually ended with Perceval's appointment as prime minister, after George III had declared him "the most straightforward man he had almost ever known." However, he found great difficulty in forming a ministry, owing to the feuds between Canning and Castlereagh. Indeed, he had to retain the post of chancellor of the exchequer himself, since he was unable to find a replacement; but his personal integrity did now allow him to accept the salary for the latter appointment. He provided strong and decisive leadership for a sometimes divided and weak government when the costly progress of the war and its economic drain on the country increased the government's unpopularity.

He saved his position after the disastrous Walcheren expedition of 1809 by forcing its leader, the Earl of Chatham, to resign from office. He also withstood the growing pressure for parliamentary reform. His budget proposals of 1810 were well received, and he insisted on the continuation of the war despite strong opposition. He dealt adroitly during the Regency Crisis of 1811 with the Prince of Wales—who held him in great dislike owing to the leading role he had taken in defending the Princess of Wales in 1805–1807—and the Prince retained him in office. He opposed the resumption of cash payments to fund the war with France, arguing successfully to the House of Commons that such a policy would destroy the capacity of the country to fund the war. Instead he emphasized the need to raise money by obtaining loans at low interest rates to finance the war. In February 1812 the government made framebreaking (of machinery) a capital offense and introduced the Watch and Ward Act in response to the Luddite disturbances in the manufacturing districts; and in April 1812 it agreed to an inquiry into the Orders in Council, whose continuation was considered increasingly harmful to the economy and to relations with the United States.

Unfortunately, on the evening of 11 May 1812, Perceval was shot in the chest in the lobby of the House of Commons and mortally wounded, thereby becoming the only British prime minister ever to be assassinated. His assassin, John Bellingham, who acted alone, was a mentally deranged bankrupt who sought government compensation for debts he had incurred in Russia. Bellingham had been angered by Perceval's refusal to introduce a petition into the House of Commons on his behalf. The assassin gave himself up immediately, stood trial at the Old Bailey, was sentenced to death, and was executed on 18 May, two days after Perceval's funeral. The House of Commons voted an annuity for Perceval's grieving wife and a grant for the support of his large family. Memorial sermons were preached across the nation, and a classical memorial to Perceval was placed in Westminster Abbey. It was a tragic end to a premiership that has been de-

scribed as the "most efficient and durable" of the five administrations that followed Pitt's resignation in 1801. Although not a great prime minister, Perceval has been described as "a capable conductor of the nation's financial business," who showed "a clear-sighted determination to support the war against Napoleonic hegemony. . . . [he] might have grown in stature had his fate allowed him a longer career" (Christie 1982, p. 209).

John A. Hargreaves

See also: Addington, Henry; Canning, George; Castlereagh, Viscount; Pitt, William (the Younger); Portland, Duke of
References and Further Reading: Christie, Ian R., 1982, *Wars and Revolutions: Britain 1760–1815* (Cambridge, MA: Harvard University Press); Gray, Denis, 1963, *Spencer Perceval, 1762–1812: The Evangelical Prime Minister* (Manchester: Manchester University Press); Thorne, R. G., 1986, *The House of Commons: 1790–1820*, vol. 4 (London: Secker & Warburg).

Pitt, William (the Elder; Earl of Chatham) (1708–1778) [PM, HS]

Pitt was a dominant figure on the British political stage during the Seven Years' War and the American War of Independence, enthralling contemporaries by his oratory and the grandeur of his national and imperial vision. He was also a flawed and paradoxical statesman, an overwhelmingly ambitious and arrogant man who could never work long with colleagues or work consistently for change. Although known as the "Great Commoner," he was not in fact a good manager of the Commons, and went to the House of Lords as soon as he became prime minister. He was a verbal advocate of liberty, but was often accused of being personally of a tyrannical disposition; and he was a spokesman for the people, but did not welcome reform and was often contemptuous of his popular support.

William Pitt (born 15 November 1708) was the second son of Robert Pitt, landowner of sizable Wiltshire estates, which were financially encumbered and became even more so under William's elder brother Thomas, who ruined his fortunes by pouring money into borough elections, trying unsuccessfully to build himself a parliamentary "interest." William had only an income of £200 a year, but in 1731, soon after leaving Oxford, he was able to purchase an ensign's commission in the horse regiment of his childless uncle, Lord Cobham.

In February 1735 Pitt first entered the Commons, standing for the family pocket borough of Old Sarum, outside Salisbury. He launched his political career as one of "Cobham's Cubs," an opposition Whig group attacking Walpole's ministry, and he soon gained a reputation as "a very pretty speaker." His first speech in Parliament, which was very well received, was in support of a place bill, to ban from the Commons those who held any place under the Crown and thus limit the scope for corrupt political control by the ministry. In April 1736 he delivered a notorious speech on the Commons' Address to the King on the Prince of Wales's marriage, which treated George II with scorn and irony. The king dismissed him soon afterward from the army, and the next year Pitt was given a place in the household of the prince, who had become a figurehead of the opposition to Walpole.

Even at this early juncture in his career, a crucial weakness of Pitt's political make-up was revealed: he was not acceptable in the royal closet, the King's inner sanctum, which was still a center of political power. He was incapable of cultivating good relations with George II and succeeded little better with George III. In opposition in the 1730s and 1740s, Pitt reserved his greatest parliamentary invective for the failures of successive ministries to attack and conquer the Bourbon powers of France and Spain, and for permitting the dominance of Hanover and German influences in British policy. In a searing attack in 1743, he not only portrayed Carteret's ministry as being enslaved to Hanover but even ridiculed the bravery and success of George II in the victory of Dettingen.

In October 1744, Pitt reaped the first reward of his public dedication to patriotism when Sarah, Duchess of Marlborough, an inveterate opponent of Walpole's, died and bequeathed Pitt £10,000. He benefited from a second estate, of around four times that sum, in January 1765, when a man unknown to him, Sir William Pynsent, inspired by Pitt's patriotic glories and

wartime leadership, left him the estate of Burton Pynsent in Somersetshire.

Pitt's first taste of high office came after the fall of Carteret, when the Pelham administration insisted on bringing him in. However, at the king's insistence, an office was found for Pitt in which he and his sovereign would not have to meet. He thus became paymaster-general of the forces in May 1746, at the age of 37. Pitt spent the next eight years learning the ways of administration and perfecting his reputation for charismatic (though not always very clear or organized) oratory. When Pelham died in 1754, George II resolutely opposed any promotion for Pitt, who saw his career stagnating as his financial difficulties mounted. In November 1754 Pitt married Lady Hester Grenville, twelve years his junior, who shared his political opinions and who was a devoted admirer of his talents. The marriage was an affectionate and successful one, which produced two daughters and three sons. Lady Hester helped Pitt manage his chronic problems of extravagance and poor financial accounting as well as his frail health, including recurrent episodes of gout and crippling bouts of depression.

A year later, while still in office as paymaster, Pitt launched a caustic denunciation of the German military subsidies in Commons, and was dismissed. In November 1756, though, the Duke of Newcastle resigned the premiership, and Pitt was brought back into office under the Duke of Devonshire and given the coveted post of secretary of state for the Southern Department. Now Pitt had a role in the conduct of a war against France; but he failed to change the pattern of reverses that he had scathingly criticized earlier. In April 1757 he was dismissed by the king, though showered with freedoms of the city by trading towns all over the country. His rhetoric had persuaded many in the country that he was the only man who should direct the war.

At the end of June 1757, Newcastle was called to form another ministry, with Pitt as secretary of state for the south. Pitt's strategic vision was the logical outcome of his years of opposition rhetoric: he opposed expensive German subsidies and costly continental warfare, and favored the use of Britain's naval power to make overseas conquests in North America, India, and the Caribbean. He had inherited a significantly enhanced naval force, and could rely on the support of the City of London and the main ports, where his personal popularity was high. The continental campaigns still had to be fought, however, and his initial plan in the autumn of 1757 for a naval expedition to harry the French coasts was a failure. Pitt's rhetoric of national power was essential to keep up public confidence and to justify the huge investment in the armed forces necessitated by war. By the end of 1758 the war in North America was going against the French, and by the autumn of 1759 the surrender of Quebec capped a triumphant year of British victories on the continent, in America, and in the East and West Indies: "Our bells are worn threadbare with ringing for victories," wrote Horace Walpole. Popular acclaim was accorded to Pitt, the man whose oratory had inspired a belief in glory and empire; but the credit should also have gone in great measure to Newcastle for his tireless and effective administration and daily political coordination.

The following October, with the accession of George III to the throne, there came a new challenge to Pitt's war effort. The young king and his chosen adviser, Lord Bute, were critical of the war and sought an early peace, whereas Chatham wanted to push France hard, using all the advantages that victory had brought, and to declare war on Spain. A year later, in October 1761, Pitt resigned, accepting a life pension of £3,000 and the creation of the title Baroness Chatham for his wife. Such was his carefully cultivated reputation for disinterested probity and for opposition to placement that these rewards were greeted with disillusionment. Effigies of Pitt were burned in the City, and his wife Hester was derided as Lady Cheat'em. Pitt's popularity soon recovered, however, and grew as he continued his attacks on the ministry's peace negotiations. He supported the 1764 motion on the Wilkes case, which condemned general warrants as illegal, and spoke passionately against the Stamp Act in the debates in January 1766; but he generally took little part in Parliament, as his health was poor for months at a time.

Despite his poor physical and mental state, he was called upon by George III in July 1766 to form a broadly based ministry after the dismissal of Rockingham. Rather than serve as head of the Treasury, Pitt decided to lead the ministry as Lord Privy Seal, which meant becoming a peer; and in August he took the title of Viscount Pitt of Burton Pynsent and first Earl of Chatham. Public support for the Great Commoner was seriously eroded by this move, which also left the ministry exposed to the Commons, where it was defended by the clever but erratic Charles Townshend and by Henry Conway, who was effective mainly within the sphere of military affairs.

The supreme self-belief and autocratic manner that made Chatham at times a mesmerizing orator were also the source of his greatest failing, a lack of ability to manage people. He had neither the personal warmth nor the respect for the abilities of others that could have made his disunited ministry work harmoniously, and his repeated illnesses kept him away from Westminster for long periods at a time. He did little to steer policy, leaving the vexed issue of American taxation to Townshend, and failing to implant in his colleagues his own desire for radical reform of the East India Company.

By the summer of 1767 Chatham had left the administration effectively in the hands of the Duke of Grafton, First Lord of the Treasury. He was so ill that for six months he conducted no business at all, though the grateful king told him, "Your name has been sufficient to enable my administration to proceed." Despite the king's earnest pleas, Chatham insisted on resigning in mid-October 1768, his ministry having thrown into high relief all his weaknesses as a peacetime leader, without adding anything to his political reputation.

Within a year, however, he had cast off his illness and joined the opposition campaign, among other things, for better treatment, short of independence, for the American colonists. Above all, in response to the government's overturning of the Middlesex elections, Chatham stood up for the rights and freedoms of electors and for constitutional reform. In the first two parliamentary sessions of Lord North's ministry, in 1770 and 1771, Chatham was once again as extreme and brilliant in opposition as he had been forty years earlier and once again galled his monarch with repeated attacks on "secret influence" and the dangers of royal power undermining the constitution. If he had been demonstrating his power and his following with a view toward holding office once more, it was not to be. Briefly, he seemed to be the obvious choice of leader if the nation went to war with Spain over the Falkland Islands; but North's ministry survived the challenge, and Chatham faded into semiretirement, speaking only rarely in the Lords.

The main issue on which he made the effort to attend debates, dramatically using such props as invalid clothing and a crutch, was America. He used his influence to argue against extreme measures and in favor of good relations with the colonies that were so valuable to Britain, yet he never clearly addressed the fundamental constitutional issues, and always opposed independence. The empire in America was his creation and his legacy, and he saw it as his mission to save it from dismemberment. For much of 1775 and 1776, Chatham was so dangerously ill as to be completely out of public life; but he returned to speak on American issues in his final year. On 7 April 1778 he went to the Lords for the last time to speak passionately but incoherently against the granting of independence to the colonists, and in the heat of debate he collapsed in a fit, which heralded his final illness. He died on 11 May 1778.

Both in office and in retirement, Chatham's prodigal spending on his properties and daily style of life was such as to astound even contemporaries used to grandeur and ostentation. The family fortunes, despite Hester's good management, were seriously embarrassed. The nation signaled its confirmation of Chatham's greatness with a parliamentary vote of £20,000 to pay off the debts he had incurred throughout his life, as well as by a funeral held in Westminster Abbey. Despite the flaws in his character and the limits of his achievements, the dead Chatham remained a hero to many in Britain who during the American war vainly sought a leader who represented national power and glory as Pitt had done in the midcentury struggle with France.

Philip Woodfine

See also: Bute, Earl of; Carteret, John; Devonshire, Duke of; Grafton, Duke of; Newcastle, Duke of; North, Lord; Pelham, Hon. Henry; Rockingham, Marquess of; Townshend, Charles (1725–1767); Walpole, Sir Robert
References and Further Reading: Birdwood, Vere (ed.), 1994, *So Dearly Loved, So Much Admired: Letters to Hester Pitt, Lady Chatham, from Her Relations and Friends, 1744–1801* (London: H.M.S.O.); Black, Jeremy, 1992, *Pitt the Elder* (Cambridge: Cambridge University Press); Middleton, Richard, 1985, *The Bells of Victory: The Pitt-Newcastle Ministry and the Conduct of the Seven Years' War* (Cambridge: Cambridge University Press); Peters, Marie, 1980, *Pitt and Popularity: The Patriot Ministry and London Opinion during the Seven Years' War* (Oxford: Clarendon); Peters, Marie, 1992, *The Elder Pitt* (London: Longman); Schweizer, Karl W. (ed.), 1993, *William Pitt, Earl of Chatham, 1798–1778: A Bibliography* (London: Greenwood); Williams, Arthur F. B., 1913, *The Life of William Pitt, Earl of Chatham* (London: Longmans).

Pitt, William (the Younger)
(1759–1806) [PM, CE]

William Pitt, the Younger, was born on 28 May 1759, the second son of William Pitt, later first Earl of Chatham, and Hester Grenville. A physically delicate but precocious child, he imbibed Whig politics from boyhood, from his father and his uncle George Grenville, both of whom held the office of prime minister in the 1760s. He received his earliest education from a private tutor and then went on to Pembroke Hall, Cambridge, graduating with an M.A. in 1776. He then trained as a barrister and joined the western assize circuit.

He soon sought election to Parliament, but failed to win the seat for Cambridge University in September 1789, trailing by 142 votes. However, at a by-election in January 1781, he was elected to the House of Commons for Sir James Lowther's pocket borough of Appleby in Westmoreland, at the age of 21. He quickly emerged as a promising orator, advocating both economic and parliamentary reform, and as a vociferous critic of Lord North, whom he blamed for the loss of the American colonies. He became chancellor of the exchequer 18 months later, at age 23, and prime minister in December 1783, at age 24, being the youngest politician ever to hold the office. He served as prime minister for over 17 years, longer than anyone else except Robert Walpole, during a period of momentous economic and social change that encompassed both the Industrial and the French revolutions. Moreover, throughout this period he combined the offices of prime minister and chancellor of the exchequer, achieving in the view of E. J. Evans an almost unrivaled "understanding of the nation's changing finances over such a long period."

When North fell in 1782, Pitt declined a subordinate role in the Rockingham ministry. After Rockingham's death, he served in Shelburne's administration as chancellor of the exchequer from July 1782 until February 1783. He was Shelburne's only effective spokesman in the House of Commons. He adopted Shelburne's plans for a reform of customs and for stricter control of public offices, but he failed to secure the support of the House of Lords for the proposed legislation.

After the resignation of Shelburne and the dismissal of the Fox-North coalition by George III, Pitt took office as prime minister and First Lord of the Treasury on 19 December 1783. His minority administration was not expected to survive long beyond the Christmas recess and was thence cynically dubbed the "mince pie" administration. However, he gradually consolidated his position before asking George III to dissolve Parliament. He then achieved a landslide victory in the ensuing general election, backed both by the exercise of royal patronage and by significant victories in many open constituencies, such as the larger borough seats and the highly populated county seats of Middlesex and Yorkshire. Pitt himself was elected for Cambridge University, heading the poll with 351 votes, and he continued to represent that constituency for the remainder of his life, facing only one further contested election in 1790.

Pitt's first ministry (December 1783–March 1801) was characterized by financial and administrative reform, in many cases involving a refinement of policies projected by his predecessors Walpole, North, and Shelburne. As a consequence of the American War, Britain had ac-

William Pitt, the Younger (engraving after the painting by Hoppner) (Library of Congress)

quired a national debt of £242.9 million. Pitt's response was to cut expenditure, improve the efficiency of tax collecting, and raise new taxes. The heaviest indirect taxes were imposed on luxuries consumed disproportionately by the better-off, such as fashionable men's hats and women's ribbons; but other taxes, on such essential items as candles, also had a detrimental impact on the poor, especially during the difficult winter months when unemployment was high.

Pitt discouraged smuggling by reducing customs duties and enabling more effective searching of vessels at sea. By 1790 the revenue from duties on wines, spirits, and tobacco had increased by between 29 percent and 63 percent over the levels collected when Pitt entered office. In 1786 Pitt revived and modified the Sinking Fund, originally devised in 1717 to reduce the national debt, under specially appointed commissioners. The scheme worked well until the unprecedented costs of the war with revolutionary France caused the national debt to escalate again from £243 million to £359 million be-

"*Britannia between death and the doctors*": death, with Napoleon's head, strides from behind the bed curtains; the doctor is William Pitt, kicking Henry Addington and stepping on Charles James Fox. (Library of Congress)

tween 1793 and 1797—so alarming the government that it suspended cash payments by the Bank of England and trebled taxes on luxuries. Indeed, by early 1798, debt repayment constituted almost one-third of total government expenditure, prompting Pitt to introduce a new tax on income and to phase out land tax. He believed economic reform was necessary to improve public administration. He reduced the use of patronage, encouraged promotion by merit, and simplified financial administration and accountability through his Consolidated Fund Act of 1787.

Influenced by the ideas of Adam Smith, Pitt regarded trade expansion within Europe as a means of compensating for the loss of the American colonies. He negotiated a wide-ranging commercial treaty with France in 1786 and entered into trade negotiations with seven other European states between 1784 and 1792. In 1785, however, opposition from English industrialists, the Irish Parliament, and the House of Lords thwarted his attempts to secure the com-

mercial union of the British Isles. Successive defeats in the Commons of his motions for parliamentary reform also caused him to abandon indefinitely further proposals after 1785. He also failed to secure the abolition of the slave trade in 1792. However, his India Act of 1784, one of his most important administrative reforms, placed the East India Company under a board of control responsible to the Crown; and his Canada Act of 1791 strengthened the position of the Anglican Church and the development of the landed aristocracy so as to make impossible any revolution on the American model. In 1788 he ended Britain's diplomatic isolation by concluding a Triple Alliance with Prussia and Holland designed to limit French influence. Exploiting the alliance, Pitt launched a successful diplomatic campaign against Spain in the dispute over Nootka Sound, Vancouver Island, leading to Spanish renunciation of claims to sovereignty over the territory.

During the French Revolution his main desire was for peace, and he has been criticized for allowing Britain to enter the war unprepared and undermanned and for spending too much time and effort on naval warfare with France in the Caribbean rather than concentrating on the Continental struggle. His strategy was to support Britain's European allies financially and militarily in direct attacks on the French, though the British expeditions to Toulon and Vendée failed miserably. The First Coalition, which Britain joined in 1793, appeared promising at the outset, but after October 1797 Britain alone among the European powers continued the war with revolutionary France; and the Second Coalition of 1798 collapsed after a couple of years. Pitt underestimated both French military capacity and the French sense of patriotic identity. Naval successes overseas were won at a heavy price, though the navy proved more successful in defending the country against invasion. However, when Pitt left office in 1801, Britain remained undefeated.

At home he has been criticized for exaggerating the danger of insurrection and consequently overreacting to popular radical movements in the 1790s. Fresh legislation restricting civil liberties was indeed introduced in most parliamentary sessions from 1792 to 1801, including the suspension of habeas corpus in 1794. However, this repressive legislation was seldom utilized and hardly constituted a regime of terror on the scale of developments in France. In contrast, his concern for the security of Ireland during the French Wars resulted in 1,500 executions of Irish rebels in 1798, and his subsequent decision to terminate the Irish Parliament produced a controversial union that exacerbated Anglo-Irish relations for over a century.

After carrying the Act of Union with Ireland, he resigned in 1801 when George III rejected Roman Catholic emancipation. The renewal of the war with France weakened the Addington administration, and Pitt returned to office for his second ministry in May 1804. Although his administration was impaired by the loss of the Grenvillites, and although Napoleon's victories at Ulm and Austerlitz effectively destroyed the Third Coalition, Pitt remained a symbol of national defiance, and he lived to hear news of the British naval victory at Trafalgar. Pitt never married, worked long hours, drank heavily, and was temperamentally aloof and introverted, but he was widely mourned by the British public after he died in 1806, at the age of 46.

J. Holland Rose in 1911 credited Pitt with promoting Britain's national revival after the devastating loss of the American colonies. E. J. Evans has emphasized the role of other factors in the transformation of Britain's economic prospects, such as the dramatic increase in overseas trade during the eighteenth century, and Britain's early lead in industrial production, which was only temporarily checked by the American War. Indeed, the value of Britain's exports almost doubled between the mid-1780s and the mid-1790s, with those to the newly independent United States increasing by 125 percent. His most recent biographer, John Ehrman, has suggested that one of Pitt's most enduring legacies was in giving "a modernising tone to the practice of government" (Ehrman 1996); and Eric Evans has acknowledged that "British government was substantially more efficient and professional" (Evans 1997) at the end of Pitt's premiership than it had been at the beginning.

The Younger Pitt combined conservative and reformist instincts in an era when party labels were confusing. Like his father, Pitt was never a party man. He believed in the maintenance of the balance between monarch, Lords, and Commons established after 1688 and dealt adroitly with the regency crisis of 1788. For the most part, up to 1801, Pitt retained the confidence of George III, with whom, in the view of Ehrman, he enjoyed a "guarded working relationship." His parliamentary authority depended more on the competence of his ministerial appointments, his skill in debate, and his support from independent members than on close party ties. "I do not wish . . . to call myself anything but an Independent Whig," he wrote to the Earl of Westmoreland in July 1779. Moreover, J. W. Derry has maintained that even following the party realignment that produced the Pitt-Portland administration, "Pitt never ceased to call himself an independent Whig" (Derry 1990, p. 33). Conventionally described by most textbooks as a Tory, Pitt may be more accurately viewed, according to Evans, as the "midwife of modern

Conservatism," which was the "legacy of second-generation Pittites"—notably Liverpool, Castlereagh, and Canning (Evans 1997).

John A. Hargreaves

See also: Addington, Henry; Canning, George; Fox, Charles James; Leeds, Duke of; North, Lord; Portland, Duke of; Shelburne, Earl of
References and Further Reading: Derry, John W., 1990, *Politics in the Age of Fox, Pitt and Liverpool* (Basingstoke, UK: Macmillan); Ehrman, John, 1969, *The Younger Pitt: The Years of Acclaim* (London: Constable); Ehrman, John, 1983, *William Pitt: The Reluctant Transition* (London: Constable); Ehrman, John, 1996, *The Younger Pitt: The Consuming Struggle* (London: Constable); Evans, Eric, 1997, *William Pitt the Younger* (London: Routledge); Mori, Jennifer, 1995, *William Pitt and the French Revolution* (Edinburgh: Keele University Press); Wright, David G., 1988, *Popular Radicalism: The Working-Class Experience, 1780–1880* (London: Longman).

Portland, Duke of (Sir William Henry Cavendish-Bentinck)
(1738–1809) [PM, HS]

Although a successful politician, Portland, who was prime minister on two occasions, in 1783 and from 1807 to 1809, was never a successful prime minister. His political career spanned fifty years and several major fluctuations in politics. He led a Whig coalition of Foxites and Northites in 1783, and an essentially Tory administration in 1807. This latter development occurred after he broke with Charles James Fox and took the conservative Whigs into an alliance with William Pitt, the Younger, and the Tories.

Portland was the grandson of William Bentinck, first Earl of Portland (1649–1709), who was born in Holland, was a page in the household of Prince William of Orange, and subsequently helped negotiate the prince's marriage to Mary, daughter of Charles II of England, in 1677. William Bentinck played a major part in the prince's invasion of England in 1688 and was active in many roles—courtly, military, and diplomatic. He became King William's most trusted agent of foreign policy.

William Henry Cavendish-Bentinck was born on 14 April 1738, the son of William Bentinck, second Duke of Portland, and Lady Margaret Cavendish Harley. He was educated at Westminster and at Christ Church, Oxford. He became M.P. for Weobly, Herefordshire, in 1760, and succeeded to the dukedom at the relatively young age of 24, in 1762. He entered Lord Rockingham's cabinet as lord chamberlain of the royal household and as privy councillor in 1765. Shortly afterward, in 1766, he married Lady Dorothy Cavendish, daughter of William, fourth Duke of Devonshire.

The political system that emerged during the 1760s was loose and shifting. It was affected in part by the personal rivalries of political leaders and the personal preferences of King George III for one set of ministers or another, as issues of a personal nature influenced the king's judgment. The disappearance of the Whig-Tory polarity of the early eighteenth century gave the king exceptional freedom to maneuver. Rockingham's brief administration, which lasted from 1765 to 1766, favored the abandonment of Grenville's Stamp Act (1765) and might thereby have avoided the conflict that led to the American War of Independence. Subsequently, in 1767, the king appointed William Pitt, the Elder, by then Earl of Chatham, to the premiership, and Parliament became divided into two groups: the King's party of government; and the Whig opposition of Rockingham, Portland, and Charles Fox. This polarization of politics intensified during the conflict with America in the 1770s.

As it became clear during 1782 that the war against America must be given up, Lord North, who had assumed leadership of the king's party effectively in 1770, resigned, and Rockingham formed an administration with the support of Chatham. On Rockingham's appointment in 1782, Portland became lord lieutenant of Ireland. The death of Rockingham in July 1781, and Shelburne's subsequent failure to win a majority for the terms of the peace treaty he had negotiated, created a crisis from which it emerged that only the followers of North and the Rockinghamites, now led by Portland and Fox, could guarantee a majority in the Commons. Portland's administration began in April 1783, and the treaty was signed in Paris the following September. This coalition was defeated in December when William Pitt, the Younger, assumed leadership of an alternative coalition more agreeable to King George III. Pitt remained in power for the remainder of his life, with the exception of Henry Addington's three-year administration (1801–1804).

During the French Revolution, Portland allied himself with Pitt, the Younger. As a reward he was appointed chancellor of the University of Oxford in 1792, and served under Pitt as home secretary between 1794 and 1801. He became a Knight of the Garter and lord lieutenant of Nottinghamshire in 1794. He greatly assisted in the passage of the Act of Union for Ireland between 1798 and 1800, and served as Lord President of the Council (Privy Council) in Addington's and Pitt's cabinets from 1801 to 1806, retiring on Pitt's death in 1806. The "Ministry of All the Talents," which succeeded Pitt's ministry, made mistake after mistake. When Pitt's friends again came to power, the difficulty was to find a prime minister under whom such rival spirits as George Canning and Castlereagh would agree to serve. Portland returned, reluctantly, to public life and served as prime minister from 1807 until he resigned, or was formally replaced, on 4 October 1809, following a life-threatening seizure. With other ministers and leading politicians clashing with the king over the issue of Catholic emancipation, Portland was the only possible candidate for the post of prime minister, although he was no longer fit for the job. He was old and had been in poor health for some time, and he died on 30 October 1809.

Kit Hardwick and Keith Laybourn

See also: Addington, Henry; Canning, George; Castlereagh, Viscount; Fox, Charles James; Grenville, George; North, Lord; Pitt, William (the Elder); Pitt, William (the Younger); Rockingham, Marquess of
References and Further Reading: Mitchell, Leslie G., 1971, *Charles James Fox and the Disintegration of the Whig Party, 1782–94* (London: Oxford University Press); O'Gorman, Francis, 1969, *The Whig Party and the French Revolution* (London: Macmillan); O'Gorman, Francis, 1975, *The Rise of Party in England: The Rockingham Whigs, 1760–82* (London: Allen and Unwin); Smith, Ernest, 1875, *Whig Principles and Party Politics: Earl Fitzwilliam and the Whig Party, 1748–1844* (Manchester: Manchester University Press).

Pulteney, Sir William (Earl of Bath)
(1684–1764) [PM]

Sir William Pulteney was for many years a commanding figure in the House of Commons, but never succeeded to the great office to which he seemed destined. After his long and ultimately successful campaign to overturn Sir Robert Walpole, Pulteney was finally offered the Treasury in February 1742 and turned it down, going instead to the Lords as Earl of Bath. When he did accept the seals of office, in February 1746, he was unable to form a ministry and was never actually head of an administration.

Pulteney was originally an ally of Walpole, and went into opposition with him from 1717 to 1720, but was already sufficiently estranged from him not to be given office when Walpole returned to the ministry. He then turned down the offer of a peerage; but in 1721 he accepted the lord lieutenancy of the East Riding of Yorkshire, in which his constituency of Hedon lay. From 1723 to 1725 he held the lucrative palace post of cofferer of the household; but he broke completely with the leading minister in April 1724, when the young Duke of Newcastle was preferred to Pulteney as secretary of state for the south. Henceforth he argued passionately in the Commons and in print that Walpole was the fount of corruption, subverting not only politicians but even the nation. With two other talented opponents—Henry St. John, Viscount Bolingbroke; and John, Lord Carteret—Pulteney formed an opposition that in late 1726 acquired a new mouthpiece, the *Craftsman* newspaper. In its heyday, up to the Excise crisis of 1733 and the 1734 election, the *Craftsman* was the most powerful agent of opposition, not least because of the regular contributions from its eminent patrons. In 1730, at the instigation of Bolingbroke, the philosopher of opposition, Pulteney joined the Tory leader Sir William Wyndham in a combined "Patriot" opposition, taking its name from the characteristic language of the *Craftsman.*

Among Pulteney's less creditable political writings of this time was the pamphlet *A Proper Reply to a Late Scurrilous Libel* (1731). The "libel" to which he was replying was a pamphlet written anonymously by Walpole's follower William Yonge, with a dedication, also anonymous, by John, Lord Hervey. Believing that the pamphlet was authored wholly by Hervey, whose reputed bisexuality was becoming steadily more notorious at this time, Pulteney attacked the man rather than the arguments. *A Proper Reply* was a very improper and personal onslaught, accusing Hervey of homosexual practices, a capital crime. Hervey promptly challenged Pulteney to a duel, which was fought on 25 January 1731, resulting in only minor cuts on both sides. In the fresh exchange of pamphlets that followed this event, Pulteney once again passed the bounds of political decency in his *An Answer to One Part of an Infamous Libel* (1731). He went so far as to repeat words that Walpole had allegedly said about the king, which angered George II so much that he struck Pulteney's name from the list of privy councillors.

Having repeatedly failed to undermine Walpole's power, even in the face of the almost nationwide furor over the Excise, Pulteney became disheartened. In a typical letter of 1735, he lamented: "It is in vain to struggle against universal Corruption and I am quite weary of the Opposition." In 1738, however, a popular outcry over the seizures of British ships in the Caribbean by the Spanish authorities gave Pulteney new heart and a chance to exercise his undoubted oratorical skills in Parliament. As Chesterfield, in his *Characters* (1777), described Pulteney at this time, "He was the most complete orator and debater in the House of Commons, eloquent, entertaining, persuasive, strong, and patriotic as occasion required, for he had arguments, wit, and tears, at his command."

Nonetheless, Pulteney again faltered in his attacks in the last year of the Walpole ministry. In June 1741, at a crucial point when the opposition coalition was counting its forces after the general election and settling strategy for the defeat of the administration, Pulteney had lost his appetite for leadership. George Bubb Dodington found him listless and inactive: "He saw no use of a meeting, or concert; would by no means undertake to write to or summon gentlemen . . . he was weary of being at the head of a party, he would rather row in the galleys, and was ab-

solutely resolved not to charge himself with taking the lead."

When Walpole resigned in February 1742, Pulteney was widely expected to become First Lord of the Treasury, and he was indeed offered the post by George II, but he refused to accept any office. His reasoning appears to have been consistent: that he had long been tired of the ungrateful labor of leading an opposition; and that now that Walpole had fallen, there was no longer any need to oppose, and he could retire to the pleasures of private life. He took the title of Earl of Bath on 14 July 1742, and was castigated in pamphlets and the press for his part in betraying his Tory allies of the Patriot alliance, who were now excluded from a share in power, despite all the earlier rhetoric of a pure administration, formed in the national interest and regardless of party.

When Lord Wilmington died in July 1743, however, Bath applied for the Treasury and was refused in favor of Henry Pelham, brother to the Duke of Newcastle. His final opportunity came in January 1746, when the Duke of Newcastle was negotiating to bring Lord Cobham's followers in to support the ministry, at the modest cost of appointing the most prominent of them, William Pitt, the Elder, secretary of war. When Pitt's appointment was vetoed by George II, the minister decided on the radical step of a mass resignation. On 19 February 1746, the secretaries of state, Lords Harrington and Newcastle, resigned the seals; they were followed the next day by Pelham and by Lord Bedford, and soon after that, by a steady stream of others. Over forty leading supporters of the administration were prepared to join the leaders, leaving almost every office of state open. George turned to Bath and Carteret (now Lord Granville), who had been strengthening his resolve against Pitt; but within forty-eight hours it had become apparent that they could not find enough supporters to form a ministry. On 13 February, Newcastle and his colleagues triumphantly resumed the seals. Bath took no further active part in politics, and retired to enjoy his considerable wealth. He died on 7 July 1764, of a fever.

Philip Woodfine

Francis Pym, 1978 (David Reed/Corbis)

See also: Carteret, John; Newcastle, Duke of; Pelham, Hon. Henry; Walpole, Sir Robert
References and Further Reading: Dickinson, Harry T. (ed.), 1998, *William Pulteney: A Proper Reply to a Late Scurrilous Libel; Intitled, Sedition and Defamation Display'd* (New York: AMS Press); Gerrard, Christine, 1994, *The Patriot Opposition to Walpole: Politics, Poetry and National Myth, 1725–1742* (Oxford: Clarendon); Halsband, Robert, 1973, *Lord Hervey: Eighteenth-Century Courtier* (Oxford: Clarendon Press); Sedgwick, Romney (ed.), 1970, *The History of Parliament: The House of Commons, 1715–1754,* vol. 2 (New York: Oxford University Press).

Pym, Francis (Lord Pym of Sandy)
(1922–) [FS]

Pym was a leading Conservative politician of the 1970s and early 1980s. Being committed to consensus politics, however, he fell afoul of Margaret Thatcher, who was committed to right-wing policies aimed at rolling back the welfare state and challenging the power of the trade unions.

Francis Leslie Pym was born on 13 February 1922, the son of Leslie Ruthven Pym and his wife, Iris. He was educated at Eton and at Sandhurst before going on to Magdalene College, Cambridge. He served in the army during World War II, and married Valerie Fortune Daglish in 1949.

Having unsuccessfully contested the Rhondda West seat in behalf of the Conservatives in 1959, Pym embarked on a parliamentary career in 1961, as M.P. for Cambridgeshire. He held that seat until 1983, when he became M.P. for Cambridgeshire Southeast, a constituency he represented until 1987. He was very much a "one-nation Tory," believing in the need to unite all social classes in the nation, which harmonized with the consensus politics of Edward Heath but not with the more confrontational politics of Margaret Thatcher.

Pym served his time as both a government and an opposition whip in the 1960s. He rose to become parliamentary secretary to the Treasury and government chief whip in Heath's ministry, between 1970 and 1973, and secretary of state for Northern Ireland between 1973 and 1974.

Out of office until Thatcher formed a government in May 1979, he was thereafter appointed secretary of defense, a post in which he served from 1979 to 1981; and chancellor of the Duchy of Lancaster, paymaster-general, and leader of the House of Commons in 1981. He was Lord President of Council between 1981 and 1982. The high point of his career came when he was appointed foreign secretary in April 1983. He did not last long in this post, though, for Thatcher saw him as a "wet," with soft-line policies. He had expressed doubt about the dangers of the Conservative Party winning too great a victory in the 1983 elections; and he was dismissed in June 1983.

After his dismissal Pym was singularly ineffective, resorting to the formation of the Centre Forward group, which produced an inconsequential book entitled *The Politics of Consent* (1984) and opposed the abolition of the Greater London Council in the Commons in the autumn of 1983. He left the Commons and was given the life peerage of Lord Sandy in the county of Bedfordshire in 1987. Since then he has filled various public roles—for example, serving as vice president of the Registered Engineers for Disaster Relief—and has worked with various industrial and commercial companies.

Keith Laybourn

See also: Heath, Edward; Thatcher, Margaret
References and Further Reading: Evans, Brendan, 1999, *Thatcherism and British Politics, 1975–1999* (Stroud, UK: Sutton).

R

Reading, Marquess of (Rufus Daniel Isaacs; Reading, Baron; Lord; Viscount; Earl of)
(1860–1935) [FS]

Rufus Daniel Isaacs, the first Marquess of Reading, was better known as lord chief justice of England and ambassador to the United States than as a politician. His term as foreign secretary in 1931 is one of the shortest on record.

Isaacs was born in London on 10 October 1860, the son of Joseph Michael Isaacs, a Jewish fruit merchant, and his wife, Sarah. He education was brief and broken; educated in Brussels between the ages of five and seven, he boarded at the Anglo-Jewish Academy at Regent's Park, and then attended University College School for a few months. He ended his education at age 14. At 15 he went to Germany and entered the family business, and later sailed around the world as a ship's boy. In 1880 he entered the London Stock Exchange as a jobber in the foreign markets; but after a disastrous period in 1884, he decided to study the law and become a barrister. He was called to the bar in November 1887. Three weeks later he married Alice Edith, the daughter of Albert Cohen, a City merchant. He quickly developed a thriving business in commercial law and was awarded silks, becoming a King's Counsel in April 1898, and thus being able to act in the major law cases of the day.

Isaacs soon began to combine law with politics. In 1900 he unsuccessfully contested North Kensington for the Liberals at the general election. In an August 1904 by-election, he was elected as M.P. for Reading. He retained that seat until he was made lord chief justice in 1913. He became solicitor general in the Asquith Liberal government in 1910, and was attorney general from 1911 to 1913, with a seat in the cabinet after 1912. He was active in helping David Lloyd George introduce his National Insurance Act in 1911.

Isaacs also was centrally involved in the famous Marconi Scandal of 1912. The English Marconi company had acquired certain monopoly rights in communications from the British government. Rufus's brother Godfrey had shares in the American Marconi Company and sold some of these to Rufus and two of his ministerial friends, one of whom was David Lloyd George. Although a select committee investigation into the Marconi affair cleared Rufus Isaacs and government ministers of having used their position and knowledge to financial advantage, Rufus Isaacs did admit that it had been a mistake to purchase the shares.

Shortly afterward, in October 1913, he became lord chief justice. He was raised to the peerage as Baron Reading in 1914. He remained lord chief justice until 1921, notably presiding at the trial for treason of Roger Casement, but was frequently employed in other activities. He led an Anglo-French mission to the United States in September 1915, in order to obtain American credits for supplies, and secured a loan of £500 million to be spent in the United States. After the United States entered World War I in April 1917, he was appointed high commissioner in Canada.

In return for his service, he was named Viscount Reading in 1916 and the Earl of Reading in 1917. In January 1918 he was made British ambassador in Washington, where he attempted to improve Anglo-American relations. While serving in this post, he was awarded honorary degrees by the universities of Harvard, Yale, Princeton, and Columbia. He returned to Britain in 1919. In 1921 he was appointed viceroy of India, a position he filled until 1926. This was at a time when Indians were demanding national independence. At first he attempted to avoid extreme measures; but he soon began to imprison the leaders of Indian resistance to British rule, whatever their position in the political spectrum. He had Mahatma Gandhi imprisoned in March 1922 and did not release him until February 1924. On his return to Britain in 1926 he was made the first Marquess of Reading. He then occupied a series of executive positions in business and industry, the most prestigious of which was the presidency of the Imperial Chemical Industries.

It was at the age of 71 that Reading attained his highest political office, serving as foreign secretary in James Ramsay MacDonald's National government, from the end of August to the beginning of November 1931. He resigned the post after the October general election. He was also leader of the House of Commons in 1931 and leader of the Liberal Party in the House of Lords between 1930 and 1935. He died on 30 December 1935.

Keith Laybourn

See also: Asquith, Herbert Henry; Lloyd George, David; MacDonald, James Ramsay
References and Further Reading: Marquand, David, 1977, *Ramsay MacDonald* (London: Cape); Reading, Lord (son), 1942, 1945, *Rufus Isaacs, First Marquess of Reading,* 2 vols. (New York: G. P. Putnam's Sons).

Rees, Lord Merlyn (Baron Merlyn-Rees of Morley and Cilyfyndd)
(1920–) [HS]

Merlyn Rees was one of the dominant politicians in the Labour governments of the 1960s and 1970s. Born in 1920, educated at Harrow Weald Grammar School and at the London School of Economics, he served in the Royal Air Force between 1941 and 1946. He was a teacher and lecturer between 1949 and 1953, before entering politics.

He was M.P. for Leeds South between 1963 and 1983, and from 1983 to 1992, for the constituency of Morley and Leeds South. Rees rose quickly in government circles. He became parliamentary private secretary to the chancellor of the exchequer in Harold Wilson's Labour government of 1964 and then parliamentary private secretary to the Ministry of Defence (Army) between 1965 and 1966. He was transferred from that army position to a similar post connected with the Royal Air Force, in which he served between 1966 and 1968. He then became undersecretary in the Home Office between November 1968 and June 1970. With the defeat of Wilson's Labour government, he was out of office for several years.

After Wilson became head of another Labour government following the general election of 1974, Rees was appointed successively secretary of state for Northern Ireland (March 1974–September 1976) and home secretary (September 1976–May 1979). He is a Welsh loyalist moderate and has been described variously, by different newspaper writers, as both "Labour's respected elder statesman" and a "fountain of ineffectual wisdom." While dealing with Northern Ireland, he secured a cease-fire with the Provisional IRA, ended detention without trial, and granted special status for political prisoners. He was also Jim Callaghan's campaign manager in the Labour leadership contest of March 1976. An elder statesman of the Labour Party by the late 1980s, he became a life peer in 1992.

Keith Laybourn

See also: Callaghan, James; Wilson, Harold
References and Further Reading: Rees, Merlyn, 1973, *The Public Sector in the Mixed Economy* (London: Batsford); ———, 1985, *Northern Ireland: A Personal Perspective* (London: Methuen).

Richmond, Duke of (Charles Lennox)
(1735–1806) [HS]

Charles Lennox was born on 22 February 1735, the third son of Charles, second Duke of Richmond, and his wife, Lady Sarah Cadogan. He was educated at Westminster School and at Leyden University, and then traveled on the Continent. He entered the army as a captain in 1753 and had risen to the rank of colonel by 1758. By 1761 he was a major general, a general by 1782, and a field marshal by 1786, although he was rarely directly involved in military ventures after

1760. He married Lady Mary Bruce, the only child of the third Earl of Ailesbury (the fourth Earl of Elgin), in 1757. He succeeded his father as the third Duke of Richmond in 1750, but did not take up his seat in the House of Lords until 1756.

Thereafter he served in a number of offices of state. He became lord lieutenant of Sussex in October 1763. However, he fell out of favor with the government and did not assume further responsibilities until August 1765, when the Marquess of Rockingham appointed him ambassador extraordinary and minister plenipotentiary at Paris. He was admitted to the Privy Council on 23 October 1765. Upon his return to England he became secretary of state for the Southern Department (a title that became that of home secretary after 1782) but occupied the position only from the end of May to the end of July 1766.

At this time Richmond became a staunch opponent of the ministries of the Duke of Grafton and Lord North, particularly in relation to their attitude toward the American colonists. He denounced the ministerial policy in America, and during the second reading of the American Prohibitory Bill in December 1775, he declared that the resistance of the American colonists was "neither treason nor rebellion, but is perfectly justifiable in every possible political and moral sense." Indeed, he put forward a motion on 7 April 1778 for the withdrawal of the troops from America. The episode ended when William Pitt, the Earl of Chatham, was struck down by a fatal illness when replying to Richmond's speech.

Richmond also supported legislative measures to redress Irish grievances and advocated a closer union among England, Ireland, and Wales. On 2 June 1780, he attempted to forward a reform bill that proposed annual parliaments, manhood suffrage, and electoral districts. Throughout that period he remained a supporter of Rockingham and the Whig grouping of M.P.s that gathered around Rockingham. Indeed, following Rockingham's death in 1782, Richmond expected to become the leader of that group of Whigs; but his advocacy of parliamentary reform barred him from such a role.

From 1783 on, he gradually drifted into the Whig/Tory coalition cabinets of William Pitt (the Younger), being given a ministerial post in the Ordnance Office. However, he was relieved of that office in February 1795. He became increasingly critical of the conduct of the French and Napoleonic Wars, and publicly condemned the humiliating peace agreement of 1802. He died on 29 December 1806. He is remembered as an effective but not a stellar politician.

Keith Laybourn

See also: Rockingham, Marquess of
References and Further Reading: Langford, Paul, 1973, *The First Rockingham Administration, 1765–6* (London: Oxford University Press).

Ridley, Sir Matthew White (Baronet; and Viscount Ridley) (1842–1904) [HS]

Sir Matthew White Ridley was a modestly successful Conservative home secretary who drew practically no attention to himself while in high office. He was born on 25 July 1842, the elder son of Sir Matthew White Ridley, fourth baronet of Blagdon, Northumberland. His mother was Cecilia Anne, eldest daughter of Sir James Parke, Baron Wensleydale. Ridley was educated at Harrow and then at Balliol College, Oxford, and was elected a fellow of All Souls College. He was married to Mary Georgiana, eldest daughter of Dudley Coutts Marjoribanks, first Lord Tweedmouth, on 10 December 1873.

Ridley embarked early on a career in politics, succeeding his father as M.P. for North Northumberland in 1868, a seat for which he was returned in 1874 and in 1880. He succeeded his father as fifth baronet in 1877. In 1878 he became undersecretary at the Home Office, and he continued in that post until 1880. He was appointed financial secretary to the Treasury in September 1885, in Lord Salisbury's first, short administration; but after his defeat in the general election that November, he resigned together with his colleagues in January 1886.

He had lost the Hexham constituency in the November 1885 election, having been forced to stand for reelection due to the redistribution of the parliamentary seats in 1885. In the July

1886 general election he was defeated again at Newcastle-on-Tyne. He was not reelected to Parliament until he won the Blackpool parliamentary by-election in August 1886. He retained this seat until he was raised to the peerage in 1900. Although he was admitted to the Privy Council in 1892, he remained a member of Parliament. His primary claim to political fame is his term as home secretary (1895–1900) in Lord Salisbury's government; but his record in this office is unremarkable. He retired from political life in 1900, becoming Viscount Ridley and contenting himself with running his estates and with a stint as chairman of the North Eastern Railway. He died on 28 November 1904.

Keith Laybourn

See also: Salisbury, Lord
References and Further Reading: Shannon, Richard, 1996, *The Age of Salisbury: The Conservative Party, 1881–1912* (London: Longman).

Rifkind, Malcolm
(1946–) [FS]

Malcolm Leslie Rifkind was born on 21 June 1946, the younger son of E. Rifkind of Edinburgh. He was educated at George Watson's College, Edinburgh, and at Edinburgh University. After graduating, he lectured at the University of Rhodesia (1967–1968) before pursuing a career in law and becoming a barrister in Scotland in 1970. In the same year he married Edith Amelia Steinberg and became M.P. for Edinburgh Central.

Rifkind's political career since he entered the House of Commons has been dominated by Scottish affairs. He was president of the Scottish Young Conservatives from 1975 to 1976 and opposition front bench spokesman on Scottish affairs at the same time; parliamentary undersecretary for Scottish affairs between 1979 and 1982; and secretary of state for Scotland between 1986 and 1990. In more recent years, he has been at the forefront of Conservative attempts to improve the party's weak political base in Scotland.

From 1979 to 1997, Rifkind was an increasingly important figure in the governments of Margaret Thatcher and John Major, filling

many different posts. He was at the Foreign and Commonwealth Office between 1982 and 1986, becoming minister in 1983. He was secretary of state for transport from 1990 to 1992 and was secretary of state for defense from 1992 to 1995. In addition, he was a member of two select committees of the House of Commons connected with European secondary legislation (1975–1976) and overseas development (1978–1979). The high point of his political career occurred when he was appointed foreign secretary in July 1995, replacing Douglas Hurd.

From time to time, Rifkind has been at the center of political decision making. Most notably, he is credited with having been among the group of ministers who told Margaret Thatcher in November 1990 that it was time for her to resign as Conservative leader and prime minister. In the 1990s he was considered pro-European, until he declared his objection to a single European currency for Europe—a position that has strongly influenced Conservative attitudes on this subject. Since the Conservative defeat in the general election of May 1997, Rifkind has continued to work within the Conservative Party to improve its political standing in Scotland.

Keith Laybourn

See also: Clarke, Kenneth; Heath, Edward; Major, John; Thatcher, Margaret
References and Further Reading: Evans, Brendan, 1999, *Thatcherism and British Popular Politics, 1975–1999* (Stroud, UK: Sutton).

Ritchie, C. T.
(Lord Ritchie of Dundee)
(1838–1906) [HS, CE]

Ritchie was almost a nonentity in politics, having enjoyed one of the shortest terms of any chancellor of the exchequer, lasting a mere 14 months and presenting only one budget. A reclusive figure, he was little known by his political colleagues and the British public. He left few political ripples in British politics, being seen more as an expert than a dynamic political figure, although he left some lasting legislative landmarks.

Charles Thomson Ritchie was born in 1838 at Broughty Ferry, on the edge of Dundee, Scotland, the son of a jute merchant and manufacturer. He was educated, until age 15, at the City of London School, before going off to work in the family firm's London office. He married at 20 and seemed set for a career as a businessman. However, in 1874, at the age of 36, he won a parliamentary seat as Conservative candidate for the two-member constituency of Tower Hamlets, in London.

A Scottish Liberal Nonconformist, Ritchie was to the left of the Conservative Party. From his seat on the backbench in Commons, he successfully promoted an 1875 bill to extend the Bank Holiday Act of 1871 to dockyard and custom house employees. He also campaigned vigorously against the continuation of the sugar bounties paid by foreign governments to sugar beet producers. He argued that such foreign bounties damaged the business prospects of London's East End sugar refiners. His argument for Britain's imposition of countervailing duties failed to persuade; but he did have the satisfaction of being appointed chairman of a select committee (of M.P.s) formed to study the issue in 1879.

When Tower Hamlets was split up as a result of the extension of the franchise and reorganization of constituencies in 1884, Ritchie moved to the single-member constituency of St. George's-in-the-East, which he won in 1885. However, he was defeated in the 1892 general election and did not return to Parliament until 1895, following his electoral victory at Croydon, near London. Despite this hiatus, Ritchie did eventually gain ministerial experience.

In the first Salisbury Conservative government (1885–1886), he was appointed financial secretary to the Admiralty. He was successful in this post, and within a year of his appointment, the construction rate of British battleships tripled. A year later, when Salisbury formed his second administration (1886–1892), Ritchie was promoted to president of the Local Government Board, a post in which he was largely responsible for the County Councils Act of 1888, which reorganized local government in Britain by making the county administration more democratic and less subject to direct domination by landowners. When Salisbury formed his third government (1895–1902), Ritchie was appointed president of the Board of Trade, thus occupying the second-ranking cabinet position, which had often served as a stepping-stone for aspirants to the post of chancellor of the exchequer. He proved a success in this role, promoting a wide variety of legislation. He introduced the Conciliation Act of 1896, under which conciliation boards were formed to settle industrial disputes, and he personally intervened to settle an eight-month engineering strike in 1898. He also created the intelligence branch of the Board of Trade to collect statistical information on commerce and labor, and he promoted a Railway Safety Act in 1900. In November 1900 he was appointed to the post of home secretary, in which he was responsible for the passage of the Factory and Workshop Act and for the Youthful Offenders Act, which was designed to develop probation as an alternative to custodial sentences.

At the end of the South African/Boer War in June 1902, Prime Minister Salisbury and Chancellor of the Exchequer Hicks Beach decided to resign. The new prime minister, Arthur James Balfour, opted for Ritchie as chancellor of the exchequer, and the appointment was duly made on 8 August 1902. From the start, however, Balfour and Ritchie were unable to develop a close working relationship. Ritchie, famed for his legislative activity, had probably become chancellor, as Balfour's secretary suggested, because he was a "hard-working minister of pedestrian methods."

Ritchie was at odds with the mood of Balfour and the cabinet. By this time he had become a fervent free trader—an attitude that did not sit well in a cabinet that was edging in the direction of mild protectionism, as indicated in the prior imposition of Hicks Beach's 1 shilling (5p) registration duty on corn imports. Ritchie was determined to remove this duty, and did so in his budget of 1903. He also announced that income tax would be reduced by 4d (1.6p) to 11d (4.4p) on the pound; this reduction, though, was lower than might have been expected, given that the Boer War was at an end.

Ritchie's budget came before Parliament at a time of intense political conflict within Conservative ranks. Shortly after the budget announcements, on 15 May 1903, Joseph Chamberlain declared his intention to raise the Imperial Preference issue. He resigned from the cabinet in September 1903 to pursue his protectionist political campaign. Ritchie resigned on 5 October 1903, along with several other free traders.

Ritchie's resignation at age 65 in effect put an end to his political career. He stayed in the House of Commons until the end of 1905, when he was raised to the House of Lords as the first Lord Ritchie of Dundee. For a time, he played a minor role in the activities of the Unionist Free Food League. He died in Biarritz on 9 January 1906.

Ritchie's political career was hardly the stuff of greatness. Nevertheless, he was a determined, prolific, and principled legislator who resigned from office largely due to his commitment to free trade in a cabinet that was divided and dithering on the issue.

Keith Laybourn

See also: Balfour, Arthur James; Gladstone, William Ewart; Hicks Beach, Sir Michael; Salisbury, Lord
References and Further Reading: Jenkins, Roy, 1998, *The Chancellors* (London: Macmillan).

Robinson, Thomas (Baron Grantham)
(1695–1770) [FS, HS]

Thomas Robinson was born in 1695, the son of William Robinson of Newby in Yorkshire and of Mary, eldest daughter of George Aislabie of Studley Royal. He was educated at Westminster School and at Trinity College, Cambridge. He then entered the diplomatic service and became secretary to the English embassy in Paris. He was one of the three English representatives at the Congress of Soissons, and in 1730 he was sent to Vienna as the English ambassador. He spent eighteen years in that post. It was during this period, in 1737, that he married Frances Worsley. As British ambassador his main tasks were to improve relations between Britain and the emperor of Austria and to protect the interests of King George II, who was also elector of Hanover. In 1740 he reminded Maria Theresa, who had just ascended to the throne of Austria, of the support that Britain had given her father

during the War of Spanish Succession. He hoped thereby to gain her support for an alliance of Austria and Britain that would counter the alliance among France, Bavaria, and Prussia.

Robinson returned to England in 1748. He had already been M.P. for Thirsk between 1727 and 1734, and now he became M.P. for Christchurch (1748–1761). He had no particular parliamentary abilities and was strongly attacked by William Pitt, the Elder; but despite these disadvantages, in 1754 he became secretary of state for the Southern Department (the post became that of home secretary in 1782) in the Whig government of the Duke of Newcastle. He did not enjoy the post and cheerfully gave it up in November 1755. He was then appointed master of the wardrobe in the royal household. He refused all subsequent offers of high office but accepted a peerage in April 1761, becoming the first Baron Grantham. He died on 30 September 1770.

Keith Laybourn

See also: Newcastle, Duke of
References and Further Reading: Browning, Reed, 1975, *The Duke of Newcastle* (New Haven, CT, and London: Yale University Press).

Rochford, Earl of (William Henry Nassau de Zuylestein)
(1717–1781) [FS, HS]

William Henry Nassau de Zuylestein was born on 17 September 1717, the eldest son of Frederick Nassau de Zuylestein, the third Earl of Rochford, and Bessy Savage, the illegitimate daughter of the third Earl Rivers. He was educated at Westminster School. He became a lord of the bedchamber in 1738, with a salary of £1,000 per year, and inherited property from an uncle, becoming the fourth Earl of Rochford. He married Lucy Young in May 1740. Being active at the court of King George II and as an envoy to the Italian and Spanish courts, he acquired significant diplomatic skills. He was lord lieutenant of Essex from 1756 to 1766, when he was appointed British ambassador in Paris. In the latter post, he warned the cabinet, with some exaggeration, of potential French aggression following the French annexation of Corsica.

Rochford was appointed secretary of state for the Northern Department on 21 October 1768 by the new prime minister, the Duke of Grafton. Rochford was something of an independent spirit, however, and his was the deciding vote that defeated Grafton's cabinet proposal to repeal the "obnoxious" American duties. Rochford's main responsibility was to deal with the treaty negotiations with Spain in 1770. These negotiations normally would have been the responsibility of Viscount Weymouth, the secretary of state for the Southern Department at this time; but Rochford switched departments with Weymouth on 17 December 1770 so as to have a hand in Spanish affairs and to organize the 1771 Convention with Spain. At this point Rochford was serving under Lord North, who had become prime minister in January 1770.

Both Grafton (FS) and Rochford (HS) resigned in October 1775, as a result of difficulties in dealing with the American colonies. Rochford retired with a annual pension of £2,500, which was quickly raised to £3,320. He gradually withdrew from active politics and died on 28 September 1781.

Keith Laybourn

See also: Grafton, Duke of; North, Lord
References and Further Reading: Whiteley, Peter, 1997, *Lord North: The Prime Minister Who Lost America* (London: Hambledon).

Rockingham, Marquess of (Lord Charles Watson-Wentworth)
(1732–1782) [PM]

A wealthy scion of the influential Yorkshire family Wentworth, and one of the most politically influential in the country, Rockingham was the leader of the "Rockingham Whigs" and the patron of Edmund Burke. It was he who first developed the concept of programmatic party action. Despite his public significance, Rockingham was a painfully shy man who rarely spoke in the House of Lords, and he held no major political office other than the premiership.

When his father died in December 1750, Rockingham inherited the family title and huge estates, at age 20. He was the eighth of ten children, and the fifth son; but his four brothers and two of his sisters had died young. Thus he inherited the family seat of Wentworth Woodhouse (among other properties), which had not quite been completed, although his father had spent lavishly on its construction over more than twenty years. The largest private house in England, with a dominating east facade that was 600 feet long, it symbolized the Wentworth family's status. The young heir, early in his public career, set up the Rockingham Club in York—the county seat and electoral center—in an attempt to translate the family's social status into political influence. Such were his political connections that he was made a Knight of the Garter by George II in May 1760, though as yet he had held no political office and had shown his loyalty only in the capacity of Lord of the Bedchamber.

Rockingham began to be courted by the Duke of Newcastle, and aligned himself with the "old Whigs," whom the new king, George III, was determined to oppose. As a county magnate with a strongly provincial power base, Rockingham was also inclined to distrust the court. He drew parliamentary support from both the Pelhamite "old corps" of aristocrats, seasoned in office and electioneering, and the "country" or "patriot" believers in purity and economy, by pressing for an end to place-holding M.P.s and patronage and secret spending. Both the Pelhamite and the Patriot traditions came together in the early years of the new reign, which was dominated by the influence of Lord Bute (the "Bute myth").

Rockingham suffered in the "massacre of the Pelhamite innocents" of 1762 to 1763, being dismissed from his prestigious regional posts as lord lieutenant of the North and West Ridings of Yorkshire and as vice admiral of Yorkshire. He commanded a following of about 100 M.P.s, though, and came to occupy a more central position in politics during the short-lived premierships of Bute and Grenville. As Newcastle was unacceptable to the king, Rockingham seemed a logical choice to deliver a viable "old corps" ministry when Grenville was dismissed. George III at first wanted Grenville to be replaced by Pitt; but when Pitt refused, the Duke of Cumberland persuaded Rockingham to form a ministry in May 1765. Rockingham served as First Lord of the Treasury, and Newcastle took office as Lord Privy Seal.

The new government was severely hampered by Pitt's hostility and refusal to cooperate in the important business of establishing policy toward America. Grenville's 1765 Stamp Act had to be enforced, appraised, and ultimately (in March 1766) repealed. In February 1766, Rockingham had laid down five resolutions on American policy that subsequently failed to pass the House of Lords. The ministry began to fall apart in April 1766, after the resignation of the Duke of Grafton, whose post of secretary of state proved difficult to fill. Unable to recruit either the followers of Bute or those of Pitt, Rockingham found it difficult to hold together his coalition. In July 1766, George III dismissed Rockingham and called on Pitt (who in the following month became the Earl of Chatham) to form a new administration. A number of Rockingham's Chathamite supporters stayed on, but Chatham treated them with disdain, and in November 1766 dismissed one of the most senior of them, Lord Edgecumbe, from his place as treasurer of the household.

Increasingly alienated from the royal court, Rockingham's now smaller party saw themselves as the heirs of the old Whig principles and the defenders of the Glorious Revolution settlement. They believed that the constitution was endangered by the corruption of the royal court, and that "secret influences" and royal favoritism were undermining the political process and had to be opposed through reform and through the setting of high moral standards in public life. At the same time, they inherited from Newcastle and the Pelhamites the knowledge that success in politics came from acting in concert. Unlike others at the time, they did not decry party politics as mere factionalism, something to be avoided; they justified and even glorified it. Edmund Burke expressed the Rockinghamite view most forcibly, and in his *Thoughts on the Present Discontents* (1770) gave full justification of men in Parliament acting together to promote their joint beliefs. Men banded together in common belief and common principles, went the argu-

ment, have a duty to contend for office and place. In pursuit of long-term goals, supporters in Parliament might occasionally have to vote as the party dictates, even if they did not approve of the measure in question.

The Rockingham Whigs were selective in choosing their battles and were not a structured opposition of the modern kind; but every year, beginning in 1774, they forced a voting division on the parliamentary address in reply to the speech from the throne. They exerted opposition sparingly but with effect. With their numbers increasing from fewer than sixty members in 1766 to around ninety in 1782, the Rockinghamites were not an alternate ministry, but they were an effective pressure group, voting their party line with considerable discipline.

Rockingham was not particularly active in Parliament after his resignation from office. He was a progressive agriculturist and had become greatly involved in the improvement of his estates. He also was passionately interested in horse racing. He did, though, consistently argue in Parliament for putting an early end to the American crisis by granting the colonists their independence; and he continuously supported the cause of "economical reform," the purification of public finances. In December 1779 Rockingham gave his authority, which was not in the event uniformly welcomed, to the cause of Christopher Wyvill's reforming Yorkshire Association, by appearing in Castle Yard at York for their first meeting. In June 1789, Lord North tried to salvage his ministry by forming a coalition with Rockingham; but the Marquess refused to come aboard unless the king accepted the principle that independence could be granted to the North American colonists. In the end, the military disappointments of the war and the refusal of George III to countenance independence made North's position untenable, and in late March 1782 he resigned to make way for an administration headed by Rockingham.

In poor health, Rockingham could neither heal the increasing divisions between his two secretaries of state, Shelburne and Fox, nor impose his party's line on Shelburne's substantial following. He did achieve some modest victories, nonetheless. Among them were parliamentary acts forbidding government contractors to sit in the Commons and removing the vote from the numerous officers of the customs and excise service, who had long been unofficial electoral agents of the government in power. Another, more ambiguous achievement was the concession to the Irish parliament of legislative independence from Westminster. In the absence of more radical reform, however, this concession was likely to provide a forum for more future debate and protest. Anglo-Irish Protestant domination was still effected by England's appointments of the lord lieutenants of Ireland; and the corruption of the Dublin Parliament and the exclusion from office of Roman Catholics were left unaddressed. Limited progress had been made in peace negotiations with America, on which Rockingham had as yet made little imprint when in late June he succumbed to a severe bout of influenza. He died on 1 July 1782. He was survived by his wife, née Mary Bright, who was not only his close companion but also his political adviser. As they had no children, Rockingham's huge estates in Yorkshire and Ireland went to his sister Anne's son William (Wentworth) Fitzwilliam, fourth Earl of Fitzwilliam. Rockingham was buried in great state in the choir of York Minster, at the heart of the county that had been his power base and had shaped his distinctive approach to politics.

Philip Woodfine

See also: Bute, Earl of; Fox, Charles James; Grafton, Duke of; Grenville, Lord; Newcastle, Duke of; North, Lord; Pitt, William (the Elder); Shelburne, Earl of

References and Further Reading: Albemarle, Earl of (ed.), 1852, *Memoirs of the Marquis of Rockingham and His Contemporaries* (London: Bentley); Guttridge, George H., 1952, *The Early Career of Lord Rockingham, 1730–1765* (Berkeley: University of California); Hoffman, Ross J. S., 1973, *The Marquis: A Study of Lord Rockingham, 1730–1782* (New York: Fordham University Press); Langford, Paul, 1973, *The First Rockingham Administration, 1765–1766* (London: Oxford University Press); O'Gorman, Francis, 1975, *The Rise of Party in England: The Rockingham Whigs, 1760–82* (London: Allen and Unwin); Thomas, Peter D. G., 1996, *John Wilkes: A Friend of Liberty* (Oxford: Clarendon).

Rosebery, Lord (Archibald Philip Primrose; Earl of Rosebery)
(1847–1929) [PM, FS]

Archibald Philip Primrose, the fifth Earl of Rosebery, was an inconsequential prime minister, as leader of a lame ministry for barely 15 months. Yet in terms of political style, he was an orator and statesman of a higher quality. As many of his biographers have noted, his premiership did not live up to expectations.

Rosebery was born on 7 May 1847, the third child of Archibald, Lord Dalmeny, and Lady Wilhelmina Stanhope. He was educated at Eton and at Christ Church, Oxford, but he did not complete his studies, due to his love of horse racing. He was born into a wealthy, landed family and generally prospered, inheriting the earldom in 1868, and marrying Hannah de Rothschild, heir to the Rothschild fortune, in 1878. As a result of these events, his holdings included estates in both England and Scotland. Rosebery reveled in gambling, the collecting of rare books, and other rarefied pleasures of the higher social strata, especially after the death of his wife in 1890. Yet the dilettante in him hid a man who seriously doubted his own abilities and who lacked the forthrightness of the great political heroes (Cromwell, Napoleon, and the Earl of Chatham) he so admired.

Rosebery entered the House of Lords in 1868, making an impression with a polished first parliamentary speech in 1871. A Whig with radical leanings, he drifted into Liberal politics. Here his obvious abilities were recognized by Gladstone, who enlisted Rosebery as manager of his Midlothian election campaign in 1880—which was a political triumph. Indeed, Rosebery was so successful that the Scottish press praised him as the person most likely to ensure that Scottish affairs would be managed more effectively. He served as undersecretary of state for home affairs between 1881 and 1883, but he never gained the cabinet post of spokesman for Scotland that he so desired. As a result, he resigned in 1883. In 1885, however, he became Lord Privy Seal—the same year that the Scottish Office was set up, complete with its own secretary, although lacking cabinet status.

Gladstone's conversion to Irish Home Rule

created political convulsions within British politics in 1885 and 1886, and the Irish Home Rule Bill of April 1886 divided the Liberal Party. Some Whigs and Unionists left the party as a result, but Rosebery, despite his Whig views, supported Gladstone. He was not particularly attracted to Irish Home Rule; instead he advocated a "Commonwealth"—an idea born during his tours of the Empire in 1883 and 1884. He also declared himself in favor of the Imperial Federation League, which was formed in 1884.

In 1886, Gladstone made Rosebery his foreign secretary, a role to which he was ideally suited. Although Rosebery was only in the post for six months before the Irish Home Rule Bill brought down Gladstone's Liberal government, he did indicate a commitment to the principles of continuity in British foreign policy, of a "free hand" in arranging diplomatic alliances for Britain in relation to the great European powers, and of refraining from foreign military engagements when the necessary resources were lacking.

Out of office for several years after the fall of Gladstone's government, Rosebery became involved in a variety of other political activities, most notably as chairman of the newly formed London county council in 1889. When Gladstone did form another ministry in August 1892, Rosebery was asked to serve again as foreign secretary. He did so until 1894. Gladstone and many in the Liberal government kept a close eye on Rosebery's actions in Uganda and Egypt during this time, having noted his imperialist leanings. Above all, Rosebery was opposed to Gladstone's wish for Britain to withdraw from Egypt. Rosebery's desire was to maintain the Empire rather than to expand it, but even this conservative attitude brought him into conflict with a significant part of Gladstone's Liberal government.

In 1894, Gladstone's second Irish Home Rule Bill was rejected by the House of Lords, prompting the prospect of his resignation. Rosebery was, with William Harcourt, one of the two obvious candidates to replace him. Supported by the majority of the Liberal Party and by the queen, Rosebery was asked to form a government on 3 March 1894, and he accepted on 5 March.

Rosebery's short-lived ministry was a failure. Both Harcourt and John Morley, a leading influence with the Liberal Party, felt slighted by his appointment, and this created serious tensions within the party. Rosebery also annoyed the supporters of Irish Home Rule within the party by clearly indicating, in several speeches, that Home Rule was not an issue that he was willing to pursue—offending both the Irish Nationalists (now divided over Parnell) and those in the Liberal Party who felt that Celtic interests should not be subject to the primacy of English interests.

Rosebery was further discredited by his attitude toward Harcourt's introduction of "death duties" in the 1894 budget. Harcourt pressed this measure through the parliamentary procedures; but Rosebery appeared reluctant to impose death duties on the rich, which might force the rich and landed interests into the hands of the Conservative Party. This led to confusion within the Liberal Party, which was further amplified by internal conflicts over foreign policy.

British foreign policy was largely based upon rivalry with France. An attempt by Britain and Belgium to prevent French access to Egypt through the Congo failed, but the British let it be known that they would regard as hostile any French incursion into the Nile. Divisions within the cabinet on such matters did not help Rosebery's administration. Rosebery's failure to deal with the Disestablishment of the Church of England in Wales and to clarify crofters' rights in Scotland made the situation worse. Eventually, on a relatively minor matter, Rosebery resigned and Parliament was dissolved. The Liberals were routed in the July 1895 general election, the Conservative and Unionists being elected with a majority of 152.

The Liberal Party had divided into various factions, despite the efforts of Rosebery to keep it together. Yet Rosebery remained its leader after the disastrous general election. He condemned the Jameson Raid in South Africa but was not forthright in his criticism of the Turkish actions over Armenia, which led Gladstone to come out of retirement and Rosebery to resign as Liberal leader in October 1896, to be replaced by Harcourt.

During the Boer War (1899–1902) Rosebery

returned to prominence, leading the "Liberal Imperialist" section of the party. He believed in the idea of an economically and socially progressive empire, and was supported in this by R. B. Haldane, Edward Grey (Grey of Fallodon), and H. H. Asquith. With this power base, he hoped to replace Henry Campbell-Bannerman, who had taken the place of Harcourt as party leader in 1898. Rosebery spoke on the issues of empire and of "national efficiency" based on social reform. In December 1901 he made a speech in which he suggested that the Liberals should abandon some of their old policies, including Home Rule. However, after the Boer War ended, Rosebery's support base dissolved, and he was forced to unite behind Campbell-Bannerman—particularly after Joseph Chamberlain launched his campaign for tariff reform and imperial preference. As class politics came to replace the old interest-group arrangements, Rosebery gradually moved farther from the political limelight.

Despite his natural political talents, Rosebery was never able to occupy the middle of the Liberal Party by balancing, or harmonizing, its various interest groups. As a result he was never a particularly effective party leader, nor a successful prime minister. By the end of World War I, he had completely left the political scene, having been devastated by the death of his son in the war in 1917, and by a stroke he suffered in 1918. He died on 21 May 1929, an almost forgotten political figure.

Keith Laybourn

See also: Asquith, Herbert Henry; Campbell-Bannerman, Sir Henry; Gladstone, William Ewart; Grey, Sir Edward; Harcourt, Sir William
References and Further Reading: Brooks, David (ed.), 1986, *The Destruction of Lord Rosebery: From the Diary of Sir Edward Hamilton, 1894–95* (London: Historian's Press); Buchan, John, 1930, *Lord Rosebery, 1847–1929* (London: Humphrey Milford); Crewe, Marquess of, 1930, *Lord Rosebery* (London: John Murray); Matthew, Henry C. G., 1973, *The Liberal Imperialist: The Ideas and Politics of a Post-Gladstonian Élite* (London: Oxford University Press); Rhodes, J. Robert, 1963, *Rosebery* (London: Weidenfeld & Nicolson); Stansky, Peter, 1964, *Ambitions and Strategies: The Struggle for Leadership of the Liberal Party in the 1890s* (Oxford: Clarendon Press).

Russell, Lord John (Earl Russell)
(1792–1878) [PM, FS, HS]

Russell was prime minister on two occasions but is best remembered for as leader of the Liberal Party for twenty years and leader of the government in the House of Commons for more than fourteen years. In many ways he exerted a dominant influence on the Liberal Party in its early, formative years.

He was born on 18 August 1792, the third son of John Russell, sixth Duke of Bedford, and of the Hon. Georgiana Byng. He was educated at home and then at Westminster public school (similar to an America private school), followed by Mr. Smith's school at Woodnesborough. Later he attended Edinburgh University. He married Adelaide, the daughter of Thomas Lister, in 1835. After Adelaide died in 1838, he married Frances Elliot, daughter of the second Earl of Minto, in 1841. She gave birth to their first child in 1850, while Russell was prime minister. (Another 150 years would pass before another British prime minister—Tony Blair—became a father while in that office.)

Russell's political career began in 1813 when he became M.P. for Tavistock, a constituency that he represented until 1817, and again from 1818 to 1820. Thereafter he was M.P. for Huntingdonshire (1820–1826), Bandon (1826–1839), Tavistock again (1830–1831), Devon (1831–1832), South Devon (1832–1835), Stroud (1835–1841), and lastly, the City of London (1841–1861). He thus represented seven different constituencies in the House of Commons in his long political career between 1813 and 1861.

Russell was greatly influenced by the Whig ideas of Charles James Fox, who held that the monarchy had to act through Parliament. He believed that the leading politicians of the day should provide political leadership and protect the liberties of the people in civil and religious matters. When Charles Grey formed his Whig administration of 1830 to 1834, Russell became paymaster of the forces and was one of the committee of four charged with the responsibility of drawing up the 1831 Reform Bill. This bill was the basis for the 1832 Reform Act, which removed nomination boroughs and created parlia-

Lord John Russell (Library of Congress)

mentary boroughs in which the M.P.s were chosen by a wider electorate.

Out of office in 1834 during the Duke of Wellington's short-lived ministry, Russell returned as home secretary (1835–1839) and then colonial secretary (1839–1841) in Melbourne's Whig administration of 1835 to 1841. As home secretary he became a great reformer. Indeed, in 1839 he pressed forward an Education Act that set up a committee of the Privy Council to administer the government's annual grants to schools. He reformed criminal law, reducing the number of offenses incurring the death penalty from 33 to 16. A supporter of minorities in the Foxite tradition, he had backed Catholic emancipation in the 1820s, and as home secretary he encouraged the use in Ireland of surplus revenues of the Anglican Church for the community as a whole—particularly the Catholic community.

It was at this time that Russell began to emerge as a politician of a different type than Lord Melbourne and Lord Palmerston, two Whig prime ministers under whom he served. Unlike these two statesmen, who preferred to rule by the consensus of Parliament, Russell was willing to take the lead. Increasingly, he was described as a Liberal, although the term did not replace *Whig* until much later. Although Russell was out of office during Sir Robert Peel's Tory administration of 1841 to 1846, it was obvious that with the retirement of Melbourne from politics Russell would become the next Whig/Liberal prime minister. Indeed, this occurred in 1846.

The split between the protectionists and the Peelite free traders in the Conservative Party in 1846, over the ending of the protective Corn Laws, provided Russell with the opportunity to become prime minister of a Whig/Liberal administration that did not enjoy a parliamentary majority. Even the 1847 general election, which increased the representation of the Whig/Liberal Party by forty seats, did not give Russell a majority over the two wings of the Conservative Party. At the same time, he could rely on the Peelites to support him only on the issue of free trade. Furthermore, some of his radical supporters demanded further parliamentary reform, economies, and the removal of state endowment of religious institutions. Others in his own party were resistant to such pressures. In effect, Russell was walking a political tightrope during the six years of his first premiership. Nevertheless, he was eager to implement a package of social and educational reforms.

In the late 1840s his government provided money for pupil teachera, which permitted children of about twelve and thirteen to train to be teachers, and grants and money for secular school textbooks. The 1848 Public Health Act established local boards of health with powers to deal with sewerage and drainage. He pressed for the reform of the Church of England, to make it more tolerant and responsive to working-class needs. In the 1850s he set up royal commissions to examine the structure of teaching at Oxford and Cambridge. Unfortunately, Russell found many of these reforms undermined. The Public Health Act of 1848 had created a General Board of Health under Edwin Chadwick, which found its authority to guide and influence local boards undermined in the 1850s. In addition, reform of the Church of England led many High Churchmen to reject his actions, especially when in his so-called Durham Letter of 1850 he referred to his Tractarian opponents as Roman Catholics. His actions offended Catholics as much as Protestants, not least because he symbolically restated the state's sovereignty in ecclesiastical matters. Indeed, the Ecclesiastical Titles Act of 1851 restated the state's nominal sovereignty in ecclesiastical matters.

The trouble that Russell found himself in with both Protestants and Catholics over religious authority was nothing, compared with his problem of Ireland. The Irish famine of 1845 to 1847 created very serious problems. In the face of nationwide starvation, which produced a massive wave of Irish migration to Britain and the United States, Russell extended the provision made to the Irish by the Poor Law; and in 1849 he encouraged the transfer of estate ownership to landlords who would invest in improving the land. Yet action in Ireland also necessitated that the Russell government withdraw habeas corpus in 1848, which alienated some sections of Irish society. In the end, many of his schemes for Ireland had to be abandoned.

Russell faced many other problems. His minority administration experienced serious financial and budgetary problems arising from the fact that its income from tariff protection was down, and thus it had to rely upon income tax. It also faced setbacks on reform. Confronted by the Chartist demand for parliamentary reform, Russell pressed his cabinet to move toward further parliamentary reform, but could not get them to accept the bringing forward of a reform bill before 1852. The government was defeated on a militia bill in 1852 and was replaced by the Conservative government of the fourteenth Earl of Derby. However, Russell reappeared as foreign secretary in December 1852, in a Whig/Liberal and Peelite government headed by the Peelite Lord Aberdeen.

Russell was unhappy with this demotion; and in 1853 he found himself demoted even further, to the role of minister without portfolio (1853–1854). He continued, ineffectively, to press for both educational and constitutional reform. He was appalled at the Crimean War. He helped bring down the Aberdeen government, resigning twice in 1855, from the posts of President of the Council (1854–1855), leader of the Commons (1855), and colonial secretary (1855). He also created problems for the Palmerston government in 1857 and 1858; but he nonetheless was appointed Palmerston's foreign secretary and served in that post from 1859 to 1865, lending his fervent support to the cause of Italian liberty. Having been left a small amount of Irish property, he was granted a peerage in 1861, becoming the first Earl Russell.

On Palmerston's death in October 1865, Russell became prime minister for the second time. As before, he placed parliamentary reform at the head of his program. He had attempted to bring a reform bill forward in 1860, but it had had to be withdrawn. In 1866 he put forward a new reform bill; but like the first, it too was defeated (in June 1867), and Russell decided to resign. Shortly afterward, in December 1867, he also resigned as Liberal leader. He never held political office again. He died a little more than a decade later, on 28 May 1878.

Although he often has been identified with the political interests of the landed constitutional Whigs, who were mainly concerned with making the monarch subject to Parliament, it is clear that Russell was in many ways one of the early Liberals committed to reform, whether parliamentary, religious, educational, or Irish national. This was evident in the late 1830s when he was home secretary. However, as prime minister he rarely held a majority in the House of Commons and found his concern for parliamentary reform thwarted by those who wanted little or no reform. Nevertheless, he bequeathed his agenda to William Gladstone and the newly emergent Liberal Party.

Keith Laybourn

See also: Aberdeen, Earl of; Derby, 14th Earl of; Gladstone, William Ewart; Grey, Sir George; Melbourne, Viscount; Palmerston, Lord; Peel, Sir Robert; Wellington, Duke of
References and Further Reading: Mandler, Peter, 1990, *Aristocratic Government in the Age of Reform: Whigs and Liberals, 1830–1852* (Oxford:

Clarendon); Parry, Jonathan, 1993, *The Rise and Fall of Liberal Government in Victorian Britain* (New Haven, CT, and London: Yale University Press); Prest, John, 1972, *Lord John Russell* (London: Macmillan).

Ryder, Richard
(1766–1832) [HS]

Richard Ryder was born on 5 July 1766, the son of Nathaniel Ryder, first Baron Harrowby, and his widow, Elizabeth Terrick. He was educated at Harrow and at St. John's College, Cambridge, and then became a student in law at Lincoln's Inn in February 1788, being called to the bar in November 1791. He entered Parliament as M.P. for Tiverton in a by-election in 1795, retaining the seat until his retirement from politics in 1830. He acted as a Welsh judge between 1804 and 1807 until he took office under the Duke of Portland in 1807, becoming lord commissioner of the Treasury. He was quickly admitted to the Privy Council and promoted to judge advocate general in November 1807. Subsequently, when Spencer Perceval became prime minister in 1809, he was promoted to the post of secretary of state for the Home Department (home secretary), with responsibility for social control at the time of the Napoleonic Wars. He held this position until June 1812, a month after the assassination of Spencer Perceval. Thereafter he continued his distinguished legal career with less active involvement in politics. He died on 18 September 1832.

Keith Laybourn

See also: Perceval, Spencer; Portland, Duke of
References and Further Reading: Gray, Denis, 1963, *Spencer Perceval: The Evangelical Prime Minister, 1762–1812* (Manchester: Manchester University Press).

S

Sackville, Viscount (Lord George Sackville Germain) (1716–1785) [AC]

George Sackville was known from 1720 to 1770 as Lord George Sackville, and from 1770 to 1782 as Lord George Germain. He was born on 26 January 1716, the third and youngest son of Lionel Cranfield Sackville, seventh Earl and first Duke of Dorset. Sackville was educated at Westminster School, and after spending some time with his father in Paris, accompanied his father to Dublin, Ireland, where he attended Trinity College, graduating with a B.A. in 1733 and an M.A. in 1734. In April 1737 he was appointed clerk to the council in Dublin, and in July he became a captain in the 6th dragoon guards, then known as the 7th or Lord Cathcart's horse guards. In 1740 he was promoted to lieutenant colonel of the 20th foot, under Major General Bragg. In 1749 he became colonel in the 12th dragoons and in 1750 colonel of his old regiment, the 6th dragoons, now renamed the 3rd Irish horse dragoons regiment.

Sackville entered the House of Commons in 1741 as M.P. for Dover, and represented that borough until 1761. After performing a tour of military service that included the battles of Dettington and Fontenoy in 1745, in which he was badly wounded, he returned to England. He was made colonel of the Lancashire fusiliers, which he joined at Inverness after the Jacobite rising of 1745, remaining in Scotland until 1747. He then returned to England, where he married Diana, daughter and coheiress of John Sambroke, in 1754. She died in 1778, leaving Sackville a widower with two sons and three daughters.

In 1751 he returned to Ireland and represented the borough of Portarlington in the Irish Parliament, at the same time retaining his English parliamentary seat. Sackville became a member of the Privy Council in 1758. During this time, he also continued his distinguished military career. However, when he hesitated to commit his forces to the battle of Minden in 1759, he was dismissed from the army. Sackville asked to be court-martialed in order to clear his name, and when this request was refused, he published an *Answer to Colonel Fitzroy*. He eventually was court-martialed, but instead of being exonerated, he was found guilty of disobeying orders and his discharge from the army was confirmed.

Despite this setback, Sackville became M.P. for Hythe, Kent, in 1761, and under the new king (George III) he was quickly restored to favor. He succeeded to his father's estates at Knowle Park in 1765, and in 1768 he was elected M.P. for East Grinstead, which he represented until he succeeded to the peerage. As a follower of Lord North he was popularly assumed to be the author of the *Letters of Junius*.

In 1770, Parliament granted him the right to be known as Lord George Germain, in accordance with the will of Lady Betty Germain. Any whiff of cowardice that might have remained due to the ignominious end of his military career was finally obliterated as a result of his duel with another M.P., Captain George Johnstone, for which he subsequently was declared a hero by none other than Horace Walpole (Horatio or Horace Walpole, fourth Earl of Oxford, 1717–1797). Germain became secretary of state for the American colonies under Lord North from 1775 to 1782, and was rewarded with a viscountcy in February 1782. Spending his late years mostly in retirement, he died at his residence in Sussex on 26 August 1785.

Kit Hardwick

See also: North, Lord
References and Further Reading: Whiteley, Peter, 1996, *Lord North: The Prime Minister Who Lost America* (London: Hambledon).

Salisbury, Lord (Robert Arthur Talbot Gascoyne-Cecil; Marquess of Salisbury)
(1830–1903) [PM, FS]

The third Marquess of Salisbury enjoyed a political career that encompassed almost half a century, from 1853 to 1902. During that period he was prime minister and foreign secretary on four occasions each. Although he greatly influenced the development of the British Empire, before the publication of Andrew Roberts's recent book *Salisbury: Victorian Titan* he had not attracted as much attention as other illustrious Conservative leaders, such as Benjamin Disraeli and A. J. Balfour.

Robert Arthur Talbot Gascoyne-Cecil (later Lord Cranborne, and then Lord Salisbury) was born on 3 February 1830 into one of Britain's oldest political dynasties. He was the son of the second Marquess of Salisbury and Frances Gascoyne. As a younger son, however, his political and social success was far from guaranteed. He was educated at Eton—an experience he detested, since he was mercilessly bullied there. Indeed, he refused to ever go to Eton as a guest speaker throughout his adult life. After graduating from Eton, he went on to Christ Church College at Oxford University, where he was elected secretary of the Oxford Union. Although he obtained only an aristocratic fourth-class degree, he was later awarded an All Souls fellowship, and ultimately, the Oxford chancellorship.

On leaving Oxford, the young Lord Robert Cecil, as he was then titled, opted to become a journalist, writing articles for the *Saturday Review* and the *Quarterly Review* as he had little prospect of inheriting title and land. He married Georgina Alderton in 1857, and the couple had an ever increasing brood of children. His various writings at this time indicate that he claimed to despise academic life, concerts, and the theater, but Andrew Roberts suggests that this was very much for show.

His journalistic activity was combined with an early involvement in parliamentary politics. He became M.P. for a family borough in 1857, and held that seat until the early 1870s. During this period he seems to have moved from being a High Tory, fixed on the rule of the Anglican Church and the rule of property, to being a rather flexible Conservative. In these early years, his interest in a ministerial career was primarily motivated by the need to earn an income; but the deaths of his elder brother and his father eventually gave him both a peerage and property. On the death of his elder brother in 1865, he became Lord Cranborne; and he succeeded his father as Marquess of Salisbury in 1868. He thus acquired the attitude of a great landowner; but he did not lose the drive to write in order to earn an income.

Salisbury's political views were, therefore, dualistic. Although he fought against the widening of the parliamentary franchise in 1867, he was a pragmatist and recognized that one of its main implications was that the Tory party had to win support in the towns. Nevertheless, as an aristocrat, he believed that "fear, awe and respect for the law" were the keys to British rule in India. Although he believed that the southern states in America should be supported in their attempt to secede from the Union, he regarded William Ewart Gladstone as an "old hypocrite" for backing Ireland's right to secede from the United Kingdom.

Between 1866 and 1867 Salisbury was secretary of state for India, but he resigned in opposition to Disraeli's campaign in favor of the Reform Bill (later, Act) of 1867, having been unable to prevent the measure's passage. After his father's death, he moved to the House of Lords. Here he watched, disapprovingly, Gladstone's reforming zeal between 1868 and 1874. Here he also matured as a politician, becoming the Conservative leader in the Lords. Disraeli appointed him foreign secretary in his second administration (1878–1880), in place of the fifteenth Earl of Derby, who had resigned as a result of Disraeli's pursuit of a belligerent policy abroad. Disraeli and Salisbury did not work closely together, largely because Salisbury disagreed with Disraeli's view of Turkey as a poten-

Lord Salisbury (Library of Congress)

tial counterweight to Russian ambitions in the Middle East.

When Disraeli died in 1881, Salisbury became one of the contenders, along with Sir Stafford Northcote in the Commons, for leadership of a future Conservative ministry. He cultivated his position well, attempting to attract right-wing dissident Liberals into the Conservative Party. In 1885 he managed to attract the Liberal Unionists away from Gladstone over the issue of Home Rule but kept them as a separate party. When Gladstone fell from power, Salisbury was asked to form a Conservative government. He served as prime minister on three separate occasions—from 1885 to 1886, 1886 to 1892, and 1895 to 1902. He also combined this post with that of foreign secretary from 1885 to 1887, 1887 to 1892, and 1895 to 1900.

During these years he was concerned with maintaining the support of Joseph Chamberlain and the Liberal Unionists, most obviously by introducing free elementary education in 1891. He attempted to thwart more radical reforms by anticipating them and promoting a watered-down alternative. This was most obvious in the case of the 1888 County Councils Act, which formed elected county councils and undermined the more radical innovations being considered by Gladstone.

As foreign secretary, Salisbury came to the conclusion that Britain's military power in Europe was declining and that its naval power in the East was overextended. In an attempt to reduce the costs of empire, he began to promote cooperation with Germany. He had come to believe that the British Empire had to be developed and protected by individual interests—a belief evidenced in 1888 by his granting of a charter to the British East Africa Company, which he expected would protect the sources of the Nile, as well as Egypt. This policy of cooperation with Germany resulted in a major redistribution of territory between Britain and Germany in 1890, whereby Britain gained Zanzibar, Kenya, and Uganda in return for handing over Heligoland and a large part of East Africa to the Germans. Nevertheless, after Bismarck fell from power in 1890, relations with Germany began to deteriorate. Britain also was unable to prevent Russia and Germany from acquiring leases of land in China.

Gladstone and the Liberal Party won the general election of 1892, but Salisbury returned at the head of another Conservative government after the 1895 general election. He remained prime minister until 1902, winning the 1900 general election, but was foreign secretary only in the first of these two administrations, from 1895 to 1900.

Joseph Chamberlain, the leader of the Liberal Unionists, was included in this government; social reform therefore was among its objectives, although Salisbury opposed the provision of old-age pensions by the state, as well as all attempts to restrict the length of the workday. He was also opposed to income tax, being unwilling to accept the premise that one social class should pay for the needs of another. However, this reticence disappeared during the Boer War at the turn of the century, when income tax doubled and the government abandoned its attempt to pay down the national debt through the Sinking Fund.

As foreign secretary, Salisbury continued to face the problem of Britain's diminishing military power. Attempts were made to win German support for Britain's restraining Russia in the Far East, in return for British naval support against France, but they came to nothing. In the end, British interests were preserved in the Far East when Lord Lansdowne, who took over from Salisbury, negotiated an alliance with Japan. In 1902, Salisbury decided to retire as prime minister, before the political and military disasters of the Boer War were exposed. He died on 22 August 1903.

How are we to assess Salisbury? Andrew Roberts, in his recent monumental biography, suggests that this leader of the "stupidest party" was a lot brighter than his bulky frame (he was six feet five inches tall) and aristocratic foibles made him look. Roberts and other recent writers consider Salisbury one of the great prime ministers of the nineteenth century. After Lord Liverpool, he held the premiership longer than any other nineteenth-century statesman; he won three general elections (1885, 1886, and 1900); he was one of the longest-serving of all foreign secretaries, often combining the role with that of prime minister; and he accomplished all of this from the House of Lords. The Boer War brought imperial and foreign affairs disasters that took a toll on his reputation, and the Conservative Party began to fracture when he left office. Nevertheless, it is possible that his skill in handling his fellow ministers and his practice of not interfering in departmental affairs helped keep the Conservative Party together in the late nineteenth century. He was undoubtedly a skillful politician and an effective premier, and recent writers seem to be coming to the opinion that he was one of the most able of Britain's prime ministers.

Keith Laybourn

See also: Churchill, Lord Randolph; Disraeli, Benjamin; Gladstone, William Ewart; Lansdowne, 5th Marquess of
References and Further Reading: Evans, Brendan, and Andrew Taylor, 1996, *From Salisbury to Major: Continuity and Change in Conservative Politics* (Manchester: Manchester University Press); Roberts, Andrew, 1999, *Salisbury: Victorian Titan* (London: Weidenfeld & Nicolson); Steele, David, 1999, *Lord Salisbury* (London: UCL Press); Taylor, Robert, 1975, *Lord Salisbury* (London: Allen Lane);
Williams, Robin H. (ed.), 1988, *The Salisbury-Balfour Correspondence, 1869–92* (Ware, UK: Hertfordshire Record Society).

Samuel, Sir Herbert (Viscount Samuel)
(1870–1963) [HS]

Sir Herbert Samuel, who became the first Viscount Samuel in 1937, was a leading figure in the Liberal Party during the early twentieth century, serving as its leader between 1931 and 1935. He was a minister in the Liberal government and wartime administrations of 1905 to 1916 and served as high commissioner of Palestine between 1920 and 1925. He was a Jew and a deeply committed Zionist. Politically, Samuel was associated with the Asquithian free-trade wing of the Liberal Party and often found himself in opposition to David Lloyd George, even though he did favor the government-inspired social reform of New Liberalism in his younger years.

Herbert Louis Samuel was born in Liverpool on 6 November 1870, the son of Edwin Samuel, a very wealthy Jewish banker, and his wife, Clara Yates. Samuel's parents moved to London in 1871, where Edwin established a partnership in Samuel & Montagu, one of the great London banks. However, Edwin died in 1877, leaving an estate of about £200,000, in addition to his holdings in Samuel & Montagu and his leasehold properties. Herbert was, therefore, raised in considerable affluence, with three brothers and a sister, by his mother.

Herbert was educated at University College School, London, and at Balliol College, Oxford, where he gained a first-class degree in modern history. While at Oxford he came under the influence of Graham Wallas, an empiricist and prominent member of the Fabian Society, which was committed to the gradual extension of state control and the improvement of social conditions. It was probably at this stage that Samuel developed his commitment to "meliorist" ideas, which he defined as those based on the assumptions that the present is an improvement over the past and that the future may be better still. He was also greatly influenced by Sidney Webb, another leading figure in the Fabian Society, who was committed to social reform. Through these personal connections, Samuel became deeply involved in the activities of a group of British radicals, including Ramsay MacDonald, Charles P. Trevelyan, and Beatrice and Sidney Webb, who met in the Rainbow Tavern in London and formed the Rainbow Circle. The group produced the *Progressive Review* between 1896 and 1897, a journal representing their views. Samuel, Trevelyan, and other Liberal Radicals wished radicalism to remain within the Liberal Party; but MacDonald and the Webbs began to favor Keir Hardie's idea that the Labour movement should focus its efforts on forming a political party that was separate from and independent of the Liberal Party.

With the acrimonious breakup of the Rainbow Circle and the demise of the *Progressive Review,* Samuel began to develop his own progressive ideas in pamphlets, and eventually in his book *Liberalism* (1902), in which he outlined many of the social reforms that were introduced by the Liberal government from the end of 1905 to 1914. Indeed, throughout the late 1890s and early twentieth century, Samuel undertook a punishing program of lectures—502 between 1893 and 1902—to shape, influence, and revive the Liberal Party organizations and attitudes. (It must be remembered that the Liberal Party was out of office between 1895 and 1905.)

Samuel entered Parliament in 1902 as Liberal M.P. for Cleveland, a seat that he held until 1918. At first he made his name because of his humanitarian concerns. Indeed, in 1903 he denounced the "barbarism" of King Leopold of the Belgians in the Congo, and in 1904–1905 he worked alongside Roger Casement on the issue; and he bitterly opposed the Conservative scheme for the importation of Chinese laborers to work in the gold mines in South Africa. This latter controversy, among others, brought down the Conservative government of Arthur Balfour in December 1905.

Between 1905 and 1909, in both the Campbell-Bannerman and Asquith governments, Samuel served as undersecretary at the Home Office. He helped draft and present social reform legislation and was closely associated with the Probation Act of 1907, which created a national system of probation officers, and with the Children's Act of 1908, which codified much of the existing legislation on the treatment and protection of children. In 1909, he was appointed chancellor of the Duchy of Lancaster, effectively a minister without a portfolio or ministry but with a cabinet membership. Thus he became the first Jew who had not converted to another religion to occupy a seat in the cabinet.

He was postmaster-general from 1910 to 1914, and again between May 1915 and January 1916, and in this role was largely responsible for the nationalization of the telephone service. He was also president of the Local Government Board from February 1914 to May 1915. His attempted reforms in that post were abandoned as a result of World War I. Serving briefly as home secretary between January and December 1916, he found himself in conflict with many former radical friends who felt that civil liberties were being flouted in pursuit of victory. The internment of Irish dissidents during this period particularly damaged his reputation in such circles. He was also deeply involved in the case of Sir Roger Casement, who was found guilty of high treason and executed on 3 August 1916, after being arrested in April 1916 as he landed from a German submarine. Samuel's ministerial and cabinet posts came to an end in December 1916, when instead of accepting an office under David Lloyd George he decided to support Asquith, the deposed prime minister, on the opposition front bench.

His primary political interest at this time was Zionism. This interest seems to have predated World War I. In 1915 he put to the cabinet the need for a British-sponsored homeland in Palestine in a memorandum entitled "The Future of Palestine," which demanded "the restoration of Jews to the land to which they are attached by ties as ancient as history itself" (Wasserstein 1992, pp. 200–202). He hoped that Palestine could provide a home for at least 3 or 4 million European Jews. Undoubtedly, he did play a part in influencing the Balfour Declaration of November 1917, a single-sentence pronouncement that stated:

His Majesty's Government view with favor the establishment in Palestine of a national home for the Jewish people, and will use their best endeavours to facilitate the achievement of this object, it being clearly understood that nothing shall be done which may prejudice the civil and religious rights of existing non-Jewish communities in Palestine, or the rights and political status enjoyed by Jews in any other country.

Samuel thus became the obvious choice as the first high commissioner in Palestine under the League of Nations mandate, a post he held from 1920 to 1925. In many ways, he laid the basis of the modern Israeli state during this formative period, although the Arab anti-Zionist riots of 1920 and 1921 did force him to restrict Jewish immigration according to the "economic absorptive capacity" of Palestine. Nevertheless, he was seen by many as a "Nehemiah leading his people home from exile" (Wasserstein, p. 249). Hymns of redemption were composed in his honor, and carpets were woven bearing his image.

When Samuel's term as high commissioner ended, he expected to retire to his house in Mount Carmel, in Palestine, to write and further develop his philosophical ideas. Instead, he was drawn again into public life as head of the Royal Commission on the Coal Industry, which was set up in August 1925 in order to examine the future of the British coal industry in light of the threatened industrial action of July 1925. The commission's report in March 1926 suggested that the industry should be rationalized; that government coal subsidies could not be continued; and that the wages of the coal miners, already much reduced in the previous five years, would have to be temporarily reduced further. The report was rejected by both the coal miners and the coal owners, and it failed to prevent the general strike of the Trades Union Congress (TUC) in favor of the coal miners, which took place between 3 and 12 May 1926. While on holiday in Italy and Switzerland, Samuel was called back by the TUC to help negotiate a settlement to the strike. His negotiations with the TUC, which led to the production of the Samuel Memorandum—largely a reiteration of the main points of the report by the Royal Commission on the Coal Industry—led the TUC, over opposition from coal miners, to call off the general strike. Baldwin's Conservative government, however, felt no need to be bound by the memorandum—and the TUC had effectively surrendered without guarantee.

In the late 1920s, Samuel was drawn back into the Liberal Party, from whose internal quarrels he had been insulated by his time in Palestine. During the 1920s he had kept close contact with Labour figures such as Beatrice and Sidney Webb, but had become rather distant from the Liberal leaders. In 1927, he became the Liberal Party's organizational chief, securing £300,000 from the Lloyd George Fund to fight the general election of May 1929 and £35,000 per year for administration. In 1929, the Liberal Party improved its position enormously over its disastrous showing at the 1924 general election, winning 59 seats instead of the 40 of 1924; and Samuel himself was elected to Parliament as M.P. for Darwen. Along with Lloyd George, he maintained a Lib-Lab arrangement that kept Ramsay MacDonald's second Labour government in office. When the Labour government fell in August 1931, Samuel was instrumental in helping form MacDonald's National government, in which he became home secretary. At this time he also became the Liberal leader. Despite Liberal losses in the October 1931 general election and many internal conflicts within the new National government, Samuel remained home secretary until the end of September 1932, when he resigned because of the continued protectionist policies that were being adopted. He remained Liberal leader until the 1935 general election, when he himself was defeated and the Liberal Party was reduced to 19 seats. Thereafter, he never held office again. After he was raised to the Lords in 1937, he occasionally spoke in the House of Lords or in BBC broadcasts. He spent the rest of his time in writing philosophical works.

Samuel will be remembered as one of the key figures in the Liberal Party as it declined during the interwar years and as a Zionist who helped lay the foundations of the state of Israel. It will probably be forgotten that he was a formative influence in the creation of the New Liberalism with its emphasis upon social reform, which David Lloyd George helped develop in the early twentieth century.

Keith Laybourn

See also: Asquith, Herbert Henry; Baldwin, Stanley; Balfour, Arthur James; Campbell-Bannerman, Sir Henry; Lloyd George, David; MacDonald, James Ramsay
References and Further Reading: Wasserstein, Bernard, 1992, *Herbert Samuel: A Political Life* (Oxford: Clarendon).

Sandwich, Earl of (John Montagu) (1718–1792) [FS]

John Montagu was born on 3 November 1718 and educated at Eton and at Trinity College, Cambridge. After touring Europe and the Orient during the years 1737 to 1739, he was elected a fellow of the Royal Historical Society in 1740. He then served in a series of military and diplomatic posts. He was appointed First Lord of the Admiralty in 1748, but was dismissed three years later after uncovering abuses and instituting stringent reforms. He was reappointed First Lord of the Admiralty and made secretary of state for the Northern Department in 1763, in the ministry of George Grenville, from which post he was removed two years later, when the second Marquess of Rockingham became prime minister. After three years as postmaster general (1768–1771), he returned to the Admiralty, although he was briefly secretary of state for the Northern Department in the government of Lord North, between December 1770 and January 1771. He misused his position and the patronage of the office to such an extent that when war broke out in 1778, the navy was found to be inadequate and the storehouses empty. He retired from public life on the fall of Lord North's administration in 1782. The Sandwich islands are named after him.

Kit Hardwick

See also: Grenville, George; North, Lord
References and Further Reading: Christie, I. R., 1958, "The Cabinet during the Grenville Administration, 1763–65," *English Historical Review* 73: 86–92; Lawson, P., 1985, "Further Reflections on the Cabinet in the Early Years of George III's Reign," *Bulletin of the Institute of Historical Research* 57: 237–240.

Lord North forces the "Intolerable Acts" down the throat of "America," while Lord Sandwich restrains her feet and peeks up her skirt, London, 1774. (Library of Congress)

Sandys, Lord Samuel (First Baron Sandys of Ombersley)
(1695–1770) [CE]

Sandys was briefly chancellor of the exchequer after the fall from power of Sir Robert Walpole in 1742, in the ministry of Spencer Compton (Lord Wilmington). However, his successful scheming against Compton backfired after the latter's government fell: when Henry Pelham became prime minister in 1743, Sandys was moved to lesser posts and gradually vanished into political obscurity.

Samuel Sandys was born on 10 August 1695, the son of Edwin Sandys, M.P. for Worcester, by Alice, the daughter of Sir James Rushout, M.P. for Northwick Park, Worcester, and the sister of Sir John Rushout. While still a child, Samuel inherited the family estates, succeeding his father in 1699 and his grandfather in 1701. He matriculated at New College, Oxford, in 1711, but did not graduate and returned to run his family estates. On 9 June 1725 he married Letitia, the daughter and coheiress of the estates of Sir Thomas Tipping, M.P. for Wheatfield, Oxfordshire. He eventually became a very substantial landowner.

Sandys, who was described as "a tall thin young gentleman" (*Dictionary of Labour Biography,* pp. 782–784), became M.P. for Worcester in 1718, and kept that seat until he was raised to the House of Lords in December 1743. At first he was closely associated with the Whig government of Sir Robert Walpole; but in 1725 he joined a group of Whigs opposed to Walpole and led by Pulteney, allegedly because he had been refused the post of secretary at war. He soon became the second-in-command to Pulteney in the opposition and also worked closely with Sir John Rushout, his brother-in-law, for the next 17 years, until Walpole was removed from office. Walpole's ministers largely survived his fall from power; but Sandys replaced Walpole as chancellor of the exchequer in February 1742, in the ministry of Spencer Compton (Lord Wilmington).

As chancellor, Sandys supported Pulteney, advocating in March 1742 the formation of a secret committee to inquire into Walpole's administration, and seeking indemnity for witnesses giving incriminating evidence against Walpole—an action that the House of Lords rejected. However, he changed his mind later that year and decided to oppose the formation of a secret committee, telling his friends that the formation of such a committee would have led King George II to dismiss the Compton ministry.

While in the post of chancellor, however, Sandys strove to thwart the policies of Spencer Compton (Lord Wilmington), who as First Lord of the Treasury was also prime minister. When Compton died in July 1743, Henry Pelham, his successor as prime minister, transferred Sandys to another post and became chancellor of the exchequer himself.

Sandys, raised to the House of Lords on 20 December 1743, briefly served as speaker in the Lords from November 1756 until July 1757 and as First Lord of Trade between March 1761 and February 1763. He also served many lesser functions, but never again won a major role in politics. He died on 21 April 1770, from injuries sustained when his carriage overturned on Highgate Hill, London.

Keith Laybourn

See also: Bute, Earl of; Compton, Spencer; Newcastle, Duke of; Pelham, Hon. Henry; Pulteney, Sir William; Walpole, Sir Robert
References and Further Reading: Sedgwick, Richard, 1970, *The House of Commons, 1715–1754,* vol. 2: *Members, E–Y* (London: H.M.S.O.).

Shelburne, Earl of (Sir William Petty)
(1737–1805) [PM, HS]

Shelburne's short ministry (1782–1783) presided over the treaty of February 1783, which accepted American independence without guaranteeing protection for British Loyalists or payment of British debts. The treaty finished off Shelburne's political ambitions; but the competing interests of Lord North and Charles James Fox might also have done so if the treaty had not.

William Petty was born on 2 May 1737, the eldest son of John, first Earl of Shelburne, and Mary Fitzmaurice. He was educated by a private tutor and at Christ Church, Oxford. He then carved out a military career, rising from lieutenant in 1757 to general in 1783. He also served from 1760 to 1761 as M.P. for Chipping Wycombe, a pocket borough seat that he obtained without electoral contest. He became the second Earl of Shelburne in 1761.

He distinguished himself early in his career, in the Battle of Minden (1759), becoming a colonel at age 23 and an aide-de-camp to George III. From the start he was committed to retaining the powers of the Crown, opposed to party politics as such, and supportive of political reforms that would widen the franchise and admit the middle classes to the electorate. As a result he aligned himself with Lord Bute, the king's favorite in the early 1760s, and with Henry Fox. These connections won him the enmity of many party or factional groups that emerged in the 1760s and had little real power in Parliament but also brought him appointments as First Lord of the Treasury in 1763, in the ministry of Lord Bute, and as secretary of state for the Southern Department (1766–1768), in the ministry of William Pitt, the Elder. He held no posts from 1768 until Lord North resigned from office in 1782.

In 1782, Shelburne was appointed secretary of state for home affairs (home secretary) in the ministry of the second Marquess of Rockingham, who died shortly after taking office. The king then (in July 1782) chose Shelburne as prime minister, rather than the Duke of Portland, the new leader of the Rockinghamites. This led to the resignation of Charles James Fox and Lord North, who opposed Shelburne's ministry. The treaty hammered out between Britain and America under Shelburne's leadership, guaranteeing American independence, was poorly received in Britain; and lacking personal influence within Parliament, Shelburne was replaced in February 1783 by William Henry Cavendish, the third Duke of Portland.

Shelburne never held high office again. He was created Marquess of Lansdowne in 1784, and throughout the 1780s and 1790s advocated an unpopular, positive policy toward France. In 1791 he praised the French National Assembly for declaring that the right to make peace or war came from the nation and not the Crown, and

urged the British government to follow this example. In 1793 he opposed the war against France and further opposed government measures to curb radicalism in Britain. In 1803, he made his last public speech, in favor of conciliation with France. He died shortly afterward, on 7 May 1805. He was survived by his second wife, Lady Louisa Fitzpatrick, daughter of the first Earl of Upper Ossory; he had previously been married to Lady Sophia Carteret, daughter of John, second Earl Granville, in 1765.

Keith Laybourn

See also: Bute, Earl of; Cartertet, John; Fox, Charles James; Fox, Henry; North, Lord; Pitt, William (the Elder); Portland, Duke of; Rockingham, Marquess of

References and Further Reading: Fitzmaurice, Lord Edmund, 1875–1876, *The Life and Times of the Earl of Shelburne* (London: Macmillan); Norris, John, 1963, *Shelburne and Reform* (London: Macmillan).

Shortt, Edward
(1862–1935) [HS]

Edward Shortt was born on 10 March 1862, the second son of Edward Shortt, vicar of St. Anthony's Church, Byker, Newcastle. He was educated at Durham School and at the University of Durham and married Isabella Stewart in 1890, the same year as he was called to the bar by the Middle Temple. He worked on the northeastern circuit and was recorder at Sunderland between 1907 and 1918. Shortt's legal career was solid but unspectacular; he was more successful in Parliament.

Shortt became Liberal M.P. for Newcastle upon Tyne in January 1910, and retained the redrawn seat (Western Division, 1918–1922) throughout his parliamentary career. He was appointed chief secretary for Ireland in April 1918, his main activity in that post being the arrest of 150 members of Sinn Fein. On 10 January 1919 he became home secretary in David Lloyd George's postwar coalition government, his main task being that of dealing with two police strikes in March and August 1919. However, his political career came to an end in October 1922, with the fall of the coalition government. Thereafter, he filled a number of public roles, the most important being that of president of the British Board of Film Censors (1929). He died on 10 November 1935.

Keith Laybourn

See also: Lloyd George, David
References and Further Reading: Wrigley, Chris, 1992, *Lloyd George* (Oxford: Blackwell).

Simon, Sir John Allsebrook (Viscount Simon of Stackpole Elidor)
(1873–1954) [FS, HS, CE]

Sir John Allsebrook Simon was one of the leading political figures of the Liberal Party during the early twentieth century. As his political career developed, he drifted from the left of the Liberal Party to the right, eventually joining the National government in 1931, leading the National Liberals into the National government and ultimately into the Conservative Party. Being strongly rooted in the Liberal tradition, Simon fulfilled the role of foreign secretary in the 1930s in an entirely nonaggressive manner, thus becoming one of the originators of the appeasement policy toward fascism. His tenure as foreign secretary has been described as "disastrous" and "surely the worst in modern times" (*Times,* 12 January 1954).

John Simon was born of Welsh parents in Manchester on 28 February 1873. He was educated at Fettes College, and in 1892 was enrolled at Wadham College, Oxford, where he studied classics. He became president of the Oxford Union, obtained a first-class degree in 1896, and was elected a fellow of All Souls College, Oxford. Two years later he was called to the bar. He was a very successful barrister, becoming King's Counsel, and in 1909, standing counsel to the University of Oxford.

By that time, Simon was already carving out a political career. In 1906 he became Liberal M.P. for the Walthamstow Division of Essex, after which he rose quickly in Liberal circles. His legal training had prepared him well for an appointment as solicitor general in 1910, a post that he held until 1913, when he became attorney general (with a seat in the cabinet). He was also appointed a privy councillor in 1912.

Like many Liberals, Simon was unhappy about Britain's involvement in World War I. He believed that peace would be best secured through international negotiations, and along with other leading Liberal figures, he seriously considered resigning from government, but did not do so. He refused the post of lord chancellor in the Asquith wartime coalition government, formed in May 1915, but accepted that of home secretary. It was a short-lived appointment, lasting only seven months; he resigned when Asquith's government introduced military conscription in 1916. This period of office had, in fact, been painful to him, since he had had to sanction the police seizure of pamphlet stock of the Union of Democratic Control, a group founded at the beginning of the Great War to protect civil liberties, among whose members were some of Simon's old friends. From 1917 on, despite his hesitancy about the Great War, he spent the rest of the war with the Royal Flying Corps in France.

Simon remained a supporter of Asquith and opposed Lloyd George's "coupon" arrangement in 1918, whereby those taking the coupon promised to support Lloyd George if he was returned as prime minister. As a result of this stance, he lost his seat in the 1918 general election. He contested the Spen Valley parliamentary by-election in November 1919 and December 1920, but faced with a pro-coalition opponent who divided the Liberal vote, he was defeated by the Labour candidate, Tom Myers. In 1922, however, the situation had changed and he was elected for Spen Valley, a seat he held until 1940, as a Liberal until 1931 and as a National Liberal thereafter.

Until 1931, Simon was firmly within Liberal ranks. He was staunchly opposed to Lloyd George because of the way he had divided the Liberal Party in December 1916; but he recognized that ideas and inspiration came back into the party when Lloyd George returned to the Liberal fold in 1923. However, the Liberal Party still remained divided—despite its attempted unity in the 1920s. The Asquithian free-trading section of the party was led by Sir Herbert Samuel in the late 1920s; David Lloyd George led his own section of the party and published many policy initiatives, encouraging state intervention in certain circumstances; and Simon led an increasingly right-wing and nationalistic section of the party. The differences between the three sections were evident on many occasions. For instance, during the General Strike of May 1926, Lloyd George condemned the actions of the Baldwin government, Sir Herbert Samuel attempted to bring about a settlement between the coal miners and the coal owners, and in the House of Commons on 6 May Sir John Simon condemned the miners' strike and the general strike. Simon went so far as to suggest that the strike was unlawful and that "every trade union leader who has advised and promoted that course of action is liable to damages to the uttermost farthing of his personal possessions." Such a comment was not surprising, for by the mid-1920s he had come to see socialism as the ultimate political evil.

In 1927 Simon was made chairman of the Indian Statutory Commission, which within the context of widespread unrest and nationalism undertook to examine the way in which constitutional progress could be achieved in India. In June 1930 the Simon Report suggested that there should be an enlarged electorate in India; more responsible government in the provinces; and a conference between the ruling princes of the native states of India, the government of India, and the British government on the future form of a central government. This report carried little weight in the context of civil unrest and disobedience in India, but it did lead to a Round Table Conference in London in November 1930. The Indian National Congress Party boycotted this conference, but the princes of the Indian states did agree to the formation of an all-Indian federation in the near future.

By 1931 Simon was disgruntled with the Liberal Party, which was propping up Ramsay MacDonald's second Labour government. In March 1931, he opposed Lloyd George's decision to continue to support the Labour government; and when that government collapsed in the financial crisis of August 1931 and the National government was formed under Ramsay MacDonald, he gave his full support to the new administration. Yet the formation of the National government was flawed by the fragmentation of the Liberal Party. David Lloyd George, the Liberal leader, stayed outside the National government and led a faction of Liberal M.P.s that was increasingly dominated by his relatives and close friends. Sir Herbert Samuel entered the National government, but withdrew with the Liberal free traders in 1932, when it became blatantly obvious that the Conservative-dominated National government was going to be staunchly protectionist. Simon joined the National government, and with about 25 supporters, formed the National Liberals—a group that formally proclaimed its separate existence on 5 October 1931. The loyalty of the Liberal National group to the National government was cemented by Simon's appointment as foreign secretary—a post he held until 1935—and by his abandonment of the principle of free trade and acceptance of protectionism.

As foreign secretary, Simon favored disarmament and noninterventionism, positions that well suited the political mood and style of MacDonald, the prime minister, as well as the goals of fascist dictators. He is rightly regarded as one of the initiators of the policy of appeasement. Simon was utterly ineffective in dealing with Japan's invasion of Manchuria in September 1931 and its creation there of the state of Manchukuo in March 1932. The League of Nations likewise did nothing to counter these developments; but Simon seemed more concerned with Japanese grievances than with those of the Chinese government. He participated in the Geneva Disarmament Conference in 1932, but found that the rivalry between France and Germany prevented any meaningful action. In 1933, he entered into a quadrilateral pact (Britain, France, Italy, and Germany) that effectively circumvented the League of Nations, agreeing to revise previous peace treaties (particularly the Treaty of Versailles) in favor of Germany. Responding to these concessions, which would pave the way for German rearmament, Hitler announced on 17 May 1933 that a European war would be "madness"—encouraging Simon to look further toward appeasement as the best means of avoiding another European conflict.

When the Disarmament Conference resumed on 14 October 1933, Simon offered a plan for five years' international supervision of arms, without disarmament or rearmament, after which there would be disarmament, bringing all nations onto an equal footing with Germany at that time. Hitler had decided not to attend the conference. Instead, he announced that he intended to withdrew Germany from the League of Nations; then he waited for a possible French invasion of the Ruhr and a Polish invasion of East Prussia. Nothing happened, and the Disarmament Conference was effectively dead, being so proclaimed in May 1934.

After this turn of events, Simon had second thoughts about disarmament. In 1935 he met with Pierre Laval, the French foreign minister, and helped produce a joint statement suggesting the need for a freely negotiated agreement between Germany and the other powers and an armaments agreement to replace the Treaty of Versailles. Yet this did not seem to attract much positive response from Hitler. On 4 March 1934, Simon issued a nine-page White Paper, the *Statement Relating to Defence,* which reiterated that Britain was committed to collective security through the League of Nations and would continue to make efforts to bring about a reduction in armaments, but that in the absence of any foreseeable agreement, Britain had to strengthen its armed forces. Simon's involvement in foreign policy then came, abruptly, to an end. Lloyd George, in a letter to Smuts on 31 July 1935, wrote, "Simon has disappeared from the Foreign Office an acknowledged failure" (Dutton 1992, p. 221).

When Baldwin replaced MacDonald as prime minister in 1935, Simon was appointed home secretary and deputy leader of the House of Commons, during which he was involved in the abdication crisis of Edward VIII and the coronation of King George VI. When Neville Chamberlain replaced Baldwin as prime minister in 1937, Simon became chancellor of the exchequer and a member of Chamberlain's inner cabinet. As chancellor he financed a substantial increase in the size of the Royal Air Force, although he tried to observe the Treasury policy of balancing the budget. Yet like Neville Chamber-

lain, he still entertained the idea that peace in Europe could be maintained by agreements with Hitler, and he endorsed the famous Munich agreement of September 1938 by which Chamberlain effectively gave Czechoslovakia up to German expansionism in order to preserve peace in Europe.

It was only after Adolf Hitler invaded Poland in September 1939 that Simon changed his mind. Up to that point he had been willing to compromise with Hitler and Mussolini; but the invasion of Poland led him and other cabinet ministers to insist that Chamberlain declare war on Germany. Thereafter, Simon played little part in the war effort. In May 1940 he became lord chancellor in Winston Churchill's wartime coalition government and was given the title of Viscount Simon of Stackpole Elidor. He retired from politics in 1945 and died on 11 January 1954 after suffering a stroke.

Simon was an excellent lawyer who relished debate. However, he lacked the ability to make wise decisions in office, and thus became associated with the policy of appeasement in the 1930s that encouraged Hitler's political expansionism. Although he held three of the four major offices of government, and might have come close to securing the post of prime minister in 1937, it is clear that his political reputation has never been of the caliber associated with Britain's great statesmen.

Keith Laybourn

See also: Baldwin, Stanley; Chamberlain, Neville; Churchill, Sir Winston; MacDonald, James Ramsay
References and Further Reading: Dutton, David, 1992, *Simon: A Political Biography of Sir John Simon* (London: Arum); Heuston, R. F. V., 1987, *Lives of the Lord Chancellors, 1940–1970* (Oxford: Clarendon); Laybourn, Keith, 1996, *The General Strike: Day by Day* (Stroud, UK: Sutton); Simon, Sir John, 1926, *The Three Speeches of Sir John Simon* (London: Macmillan).

Snowden, Philip (Viscount Snowden of Ickornshaw)
(1864–1937) [CE]

Philip Snowden was a profoundly controversial figure in the early years of the British labor movement. His name is closely associated with that of Ramsay MacDonald in the "betrayal" of 1931, which saw the collapse of the second Labour government, an event that many construed as having arisen from his policies as Labour's first chancellor of the exchequer.

Snowden was born on 18 July 1864, in the remote Pennine moorland parish of Cowling, near Keighley, in the West Riding of Yorkshire. He was raised in a small textile town where Nonconformity, particularly Wesleyan Methodism, shaped community life. He received a basic elementary education, worked as a clerk, and eventually joined the civil service. He was forced to leave his post due to a bone deformity that resulted either from an accident or an illness; and while he was recuperating, he became involved in the activities of the Liberal Party. In January 1895 he began to participate in the Independent Labour Party, which was active in the West Riding.

In local politics, Snowden was elected to the Cowling school board and Keighley town council. He was also the editor of the *Keighley Labour Journal*. Nonetheless, it is for his parliamentary activity that he is most famous. After two unsuccessful parliamentary contests, he was elected M.P. for Blackburn in 1906, and was twice re-elected in 1910. However, his opposition to World War I led to his defeat at Blackburn in the 1918 general election. Nevertheless, he returned to Parliament as M.P. for Colne Valley in the 1922 general election, and maintained that seat through four general elections until he was raised to the House of Lords as Lord Snowden of Ickornshaw, in November 1931. During his time in the Commons, Snowden was chancellor of the exchequer in the first two Labour governments, in 1924 and from 1929 to 1931. As Viscount Snowden of Ickornshaw, he was briefly a member of Ramsay MacDonald's National government, acting as Lord Privy Seal until his resignation on 28 September 1932.

Throughout his life Snowden adhered to radical Liberal sentiments. He opposed World War I, was a dedicated free trader, and abhorred borrowing. His economic policies were those of an old Gladstonian Liberal. His wife, Ethel Annakin, whom he married in 1905, contributed to his favorable views on women's suffrage. He was a staunch member of the Independent Labour Party (ILP) and acted as its chairman and treasurer at various times between 1900 and 1921. During World War I, he also mounted the ILP's Peace Campaign of 1917 and attended the convention of the Workmen's and Soldiers' Council, held at Leeds in June 1917, at which a mixture of Marxists and socialists sought to bring about international peace in the wake of the first Russian Revolution of 1917.

From 1922 on, as M.P. for Colne Valley, Snowden made the Labour Party his political home. He was frustrated at Ramsay MacDonald's return as Labour's parliamentary leader in 1922, but served under him as chancellor of the exchequer and shadow chancellor. In the former role he gave free rein to his notion of balancing the budget, reducing the national debt, and if necessary, deflating the economy. In 1924 he was alarmed at the rhetoric of his fellow cabinet ministers, which gave the impression of great increases in expenditure when, in fact, little extra was being spent.

Although his tenacity brought him some personal success, and Britain some economic savings at the conference on war reparations in 1929, it is clear that his policies were inappropriate to the economic climate of 1929–1931. The Wall Street crash had reverberated around the world and led to a rise in unemployment in Britain, which increased government expenditure enormously. The enormous deficit of £100–£170 million—representing between a quarter and a fifth of the national budget—placed a severe downward pressure on the pound, resulting in a serious economic crisis. Snowden, concerned about sound finance, advocated the twin policies of a 10 percent cut in unemployment benefit and increased taxation on the middle classes (which he referred to as "equality of sacrifice"). The Labour government was deeply divided on the cuts, even though Snowden maintained that they were required by the international bankers in order to justify the loans to Britain needed to restore economic confidence in the pound. The indecisive vote on the benefit cuts on 23 August 1931, and the fact that the tax increases seemed to have been abandoned, led to the resignation of the second Labour government and the formation of the

National government on 24 August 1931, in which Snowden was appointed Lord Privy Seal.

Snowden became alarmed when Britain was taken off the gold standard on 21 September 1931, but he assured himself that it was only a temporary situation and not the basis of a move toward protectionism. Yet less than a year later, when it became clear to him that the government had indeed abandoned free-trade policies, Snowden resigned. Although he continued thereafter to launch personal attacks on MacDonald from his seat in the Lords, his political activity was ineffective. He died of a heart attack, following a long illness, on 15 May 1937.

Keith Laybourn

See also: Baldwin, Stanley; Chamberlain, Neville; Clynes, John Richard; MacDonald, James Ramsay; Samuel, Sir Herbert; Simon, Sir John
References and Further Reading: Cross, Colin, 1966, *Philip Snowden* (London: Barrie & Rockliff); Laybourn, Keith, 1988, *Philip Snowden: A Biography, 1864–1937* (Aldershot, UK: Temple Smith); Laybourn, Keith, and David James (eds.), 1987, *Philip Snowden* (Bradford, UK: Bradford Libraries and Information Service); Snowden, Philip, 1934, *An Autobiography* (London: Nicholson & Watson).

Somervell, Sir Donald Bradley (Lord Somervell of Harrow)
(1889–1960) [HS]

Donald Bradley Somervell, who was briefly home secretary in 1945, was born at Harrow on 24 August 1889, the second son of Robert Somervell, master and bursar of Harrow School, and his wife, Octavia Paulina, daughter of the Rev. John Churchill. He was educated at Harrow and then at Magdalen College, Oxford, where he graduated with first-class honors in chemistry. In 1912 he was elected a fellow of All Souls, Oxford. He began to study law at the Inner Temple, but World War I interrupted his studies. During the war he served in India (1914–1917) and Mesopotamia (1917–1919). He was called to the bar in his absence, in 1916, and after the war he became involved in work connected with the commercial clauses of the Treaty of Versailles. He took silk (became King's Counsel) in 1929.

Politically he had been sympathetic to the Liberal cause; but faced with the Liberal Party's decline and given his admiration for Stanley Baldwin, he was soon attracted to the Conservative Party. He was defeated at Crewe in the 1929 general election, but won that seat by narrow majorities in both 1931 and 1935. He was knighted in 1933. In 1936 he became attorney general (law officer to various ministries) in Baldwin's National government, retaining that position for a decade, until 1946. In 1938 he became a member of the Privy Council. During this period he was supportive of Neville Chamberlain's attempt to appease Hitler at Munich. He was involved in preparing many statutory instruments during World War II, most obviously the War Damages Act. Somervell served as home secretary between 25 May and 2 August 1945, in Winston Churchill's caretaker government (between the end of the wartime coalition government and the formation of the first Attlee Labour government). Labour's victory brought an end to his modest political career, but he continued in his legal one, acting as Lord Justice of Appeal between 1946 and 1954. He died in London on 18 November 1960.

Keith Laybourn

See also: Baldwin, Stanley; Chamberlain, Neville; Churchill, Sir Winston
References and Further Reading: Charmley, John, 1993, *Churchill: The End of Glory* (New York: Harcourt Brace).

Soskice, Sir Frank (Baron Stow Hill)
(1902–1979) [HS]

Sir Frank Soskice enjoyed a brief period as home secretary in the first of Harold Wilson's Labour governments. Although he possessed a fine legal mind, his record as home secretary reveals an obvious lack of ability for political decision making.

Soskice was born in Geneva on 23 July 1902. His father, David Vladimir Soskice, was a Russian liberal, and his mother, Julia Hueffer, was a granddaughter of Ford Madox Brown, the pre-Raphaelite painter. His father had been a member of Kerensky's secretariat at the time of the

Russian revolutions of 1917. Frank was educated at St. Paul's School and at Balliol College, Oxford. After graduating from Oxford, he went into law and was called to the bar of the Inner Temple in 1926. During World War II, he served in the army. In the 1945 general election, he became M.P. for Birkenhead East, which he represented until 1945. He then represented Sheffield Neepsend from 1950 to 1955, and after a break, Newport from 1956 to 1966.

Soskice's first government office came in August 1945, when he was appointed solicitor general in Attlee's first Labour government. He was briefly promoted to attorney general in the second Attlee government, serving as the government's supreme legal official from April 1951 until October 1951. As a result of his attainment of this office, he was given the customary knighthood in 1945. During the 1950s he became a close friend of Hugh Gaitskell, Labour leader from 1955 until 1963, and was part of the "Hampstead set" of friends that Gaitskell gathered around him. In fact, he lived about 200 yards from Gaitskell's house in Hampstead, in a remarkably impressive building on Church Row.

When Harold Wilson (Labour leader after Gaitskell's death in 1963) became prime minister of a new Labour government in 1964, Soskice was appointed home secretary. He was obsessed with legal procedure and precedent, however, and his efforts at political decision making were therefore highly ineffective. He placed an immigration control bill that followed from the Conservative Commonwealth Immigrants Act of 1962 in jeopardy while it was still in committee, on the grounds that immigration controls were being widely evaded and that he was attempting to tighten the loopholes. The white paper he had produced suggested the need to limit immigration to 8,500 professional and skilled workers per year through the allocation of vouchers. In 1965 he introduced the Race Relations Act, which outlawed direct discrimination on grounds of color, race, or national or ethnic origin in some public places; but the board set up to implement this law was given insufficient power and resources to do its job. Beleaguered in his post, Soskice resigned on the grounds of ill health on 23 December 1965. He briefly took up the post of Lord Privy Seal, but left the House of Commons in 1966, after which he was raised to the House of Lords as Baron Stow Hill. He participated little in parliamentary politics after this point, focusing instead on professional interests. He died on 1 January 1979.

Keith Laybourn

See also: Attlee, Clement; Gaitskell, Hugh; Wilson, Harold
References and Further Reading: Harmer, Harry, 1999, *The Longman Companion to the Labour Party, 1900–1998* (New York: Addison Wesley Longman); Jenkins, Roy, 1991, *A Life at the Centre* (London: Macmillan).

Spring-Rice, Thomas (Baron Monteagle of Brandon in Kerry)
(1790–1866) [CE]

Thomas Spring-Rice was born at Limerick on 8 February 1790, the elder son of Stephen Edward Rice and Catherine, heiress of Thomas Spring. He went to Trinity College, Cambridge, and then studied law, but was never called to the bar. He became Whig M.P. for Limerick in 1820, and represented it until 1832, when he became M.P. for Cambridge. He held the latter seat until he was elevated to the peerage in 1839.

Considered an expert on Irish affairs, Spring-Rice became undersecretary to the Marquess of Lansdowne at the Home Office in 1827, and he was responsible for most of the subsequent Irish reforms. He left office in January 1828 when the Duke of Wellington became prime minister in place of George Canning. Spring-Rice then became secretary of the Treasury in Earl Grey's administration in 1830, holding the post until 1834. In 1834 he restated in the House of Commons the unionist case against Daniel O'Connell. In the summer of 1834, he became secretary of state for war and the colonies in Lord Melbourne's first ministry. He became chancellor of the exchequer in April 1835, in Lord Melbourne's second administration, and held that office until September 1839. It was a thankless task, for the government majority was too small to permit him to deal effectively with the deficit budgets that he faced.

Spring-Rice's only major achievement was the introduction of the penny-postage scheme in July 1839. In September 1839 he was created Baron Monteagle, after which he practically withdrew from public life. He died on 7 February 1866 at Mount Trenchard, near Limerick.

Keith Laybourn

See also: Grey, Lord; Melbourne, Viscount
References and Further Reading: Ziegler, Philip, 1982, *Melbourne* (New York: Atheneum).

Stewart, Michael (Baron Stewart of Fulham)
(1906–1990) [FS]

Robert Michael Maitland Stewart was born on 6 November 1906, the son of Robert Wallace Stewart and his wife, Eva. He was educated at Christ's Hospital and then at St. John's College, Oxford, where he became president of the Oxford Union in 1929. In 1931 he began work as an assistant master at Merchant Taylors' School in 1931, soon moved to the Coopers' Company School, and then became a lecturer for the Workers' Educational Association, where he remained until 1942. He married Mary Elizabeth Birkinshaw in 1941. In 1942 he entered the Army Intelligence Corps, but transferred to the Army Educational Corps in 1943, where he was commissioned and promoted to the rank of captain.

Stewart revealed an interest in parliamentary politics in the 1930s, unsuccessfully contesting the West Lewisham seat for Labour in 1931 and 1935. He did win a seat as Labour M.P. for Fulham East in 1945, Fulham in 1955, and Hammersmith Fulham in 1974, holding the latter until 1979. In the 1945 Labour government he became vice-chamberlain of His Majesty's household (1946–1947) and comptroller of His Majesty's household (1946–1947). From 1947 to 1951, he served as undersecretary of state for war. In May 1951, Attlee, the Labour leader and prime minister, appointed him parliamentary secretary to the Ministry of Supply; but Stewart's tenure in this post ended with the collapse of the Labour government the following October.

With Labour out of office between 1951 and 1964, Stewart consolidated his position within the Labour Party. During this time he also

Foreign Secretary Michael Stewart with the Laotian prime minister in London, 1965 (Hulton-Deutsch Collection/Corbis)

joined the ranks of those opposed to Britain's entry into the Common Market, in the debate that divided the Labour Party at the beginning of the 1960s. He rose quickly through the ministerial ranks after Harold Wilson formed his first Labour government in 1964. Stewart was appointed secretary of state for education and science in 1964, secretary of state for foreign affairs in January 1965, and secretary of state for economic affairs, in a straight swap with George Brown, in 1966, retaining the latter post until 1968. He again served as secretary of state for foreign and commonwealth affairs (FS) from March 1968 to June 1970. One of his major tasks as foreign secretary was to deal with the issues of white rule and national independence in Southern Rhodesia, Ian Smith having declared Rhodesian independence from the British Commonwealth and British control.

From 1975 to 1976, Stewart was a member of the European Parliament. In 1979 he became a life peer, as Baron Stewart of Fulham. He died on 10 March 1990.

Keith Laybourn

See also: Attlee, Clement; Brown, George; Wilson, Harold
References and Further Reading: Pimlott, Ben, 1993, *Harold Wilson* (London: HarperCollins); Stewart, Michael, 1977, *The Jekyll and Hyde Years* (London: Dent).

Stormont, Viscount (David Murray; Earl of Mansfield) (1727–1796) [HS]

David Murray, the second Earl of Mansfield, was born on 9 October 1727 to David, sixth Viscount Stormont, and Anne, only daughter of John Stewart. He was educated at Westminster and at Christ Church, Oxford. In 1748, his father died, and he became the seventh Viscount Stormont, an Irish title that entitled him to a seat in the House of Lords upon election. He soon entered the diplomatic service and was attached to the British embassy in Paris in 1751. He also spent time in various German states and in Poland and Austria in the 1760s, observing firsthand the rule of Frederick the Great, Maria Theresa, and the Emperor Joseph. He became a member of the Privy Council in 1763. In the 1760s he also was appointed lord justice general of Scotland.

However, his main claim to fame is that he became secretary of state for the Northern Department (from 1782, known as secretary of state for foreign affairs) in 1779, holding that post in the ministry of Lord North and resigning with North in March 1782. In 1794 he became president of the Privy Council.

In 1793 he succeeded to the title of the second Earl of Mansfield, of Caen Wood, Middlesex, on the death of his uncle William Murray, the first Earl of Mansfield. He died on 9 September 1796, and is buried next to the first Earl of Mansfield, in the North Cross, Westminster Abbey.

Keith Laybourn

See also: North, Lord
References and Further Reading: Whiteley, Peter, 1997, *Lord North: The Prime Minister Who Lost America* (London: Hambledon).

Straw, Jack (John Whitaker) (1946–) [HS]

Jack Straw first drew attention to himself as a radical university student leader at Leeds in the 1960s and as president of the National Union of Students between 1969 and 1971. Yet as he has risen in Labour and government circles, he has become less radical and has drifted to the right of the Labour Party, becoming a determined and uncompromising figure in the fight against crime.

He was born 3 August 1946 at Buckhurst Hill, Essex, and educated at Brentwood School, at the University of Leeds, and at the Inns of Court, School of Law. He was called to the bar in 1972. He is married and has two children. Before entering Parliament, Straw worked as a barrister and a political adviser to Barbara Castle and Peter Shore.

Straw's parliamentary career began in 1979 when he became M.P. for Blackburn, the seat he has represented ever since. He was appointed opposition spokesman on treasury and economic

Home Secretary Jack Straw arrives at Downing Street, December 1998. (AFP/Corbis)

affairs (1980–1983) and then opposition spokesman on the Environment (1983–1987). Rising swiftly, he served as shadow education secretary between 1987 and 1992 and as shadow environment secretary from 1992 to 1994. He then became shadow home secretary in 1994, becoming official home secretary upon Labour's general election victory in May 1997. One of his most controversial moves in this office—a move that many interpreted as a signal of his drift toward the Conservative policies of Michael Howard, the previous home secretary—was the adoption, on 12 January 1999, of a policy aimed at ensuring that those convicted three times of burglary are given at minimum a three-year prison sentence. He also has been involved more recently in the controversy surrounding the definition of the legal use of force to defend one's home and property against burglars.

Keith Laybourn

See also: Blair, Tony; Brown, Gordon; Cook, Robin
References and Further Reading: Anderson, Paul, and Nyta Mann, 1997, *Safety First: The Making of New Labour* (London: Granta); Jones, Tudor, 1997, *Remaking the Labour Party: From Gaitskell to Blair* (London: Routledge).

Sturges-Bourne, William
(1769–1845) [HS]

William Sturges-Bourne was born on 7 November 1769, the only son of Rev. John Sturges, of Winchester, and Judith, daughter of Richard Bourne, of Worcester. He was educated at a private school near Winchester and at Christ Church, Oxford. He then pursued a legal career and was called to the bar at Lincoln's Inn in November 1793.

He became M.P. for Hastings in July 1798 and later represented Christchurch (1802–1812 and 1818–1826), Bandon (1815–1818), Ashburton (1826–1830), and Milburne Port (1830–1831). On the death of his uncle Francis Bourne in 1803, he assumed the name Bourne as a condition of his inheritance.

Sturges-Bourne filled many minor ministerial and administrative posts. He was a joint secretary of the Treasury from 1804 to 1806; a lord of the Treasury from 1807 to 1809; and an unpaid commissioner for Indian affairs in 1814,

also being raised to the Privy Council at that time. In 1818 he gave his name to the Sturges-Bourne Act, which rearranged the voting rights in vestries in order to favor property owners, who would thus gain more control over the local Poor Law arrangements. In April 1827 he accepted George Canning's offer of the post of home secretary, but resigned from this post a few months later, in July, allowing the third Marquess of Lansdowne to take his place and accepting the alternative position of commissioner of woods and forests, which permitted him to retain his seat in the cabinet. In January 1828 he resigned all of his offices, and in 1831 he retired from the House of Commons. He died on 1 February 1845.

Keith Laybourn

See also: Canning, George; Liverpool, Earl of
References and Further Reading: Hinde, Wende, 1973, *George Canning* (London: Collins).

Suffolk and Berkshire, Earl of (Henry Howard)
(1739–1779) [FS]

Henry Bowes Howard, twelfth Earl of Berkshire, was born either on 10 May or on 16 May 1739, according to *The Complete Peerage*. He is one of only two secretaries of state not to appear in the *Dictionary of National Biography*. He succeeded his cousin on 22 April 1745 as Earl of Suffolk and Berkshire. Howard was educated at Eton (1746–1756) and matriculated at Magdalen College, Oxford, in 1757, gaining an M.A. in 1759. He became a doctor of civil law in March 1761.

He was the bearer of the second sword at the coronation of King George III and served as High Steward of Malmesbury between 1763 and 1767 and as Deputy Earl Marshall between 1763 and 1765. On 25 May 1764, he was married to Maria Constantia, only daughter of Robert, first Viscount Hampden. She died in childbirth less than three years later, on 8 February 1767.

Howard was appointed a member of the Privy Council on 22 January 1771 and served as Lord Privy Seal from January to June 1771. He was then appointed secretary of state for the north in Lord North's administration (North was First Lord of the Treasury, and thus prime minister, from 1770 to 1782), in June 1771, and he remained in that office for the rest of his short life. His tenure of eight years was longer than that of many of his predecessors and successors in this office.

Howard married for the second time, on 14 August 1777, to his cousin Charlotte, first daughter of Heneage, third Earl of Aylesford. He was elected a Knight of the Garter in 1778, but was never installed because of illness and died at the age of 39, on 7 March 1779, at Bath, and was buried on 20 March 1779, at Charlton.

Kit Hardwick

See also: North, Lord
References and Further Reading: Cannon, John A., 1970, *Lord North: The Noble Lord of the Blue Ribbon* (London: Historical Association); Thomas, Peter, 1976, *Lord North* (London: Allen Lane); Whiteley, Peter, 1997, *Lord North: The Prime Minister Who Lost America* (London: Hambledon).

Sydney, Viscount (Thomas Townshend)
(1733–1800) [HS]

Thomas Townshend, the first Viscount Sydney, was the only son of Thomas Townshend by his wife Albinia. He was educated at Clare College, Cambridge, where in 1753 he graduated with an M.A. He was elected M.P. for Whitchurch, Hampshire, in 1754, and represented that borough until his elevation to the peerage in 1783.

He was a supporter of William Pitt (the Elder), Earl of Chatham, who appointed him to a minor post in 1760, the same year he married Elizabeth Powys. However, he was dismissed two years later, as his conduct did not satisfy the "king's friends." In 1765 he was appointed Treasury lord in the ministry of the second Marquess of Rockingham. In 1767 he became joint paymaster and a privy councillor, but resigned from the position of joint paymaster in 1768 rather than be transferred to another post to make way for an appointee of the Duke of Grafton. He opposed the unseating of Wilkes from the House

of Commons in 1769, and declined to become speaker of the House of Commons in 1770, remaining in opposition to Lord North and his friends.

In March 1782, Townshend was returned to office as secretary at war, responsible for presenting army and naval estimates to the House of Commons, in the ministry of the Marquess of Rockingham. On the death of Rockingham four months later, he sided with the Earl of Shelburne (rather than Charles James Fox), whom he succeeded as home secretary (July 1782–April 1783) when the other became prime minister. As home secretary he was considered to have made an excellent defense of the peace terms concluded with the American colonists in February 1783.

He was created Baron Sydney the following month, in March 1783, and became secretary of the Home Department again, this time under William Pitt, the Younger, on 23 December, remaining in that post until June 1789. This appointment was, perhaps, predictable, since his second daughter had married John Pitt (the brother of William Pitt, the Elder, and uncle of William Pitt, the Younger, who became the second Earl of Chatham) in 1783.

Though Sydney's subsequent career in the House of Lords was unspectacular, he is remembered as having been instrumental in setting up a new convict colony in New South Wales, Australia, to take the place of those lost to American independence. The town founded in 1788 at Port Jackson was named Sydney in his honor. On his resignation from office following a disagreement with Pitt in 1789, he was created Viscount Sydney and awarded a pension of £2,500 a year. He died on 30 June 1800.

Kit Hardwick and Keith Laybourn

See also: Grafton, Duke of; North, Lord; Pitt, William (the Elder); Pitt, William (the Younger); Rockingham, Marquess of; Shelburne, Earl of
References and Further Reading: Ehrman, John, 1969, *William Pitt: The Years of Acclaim* (London: Constable).

T

Temple, Earl of (George Nugent-Temple-Grenville; Marquess of Buckingham)
(1753–1813) [HS]

George Nugent-Temple-Grenville, the third Earl of Temple, had one of the shortest periods in office of any leading politician, being home secretary for less than four days in the first ministry of William Pitt, the Younger. He was born on 17 June 1753, the second son of George Grenville and Elizabeth, daughter of Sir William Wyndham, and was educated at Eton and at Christ Church, Oxford, but did not obtain a degree.

In October 1774 he was elected as one of the M.P.s for Buckinghamshire. He was initially a supporter of Lord North's government, and in 1776 backed North's German treaties to hire troops to coerce the American colonies, having "no doubt of the right of Parliament to tax America" (*Dictionary of National Biography*, p. 560). Later, he did moderate some measures taken against the American colonies. He succeeded his uncle as the second Earl Temple in September 1779, and soon afterward assumed the names of Nugent and Temple.

Lord Temple's political career began to rise with the downfall of the ministry of Lord North in 1782. Temple became lord lieutenant of Buckinghamshire in March 1782, and on 31 July 1782 was made both lord lieutenant of Ireland and a member of the Privy Council. This was in the short-lived government of the Earl of Shelburne, who had been appointed prime minister by the king, having been chosen over Lord Portland, the new leader of the Rockinghamite section of the Whigs. Temple found the Irish situation ominous, and he helped to introduce a new constitution for Ireland in 1782. He left his Irish office in 1783, with the end of Shelburne's ministry, but returned to government as secretary of state for the Home Department in the ministry of William Pitt, the Younger. He accepted this post on 19 December 1783 and resigned it on the 22 December—allegedly because he had used the king's name to influence legislation, but possibly because he was denied a dukedom. The latter explanation is supported by a later statement made by Horace Walpole, who wrote that Temple had "many disgusting qualities, as pride, obstinacy, and want of truth, with natural propensity to avarice" (ibid., p. 561).

On 4 December 1784, Temple was created the Marquess of Buckingham. He became lord lieutenant of Ireland again in November 1787, but lost that position in 1789 under accusations of financial mismanagement. In the meantime, he had succeeded to the Irish earldom of Nugent in October 1788. Thereafter, he gradually retired from politics, but maintained his interest and involvement in Irish affairs. He was colonel of the Buckinghamshire militia in Ireland at the time of the Irish insurrection of 1798, and remained a strong supporter of Britain's union with Ireland. He died on 11 February 1813.

Keith Laybourn

See also: North, Lord; Pitt, William (the Younger); Shelburne, Earl of
References and Further Reading: Sack, James, 1993, *From Jacobite to Conservative: Reaction and Orthodoxy in Britain, c. 1760–1832* (Cambridge: Cambridge University Press).

Thatcher, Margaret (Lady Thatcher; Baroness Thatcher of Kesteven)
(1925–) [PM]

Thatcher was Britain's first, and only, female prime minister. A powerful and determined politician, she stood for limited, firm government; the rolling back of the welfare state; the end of consensus politics; and a staunchly anti-federalist approach to the European Union. These policy tenets became the foundation of a new British political ideology, popularly labeled "Thatcherism." Thatcher was also the longest-serving prime minister of the twentieth century and the only prime minister ever to have been removed from office in a leadership contest determined by party M.P.s. She was the first head of government since Lord Liverpool (the longest continuously serving prime minister of the nineteenth and twentieth centuries) to have won three successive general elections. Her tenure as prime minister (1979–1990) transformed British politics.

Margaret Hilda Roberts was born on 13 October 1925, the younger daughter of Alfred Roberts and Beatrice Stephenson, a lower-middle-class couple who operated a small grocery store. She was raised as a Methodist. Her father, an ex-Liberal who became an Independent councillor and mayor of Grantham, in Lincolnshire, greatly influenced her outlook with his emphasis on thriftiness and his staunch belief in the free-market economy. She was educated at Kesteven and at Grantham Grammar School, and from there went on to Somerville College, Oxford, where she graduated with second-class honors in chemistry. She worked for a period in commercial and industrial chemistry (1947–1951) and then married fellow Methodist Denis Thatcher in 1951, by whom she had twins in 1953. During these years Thatcher had been studying law, and she passed her exams to become a lawyer also in 1953, after which she practiced in the field of tax law for a few years.

Thatcher's active interest in politics began at Oxford, and after her graduation she quickly became involved in parliamentary politics. She lost her bid for the Dartford constituency in the general elections of 1950 and 1951 but secured the Conservative candidacy for Finchley in 1958 and represented that seat from 1959 to 1992, when she was raised to the House of Lords.

She was appointed to a minor post in October 1961 and then served successively as Conservative Party spokesman on pensions, hous-

Prime Minister Margaret Thatcher at the Conservative Party conference in Brighton, 12 October 1984, after the IRA tried to assassinate her with a bomb (Bettmann/Corbis)

ing, energy, transport, education, and the environment between 1961 and 1970. She became a member of the shadow cabinet in 1967. She was appointed secretary of state at the Department of Education and Science in the government of Edward Heath and served in that post from June 1970 to February 1974. She campaigned for the extension of nursery education, but in general felt that the Ministry of Education was "self-righteously socialist" and was spending too much money on education (Evans 1999, p. 106). Not surprisingly, she earned a reputation as a "cutting minister" when she transferred a small amount of money from the provision of school milk to science. The furor that ensued gave birth to the catchphrase "Thatcher the milk snatcher." At that point Thatcher seemed widely unpopular; and with the defeat of the Conservatives in the general elections in 1974, it appeared that her political star was on the wane. Yet she stood against Edward Heath for the leadership of the Conservative Party in 1975 and won by 130 votes to 119, in what was effectively a backbench revolt against Heath.

As opposition leader (1975–1979), Thatcher moved gradually to replace the old Heathite, "one-nation" Tories, who believed that the welfare state should help to ensure that all people in Britain enjoyed a basic standard of living. It contrasted with Thatcher's view that the welfare state should be "rolled back" and inequality generated in order to stimulate British economy. She worked with figures from the New Right, such as Sir Keith Joseph and Rhodes Boyson, who were advocating the free-market ideas of writers such as Milton Friedman and Friedrich A. Hayek. She herself had been influenced by similar ideas expressed by her father, and she immediately identified with this New Right group when she became vice chair of the Centre for Policy Studies in June 1974.

Her moment for introducing these ideas into policy came after she won the 1979 general election, defeating a deeply unpopular Labour government led by James Callaghan. Her performance during her first ministry (1979–1983) lacked political finesse but displayed determination, particularly in ushering out the old Heathite Tories, such as Francis Pym. Faced with inflation well in excess of 20 percent per annum, she moved to redistribute income in favor of the rich (via Geoffrey Howe's tax-cutting budget of 1979) and then to control the supply of money. She supported the 1981 budget, which actually called for an increase in taxes at a time when the country was in the depths of a recession. As a result, the number of unemployed, which was just over 1 million in May 1979, rose rapidly to more than 3 million by 1983.

Thatcher's government became deeply unpopular and was soon falling behind the Labour and Liberal parties in opinion polls, and struggling to keep ahead of the Social Democrats. However, Thatcher's government won the 1983 general election—largely due to the successful Falklands War, in which Britain retook the Falkland Islands from Argentina in the spring and summer of 1982. As a result of this British military success, her popularity rose to 80 percent in the opinion polls. Other factors also helped Thatcher secure her second general electoral victory. The most obvious was that inflation had fallen from 21.8 percent in April 1980 to 3.7 percent in June 1983, revealing the success of her antiinflationary policies.

Thatcher's second ministry (1983–1987) was far more successful than her first. As time wore on, Thatcher became increasingly committed to the privatization of public services and the reduction of public expenditure, particularly expenditure on the welfare state. Thatcher pressed forward a range of measures designed to reduce the power of the trade unions—a power that she perceived as a bulwark defending the structures of government control and intervention. Her governments introduced eight acts between 1979 and 1990 (the most significant being the Employment Acts of 1980, 1982, 1988, 1989, and 1990, and the Trade Union Act of 1984) that were designed to weaken trade union power, deregulate the economy, and remove the checks on British employment that Thatcher and her colleagues held responsible for the relative economic decline of Britain since World War II.

The 1980 Employment Act introduced a limited definition of legal picketing, and the 1982 act permitted closed trade union shops only where 85 percent of the workforce favored it. The 1984 Trade Union Act compelled trade unions to hold secret ballots, with preference given to postal secret ballots, before initiating any industrial action. These and other measures were a direct challenge to established trade union rights. Conflict erupted around this issue with the coal miners' strike of 10 March 1984 to 5 March 1985, which was called in response to the closure of a number of pits. The miners were eventually defeated—partly by the intransigence of Arthur Scargill, their leader, who succeeded in dividing the mining unions, but also by the Conservative government's use of the law to restrict and punish the National Union of Mineworkers. Thatcher was determined that the miners would not bring down her government as they had Heath's in February 1974. After the strike, British trade unionism recognized the need to restructure its policies in a less confrontational mode.

Thatcher was equally fortunate in other political developments. On 12 October 1984 she narrowly missed death when an IRA bomb exploded at the Grand Hotel in Brighton during the Conservative Party Conference, killing 5 people and injuring 32. She survived to help broker the Anglo-Irish Agreement of 1985, which allowed the Irish Republic a role in the politics of Northern Ireland; and she was able to play a supporting role when Soviet leader Mikhail Gorbachev began making moves toward ending the Cold War, in late 1984 and early 1985. However, Thatcher's apparent invincibility and good fortune were tested by the Westland affair, which took place in 1985 and 1986.

After a prolonged debate over the future of the financially troubled Westland Helicopter Company—which Thatcher thought could be saved only by a merger with the American firm of Sikorsky—Michael Heseltine, the minister of defense, resigned on 9 January 1986. The Westland issue raised matters of national defense and the conduct of the cabinet business by Thatcher. Heseltine's resignation in itself was damaging; and the subsequent public debate, in which Heseltine accused Thatcher of adopting a presidential style of government and of deliberately leaking information, was even more so. These accusations led to a government defense that brought down Home Secretary Leon Brittan, who resigned in response to charges that he had knowingly misled the House of Commons. The Westland affair could have damaged Thatcher's political future as well; but in the end, an overall improvement in the national economy, cuts in income tax, and continued problems within the Labour Party ensured her victory in the general election of June 1987.

Thatcher began her third term (1987–1990) in a seemingly unassailable position, with the economy doing well, income tax reduced to 40 percent by 1988, and a surplus for use in increased public spending. Yet in November 1990 she resigned and was replaced by John Major as Conservative leader and prime minister.

Her resignation as prime minister was prompted by a number of events. The economic situation of the country began to worsen in the late 1980s. At the same time, her party and some of her supporters began to doubt her policies on Europe. On 20 September 1988 she made a speech to a European Economic Community meeting in Bruges, in which she declared her opposition to any diminution of the sovereignty of the United Kingdom. This speech strengthened her reputation for toughness, which had won Britain reductions in its assessed financial contributions to Europe between 1984 and 1986; but it also brought her into conflict with the pro-Europe section of her party, led by Kenneth Clarke, as well as with the many sectors of industry that favored the European Union.

Perhaps even more important in precipitating her resignation was her introduction of the poll tax. Having committed herself to abolishing property-based rates, Thatcher advocated a system (officially known as the Community Charge; popularly, as the poll tax) whereby every adult paid the same local rates for the same local services. The scheme was first introduced in Scotland, in 1989, where it was considered unjust because it required "a widow in her flat to pay the same as a lord in his castle" (Evans 1999, pp. 115–116). Yet the Conservative Party Conference insisted upon its introduction in England and Wales (1990); but the opposition to it was intense, as manifested both in public demonstrations (the most important being in London on 31 March 1990) and in nonpayment of taxes. When John Major replaced Thatcher as prime minister, he quickly abandoned the poll tax and returned to the old property-based system of raising money for local authorities.

Thatcher's resignation brought a dramatic end to her political career. Under Conservative Party rules, the leadership could be contested every year. In 1989, a backbench candidate lost to Thatcher, 314 votes to 33. In November 1990, after she had been attacked by Geoffrey Howe, who had just resigned as foreign secretary, Michael Heseltine decided to challenge Thatcher's leadership. She obtained 204 votes to Heseltine's 152, but fell four votes short of the majority required for outright victory in the first round. Pressured to resign by various ministers, including Kenneth Clarke, she finally did so. Her resignation resulted in a brief rise of support for the Conservative Party in the opinion polls.

In 1992, Thatcher accepted a life peerage in the House of Lords as Baroness Thatcher of Kesteven. She has since remained a presence in Conservative politics, steadily opposing Britain's closer involvement with the European Economic Community, and in 1997, endorsing William Hague's leadership of the Conservative Party.

As prime minister, Thatcher presided over the breakup of the general consensus that had existed in parliamentary politics since 1945. In particular, her ministry removed the close links between trade unions and government, challenged the welfare state, and promoted the privatization of government-owned public services and industry. Above all, her period in office inculcated in the British a more free-market-friendly attitude and established in the minds of the British public that lower rates of taxation would allow individuals, and not the government and public service institutions, to determine supply and demand conditions of the market. Thatcher's survival at the top of British politics may have owed much to fortunate events such as the Falklands War and the miners' strike, which demonstrated her toughness and won her patriotic support. But whatever the reasons for her political longevity, her impact on the politics of John Major, her Conservative successor, and of Tony Blair and New Labour has been enormous.

Keith Laybourn

See also: Baker, Kenneth; Blair, Tony; Brittan, Sir Leon; Clarke, Kenneth; Heath, Edward; Howe, Sir Geoffrey; Whitelaw, William
References and Further Reading: Evans, Brendan, 1999, *Thatcherism and British Politics, 1975–1999* (Stroud, UK: Sutton); Thatcher, Margaret, 1993, *The Downing Street Years* (London: HarperCollins); Young, Hugo, 1991, *One of Us: A Biography of Margaret Thatcher* (London: Macmillan).

Thorneycroft, Peter (Baron Thorneycroft of Dunston) (1909–1994) [CE]

Thorneycroft was a controversial chancellor of the exchequer in Harold Macmillan's Conservative government in the late 1950s. He was dismissed by Macmillan in 1957 because he in-

sisted on making cuts in the financial support for the welfare state. Although he returned to government later and became one of the greatly respected, even revered, figures in the Conservative Party, his political career was effectively at an end.

George Edward Peter Thorneycroft was born on 26 July 1909, the son of Major George Edward Mervyn Thorneycroft and his wife, Dorothy. He was educated at Eton and at the Royal Military Academy, Woolwich. He was commissioned into the Royal Artillery in 1931, but resigned in 1933. He was called to the bar while at the Inner Temple, in 1935. He practiced law at Birmingham, on the Oxford circuit, and in 1938 he married Sheila Wells Page. They divorced in 1949, and he married the Countess Carla Roberts.

Thorneycroft's parliamentary career began when he became Conservative M.P. for Stafford in 1938, a seat he held until 1945. He then became Conservative M.P. for Monmouth (1945), holding that seat until 1966, when he was raised to the House of Lords as Baron Thorneycroft, a life peer.

His ministerial career began early, with a brief appointment as parliamentary secretary to the minister of transport in 1945. He served as president of the Board of Trade from 1951 to 1957, in the Conservative ministries of Winston Churchill, Sir Anthony Eden, and Harold Macmillan. In 1957 he was appointed chancellor of the exchequer. When as chancellor he decided to cut expenditure on the welfare state in an attempt to reduce inflation, he encountered strong opposition from Macmillan. The resulting conflict led to the resignation not only of Thorneycroft but also of Nigel Birch and Enoch Powell (Birch was a junior minister at the Air Ministry and Powell was a parliamentary secretary in the Department of Local Government) in January 1958. Thorneycroft was replaced as chancellor by Derick Heathcoat Amory.

Thorneycroft later returned to government as minister of aviation between 1960 and 1962. He then served as minister of state for defense in 1962 and as secretary of state for defense between April and October 1964, before losing his post with the electoral victory of Harold Wilson's Labour government. Although he played no role in government after 1964, he retained an active interest in politics, chairing the Conservative Party between 1975 and 1981, and serving as one of Margaret Thatcher's early political advisers. In his later years he also worked in the private sector, acting as chairman of British Reserve Insurance from 1980 to 1987, and as president of Pirelli General from 1987 to 1994. He died in 1994.

Keith Laybourn

See also: Churchill, Sir Winston; Eden, Sir Anthony; Macmillan, Harold
References and Further Reading: Lamb, Richard, 1995, *The Macmillan Years, 1957–1963* (London: John Murray).

Townshend, Charles (Viscount Townshend)
(1674–1738) [FS]

Charles Townshend was the son of Horatio, the first Viscount Townshend, from whom he inherited the peerage in 1687. He was educated at Eton and at King's College, Cambridge, and subsequently completed his education by traveling abroad. Though born and raised a Tory, he later joined the Whig junta and supported religious liberty against the Occasional Conformity Bill, which imposed conformity to the view of the Church of England.

Townshend helped negotiate the Treaty of Union with Scotland in 1706 and was appointed a privy councillor in 1707. He was ambassador plenipotentiary to the Netherlands in 1709. In 1710 he negotiated a treaty with the Dutch States General (Parliament) that guaranteed the Hanoverian succession to the English crown, as well as a number of other conventions guaranteeing the security of the Empire. With a change in government in 1711, he was recalled and voted an enemy of the country for having exceeded his instructions in negotiating the barrier treaty (against the return of James Stuart) and for having subsequently aided agitation for the repeal of the union between England and Scotland.

He was reinstated on the accession of King George I and was appointed secretary of state for the Northern Department (the post of foreign secretary, after 1782). Townshend used his connections at court to secure the post of paymaster general for Sir Robert Walpole, whose sister he married in 1713. Townshend was involved in the proceedings against the negotiators of the Treaty of Utrecht, and he moved harshly and swiftly to suppress the 1715 Jacobite uprising against English rule. He cooperated with (James) Stanhope, first Earl of Stanhope, in foreign policy, making a definite barrier treaty and an alliance with the Austrian emperor in 1716, but lost his post after he was accused by Charles Spencer, the earl of Sunderland, of obstructing the French alliance and of plotting to replace King George I with his son, the Prince of Wales.

Out of favor with the king's favorites, Townshend was relegated to the post of lord lieutenant of Ireland in 1717; but he lost this post also, on suspicion of not being wholeheartedly in support of the government. He regained office in 1720 as president of the Privy Council in the administration of Stanhope; and after Stanhope's death the following year, he again became secretary of the Northern Department. He played a wise and patient role in the uncovering and prosecution of the Jacobite Atterbury plotters. He remained at the center of politics for the next decade, obtaining partial restitution for Henry St. John, Viscount Bolingbroke (1678–1751), who had lost some prestige in Parliament and with King George I because of his negotiations on the Spanish succession, and thwarting John Carteret's political schemes in alliance with the Duchess of Kendal, a mistress of King George I, in 1723.

In foreign affairs, he was dissatisfied with Austria, and negotiated the Treaty of Hanover with Russia and France in 1725. He went further, and forced the Austrian emperor to end his alliance with Spain in 1727. Having been misled by a spurious version of the Austro-Spanish treaty, he also negotiated a subsidiary treaty with the Duke of Brunswick-Wolfenbüttel. Townshend brought the Hanoverian League to the side of Spain and agreed to the Treaty of Seville in 1729, which paved the way for an alliance between France and Spain, thus jeopardizing the peace of Europe by further reducing Austria's influence. When the king of Prussia sided with the Austrian emperor, Townshend proposed war, but he was overruled by Walpole and Queen Caroline. He resigned in 1730 and thereafter devoted himself to agriculture at Rainham, Norfolk, where he was popularly dubbed "Turnip Townshend," due to his practice of feeding his cattle turnips through the winter months. He also became known for his innovations in the method of field rotation. He died in 1738.

Kit Hardwick

See also: Carteret, John
References and Further Reading: Black, Jeremy, 1985, *British Foreign Policy in the Age of Walpole* (Edinburgh: John Donald).

Townshend, Charles
(1725–1767) [CE]

Charles Townshend is remembered for the Stamp Act and related legislation imposed on the American colonies in 1767, which led to the American War of Independence. If Lord North lost America, Townshend started the process.

Townshend was born on 29 August 1725, the second son of Charles, third Viscount Townshend, by his wife Etheldreda (Audrey) Harrison. He was educated at Leyden, where his schoolmates were John Wilkes and William Dowdeswell, and then at Oxford University. On 15 August 1755 he married Caroline, the eldest daughter and coheir of John Campbell (the second Duke of Argyll), and the widow of Francis Scott, earl of Dalkeith.

Townshend began his parliamentary career in 1727 when he became M.P. for Great Yarmouth. In Parliament, he developed an association with George Montagu Dunk, the second Earl of Halifax, who became president of the Board of Trade in 1748 and offered Townshend a post in his department. On the death of Prime Minister Henry Pelham in March 1754, Townshend was made a Lord of the Admiralty, and soon afterward, in April 1754, was elected M.P. for Saltash. However, his period in office was brief; he resigned in 1755, and later, in December of that year, publicly attacked the policy of the prime minister, now the Duke of Newcastle, of employing German mercenaries.

Townshend became treasurer of the chamber and a member of the Privy Council in the brief ministry (1756–1757) of William Cavendish, the fourth Duke of Devonshire, and remained in that post throughout the ministry of William Pitt, the Elder (1757–1761). In March 1761 he was appointed secretary at war under Pitt, a post that mainly involved the presentation of military and naval estimates to Parliament.

In the general election of March 1761, Townshend became M.P. for Harwich. He retained his post as secretary at war when Pitt resigned that October; but he himself resigned in 1762, when the third Earl of Bute was prime minister, largely because he expected Pitt to return to power. This did not occur, and Townshend therefore accepted the post of president of the Board of Trade in February 1763. When George Grenville replaced Bute as prime minister in April 1763, Townshend again resigned from the government, refusing the offer of the position of First Lord of the Admiralty. He became a staunch critic of the Grenville administration; but in May 1765, on the dismissal of Henry Fox from office, he became paymaster general, retaining the post through the succeeding ministry of the second Marquess of Rockingham. Townshend's fortunes improved after Pitt agreed to form a second ministry in August 1766, and Townshend was appointed chancellor of the exchequer.

Pitt was ill at this stage and moved to the House of Lords as the first Earl of Chatham. This left Townshend as the effective leader of government in the House of Commons, which soon led to conflict between him and Chatham. This conflict was most obviously revealed in the fact that Townshend declared that the East India Company had a right to territorial revenue in India, whereas Chatham had declared his intent to deprive it of such rights.

In January 1767, Townshend presented his first budget to Parliament. It included the usual land tax of four shillings in the pound; but his opponents, mainly Grenville and Dowdeswell, insisted that the tax be reduced to three shillings. The government might well have resigned in such a situation; but instead Townshend decided that he would raise the shortfall by resurrecting the Stamp Act, which had been repealed a few months earlier by the Grenville ministry. In May 1767 he introduced the necessary legislative measures, suspending the legislative functions of the New York assembly, setting up commissioners of customs in the American colonies to superintend the new laws relating to trade, and imposing a port duty on glass, red and white lead, painters' colors, paper, and tea. In response, the Americans formed anti-importation associations, and riots broke out. However, Townshend did not live to see the consequences of his actions; he died on 4 September 1767, at the age of 42. The one abiding memory of him is that in order to raise a mere £40,000 he had begun the process that led to the American War of Independence.

Keith Laybourn

See also: Bute, Earl of; Devonshire, Duke of; Dowdeswell, William; Grenville, George; Halifax, Earl of; Newcastle, Duke of; Pelham, Hon. Henry; Pitt, William (the Elder); Rockingham, Marquess of

References and Further Reading: Black, Jeremy, 1992, *The Elder Pitt* (Cambridge: Cambridge University Press).

Waddington, David Charles (Lord Waddington of Read, County of Lancaster)
(1929–) [HS]

David Charles Waddington, the son of Charles Waddington and Minnie Hugh Waddington, was born on 2 August 1929. He was educated at Sedbergh Grammar School and Hertford College, Oxford. After graduating from Oxford, he pursued a legal career at first, being called to the bar at Gray's Inn in 1951; but he then entered the army, rising to the rank of captain. In 1958, while in the army, he married Gillian Rosemary Green. He eventually returned to his legal career, becoming a recorder of the Crown Court in 1972 and receiving other honors over the years.

Waddington's political interests had begun at Oxford, where he was president of the Oxford University Conservative Association. He unsuccessfully contested the constituencies of Farnworth in 1955, Nelson and Colne in 1964, and Heywood and Royton in 1966, before becoming M.P. for Nelson and Colne in 1968. He was out of Parliament from 1974 to 1979, but returned as M.P. for Clitheroe in 1979, and then for Ribble Valley in 1983, holding the latter seat until 1990, when he was made a life peer.

Waddington's ministerial career was confined to the years of the Margaret Thatcher premiership. He was a lord commissioner at the Treasury between 1979 and 1981, parliamentary undersecretary of state at the Department of Employment between 1981 and 1983, minister of state at the Home Office between 1983 and 1987, parliamentary secretary to the Treasury and government chief whip from 1987 to 1989, and secretary of state at the Home Office (home secretary) from 1989 to 1990. His period as home secretary was cut short when Thatcher was forced to retire as Conservative leader and prime minister and was replaced by John Major.

He was raised to the House of Lords in 1990, and became Lord Privy Seal and leader of the House of Lords, a position he held until 1992. From 1992 to 1997 he was governor and commander in chief of Bermuda.

Keith Laybourn

See also: Thatcher, Margaret
References and Further Reading: Evans, Brendan, 1999, *Thatcherism and British Politics, 1975–1999* (Stroud, UK: Sutton).

Waldegrave, James (Earl of Waldegrave)
(1715–1763) [PM]

Lord Waldegrave never led a faction or actively sought high office, yet at the time of his early death he had been so long known and respected in the political world that he was being talked of as the next prime minister. Had he lived, he might have brought stability to government in the 1760s. His one attempt to form an administration, in June 1757, was undertaken out of respect for the aging George II, and it soon ended in failure.

Waldegrave came from a Catholic family of Stuart loyalists. His grandmother, Lady Henrietta Fitzjames, was the daughter of James II by his mistress, Arabella Churchill, and the barony of Waldegrave was created by James II in January 1686. Waldegrave's father, having despaired of founding a Catholic faction that was sincerely Hanoverian, had converted to the Anglican faith in February 1722. In September 1729, he was created Viscount Chewton of Chewton and first Earl Waldegrave by George II. After the elder Waldegrave (who also was named James) died of dropsy in April 1741, his son inherited both titles.

The second earl (born 17 March 1715) was only 26 when he inherited the family title, but he at once began to play an active part in the Lords, defending Sir Robert Walpole against an impeachment, one of the articles of which was the charge that Walpole had appointed a close relative of the Pretender (Waldegrave's father) British ambassador in Paris. From 1743 to 1752 Waldegrave held the relatively modest court post of Lord of the Bedchamber, attending regularly on the king, who had become attached to the young peer. All surviving comments on Waldegrave agree on his honesty and charm of manner, his unusual lack of malice or sharpness even toward those who opposed him in politics. He was inclined to enjoy the company of the nation's political elite in their convivial moments rather than their business hours, and was thus a stalwart of White's, the leading Whig club, notorious for its gaming and reckless wagers. When in autumn 1750 George II personally proposed Waldegrave for the office of secretary of state, Henry Pelham opposed him, confiding to his brother the Duke of Newcastle that the earl was "as good-natured, worthy, and sensible a man as any in the kingdom, but totally surrendered to his pleasures."

In 1751, when the Prince of Wales died and the Duchy of Cornwall reverted to the Crown, George marked out Waldegrave for his personal favor, appointing him Lord Warden of the Stannaries—a post with valuable powers of patronage that made its holder useful to the ministry. In December 1752, Waldegrave accepted the position of governor to the young Prince of Wales, with overall responsibility for the education of the heir to the throne. His friend, the young Horace Walpole, described his reluctance to accept this charge: "The Earl was very averse to it: he was a man of pleasure, understood the court, was firm in the King's favor, easy in his circumstances, and at once undesirous of rising, and afraid to fall." Waldegrave understood that his standing at court would likely determine his future career after Prince George became king. In the event, although the two did not develop the kind of friendship that the prince enjoyed

with Waldegrave's successor, Lord Bute, Waldegrave was on quite good terms with his royal charge. In contrast, the dowager princess, George's mother, was always cool toward him; after 1755, her coolness noticeably grew as Bute came into favor and as Pitt became more clearly the political leader of the reversionary interest, those who attended the Prince's court at Leicester House and hoped to gain when the throne reverted to him.

In September 1756, Waldegrave was permitted to resign his governor's post, having sometime earlier lost the confidence of the prince. Soon afterward, toward the end of October, Newcastle resigned from the Treasury, and Waldegrave followed him into political exile. George II was compelled to accept a ministry headed by the Duke of Devonshire, with Pitt—whom the king detested—as secretary of state. His attempts to replace this grouping with a different ministry (minus Pitt) created an anomalous situation. The ministers were dismissed at the end of the parliamentary session in April 1757 and not replaced, while the king attempted to persuade Newcastle to form a ministry that excluded the Leicester House faction. In the end, Newcastle declared unequivocally that he could govern only by bringing in Pitt and his supporters.

On 8 June the king called on Henry Fox, Newcastle's rival and Waldegrave's friend, to form an administration, with Waldegrave at the Treasury. With little hope of success, Waldegrave acceded to the king's direct command to take the post. He noted in his *Memoirs* that he was "partly moved by [George's] Distress, partly yielding to his Persuasion, or perhaps fired by some latent Spark of Pride or Ambition." With the next day came a stream of resignations by followers of Newcastle, reminiscent of the mass resignation of February 1746, and having the same effect of forcing the king's hand. On 11 June, Waldegrave advised the king to come to terms with Pitt and Newcastle, and his brief bid for the premiership was over. In July he was rewarded with the Garter, in an unusual single ceremony of investiture—a sign of the king's high regard for him.

Waldegrave's friendship with the king's

younger son the Duke of Cumberland also continued, but he had little to do in Parliament after this period. It was a time of greater personal happiness, however; for in May 1759, at the age of 44, he married Maria Walpole, niece of his friend Horace and illegitimate daughter of Sir Edward Walpole and his lifelong mistress, Dorothy Clement. Although she was half his age, Maria evidently made a devoted wife, and within a short time they had three daughters. When his former pupil came to the throne in 1760, Waldegrave was for a time an influential court insider, but the rise of Bute prevented his taking a leading political role. There was talk of offering him his father's old post as ambassador to Paris. The offer was made, and duly refused, on 29 March 1763. The next day, Waldegrave fell ill of smallpox, of which he died on 8 April at the age of 48. Always placid, amiable, and widely liked, Waldegrave had matured by 1763 into a figure who might well have commanded respect and assent had he survived to form a ministry after the resignation of Bute—which by coincidence took place on the very day of Waldegrave's death.

Philip Woodfine

See also: Bute, Earl of; Newcastle, Duke of; Pelham, Hon. Henry
References and Further Reading: Clark, Jonathan C. D., 1982, *The Dynamics of Change: The Crisis of the 1750s and English Party Systems* (Cambridge: Cambridge University Press); Clark, Jonathan C. D. (ed.), 1988, *The Memoirs and Speeches of James, 2nd Earl Waldegrave, 1742–1763* (Cambridge: Cambridge University Press).

Walpole, Sir Robert (Earl of Orford)
(1676–1745) [PM, CE]

Generally accepted as the man who shaped the modern role of prime minister, Sir Robert Walpole was the dominant force in party politics and national government for more than twenty years, between 1721 and 1742. A large man with enormous self-confidence, he nonetheless leaned heavily upon the support of monarchs George I and George II. This support, together with his control of Parliament through the skillful distribution of places and a firm discipline over those who held them, gave him a power that his contemporaries attacked by abusing him as a would-be prime minister. The label was pejorative, implying that he was usurping unconstitutional powers, as overweening royal favorites had done in earlier reigns. He was regularly compared to Henry VIII's minister Cardinal Wolsey; to Piers Gaveston, the favorite of Edward II; and even to Sejanus, the favorite of the emperor Tiberius. Despite the denunciations of his unique corruption and baneful impact, Walpole was hailed after his death, even by many of his critics, as a statesman of rare abilities who had presided over a period of peace and prosperity.

Walpole's crucial contribution to the development of the prime ministerial office stemmed from his decision to remain a commoner, whereas previous leading officers of state had chosen elevation to the Lords. Based in the House of Commons, Walpole found himself answerable for all of the policies of his ministry and their consequences. He therefore insisted on having a hand in all departments of the administration. Crucially, in so doing he had the support of the King, whose authority might very occasionally be challenged by Parliament but was paramount in everyday matters. Equally crucial was the extensive control enjoyed by the head of the Treasury over patronage to be distributed by the Crown, and over secret service funds.

Walpole was born on 26 August 1676, the third son of Robert Walpole of Houghton, in Norfolk, who was M.P. for Castle Rising, a seat that Walpole inherited in 1701. Eight of his sixteen brothers and sisters died in their first years of life, four of them as babies, and his two older brothers died as young men. When his eldest brother, Edward, died in February 1697, Walpole was plucked from his Cambridge studies after only two years to take Edward's place in managing the affairs of his ailing father. He was married in July 1700, to Catherine Shorter, the attractive and extravagant daughter of a wealthy Baltic timber merchant, and that November his father died.

The young heir entered Parliament in January 1701, in the Whig interest; and from July

Robert Walpole, Earl of Orford (Library of Congress)

1705 on, he represented the borough of King's Lynn, for the remainder of his public career. Walpole rose early to high office. By February 1708 he already held the post of secretary of war, which provided both valuable administrative experience and the profits needed to support his chosen style of living. That post also gave him a taste of political persecution, with the Tories in power. Walpole found himself expelled from the Commons and imprisoned in the Tower from January to July 1712, for alleged corruption over a forage contract.

He was reelected for King's Lynn in August 1713, and after George I ascended the throne, Walpole came into the new ministry as paymaster general of the forces. His enduring contribution to public finance at this time was to introduce a Sinking Fund to redeem the national debt. He was closely allied with his brother-in-law Charles and with Viscount Townshend, who headed the new ministry. Soon outflanked by Charles Spencer, third Earl of Sunderland, and James, first Earl of Stanhope, however, the brothers-in-law left office in April 1717, when Townshend was dismissed. They went on to

shape a formal opposition to the ministry of the day, designed systematically to hinder the business of the administration and lead to their own reinstatement—which duly occurred in April 1720. Grouped around the court of the Prince of Wales and cooperating closely with the Tories as well as Country Whigs, Walpole and his colleagues showed what could be done to embarrass the king's ministers and limit their scope for action. Oppositions formed later in the reign of George II followed the pattern established by this one.

Brought back into favor just as the South Sea investment bubble burst, Walpole was soon warding off the national outcry against the government and even the king for their involvement in the scandal. For his success in this effort he earned the enduring nickname of Screen Master. But he also restored public confidence in the state of the national finances and enhanced his reputation as a man who understood revenue and financial matters. There was a certain amount of luck involved in this success, as there was in the sudden deaths of his two leading rivals, Stanhope and Sunderland, in 1721 and 1722, respectively; but Walpole had the successful politician's gift of seizing luck and using it.

In April 1721, he was appointed both First Lord of the Treasury and chancellor of the exchequer. After April 1722, with Sunderland dead, he was beyond dispute the first servant of the king, and leader both of the ministry and of Parliament. These were the years, too, in which Walpole began the design and building of a great Palladian mansion, Houghton Hall, which was progressively filled with the finest commissioned furniture and adorned with an art collection that had been assembled over the years with a true collector's avidity and discernment, and at enormous cost. From the late 1720s on, opponents had only to point to his princely manner of living to demonstrate their case that his wealth was corruptly garnered from the public purse and that he was setting himself up as a colossus, a dominating "prime and sole minister."

Against expectations, Walpole's power survived the death of George I in June 1727 and the accession of George II, who as Prince of

Wales had opposed his father's chief minister. Walpole had cultivated the Princess of Wales, who as Queen Caroline became his supporter and advocate with the new king. The relative position of Townshend—who earlier had enjoyed the favor of George's influential mistress, the Duchess of Kendal—was reversed in the new reign; and by 1730, Townshend, who resented having become the subordinate partner in the relationship, resigned. By this time, an extensive opposition was emerging. Since 1725, William Pulteney and Henry St. John, Viscount Bolingbroke, along with John, Lord Carteret, had been building a coalition that advocated a "patriot" stance against the alleged corruption and self-interest of Walpole, Townshend, and their cronies. By 1730, there was an official pact between opposition Whigs and Tories, and the rest of Walpole's period in office was marked by a sustained and inventive campaign of opposition not only in Parliament but in newspapers, pamphlets, and graphic satirical prints.

The existence of this permanent opposition in turn shaped Walpole's handling of government and policy formation. The essence of his approach was to do as little as possible to reform any abuse that could be tolerated, and to introduce as few controversial measures as possible. When the Excise Bill of 1733 unexpectedly met with huge popular resistance, the minister withdrew the measure rather than force through a reform that he believed was sound. In finance, his aim was to keep down the level of taxes on the landowning political classes, and in foreign policy to maintain peace and therefore economy. Wars were not only costly in lives and in money, but they also might lead to discontent with the bias of George I and George II, who viewed European diplomacy through the eyes of Hanoverian electors and were not above using the power and finances of the British state to further their interests in their North German homeland. Wars also gave opportunities to Jacobites at home and abroad to plan an invasion to restore the Stuart dynasty. Throughout his career Walpole devoted time, energy, and money to countering Jacobitism in all its forms, through costly intelligence systems and not least through avoiding an open rupture with the leading

Catholic powers in Europe. Walpole did all that he could to maintain peace with France, and in 1733 he succeeded—against the inclinations of some of his colleagues and of George II—in keeping British troops out of the War of Polish Succession. He was unable in October 1739 to exert the same influence, and Britain declared war on Spain—the action that the Patriot opposition had been clamoring for.

Despite his long hold on power and on the favor of the king, Walpole was not invulnerable; and his colleagues began, especially after the death of Queen Caroline in November 1737, to plan for their own survival in case he should fall. Personal grief made him less effective in managing people and affairs. In August 1737, his wife had died. A little more than three months later, he married the true love of his life, Maria (Molly) Skerrett, nearly twenty-six years his junior and his mistress of fourteen years. Tragically, in June 1738, Molly died in childbirth. Later that year he was still able to throw himself into the demanding detail of negotiations to resolve Anglo-Spanish differences; but in private he frequently commented on how tired he was of maintaining the preeminence that he had enjoyed so long.

The war with Spain marked an important turning point in his hold on power. Not cut out, as he said himself, to "bear the truncheon," Walpole was increasingly at odds with his leading cabinet colleagues, the Duke of Newcastle and Lord Hardwicke, and was forced to defend the conduct of a war in the Caribbean that he had not wanted and that he feared would open the way for a Jacobite invasion to restore the Stuart dynasty. Though the ministry won a majority in the 1741 general election, it was fatally undermined by electoral losses in Cornwall and Scotland, due, respectively, to the influence of the Prince of Wales and the Duke of Argyll. Walpole had a formal parliamentary majority of 19 in December 1741, but his support quickly evaporated in successive struggles to decide contested elections. He spent the Christmas recess in an unsuccessful bid to achieve a compromise with the Prince of Wales. It became increasingly clear that all of his leading cabinet colleagues saw his fall as inevitable.

In the end, George II reluctantly agreed to accept Walpole's resignation, and on 6 February 1742 made him Earl of Orford, refusing to allow the fallen minister to kneel and kiss his hands but instead embracing him in a rare gesture of royal affection. Walpole's illegitimate daughter by Molly Skerrett, by special patent of precedence, became Lady Maria Walpole, the rank to which her father's elevation would have entitled her had she been his legitimate heir. Walpole also was granted a pension of £4,000 a year, which he dared not accept until 1744, by which time the initial angry public reaction to the grant had faded.

Walpole had abilities that seemed the more salient as disillusion set in with the Patriot opponents who had overthrown him. His understanding of public finance was manifested in a number of pamphlet publications and in his ability to hold the attention of even a hostile House while elucidating financial legislation. As a Commons speaker, he was clear and intuitive in reading the temper of his listeners: Lord Chesterfield, who spent many years as Walpole's opponent, called him "the best parliament-man, and the ablest manager of Parliament, that I believe ever lived." His influence at court was not due to the conventional abilities of the courtier: his bluff Norfolk manner, partly cultivated as a means of making himself more accessible to ordinary M.P.s, was too habitual to be put aside except in the most formal interviews with the king and queen. Queen Caroline in particular was often offended by his indelicate jokes and his coarse speech. Rather, it was his reading of policy issues and practicalities, and his unfailing attention to the interests of the Crown, that ensured his success in the royal closet.

A final factor in Walpole's successful management was undoubtedly his thoroughgoing mastery of the various techniques used to acquire political support. He entered government at a period when the inner structure of politics was shaped by patronage and by the complex mesh of rewards and mutual obligations which it created, from Westminster to the most remote borough. He exploited this structure unabashedly, granting rewards, offering incentives, and meting out punishments whenever a place or pension or favor did not bring the expected loyalty. Money was not the only reason for his success, but it was an important means of his management. As his son Horace later remarked, Walpole dipped in corruption up to the elbow. In his final years he retained considerable influence behind the scenes, advising the king and guiding his former colleagues, especially Henry Pelham, on how to conduct themselves and handle their sovereign. Walpole's health, though, had never been good, and he was subject to recurrent bouts of violent illness, which seem to have been aggravated by his increasing obesity (which had attracted comment and caricature even ten years before his resignation). In the end, he fell victim to a then-fashionable belief in a harsh, lye-based remedy for the crippling kidney stones from which he suffered. He died on 18 March 1745, at his house on Arlington Street in London, having traveled there in great pain from Norfolk in response to a summons from the king.

Philip Woodfine

See also: Compton, Spencer; Newcastle, Duke of; Pelham, Hon. Henry; Pulteney, Sir William
References and Further Reading: Black, Jeremy M. (ed.), 1984, *Britain in the Age of Walpole* (London: Macmillan Education); ——, 1990, *Robert Walpole and the Nature of Politics in Early-Eighteenth-Century England* (Basingstoke, UK: Macmillan Education); Dickinson, Harry T., 1973, *Walpole and the Whig Supremacy* (London: English Universities Press); Hervey, John (Lord), 1931, *Memoirs,* 3 vols. (London: Eyre & Spottiswoode); Hill, Brian W., 1989, *Sir Robert Walpole, 'Sole and Prime Minister'* (London: Hamilton); Plumb, John H., 1956 and 1969, *Sir Robert Walpole,* 2 vols. (London: Cresset Press).

Walpole, Spencer Horatio
(1806–1898) [HS]

Spencer Walpole is famous as the home secretary at the time of the parliamentary reform agitation in 1866 and 1867; he was involved in the attempt to deny the reform agitators the right of meeting in Hyde Park. These events eventually brought the political career of this three-time home secretary to an ignominious end.

Walpole was born in 11 September 1806, the second son of Thomas Walpole and his wife, Margaret, the youngest daughter of John Perceval, second Earl of Egmont. His great-grandfather was Horatio Walpole, and his maternal grandfather was Spencer Perceval, the prime minister. Walpole was educated at Eton and at Trinity College, Cambridge, and then went into law, being called to the bar at Lincoln's Inn Field in 1831. He married his first cousin Isabella, fourth daughter of Spencer Perceval, on 6 October 1835. In 1846 he became Queen's Counsel. He continued with his legal career until 1852, but his attention was increasingly absorbed by politics.

Walpole became M.P. for Midhurst in 1846—where his cousin the third Earl of Egmont exercised political influence—and held that seat until 1856, when he became M.P. for Cambridge, which he represented until 1882. He quickly earned a reputation as a good speaker.

In February 1852, he was appointed home secretary in Lord Derby's Conservative ministry. This was a brief period of office, ending in December 1852, but he managed to initiate a reform of the militia. He became home secretary again when the fourteenth Earl of Derby formed a government in February 1858, but resigned in early 1859 in opposition to the Derby cabinet's decision to support the introduction of a parliamentary reform bill.

He accepted yet a third appointment as home secretary, in Lord Derby's third ministry in June 1866, and was immediately faced by a problem: the National Reform League was organizing a march to, and a meeting in, Hyde Park on 23 July 1866. In cabinet discussions, he maintained that the procession and meeting were legal and could not be stopped, and advised that they be halted only if the assembly became disorderly. His advice was overruled by the cabinet on 19 July, and Sir Richard Meyne, the chief commissioner of police, was ordered to shut the gates of the park on the day of the demonstration. This act provoked violence on 23 and 24 July. On 25 July, representatives of the Reform League met with Walpole, who advised them to put in writing their request to hold a meeting in Hyde Park on Monday, 30 July. They did so, but the request was denied; the government suggested as an alternative that the meeting be held at Primrose Hill. This offer was not accepted.

The Reform League called another meeting to be held in Hyde Park on 6 May 1867. On 1 May, the government issued a notice denying permission for the meeting; but when the meeting took place anyway, the police and authorities took no action to stop it. This was a humiliation for the government, and even though Lord Derby defended Walpole—who had, after all, done what he could to dissuade the cabinet from its folly—it was clear that he had to resign, which he did on 16 May. He remained a member of the cabinet until Benjamin Disraeli restructured it in February 1868. That was the end of Walpole's career at the top of British politics, although he continued as an M.P. until 1882 and filled many public posts. He died on 22 May 1898.

Keith Laybourn

See also: Derby, 14th Earl of; Disraeli, Benjamin
References and Further Reading: Harrison, Royden, 1965, *Before the Socialists* (London: Routledge & Kegan Paul).

Wellesley, Richard Colley (Marquess of Wellesley) (1760–1842) [FS]

Richard Colley Wellesley, one of the great politicians of his day, was born on 20 June 1760, the eldest son of Garrett Wellesley, first Viscount Wellesley of Dangon Castle and Earl of Mornington in the County of Meath, Ireland. Richard's mother was Anne, eldest daughter of Arthur Hill-Trevor, first Viscount of Dungannon. Arthur Wellesley, the Duke of Wellington, was Richard's younger brother.

Wellesley was educated at Harrow, at Eton, and at Christ Church, Oxford. On the death of his father in 1781, he cut short his studies at Oxford in order to run the family estates in Ireland and to supervise the education of his five other brothers. He entered the Irish House of Peers in 1781 as the second Viscount Wellesley and Earl of Mornington, and in 1784 became M.P. for the seat of Beeralston in Devonshire. He was subsequently elected for the rotten, or corrupt, borough of Old Sarum in 1787, 1790, and 1796.

Politically, he was a supporter of William Pitt, the Younger, favoring controls on the slave trade; but he opposed parliamentary reform in 1793. He was appointed a member of the Board of Control for Indian affairs in 1793, thus beginning his long political association with the Indian subcontinent. He then married Hyacinthe Gabrielle, daughter of Pierre Roland of Paris, with whom he had lived for nine years and by whom he had had children. In 1797, when he became governor of Madras, he decided against taking her to India with him, which led to their subsequent estrangement.

Wellesley went to India at a difficult period in the development of British rule in India, when it was subject to attack and subversion by the forces of Tippu Sahib, headquartered in southern India (in Mysore), and of Zaman Shah in Kabul, Afghanistan, both of whom were supported by the French. As a result, Wellesley was moved to ensure the removal of French influence from India, and he mounted a military expedition (in 1799) against Tippu Sahib that was partly organized by his brother Arthur (then Col. Wellesley), the future Duke of Wellington. Ultimately, Wellesley built up Hindu power in Mysore and formed numerous alliances that ensured British control of India. As a reward for his military and diplomatic achievements, he was created the Marquess Wellesley of Norragh in the Irish peerage. Although he saw this as an inadequate reward for his achievements (he had foregone £100,000 of booty from the military campaigns), he remained in India and continued to work to establish British rule by building up relations with the various *nawab*s through a system of subsidiary alliances. This method allowed the British government to avoid the forcible annexation of many territories. French influence was largely liquidated by 1803; but there were still problems with some states, and military expeditions continued until 1805. After asking to be relieved of his command on several occasions, he eventually left India on 15 August 1805 and landed in England in 1806.

Once in England, Wellesley found himself under attack in Parliament by those who suggested that his actions were responsible for some of the rebellions against British rule in India.

Nevertheless, in 1808, the House of Commons endorsed his policy in India, and the motion of impeachment against him for mishandling Indian affairs was dropped. Being among the Irish peers voted into the English House of Lords, he spoke there for the first time on 8 February 1808. Then, in 1809, he was sent to Seville as an ambassador extraordinary, in order to organize relations with the Spanish junta to enable his brother, Sir Arthur Wellesley, to carry out military campaigns in Spain. The high point of these campaigns was Sir Arthur Wellesley's victory at Talavera in July 1809. Shortly afterward, with the resignation of George Canning from the government as a result of his duel with Castlereagh, Wellesley became foreign secretary in the government of Spencer Perceval.

Wellesley served in that post from December 1809 until February 1812. He assumed the office at a time when Britain was isolated in Europe. Napoleon had established alliances with most other European nations and was threatening British trade through his Berlin and Milan decrees. Relations between the United States and Britain had broken down, and there were grave doubts in England about the wisdom of the Peninsular War. Wellesley's own relations with Spencer Perceval were not good, and his absence from many cabinet meetings prepared the way for his resignation. However, the assassination of Perceval on 11 May 1812 led the prince regent to ask Lord Wellesley to form a government, bringing together the leading figures from the Tory and Whig parties. He was unable to do so; instead, Lord Liverpool formed a Tory ministry.

Wellesley was out of office from 1812 to 1821. During this period he began to drift away from the politics of his brother, Wellington, whose career he had supported in both India and Spain. Wellesley supported free trade, whereas Wellington supported protection. On the Irish question, Wellesley pressed for the removal of Irish disabilities; until 1829, Wellington refused to support such a measure. In foreign policy, Wellesley wanted Napoleon to be allowed to assume the throne of France, whereas Wellington wanted what became the Waterloo campaign.

In 1821, Wellesley was offered, and accepted, the post of lord lieutenant of Ireland. Since he was known to favor Roman Catholic emancipation, he was popular with the Catholics, although he was obviously opposed by the Protestant Orangemen. Despite all the violence that accompanied British rule in Ireland, Wellesley attempted to maintain a policy of conciliation under Lord Liverpool and George Canning; but he resigned after Canning's death and the emergence of his brother as prime minister, for Wellington supported the Protestant ascendancy. Up to that point, Wellesley had reorganized the Irish police, reformed the magistracy, attempted to reduce party prejudice, and had raised money to relieve the acute poverty of the early 1820s. Unlike Sir Robert Peel—a pronounced anti-Catholic who was involved both in Ireland and as home secretary in the 1820s—Wellesley was fair-minded. His second marriage in 1825, to Marianne Patterson, an American Roman Catholic widow, confirmed Wellesley's pro-Catholic credentials. She was the granddaughter of Charles Carroll, who at his death in 1832 was the last surviving signatory of the American Declaration of Independence.

Wellesley was out of office for four years. During that time he remained active in Parliament and voted in favor of the Reform Bill of 1832, having reversed his attitude toward parliamentary reform in 1793. After the bill was passed, he was asked by Earl Grey, the prime minister, to be lord steward of the royal household. From 1832 to 1834, Wellesley also served again as lord lieutenant of Ireland. He continued with his conciliatory policy toward Ireland and pushed for more Roman Catholics to be incorporated into the civil service. After 1834 he gradually withdrew from active politics. He died on 26 September 1842.

Wellesley was a remarkably gifted politician. He was one of the great figures who consolidated British power in India. His service in Spain helped ensure the success of the Peninsular War, and his policy on Ireland was enlightened and statesmanlike. His role as foreign secretary was possibly the least successful part of his career. Nevertheless, he was one of the great politicians of his day, and only narrowly missed becoming prime minister.

Keith Laybourn

See also: Canning, George; Liverpool, Earl of; Perceval, Spencer; Wellington, Duke of
References and Further Reading: Gray, Denis, 1963, *Spencer Perceval: The Evangelical Prime Minister* (Manchester: Manchester University Press); Jones, Wilbur, 1967, *Prosperity Robinson: The Life and Times of Viscount Goderich, 1782–1859* (London: Macmillan); Pakenham, Elizabeth, Countess of Longford, 1975, *Wellington: Pillar of State* (St. Albans:: Panther); Smith, Ernest, 1990, *Lord Grey, 1764–1845* (Oxford: Clarendon).

Wellington, Duke of (Hon. Sir Arthur Wellesley [Originally Wesley]) (1769–1852) [PM, FS, HS]

Arthur Wesley (later Wellesley) was born on 1 May 1769 in Dublin, the fifth son of Garrett Wesley, the first Earl of Mornington. Although his father's extravagant lifestyle and preoccupation with musical composition conveyed an impression of financial instability to his contemporaries, recent research by Professor Peter Jupp has revealed that his estates, amounting to over 16,000 acres with an annual yield of £8,000, placed him securely within the Anglo-Irish (aristocratic) landed elite. After his early education in Ireland, the young Arthur went to preparatory school in London. Just a few months after his father's death in 1781, he entered Eton, but he showed little promise as a classical scholar, and suffered the humiliation of premature removal after three years. His widowed mother considered him "food for powder and nothing more" (*Dictionary of National Biography*, p. 1081) and he was sent to a military academy in Angers, in western France, where his most enduring accomplishment was perfecting his spoken and written French, which were later to prove valuable assets in war and diplomacy.

In 1787, when Arthur was 18, his brother the second Earl of Mornington purchased him a commission as an ensign in the army, and he was soon also appointed aide-de-camp to the Irish viceroy. In 1790 he succeeded another brother as member of the Irish Parliament for the family seat of Trim, which he represented until 1797. Purchasing his way through the upper echelons of the army without experienc-

Duke of Wellington (Michael Nicholson/Corbis)

edge for his masterly despatches and letters." He also gained a reputation for personal asceticism and good humor.

The unexpected arrival of Arthur's eldest brother, Richard Wellesley (as the family now spelled its name), as viceroy in May 1798 enabled him to exploit his military talents to the full. He commanded a division against the formidable Tippu Sahib, sultan of Mysore, and became governor of Serengipatam (1799) and commander in chief of the British forces in Mysore. His victories, especially in Assaye (1803), where he had daringly attacked over 40,000 well-equipped Maratha troops, resulted in a peace that he himself negotiated. He left India in 1805 with the rank of major general, a knighthood, and sufficient prize money to confidently seek the hand of the now somewhat faded Kitty Pakenham, whom he married in 1806. He also determined to try his fortunes in the European war against Napoleon Bonaparte, which had resumed in 1803 after the short-lived peace of Amiens. His biographer, Elizabeth Longford, has maintained that all of the successful attributes that he later exhibited on European battlefields were developed in India, notably his "decision, common sense, and attention to detail; his care of his troops and their supplies; and his good relations with the civilian population." She has argued that Napoleon was unwise in later dismissing Arthur as a mere "sepoy general."

Both his singularly unhappy marriage, which ended with the death of Kitty in 1831, and his new military assignments, which included an abortive expedition to Hanover followed by a brigade posting at Hastings, proved disappointing. He was advised by Castlereagh to seek election as M.P. for Rye at a by-election in April 1806, in order to defend his brother's Indian record, which he did, successfully. He later served as M.P. for Mitchell in Cornwall and Newport on the Isle of Wight.

His acceptance of the office of chief secretary for Ireland in the Duke of Portland's ministry in 1807 proved the key to his future military success. As a ministerial colleague of the war minister Castlereagh, he was in a strong position to secure any command that became available. On a brief military expedition to Copenhagen in the

ing military service, he was promoted successively to captain, major, and lieutenant-colonel between 1791 and 1793. His official income remained modest, however, and he accumulated considerable debts from his heavy gambling. Indeed, when the impecunious and unambitious young soldier proposed marriage to Catherine (Kitty) Pakenham, the third daughter of the Earl of Longford, in 1792, and again in 1794, he was rejected on both occasions.

The outbreak of war with revolutionary France proved a turning point in Wesley's career. He saw active service for the first time in Flanders, in the 33rd Foot, in 1794 and 1795. On his return to Dublin, he sold his officer's commission to pay off his debts. Only after failing to find civil employment did he decide in 1796 to go with his regiment to India, hoping to accumulate a sufficient fortune there with which to enhance his marriage prospects. In India he determined to remedy the deficiencies in his education through avid reading, particularly of the works of Jonathan Swift, which Neville Thompson has argued may have provided "the sardonic summer of 1807, he defeated a small Danish force; and following a Portuguese revolt against Napoleon in 1808, he was dispatched to the Iberian Peninsula, where his infantry defeated General Andoche Junot at Vimeiro. The intervention of two cautious superior British officers prevented his pursuit of the retreating French army, however; and Junot's army was repatriated by the controversial Convention of Cintra, an armistice arranged by Wellesley. Exonerated of the charge that he had no right to arrange such an armistice by a subsequent court of inquiry, Wellesley resumed his duties as chief secretary of Ireland; but he persuaded the government to allow him to renew hostilities with the French after the British evacuation from Spain in 1809, following the death of Sir John Moore at Corunna. He argued that Portugal could still be held.

The British decision to send Wellesley to Portugal with an expeditionary force proved crucial to the ultimate defeat of Napoleon. Having resigned as chief secretary of Ireland, Wellesley landed at Lisbon, captured Oporto, and drove the French back into Spain. A brilliant commander, he remained undefeated throughout the Peninsular War, constructing impregnable defensive fortifications at Torres Vedras and achieving notable victories at Talavera (1809), Bussaco (1810), Salamanca (1812), and Vittoria (1813), by pursuing brilliant aggressive tactics. In 1814 he invaded France; and on 18 June 1815, at the Battle of Waterloo, in which Napoleon was finally defeated, confirmed his status as the greatest British general since the Duke of Marlborough. Elevated to the peerage as Viscount Wellington of Talavera, he was created successively earl and marquess in 1812, and in 1814, duke. At the Convention of Paris he was appointed commander of the allied army of occupation. He greatly assisted Castlereagh in the complex diplomacy of the postwar era, opposing a punitive peace settlement and instead organizing loans to help stabilize French finances, and advocating the withdrawal of the army of occupation in 1818.

Returning to Britain but reluctant to become embroiled in party politics, he was persuaded to join Liverpool's cabinet in 1818 as Master General of the Ordnance by Castlereagh, to whom he remained indebted for securing his command in the Iberian Peninsula. He made it a precondition of accepting office, however, that he retain the right to adopt a nonpartisan approach, even to the point of remaining in office should the government resign. During his early years in the cabinet, notwithstanding his illustrious international reputation, he remained relatively inconspicuous. He assumed a more prominent role in cabinet following the suicide of his friend and patron Lord Castlereagh in 1822. A strong supporter of the Congress system, he took Castlereagh's place at the Congress of Verona in 1822. At Liverpool's request, he also persuaded George IV, who stood in awe of the victor of Waterloo, to appoint Canning as foreign secretary.

Ironically, Canning's return to the cabinet produced a growing friction between the two men, which resulted in the emergence of Wellington as unofficial leader of an anti-Canning faction within the government, with a larger number of adherents among backbenchers and outside Parliament. Wellington, with his more forthright and straightforward negotiation style, failed to appreciate Canning's more subtle approach to the conduct of foreign policy and found his flamboyant appeals to the press and public opinion irritating. He remained acutely sensitive to any potential threat to the alliance of European monarchists that had brought peace in Europe in 1815. But Wellington himself had failed to heal the dissension among the European allies at Verona; and his later diplomatic mission to Russia in 1826 failed to prevent Russian intervention on the Eastern question in support of the Ottoman Empire against Greece. On the Irish problem, Wellington resented Canning's persistent attempts to make the issue of Roman Catholic emancipation one of government policy. When Canning became prime minister in April 1827, Wellington became his most formidable opponent. This conflict culminated when Peel led a mass exodus from the government of those who feared that the Protestant ascendancy in Ireland had been jeopardized.

After the death of Canning, Wellington resumed his army command; but following the failure of the Goderich ministry, he was summoned by George IV to become prime minister in January 1828. In a bid to reunite the Tory party, he invited the Canningites led by Huskisson to serve in his administration. He proceeded to remove the Test and Corporation Acts, which had penalized Nonconformists and mitigated the effect of the Corn Laws. When further crisis erupted in Ireland following Daniel O'Connell's victory at the County Clare by-election in July 1828, he came to the conclusion that the only way to prevent any risk of civil war was to grant Roman Catholic emancipation. His success in convincing George IV, Peel, and the majority of the Tories of the need for Roman Catholic emancipation, without the support of any great movement of public opinion on the British mainland, was achieved with the planning and precision of a military campaign and remains his greatest political achievement. However, in the process he alienated the ultra-Tories; and he made matters worse by fighting a duel in defense of his integrity with one of their leading protagonists, Lord Winchilsea, on 21 March 1829, in which both combatants deliberately declined to aim their fire at their targets.

Thereafter Wellington's leadership of the government was marked by a draining away of support, as the Canningites became increasingly disillusioned by his apparent indifference to the prevalent economic distress in the spring of 1830, his lack of initiative in fiscal reform, and his intransigent opposition to parliamentary reform. In the end, his ill-judged defense of the unreformed electoral system on 2 November, which was intended to clarify his own position and thereby reunite the party behind him, led to the defeat of his government in the House of Commons and to his resignation on 22 November 1830.

Wellington's determination while in the opposition to thwart the passage of the Whig Reform Bill in the House of Lords made him unpopular with radicals, mobs of whom twice smashed the windows of Aspley House, his London home, before he had iron shutters put up (earning himself the pejorative nickname Iron Duke). After Earl Grey's resignation in May 1832 and Wellington's failure to form an alternative government, Wellington mustered sufficient influence over the Tory peers to enable the reform bill's passage through the House of Lords without the threatened creation of additional Whig peers.

When the first reformed Parliament met in January 1833, Wellington and Peel determined to oppose the Whig government only if some vital principle came under attack. In 1834, during the crisis provoked by Melbourne's resignation, Wellington became a caretaker prime minister for three weeks, also holding provisionally the offices of home secretary, foreign secretary, and secretary of war for the colonies. His magnanimous insistence that Peel, who was taking a holiday in Italy, should form the next Tory administration proved a turning point in the reconstruction of the Conservative Party. Wellington continued to serve as foreign secretary, his last great ministerial post, until the fall of Peel's first administration in April 1835. During his tenure, he negotiated the Eliot Convention with the commanders of the rival armies in the Carlist War in Spain, putting an end to the systematic shooting of prisoners of war and providing for the periodic exchange of captives.

After 1835, Wellington retained an important consultative role as leader of the opposition in the House of Lords, but again ruled himself out of high office when summoned to form an administration by the young Queen Victoria on the advice of Lord Melbourne in 1839—partly because of his conviction that the prime minister should sit in the House of Commons. He later served as a minister without portfolio in Peel's second administration (1841–1846), exerting a powerful political influence and helping to secure the repeal of the Corn Laws in 1846. The fall of Peel on 29 June 1846 marked the end of Wellington's political career; Wellington felt that he could not lead the opposition to the incoming Whig administration in the House of Lords. He opted instead to continue as commander in chief of the army (a post he had held since 1842). In this role he was criticized for failing to initiate urgently needed military reforms; but his calm and confident handling of the Chartist demonstration in London in 1848 prevented the outbreak of violence.

Wellington died of a stroke at Walmer Castle, his residence in Kent, as Lord Warden of the Cinque Ports on 14 September 1852. He was mourned as an outstanding soldier, the only professional soldier ever to become a British prime minister, and a distinguished public servant. Queen Victoria wrote of him after his death, "For this country, and for us, his loss is irreparable." After a monumental state funeral he was buried in St. Paul's Cathedral.

Although he occasionally has been criticized as an overcautious general, his intuitive genius for discerning when to adopt defensive strategies and when to resort to aggressive tactics is now widely recognized. His political reputation has been more controversial. He has been variously condemned as "Britain's worst nineteenth-century prime minister" and praised for his leadership of an administration that was "one of the most economical and reforming of the century, given its short duration." His political attitudes were essentially those of an Anglo-Irish aristocrat who distrusted democracy and ignored public opinion. (He reportedly confided to Mrs. Arbuthnot in 1831, "The people are rotten to the core.") A rigid upholder of the law and the constitution, he believed passionately that the defense of Britain's privileged institutions was the best guarantee of the social order.

Although he possessed such admirable qualities as courage, common sense, determination, and great administrative ability, which made him well-equipped to achieve political success, he expressed little enthusiasm for the politics of high office, informing the Prince of Orange, shortly after becoming prime minister in January 1828, that it was an office "for the performance of the duties of which I am not qualified, and they are very disagreeable to me." He lacked skill in parliamentary debates, in which he rarely spoke, and in managing his cabinet colleagues. He remained throughout his life a soldier at heart, instinctively authoritarian, intolerant of criticism, indifferent to public opinion, and occasionally bad-tempered and peevish. His former Spanish ally, General Alava, famously declared, "The Duke of Wellington ought never to have had anything to do with politics." More recently, Norman Gash has concurred that "he

damaged his reputation by his subsequent incursion into politics." F. C. Mather has asserted, in contrast, that Wellington's role in shaping foreign policy has been "harshly judged and for the post-1832 era, almost ignored." Arguing that he was more pacific than either Palmerston or Peel, he has concluded that Wellington "deserves credit which has seldom been accorded to him for his efforts to limit and preserve the peace of Europe when it was threatened."

John A. Hargreaves

See also: Canning, George; Castlereagh, Viscount; Liverpool, Earl of; Peel, Sir Robert; Perceval, Spencer; Portland, Duke of
References and Further Reading: Gash, Norman (ed.), 1990, *Wellington* (Manchester: University of Manchester); Jupp, P., 1998, *British Politics on the Eve of Reform: The Duke of Wellington's Administration, 1828–1830* (Manchester: University of Manchester); Mather, F. C., 1986, *Achilles or Nestor? The Duke of Wellington in British Politics after the Great Reform Act* (Southampton: University of Southampton); Pakenham, Elizabeth, Countess of Longford, 1969, *Wellington: The Years of the Sword* (London: Weidenfeld & Nicolson); Pakenham, Elizabeth, Countess of Longford, 1975, *Pillar of State* (St. Albans: Panther); Thompson, Neville, 1986, *Wellington after Waterloo* (London: Routledge & Kegan Paul).

Weymouth, Viscount (Thomas Thynne; Marquess of Bath)
(1734–1796) [FS, HS]

Thomas Thynne, the third Viscount Weymouth and first Marquess of Bath, was considered by many of his contemporaries an indolent figure of limited political ability, even though he was secretary of state for two different departments during his career. He was born on 13 September 1734, the eldest son of Thomas, second Viscount Weymouth, by his wife, Louisa, the daughter of John Carteret, Earl Granville. Thynne was educated at St. John's College, Cambridge, and then went to the Continent. He succeeded to the title of third Viscount Weymouth in 1751, after which he embarked on a life of dissipation. During this period, he also employed Lancelot Brown (Capability Brown) to redesign the gardens at Longleat. He married Elizabeth Cavendish Bentinck, the elder daughter of the second Duke of Portland and sister of the third Duke of Portland (who later became prime minister), in May 1759.

Weymouth's early political career was uneven. He filled a number of royal household posts, and in 1765 briefly served as viceroy of Ireland, but never set foot on Irish soil. He quickly aligned himself with the political groups emerging around the fourth Duke of Bedford at this time, gaining a political advantage from these connections when the Bedford faction made it a condition of its support for the ministry of the Duke of Grafton, who effectively shared power with William Pitt (the Earl of Chatham), that Weymouth should be made one of the two secretaries of state. As a result he became secretary of state for the Northern Department (the post of foreign secretary, after 1782) in January 1768. In this office, Weymouth declared an interest in maintaining British naval power in the Mediterranean. Under the personal direction of George III, he also advocated harsh measures in dealing with the Wilkes riots, which occurred in 1768 and 1769 in the London area as a result of John Wilkes's continued challenge to the government's suppression of the press and Wilkes's own attempt to get into Parliament.

On the resignation of Shelburne, in October 1768, Weymouth was transferred to the post of secretary of state for the Southern Department (the post of home secretary, after 1782), where he remained until December 1779, his main achievement being the signing of an agreement with the East India Company to restrict the size of its dividends. He was also involved in dealing with minor naval disputes with France and in disputing the ownership of the Falkland Islands with Spain. The Spanish authorities in Buenos Aires had driven British settlers out of Port Egmont, and Weymouth demanded their return, on threat of war, which led France to mediate. At this point Weymouth resigned, possibly as a result of pressure from the Earl of Hillsborough, who was secretary of state for the American colonies at that time. In the event, Spain recognized Britain's claim to the Falklands in 1771.

While out of office Weymouth did not join the opposition, but he did often pursue an independent line. He was considered for a number of posts, which he rejected. He eventually accepted the post of secretary of state for the Southern Department on 10 November 1775, and for the next four years generally conducted the government business in the House of Lords. In particular, he defended government action in the American colonies and opposed efforts to bring the American war to an end. He attacked a motion by the Earl of Chatham (William Pitt, the Elder) to put an end to the war, on 30 May 1777, as ill-timed. Matters got worse when he announced on 5 March 1782 that there was no treaty between France and the deputies of the American Congress, and then had to announce on 17 March that such a treaty did exist, and had to call for a vote of support for the king from Parliament.

In the summer of 1778, Weymouth became centrally involved in negotiations to replace the ministry of Lord North, who wished to retire from the premiership. He negotiated with the Pittite Duke of Grafton and the Whig Marquess of Rockingham to form a coalition. Yet, despite constant negotiations throughout 1778 and 1779, Weymouth was unable to secure the formation of a coalition government to replace Lord North's ministry, and North continued as prime minister until 1782. In March 1779, while still serving as secretary of state for the Southern Department, Weymouth also became secretary of state for the north. However, dissatisfied with his efforts to form a coalition government, and opposed to the continuance of the war in America, he resigned as secretary of state for the Northern Department on 21 October 1779, and as secretary of state for the Southern Department a month later (on 25 November 1779). He never held senior office again, although he did hold some minor posts. On 25 August 1789 he was created Marquess of Bath, and in August 1793 he was appointed a member of the Board of Agriculture. He died on 19 November 1796, a largely forgotten political figure.

Keith Laybourn

See also: Fox, Charles James; Grafton, Duke of; Hillsborough, Earl of; North, Lord; Pitt, William (the Elder); Rockingham, Marquess of; Shelburne, Earl of

References and Further Reading: Whiteley, Peter, 1997, *Lord North: The Prime Minister Who Lost America* (London: Hambledon).

Whitelaw, William
(Baron Whitelaw of Penrith)
(1918–1999) [HS]

Whitelaw is best remembered as an old-consensus Conservative who was, nevertheless, something of a mentor for Margaret Thatcher, who once declared, "Every Prime Minister needs a Willie" (Evans 1999, p. 76). A loyal supporter of Thatcher, he was appointed deputy prime minister in 1983, chairing the Cabinet Committee (known as the "Star Chamber"), which arbitrated on spending estimates between ministers and the Treasury. As a "one-nation Conservative" (committed to uniting all the social classes of the nation) supporter of Edward Heath in the early 1970s and an opponent of monetarism, he was an unlikely Thatcherite. Yet he helped remove the remnants of the one-nation section of the Conservative Party from high office while serving under Thatcher. Many cabinet ministers at the time saw him as a restraining hand on Thatcher; after his retirement from government in 1987, as a result of ill health, they felt that her political judgment was impaired. Whitelaw was also famous throughout his political career for his idiosyncratic statements—most famously, in 1974, his observation that the Labour Party was "going around the country stirring up apathy" (Evans 1999, p. 33).

William Stephen Ian Whitelaw was born on 28 June 1918, the son of William Alexander Whitelaw. He was educated at Winchester College and at Trinity College, Cambridge, where he obtained a third in law and a second in history. On leaving Cambridge, he entered the army as a regular officer in the Scots Guards, in which he served from 1939 to 1947. He married Cecilia Sprot in 1943. After leaving the army, he became a farmer and landowner and was active in local politics.

He contested the East Dumbartonshire seat for the Conservatives in the 1950 and 1951 general elections, but did not enter the House of Commons until 1955, when he became Conservative M.P. for Penrith and for the Border Division of Cumberland, which he held until 1983, when he was raised to the House of Lords.

His ministerial career was impressive. He became parliamentary private secretary to the president of the Board of Trade in 1956, and to the chancellor of the exchequer in 1957, remaining in the latter position until 1958. Between 1959 and 1961 he was assistant government whip, and from 1961 to 1962, a lord commissioner of the Treasury. He was parliamentary secretary to the Ministry of Labour from July 1962 to October 1964, and from then until June 1970 was opposition chief whip, dealing with divisive issues such as immigration and the moves for "white-dominated" independence in Southern Rhodesia.

In Edward Heath's government of the early 1970s he was Lord President of the Council and leader of the House of Commons (1970–1972), secretary of state for Northern Ireland (1972–1973), and secretary of state for employment (1973–1974). In the Northern Ireland post he had the responsibility of bringing together the leading political representatives from both communities in a power-sharing administration responsible to the newly elected Assembly in 1973, although this coalition failed six months later. In opposition once again, following the Conservative defeat in the general election of 1974, Whitelaw acted as chairman of the Conservative Party (1974–1975) and as deputy leader of the opposition and spokesman on home affairs (1975–1979).

When Margaret Thatcher's Conservative Party won the general election of May 1979, Whitelaw predictably became home secretary (1979–1983). In this role he increased police pay, recruited an additional 10,000 police officers, and began the biggest prison-building and -improvement program of the century. Yet his main responsibility appeared to be to temper Thatcher's political rashness. He continued to influence Thatcher after he was raised to the House of Lords in 1983, as Lord President of the Council and leader of the House of Lords (1983–1988). He apparently kept the unofficial title of deputy prime minister, acquired in 1983, until 1991.

After his 1987 retirement, unlike many ex-ministers, Whitelaw did not devote himself to improving his financial fortunes by moving into the business sector but instead offered his services to public bodies, such as the Cumbria

Tourist Board, of which he became president in 1988. He died on 1 July 1999.

Keith Laybourn

See also: Heath, Edward; Lawson, Nigel; Pym, Francis; Thatcher, Margaret

References and Further Reading: Evans, Brendan, 1999, *Thatcherism and British Politics, 1975–1999* (Stroud, UK: Sutton); Whitelaw, W., 1989, *The Whitelaw Memoirs* (London: Headline).

Wilson, Harold (Lord Wilson of Rievaulx)
[1916–1995] [PM]

Wilson was prime minister between 1964 and 1970, and again between 1974 and 1976. He was the first Labour Party leader to win four general elections, and at his retirement in 1976 was Labour's longest-serving prime minister. However, his premierships occurred at a time when Britain was facing serious economic difficulties, and they were dominated by major social and industrial problems. As a result, Wilson tends to be seen in two contrasting lights: on the one hand he is projected as a master of expediency, and indeed intrigue, who was not to be trusted; and on the other, as the man who brought stability to British society in a period when Britain faced serious difficulties with foreign trade and international finance.

James Harold Wilson was born on 11 March 1916 into a lower-middle-class family, the son of John Herbert and Ethel Wilson. His father was an industrial chemist at Hollidays in Huddersfield. Harold was educated at Royds Hall Secondary School in Huddersfield, where he was an outstanding pupil. He was greatly influenced in these early years by the Nonconformist radicalism of his grandfather. He subsequently attended Jesus College, Oxford, where he graduated with first-class honors. It was here that his political education began. At first he was a member of the Liberal Club; but by the end of the 1930s, he had drifted toward Labour, although he never became a member of the prestigious Labour Club at Oxford, which had produced future Labour political figures such as Anthony Crosland and Denis Healey. His views at this time seem to have been greatly influenced by G. D. H. Cole, one of Oxford's foremost socialist intellectuals. In 1939 he married Gladys Mary Baldwin, the daughter of the Rev. D. Baldwin. At this time he was a junior academic at Oxford and a research assistant to William Beveridge. During World War II, he filled several posts in the civil service and then served as director of economics and statistics at the Ministry of Fuel and Power between 1943 and 1944.

Wilson rose to political prominence after the 1945 general election, when he was elected as M.P. for Ormskirk. He held this seat until 1950, when he switched to Huyton, which he represented until his retirement from the House of Commons in 1983. Once in the House of Commons, he rose quickly in the government ranks. He was parliamentary secretary to the minister of works between 1945 and 1947, in the first Attlee Labour government. He then became secretary for overseas trade in 1947, before being appointed president of the Board of Trade, a post that he held from 1947 to 1951 and that gave him a place in the cabinet. This was a remarkable achievement for someone who had no grounding within the Labour Party and who had little practical experience of the power and influence of the trade union movement.

What was even more surprising was his attachment to Aneurin Bevan, one of the leading political figures in the Labour Party and the founder of the National Health Service. In April 1951 he joined Bevan and John Freeman in resigning from the cabinet over the threat of the government to impose national health charges and in order to "fight for the soul of the Labour Party" (Laybourn 1997, p. 147). With Bevan and Freeman, Wilson joined Keep Left, a left-wing grouping within the Labour Party that was committed to long-term planning for socialism and to creating a "third force" of European nations to act as a buffer between the United States and the Soviet Union. Keep Left became the basis of the Bevanite split within the Labour Party in the early and mid-1950s.

In 1954, Wilson replaced Bevan in the Labour shadow cabinet, taking on the responsibilities for foreign policy and defense. To many political observers, this action suggested that Wilson was a pragmatist who cared little for principle. Wilson nonetheless lacked the social

Harold Wilson meets the Beatles, March 19, 1964. (Hulton-Deutsch Collection/Corbis)

and intellectual connections that Hugh Gaitskell, Anthony Crosland, and the Gaitskellites acquired in the Labour Club at Oxford. From a different cultural background, Wilson had a strained relationship with Gaitskell, who became Labour leader in 1955. Indeed, Gaitskell's unsuccessful attempt to get the party to change Clause Four, and his opposition in 1960 to unilateral nuclear disarmament, provoked Wilson into a leadership challenge aimed partly at forestalling other rivals to Gaitskell. Wilson was roundly defeated by 166 votes to 81, but he had made his mark as a potential new leader.

Gaitskell's death in 1963 led to a leadership contest that ended when Wilson was elected Labour Party leader, defeating George Brown and James Callaghan. Wilson clearly benefited from the fact that he was not closely attached to the trade unions or to the middle-class Gaitskel-

lites. In 1964 he won a narrow victory in the general election, at which he offered the vision of a newly egalitarian Britain based on a scientific and technological revolution and a wide range of social welfare measures.

Wilson's government inherited a balance-of-trade deficit of around £600 million, and found it difficult to achieve its objectives faced with both a poor financial and weak political position. Even so, Labour was able to obtain a majority of almost 100 seats in the general election of March 1966. The omens looked good for the new Labour government, with public opinion buoyed by an upsurge in patriotism after England won the World Cup at football. However, the economic situation soon deteriorated further, due in part to a prolonged seamen's strike. The pound sterling remained under pressure, necessitating a rather belated devaluation in November 1967, which further constrained the economic growth policies of Wilson's government. Trade unions were resistant to wage controls and curbs on unofficial strike activity of the kind discussed by Barbara Castle in her white paper *In Place of Strife* (1969), and the attempt to impose such measures created intense conflict within the Labour movement. Despite these difficulties, the Wilson government did introduce progressive legislation guaranteeing sexual and racial equality.

Wilson's government also had a bumpy ride in foreign affairs. The European Economic Community (EEC) rebuffed Britain's renewed efforts in 1967 to obtain membership. Wilson's attempt to mediate in the Vietnam War was unsuccessful. And the white government of Rhodesia unilaterally declared independence from the British Commonwealth.

Wilson called a general election for June 1970, at a time when the economy seemed to be recovering. He appealed to the electorate to give him a mandate to implement the necessary social measures, which he believed he had earned by "two years of hard slog." However, the Conservatives were elected instead, under Edward Heath. Wilson was now leader of a Labour Party in opposition, which began to split between the political left and right. The party was divided on many issues—most obviously, on joining the EEC, which the left opposed and the right, led by Roy Jenkins, supported. However, Labour as a whole generally drifted leftward, as was reflected in the radical commitments envisaged within the "Labour Programme 1973," which included major extensions to public ownership. Wilson was not particularly happy with this trend; but he fought, and won, the general election of February 1974 on the issues of inflation and rising unemployment. However, his new ministry was a minority government; and it did not secure a majority until the general election of October 1974, when it won a majority of only three seats.

Wilson was now a much less active leader than he had been in the 1960s. Nevertheless, he was involved in many important developments. He resolved the left and right split over joining the Common Market (the EEC) by calling a national referendum, which, by two to one, voted

in favor of joining. He scrapped the incomes policy of the Heath government and negotiated a "social contract" with the trade unions, attempting to regulate wage bargaining in return for an extension of welfare benefits to be paid out of increased taxation on the rich and by large-scale borrowing. However, the world economic crisis of 1975 created problems for Britain and forced Denis Healey, then chancellor of the exchequer, to increase taxation in his April 1975 budget. Thus, the government failed to honor its part of the social contract.

The Wilson government began to falter and was defeated in the House of Commons on two occasions in March 1976. It was at this point that Wilson, at age 60, announced his resignation. There are many possible reasons for this. He had long ago suggested that he might retire at 60, although few took him seriously. There is also the possibility that he became frustrated with a possible long-term campaign against him by members of the security services who believed him to be a Soviet stooge. Perhaps he was just tired of the strain of the economic problems that every one of his governments had faced. Whatever the reason, he retired to the backbench until 1983. He was then immediately raised to the House of Lords as Lord Wilson of Rievaulx, but he was not a particularly prominent or active member of the Lords. He suffered from serious health problems later in life, and died on 24 May 1995.

Wilson is a perplexing political character. On the one hand, he had immense political skills and often has been regarded as a master political tactician. On the other hand, one has to recognize that his four Labour governments, talented as they were, never became the reforming and socialist agencies they were intended to be (although largely because of the acute economic situation each one faced). There were some important reforms, particularly in the late 1960s, and Wilson managed to keep the left and the right wings of a deeply divided party together in a period of significant tension. Perhaps he was, of all Labour's prime ministers, the best at crisis management and compromise, belonging to neither section of the party. It may be that his great contribution was to keep the Labour Party together, although he was unable to reshape it in the way some of his successors have been able to do.

Keith Laybourn

See also: Attlee, Clement; Bevin, Ernest; Brown, George; Callaghan, James; Crosland, Tony; Gaitskell, Hugh; Healey, Denis; Heath, Edward; Jenkins, Roy

References and Further Reading: Foot, Paul, 1968, *The Politics of Harold Wilson* (Harmondsworth, UK: Penguin Books); Laybourn, Keith, 1997, *The Rise of Socialism in Britain* (Stroud, UK: Sutton); Morgan, Austen, 1992, *Harold Wilson* (London: Pluto Press); Pimlott, Ben, 1992, *Harold Wilson* (London: HarperCollins); Wilson, Harold, 1971, *The Labour Government, 1964–1970: A Personal Record* (London: Weidenfeld & Nicolson); ——, 1979, *Final Term: The Labour Government, 1974–1976* (London: Weidenfeld & Nicolson).

Wood, Sir Charles (Viscount Halifax of Monk Bretton)
(1800–1885) [CE]

Sir Charles Wood was born on 20 December 1800, the eldest son of Sir Francis Lindley Wood, the second Baron Halifax, and his wife, Anne, the daughter of Samuel Buck. He was educated at Eton and at Oriel College, Oxford. Soon afterward he entered politics and was elected Liberal M.P. for Grimsby in 1826. He was subsequently elected M.P. for Wareham in 1831, and for Halifax in December 1832.

Wood's government career began in August 1832 when he was appointed joint secretary to the Treasury in Lord Grey's government. The second Earl Grey was his father-in-law, for Wood had married Mary, Grey's fifth daughter, on 29 July 1829. Wood resigned from the post in November 1834, and became secretary to the Admiralty in April 1835. He was a rather moderate Whig and was not convinced of the need to repeal the Corn Laws until 1844. He also opposed, with John Bright, the age and hours restrictions imposed on children and women by the 1844 Factory Act. He became chancellor of the exchequer under Lord John Russell in July 1846, simultaneously becoming a member of the Privy Council; and shortly afterward, he succeeded to the baronetcy on his father's death.

Wood's stewardship as chancellor of the exchequer, a post he held until February 1852, was not impressive. The poor financial position of the nation, plus the Irish famines, created serious economic problems for him, and he had to introduce three budgets in 1848. He was opposed to introducing new expenditure and new taxes and did little to alleviate the Irish famine. He resigned with the rest of the Russell government on 27 February 1852, but found a place in the succeeding government of Lord Aberdeen, as president of the Board of Control connected with Indian affairs. In this office he pressed forward the India Act of 1853.

On 8 February 1855 he became a member of Lord Palmerston's cabinet as First Lord of the Admiralty, compelling Parliament to keep up the size of the navy after the conclusion of the Crimean War. Wood resigned this office in 1858. In 1859 he became secretary of state for India and spent the next few years organizing the government and finances of India in the wake of the demise of the East India Company. He promoted acts for limiting the number of European troops in India (1859), for reorganizing the Indian army (1860), and for regulating the legislative council and high court of India (1861). His reforms built up Indian debts, but his budgets of 1864 and 1865 led to improved finance and the removal of those debts. He eventually resigned from the Indian secretaryship, on the grounds of ill health, on 16 February 1866.

In 1865 Wood lost his parliamentary seat at Halifax but was elected for Ripon. On 21 February 1866 he was raised to the peerage as Viscount Halifax of Monk Bretton (near Barnsley, in Yorkshire), after which he gradually withdrew from active politics, although he was Lord Privy Seal from July 1870 to February 1874. He died on 8 August 1885.

Keith Laybourn

See also: Grey, Lord
References and Further Reading: Prest, John, 1972, *Lord John Russell* (London: Macmillan); Smith, Ernest, 1990, *Lord Grey, 1764–1845* (Oxford: Clarendon).

Wood, Sir Kingsley
(1881–1943) [CE]

Wood was chancellor of the exchequer during the early years of World War II. Although he introduced Keynesian expansionist and contractionist policies to deal with war finance, today he is an almost-forgotten Conservative politician.

Howard Kingsley Wood was born at Hull on 19 August 1881, the son of a Wesleyan minister, the Rev. Arthur Wood. Soon after Howard's birth, the family moved to the Wesley Chapel, Finsbury Road, London. Kingsley Wood was educated at the Central Federation Boys' School, London, a Wesleyan school, and became an articled solicitor in 1903. He married Agnes Lilian, daughter of Henry Frederick Fawcett, in 1905. At about this time he also set up his own City firm—Kingsley Wood, Williams, Murphy and Ross—which specialized in industrial insurance law. After the 1911 National Insurance Act was passed, he became involved in bringing companies into the plan and held numerous positions on industrial insurance bodies in London. As a result of his work he was knighted in 1918.

Wood's political career began in 1911, when he was elected for Woolwich to the London county council. He remained a member of that body until 1919. In 1918 he was elected Conservative M.P. for Woolwich, which he represented, without interruption, until his death in 1943. As a talented Conservative M.P. in a period of Conservative political dominance, he rose quickly through the government ranks. Between 1919 and 1922 he was parliamentary private secretary (a voluntary post) to the minister of health in the coalition government of 1918 to 1922. He then became private secretary (a paid government post) to the minister of health (Neville Chamberlain) in the Conservative government of 1924 to 1929. During this period he also acted as civil commissioner of the northern district of Britain during the General Strike of 1926, the country having been divided into ten districts and London for the civil administration of the nation. He was also made a privy councillor in 1928—an unusual honor for a private secretary.

Ramsay MacDonald formed a Labour government in 1929, which lasted until 1931; during this hiatus, Wood was excluded from the administration. However, when MacDonald formed a National government in August 1931, Wood was appointed to a variety of government posts. At first, in 1931, he was appointed private secretary to the Board of Education; but almost immediately, he was promoted to the office of postmaster-general. He attempted to make the Post Office more effective financially, negotiating a new financial arrangement with the Treasury that fixed the sum the Post Office contributed to national finances and allowed it to keep any profits above that figure for reinvestment. He also built up the telephone section of the Post Office.

Wood's work earned him a place in the cabinet in 1933 and eventually a promotion to minister of health (1935–1938). In this office he pushed for improvements in public health and for improved housing standards. In 1938 he was elected to succeed Stanley Baldwin as Grand Master of the Primrose League, an organization named after Disraeli's favorite flower. The league was one of the most important, keeping the Conservative rank and file, particularly women, united. In the same year, he became secretary of state for air, presiding over a buildup of the air force. During his tenure in that post, Britain's monthly production of front-line aircraft increased from 80 (in March 1938) to 546 (in April 1940). Having accomplished that task, he decided to accept an appointment as Lord Privy Seal, which came with a less exhausting workload. It was in this capacity, in May 1940, that he was largely responsible for informing his close friend, Prime Minister Neville Chamberlain, that he should resign in favor of Winston Churchill.

To accomplish its mandate, Churchill's wartime coalition government of necessity included Labour, Liberals, and anti-appeasement Conservatives acting in ministerial roles. Despite Wood's close association with Neville Chamberlain, he was given the post of chancellor of the exchequer. At first he was not given membership in the small wartime cabinet, but he did become a cabinet member in October 1940. He lost his cabinet status, however, in the ministerial reshuffle of February 1942.

Wood was a competent chancellor, and introduced four wartime budgets. The first, in July 1940, implemented the purchase tax that his predecessor, Sir John Simon, had announced, and introduced new measures to deduct income tax at the source. Around this time, he also set up a council of economic advisers, through which the ideas of John Maynard Keynes became central to Britain's wartime and postwar economic policy making.

Wood's 1941 budget was greatly influenced by Keynesian ideas, having been based on the principle that state spending should expand when demand is low and should contract when demand is high. In order to finance the war effort, Wood raised income tax to 10s (50p) in the pound; lowered tax exemptions; and included the majority of British citizens, for the first time, among income tax payers. These policies were made palatable, in the context of war, by the creation of postwar credits whereby people were being forced to save money for the government to borrow. The 1942 and 1943 budgets followed the same general lines. In 1943 the state spent more than £5.6 billion, half of it financed out of taxation. There was, of course, much wartime demand, with potential for inflation. However, a series of food-subsidy programs ensured that wartime prices did not rise more than 30 percent above the levels prevailing in the prewar years. Wood also introduced the pay-as-you-earn (PAYE) scheme, which taxed wage earners on their weekly or monthly income, which has since become the core of the tax system in Britain.

Wood died, unexpectedly, while still in office, on 21 September 1943. Since his death, he has been largely forgotten. Yet although he was never a major player in British politics, he was more than the competent solicitor and stolid administrator that he has sometimes been presented as.

Keith Laybourn

See also: Baldwin, Stanley; Chamberlain, Neville; Churchill, Sir Winston; Simon, Sir John
References and Further Reading: Jenkins, Roy, 1998, *The Chancellors* (London: Macmillan).

Y

Yorke, Charles Philip
(1764–1834) [HS]

Charles Philip Yorke was born 12 March 1764, the elder son of Charles Yorke by his second wife. His father was the elder brother of Sir Joseph Sydney Yorke and half brother of Philip Yorke, third Earl of Hardwicke. Charles was educated at Harrow and at St. John's College, Cambridge, graduating with an M.A. in 1783. He then trained to be a barrister, and was called to the bar from the Middle Temple in 1787. In 1790 he married Harriott Manningham. The marriage was childless, and after Charles's death the earldom of Hardwicke passed to Charles Philip Yorke, the son of his younger brother.

Yorke was M.P. for Cambridge from 1790 to 1810, but lost that seat in 1810. He was immediately elected as M.P. for St. Germains, a seat that he exchanged in 1812 for the Liskeard seat, which he held until 1818. In his 28 years in the House of Commons, he became a strong opponent of William Pitt, the Younger, and of equality and emancipation for Catholics.

In 1801 he became a member of the Privy Council and accepted the post of secretary at war, which meant presenting army estimates to Parliament, in Henry Addington's administration (1801–1804). He performed poorly in this office and was transferred to the post of home secretary in August 1803, in which he served until May 1804, when Pitt formed a new ministry.

Thereafter, Yorke spoke frequently in Parliament, defending many of the military expeditions launched by the governments of Lord Grenville (1806–1807), the third Duke of Portland (1807–1809), and Spencer Perceval (1809–1812). Early in 1810, Yorke became one of the tellers of the exchequer, which brought him an income of £2,700 per year, improving his parlous financial situation.

At this time he also enforced the parliamentary standing orders excluding the press from the House of Commons—one of the factors that led the British Forum Debating Society to suggest that the freedom of the press was being attacked. The society's vigorous campaign against this action helped precipitate the riots on 6 April 1810, during which windows in Yorke's house were smashed. Later that month Perceval moved Yorke into the cabinet as First Lord of the Admiralty, a post he held for about 18 months before resigning on the grounds of poor health. Yorke continued to play an active part in the House of Commons for some years, but retired from public life in 1818. He died on 13 March 1834.

See also: Addington, Henry; Canning, George; Castlereagh, Viscount; Grenville, Lord; Perceval, Spencer; Pitt, William (the Younger); Portland, Duke of
References and Further Reading: Ziegler, Philip, 1965, *Addington* (New York: John Day).

CHRONOLOGICAL LIST OF LEADERS
BY CABINET OFFICE

PRIME MINISTERS

1. Sir Robert Walpole, April 1721–February 1742
2. Spencer Compton, February 1742–July 1743
3. Hon. Henry Pelham, August 1743–February 1746
4. Sir William Pulteney, February 1746
5. Hon. Henry Pelham, February 1746–March 1754
6. Duke of Newcastle, March 1754–October 1756
7. Duke of Devonshire, November 1756–May 1757
8. James Waldegrave, June 1757
9. Duke of Newcastle, July 1757–October 1762[1]
10. Earl of Bute, May 1762–April 1763
11. George Grenville, April 1763–July 1765
12. Marquess of Rockingham, July 1765–July 1766
13. William Pitt, the Elder, July 1766–October 1768
14. Duke of Grafton, October 1768–January 1770
15. Lord North, January 1770–March 1782
16. Marquess of Rockingham, March 1782–July 1782
17. Earl of Shelburne, July 1782–February 1783
18. Duke of Portland, April 1783–December 1783
19. William Pitt, the Younger, December 1783–March 1801
20. Henry Addington, March 1801–April 1804
21. William Pitt, the Younger, May 1804–January 1806
22. Lord Grenville, February 1806–March 1807
23. Duke of Portland, March 1807–October 1809
24. Spencer Perceval, October 1809–May 1812
25. Earl of Liverpool, June 1812–February 1827
26. George Canning, April 1827–August 1827
27. Viscount Goderich, August 1827–January 1828
28. Duke of Wellington, January 1828–November 1830
29. Lord Grey, November 1830–July 1834
30. Viscount Melbourne, July 1834–November 1834
31. Duke of Wellington, November 1834–December 1834
32. Sir Robert Peel, December 1834–April 1835
33. Viscount Melbourne, April 1835–August 1841
34. Sir Robert Peel, August 1841–June 1846
35. Lord John Russell, June 1846–February 1852
36. 14th Earl of Derby, February 1852–December 1852
37. Earl of Aberdeen, December 1852–February 1855
38. Lord Palmerston, February 1855–February 1858
39. 14th Earl of Derby, February 1858–June 1859
40. Lord Palmerston, June 1859–October 1865
41. Lord John Russell, October 1865–June 1866
42. 14th Earl of Derby, June 1866–February 1868
43. Benjamin Disraeli, February 1868–November 1868
44. William Ewart Gladstone, December 1868–February 1874
45. Benjamin Disraeli, February 1874–April 1880
46. William Ewart Gladstone, April 1880–June 1885
47. Lord Salisbury, June 1885–January 1886
48. William Ewart Gladstone, February 1886–July 1886
49. Lord Salisbury, July 1886–August 1892
50. William Ewart Gladstone, August 1892–March 1894

51. Lord Rosebery, March 1894–June 1895
52. Lord Salisbury, June 1895–July 1902
53. Arthur James Balfour, July 1902–December 1905
54. Sir Henry Campbell-Bannerman, December 1905–April 1908
55. Herbert Henry Asquith, April 1908–December 1916
56. David Lloyd George, December 1916–October 1922
57. Andrew Bonar Law, October 1922–May 1923
58. Stanley Baldwin, May 1923–January 1924
59. James Ramsay MacDonald, January 1924–November 1924
60. Stanley Baldwin, November 1924–June 1929
61. James Ramsay MacDonald, June 1929–June 1935
62. Stanley Baldwin, June 1935–May 1937
63. Neville Chamberlain, May 1937–May 1940
64. Sir Winston Churchill, May 1940–July 1945
65. Clement Attlee, July 1945–October 1951
66. Sir Winston Churchill, October 1951–April 1955
67. Sir Anthony Eden, April 1955–January 1957
68. Harold Macmillan, January 1957–October 1963
69. Sir Alec Douglas Home, October 1963–October 1964
70. Harold Wilson, October 1964–June 1970
71. Edward Heath, June 1970–March 1974
72. Harold Wilson, March 1974–April 1976
73. James Callaghan, April 1976–May 1979
74. Margaret Thatcher, May 1979–November 1990
75. John Major, November 1990–May 1997
76. Tony Blair, May 1997–

CHANCELLORS OF THE EXCHEQUER[2]

1. Sir Robert Walpole, April 1721–February 1742
2. Lord Samuel Sandys, February 1742–December 1743
3. Hon. Henry Pelham, December 1743–March 1754
4. Henry Bilson Legge, April 1754–November 1756
5. Henry Bilson Legge, November 1756–April/May 1757
6. Lord Mansfield, April/May 1757–June 1757
7. Henry Bilson Legge, July 1757–March 1761

8. Viscount Barrington, March 1761–May 1762
9. Lord Le Despenser, May 1762–April 1763
10. George Grenville, April 1763–July 1765
11. William Dowdeswell, July 1765–August 1766
12. Charles Townshend, August 1766–September 1767
13. Lord Mansfield, September 1767–April 1772
14. Lord John Cavendish, April 1772–July 1782
15. William Pitt, the Younger, July 1782–April 1783
16. Lord John Cavendish, April 1783–December 1783
17. William Pitt, the Younger, December 1783–March 1801
18. Henry Addington, March 1801–May 1804
19. William Pitt, the Younger, May 1804–February 1806
20. 3d Marquess of Lansdowne, February 1806–March 1807
21. Spencer Perceval, March 1807–June 1812
22. Lord Bexley, June 1812–January 1823
23. Viscount Goderich, January 1823–April 1827
24. George Canning, April 1827–September 1827
25. John Charles Herries, September 1827–January 1828
26. Henry Goulburn, January 1828–November 1830
27. Henry Althorp, November 1830–July 1834
28. Sir Robert Peel, December 1834–April 1835
29. Thomas Spring-Rice, April 1835–August 1839
30. Sir Francis Thornhill Baring, August 1839–September 1841
31. Henry Goulburn, September 1841–July 1846
32. Sir Charles Wood, July 1846–February 1852
33. Benjamin Disraeli, February 1852–December 1852
34. William Ewart Gladstone, December 1852–March 1855
35. Sir George Cornewall Lewis, March 1855–February 1858
36. Benjamin Disraeli, February 1858–June 1859
37. William Ewart Gladstone, June 1859–July 1866
38. Benjamin Disraeli, July 1866–February 1868
39. George Ward Hunt, February 1868–December 1868
40. Sir Robert Lowe, December 1868–August 1873
41. William Ewart Gladstone, August 1873–February 1874

42. Sir Stafford Northcote, February 1874–April 1880
43. William Ewart Gladstone, April 1880–December 1882
44. Hugh Childers, December 1882–June 1885
45. Sir Michael Hicks Beach, June 1885–February 1886
46. Sir William Harcourt, February 1886–August 1886
47. Lord Randolph Churchill, August 1886–January 1887
48. George Joachim Goschen, January 1887–August 1892
49. Sir William Harcourt, August 1892–June 1895
50. Sir Michael Hicks Beach, June 1895–August 1902
51. Charles Thomson Ritchie, August 1902–October 1903
52. Austen Chamberlain, October 1903–December 1905
53. Herbert Henry Asquith, December 1905–April 1908
54. David Lloyd George, April 1908–May 1915
55. Reginald McKenna, May 1915–December 1916
56. Andrew Bonar Law, December 1916–January 1919
57. Austen Chamberlain, January 1919–April 1921
58. Sir Robert Horne, April 1921–October 1922
59. Stanley Baldwin, October 1922–August 1923
60. Neville Chamberlain, August 1923–January 1924
61. Philip Snowden, January 1924–November 1924
62. Sir Winston Churchill, November 1924–June 1929
63. Philip Snowden, June 1929–November 1931
64. Neville Chamberlain, November 1931–May 1937
65. Sir John Simon, May 1937–May 1940
66. Sir Kingsley Wood, May 1940–September 1943
67. Sir John Anderson, September 1943–July 1945
68. Hugh Dalton, July 1945–November 1947
69. Sir Stafford Cripps, November 1947–October 1950
70. Hugh Gaitskell, October 1950–October 1951

71. Richard Austen Butler, October 1951–December 1955
72. Harold Macmillan, December 1955–January 1957
73. Peter Thorneycroft, January 1957–January 1958
74. Derick Heathcoat Amory, January 1958–July 1960
75. Selwyn Lloyd, July 1960–July 1962
76. Reginald Maudling, July 1962–October 1964
77. James Callaghan, October 1964–November 1967
78. Roy Jenkins, November 1967–June 1970
79. Iain Macleod, June 1970–July 1970
80. Anthony Barber, July 1970–March 1974
81. Denis Healey, March 1974–May 1979
82. Sir Geoffrey Howe, May 1979–June 1983
83. Nigel Lawson, June 1983–October 1989
84. John Major, October 1989–November 1990
85. Norman Lamont, November 1990–May 1993
86. Kenneth Clarke, May 1993–May 1997
87. Gordon Brown, May 1997–

FOREIGN SECRETARIES[3]

1. Charles Townshend (Viscount), February 1721–May 1730
2. Earl Harrington, June 1730–February 1742
3. John Carteret, February 1742–November 1744
4. Earl Harrington, November 1744–February 1746
5. Earl Harrington, February 1746–October 1746
6. Earl of Chesterfield, October 1746–February 1748
7. Duke of Newcastle, February 1748–March 1754
8. Earl of Holderness, March 1754–March 1761
9. Earl of Bute, March 1761–May 1762
10. George Grenville, May 1762–October 1762
11. Earl of Halifax, October 1762–September 1763
12. Earl of Sandwich, September 1763–July 1765
13. Duke of Grafton, July 1765–May 1766
14. Henry Seymour Conway, May 1766–January 1768
15. Viscount Weymouth, January 1768–October 1768
16. Earl of Rochford, October 1768–December 1770
17. Earl of Sandwich, December 1770–January 1771

18. Earl of Halifax, January 1771–June 1771
19. Earl of Suffolk and Berkshire, June 1771–March 1779
20. Viscount Weymouth, March 1779–October 1779
21. Viscount Stormont, October 1779–March 1782
22. Charles James Fox, March 1782–July 1782
23. Lord Grantham, July 1782–April 1783
24. Charles James Fox, April 1783–December 1783
25. Earl of Temple, December 1783
26. Duke of Leeds, December 1783–April 1791
27. Lord Grenville, April 1791–February 1801
28. Earl of Liverpool, February 1801–May 1804
29. Lord Harrowby, May 1804–December 1804
30. Lord Mulgrave, January 1805–February 1806
31. Charles James Fox, February 1806–September 1806
32. Lord Grey, September 1806–March 1807
33. George Canning, March 1807–October 1809
34. Henry Bathurst, October 1809–December 1809
35. Richard Colley Wellesley, December 1809–January 1812
36. Viscount Castlereagh, February 1812–September 1822
37. George Canning, September 1822–April 1827
38. Viscount Dudley, April 1827–May 1828
39. Earl of Aberdeen, May 1828–November 1830
40. Lord Palmerston, November 1830–July 1834
41. Duke of Wellington, November 1834–April 1835
42. Lord Palmerston, April 1835–August 1841
43. Earl of Aberdeen, September 1841–July 1846
44. Lord Palmerston, July 1846–December 1851
45. Earl Granville, December 1851–February 1852
46. Earl of Malmesbury, February 1852–December 1852
47. Lord John Russell, December 1852–February 1853
48. Earl of Clarendon, February 1853–February 1858
49. Earl of Malmesbury, February 1858–June 1859
50. Lord John Russell, June 1859–October 1865
51. Earl of Clarendon, November 1865–July 1866
52. 15th Earl of Derby, July 1866–December 1868
53. Earl of Clarendon, December 1868–July 1870
54. Earl Granville, July 1870–February 1874
55. 15th Earl of Derby, February 1874–April 1878
56. Lord Salisbury, April 1878–April 1880
57. Earl Granville, April 1880–June 1885
58. Lord Salisbury, June 1885–February 1886
59. Lord Rosebery, February 1886–July 1886
60. Sir Stafford Northcote, August 1886–January 1887
61. Lord Salisbury, January 1887–August 1892
62. Lord Rosebery, August 1892–March 1894
63. Earl of Kimberley, March 1894–June 1895
64. Lord Salisbury, June 1895–November 1900
65. 5th Marquess of Lansdowne, November 1900–December 1905
66. Sir Edward Grey, December 1905–December 1916
67. Arthur James Balfour, December 1916–October 1919
68. Lord Curzon, October 1919–January 1924
69. James Ramsay MacDonald, January 1924–November 1924
70. Austen Chamberlain, November 1924–June 1929
71. Arthur Henderson, June 1929–August 1931
72. Marquess of Reading, August 1931–November 1931
73. Sir John Simon, November 1931–June 1935
74. Sir Samuel Hoare, June 1935–December 1935
75. Sir Anthony Eden, December 1935–February 1938
76. Lord Halifax, February 1838–December 1940
77. Sir Anthony Eden, December 1940–July 1945
78. Ernest Bevin, July 1945–March 1951
79. Herbert Morrison, March 1951–October 1951
80. Sir Anthony Eden, October 1951–April 1955
81. Harold Macmillan, April 1955–December 1955
82. Selwyn Lloyd, December 1955–July 1960
83. Sir Alec Douglas Home, July 1960–October 1963
84. Richard Austen Butler, October 1963–October 1964

85. Patrick C. Gordon Walker, October 1964–January 1965
86. Michael Stewart, January 1965–August 1966
87. George Brown, August 1966–March 1968
88. Michael Stewart, March 1968–June 1970
89. Sir Alec Douglas Home, June 1970–March 1974
90. James Callaghan, March 1974–April 1976
91. Tony Crosland, April 1976–February 1977
92. David Anthony Owen, February 1977–May 1979
93. Lord Carrington, May 1979–April 1982
94. Francis Pym, April 1982–June 1983
95. Sir Geoffrey Howe, June 1983–July 1989
96. John Major, July 1989–October 1989
97. Douglas Hurd, October 1989–July 1995
98. Malcolm Rifkind, July 1995–May 1997
99. Robin Cook, May 1997–

HOME SECRETARIES[4]

1. Duke of Newcastle, April 1724–February 1746
2. Duke of Newcastle, February 1746–February 1748
3. Duke of Bedford, February 1748–June 1751
4. Earl of Holderness, June 1751–March 1754
5. Thomas Robinson, March 1754–October 1755
6. Henry Fox, November 1755–November 1756
7. William Pitt, the Elder, December 1756–April 1757
8. William Pitt, the Elder, June 1757–October 1761
9. Earl of Egremont, October 1761–September 1763
10. Earl of Halifax, September 1763–July 1765
11. Henry Seymour Conway, July 1765–May 1766
12. Duke of Richmond, May 1766–July 1766
13. Earl of Shelburne, July 1766–October 1768
14. Viscount Weymouth, October 1768–December 1770
15. Earl of Rochford, December 1770–November 1775
16. Viscount Weymouth, November 1775–November 1779
17. Earl of Hillsborough, November 1779–March 1782
18. Earl of Shelburne, March 1782–July 1782
19. Viscount Sydney, July 1782–April 1783
20. Lord North, April 1783–December 1783
21. Earl of Temple, December 1783
22. Viscount Sydney, December 1783–June 1789
23. Lord Grenville, June 1789–June 1791
24. Henry Dundas, June 1791–July 1794
25. Duke of Portland, July 1794–July 1801
26. Lord Pelham, July 1801–August 1803
27. Charles Philip Yorke, August 1803–May 1804
28. Earl of Liverpool, May 1804–February 1806
29. Henry Althorp, February 1806–March 1807
30. Earl of Liverpool, March 1807–November 1809
31. Richard Ryder, November 1809–June 1812
32. Henry Addington, June 1812–January 1822
33. Sir Robert Peel, January 1822–April 1827
34. William Sturges-Bourne, April 1827–July 1827
35. 3rd Marquess of Lansdowne, July 1827–January 1828
36. Sir Robert Peel, January 1828–November 1830
37. Viscount Melbourne, November 1830–July 1834
38. Viscount Duncannon, July 1834–December 1834
39. Henry Goulburn, December 1834–April 1835
40. Lord John Russell, April 1835–August 1839
41. Marquess of Normanby, August 1839–September 1841
42. Sir James Graham, September 1841–July 1846
43. Sir George Grey, July 1846–February 1852
44. Spencer Horatio Walpole, February 1852–February 1855
45. Sir George Grey, February 1855–February 1858
46. Spencer Horatio Walpole, February 1858–March 1859
47. Thomas H. S. S. Estcourt, March 1859–June 1859
48. Sir George Cornewall Lewis, June 1859–July 1861
49. Sir George Grey, July 1861–July 1866
50. Spencer Horatio Walpole, July 1866–May 1867
51. Gathorne Hardy, May 1867–December 1868
52. Henry Austin Bruce, December 1868–August 1873
53. Sir Robert Lowe, August 1873–February 1874

54. Sir Richard Assheton Cross, February 1874–April 1880
55. Sir William Harcourt, April 1880–June 1885
56. Sir Richard Assheton Cross, June 1885–February 1886
57. Hugh Childers, February 1886–August 1886
58. Henry Matthews, August 1886–August 1892
59. Herbert Henry Asquith, August 1892–June 1895
60. Sir Matthew White Ridley, June 1895–November 1900
61. Charles Thomson Ritchie, November 1900–August 1902
62. Aretas Akers-Douglas, August 1902–December 1905
63. Herbert Gladstone, December 1905–April 1908
64. Sir Winston Churchill, April 1908–October 1911
65. Reginald McKenna, October 1911–May 1915
66. Sir John Simon, May 1915–January 1916
67. Sir Herbert Samuel, January 1916–December 1916
68. Sir George Cave, December 1916–January 1919
69. Edward Shortt, January 1919–October 1922
70. W. C. Bridgeman, October 1922–January 1924
71. Arthur Henderson, January 1924–November 1924
72. William Joynson-Hicks, November 1924–June 1929
73. John Richard Clynes, June 1929–August 1931
74. Sir Herbert Samuel, August 1931–September 1932
75. Sir John Gilmour, September 1932–June 1935
76. Sir John Simon, June 1935–May 1937
77. Sir Samuel Hoare, May 1937–September 1939

78. Sir John Anderson, September 1939–October 1940
79. Herbert Morrison, October 1940–May 1945
80. Sir Donald Bradley Somervell, May 1945–August 1945
81. James Chuter-Ede, August 1945–October 1951
82. Sir David Patrick Maxwell Fyfe, October 1951–October 1954
83. Gwilym Lloyd-George, October 1954–January 1957
84. Richard Austen Butler, January 1957–July 1962
85. Henry Brooke, July 1962–October 1964
86. Sir Frank Soskice, October 1964–December 1965
87. Roy Jenkins, December 1965–November 1967
88. James Callaghan, November 1967–June 1970
89. Reginald Maudling, June 1970–July 1972
90. Robert Carr, July 1972–March 1974
91. Roy Jenkins, March 1974–September 1976
92. Lord Merlyn Rees, September 1976–May 1979
93. William Whitelaw, May 1979–June 1983
94. Sir Leon Brittan, June 1983–September 1985
95. Douglas Hurd, September 1985–October 1989
96. David Charles Waddington, October 1989–November 1990
97. Kenneth Baker, November 1990–April 1992
98. Kenneth Clarke, April 1992–May 1993
99. Michael Howard, May 1993–May 1997
100. Jack Straw, May 1997–

SECRETARIES OF STATE FOR THE AMERICAN COLONIES

1. Earl of Hillsborough, January 1768–August 1772
2. Earl of Dartmouth, August 1772–November 1775
3. Viscount Sackville, November 1775–February 1782
4. Welbore Ellis, February 1782–March 1782

---

[1]William Pitt, the Elder, was unofficial acting prime minister from October 1760 to May 1762.

[2]Sometimes combined with the post of First Lord of the Treasury, the normal position of the prime minister.

[3]The title emerged in 1782 to replace the title of secretary of the Northern Department, and Charles James Fox was properly the first foreign secretary.

[4]The title of home secretary was used from 1782 and replaced that of secretary of the Southern Department.

BIBLIOGRAPHY

Addison, Paul. 1992. *Churchill on the Home Front 1900–1955* (London: Cape).

Albemarle, Earl of (ed.). 1852. *Memoirs of the Marquis of Rockingham and His Contemporaries* (London: Bentley).

Anderson, Paul, and Nyta Mann. 1997. *Safety First: The Making of New Labour* (London: Granta).

Anson, Sir William R. (ed.). 1898. *Autobiography and Political Correspondence of Augustus Henry Third Duke of Grafton K.G.* (London: Murray).

Asquith, Herbert H. 1928. *Memories and Reflections,* 2 vols. (Boston: Little, Brown).

Attlee, Clement R. 1935. *The Will and the Way to Socialism* (London: Methuen).

Baker, Kenneth. 1993. *Kenneth Baker: The Turbulent Years: My Life in Politics* (London: Faber and Faber).

Baldwin, Stanley. 1971. *On England, and Other Addresses* (Freeport, NY: Books for Libraries Press).

Ball, Stuart. 1988. *Baldwin and the Conservative Party: The Crisis of 1929–1931* (New Haven, CT: Yale University Press).

Barker, Bernard (ed.). 1972. *Ramsay MacDonald's Political Writings* (London: Allen Lane).

Beales. D. 1974. "Peel, Russell, and Reform," *Historical Journal,* 17.

Beckett, Francis. 1996. *Clem Attlee: A Biography* (London: Richard Cohen).

Beckett, John. 1994. *The Rise and Fall of the Grenvilles, Dukes of Buckingham and Chandos, 1710–1921* (Manchester: Manchester University Press).

Bellamy, Joyce M., and John Saville (eds.). 1972. *Dictionary of Labour Biography* (Clifton, NJ: A. M. Kelley).

Bigelow, John (ed.). 1879. *Life of Benjamin Franklin* (Philadelphia: Lippincott).

Birdwood, Vere (ed.). 1994. *So Dearly Loved, So Much Admired: Letters to Hester Pitt, Lady Chatham, from Her Relations and Friends, 1744–1801* (London: H.M.S.O.).

Birkenhead, Frederick, Earl of. 1965. *Halifax: The Life of Lord Halifax* (London: Hamish Hamilton).

Birrell, Francis. 1933. *Gladstone* (London: Duckworth).

Black, Jeremy. 1985. *British Foreign Policy in the Age of Walpole* (Edinburgh: John Donald).

———. 1990. *British Politics from Walpole to Pitt, 1742–1789* (Basingstoke, UK: Macmillan).

———. 1992. *Pitt the Elder* (Cambridge: Cambridge University Press).

———. 1993. *The Politics of Britain, 1688–1801* (Manchester: Manchester University Press).

———. 1994. *British Foreign Policy in the Age of Revolutions, 1783–1793* (Cambridge: Cambridge University Press).

Black, Jeremy (ed.). 1984. *Britain in the Age of Walpole* (London: Macmillan).

———. 1990. *British Politics and Society from Walpole to Pitt* (Basingstoke, UK: Macmillan).

———. 1990. *Robert Walpole and the Nature of Politics in Early-Eighteenth-Century England* (Basingstoke, UK: Macmillan Education).

Blair, Tony. 1996. *New Britain: My Vision of a Young Country* (London: Fourth Estate).

Blake, Robert, Lord Blake. 1955. *The Unknown Prime Minister: The Life and Times of Andrew Bonar Law, 1858–1923* (London: Eyre & Spottiswoode).

———. 1966 and 1969. *Disraeli.* (London: Eyre & Spottiswoode).

———. 1985. *The Conservative Party from Peel to Thatcher* (London: Metheun).

Blake, Robert, and William R. Louis (eds.). 1993, 1996. *Churchill* (New York: W. W. Norton).

Bourne, Kenneth. 1982. *Palmerston: The Early Years, 1784–1841* (London: Allen Lane).

Brewer, J. 1973. "The Misfortunes of Lord Bute: A Case Study in Eighteenth-Century Political Argument and Public Opinion," *Historical Journal* 16: 3–44.

Brewer, John. 1976. *Party Ideology and Popular Politics at the Accession of George III* (Cambridge: Cambridge University Press).

Briggs, A. 1974. "Peel," in Herbert von Thal (ed.), *The Prime Ministers,* vol. 1 (London: Allen and Unwin).

Brivati, Brian. 1996. *Hugh Gaitskell: A Biography* (London: Richard Cohen).

Brock, Michael. 1973. *The Great Reform Act of 1832* (London: Hutchinson).

Brock, William R. 1941 and 1967. *Lord Liverpool and Liberal Toryism* (Cambridge: Cambridge University Press).

Brooks, David (ed.). 1986. *The Destruction of Lord Rosebery: From the Diary of Sir Edward Hamilton, 1894–95* (London: Historians' Press).

Brown, George. 1971, 1972, and 1975. *In My Way* (London: Gollancz).

Brown, Peter D., and Karl W. Schweizer (eds.). 1982. *The Devonshire Diary, William Cavendish, Fourth Duke of Devonshire, Memoranda and State of Affairs, 1759–1762* (London: Office of the Royal Historical Society, University College London).

Browning, Reed. 1975. *The Duke of Newcastle* (New Haven, CT, and London: Yale University Press).

Bruce-Gardyne, Jock. 1984. *Mrs. Thatcher's First Administration* (London: Macmillan).

Bryant, Chris. 1992. *Stafford Cripps the First Modern Chancellor* (London: Hodder & Stoughton).

Buchan, John. 1930. *Lord Rosebery, 1847–1929* (London: Humphrey Milford).

Bullock, Alan. 1960 and 1967. *The Life and Times of Ernest Bevin,* 2 vols. (London: Heinemann).

———. 1983. *Ernest Bevin: Foreign Secretary 1945–1951* (Oxford: Oxford University Press).

Butler, Lord. 1971. *The Art of the Possible* (London: Hamilton).

Butterfield, Herbert. 1949. *Lord North and the People, 1779–80* (London: G. Bell & Sons).

Callaghan, James. 1987. *Time and Chance* (London: Collins).

Campbell, John. 1993. *Edward Heath: A Biography* (London: Pimlico).

Cannadine, David (ed.). 1996. *Blood, Toil, Tears and Sweat: The Speeches of Winston Churchill* (London: Penguin).

Cannon, John. 1969. *The Fox-North Coalition: Crisis of the Constitution, 1782–1784* (London: Cambridge).

———. 1970. *Lord North: The Noble Lord of the Blue Ribbon* (London: Historical Association).

Cannon, John (ed.). 1978. *The Letters of Junius* (Oxford and New York: Oxford University Press).

Carlton, David. 1970. *MacDonald versus Henderson* (London: Macmillan).

———. 1981. *Anthony Eden: A Biography* (London: Allen Lane).

———. 1989. *Britain and the Suez Crisis* (Oxford: Basil Blackwell).

Cave, Lady. 1931. *Lord Cave: A Memoir* (London: J. Murray).

Chamberlain, Muriel E. 1983. *Lord Aberdeen: A Political Biography* (London and New York: Longman).

———. 1987. *Lord Palmerston* (London: Cardiff GPC).

Charmley, John. 1989. *Chamberlain and the Lost Peace* (London: Hodder & Stoughton).

———. 1993. *Churchill: The End of Glory* (London: Hodder & Stoughton).

Christie, Ian R. 1958. "The Cabinet during the Grenville Administration, 1763–65," *English Historical Review* 73: 86–92.

———. 1958. *The End of North's Ministry, 1780–1782* (London: Macmillan).

———. 1982. *Wars and Revolutions: Britain, 1760–1815* (Cambridge, MA: Harvard University Press).

Clark, Jonathan C. D. 1982. *The Dynamics of Change: The Crisis of the 1750s and English Party Systems* (Cambridge: Cambridge University Press).

Clark, Jonathan C. D. (ed.). 1988. *The Memoirs and Speeches of James, 2nd Earl Waldegrave, 1742–1763* (Cambridge: Cambridge University Press).

Clarke, Peter. 1991. *A Question of Leadership* (London: Penguin).

Clynes, John R. 1937. *Memoirs,* 2 vols. (London: Hutchinson).

———. 1940. *When I Remember* (London: Macmillan).

Coleman, Bruce. 1988. *Conservatism and the Conservative Party in Nineteenth-Century Britain* (London: Edward Arnold).

Conacher, James. 1968. *The Aberdeen Coalition 1852–1855* (Cambridge: University Press).

———. 1987. *Britain and the Crimea, 1855–56: Problems of War and Peace* (New York: St. Martin's).

Cook, Margaret. 1999. *A Slight and Delicate Creature* (London: Weidenfeld & Nicolson).

Cooke, Colin. 1957. *The Life of Richard Stafford Cripps* (London: Hodder & Stoughton).

Cookson, J. E. 1975. *Lord Liverpool's Administration: The Crucial Years, 1815–22* (Hamden, CT: Archon Books).

Cosgrave, Patrick. 1981. *R. A. Butler: An English Life* (London: Quartet Books).

Crewe, Marquess of. 1930. *Lord Rosebery* (London: John Murray).

Cross, Colin. 1966. *Philip Snowden* (London: Barrie & Rockliff).

Cross, J. A. 1977. *Sir Samuel Hoare: A Political Biography* (London: Cape).

Dalton, E. Hugh. 1953. *Call Back Yesterday* (London: Frederick Muller).

———. 1957. *The Fateful Years* (London: Frederick Muller).

———. 1962. *High Tide and After* (London: Frederick Muller).

Derby, Edward H., and John R. Vincent. 1978. *Disraeli, Derby and the Conservative Party: Journals of Lord Stanley, 1849–1869* (Hassocks, UK: Harvester Press).

Derry, John W. 1990. *Politics in the Age of Fox, Pitt and Liverpool* (Basingstoke, UK: Macmillan).

———. 1992. *Charles, Earl Grey: Aristocratic Reformer* (Oxford, UK, and Cambridge, MA: Basil Blackwell).

Dickie, John. 1964. *The Uncommon Commoner: A Study of Sir Alec Douglas Home* (London: Pall Mall Press).

Dickinson, Harry T. 1973. *Walpole and the Whig Supremacy* (London: English Universities Press).

———. 1985. *British Radicalism and the French Revolution, 1789–1815* (Oxford: Blackwell).

———. 1989. *Britain and the French Revolution, 1789–1815* (Basingstoke, UK: Macmillan).

Dickinson, Harry T. (ed.). 1998. *Britain and the American Revolution* (London: Longman).

———. 1998. *William Pulteney: A Proper Reply to a Late Scurrilous Libel; Intitled, Sedition and Defamation Display'd* (New York: AMS Press).

Dixon, Peter. 1976. *Canning: Politician and Statesman* (London. Weidenfeld and Nicolson).

Donoughue, Bernard. 1987. *Prime Minister: The Conduct of Policy under Harold Wilson and James Callaghan* (London: Cape).

Donoghue, Bernard, and G. W. Jones. 1973. *Herbert Morrison: Portrait of a Politician* (London: Weidenfeld & Nicolson).

Draper, Derek. 1997. *Blair's Hundred Days* (London: Faber and Faber).

Dutton, David. 1986. *Austen Chamberlain: Gentleman in Politics* (New Brunswick, NJ: Transaction Books).

———. 1992. *Simon: A Political Biography of Sir John Simon* (London: Arum).

———. 1996. *Anthony Eden: A Life and Reputation* (London: Arnold).

Eastwood, D. 1992. "Peel and the Tory Party Reconsidered," *History Today* 42.

Eccleshall, Robert, and Graham Walker (eds.). 1998. *Biographical Dictionary of British Prime Ministers* (London: Routledge).

Egremont, Max. 1980. *Balfour: A Life of Arthur James Balfour* (London: Collins).

Ehrman, John. 1969. *The Younger Pitt: The Years of Acclaim* (London: Constable).

———. 1983. *William Pitt: The Reluctant Transition* (London: Constable).

———. 1996. *The Younger Pitt: The Consuming Struggle* (London: Constable).

Ensor, Robert K. 1936. *England, 1870–1914* (Oxford: Oxford University Press).

Evans, Brendan. 1999. *Thatcherism and British Politics 1975–1999* (Stroud, UK: Sutton).

Evans, Brendan, and Andrew Taylor. 1996. *From Salisbury to Major: Continuity and Change in Conservative Politics* (Manchester: Manchester University Press).

Evans, Eric. 1989. *Britain before the Reform Act: Politics and Society, 1815–1832* (London: Longman).

———. 1997. *William Pitt the Younger* (London: Routledge).

Evans, Harold. 1981. *Downing Street Diary: The Macmillan Years, 1957–1963* (London: Hodder & Stoughton).

Feuchtwanger, E. J. 1975. *Gladstone* (London: Allen Lane).

Fisher, Nigel. 1973. *Iain Macleod* (London: Andre Deutsch).

———. 1982. *Harold Macmillan* (London: Weidenfeld and Nicolson).

Fitzmaurice, Lord Edmund. 1875–1876. *The Life and Times of the Earl of Shelburne* (London: Macmillan).

Foot, Paul. 1968. *The Politics of Harold Wilson* (Harmondsworth, UK: Penguin Books).

Foster, Robert F. 1981. *Lord Randolph Churchill: A Political Life* (Oxford: Clarendon Press).

Franklin, Colin. 1993. *Lord Chesterfield: His Character and Characters* (Aldershot: Scolar).

Gardiner, Alfred G. 1923. *The Life of Sir William Harcourt*, 2 vols. (London: Constable).

Gash, Norman. 1961 and 1972. *Mr. Secretary Peel: The Life of Sir Robert Peel to 1830* (London: Longman).

———. 1984. *Lord Liverpool* (London: Weidenfeld & Nicolson).

Gash, Norman (ed.). 1990. *Wellington* (Manchester: University of Manchester).

Gerrard, Christine. 1994. *The Patriot Opposition to Walpole: Politics, Poetry and National Myth, 1725–1742* (Oxford: Clarendon).

Gilbert, Bentley B. 1987, 1992. *David Lloyd George: A Political Life*, 2 vols. (London: Batsford).

Gilbert, Martin. 1971–1988. *Winston S. Churchill*, 8 vols. (London: Heinemann).

Gray, Denis. 1963. *Spencer Perceval, 1762–1812:*

The Evangelical Prime Minister (Manchester: Manchester University Press).

Grenville, J. A. S. 1964. *Lord Salisbury and Foreign Policy: The Close of the Nineteenth Century* (London: Athlone Press).

Grey of Fallodon, Viscount. 1925. *Twenty-Five Years, 1892–1916,* 2 vols. (New York: Frederick A. Stokes).

Grigg, John. 1973, 1978, 1985. *Lloyd George,* 3 vols. (London: Methuen).

Guttridge, George H. 1952. *The Early Career of Lord Rockingham, 1730–1765* (Berkeley: University of California).

Halsband, Robert. 1973. *Lord Hervey: Eighteenth-Century Courtier* (Oxford: Clarendon Press).

Hamilton, Mary A. 1938. *Arthur Henderson* (London: William Heinemann).

Harmer, Harry. 1999. *The Longman Companion to the Labour Party, 1900–1998* (New York: Addison Wesley Longman).

Harris, J. F., and C. Hazlehurst. 1970. "Campbell-Bannerman as Prime Minister," *History* 55.

Harris, Kenneth. 1987. *David Owen* (London: Weidenfeld & Nicolson).

Harris, R., and B. Sewill. 1975. *British Economic Policy, 1970–74: Two Views* (London: Institute of Economic Affairs).

Harrison, Robert. 1995. *Gladstone's Imperialism in Egypt: Techniques of Domination* (London: Greenwood Press).

Harrison, Royden. 1965. *Before the Socialists* (London: Routledge & Kegan Paul).

Harvey, Arnold D. 1999. *Lord Grenville, 1759–1834: A Bibliography* (Westport, CT: Meckler).

Healey, Denis. 1989. *The Time of My Life* (London: Michael Joseph).

Hervey, John (Lord). 1931. *Memoirs,* 3 vols. (London: Eyre & Spottiswoode).

Heuston, R. F. V. 1987. *Lives of the Lord Chancellors, 1940–1970* (Oxford: Clarendon).

Hill, Brian W. 1989. *Sir Robert Walpole, 'Sole and Prime Minister'* (London: Hamilton).

Hilton, B. 1993. "The Ripening of Robert Peel," in Michael Bentley (ed.), *Public and Private Doctrine: Essays in British History Presented to Maurice Cowling* (Cambridge: Cambridge University Press).

Hinde, Wendy. 1973 and 1989. *George Canning* (London: Collins).

Hinsley, F. H. (ed.). 1977. *British Foreign Policy under Sir Edward Grey* (Cambridge and New York: Cambridge University Press).

Hoffman, Ross J. S. 1973. *The Marquis: A Study of Lord Rockingham, 1730–1782* (New York: Fordham University Press).

Holmes, Martin. 1982. *Political Pressure and Economic Policy: British Government, 1970–1974* (London and Boston: Butterworth).

Home, Lord Alec. 1976. *The Way the Wind Blows* (London: Collins).

Horne, Alistair. 1988. *Macmillan, 1894–1956* (London: Macmillan).

Howard, Anthony. 1987. *RAB: The Life of R. A. Butler* (London: J. Cape).

Howe, Sir Geoffrey. 1994. *Conflict of Loyalty* (London: Macmillan).

Hyde, Harford M. 1973. *Baldwin: The Unexpected Prime Minister* (London: Hart-Davis MacGibbon).

Iremonger, Lucille. 1978. *Lord Aberdeen: A Biography of the Fourth Earl of Aberdeen* (London: Collins).

Jagger, Peter J. 1991. *Gladstone: The Making of a Christian Politician* (Allison Park, PA: Pickwick Publications).

Jagger, Peter J. (ed.). 1998. *Gladstone* (London: Hambledon).

James, Robert Rhodes. 1951. *Lord Randolph Churchill* (London: Hamilton).

———. 1963. *Rosebery* (London: Weidenfeld and Nicolson).

——— (ed.). 1974. *Winston S. Churchill: His Complete Speeches, 1897–1963* (New York: Chelsea House Publishers).

———. 1986. *Anthony Eden* (London: Weidenfeld & Nicolson).

Jefferys, Kevin. 1999. *Anthony Crosland: A New Biography* (London: Richard Cohen).

Jefferys, Kevin (ed.). 1999. *Leading Labour: From Keir Hardie to Tony Blair* (London: I. B. Tauris).

Jenkins, Edwin A. 1933. *From Foundry to Foreign Office* (London: Grayson & Grayson).

Jenkins, Roy. 1964. *Asquith* (London: Collins).

———. 1991. *A Life at the Centre* (London: Macmillan).

———. 1995. *Gladstone* (London: Macmillan).

———. 1998. *The Chancellors* (London: Macmillan).

Jones, Tudor. 1997. *Remaking the Labour Party: From Gaitskell to Blair* (London: Routledge).

Jones, Wilbur D. 1956. *Lord Derby and Victorian Conservatism* (Oxford: Basil Blackwell).

———. 1967. *"Prosperity Robinson": The Life of Viscount Goderich, 1782–1859* (London: Macmillan).

Junor, Penny. 1996. *John Major: From Brixton to Downing Street* (London: Penguin).

Jupp, Peter. 1985. *Lord Grenville* (Oxford: Clarendon Press).

———. 1998. *British Politics on the Eve of Reform:*

The Duke of Wellington's Administration, 1828–1830 (Manchester: University of Manchester).

Kelch, Ray A. 1974. *Newcastle: A Duke without Money* (London: Routledge & Kegan Paul).

Kilmuir, Earl of, David P. 1964. *Political Adventures* (London: Weidenfeld & Nicolson).

Knight, R. 1986. "Harold Macmillan and the Cossacks: Was There a Klagenfurt Conspiracy?" *Intelligence and National Security* 1: 234–254.

Koss, Stephen. 1976. *Asquith* (New York: St. Martin's).

Lamb, Richard. 1987. *The Failure of the Eden Government* (London: Sidgwick & Jackson).

———. 1995. *The Macmillan Years, 1957–1963: The Emerging Truth* (London: John Murray).

Langford, Paul. 1973. *The First Rockingham Administration, 1765–1766* (London: Oxford University Press).

———. 1989. *A Polite and Commercial People: England, 1727–1783* (Oxford: Clarendon Press).

Lawson, Nigel. 1992. *The View from No. 11: Memoirs of a Tory Radical* (London: Corgi).

Lawson, P. 1985. "Further Reflections on the Cabinet in the Early Years of George III's Reign," *Bulletin of the Institute of Historical Research* 57: 237–240.

Lawson, Philip. 1984. *George Grenville: A Political Life* (Oxford: Clarendon Press).

Laybourn, Keith. 1988. *Philip Snowden: A Biography, 1864–1937* (Aldershot, UK: Temple Smith).

———. 1988. *The Rise of Labour* (London: Edward Arnold).

———. 1996. *The General Strike: Day by Day* (Stroud, UK: Sutton).

———. 1997. *The Rise of Socialism in Britain* (Stroud, UK: Sutton).

———. 2000. *A Century of Labour: A History of the Labour Party, 1900–2000.* (Stroud, UK: Sutton).

Laybourn, Keith, and David James (eds.). 1987. *Philip Snowden: The First Labour Chancellor of the Exchequer* (Bradford, UK: Bradford Libraries and Information Service).

Leventhal, Fred M. 1989. *Arthur Henderson* (Manchester: Manchester University Press).

Lloyd, J. S. B. 1976. *Mr. Speaker, Sir* (London: Cape).

Lloyd George, Earl David. 1933–1936. *War Memoirs* (London: Ivor Nicholson & Watson).

Mackay, Ruddock. 1985. *Balfour, Intellectual Statesman* (Oxford: Oxford University Press).

Macmillan, Harold. 1933. *Reconstruction: A Plea for National Unity* (London: Macmillan).

———. 1966. *Winds of Change, 1914–1939* (London: Macmillan).

———. 1967. *The Blast of War, 1939–1945* (London: Macmillan).

———. 1969. *Tides of Fortune, 1945–1955* (London: Macmillan).

———. 1971. *Riding the Storm, 1956–1959* (London: Macmillan).

———. 1972. *Pointing the Way, 1959–1961* (London: Macmillan).

———. 1973. *At the End of the Day, 1961–1963* (London: Macmillan).

———. 1984. *War Diaries* (London: Macmillan).

Magnus, Philip. 1954. *Gladstone* (London: Murray).

Major, John. 1999. *John Major: The Autobiography* (London: HarperCollins).

Mallet, Sir Charles E. 1932. *Herbert Gladstone: A Memoir* (London: Hutchinson).

Mandelson, Peter, and Roger Liddle. 1996. *The Blair Revolution—Can New Labour Now Deliver?* (London: Faber and Faber).

Mandler, Peter. 1990. *Aristocratic Government in the Age of Reform: Whigs and Liberals, 1830–1852* (Oxford: Clarendon Press).

Margach, James. 1984. *The Anatomy of Power* (London: W. H. Allen).

Marquand, David. 1977. *Ramsay MacDonald* (London: Cape).

Marsh, Peter. 1978. *The Discipline of Popular Government: Lord Salisbury's Domestic Statecraft, 1881–1902* (Hassocks, UK: Harvester Press).

Marshall, Dorothy. 1975. *Lord Melbourne* (London: Weidenfeld & Nicolson).

Mather, F. C. 1986. *Achilles or Nestor? The Duke of Wellington in British Politics after the Great Reform Act* (Southampton: University of Southampton).

Matthew, Henry C. G. 1973. *The Liberal Imperialist: The Ideas and Politics of a Post-Gladstonian Élite* (London: Oxford University Press).

———. 1986. *Gladstone, 1809–1875* (Oxford: Oxford University Press).

———. 1995. *Gladstone, 1875–1898* (Oxford: Oxford University Press).

Maudling, Reginald. 1978. *Memoirs* (London: Sidgwick and Jackson).

McCallum, Ronald B. 1936. *Asquith* (London: Duckworth).

McDermott, Geoffrey. 1982. *Leader Lost: A Biography of Hugh Gaitskell* (London: Leslie Frewin).

Middlemass, Robert Keith, and Anthony John Lane Barnes. 1969. *Baldwin: A Biography* (London: Weidenfeld & Nicolson).

Middleton, Richard. 1985. *The Bells of Victory: The Pitt-Newcastle Ministry and the Conduct of the*

Seven Years War (Cambridge: Cambridge University Press).

Mitchell, Austin. 1967. *The Whigs in Opposition, 1815–1830* (Oxford: Clarendon Press).

Mitchell, Leslie G. 1971. *Charles James Fox and the Disintegration of the Whig Party, 1782–94* (London: Oxford University Press).

———. 1997. *Charles James Fox* (Oxford and New York: Oxford University Press).

Morgan, Austen. 1992. *Harold Wilson* (London: Pluto Press).

Morgan, Kenneth O. 1974. *Lloyd George* (London: Weidenfeld & Nicolson).

———. 1984. *Labour in Power 1945–1951* (Oxford: Oxford University Press).

———. 1987. *Labour People* (Oxford: Oxford University Press).

———. 1997 and 1999. *Callaghan: A Life* (Oxford: Oxford University Press).

Mori, Jennifer. 1995. *William Pitt and the French Revolution* (Edinburgh: Keele University Press).

Morley, John. 1903. *Life of Gladstone* (New York and London: Macmillan).

Morrison, Herbert. 1933. *Socialisation and Transport.* (London: Constable).

———. 1943. *Looking Ahead* (London: Hodder & Stoughton).

———. 1949. *How London Is Governed* (London: People's Universities Press).

———. 1960. *Herbert Morrison: An Autobiography of Lord Morrison of Lambeth, PC, CH* (London: Odhams Press).

Namier, Sir Lewis. 1961. *England in the Age of the American Revolution* (London: Macmillan).

Newbould, I. 1983. "Peel and the Conservative Party, 1832–1841: A Study in Failure," *English Historical Review* 98.

Newbould, Ian. 1990. *Whiggery and Reform, 1830–1841: The Politics of Government* (Stanford, CA: Stanford University Press).

Norris, John. 1963. *Shelburne and Reform* (London: Macmillan).

O'Gorman, Francis. 1969. *The Whig Party and the French Revolution* (London: Macmillan).

———. 1975. *The Rise of Party in England: The Rockingham Whigs, 1760–1782* (London: Allen and Unwin).

Owen, David. 1991. *Time to Declare* (London: Joseph).

Owen, John B. 1957 and 1971. *The Rise of the Pelhams* (London: Methuen).

Packer, Ian. 1998. *Lloyd George* (Basingstoke, UK: Macmillan).

Pakenham, Elizabeth, Countess of Longford. 1969.

Wellington: The Years of the Sword (London: Weidenfeld & Nicolson).

———. 1975. *Wellington: Pillar of State* (St. Albans: Panther).

Panitch, Leo, and C. Leys. 1997. *The End of Parliamentary Socialism: From New Left to New Labour* (London: Verso).

Parker, James G. 1991. *Lord Curzon: 1859–1925* (New York: Greenwood Press).

Parry, Jonathan. 1993. *The Rise and Fall of Liberal Government in Victorian Britain* (New Haven, CT, and London: Yale University Press).

Partridge, Michael S., and Karen Partridge. 1994. *Lord Palmerston, 1784–1865: A Biography* (London: Greenwood).

Pearce, Robert. 1996. *Attlee* (London: Longman).

Pearson, John. 1983. *Stags and Serpents: The Story of the House of Cavendish and the Dukes of Devonshire* (London: Macmillan).

Peters, Marie. 1980. *Pitt and Popularity: The Patriot Ministry and London Opinion during the Seven Years' War* (Oxford: Clarendon).

———. 1992. *The Elder Pitt* (London: Longman).

Pimlott, Ben. 1988. "Is the Postwar Consensus a Myth?" *Contemporary Record* 2 (Summer).: 12–14.

———. 1985. *Hugh Dalton* (London: Cape).

———. 1992. *Harold Wilson* (London: HarperCollins).

Pimlott, Ben (ed.). 1986. *The Political Diary of Hugh Dalton, 1918–40, 1945–60* (London: Cape).

———. 1986. *The Second World War Diary of Hugh Dalton 1940–45* (London: Cape).

Plowright, John. 1996. *Regency England: The Age of Lord Liverpool* (London: Routledge).

Plumb, John H. 1956 and 1969. *Sir Robert Walpole*, 2 vols. (London: Cresset Press).

Prest, John. 1972. *Lord John Russell* (London: Macmillan).

Pugh, Martin. 1988. *Lloyd George* (London: Longman).

Ramsden, John. 1978. *The Age of Balfour and Baldwin: 1902–1940* (London: Longman).

———. 1978. *The History of the Conservative Party: The Age of Balfour and Baldwin* (London: Longman).

———. 1998. *An Appetite for Power: A History of the Conservative Party since 1830* (London: HarperCollins).

Read, Donald. 1987. *Peel and the Victorians* (Oxford: Basil Blackwell).

Reading, Lord (son). 1942, 1945. *Rufus Isaacs, First Marquess of Reading*, 2 vols. (New York: G. P. Putnam's Sons).

Rees, Merlyn. 1973. *The Public Sector in the Mixed Economy* (London: Batsford).

———. 1985. *Northern Ireland: A Personal Perspective* (London: Methuen).

Rentoul, John. 1992. *Tony Blair* (London: Warner Books).

Ridley, Jasper. 1970. *Lord Palmerston* (London: Constable).

Robbins, Keith. 1971. *Sir Edward Grey: A Biography of Lord Grey of Fallodon* (London: Cassell).

———. 1991. *Churchill* (London: Longman).

Roberts, Andrew. 1991. *The Holy Fox: A Biography of Lord Halifax* (London: Weidenfeld and Nicolson).

———. 1999. *Salisbury: Victorian Titan* (London: Weidenfeld & Nicolson).

Rolo, Paul J. V. 1965. *George Canning: Three Biographical Studies* (London: Macmillan).

Rothwell, Victor. 1991. *Anthony Eden: A Political Biography 1931–1957* (Manchester: Manchester University Press).

Rowland, Peter. 1968. *The Last Liberal Governments: The Promised Land, 1905–10* (London: Barrie & Rockliff).

———. 1975. *Lloyd George* (London: Barrie & Jenkins).

Russell, Alan K. 1973. *Liberal Landslide: The General Election of 1906* (Hamden, CT: Archon Books).

Sack, James. 1993. *From Jacobite to Conservative: Reaction and Orthodoxy in Britain, c. 1760–1832* (Cambridge: Cambridge University Press).

Sampson, Anthony. 1967. *Macmillan: A Study in Ambiguity* (London: Allen Lane).

Schweitzer, David. 1991. *Charles James Fox, 1749–1806: A Bibliography* (New York: Greenwood).

Schweizer, Karl W. 1988. *Lord Bute: Essays in Reinterpretation* (Leicester: Leicester University Press).

Schweizer, Karl W. (ed.). 1993. *William Pitt, Earl of Chatham, 1798–1778: A Bibliography* (London: Greenwood).

Searle, Geoffrey. 1990. *The Quest for National Efficiency: A Study in British Politics and Political Thought, 1899–1914* (London: Ashfield Press).

Sedgwick, Richard. 1970. *The House of Commons, 1715–1754,* vol. 2, *Members, E-Y* (London: H.M.S.O.).

Sedgwick, Romney (ed.). 1931. *Memoirs of the Reign of King George II* (London: Eyre & Spottiswoode).

———. 1970. *The History of Parliament: The House of Commons, 1715–1754* (New York: Oxford University Press).

Seldon, Anthony, and Stuart Ball. 1996. *The Heath Government 1970–1974: A Reappraisal* (London: Longman).

Self, Robert (ed.). 1996. *The Austen Chamberlain Diary Letters* (London: Cambridge University Press).

Shannon, Catherine. 1988. *Arthur James Balfour and Ireland, 1874–1922* (Washington, DC: Catholic University of America Press).

Shannon, Richard. 1982. *Gladstone,* vol. I: *1809–1865* (London: Hamilton).

———. 1992. *The Age of Disraeli, 1868–1881: The Rise of Tory Democracy* (London: Longman).

———. 1996. *The Age of Salisbury: The Conservative Party, 1881–1912* (London: Longman).

Simon, Brian. 1960. *Studies in the History of Education, 1780–1870* (London: Lawrence & Wishart).

Simon, Sir John. 1926. *The Three Speeches of Sir John Simon* (London: Macmillan).

Smith, Ernest. 1975. *Whig Principles and Party Politics: Earl Fitzwilliam and the Whig Party, 1748–1844* (Manchester: Manchester University Press).

———. 1990. *Lord Grey, 1764–1845* (Oxford: Clarendon Press; New York: Oxford University Press).

Smith, Francis. 1966. *The Making of the Second Reform Bill* (Cambridge: Cambridge University Press).

Smith, Paul. 1967. *Disraelian Conservatism and Social Reform* (London: Routledge & Kegan Paul).

Smith, William J. (ed.). 1852–1853. *The Grenville Papers: Being the Correspondence of Richard Grenville, Earl Temple, KG and the Rt. Hon. George Grenville, Their Friends and Contemporaries* (New York: AMS Press [reprint]).

Snowden, Philip. 1934. *An Autobiography* (London: Nicholson & Watson).

Southgate, Donald. 1966. '*The Most English Minister. . . .': The Policies and Politics of Palmerston* (London: Macmillan).

Spender, John A., and Cyril Asquith. 1932. *The Life of Lord Oxford and Asquith* (London: Hutchinson).

Stansky, Peter. 1964. *Ambitions and Strategies: The Struggle for Leadership of the Liberal Party in the 1890s* (Oxford: Clarendon Press).

Stansky, Peter (ed.). 1973. *Churchill: A Profile* (New York: Hill and Wang).

Steele, David. 1999. *Lord Salisbury* (London: UCL Press).

Stewart, Michael. 1977. *The Jekyll and Hyde Years* (London: Dent).

Stewart, Robert. 1971. *The Politics of Protection: Lord Derby and the Protectionist Party, 1841–1852* (London: Cambridge University Press).

————. 1978. *The Foundation of the Conservative Party, 1830–1867* (London: Longman).

Taylor, A. J. P., et.al. 1969. *Churchill: Four Faces of the Man* (London: Allen Lane).

Taylor, Robert. 1975. *Lord Salisbury* (London: Allen Lane).

Thatcher, Margaret. 1993. *The Downing Street Years* (London: HarperCollins).

Thomas, Peter D. G. 1971. *The House of Commons in the Eighteenth Century* (Oxford: Clarendon Press).

————. 1976. *Lord North* (London: Allen Lane).

————. 1996. *John Wilkes: A Friend of Liberty* (Oxford: Clarendon).

Thompson, Neville. 1986. *Wellington after Waterloo* (London: Routledge & Kegan Paul).

Thorne, R. G. 1986. *The House of Commons: 1790–1820,* vol. 4 (London: Secker & Warburg).

Thorpe, D. R. 1980. *The Uncrowned Prime Minister* (London: Darkhorse Publishing).

Tirastsoo, Nick (ed.). 1991. *The Attlee Years* (London: Pinter Publishers).

Turner, John. 1992. *British Politics and the Great War: Coalition and Conflict, 1915–1918* (New Haven, CT: Yale University Press).

————. 1994. *Macmillan* (London: Longman).

Turner, Michael. 2000. *The Age of Unease* (Stroud, UK: Sutton).

Valentine, Alan. 1967. *Lord North,* 2 vols. (Norman: University of Oklahoma Press).

Vincent, John. 1990. *Disraeli* (Oxford: Oxford University Press).

Vincent, John (ed.). 1994. *A Selection from the Diaries of Edward Henry Stanley, 15th Earl of Derby (1826–1893): Between September 1869 and March 1878* (London: Royal Historical Society).

Walpole, Horace, in John Brook (ed.). 1985. *Memoirs of King George II* (New Haven, CT: Yale University Press).

Wasserstein, Bernard. 1992. *Herbert Samuel: A Political Life* (Oxford: Clarendon).

Weiler, Peter. 1993. *Ernest Bevin* (Manchester: Manchester University Press).

Weir, Lauchlan M. 1938. *The Tragedy of Ramsay MacDonald* (London: Secker & Warburg).

Wheeler-Bennett, John W. 1962. *John Anderson, Viscount Waverley* (New York: St. Martin's).

Whitelaw, William. 1989. *The Whitelaw Memoirs* (London: Headline).

Whiteley, Peter. 1996. *Lord North: The Prime Minister Who Lost America* (London: Hambledon).

Wiggin, Lewis M. 1958. *The Faction of Cousins: A Political Account of the Grenvilles, 1733–1763* (New Haven, CT: Yale University Press).

Wilkes, John W. 1964. *A Whig in Power: The Political Career of Henry Pelham* (Evanston, IL: Northwestern University Press).

Williams, Arthur F. B. 1913. *The Life of William Pitt, Earl of Chatham* (London: Longmans).

Williams, Philip M. 1979. *Hugh Gaitskell: A Political Biography* (London: Cape).

Williams, Robin H. (ed.). 1988. *The Salisbury-Balfour Correspondence, 1869–92* (Ware, UK: Hertfordshire Record Society).

Williamson, Philip. 1992. *National Crisis and National Government: British Politics, the Economy and Empire, 1926–1932* (Cambridge: Cambridge University Press).

————. 1999. *Stanley Baldwin: Conservative Leadership and National Values* (Cambridge: Cambridge University Press).

Williamson, Philip (ed.). 1988. *The Modernisation of the Conservative Politics: The Diaries and Letters of William Bridgeman, 1904–1935* (London: Historians' Press).

Wilson, Harold. 1971. *The Labour Government, 1964–1970: A Personal Record* (London: Weidenfeld & Nicolson).

————. 1979. *Final Term: The Labour Government, 1974–1976* (London: Weidenfeld & Nicolson).

Wilson, John. 1973. *CB: A Life of Sir Henry Campbell-Bannerman* (London: Constable).

Wright, David G. 1988. *Popular Radicalism: The Working-Class Experience, 1780–1880* (London: Longman).

Wright, J. (ed.). 1841–1843. *Sir Henry Cavendish's Debates of the House of Commons during the Thirteenth Parliament of Great Britain,* 2 vols (London: Longmans).

Wrigley, Chris. 1992. *Lloyd George* (Oxford: Blackwell).

————. 1999. *Arthur Henderson* (Cardiff: GPC Books).

Young, George. 1952. *Stanley Baldwin* (London: Hart-Davis).

Young, Hugo. 1991. *One of Us: A Biography of Margaret Thatcher* (London: Macmillan).

Young, Kenneth. 1970. *Sir Alec Douglas-Home* (London: Dent).

Zebel, Sydney. 1973. *Balfour: A Political Biography* (Cambridge: Cambridge University Press).

Ziegler, Philip. 1965. *Addington* (New York: John Day).

————. 1982. *Melbourne* (London: Collins).

INDEX

Rodgers, Bill, 160, 188, 247
Roman Catholic bishops, in
    England, 128
Roman Catholics, in Ireland, 24,
    110, 128, 135, 145, 238,
    260
  emancipation of, 3, 5, 57, 62,
    100, 110, 131, 135, 194, 204,
    253, 255, 260, 284, 323, 325,
    326, 337
Roosevelt, Franklin D., 79,
    78(photo), 154
Roosevelt, Theodore, 196
Rosebery, Lord (Earl of Rosebery),
    55, **281–283**
  government of, 9, 125, 149, 156,
    192
Rothermere, Lord, 23, 67
Rushout, Sir John, 294
Russell, Lord John (Earl Russell), 2,
    6, 100, 110, 127, 148, 211,
    231, 252, 253, **283–286,**
    284(photo)
  government of, 27, 81, 128, 133,
    139, 140, 149, 194, 202, 250,
    251, 333
Russell, John. See Bedford, Duke
    of; Russell, Lord John
Russia
  18th century, 200
  19th century, 2, 63, 81, 107,
    141, 157, 250, 252, 253, 325
  20th century, 149, 156, 223
  See also Soviet Union
Russo-Turkish War (1877), 107
Rutland, Duke of, 137
Ryder, Dudley. See Harrowby, Lord
Ryder, Richard, **286**

Sacheverell, Henry, 85
Sackville, Viscount (Lord George
    Sackville), **287–288**
St. Aldwyn, Viscount. See Hicks
    Beach, Sir Michael
St. Cyres, Viscount. See Northcote,
    Sir Stafford
St. John, Henry. See Bolingbroke,
    Viscount
Salisbury, Marquess of, 55, 75, 107,
    242, **288–290,** 289(photo)
  government of, 5, 24, 76, 92, 93,
    134, 157, 170, 195–196, 227,
    242, 243, 275, 276, 277
Samuel, Sir Herbert (Viscount
    Samuel), 22, 189, 213,
    290–293, 296, 297

Sandon, Viscount. See Harrowby,
    Lord
Sandwich, Earl of, 143, 199, **293,**
    293(photo)
Sandys, Samuel (First Baron Sandys
    of Ombersley), **294**
Scarsdale, Viscount. See Curzon,
    Lord
Scotland
  18th century, 312
  20th century, 36–37, 54, 124,
    177, 276
Selwyn-Lloyd, Lord. See Lloyd,
    Selwyn
Serbs, 19th century, 107
Seven Years' War (1756–1763), 29,
    47, 104, 116, 201, 236
Sex discrimination, 187
Shelburne, Earl of, 116, 241,
    294–295
  government of, 120–121, 137,
    140, 305, 307
Sherbrooke, Viscount. See Lowe, Sir
    Robert
Shinwell, Emmanuel, 216
Shore, Peter, 304
Shortt, Edward, **295**
Sidmouth, Viscount. See
    Addington, Henry
Sidney Street siege (1911), 77
Sierra Leone, 87
Silk, taking, 63, 300
Simon, Sir John Allsebrook
    (Viscount Simon of Stackpole
    Elidor), 70, **296–298,** 335
Single European Act (1985), 181,
    198
Sinking Fund, 4, 74, 178, 242,
    265, 318
Sinn Fein, 35, 36
Sinope, massacre at (1853), 2–3,
    81, 252
Slater, Oscar, 124
Slavery, slave trade, 100, 131, 145,
    150, 194, 204, 237, 250,
    260
Smith, F. E., 77
Smith, John, 33, 87
Smith, W. H., 169
Smog pollution, 20th century, 42
Snowden, Philip (Viscount
    Snowden of Ickornshaw), 178,
    196, 216, **298–300**
Social Democratic Federation, 213,
    232
Social Democratic Party, 36, 163,

188, 247–248. See also
    Democratic Socialist Party
Social insurance, 13
Social and Liberal Democratic
    Party, 188
Social welfare
  19th century, 92, 106, 289
  20th century, 10, 13, 20, 34, 35,
    38, 45, 49, 77, 206, 218, 220,
    221, 309, 311, 329
  See also Health services; Housing;
    Poor law
Socialists, 83, 88–89, 90, 91, 123,
    213, 214, 216, 232, 330
Socialization. See Public ownership
    of industry
Solicitor generalship, 179
Somervell, Sir Donald Bradley
    (Lord Somervell of Harrow),
    300
Soskice, Sir Frank, **300–301**
South Africa, 10, 24, 43–44, 102,
    126, 191–192, 291
Southern Rhodesia, 177, 246, 302,
    329, 332
Soviet Union, 53, 79, 89, 113, 114,
    154, 159, 160, 175, 181,
    189–190, 205, 216, 219, 221
Spain
  18th century, 73, 116, 157–158,
    266, 279, 312, 319, 322
  19th century, 57, 62, 145, 233,
    250, 326
  20th century, 13, 78, 174
Spencer, Charles (Earl of
    Sunderland), 318
Spencer, John Charles (Earl
    Spencer). See Althorp, Henry
Spring-Rice, Thomas, 150,
    301–302
Stalin, Joseph, 78(photo)
Stamp Act (1765), 29, 143, 237,
    314
Stanhope, James (Earl of Stanhope),
    312, 318
Stanhope, Philip Dormer. See
    Chesterfield, Earl of
Stanhope, William. See Harrington,
    Earl
Stanley, Hon. Sir Edward George
    Geoffrey Smith (Baron
    Stanley; Lord Derby). See
    Derby, 14th Earl of
Stanley, Edward Henry (Lord
    Stanley). See Derby, 15th Earl
    of

ABOUT THE EDITOR
AND CONTRIBUTORS

KEITH LAYBOURN is professor of history at the University of Huddersfield and a Fellow of the Royal Historical Society. He has published twenty-seven books and more than fifty articles. Recently he has written *Under the Red Flag* (1999), *Modern Britain since 1906* (1999), and *A Century of Labour: A History of the Labour Party, 1900–2000* (2000) and has edited *Representation and Reality of War* (1999). He also edits the *Annual Bulletin of Historical Literature.*

KIT HARDWICK teaches at the University of Huddersfield. His doctoral dissertation was on Brian Jackson, the founder of the open- and wider-learning movement in Britain.

JOHN A. HARGREAVES is head of history, Howden Clough School, Batley, West Yorkshire, and editor of the *Transactions of the Halifax Antiquarian Society.* He is an Associate of the Royal Historical Society and has twice won the Yorkshire history prize. Among his publications are books on Luddism and the history of Halifax, West Yorkshire.

JOHN O'CONNELL is a retired professor and former dean of the School of Music and Humanities at the University of Huddersfield. In recent years he has been writing a history of the university.

PHILIP WOODFINE is reader in history at the University of Huddersfield and a Fellow of the Royal Historical Society. He is the author of *Britannia's Glories: The Walpole Ministry and the 1739 War with Spain* (1998) and co-editor (with Jeremy Black) of *The British Navy and the Use of Naval Power in the Eighteenth Century.* (1988). He is currently working on a biography of Sir Robert Walpole.

CHRIS WRIGLEY is professor of British history at the University of Nottingham, Fellow of the Royal Historical Society, and president of the Historical Association. Among his many publications are *David Lloyd George and the British Labour Movement* (1976), *A History of British Industrial Relations,* 3 volumes (1982, 1993, and 1996), and *Arthur Henderson* (1990).